POCKETS

THESAURUS

D1059377

DK PUBLISHING

LONDON, NEW YORK,
MELBOURNE, MUNICH, and DELHI

Produced for Dorling Kindersley by
PAGEOne, Cairn House, Elgiva Lane, Chesham,
Buckinghamshire HP5 2JD

PAGEOne team Chris Clark, Helen Parker
DK Managing editor Jane Yorke
Dictionary editor Sheila Dignen
US editor Iris Rosoff
Dictionary compilers Roz Combley, Jessica Feinstein,
Fred McDonald, Elaine Pollard,
Laura Wedgeworth, John Williams

Second American Edition, 2003
Published in the United States by
DK Publishing, Inc.,
375 Hudson Street,
New York, New York 10014

06 07 08 10 9 8 7 6

Copyright © 2003 Dorling Kindersley Limited
All rights reserved under International and Pan-American Copyright Conventions. No part of this publication may be reproduced, stored in a retrieval system, or transmitted in any form or by any means, electronic, mechanical, photocopying, recording or otherwise, without the prior written permission of the copyright owner.
Published in Great Britain by Dorling Kindersley Limited.

A Cataloging-in-Publication record for the First American Edition of this book is available from the Library of Congress.

ISBN-13: 978-0-7894-9600-3

ISBN-10: 0-7894-9600-3

Printed and bound in Italy by LEGOPRINT

See our complete product line at
www.dk.com

THE AIM OF THIS BOOK

The aim of a thesaurus wordfinder is to provide lists of useful synonyms or near synonyms. If you have a particular word in mind, but feel that it is not quite the word that you want to use – for example, because you have already used it once in a piece of writing, or it does not convey the exact meaning that you wish to impart – you can look the word up in this thesaurus and find a list of other words that mean the same thing, or nearly the same. You can then select the one word most appropriate for your needs. The thesaurus includes phrases as well as single words where it is felt that these may be useful. For example, the entry at dance (verb) includes not only verbs such as "jive," "twirl," and "waltz," but also phrases such as "do a jig," "leap about," and "shake a leg."

ARRANGEMENT OF ENTRIES

1 This thesaurus is arranged in strict alphabetical order. The main entries are listed in alphabetical order, and individual synonyms within the entries are also arranged in alphabetical order.

2 Different parts of speech are included as separate headwords. For example, **fence** (noun) is listed as a separate entry from **fence** (verb). They are listed next to each other in the thesaurus:

fence *n* barricade, barrier, defense, fencing, hedge, hurdle, paling, palisade, railings, rampart, stockade, wall, wire

fence *v* bound, circumscribe, confine, coop, encircle, enclose, hedge, pen, surround

3 Plural and singular nouns are listed separately. For example, **arms** (weapons) is listed as a separate entry from **arm**.

4 Parts of speech are given immediately after the headword. The following abbreviations are used throughout the wordfinder:

n	noun
v	verb
adj	adjective
adv	adverb
prep	preposition
conj	conjunction

5 Where a word has more than one meaning, each meaning is numbered and, where there is a possibility of confusion, a brief definition or example is given to make it clear which meaning is being dealt with. The following abbreviations are used throughout the book:

sb	somebody
sth	something

6 Where a particular synonym is an informal or technical word, this is indicated immediately after the synonym in question. The following labels are used throughout the book:

inf	informal
sl	slang
tech	technical

For example, at the entry for **abnormal**, the synonym "kinky" is labeled as informal and "wacko" is labeled as slang.

abnormal *adj* aberrant, anomalous, atypical, bizarre, deviant, eccentric, erratic, exceptional, extraordinary, idiosyncratic, irregular, kinky *inf*, odd, peculiar, perverse, perverted, queer, singular, strange, unexpected, unnatural, unorthodox, unusual, wacko *sl*, weird; ***opp*** normal

7 Where a word has a clear or useful opposite, this is given at the end of the list of synonyms. Sometimes more than one opposite may be given if it is useful. For example:

noisy *adj* blaring, blasting, boisterous, deafening, ear-splitting, loud, piercing, raucous, riotous, rowdy; ***opp*** quiet, silent

THESAURUS

abandon *v* **1** (leave sb) desert, ditch *inf*, dump *inf*, forsake, jilt, leave, leave behind, maroon, run out on *inf*, strand, throw over *inf*. **2** (leave a place) depart from, evacuate, go away from, quit, vacate, withdraw. **3** (give sth away) cede, deliver, forfeit, give up, renounce, relinquish, resign, surrender, waive, yield. **4 abandon yourself to** give yourself up to, give way to, indulge in, lose yourself in, lose yourself to

abashed *adj* ashamed, discomfited, disconcerted, embarrassed, humiliated, mortified, shamefaced; ***opp*** unabashed

abate v die down, diminish, ease, fade, lessen, let up, subside

abbreviate *v* abridge, clip, compress, condense, crop, curtail, cut, cut down, précis, prune, reduce, shorten, summarize, trim, truncate; ***opp*** lengthen

abbreviation *n* contraction, shortened form

abdicate *v* **1** (give up throne) cede, give up, quit, renounce, resign, retire, stand down, step down *inf*, vacate, waive, yield. **2** (give up responsibility) cast aside, disown, give up, refuse, relinquish, renounce, repudiate, surrender, turn your back on, wash your hands of

abduct *v* carry off, hold for ransom, kidnap, make off with, run away with, run off with, seize, snatch *inf*

abhor *v* abominate, detest, dislike, hate, loathe, recoil from, shrink from, shudder at

abhorrent *adj* abominable, detestable, disgusting, distasteful, execrable, hated, hateful, horrible, horrid, loathsome, nauseating, obnoxious, odious, offensive, repellent, repugnant, repulsive, revolting

abide *v* **1** accept, bear, endure, put up with, stand, stomach, suffer, tolerate. **2 abide by** adhere to, agree to, comply with, conform to, follow, keep to, obey, observe, stand by, stick to, submit to

ability *n* adeptness, adroitness, aptitude, bent, capability, capacity, cleverness, competence, competency, expertise, expertness, facility, faculty, flair, gift, knack, know-how *inf*, power, proficiency, prowess, skill, talent

abject *adj* **1** (of conditions) deplorable, hopeless, miserable, pathetic, pitiable, piteous, wretched. **2** (of people) base, contemptible, cringing, despicable, groveling, ignominious, ingratiating, low, mean, obsequious, servile, slavish, sniveling, submissive, sycophantic, toadying, vile, worthless, wretched

ablaze *adj* **1** (on fire) afire, alight, blazing, burning, fiery, flaming, ignited, lighted, on fire, raging. 2 (full of light) aglow, bright, brilliant, flashing, gleaming, glowing, illuminated, incandescent, lit up, luminous, radiant, shimmering, sparkling

able *adj* accomplished, adept, capable, clever, competent, experienced, expert, gifted, masterly, proficient, qualified, skilled, strong, talented

abnormal *adj* aberrant, anomalous, atypical, bizarre, deviant, eccentric, erratic, exceptional, extraordinary, idiosyncratic, irregular, kinky *inf*, odd, peculiar, perverse, perverted, queer, singular, strange, unexpected, unnatural, unorthodox, unusual, wacko *sl*, weird; ***opp*** normal

abolish *v* annul, ax, cancel, destroy, do away with, eliminate, end, eradicate, extinguish, get rid of, nullify, put an end to, quash, rescind, revoke, stamp out, stop, terminate, wipe out

abominable *adj* abhorrent, contemptible, despicable, detestable, disgusting, foul, hateful, horrible, horrid, loathsome, nasty, obnoxious, odious, offensive, repellent, revolting, terrible, vile, wretched

abort *v* 1 (end pregnancy) have a miscarriage, miscarry, terminate. 2 (end mission) call off, come to a halt, end, fail, halt, stop, terminate

abortion *n* miscarriage, termination

abortive *adj* failed, fruitless, futile, ineffective, ineffectual, pointless, unproductive, unsuccessful, useless, vain, worthless; ***opp*** successful

abound *v* 1 (be full of) be alive with, be crawling with *inf*, be full of, overflow with, swarm with, teem with. 2 (be plentiful) be plentiful, flourish, thrive

abrasive *adj* 1 (rubbing a surface) caustic, chafing, coarse, corrosive, eroding, harsh, rough, sharp. 2 (of people) aggressive, biting, cutting, grating, harsh, hurtful, nasty, rough, sharp, unpleasant

abridge *v* abbreviate, compress, condense, cut, cut down, précis, prune, reduce, shorten, summarize, trim, truncate

abrupt *adj* 1 (rude) blunt, brisk, brusque, curt, direct, gruff, impolite, rough, rude, short, snappish, terse, uncivil, ungracious. 2 (sudden) hasty, hurried, instantaneous, quick, rapid, sharp, sudden, swift, unexpected, unforeseen

abscond *v* bolt, decamp, disappear, escape, flee, make a quick getaway, make off, run away, run for it, slip away, sneak away, steal away, take flight, take to your heels

absence *n* 1 (person missing) absenteeism, non-attendance, non-appearance, truancy; ***opp*** presence. 2 (thing missing) deficiency, lack, need, omission, privation, want

absent *adj* 1 (not present) away, elsewhere, gone, lacking, missing, not present, off, out, unavailable, wanting; ***opp*** present. 2 (not paying attention) absentminded, blank, day-dreaming, distracted, dreaming, dreamy, empty, far-away, inattentive, oblivious, preoccupied, unaware, unconscious, vacant, vague

absentminded *adj* absorbed, abstracted, bemused, distracted, dreaming, engrossed, forgetful, preoccupied, unaware, vague

absolute *adj* 1 (complete) complete, downright, entire, out-and-out, outright, perfect, pure, sheer, thorough, total, unmitigated, unqualified, utter. 2 (definite) categorical, certain, conclusive, decided, definite, positive, sure, undoubted, unequivocal, unquestionable. 3 (absolute power) authoritarian, autocratic, despotic, dictatorial, full, sovereign, supreme, unbounded, unconditional, unlimited, unqualified, unrestrained

absolutely *adv* 1 (completely) completely, entirely, fully, perfectly, totally, utterly, wholly. 2 (definitely) certainly, definitely, positively, surely, truly, undoubtedly, unequivocally, unquestionably, unreservedly, without a doubt

absolve *v* acquit, clear, discharge, exempt, excuse, exonerate, forgive, free, liberate, let off, pardon, release, reprieve, set free, vindicate

absorb *v* 1 (take in substance) assimilate, digest, draw in, draw up, mop up, soak up, sop up, suck up, take in. 2 (engross) captivate, engage, engross, enthrall, fascinate, immerse, involve, occupy, preoccupy, rivet. 3 (take over) appropriate, incorporate, swallow, take over

absorbed *adj* captivated, engrossed, fascinated, fixed, held, immersed, involved, lost, occupied, preoccupied, rapt, riveted, spellbound

absorbing *adj* captivating, fascinating, gripping, intriguing, riveting, spellbinding

abstain *v* 1 avoid, decline, deny yourself, desist, forbear, forgo, give up, go without, hold back, refrain, refuse, renounce, shun. 2 (not drink) be on the wagon *inf*, be teetotal, take the pledge

abstemious *adj* abstinent, austere, frugal, moderate, puritanical, self-denying, sober, sparing, temperate

abstract *adj* 1 abstruse, complex, conceptual, deep, general, intellectual, metaphysical, obscure, philosophical, theoretical. 2 (art) non-representational, nonrealistic, symbolic, unrealistic

abstract *n* digest, outline, précis, resume, summary, synopsis

abstract *v* detach, extract, isolate, remove, separate, take away, take out, withdraw

absurd *adj* crazy, daft *inf*, farcical, foolish, idiotic, illogical, inane, hare-brained, laughable, ludicrous, nonsensical, paradoxical, preposterous, ridiculous, risible, silly, stupid, surreal, zany

abundance *n* affluence, bountifulness, copiousness, heaps *inf*, loads *inf*, plentifulness, plenty, profusion, stacks *inf*, tons *inf*

abundant *adj* ample, bounteous, bountiful, copious, flourishing, full, generous, great, huge, large, lavish, liberal, luxuriant, overflowing, plentiful, profuse, rampant, rich, teeming

abuse *n* 1 (wrong use) corruption, misapplication, mishandling, misuse. 2 (cruel behavior) beating, cruelty, exploitation, harm, ill-treatment, maltreatment, mistreatment, oppression, torture, wrongdoing.

3 (insults) blame, censure, curses, cursing, defamation, expletives, insults, invective, obscenity, rebuke, reproach, revilement, slander, swearing, swear-words, upbraiding, vilification, vituperation

abuse *v* 1 (use sth wrongly) misapply, mishandle, misuse. 2 (behave cruelly to sb) batter, beat, harm, hurt, ill-treat, ill-use, injure, maltreat, manhandle, mistreat, molest, oppress, torture. 3 (insult) blame, call sb names *inf*, castigate, censure, criticize, curse, denigrate, disparage, insult, malign, rebuke, revile, scold, smear, swear, upbraid, vilify

abusive *adj* acrimonious, angry, censorious, critical, cruel, disparaging, hurtful, insulting, libelous, obscene, offensive, rude, scornful, slanderous

abysmal *adj* appalling, awful *inf*, bad, deplorable, dreadful, dire, lousy, poor, terrible

abyss *n* bottomless pit, chasm, depths, gulf, hole, pit, void

academic *adj* 1 (to do with education) educational, instructional, pedagogical, scholastic. 2 (of a person) bookish, brainy *inf*, cerebral, cultured, erudite, high-brow, intellectual, learned, literary, scholarly, studious, well-read. 3 (theoretical) abstract, conjectural, hypothetical, impractical, speculative, theoretical

academic *n* don, fellow, lecturer, pedagogue, professor, pupil, scholar, student, teacher, thinker, tutor

accelerate *v* 1 go faster, hurry, pick up speed, speed up; ***opp*** slow down. 2 (make sth go faster) advance, expedite, hasten, precipitate, speed up, spur on, stimulate

accent *n* 1 (way of talking) articulation, brogue, cadence, dialect, enunciation, inflection, intonation, modulation, pronunciation, tone. 2 (stress) accentuation, emphasis, force, stress. 3 (written mark) acute accent, cedilla, circumflex, diacritic, grave accent, mark, sign, tilde, umlaut

accept *v* 1 accede, acknowledge, acquiesce, admit, agree, approve, assume, buy *sl*, comply, concur, consent, cooperate, go along with, take on, undertake. 2 (receive) acquire, come by, gain, get, obtain, receive, secure, take. 3 (tolerate) put up with, stand, submit to, suffer, take, tolerate. 4 (believe) be convinced, believe, credit, have faith, trust

acceptable *adj* 1 (welcome) agreeable, delightful, desirable, gratifying, pleasing, welcome. 2 (satisfactory) adequate, admissible, all right, fair, moderate, OK, okay, passable, satisfactory, so-so *inf*, tolerable. 3 (of risks) admissible, allowable, bearable, supportable, tolerable

accepted *adj* acknowledged, admitted, agreed, approved, authorized, conventional, customary, normal, recognized, standard, time-honored, traditional, usual

access *n* accessibility, admission, admittance, entrance, entrée, entry, right of entry, way in

accessible *adj* 1 (able to be reached) available, exposed, get-at-able *inf*, handy, near, nearby, obtainable, on hand, open, reachable, within reach. **2** (able to be understood) comprehensible, fathomable, intelligible, understandable. **3** (of a person) affable, agreeable, approachable, available, cordial, easy-going, friendly, informal, obliging

accessory *n* **1** addition, add-on, adjunct, appendage, attachment, component, extra, supplement. **2** (crime) accomplice, assistant, associate, confederate, helper, partner

accident *n* **1** blunder, calamity, catastrophe, disaster, mishap, misfortune, tragedy. **2** (road accident) collision, crash, pile-up, smash. **3** (chance) chance, coincidence, fate, fluke *inf*, fortune, hazard, luck, serendipity, twist of fate

accidental *adj* arbitrary, chance, coincidental, fortuitous, fortunate, inadvertent, lucky, random, unexpected, unforeseen, unintentional, unplanned, unpremeditated, unwitting

accidentally *adv* by accident, by chance, by mistake, inadvertently, unintentionally, unwittingly

acclaim *v* announce, applaud, approve, celebrate, cheer, clap, commend, declare, exalt, extol, hail, honor, praise, proclaim, salute, welcome

acclimatize *v* accommodate, accustom, adapt, adjust, become seasoned, familiarize yourself, get used to, habituate yourself

accommodate *v* **1** (give a room to) board, cater for, entertain, house, lodge, put up, shelter, take in. **2** (help) aid, assist, help, lend a hand, meet sb's needs, oblige, do sb a favor. **3** (give sth to sb) equip, furnish, grant, oblige, provide, serve, supply. **4** (adapt) accustom, adapt, adjust, conform

accommodating *adj* agreeable, complaisant, compliant, considerate, cooperative, helpful, hospitable, kind, obliging, polite, unselfish, willing

accommodation *n* board, digs *inf*, home, housing, lodging, pied-à-terre, premises, quarters, shelter

accompany *v* **1** attend, chaperon, conduct, escort, go with, guide, tag along with *inf*, travel with. **2** (musically) provide backing for, play for, support

accomplice *n* accessory, ally, assistant, collaborator, colleague, confederate, conspirator, friend, helper, henchman, mate, right-hand man, sidekick *inf*

accomplish *v* achieve, attain, bring about, bring off, carry off, do, effect, execute, finish, fulfill, perform, produce, realize, succeed

accomplished *adj* able, adept, capable, competent, consummate, deft, expert, gifted, masterly, polished, practiced, proficient, skillful, skilled, talented

accomplishment *n* **1** (talent) ability, achievement, attainment, capability, proficiency, skill, talent. **2** (thing done) achievement, act, attainment, coup, deed, exploit, feat, success, triumph

accost *v* address, buttonhole *inf*, confront, grab, greet, hail, nab *inf*, salute, speak to

account *n* **1** (report) chronicle, description, explanation, history, portrayal, record, report, statement, story, tale. **2 accounts** balance, balance sheet, books, reckoning, tally

account for *v* explain, give reasons

for, justify

accountable *adj* answerable, liable, responsible

accrue *v* accumulate, amass, build up, collect, gather, grow, increase, mount up

accumulate *v* accrue, amass, assemble, build up, collect, gather, grow, hoard, increase, pile up, stash away *inf*, stockpile

accumulation *n* buildup, collection, heap, hoard, mass, pile, stack, stock, stockpile, store, supply

accuracy *n* authenticity, carefulness, correctness, exactness, faithfulness, meticulousness, precision, rightness, truth, truthfulness, validity, veracity; ***opp*** inaccuracy

accurate *adj* careful, correct, exact, faithful, literal, meticulous, precise, reliable, right, scrupulous, sound, spot on *inf*, strict, sure, true, truthful, valid; ***opp*** inaccurate

accusation *n* allegation, blame, charge, complaint, denouncement, indictment, recrimination, summons

accuse *v* arraign, blame, censure, charge, condemn, denounce, hold sb responsible, point the finger at *inf*

accustomed *adj* 1 (usual) common, customary, established, fixed, general, habitual, normal, ordinary, regular, routine, set, typical, usual.
2 accustomed to given to, in the habit of, seasoned, trained, used to

ache *n* discomfort, hurt, pain, pang, smarting, soreness, throb, twinge

ache *v* be painful, be sore, hurt, pound, smart, sting, throb

achieve *v* accomplish, acquire, arrive at, attain, bring about, carry out, do, earn, effect, engineer, execute, finish, fulfill, gain, get, manage, obtain, perform, procure, reach, realize, win

achievement *n* accomplishment, act, action, attainment, deed, exploit, feat

acid *adj* 1 (taste) acrid, biting, bitter, pungent, sharp, sour, tangy, tart, vinegary. 2 (remarks) acerbic, caustic, cutting, sarcastic, sharp, vitriolic

acknowledge *v* 1 (notice sb) address, greet, hail, notice, recognize, respond, say hello to *inf*. 2 (answer a letter) answer, reply, respond. 3 (admit sth) accept, admit, allow, concede, own, recognize

acknowledgment *n* acceptance, admission, agreement, answer, appreciation, notice, reaction, recognition, reply, response

acquaintance *n* 1 (person) associate, colleague, contact. 2 (knowledge) awareness, familiarity, knowledge, understanding

acquainted *adj* aware, conscious, familiar, informed, privy to

acquiesce *v* accept, agree, assent, bow, comply, concur, consent, go along with, submit, yield

acquire *v* amass, appropriate, buy, collect, come by, gain, gather, get, earn, obtain, pick up, procure, purchase, receive, win

acquisition *n* addition, buy, gain, possession, prize, property, purchase

acquit *v* absolve, clear, discharge, exonerate, find innocent, free, let off *inf*, liberate, reprieve, set free, vindicate

acrimonious *adj* acerbic, bad-tempered, bitter, caustic, cutting, harsh, hostile, hot-tempered, petulant, quarrelsome, rancorous, sarcastic, spiteful, unpleasant, vitriolic

act *n* **1** (thing done) accomplishment, achievement, action, deed, exploit, feat, move. **2** (law) bill, decree, edict, judgment, law, measure, ruling, statute. **3** (piece of entertainment) item, performance, routine, sketch, skit, show, turn. **4** (pretending) affectation, fake, feigning, front, pose, pretense, sham, show

act *v* **1** (do sth) be active, do sth, function, get involved, move, react, strike, take action, take steps. **2** (behave) behave, carry on. **3** (perform on stage) act out, appear as, be an actor, be an actress, dramatize, enact, mime, perform, play, play a part, portray, represent, take a part, tread the boards *inf*. **4** (have an effect) operate, take effect, work. **5** (pretend) affect, dissemble, fake, feign, pose, pretend, put on

acting *adj* deputy, fill-in *inf*, interim, pro tem, provisional, stopgap, substitute, surrogate, temporary, vice-

action *n* **1** accomplishment, achievement, act, deed, effort, endeavor, initiative, maneuver, measure, move, operation, step. **2** activity, energy, force, forcefulness, get-up-and-go *inf*, liveliness, spirit, vigor, vim, vitality. **3 the action** activity, bustle, drama, events, excitement, goings-on *inf*, happenings, incidents. **4** (war) battle, combat, conflict, fighting, warfare. **5** (legal) case, lawsuit, litigation, proceedings

activate *v* arouse, energize, excite, fire, galvanize, initiate, kick-start, mobilize, motivate, prod, prompt, rouse, set going, set off, start, stimulate, switch on, trigger, turn on

active *adj* **1** animated, bustling, busy, dynamic, energetic, enthusiastic, hyperactive, industrious, lively, mobile, nimble, on the go *inf*, on the move *inf*, quick, sprightly, spry, vibrant, vigorous, vivacious. **2** effective, effectual, functioning, in force, live, moving, operating, operative, potent, powerful, running, working

activist *n* campaigner, lobbyist, man of action, militant, woman of action

activity *n* **1** (things happening) action, bustle, comings and goings *inf*, commotion, flurry, hurly-burly, hustle and bustle, industry, life, movement, stir, toing and froing *inf*, tumult. **2** (sth that you do) enterprise, hobby, job, occupation, pastime, project, pursuit, scheme, task, undertaking, venture, work

actor, actress *n* artist, artiste, lead, leading man, leading woman, performer, play-actor, player, star, starlet, supporting actor, Thespian, tragedian, trouper

actual *adj* authentic, bona fide, confirmed, definite, genuine, indisputable, legitimate, physical, real, tangible, true, undeniable, verified, veritable

actually *adv* as a matter of fact, indeed, in fact, in truth, literally, really, truly

acute *adj* **1** alert, astute, canny, clever, discerning, incisive, intuitive, keen, observant, penetrating, perceptive, perspicacious, quick, sharp, smart. **2** (of senses) discerning, keen, sensitive, sharp; ***opp*** dull. **3** (very great) critical, dangerous, grave, great, pressing, serious, severe, urgent, vital. **4** (of pain) excruciating, fierce, intense, piercing, racking, sharp, stabbing, shooting, sudden, violent

adamant *adj* determined, firm, inflexible, intransigent, obdurate, resolute, stubborn, unbending, uncompromising, unyielding

adapt *v* **1** adjust, alter, change, convert, modify, remodel, reorganize, reshape, tailor, transform. **2** (get used to) accommodate, adjust, become conditioned, become hardened, conform, familiarize yourself, get used to, habituate yourself

adaptable *adj* adjustable, convertible, flexible, malleable, modifiable, pliant, resilient, variable, versatile

add *v* **1** attach, affix, append, combine, include, integrate, join, tack on *inf*. **2** (figures) add up, compute, count, reckon, total, tot up *inf*

addict *n* **1** (drug addict) abuser, dope-fiend *sl*, freak *inf*, junkie *inf*, user. **2** (sb who is keen on sth) buff *inf*, devotee, enthusiast, fan, follower, freak *inf*, nut *inf*

addicted *adj* dependent, hooked *inf*, obsessed

addiction *n* compulsion, craving, dependence, dependency, fixation, habit, obsession

addition *n* adjunct, appendage, appendix, attachment, augmentation, enlargement, extension, extra, gain, increase, increment, supplement

additional *adj* added, extra, fresh, further, more, new, other, supplementary

address *n* **1** (place where sb lives) abode, domicile, dwelling, home, house, location, lodging, pad *sl*, residence. **2** (speech) lecture, oration, sermon, speech, talk

address *v* **1** (give a speech) lecture, preach, sermonize, speak, spout *inf*, talk. **2** (talk to) buttonhole *inf*, engage sb in conversation, greet, hail, salute, speak to, talk to

adept *adj* able, accomplished, adroit, clever, dexterous, expert, practiced, proficient, skillful, skilled

adequate *adj* acceptable, ample, competent, enough, fair, mediocre, middling, OK, passable, presentable, reasonable, satisfactory, sufficient, suitable

adhere *v* attach, bind, bond, cling, fix, stick

adjacent *adj* abutting, adjoining, alongside, attached, bordering, close, near, neighboring, touching

adjoining *adj* abutting, adjacent, attached, bordering, connected, connecting, joining, next door, neighboring, touching

adjourn *v* break off, delay, interrupt, postpone, put off, suspend

adjournment *n* break, delay, interruption, pause, postponement, recess

adjudicate *v* arbitrate, decide, determine, give a ruling, judge, referee, settle, umpire

adjust *v* **1** adapt, alter, change, modify,

move, position, put right, rearrange, remodel, set, tailor, tune, vary. **2** (adjust to a situation) acclimatize, assimilate, become accustomed, conform, get used to, settle

adjustment *n* alteration, change, modification, rearrangement, rectification, repair, setting, tuning

ad-lib *v* extemporize, improvise, make up, speak impromptu, speak off the cuff

administration *n* **1** (managing sth) control, management, overseeing, running, supervision. **2** (government) executive, governing body, government, ministry, regime

administrative *adj* controlling, directorial, executive, governmental, management, managerial, organizational, regulatory, supervisory

admirable *adj* commendable, creditable, estimable, exemplary, fine, good, great, honorable, laudable, marvelous, praiseworthy, wonderful, worthy

admiration *n* adoration, appreciation, approval, awe, esteem, praise, regard, respect, veneration, wonder

admire *v* applaud, approve, carry a torch for *inf*, esteem, have a high opinion of, hero-worship, idolize, like, look up to, love, praise, respect, revere, sing the praises of, think highly of, value, venerate, wonder at, worship

admirer *n* **1** beau, boyfriend, girlfriend, lover, suitor, sweetheart. **2** aficionado, devotee, disciple, enthusiast, fan, follower, freak *inf*, supporter, worshipper

admissible *adj* acceptable, allowable, allowed, permissible, permitted, tolerated

admission *n* **1** (getting in) access, admittance, entrance, entry, right of entry, ticket. **2** (admitting sth) acceptance, acknowledgement, avowal, confession, declaration, profession, revelation; ***opp*** denial

admit *v* **1** (let in) accept, allow in, give access, give admission to, grant access, let in, permit entry, receive, take in. **2** (admit that sth is true) accept, acknowledge, allow, concede, confess, declare, own, own up, recognize, reveal; ***opp*** deny

adolescent *adj* boyish, childish, girlish, immature, juvenile, pubescent, puerile, teenage, young, youthful

adolescent *n* teenager, young man, young person, young woman, youngster, youth

adopt *v* **1** accept, approve, assume, back, champion, choose, endorse, espouse, follow, ratify, sanction, select, support, take on, take up. **2** (adopt a child) foster, take care of, take in

adorable *adj* appealing, attractive, captivating, charming, cute, darling, dear, delightful, gorgeous, lovable, sweet

adore *v* cherish, dote on, idolize, love, praise, revere, worship

adorn *v* beautify, bedeck, deck, decorate, embellish, enhance, festoon, garnish, ornament, trim

adult *adj* full-grown, full-size, fully developed, fully grown, grown-up, mature, of age; ***opp*** immature

adulterate *v* contaminate, debase, degrade, dilute, pollute, spoil, taint, thin, water down, weaken

adultery *n* a bit on the side, extramarital affair, infidelity, unfaithfulness

advance *n* breakthrough, development, finding, improvement, invention, progress

advance *v* **1** (move) come forward, forge ahead, gain ground, go ahead, go forward, make headway, move along, move forward, press on, proceed, push forward, push on *inf*; ***opp*** retreat. **2** (quicken) accelerate, expedite, forward, hasten, quicken, speed up, step up. **3** (develop) develop, evolve, flourish, grow, improve, progress, thrive. **4** (lend money) give, lend, loan, provide, supply on credit. **5** (put forward a theory) offer, propose, put forward, recommend, submit, suggest. **6** (help) assist, benefit, boost, facilitate, further, promote

advantage *n* **1** asset, benefit, blessing, boon, convenience, gain, good point, help. **2** (have an advantage over sb) edge, head start *inf*, lead, power, superiority, supremacy, upper hand

advantageous *adj* beneficial, constructive, convenient, helpful, invaluable, positive, profitable, useful, valuable, worthwhile

adventure *n* **1** (sth exciting that happens) escapade, experience, exploit, incident, occurrence. **2** (go out looking for adventure) danger, excitement, peril, risk, uncertainty

adventurous *adj* **1** bold, brave, courageous, daredevil, daring, intrepid; ***opp*** cautious. **2** challenging, dangerous, difficult, exciting, hazardous, precarious, perilous, risky

adversary *n* antagonist, competitor, enemy, foe, opponent, rival

adverse *adj* **1** (bad conditions) bad, disadvantageous, dreadful, inauspicious, unfavorable, unlucky; ***opp*** favorable. **2** (unkind) antagonistic, critical, derogatory, hostile, hurtful, negative, unfavorable, unfriendly, unkind, unsympathetic

adversity *n* affliction, bad luck, calamity, disaster, hardship, ill luck, misfortune, sorrow, suffering, tribulation, woe

advertise *v* **1** (try to sell sth) market, plug *inf*, promote, publicize, push *inf*, tout. **2** (tell people sth) advise, announce, broadcast, make known, notify, proclaim, publish

advertisement *n* advert *inf*, announcement, blurb *inf*, commercial, notice, poster, promotion, publicity, sign, small ad *inf*

advice *n* counsel, counseling, guidance, help, idea, opinion, recommendation, suggestion, tip, warning

advisable *adj* appropriate, desirable, expedient, judicious, politic, prudent, recommended, seemly, sensible, wise

advise *v* advocate, argue for/against caution, counsel, encourage, exhort, give guidance, guide, help, prescribe, recommend, suggest, urge, warn

adviser *n* confidant, confidante, consultant, coach, counselor, guide, mentor

advocate *n* backer, champion, fan *inf*, promoter, spokesman, spokesperson, spokeswoman, supporter

advocate *v* advise, argue for, back, campaign for, champion, endorse, plead for, promote, recommend, speak for, uphold, urge

affair *n* **1** activity, business, case, episode, happening, issue, matter, project, question, subject, thing, topic. **2** attachment, bit on the side *inf*, intrigue, involvement, liaison, love affair, relationship, romance

affect *v* **1** (have an effect on) act on, alter, change, have an effect on, have an impact on, impinge on, influence, sway, transform. **2** (upset) concern, distress, disturb, grieve, hit *inf*, move, stir, touch, trouble, upset. **3** (put on) adopt, assume, fake, feign, pretend, put on *inf*, simulate

affectation *n* airs, airs and graces, facade, insincerity, mannerism, pose, posturing, pretense, pretension, sham, show, simulation

affected *adj* **1** (not real) artificial, contrived, fake, feigned, insincere, put on *inf*, simulated, studied, unnatural; ***opp*** natural. **2** (of style) high-flown, ostentatious, pompous, precious, pretentious

affection *n* devotion, fondness, friendliness, friendship, liking, love, soft spot *inf*, tenderness, warmth

affectionate *adj* caring, fond, friendly, kind, loving, tender, warm, warm-hearted

affinity *n* closeness, compatibility, connection, kinship, likeness, liking, relationship, resemblance, similarity, sympathy

affirm *v* assert, attest, avow, certify, confirm, declare, say, state, swear, testify

afflict *v* bother, cause suffering to, distress, grieve, harm, hurt, plague, rack, torment, torture, trouble, try, vex, worry

affliction *n* distress, grief, hardship, misery, misfortune, ordeal, pain, scourge, sorrow, suffering, torment, trouble, woe, wretchedness

affluent *adj* **1** (people) flush *inf*, loaded *inf*, moneyed, opulent, prosperous, rich, wealthy, well-heeled *inf*, well-off, well-to-do; ***opp*** poor. **2** (life style) comfortable, expensive, lavish, luxurious, opulent, pampered, sumptuous

afford *v* **1** (be able to buy sth) find money for, have the means for, meet the expense of, pay for, spare the price of. **2** (be able to stand sth happening) bear, sustain, stand. **3** (give) bestow, furnish, give, offer, provide, supply

affront *n* aspersion, indignity, insult, outrage, provocation, slight, slur, snub, slap in the face *inf*

afraid *adj* alarmed, anxious, apprehensive, chicken *inf*, fearful, frightened, horror-struck, nervous, panic-stricken, scared, terrified, terror-stricken, timid, worried; ***opp*** fearless

age *n* **1** (period of history) date, days, epoch, era, generation, period, time. **2** (old age) advancing years, declining years, dotage, maturity, old age, senescence, senility, seniority. **3** (a long time) aeon, eternity, hours on end, lifetime, long time

age *v* become obsolete, decline, degenerate, deteriorate, get older, grow older, look older, mature, mellow, ripen, wither

aged *adj* ancient, antique, decrepit, elderly, getting on *inf*, gray, in your dotage, long in the tooth *inf*, old, past it *inf*, senile

agency *n* bureau, business, company, department, office, organization
agenda *n* list, plan, program, schedule, scheme, timetable
agent *n* **1** broker, delegate, emissary, envoy, executor, go-between, intermediary, middleman, negotiator, proxy, rep *inf*, representative, spokesman, spokeswoman. **2** mole *inf*, spook *inf*, spy
aggravate *v* **1** compound, exacerbate, heighten, inflame, intensify, make worse, worsen. **2** (*inf*) (annoy sb) annoy, exasperate, get on sb's nerves, hassle *inf*, irritate, provoke, rub sb the wrong way
aggression *n* attack, assault, hostility, invasion, offensive, onslaught, raid
aggressive *adj* argumentative, assertive, attacking, belligerent, forceful, hostile, provocative, pugnacious, pushy *inf*, quarrelsome, warlike
aggrieved *adj* distressed, hurt, ill-used, injured, peeved *inf*, piqued, resentful, unhappy, upset, wronged
agile *adj* acrobatic, active, fit, graceful, lithe, mobile, nimble, quick, sprightly, spry, supple
agility *n* activity, fitness, sprightliness, suppleness
agitated *adj* alarmed, anxious, confused, disconcerted, disturbed, excited, fazed, flustered, nervous, nervy, unnerved, unsettled, upset, worked up, worried; ***opp*** calm
agonize *v* deliberate, fret, labor, struggle, suffer, worry, wrestle
agonizing *adj* distressing, excruciating, harrowing, painful, racking, tormenting
agony *n* anguish, distress, hurt, misery, pain, suffering, torment, torture, woe
agree *v* **1** accept, acknowledge, acquiesce, admit, allow, concede, consent, grant, promise. **2** (two people agree) accord, be of the same mind, concur, get on, see eye to eye *inf*. **3** (figures) add up, match, tally
agreeable *adj* **1** amiable, charming, congenial, delightful, friendly, lovely, nice, pleasant, satisfying, to your liking; ***opp*** disagreeable. **2** (willing to do sth) accommodating, amenable, compliant, consenting, well-disposed, willing; ***opp*** unwilling
agreement *n* **1** accord, affinity, compatibility, concord, concurrence, congruity, consensus, harmony, unanimity, union. **2** (a deal) arrangement, bargain, contract, deal *inf*, pact, pledge, treaty, truce, understanding
aid *n* assistance, cooperation, encouragement, guidance, help, support
aid *v* abet, assist, benefit, encourage, facilitate, help, lend a hand, relieve, support
aim *n* ambition, aspiration, desire, dream, end, focus, goal, hope, intention, objective, plan, target, wish
aim *v* **1** (aim at sth) beam, direct, focus, line up, point, take aim, train, zero in. **2** (try to do sth) aspire, attempt, endeavor, hope, intend, resolve, seek, set your sights on, strive
air *n* **1** (space above earth) atmosphere, heavens, sky, space. **2** (breeze) blast, breath of air, breeze, draft, fresh air, oxygen, puff, ventilation, waft, wind. **3** (impression) appearance, aspect, atmosphere, aura, bearing, character,

characteristic, demeanor, effect, feeling, flavor, look, manner, mood, quality, tone, vibes *inf*. **4** (tune) melody, theme, tune, song

air *v* **1** (air an opinion) communicate, declare, disclose, divulge, express, give vent to, make known, reveal, say, state, tell, voice. **2** (air a room or clothes) dry, freshen, ventilate

alarm *n* **1** angst, anxiety, apprehension, consternation, dismay, fear, fright, horror, nervousness, panic, shock, terror, uneasiness, worry; ***opp*** calmness, composure. **2** bell, distress signal, fire alarm, flare, red alert, siren, warning

alarm *v* daunt, dismay, distress, frighten, make sb nervous, panic, perturb, scare, scare sb stiff *inf*, shake, terrify, trouble, unnerve, worry

alarmed *adj* anxious, apprehensive, concerned, dismayed, fearful, frightened, horrified, nervous, perturbed, shocked, terrified, uneasy, worried; ***opp*** calm, collected, composed, cool

alarming *adj*, daunting, distressing, disturbing, dreadful, frightening, scary, shocking, startling, ominous, terrifying, unnerving, worrying; ***opp*** reassuring

alcoholic *n* alky *slang*, dipsomaniac, drunk, drunkard, hard drinker, heavy drinker, wino *slang*

alert *adj* **1** (ready to respond) attentive, awake, eagle-eyed, on your guard, on your toes, prepared, ready, sharp-eyed, vigilant, wary, watchful, wide-awake; ***opp*** off guard. **2** (with a lively mind) bright, lively, on the ball *inf*, perceptive, quick, quick off the mark, sharp-witted, with your wits about you; ***opp*** slow. **3 alert to** alive to, aware of, clued up on *inf*, conscious of, sensitive to

alert *n* alarm, danger signal, emergency, flare, mayday, red-alert, signal, siren, warning

alert *v* advise, draw sb's attention to, notify, raise the alarm, tip sb off, warn

alibi *n* defense, excuse, explanation, justification, pretext, reason

alien *adj* extraterrestrial, foreign, outlandish, strange, unfamiliar, unnatural, weird; ***opp*** familiar

alight *v* dismount, disembark, get down, get off, get out. **2** land, come down, settle, perch

alight *adj* **1** (burning) aflame, blazing, burning, flaming, lit, on fire; ***opp*** burnt out, dead, extinguished, out. **2** (lit up) bright, glowing, illuminated, lit up, radiant, shining; ***opp*** dark, dead, dim, dull

alike *adj* cast in the same mold, comparable, duplicate, equivalent, identical, like, like peas in a pod, much the same, parallel, resembling, similar, the same, twin, uniform; ***opp*** different, dissimilar, unlike

alive *adj* **1** alive and kicking, animate, breathing, in the land of the living *inf*, living; ***opp*** dead, deceased, lifeless. **2** (continuing) continuing, current, in action, in existence, in operation, on-going; ***opp*** dead, defunct. **3** (lively, energetic) active, alert, energetic, full of life, lively, sprightly, vibrant, vigorous, vivacious; ***opp*** dead, dull, lifeless. **4** (alive to a problem) aware of, alert to, conscious of, sensitive to. **5** (alive with people, insects) bustling, crawling, heaving, swarming, teeming

allay *v* alleviate, assuage, calm, diminish, lessen, pacify, quell, reduce, relieve, soothe; ***opp*** exacerbate, make worse, inflame

allegation *n* accusation, assertion, charge, claim

allege *v* accuse, assert, aver, contend, claim, declare, insist, maintain, profess, say, state, suggest

allergic *adj* hypersensitive, sensitive, susceptible

allergy *n* allergic reaction, hypersensitivity, sensitivity, susceptibility

alleviate *v* allay, assuage, deaden, ease, lessen, mitigate, moderate, reduce, relieve, soothe; ***opp*** exacerbate, make worse

alliance *n* affiliation, agreement, association, coalition, confederation, federation, league, marriage, pact, partnership, relationship, treaty, union; ***opp*** divorce, separation

allied *adj* associated, connected, linked, related, similar

allocate *v* allot, assign, dish out *inf*, distribute, dole out *inf*, earmark, give, give out, grant, set aside, share out

allot *v* allocate, assign, dish out *inf*, distribute, dole out *inf*, earmark, give, give out, grant, set aside, share out

all-out *adj* complete, determined, full, maximum, no-holds-barred, thorough, total, unmitigated, utmost, wholehearted, wholesale

allow *v* **1** (permit) approve, authorize, give sb the go-ahead *inf*, give sb the green light, let, permit, sanction. **2** (allocate) allocate, allot, assign, give, grant, set aside. **3** (take sth into account) bear sth in mind, make allowances for, make provision for, take into account, take into consideration, provide for. **4** (accept that) accept, acknowledge, admit, concede, confess, grant

allowance *n* **1** grant, maintenance, payment, pocket money, remittance, stipend. **2** allocation, quota, ration, share

allude to *v* hint at, imply, mention, refer to, suggest, touch upon

allusion *n* hint, implication, insinuation, intimation, mention, reference, remark, suggestion

ally *n* accomplice, associate, collaborator, colleague, co-worker, friend, helper, partner in crime, sidekick; ***opp*** enemy

alone *adj*, *adv* **1** apart, by yourself, detached, isolated, lone, separate, solitary, unaccompanied, unattended. **2** (without help) by yourself, single-handed, solo, unassisted, unaided. **3** abandoned, deserted, forsaken, lonely. **4** (you alone, this alone) exclusively, just, nothing but, purely, only, simply, solely

aloof *adj* cold, cool, distant, haughty, inaccessible, indifferent, reserved, standoffish, unapproachable, unfriendly, unsociable; ***opp*** friendly, sociable, warm

aloud *adv* audibly, clearly, distinctly, out loud, plainly; ***opp*** silently, to yourself

alter *v* adapt, adjust, amend, change, convert, do sth differently, make sth different, modify, remodel, reshape, revise, transform, vary

alteration *n* adaptation, adjustment, amendment, change, conversion, difference, modification, revision, transformation, variation
alternate *adj* alternating, every other, every second, turn and turn about
alternate *v* follow in turn, intersperse, rotate, take turns, vary
alternative *n* choice, option, other, substitute
always *adv* 1 (every time) consistently, every time, invariably, without exception, without fail. 2 (continually) continually, constantly, incessantly, interminably, perpetually, repeatedly. 3 (forever) eternally, endlessly, forever, forever more
amalgamate *v* combine, fuse, incorporate, integrate, join, link, merge, mix, unify, unite; ***opp*** separate, split
amalgamation *n* combination, fusion, incorporation, integration, linking, joining, merger, unification; ***opp*** separation
amass *v* accumulate, assemble, collect, gather together, hoard, save, stash away *inf*, stockpile, store away
amaze *v* astonish, astound, bowl sb over *inf*, dumbfound, floor *inf*, leave sb speechless, shock, stagger, stun, surprise, take sb's breath away
amazed *adj* astonished, astounded, bowled over *inf*, dumbfounded, floored *inf*, left speechless, shocked, staggered, stunned, surprised, thunderstruck
amazement *n* astonishment, awe, surprise, shock, wonder
amazing *adj* 1 (very good) brilliant, excellent, fabulous, fantastic, great, incredible, marvelous, superb, terrific, tremendous, wonderful. 2 (surprising) astonishing, astounding, shocking, staggering, stunning, surprising
ambassador *n* attaché, consul, diplomat, emissary, envoy, representative
ambiguous *adj* cryptic, double-edged, enigmatic, equivocal, obscure, puzzling, unclear, vague, with a double meaning; ***opp*** clear, plain, obvious, unequivocal
ambition *n* 1 determination, drive, enterprise, get-up-and-go *inf*, motivation; ***opp*** apathy, indifference. 2 aim, aspiration, desire, dream, goal, objective
ambitious *adj* 1 determined, eager, enterprising, go-ahead, keen, motivated. 2 challenging, demanding, difficult
ambush *n* surprise attack, trap
ambush *v* attack, lie in wait for, trap, waylay
amenable *adj* accommodating, agreeable, flexible, open to persuasion, open to suggestion, responsive
amend *v* adjust, alter, change, correct, improve, modify, revise
amendment *n* addendum, adjustment, alteration, change, correction, improvement, modification, revision
amenity *n* facility, feature, resource, service
amiable *adj* affable, agreeable, approachable, endearing, engaging, friendly, genial, good-natured, kindly, likeable, pleasant, sociable
amicable *adj* amiable, civil, cordial, courteous, friendly, good-humored, good-natured, harmonious, peaceable
ammunition *n* ammo *inf*, armaments,

bombs, bullets, cartridges, explosives, grenades, missiles, munitions, pellets, rounds, shot

amnesty *n* dispensation, forgiveness, immunity, pardon, remission, reprieve

amorous *adj* adoring, ardent, doting, enamored, erotic, in love, lecherous, lovesick, loving, lustful, passionate, randy, sexual, sexy

amount *n* 1 degree, extent, magnitude, quantity, number, size, value, volume. 2 lot, measure, sum, sum total, total

amount to *v* 1 add up to, come to, equal, make, run to, total. 2 add up to, be equivalent to, be tantamount to, be the same as, mean

ample *adj* 1 adequate, enough, more than enough, plenty, sufficient. 2 abundant, generous, lavish, plentiful. 3 big, expansive, full, large, roomy, spacious, substantial, voluminous

amplify *v* 1 boost, intensify, increase, magnify, make louder, strengthen. 2 develop, elaborate on, enlarge on, expound, flesh out, go into details, say more about

amputate *v* chop off, cut off, lop off, remove, sever

amuse *v* 1 entertain, make sb laugh, make sb smile, regale sb with. 2 (find sth to do) entertain, keep sb happy, occupy

amused *adj* 1 entertained, tickled, tickled pink. 2 absorbed, engrossed, entertained, occupied

amusement *n* 1 delight, enjoyment, hilarity, laughter, pleasure. 2 diversion, entertainment, occupation, recreation

amusing *adj* comical, droll, funny, hilarious, humorous, ludicrous, ridiculous, witty

analogy *n* correlation, correspondence, parallel, resemblance, similarity

analysis *n* 1 examination, study, investigation, evaluation. 2 (of blood sample) test, breakdown

analytical *adj* detailed, diagnostic, methodical, investigative, systematic

analyze *v* 1 evaluate, examine, investigate, study, work out. 2 (analyze a blood sample) break down, do an analysis of, separate out, test

anarchic *adj* chaotic, disorderly, lawless, rebellious, uncontrolled, undisciplined, unpredictable; ***opp*** orderly

anarchy *n* anarchism, chaos, disorder, lawlessness, rebellion

ancestor *n* family, forbear, forefather, previous generation

ancient *adj* 1 (very old) aged, aging, antiquated, elderly, old. 2 (old-fashioned) antiquated, archaic, behind the times, dated, obsolete, old-fashioned, old hat, outmoded, out-of-date, passé; ***opp*** latest, modern, up-to-date. 3 (in early history) early, prehistoric, primeval, primitive, primordial

anecdote *n* account, cautionary tale, reminiscence, story, tale

angel *n* 1 cherub, seraph, archangel. 2 dear, gem, marvel, saint, star, treasure

anger *n* annoyance, exasperation, displeasure, fury, irritation, outrage, rage, temper

angle *n* 1 bend, corner, crook, fork, point. 2 approach, aspect, direction, point of view, position, perspective, side, slant, standpoint, viewpoint

angry *adj* annoyed, cross, mad, fuming, furious, heated, hopping mad, hot under the collar, incensed, infuriated, irate, irritated, mad, outraged, uptight *inf*; ***opp*** calm, laid-back

anguish *n* agony, distress, grief, heartbreak, misery, pain, sorrow, suffering, torment, trauma

animal *n* beast, creature, mammal

animated *adj* **1** enthusiastic, excited, lively, impassioned, passionate, vehement, vigorous. **2** cartoon, lifelike, moving

animosity *n* acrimony, antagonism, bad feeling, bitterness, conflict, disapproval, distaste, hatred, hostility, loathing, rancor, resentment

annihilate *v* decimate, defeat, destroy, eradicate, exterminate, extinguish, liquidate, take out, wipe out

announce *v* declare, give out, go public on, make known, publicize, publish, release, reveal, say

announcement *n* bulletin, communiqué, declaration, disclosure, notice, statement, press release, pronouncement, report, revelation

annoy *v* aggravate, anger, bother, exasperate, get on sb's nerves, get to sb *inf*, infuriate, hassle *inf*, irritate, madden, make sb mad, pester, vex

annoyance *n* **1** anger, displeasure, infuriation, irritation. **2** (nuisance) bind *inf*, bother, hassle *inf*, nuisance, pain *inf*, pain in the neck *inf*, pest, pig *inf*

annoyed *adj* angry, cross, exasperated, fuming, furious, hopping mad, hot under the collar, incensed, infuriated, irate, irritated, mad, outraged, uptight *inf*

annoying *adj* aggravating, exasperating, galling, infuriating, irritating, maddening, tiresome, troublesome

annual *adj* once a year, yearly

anomaly *n* abnormality, fluke *inf*, freak, inconsistency, irregularity, oddity, peculiarity, quirk, rarity, unusual occurrence

anonymous *adj* nameless, unassigned, unidentified, unknown, unsigned

answer *n* **1** reply, response, retort. **2** explanation, solution

answer *v* **1** acknowledge, react to, reply, respond to, retort. **2** find a solution to, resolve, solve. **3** (satisfy a need) fit the bill, fulfill, meet, satisfy, suit

answerable *adj* accountable, responsible

antagonistic *adj* against, aggressive, anti, disapproving, hostile, in opposition to, on the other side, opposed

antagonize *v* alienate, annoy, bother, estrange, infuriate, irritate, offend, pester, rub sb the wrong way *inf*

anthology *n* collected works, collection, compendium, compilation, selection

anticipate *v* assume, count on, expect, forecast, foresee, look forward to, predict, think of in advance

anticlimax *n* bathos, comedown, failure, fiasco, flop, disappointment, letdown, wash-out *inf*

antics *n* messing about, mischief, shenanigans, silliness, tomfoolery, tricks

antidote *n* antitoxin, antivenin, cure, remedy

antiquated *adj* **1** aged, ancient, elderly, old. **2** (old-fashioned) ancient, archaic, behind the times, dated, obsolete, old-fashioned, old hat, out-of-date, outmoded, passé; ***opp*** latest, modern, up-to-date

antique *adj* antiquarian, classic, old, veteran, vintage

antisocial *n* **1** (of people) cold, standoffish, unapproachable, unfriendly, unsociable, withdrawn; ***opp*** friendly, gregarious. **2** (of behavior) offensive, unacceptable

anxiety *adj* angst, apprehension, bother, concern, hang-up *inf*, misgiving, nervousness, stress, tension, trauma, uneasiness, worry

anxious *adj* apprehensive, bothered, concerned, nervous, on tenterhooks, stressed-out, tense, uneasy, worried; ***opp*** calm, cool, laid-back, relaxed

apartment *n* living quarters, penthouse, pied-à-terre, room, rooms, studio flat

apathetic *adj* indifferent, lazy, lethargic, listless, uninterested

apathy *n* indifference, laziness, lethargy, listlessness

apologetic *adj* contrite, repentant, remorseful, sorry

apologize *v* eat crow *inf*, eat humble pie *inf*, eat your words, grovel *inf*, make an apology, say sorry, take back what you said

apology *n* confession, excuse, expression of regret

appall *v* disgust, dismay, horrify, outrage, shock

appalled *adj* disgusted, dismayed, horrified, outraged, shocked

appalling *adj* atrocious, awful, disgusting, dreadful, foul, ghastly, grim, hideous, horrendous, horrible, horrific, horrifying, outrageous, really bad, shocking, terrible

apparatus *n* contraption, device, equipment, gear, tackle

apparent *adj* **1** clear, evident, noticeable, obvious, plain, visible, unmistakable. **2** ostensible, outward, seeming, superficial

apparently *adv* evidently, rumor has it that, seemingly

appeal *n* **1** application, call, entreaty, petition, plea, request, suit. **2** attraction, charm, fascination, interest

appeal *v* **1** ask for, beg for, call for, implore, petition for, put in a request for, request. **2** (seem attractive or interesting) attract, draw, fascinate, interest, please, tempt

appealing *adj* attractive, fascinating, interesting, pleasing, tempting

appear *v* **1** arrive, come into view, come out, come to light, crop up, emerge, materialize, pop up, show up, turn up. **2** look like, seem. **3** (in a show) perform, play, star, take part

appearance *n* **1** arrival, emergence, materialization. **2** air, aspect, demeanor, dress, expression, impression, look. **3** (illusion) front, guise, illusion, outward appearance, pretense, show

appease *v* calm down, mollify, pacify, placate, soften up, soothe

appendix *n* addendum, addition, adjunct, codicil, supplement

appetite *n* craving, desire, hunger, keenness, relish, stomach, will

appetizing *adj* delicious, inviting, mouth-watering, tasty

applaud *v* **1** clap, bring the house down, give a standing ovation to, give sb a big hand, give sb a round of applause, put your hands together for, raise the roof.

2 approve, commend, have great admiration for, praise, support, welcome

applause *n* clapping, curtain call, encore, ovation

applicable *adj* apposite, appropriate, pertinent, relevant, suitable, to the point, valid

applicant *n* candidate, claimant, interviewee

application *n* claim, form, petition, request

apply *v* 1 (be relevant) appertain, be applicable, be appropriate, be relevant, be valid, concern, involve, pertain, relate. 2 (use) carry out, employ, implement, make use of, put into operation, put into practice, use, utilize. 3 (apply medication, glue) cover with, put on, rub in, spread on

appoint *v* choose, elect, employ, name, nominate, put into office, select, sign, take on

appointment *n* 1 date, engagement, meeting, rendezvous. 2 job, office, position, post, role, situation, situation vacant

apportion *v* allocate, dish out *inf*, dispense, distribute, divide up, dole out *inf*, hand out, share out

appraise *v* assess, cast your eye over, evaluate, give sth the once-over *inf*, judge, review, size up *inf*

appreciable *adj* apparent, considerable, discernible, noticeable, significant, substantial

appreciate *v* 1 (be grateful) be appreciative of, be grateful for, be thankful for, value. 2 (appreciate art, good food) like, prize, rate, rate highly, respect, think a lot of, value. 3 (realize) accept, be aware of, be conscious of, realize, recognize, understand

appreciation *n* 1 gratitude, thanks. 2 (understanding) acceptance, awareness, realization, recognition, understanding

appreciative *adj* 1 grateful, pleased, thankful. 2 admiring, enthusiastic, supportive

apprehend *v* arrest, capture, detain, nail *inf*, nick *inf*, pick up *inf*, run in *inf*, take in, take in for questioning, take into custody

apprehension *n* 1 alarm, anxiety, butterflies in the stomach, concern, disquiet, doubt, fear, foreboding, misgiving, mistrust, nervousness, presentiment, the heebie-jeebies, the shakes, trepidation, unease, uneasiness, worry. 2 arrest, capture, detention, seizure. 3 appreciation, awareness, comprehension, conception, discernment, grasp, perception, realization, recognition, understanding

apprehensive *adj* afraid, alarmed, anxious, concerned, fearful, frightened, mistrustful, nervous, scared, uneasy, worried

approach *n* 1 (coming nearer) advance, advancing, advent, arrival, nearing. 2 (to a place) access road, avenue, drive, driveway, entrance, entry, passage, path, road, way. 3 (to a person) advances, appeal, application, invitation, overtures, proposal, proposition. 4 (to doing something) attitude, course, manner, means, method, mode, procedure, style, technique, way

approach *v* 1 advance, arrive, catch up,

come close, come near, come to, draw near, gain on, go towards, meet, move towards, near, reach. **2** (talk to sb) address, greet, hail, speak to, start talking to. **3** (ask sb for sth) appeal, apply, ask, broach the matter with, chat up *inf*, make advances, make a proposal, make overtures, proposition, solicit, sound out, suggest to. **4** (do sth) begin, commence, embark on, make a start on, set about, tackle, undertake. **5** approximate, be close to, be like, be near to, be comparable with, be similar to, come close to, come near to, compare with, resemble, suggest

approachable *adj* accessible, affable, amicable, easygoing, friendly, informal, kind, open, relaxed, sympathetic, understanding, well-disposed; ***opp*** aloof, severe, stuffy

appropriate *adj* apposite, apt, becoming, befitting, belonging, correct, fit, fitting, going well with, pertinent, proper, relevant, right, suitable, to the point, to the purpose, well-suited, well-timed

approval *n* **1** (liking) acceptance, acclaim, acclamation, admiration, applause, appreciation, approbation, commendation, esteem, favor, good opinion, high regard, liking, praise, regard, respect. **2** (agreement) acceptance, acquiescence, agreement, assent, authorization, blessing, confirmation, consent, endorsement, leave, mandate, permission, ratification, sanction, the go-ahead *inf*, the green light *inf*, the okay *inf*

approve *v* **1** acclaim, admire, applaud, appreciate, be pleased with, commend, esteem, favor, have a good/high opinion of, have a high regard for, like, praise, regard highly, respect, think highly of, think well of. **2** accept, agree to, authorize, consent to, endorse, give the go-ahead *inf*, give the green light to *inf*, give the nod to *inf*, give the OK to *inf*, give your backing to, give your blessing to, go along with, pass, permit, ratify, recommend, sanction, validate

approximate *adj* estimated, imprecise, inexact, loose, rough

approximately *adv* **1** about, around, close to, give or take *inf*, in the region of, just about, loosely, more or less, not far off, or so, roughly. **2** (with dates) circa

approximation *n* conjecture, ballpark figure *inf*, estimate, guess, guesstimate *inf*, guesswork, rough calculation, rough figure, rough idea

apt *adj* **1** applicable, appropriate, apposite, correct, felicitous, fitting, pertinent, proper, relevant, suitable, to the point. **2** able, adept, astute, bright, clever, competent, gifted, intelligent, quick, quick to learn, sharp, smart, talented. **3 apt to** given, inclined, liable, likely, of a mind, prone

aptitude *n* ability, faculty, flair, gift, knack, quickness, talent

arbitrary *adj* erratic, irrational, personal, random, subjective

arbitrate *v* adjudicate, decide, determine, judge, mediate, settle

arbitration *n* adjudication, decision, judgment, settlement

archaic *adj* ancient, behind the times, old, old-fashioned, outdated, outmoded

ardent *adj* eager, emotional, enthusiastic, fervent, intense, keen, passionate, zealous

arduous *adj* back-breaking, demanding, exhausting, grueling, hard, strenuous, taxing, tiring, uphill, wearying; ***opp*** easy

area *n* **1** district, environment, neighborhood, patch *inf*, quarter, region, sector, space, surroundings, territory, turf *sl*. **2** acreage, expanse, extent, measurements, size. **3** (of knowledge) branch, discipline, field, province, realm, sphere, world

arena *n* **1** amphitheater, field, ground, ring, stadium. **2** battleground, domain, realm, scene, sphere

argue *v* **1** be at each other's throats, bicker, clash, disagree, fall out *inf*, feud, fight, have a bone to pick with sb, have a row, pick a fight, quarrel, squabble, wrangle. **2** debate, discuss, dispute, reason, remonstrate. **3** assert, claim, insist, put forward, say, state, suggest

argument *n* **1** clash, controversy, difference of opinion, disagreement, discussion, dispute, feud, fight, quarrel, row, showdown, squabble, tiff. **2** assertion, case, claim, contention, hypothesis, idea, plea, proposition, reasoning, reasons, statement, view

argumentative *adj* awkward, belligerent, combative, contrary, difficult, opinionated, quarrelsome

arid *adj* desert, dried up, dry, parched, waterless

arise *v* **1** appear, begin, come up, come to light, crop up *inf*, emerge, happen, occur, originate. **2** be caused by, be the result of, come of, come out of, follow, proceed, result, spring from, stem from. **3** get out of bed, get to your feet, get up, stand up

aristocrat *n* grandee, lady, lord, nob *sl*, noble, nobleman, noblewoman, patrician, peer, peeress

aristocratic *adj* blue-blooded, elite, noble, posh *inf*, privileged, upper-class, titled, well-born

arm *n* **1** appendage, limb, upper limb. **2** branch, department, division, extension, offshoot, section, sector

arm *v* **1** equip, fit with, issue with, provide, supply. **2** (prepare yourself) brace, fortify, gird your loins, prepare, steel

armed *adj* **1** (carrying weapons) in arms, tooled up *slang*, under arms. **2** equipped, fortified, prepared, primed, provided, ready, strengthened,

armored *adj* armor-plated, bombproof, bulletproof, fortified, protected, strengthened

arms *n* **1** armaments, firearms, guns, ordnance, weaponry, weapons. **2** coat of arms, crest, emblem, escutcheon, insignia, shield

army *n* **1** armed forces, forces, land force, soldiers, the military, troops. **2** crowd, horde, host, mob, multitude, pack, swarm, throng

aroma *n* bouquet, fragrance, odor, perfume, scent, smell

aromatic *adj* fragrant, perfumed, piquant, pungent, scented, sweet-smelling

arouse *v* **1** awake, rouse, waken, wake up. **2** agitate, animate, egg on, enliven, excite, goad, incense, inflame, provoke, spur on, wind up *inf*. **3** cause, foster, induce, kindle, provoke, set off, sow the seeds of, stimulate, stir up, trigger, whip up. **4** excite, stimulate, turn on *inf*

arrange *v* **1** align, classify, grade, group, lay out, line up, order, organize, put in order, rank, set out, sort, sort out, tidy. **2** agree, decide, fix up, make a date, make an appointment, make arrangements, organize, pencil in, plan, schedule, settle on , set up. **3** (music) adapt, orchestrate, score, set to music

arrangement *n* **1** alignment, array, classification, design, display, formation, grouping, layout, line-up, order, organization, pattern, ranking, set-up, structure, system. **2** agreement, appointment, date, plan, preparations. **3** adaptation, interpretation, orchestration, score, version

array *n* arrangement, collection, display, formation, group, line-up, presentation

array *v* arrange, assemble, draw up, group, line up, order, organize, place, position, range, rank

arrival *n* **1** appearance, approach, beginning, coming, dawn, entrance, entry. **2** (a person) immigrant, newcomer, visitor

arrive *v* appear, come, come along, come on the scene, enter, get here/there, make an entrance, put in an appearance, reach, roll up *inf*, show up *inf*, turn up

arrogant *adj* big-headed, boastful, brash, cavalier, cocky *inf*, conceited, contemptuous, disdainful, egotistical, haughty, high-and-mighty, high-handed, lordly, overbearing, patronizing, pompous, proud, scornful, self-important, smug, superior, supercilious, vain

arrow *n* **1** bolt, dart, shaft. **2** indicator, marker, pointer

art *n* **1** knack, knowledge, method, skill, technique, trick. **2** aptitude, artistry, craft, craftsmanship, dexterity, expertise, ingenuity, proficiency, skillfulness, skill. **3** craft, culture, fine art, the arts

article *n* **1** artifact, item, object, piece, thing, unit. **2** (in a newspaper) account, essay, feature, item, piece, report, story, write up

articulate *v* enunciate, express, pronounce, say, speak, state, talk, utter, voice

articulate *adj* **1** (of a person) eloquent, expressive, fluent, having the gift of the gab *inf*, lucid, silver-tongued; ***opp*** inarticulate. **2** (of language) clear, coherent, comprehensible, eloquent, fluent, intelligible, lucid, understandable

artificial *adj* **1** man-made, manufactured, synthetic; ***opp*** real, natural. **2** bogus, counterfeit, ersatz, fake, false, imitation, mock, phony, pseudo-, sham, simulated; ***opp*** real, genuine. **3** affected, assumed, fake, false, feigned, forced, insincere, put on, unnatural, unreal; ***opp*** real, genuine

artistic *adj* **1** (of people) accomplished, creative, cultured, gifted, talented. **2** attractive, beautiful, decorative, elegant, esthetic, exquisite, graceful, ornamental, stylish, tasteful

artistry *n* **1** ability, brilliance, creativity, expertise, flair, gift, proficiency, skill, talent, virtuosity. **2** art, craftsmanship, style, workmanship

ascend *v* climb, climb up, float up, fly up,

gain height, go up, lift off, mount, move up, rise, scale, soar, take off; ***opp*** descend

ascent *n* climb, gradient, hill, incline, ramp, rise, slope; ***opp*** descent

ascertain *v* **1** determine, discover, establish, ferret out *inf*, find out, get to know, learn. **2** confirm, establish, identify, make certain, make sure, settle, verify

ascetic *adj* abstemious, abstinent, austere, celibate, chaste, frugal, harsh, hermit-like, plain, puritanical, restrained, rigorous, self-denying, self-disciplined, severe, simple, Spartan, strict, temperate

ascribe *v* assign, attribute, blame, charge, credit sb with, give credit to, impute, put down, refer, set down

ashamed *adj* apologetic, chastened, conscience-stricken, contrite, embarrassed, guilty, humiliated, mortified, red-faced, remorseful, repentant, shamefaced, sheepish, sorry, unable to look sb in the face

ask *v* **1** (ask questions) ask around, canvass, enquire, inquire, make inquiries, query, question. **2** (question sb) fire questions at, give sb the third degree *inf*, grill *inf*, interrogate, interview, pick sb's brains, put sb on the spot *inf*, question, quiz. **3** (ask for sth) appeal, apply, beg, beseech, call upon, claim, demand, implore, petition, plead, pray, request, seek, solicit. **4** invite, summon

asleep *adj* catnapping, comatose, dead to the world *inf*, dormant, dozing, having a nap, having a snooze, hibernating, out like a light, resting, sleeping, slumbering, snoozing; ***opp*** awake

aspect *n* **1** angle, face, feature, part, side, slant, standpoint, viewpoint. **2** air, appearance, attitude, bearing, demeanor, expression, look, manner, mien

aspiration *n* aim, ambition, desire, dream, goal, hankering, hope, intention, longing, objective, purpose, wish, yearning

aspire *v* aim, be ambitious, desire, dream of, hanker after *inf*, hope, long, pursue, seek, set your sights on, wish, yearn

aspiring *adj* ambitious, budding, eager, hopeful, potential, striving, wannabe *inf*, would-be

assail *v* **1** (attack) assault, attack, bombard, fall on, lay into, pelt, set about, set on. **2** (criticize) abuse, berate, blast, criticize, harangue, lambast, malign, pillory, put down, revile, vilify

assassin *n* contract killer, executioner, hit man *inf*, killer, murderer, slayer

assassinate *v* eliminate, execute, hit *slang*, kill, liquidate, murder, slay

assault *n* **1** act of aggression, attack, invasion, offensive, raid, strike. **2** assault and battery, mugging, rape

assault *v* **1** (a place) assail, attack, invade, storm. **2** (a person) attack, fly at *inf*, hit, lay into *inf*, set about *inf*, set upon, work over *inf*. **3** (sexually) grope, interfere with, molest, rape, sexually assault

assemble *v* **1** (of people) call together, come together, congregate, convene, flock, gather, get together, herd together, marshal, meet, muster, rally, round up. **2** (of things) amass, bring together, collect, gather, get together, pile up. **3** (put parts together) build, cobble together *inf*, connect, construct, erect, fabricate, fit together, join, make, piece together, put together, set up

assembly *n* **1** body, company, congregation, convention, council, crowd, flock, gathering, group, mass, meeting, throng. **2** accumulation, collection

assert *v* **1** affirm, allege, announce, argue, claim, contend, declare, insist, maintain, profess, say, state, stress. **2 assert yourself** act confidently, be assertive, exert your influence, insist, make your presence felt, put your foot down, stand firm, stand up for yourself, stick up for yourself, stick to your guns

assertion *n* affirmation, allegation, argument, claim, contention, declaration, insistence, pronouncement, statement

assertive *adj* **1** confident, decided, definite, emphatic, firm, forceful, insistent, positive, self-assured, strong-willed. **2** bossy, dogmatic, domineering, not backward in coming forward *inf*, opinionated, peremptory, pushy *inf*, stubborn, uncompromising

assess *v* appraise, calculate, determine, estimate, evaluate, gauge, judge, price, rate, reckon, size up *inf*, value, weigh up

assessment *n* appraisal, estimate, estimation, gauging, judgment, rating, valuation

asset *n* advantage, benefit, blessing, boon, godsend, help, resource, support

assets *n* capital, estate, funds, goods, means, money, possessions, property, reserves, resources, wealth

assign *v* **1** (to a job) appoint, choose, commission, designate, name, nominate, select. **2** (give) allocate, allot, consign, give, share out

assimilate *v* **1** (absorb) absorb, digest, incorporate, take in. **2** (fit in) adapt, become adjusted, become like, blend in, conform with, fit in

assist *v* **1** (help) aid, collaborate, cooperate with, help, help out, lend a hand, play a part, rally round *inf*, succor, support, work; ***opp*** hinder. **2** (make easier) expedite, facilitate, further, help, make easier; ***opp*** hinder

assistance *n* **1** a hand, a helping hand, aid, benefit, collaboration, cooperation, help, support; ***opp*** hindrance. **2** (financial) aid, backing, back-up, help, patronage, reinforcement, sponsorship, subsidy, support

assistant *n* **1** (colleague) accessory, accomplice, ally, associate, collaborator, colleague, comrade, helper, partner. **2** (subordinate) aide, auxiliary, deputy, helper, henchman, mate, personal assistant, right-hand man, right-hand woman, second in command, secretary, subordinate

associate *n* ally, colleague, companion, comrade, co-worker, follower, friend, mate, partner, workmate

associate *v* **1** (in the mind) connect, couple, link, relate, think of together, tie in, tie up *inf*. **2** (of people) ally yourself, band together, be friends, fraternize, gang up *inf*, get pally with *inf*, go round with, hang out *inf*, hobnob, join up, keep company, make friends, mingle, mix, pal up, socialize. **3** (of organizations) affiliate, ally, amalgamate, attach, combine, connect, join, link up, unite, yoke

association *n* **1** (group) alliance, band, body, brotherhood, cartel, clique, club, coalition, company, confederacy, confederation, cooperative, corporation, federation, firm, fraternity, gang, group, league, order, organization, partnership, society, syndicate, union. **2** (joining) amalgamation, blend, combination, connection, mixture, pairing, relation, tie in, union

assorted *adj* different, diverse, heterogeneous, miscellaneous, mixed, motley, multifarious, sundry, varied, various

assortment *n* choice, collection, hotchpotch, jumble, medley, miscellany, mishmash, mixed bag *inf*, mixture, range, selection, variety

assume *v* **1** believe, deduce, expect, fancy, guess, have a hunch *inf*, have an idea, imagine, infer, presume, presuppose, reckon, surmise, suspect, take for granted, think, understand. **2** (assume responsibility) accept, shoulder, take on, take up, take on yourself, undertake. **3** affect, feign, pretend, put on, simulate

assumption *n* belief, conjecture, expectation, guess, hunch *inf*, hypothesis, inference, premise, presumption, surmise, suspicion, theory

assurance *n* **1** certainty, confidence, coolness, self-assurance, self-confidence, nerve, poise. **2** guarantee, oath, pledge, promise, vow, word, word of honor. **3** insurance

assure *v* convince, give your word, guarantee, persuade, promise, reassure, soothe, swear, vow

astonish *v* amaze, astound, bewilder, daze, dazzle, shock, stagger, stun, stupefy, surprise, take your breath away

astonished *adj* amazed, astounded, dumbfounded, shocked, speechless, staggered, surprised, taken aback

astonishing *adj* amazing, astounding, bewildering, breathtaking, hard to believe, mind-boggling *inf*, shocking, striking, stunning, surprising

astonishment *n* amazement, bewilderment, confusion, disbelief, shock, surprise, wonder

astounding *adj* amazing, astonishing, awe-inspiring, bewildering, impressive, staggering, striking, surprising

astute *adj* artful, calculating, canny, clever, crafty, cunning, discerning, knowing, nobody's fool, perceptive, sharp, shrewd, wily

asylum *n* a haven, protection, refuge, safety, sanctuary, shelter

atheist *n* free-thinker, non-believer, unbeliever

athlete *n* **1** competitor, contender, fitness fanatic, fitness freak *inf*, gymnast, player, runner, sportsman, sportsperson, sportswoman. **2** (in particular events) decathlete, distance runner, heptathlete, high jumper, long jumper, sprinter, triple jumper

athletic *adj* active, brawny, energetic, fit, muscular, powerful, robust, sporty, strapping, strong, sturdy, well-built

atmosphere *n* **1** (around the earth) air, ionosphere, sky, stratosphere. **2** (general mood) air, ambience, aura, character, climate, feel, feeling, flavor, mood, quality, spirit, tone, vibes *inf*

atrocious *adj* abominable, appalling, awful, bad, dreadful, ghastly, grim, horrendous *inf*, horrible, horrific, terrible, unspeakable

atrocity *n* abomination, barbarity, bloodbath, brutality, crime against humanity, killing, massacre, outrage, slaughter, war crime

attach *v* add, add on, affix, append, connect, couple, fasten, fit, fix, hitch, hitch up, hook up, join, link, pin, secure, stick, tie; ***opp*** detach

attachment *n* 1 (thing attached) accessory, accoutrement, addition, add-on, adjunct, affix, extension. 2 (feeling) affection, affinity, bond, devotion, emotional tie, fondness, friendship, liking, love, loyalty, tenderness

attack *n* 1 act of aggression, assault, incursion, invasion, onslaught, raid, storming. 2 (against person) assault, beating, mugging, rape

attack *v* 1 invade, raid, storm. 2 (attack a person) assail, assault, beat, beat up, lay into, mug, rape

attacker *n* 1 aggressor, invader, raider. 2 assailant, mugger, rapist. 3 (in sport) forward, goalscorer, striker

attain *v* achieve, accomplish, acquire, arrive at, earn, fulfill, gain, get, obtain, reach, realize, secure, win

attempt *n* crack *inf*, effort, endeavor, go, shot, stab *inf*, try

attempt *v* aim, do your best, endeavor, give it a whirl *inf*, have a bash at *inf*, have a crack at *inf*, have a go at, have a shot at, have a stab at *inf*, make an effort, seek, set out, strive, take it upon yourself, try, undertake, venture

attend *v* 1 (be at a place) be present at, go to, visit. 2 (serve sb) accompany, escort, help, serve, wait on, wait on sb hand and foot. 3 **attend to** deal with, do, handle, see to, set your mind to

attendant *n* aide, assistant, butler, companion, equerry, escort, guard, helper, lackey, lady-in-waiting, minder *inf*, servant, squire, steward, usher, valet

attention *n* 1 attentiveness, awareness, concentration, consideration, heed, notice, observation, regard, scrutiny, thought. 2 (medical) care, therapy, treatment. 3 **attentions** attendance, civilities, compliments, concern, courtesies, gallantry, ministrations, respects

attentive *adj* 1 alert, all ears *inf*, awake, aware, heedful, listening, looking, mindful, observant, on guard, on the lookout, on your guard, vigilant, watchful, watching, wide awake; ***opp*** inattentive. 2 (considerate) chivalrous, concerned, conscientious, considerate, courteous, dancing attendance, gallant, gracious, kind, obliging, polite, respectful, thoughtful

attitude *n* 1 (mental) approach, disposition, feeling, opinion, outlook. 2 (physical) pose, position, posture

attract *v* allure, bewitch, captivate, charm, draw, enchant, entice, fascinate, interest, intrigue, pull, seduce, tempt; ***opp*** repel

attractive *adj* 1 (of person) alluring, beautiful, captivating, comely, enchanting, good-looking, gorgeous, handsome, lovely, pretty, seductive, sexy, striking, stunning; ***opp*** repulsive. **2** (of things, qualities) agreeable, appealing, charming, engaging, fascinating, fetching, interesting, inviting, nice, pleasant, pleasing, tempting

attribute *n* aspect, characteristic, facet, feature, hallmark, mark, property, quality, virtue

attribute *v* ascribe, assign, charge, credit, impute, lay at the door of, put down to

audacious *adj* adventurous, bold, brave, cheeky, intrepid, reckless, risky

audible *adj* clear, discernible, distinct, perceptible, within earshot, within hearing

audience *n* **1** assembly, congregation, crowd, fans, gallery, house, listeners, public, spectators, turnout, viewers. **2** (for particular views or publications) aficionados, devotees, fans, following, market, public. **3** (meeting with important person) consultation, reception, hearing, interview, meeting

audit *n* bookkeeping, check, examination, inspection, monitoring, review, scrutiny

audit *v* check, examine, go through, inspect, monitor, oversee, review, scrutinize

auspicious *adj* bright, encouraging, favorable, felicitous, rosy, good, hopeful, opportune, promising, propitious, timely; ***opp*** inauspicious

austere *adj* **1** (of place, conditions) hard, harsh, plain, spare, spartan. **2** (of person) abstemious, ascetic, forbidding, frugal, puritan, sober, solemn, stern, strict

austerity *n* belt-tightening, frugality, hardship, poverty, recession, straitened circumstances

authentic *adj* authenticated, bona fide, genuine, kosher *inf*, real, true

author *n* authoress, biographer, composer, creator, dramatist, essayist, journalist, librettist, lyricist, novelist, originator, playwright, poet, poetess, songwriter, writer

authoritarian *adj* autocratic, despotic, dictatorial, disciplinarian, dominant, dominating, domineering, imperious, strict, totalitarian, tyrannical, undemocratic

authority *n* **1** (power to command or decide) command, competence, control, charge, dominion, influence, jurisdiction, power, prerogative, remit, rule, sovereignty, supremacy. **2** (the right to do sth) authorization, clearance, license, permission, right, sanction, warrant. **3** (controlling body) board, body, executive, institution, local authority, regulator, regulatory body. **4** (person with special knowledge) expert, fount of knowledge, pundit, scholar, source, specialist, witness

authorize *v* agree to, allow, approve, assent to, clear, countenance, empower, enable, entitle, give the go-ahead to, give the green light to, let, license, permit, sanction

autocratic *adj* absolutist, authoritarian, despotic, dictatorial, dominant, dominating, domineering, imperious, tyrannical, undemocratic

automatic *adj* **1** (of machines) mechanical, electronic, remote-control; ***opp*** manual. **2** (happening by itself)

instinctive, involuntary, unconscious
autonomous *adj* free, independent, self-contained, self-governing, sovereign
available *adj* accessible, free, handy, in plentiful supply, obtainable, on hand, on tap *inf*, ready, to be had, to hand, vacant
avarice *n* acquisitiveness, greed, meanness, miserliness, parsimony, selfishness, stinginess *inf*
avenge *v* get back at, retaliate against, take vengeance on, take revenge on
avenue *n* **1** boulevard, path, road, street, thoroughfare. **2** choice, opening; opportunity, possibility
average *adj* everyday, medium, middle-sized, middling, moderate, normal, ordinary, run-of-the-mill, standard, typical, unexceptional, usual
average *n* median, mean, midpoint, norm, standard
averse *adj* antipathetic, disinclined, hostile, ill-disposed, loath; opposed, reluctant, unfavorable, unwilling
aversion *n* abhorrence, animosity, antipathy, detestation, disinclination, dislike, disgust, distaste, hate, hatred, horror, hostility, loathing, opposition, reluctance, repugnance, repulsion, revulsion, unwillingness
avert *v* avoid, prevent, stop, turn aside, turn away
avid *adj* eager, enthusiastic, greedy, hungry, keen, thirsty
avoid *v* **1** elude, escape, evade, keep away from, shirk, shun, stay away from. **2** (not do sth) abstain from, get out of, refrain from
avoidable *adj* escapable, preventable, unnecessary
await *v* anticipate, expect, wait for
awake *adj* alert, aware, compos mentis *inf*, conscious, vigilant, wide awake; ***opp*** asleep
awaken *v* rouse, wake, wake up
award *n* **1** (for achievement) decoration, presentation, prize, reward, trophy. **2** (legally or officially granted) adjudication, compensation, damages, grant, order
award *v* accord, allot, assign, bestow, confer, endow, give, grant, hand out, present
aware *adj* **1** attentive, alert, awake, conscious. **2 aware of** able to recognize, alive to, conscious of, conversant with, familiar with, mindful of, wise to
awareness *n* cognition, cognizance, consciousness, perception, recognition
awe *n* admiration, adoration, amazement, fear, wonder
awesome *adj* amazing, astonishing, awe-inspiring, incredible, magnificent, marvelous, stupendous, unbelievable, wonderful
awful *adj* abominable, appalling, atrocious, bad, deplorable, devastating, disgusting, dire, dreadful, frightful, ghastly, grim, hideous, horrendous *inf*, horrible, horrific, shocking, sickening, terrible, unspeakable; ***opp*** great, terrific, wonderful
awfully *adj* dreadfully, extremely, frightfully, horrendously *inf*, incredibly, really, terribly, unspeakably, very
awkward *adj* **1** (of a person) clumsy, embarrassed, ill-at-ease, maladroit, nervous, uncoordinated, ungainly. **2** (of a problem, situation) difficult,

embarrassing, thorny, tricky

awkwardness *n* clumsiness, embarrassment, nervousness

ax *v* abolish, dismiss, do away with, fire, get rid of, give sb the boot *inf*, kick out *inf*, make redundant, remove, repeal, sack

baby *n* babe, babe in arms, child, infant, neonate *tech*, newborn, tiny tot, toddler, tot, young child

back *n* **1** end, hind quarters, rear, rear end, reverse, stern, tail; ***opp*** front. **2** backbone, spine

back *v* **1** (give or express support for) advocate, agree with, approve, approve of, back up, bet on, champion, encourage, endorse, favor, finance, invest in, sanction, second, side with, sponsor, subsidize, support, underwrite. **2** (move backwards) back away, back up, backtrack, retreat, reverse. **3 back down** back off, backpedal, backtrack, climb down, concede, give in, give way, retreat, submit, surrender, withdraw, yield. **4 back out of** abandon, back away from, cancel, chicken out of *inf*, get cold feet about, go back on, have second thoughts about, renege on, welsh on, withdraw from. **5 back up** (back up a statement) confirm, corroborate, prove, substantiate, support

backer *n* advocate, benefactor, champion, investor, patron, promoter, punter, sponsor, supporter, underwriter

backfire *v* blow up in sb's face, boomerang, fail, go wrong, miscarry, misfire, rebound

background *n* **1** (of a picture) backdrop, decor, distance, hinterland, middle distance, scenery. **2** (of a person) breeding, credentials, culture, education, experience, life history, origins, past, qualifications, upbringing. **3** (of events, situation) circumstances, context, events leading up to, history

backing *n* agreement, aid, approval, assistance, cooperation, endorsement, finance, help, helping hand, encouragement, sponsorship, support

backward *adj* **1** primitive, uncivilized, underdeveloped, undeveloped, unsophisticated. **2** (of a person) educationally subnormal, mentally retarded, retarded, slow, subnormal, with special needs

bad *adj* **1** (of low quality) appalling, atrocious, awful, defective, deficient, dreadful, faulty, imperfect, inferior, lousy *inf*, low-quality, mediocre, poor, rotten, substandard, terrible, useless, worthless; ***opp*** good. **2** (not what is wanted or needed) adverse, difficult, disagreeable, distressing, grim, inadequate, inappropriate, incorrect, nasty, unacceptable, uncomfortable, undesirable, unfavorable, unfortunate, unlucky, unnecessary, unpleasant, unsuitable, unwanted, unsatisfactory, unwelcome, wrong; ***opp*** good. **3** (bad accident or illness) acute, chronic, critical, disastrous, dreadful, grave, serious, severe, terrible. **4** (causing damage or harm) damaging, dangerous, deleterious, destructive, detrimental, harmful, injurious, noxious, poisonous, ruinous, unhealthy; ***opp*** good. **5** (of a person) badly behaved, base, corrupt, criminal, crooked, delinquent, depraved, dishonest, dishonorable, evil, immoral, nasty *inf*, naughty, sinful, unruly, unscrupulous, vile, villainous, wicked; ***opp*** good. **6** (of food) contaminated, decaying, festering, moldy, off, putrescent, putrid, rancid, rotten, sour, spoiled, tainted. **7 not bad** acceptable, adequate, all right, average, fair, moderate, OK *inf*, passable, satisfactory, so-so *inf*, tolerable

baffle *v* bamboozle, bewilder, confound, confuse, flummox, have sb scratching his head, mystify, nonplus, perplex, puzzle, stump

bag *n* basket, case, container, handbag, holdall, rucksack, sack, satchel, shopping bag, shoulder bag

baggage *n* bags, belongings, cases, gear, kit, luggage, suitcases, things

balance *n* **1** (personal quality) composure, equanimity, even-handedness, fairness, level-headedness, objectivity, poise, stability, steadiness. **2** (between different factors or interests) balance of power, correspondence, due proportion, equality, equilibrium, equity, parity, symmetry. **3** (machine) scales, weighing machine. **4** (sum of money) difference, outstanding amount, remainder, residue, rest; ***opp*** deposit. **5 in the balance** at a crisis, at a crossroads, at a turning point, critical, finely balanced, uncertain, undecided. **6 on balance** all in all, all things considered, on the whole, taking everything into account, taking everything into consideration, when all's said and done

balance *v* **1** (place carefully) adjust, perch, place/put carefully, stabilize, steady. **2** (balance different factors or interests) counterbalance, equalize, give equal weight to, offset, weigh, weigh up. **3** (of figures, amounts) add up, balance out, balance up, correspond, match

balanced *adj* evenhanded, fair, objective, unbiased

bald *adj* bald as a coot, bald-headed, bare, hairless, receding, thin on top, with thinning hair

ballot *n* election, franchise, plebiscite, poll, polling, referendum, vote, voting

ban *n* boycott, censorship, embargo, moratorium, prohibition, suppression, taboo, veto

ban *v* abolish, banish, bar, criminalize, debar, end, exclude, forbid, make illegal, outlaw, prohibit, proscribe, put an end to, put a stop to, stop, suppress, veto

banal *adj* bland, clichéd, common, commonplace, everyday, hackneyed, humdrum, meaningless, ordinary, pedestrian, stale, tired, trite, trivial, vapid

band *n* **1** (of people) bevy, brigade, bunch, clique, company, crew *inf*, gang, group, mob, pack, set, troop. **2** (of musicians) brass band, combo *inf*, ensemble, group, orchestra. **3** (narrow piece) bar, line, ribbon, sash, streak, strip, stripe

bandit *n* brigand, highwayman, outlaw, robber, thief

bang *n* boom, detonation, explosion, gunshot, thud, thump

banish *v* **1** (banish a person) ban, bar, boot out *inf*, cast out, deport, drive away, eject, evict, exclude, exile, expel, kick out *inf*, throw out. **2** (banish a feeling) dismiss, dispel, get rid of, shake off

bank *n* **1** (where money is kept) building society, depository, financial institution, investment bank, merchant bank, reserve, savings and loan association, savings bank. **2** (of a river) embankment, riverside, shore, verge, waterside, waterfront, water's edge

bank *v* **1** (put money in an account) deposit, pay in

bank on count on, depend on, expect, rely on

bankrupt *adj* broke *inf*, bust, cleaned out *inf*, failed, in liquidation *tech*, insolvent *tech*, penniless, poor, ruined, without a penny to your name

banner *n* colors, flag, pennant, placard, standard, streamer

banquet *n* blow-out *inf*, dinner, dinner party, feast, formal dinner, repast

banter *n* chaff, gossip, idle chat, joking, joshing, patter, small talk, talk, teasing

baptize *v* christen, name

bar *n* **1** (piece of metal) barrier, bolt, ingot, rail, rod. **2** (for drinking) club, lounge, lounge bar, pub, public bar, saloon. **3** (sth that prevents progress) barrier, glass ceiling, hindrance, obstacle

bar *v* ban, exclude, forbid, keep out, prevent, prohibit, rule out

barbarian *n* boor, brute, hooligan, lout, monster, ruffian, savage

barbaric *adj* barbarous, brutal, cruel, primitive, savage, uncivilized, uncouth, wild

bare *adj* **1** (without clothes) exposed, in the buff *inf*, in the nude, in your birthday suit *inf*, naked, nude, stark naked, stripped, unclothed, undressed, with nothing on; ***opp*** clothed, dressed. **2** (of a room) austere, empty, plain, spare, unfurnished, vacant. **3** (of landscape) austere, barren, bleak, desolate, empty, exposed, exposed to the elements, featureless, open, scanty, stark, treeless

barefaced *adj* audacious, blatant, bold, brash, brazen, glaring, impudent, open, patent, shameless, undisguised

barely *adv* by the skin of your teeth, hardly, just, only just, scarcely

bargain *n* **1** agreement, arrangement, contract, deal, negotiation, pact, pledge, transaction, treaty, understanding. **2** (sth cheap) discount, good buy, good deal, good value, give-away, reduction. **3 into the bargain** also, as well, besides, in addition, moreover

bargain *v* agree, negotiate, transact

bark *v* bay, growl, howl, snarl, woof, yap, yelp

barrage *n* **1** (of gunfire) battery, bombardment, salvo, shelling, volley, wall of fire. **2** (of abuse, criticism) burst, hail, onslaught, storm, stream, torrent

barren *adj* **1** childless, infertile, sterile; ***opp*** fertile. **2** arid, desert, desolate, infertile, unfruitful, unproductive, waste; ***opp*** fertile

barricade *n* bar, barrier, blockade, bulwark, obstacle, obstruction, palisade, rampart, roadblock, stockade

barrier *n* **1** bar, barricade, blockade, fence, obstacle, obstruction, railing, roadblock, wall. **2** (to achieving sth) check, handicap, hurdle, impediment, limitation, obstacle, restraint, restriction, stumbling block

base *adj* contemptible, corrupt, debased, depraved, despicable, dishonorable, disreputable, dissolute, evil, foul, ignoble, immoral, low, reprobate, scandalous, shameful, sinful, sordid, unprincipled, vile, villainous, vulgar, wicked

base *n* **1** bed, bottom, foot, foundation, pedestal, rest, stand, support; ***opp*** top. **2** basis, core, essence, essentials, heart, key, origin, principal, root, source. **3** camp, headquarters, post, settlement, starting point, station

base *v* build, construct, derive, establish, fasten, form, found, ground, hinge, rest, root

bash *n* attempt, crack *inf*, go *inf*, shot *inf*, stab *inf*, try

bash *v* bang, belt *inf*, biff *inf*, crash, deck *inf*, hit, punch, smash, sock *inf* , strike, wallop *inf*, whack

basic *adj* central, elementary, essential, fundamental, indispensable, intrinsic, key, necessary, primary, rudimentary, underlying, vital; ***opp*** peripheral

basically *adv* at bottom, at heart, essentially, firstly, for the most part, fundamentally, inherently, in the main, intrinsically, mainly, mostly, primarily

basics *n* brass tacks *inf*, core, essentials, facts, fundamentals, hard facts, nitty-gritty *inf*, nuts and bolts, practicalities, principles, realities, rudiments

basis *n* base, footing, foundation, grounds, reasoning, support

bask *v* **1** laze, lie, loll, lounge, relax, sunbathe. **2** delight, rejoice, revel, savor, take pleasure

batch *n* accumulation, amount, collection, crowd, group, lot, mass, pack, quantity, set

bath *n* dip, douche, shower, soak, soaping, wash

bathe *v* clean, cleanse, immerse, moisten, rinse, soak, steep, wash, wet

batter *v* **1** (of a person) abuse, assault, bash *inf*, beat, clobber *inf*, hit, smack, whack. **2** (of the weather) buffet, lash, pelt, pound, pummel, smash, thrash, wallop *inf*, whack *inf*

battle *n* action, affray, attack, campaign, clash, combat, conflict, confrontation, contest, encounter, engagement, fight, fray, hostilities, scuffle, skirmish, struggle, tussle, war, warfare

battle *v* **1** contend, fight, strive, struggle. **2** (argue) argue, bicker, disagree, dispute, feud, fight, have a row, quarrel, row *inf*, squabble, wrangle

bawdy *adj* blue, coarse, crude, dirty, disgusting, filthy, gross, indecent, indelicate, lascivious, lecherous, lewd, licentious, naughty, obscene, pornographic, prurient, racy, risqué, rude, smutty, salacious, steamy *inf*, suggestive, ribald, vulgar

bawl *v* **1** bellow, call, cry, howl, roar, scream, screech, shout, yell. **2** blubber, cry, snivel, sob, squall, wail, weep

bay *n* 1 cove, gulf, harbor, inlet, sound. 2 alcove, niche, nook, opening, recess

beach *n* coast, coastline, sand, seashore, seaside, water's edge

beacon *n* beam, bonfire, flare, lighthouse, sign, signal, warning light, watchtower

beam *n* 1 board, girder, joist, plank, rafter, support, timber. 2 flash, gleam, glimmer, glint, glow, ray, shaft, streak, stream

beam *v* 1 emit, glare, gleam, glitter, glow, radiate, shine. 2 grin, smile

bear *v* 1 bring, carry, convey, fetch, move, take, tote, transport. 2 endure, put up with, stand, stomach, suffer, tolerate, undergo. 3 (bear a child, bear fruit) beget, breed, bring forth, engender, give birth to, produce, yield

bearable *adj* acceptable, endurable, manageable, passable, sufferable, sustainable, tolerable; ***opp*** unbearable

bearing *n* 1 (sb's bearing) air, aspect, attitude, behavior, demeanor, manner, mien, posture. 2 (a ship's bearing) course, direction. 3 (have a bearing on) connection, pertinence, relation, relevance

bearings *n* course, direction, location, orientation, position, situation, track, way, whereabouts

beast *n* 1 (animal) animal, brute, creature, monster. 2 (person) animal, barbarian, brute, fiend, monster, ogre, sadist, savage

beat *v* 1 bang, batter, buffet, hammer, hit, knock, pound, pummel, strike, thrash. 2 (beat up a person) abuse, assault, bash *inf*, beat up, clobber *inf*, hit, knock about *inf*, lay into, punch, rough up *inf*, slap, smack, strike, thrash, thump, wallop *inf*, work over *inf*. 3 conquer, defeat, lick *inf*, master, outdo, overcome, quash, rout, subdue, surpass, thrash *inf*, vanquish, walk all over *inf*

beautiful *adj* alluring, appealing, attractive, becoming, charming, comely, delightful, elegant, exquisite, fair, fine, glamorous, good-looking, gorgeous, graceful, handsome, lovely, pleasant, pleasing, pretty, radiant, ravishing, seemly, stunning; ***opp*** ugly

beauty *n* 1 allure, appeal, attractiveness, bloom, charm, elegance, fairness, glamour, good looks, grace, handsomeness, loveliness, prettiness, seemliness; ***opp*** ugliness. 2 belle, charmer, femme fatale, goddess, knockout *inf*, seductress, stunner *inf*

beckon *v* bid, call, gesticulate, gesture, motion, nod, signal, summon, wave

becoming *adj* attractive, comely, chic, elegant, flattering, graceful, handsome, lovely, neat, pretty, stylish, tasteful; ***opp*** ugly

bedlam *n* chaos, clamor, commotion, disarray, disorder, furor, hubbub, hullabaloo, pandemonium, tumult, turmoil, uproar; ***opp*** calm

bedraggled *adj* dirty, disheveled, disordered, drenched, messy, muddied, muddy, soaking, sodden, soiled, stained, sullied, tatty, unkempt, untidy; ***opp*** tidy

befall *v* arise, chance, come about, crop up, ensue, follow, happen, materialize, occur, result, take place, transpire

beg *v* 1 ask for, beseech, entreat, implore, importune, plead, request. 2 (for money) cadge *inf*, scrounge, sponge *inf*

beggar *n* down-and-out, mendicant,

scrounger *inf*, sponger *inf*, tramp, vagrant

begin *v* commence, get going, get the ball rolling, get the show on the road, inaugurate, initiate, instigate, institute, kick off, set about, set in motion, set on foot, start; ***opp*** end, finish

beginner *n* amateur, apprentice, fledgling, fresher, freshman, learner, new recruit, novice, probationer, rookie, trainee; ***opp*** expert

beginning *n* **1** (earliest time) birth, commencement, dawn, emergence, inauguration, inception, initiation, onset, outset, start, starting point; ***opp*** end, finish. **2** (of a book) foreword, introduction, opening, preface, prelude, start, starting point; ***opp*** end

begrudge *v* be jealous, envy, grudge, not be happy about, resent

behave *v* **1** act, function, operate, perform, work. **2** acquit yourself well, be good, behave yourself, be on your best behavior, mind your manners; ***opp*** misbehave

behavior *n* **1** actions, conduct, demeanor, deportment, manner, manners, ways. **2** (of a machine) action, functioning, operation, performance, reaction, response

being *n* animal, beast, body, creature, entity, human, human being, individual, living thing, man, mortal, person

belief *n* **1** conviction, feeling, impression, judgment, notion, opinion, persuasion, way of thinking, theory, thinking, view, viewpoint. **2** credo, creed, doctrine, dogma, faith, ideology, teaching

believable *adj* acceptable, conceivable, credible, imaginable, likely, not beyond the realms of possibility, plausible, possible, probable, reliable, trustworthy; ***opp*** implausible

believe *v* **1** accept, be certain of, be convinced of, buy *inf*, fall for *inf*, have faith in, swallow *inf*, swear by, trust. **2** assume, be of the opinion that, consider, gather, guess, have an opinion, imagine, judge, postulate, presume, reckon, speculate, suppose, think, understand

believer *n* adherent, devotee, disciple, follower, supporter

bellow *v* bawl, call, clamor, cry, holler, howl, roar, scream, screech, shout, shriek, yell

belong *v* **1 belong to** be at the disposal of, be held by, be owned by, be the property of. **2 belong to** be affiliated with, be allied with, be a member of, be associated with, be included in. **3** attach to, be connected with, be part of, fit, go with, relate to, relevant to

belongings *n* effects, gear, goods, property, possessions, stuff, things

beloved *adj* adored, cherished, darling, dear, dearest, idolized, loved, precious, prized, sweet, treasured, worshipped

belt *n* band, cummerbund, girdle, girth, sash, strap, waistband

bench *n* **1** form, pew, seat. **2** counter, table, workbench, worktable. **3** (in a court) bar, court, courtroom, judge, judiciary, magistrate, tribunal

bend *n* angle, arc, corner, crook, curve, hook, loop, spiral, turn, twist

bend *v* **1** arch, bow, buckle, contort, crook, curl, curve, flex, turn, twist, warp. **2** (a road bends) curve, deviate, diverge, go round, swerve, turn, twist, veer.

3 (a person bends) crouch, hunch, lean, stoop

beneficial *adj* advantageous, favorable, good, helpful, profitable, useful, valuable; ***opp*** harmful

benefit *n* advantage, aid, asset, assistance, blessing, boon, favor, fringe benefit, gain, good, help, perk, profit; ***opp*** disadvantage

benefit *v* advance, advantage, aid, assist, avail, be an advantage to, better, contribute to, enhance, further, help, improve, profit, promote, serve; ***opp*** harm

benevolent *adj* altruistic, amiable, caring, compassionate, considerate, friendly, generous, helpful, humane, kind, kind-hearted, magnanimous, obliging, sympathetic, thoughtful, warm-hearted; ***opp*** unkind

benign *adj* **1** amiable, benevolent, cordial, friendly, generous, genial, gentle, kind, sympathetic; ***opp*** unkind. **2** (of a tumor) curable, harmless, innocent, nondangerous, nonmalignant, treatable; ***opp*** malignant

bent *adj* **1** angled, arched, bowed, contorted, crooked, curved, hunched, stooped, twisted, warped; ***opp*** straight. **2 bent on** determined, insistent, resolved, set. **3** ability, aptitude, capacity, flair, forte, gift, inclination, knack, leaning, penchant, predisposition, proclivity, talent

bequeath *v* bestow, cede, commit, consign, endow, entrust, give, grant, hand down, leave to, pass on, will

bequest *n* estate, gift, heritage, inheritance, legacy, settlement, trust

bereavement *n* death, deprivation, loss, passing

berserk *adj* crazed, crazy, frenzied, hysterical, insane, mad, manic, rabid, raging, raving, uncontrollable, violent, wild; ***opp*** calm

berth *n* **1** bed, bunk, sleeping accommodation. **2** anchorage, dock, harbor, mooring, pier, port, quay, wharf

besiege *v* beleaguer, beset, blockade, encircle, encompass, lay siege to, surround

besotted *adj* doting, infatuated, in love, smitten, spellbound; ***opp*** indifferent

best *adj* chief, cream, elite, finest, first, first-class, first-rate, foremost, greatest, highest, leading, most fitting, most suitable, outstanding, pick, pre-eminent, prime, right, supreme, top, unsurpassed; ***opp*** worst

bet *n* gamble, pledge, risk, speculation, stake, venture, wager

bet *v* gamble, pledge, risk, speculate, stake, venture, wager

betray *v* blow the whistle on, break your promise, double-cross *inf*, inform on, sell out *inf*, stab sb in the back, swindle, tell on *inf*

betrayal *n* back-stabbing *inf*, breach of faith, disloyalty, double-dealing, duplicity, falseness, treachery, treason, subversion, trickery; ***opp*** loyalty

beware *v* avoid, be careful, be on the alert, be on the lookout, be on your guard, heed, look out, mind, steer clear of, take heed, watch out

bewildered *adj* baffled, bemused, confused, dazed, disconcerted, flummoxed, muddled, mystified, nonplussed, perplexed, puzzled, startled, surprised, taken aback, thrown off balance

bewildering *adj* baffling, confusing, disconcerting, mystifying, perplexing, puzzling, startling, surprising

bewitched *adj* beguiled, captivated, charmed, enchanted, enraptured, entranced, fascinated, mesmerized, spellbound; ***opp*** indifferent

bias *n* **1** bigotry, favoritism, narrow-mindedness, one-sidedness, partiality, prejudice, unfairness. **2** bent, inclination, leaning, penchant, predisposition, propensity, tendency

biased *adj* distorted, one-sided, partial, prejudiced, slanted, weighted; ***opp*** impartial

bicker *v* argue, disagree, dispute, fall out, feud, fight, have a row, quarrel, squabble

bid *n* **1** offer, price, proposal, proposition, submission, sum, tender. **2** attempt, effort, try, venture

bid *v* **1** (bid money) offer, proffer, propose, put forward, submit, tender. **2** (bid sb farewell, good-day) call, greet, say, tell, wish. **3** (bid sb do sth) ask, charge, command, demand, direct, enjoin, instruct, invite, order, require, solicit, summon, tell

big *adj* **1** (in size) beefy, bulky, burly, colossal, enormous, extensive, gigantic, great, huge, hulking, immense, large, mammoth, massive, muscular, prodigious, sizable, spacious, strapping, thickset, substantial, tall, vast, voluminous; ***opp*** small. **2** (in importance) eminent, important, leading, main, momentous, powerful, principal, prominent, serious, significant, valuable, weighty; ***opp*** small. **3** (in generosity) altruistic, benevolent, generous, gracious, kind, heroic, magnanimous, unselfish; ***opp*** petty, selfish

bigot *n* chauvinist, dogmatist, fanatic, homophobic, racist, sexist

bigoted *adj* dogmatic, fanatical, homophobic, intolerant, narrow-minded, opinionated, prejudiced, racist, sexist

bill *n* **1** account, charges, check, invoice, statement, tally. **2** act, measure, piece of legislation, proposal

bill *v* charge, debit, invoice

bind *v* **1** attach, chain, fasten, fetter, glue, hitch, lash, paste, secure, stick, strap, tether, tie. **2** (make sb do sth) compel, constrain, force, impel, obligate, oblige, prescribe. **3** (make doing sth difficult) confine, detain, hamper, hinder, inhibit, restrain, restrict; ***opp*** help. **4** (bind a wound) bandage, cover, dress, strap

binding *adj* compulsory, irrevocable, mandatory, obligatory, unalterable

biography *n* account, life, life story, memoir, memoirs, profile

birth *n* **1** childbirth, confinement, delivery, nativity, parturition. **2** beginning, beginnings, commencement, emergence, genesis, origin, rise, start, source. **3** ancestry, background, blood, breeding, descent, extraction, family, genealogy, heritage, line, lineage, origin, parentage, pedigree, race, stock

bit *n* chip, chunk, crumb, flake, fragment,

grain, iota, jot, lump, mite, morsel, part, particle, piece, scrap, shred, sliver, speck, trace, whit

bitchy *adj* backbiting, catty, cruel, malicious, mean, nasty, rancorous, snide, spiteful, venomous, vicious, vindictive, waspish

bite *n* 1 nibble, nip, puncture. 2 morsel, mouthful, snack. 3 edge, piquancy, punch, pungency, spice, spiciness

bite *v* chew, champ, crunch, gnaw, masticate, munch, nibble, nip, pierce, pinch, snap, tear

biting *adj* 1 (of wind) bitter, cold, cutting, freezing, harsh, nipping, penetrating, piercing, stinging. 2 (of remarks) acid, caustic, cutting, sarcastic, scathing, sharp, stinging, trenchant, vitriolic

bitter *adj* 1 (of taste) acid, acrid, astringent, pungent, sharp, sour, tart, unsweetened, vinegary. 2 acrimonious, angry, begrudging, embittered, hostile, hurt, morose, piqued, rancorous, resentful, sore, sour, sullen

bizarre *adj* abnormal, curious, eccentric, extraordinary, fantastic, freakish, grotesque, ludicrous, odd, oddball *inf*, offbeat, outlandish, outré, peculiar, queer, strange, unconventional, unusual, way-out *inf*, wacky *inf*, weird; ***opp*** normal

black *adj* 1 coal-black, dark, dusky, ebony, inky, jet, murky, pitch-black, raven, sable, starless, swarthy. 2 dark, depressing, dismal, distressing, doleful, foreboding, funereal, gloomy, hopeless, lugubrious, melancholy, mournful, pessimistic, ominous, sad, somber. 3 bad, devilish, diabolic, evil, foul, heinous, iniquitous, nefarious, villainous, wicked

blacklist *v* ban, bar, boycott, debar, exclude, expel, ostracize, proscribe, reject

blackmail *v* extort, exact, extract, force, hold to ransom, intimidate, threaten

blame *n* 1 accountability, culpability, fault, guilt, liability, onus, responsibility. 2 accusation, castigation, censure, charge, condemnation, incrimination, indictment, recrimination, reprimand, reproof

blame *v* accuse, censure, charge, condemn, hold accountable, hold to account, indict, find fault with, find guilty, reprehend, reprimand, reproach, reprove, take to task; ***opp*** absolve

blameless *adj* above suspicion, beyond reproach, faultless, guiltless, innocent, in the clear, irreproachable, not to blame, perfect, stainless, unblemished, unimpeachable, upright, virtuous

bland *adj* 1 (of flavor) boring, dull, flavorless, insipid, mild, plain, tasteless, weak. 2 (of a person, remarks) boring, dull, insipid, middle-of-the-road, mediocre, nondescript, neutral, safe, uncontroversial, uninspiring, uninteresting, vapid

blank *adj* 1 bare, clean, clear, empty, plain, spotless, unfilled, unmarked, vacant, void, white. 2 at a loss, baffled, bewildered, confounded, confused, expressionless, nonplussed, perplexed, puzzled, uncomprehending

blare *v* bellow, blast, boom, honk, hoot, peal, resound, roar, trumpet

blasé *adj* apathetic, bored, casual, indifferent, jaded, laid-back, lukewarm, nonchalant, phlegmatic, offhand, relaxed, unconcerned, unenthusiastic, unimpressed, uninterested, unmoved, unperturbed, weary, world-weary

blaspheme *v* curse, damn, desecrate, profane, swear

blasphemous *adj* godless, impious, irreverent, profane, sacrilegious, ungodly, unholy

blast *n* **1** bang, blowing-up, boom, crash, detonation, explosion, salvo, volley. **2** blare, boom, honk, hoot, peal, trumpeting, wail

blast *v* **1** bomb, blow up, demolish, destroy, detonate, explode, fire, fire-bomb, raze, ruin, shatter. **2** blare, boom, honk, hoot, peal, sound, trumpet, wail

blatant *adj* brazen, conspicuous, flagrant, glaring, naked, obvious, open, ostentatious, outright, overt, prominent, shameless, sheer, unashamed, unconcealed

blaze *n* **1** bonfire, conflagration, fire, flame, flames, inferno. **2** beam, brilliance, flare, flash, glare

blaze *v* **1** (of a fire) be ablaze, burn, burst into flames, catch fire, flame, glow. **2** (of light) be ablaze, burn, beam, flare, flash, glare, gleam, glow, shine

bleach *v* blanch, fade, pale, peroxide, lighten, take the color out of, whiten

bleak *adj* **1** bare, barren, desolate, exposed, open, raw, unsheltered, waste, windswept. **2** cheerless, dark, depressing, dismal, drab, dreary, gloomy, grim, hopeless, joyless, miserable, somber, unpromising, wretched

bleary *adj* blurred, blurry, clouded, dim, fogged, foggy, fuzzy, hazy, indistinct, misty, unclear; ***opp*** clear

blemish *n* **1** (on skin) blotch, defect, disfigurement, fault, flaw, imperfection, mark, mole, patch, scab, scar, smudge, speck, spot, stain, taint. **2** (on character) blot, defect, disgrace, dishonor, fault, flaw, imperfection, stain, taint

blemished *adj* blotted, blotchy, defective, disfigured, faulty, flawed, imperfect, marked, patchy, smudged, speckled, spotted, spotty, stained, tainted; ***opp*** clear

blend *n* alloy, amalgam, amalgamation, combination, composite, compound, cross, fusion, mix, mixture, synthesis, union

blend *v* amalgamate, coalesce, combine, cross, fuse, merge, mingle, mix, synthesize, unite

bless *v* **1** consecrate, dedicate, exalt, extol, glorify, praise, sanctify, thank. **2** (bless sb with sth) bestow, endow, favor, grace, grant, provide. **3** approve, be in favor, condone, consent, endorse, sanction, support

blessed *adj* **1** adored, beatified, consecrated, divine, exalted, hallowed, holy, sanctified, sacred. **2** (blessed with sth) endowed, favored, fortunate, gifted, lucky

blessing *n* **1** benediction, benison, consecration, dedication, grace, invocation, praise, thanksgiving. **2** approval, assent, backing, consent, endorsement, permission, sanction, support. **3** advantage, benefit, boon, endowment, gift, godsend, good fortune, favor, windfall

blight *n* **1** affliction, bane, cancer, curse, pestilence, plague, scourge, woe.

2 (in plants) canker, disease, fungus, infestation, mildew, pest, pestilence, rot

blight *v* 1 afflict, blast, crush, curse, dash, destroy, kill, ruin, wreck. 2 (blight a plant) blast, destroy, infest, kill, rot, shrivel, wither

blind *adj* 1 sightless, unseeing, visually impaired. 2 dense, heedless, ignorant, inattentive, insensitive, neglectful, oblivious, unaware, unconscious, unmindful, unobservant

bliss *n* delight, ecstasy, elation, euphoria, gladness, happiness, heaven, joy, paradise, pleasure, rapture

blissful *adj* delightful, ecstatic, euphoric, happy, heavenly, joyful, rapturous, wonderful

blitz *n* assault, attack, blitzkrieg, bombardment, bombing, offensive, onslaught, raid, strike

bloated *adj* dilated, distended, enlarged, full, inflated, puffed up, swollen

blob *n* ball, bead, dab, dollop, drop, droplet, glob, globule, lump, mass

block *n* bar, brick, cake, chunk, cube, hunk, lump, ingot, piece, rectangle, square, wedge

block *v* 1 choke, clog, close, obstruct, plug, stop up. 2 bar, check, hinder, impede, obstruct, prevent, stop, thwart

blockage *n* bar, barrier, clog, impediment, jam, obstacle, obstruction, occlusion, plug, stoppage

blond(e) *adj* fair, fair-haired, flaxen, golden, golden-haired

blood *n* 1 gore, lifeblood, vital fluids. 2 ancestry, birth, descent, extraction, family, genealogy, heritage, kindred, kinship, line, lineage, origin, parentage, pedigree, race, relation, relative, stock, strain

bloodshed *n* blood bath, bloodletting, butchery, carnage, gore, killing, massacre, murder, slaughter, slaying, violence, war

bloodthirsty *adj* barbaric, barbarous, brutal, cruel, ferocious, murderous, ruthless, sadistic, savage, vicious, violent, warlike

bloody *adj* 1 bleeding, bloodstained, blood-soaked, blood-spattered, gory. 2 barbaric, barbarous, bloodthirsty, brutal, gory, murderous, sadistic, savage, vicious, violent

bloom *n* 1 blossom, blossoming, bud, flower. 2 blush, flush, freshness, glow, health, luster, radiance, rosiness

bloom *v* 1 be in bloom, be in blossom, be in flower, blossom, bud, burgeon, flower, open. 2 (of a person) blossom, flourish, glow, thrive

blossom *n* bloom, blossoming, bud, flower

blossom *v* 1 be in bloom, be in blossom, be in flower, bud, burgeon, flower, open. 2 (of a person) bloom, flourish, glow, thrive

blot *n* 1 blemish, blotch, blur, dot, mark, patch, smudge, speck, spatter, speckle, spot, stain. 2 (on reputation) blemish, blur, defect, disgrace, dishonor, fault, flaw, imperfection, stain, taint

blow *n* 1 bang, bash, buffet, clout, hit, knock, punch, rap, slap, smack, stroke, thump, thwack, wallop *inf*, whack. 2 bombshell, calamity, catastrophe, disappointment, disaster, jolt, letdown, misfortune, reverse, setback, shock, upset

blow *v* **1** blast, breathe, exhale, fan, huff, pant, puff. **2** (move by air, wind) buffet, flap, flutter, sweep, toss, waft, wave, whirl, whisk. **3** pipe, play, sound, toot. **4 blow up** blast, bomb, burst, detonate, fire, explode, go off, pop, rupture, shatter

blue adj **1** azure, cobalt, indigo, navy, sapphire, sky-blue, turquoise, ultramarine. **2** dejected, depressed, despondent, down *inf*, downcast, downhearted, fed up *inf*, gloomy, glum, low, melancholy, miserable, sad, unhappy; ***opp*** happy

blues *n* dejection, depression, despondency, doldrums, dumps *inf*, gloom, gloominess, glumness, low spirits, melancholy, misery, sadness, unhappiness

bluff *v* con, deceive, delude, fake, feign, hoax, lie, mislead, pretend, put it on, sham, take in, trick

blunder *n* boob *inf*, error, faux pas, gaffe, mistake, oversight, slip

blunt *adj* **1** dull, rounded, unsharpened; ***opp*** sharp. **2** abrupt, bluff, brusque, candid, direct, forthright, frank, honest, outspoken, plainspoken, straight, straightforward, tactless, to the point

blur *n* dimness, fog, haze, indistinctness, mist, obscurity, smear, smudge

blur *v* blotch, cloud, darken, dim, fog, mask, mist up, obscure, smear, smudge, steam up, veil

blurred *adj* bleary, blurry, clouded, dim, faint, fogged, foggy, fuzzy, hazy, indistinct, misty, nebulous, obscure, out of focus, smeared, smudged, unclear, vague; ***opp*** clear

blurt out *v* babble, blab, cry, disclose, exclaim, let out, let slip, reveal, say, spill the beans *inf*, tattle, tell

blush *v* color, flush, go pink, go red, redden, turn pink, turn red

board *n* **1** beam, panel, plank, slat, timber. **2** body, committee, council, directorate, directors, panel, trustees

board *v* **1** embark, enter, go aboard, go on board, mount. **2** accommodate, feed, house, lodge, put up, quarter, take in

boast *n* **1** bluster, bragging, crowing, exaggeration, self-congratulation, showing off, swagger, swank. **2** gem, jewel, pride, pride and joy, treasure

boast *v* **1** blow your own trumpet *inf*, bluster, brag, crow, exaggerate, show off, strut, swagger, swank, talk big *inf*, vaunt. **2** enjoy, have, own, possess, pride yourself on

bodily *adj* carnal, corporal, corporeal, fleshly, material, physical

body *n* **1** build, figure, form, flesh, frame, physique, shape, torso, trunk. **2** cadaver, carcass, corpse, dead body, remains. **3** bulk, essence, main part, majority, mass, material, matter, substance. **4** association, authority, band, committee, company, corporation, group, organization, society

bog *n* fen, marsh, mire, morass, quagmire, swamp, wetland

boggy *adj* marshy, muddy, soft, swampy, wet

bogus *adj* artificial, counterfeit, dummy, ersatz, fake, false, forged, fraudulent, imitation, mock, phony *inf*, pseudo, sham, spurious; ***opp*** genuine

boil *n* blister, carbuncle, pustule, spot, swelling
boil *v* bubble, come to the boil, cook, churn, foam, froth, seethe, simmer, steam, stew
boiling *adj* baking, blistering, hot, roasting, scorching, searing, sweltering; ***opp*** freezing
boisterous *adj* bouncy, exuberant, lively, loud, noisy, riotous, rollicking, rough, rowdy, spirited, unruly, uproarious, wild
bold *adj* **1** adventurous, audacious, brash, brave, cheeky, courageous, daring, dauntless, enterprising, fearless, intrepid, presumptuous, valiant; ***opp*** timid. **2** bright, colorful, conspicuous, eye-catching, flashy, loud, lurid, prominent, showy, striking, strong, vivid; ***opp*** muted
bolster *v* aid, assist, boost, brace, buoy up, buttress, help, hold up, maintain, prop up, reinforce, shore up, strengthen, support
bolt *n* **1** bar, catch, fastener, latch, lock. **2** peg, pin, rivet, rod
bolt *v* **1** abscond, bound, dart, dash, escape, flee, fly, hurtle, leap, run, rush, sprint. **2** bar, fasten, lock, secure. **3** (bolt food) cram, devour, down, gobble, gulp, guzzle, stuff, wolf
bomb *n* blast, booby-trap, charge, device, explosive, grenade, incendiary, mine, shell, torpedo
bomb *v* attack, blast, blitz, blow up, bombard, booby-trap, destroy, detonate, explode, fire, firebomb, shell, torpedo
bombard *v* **1** assault, attack, blast, blitz, bomb, fire on, open fire, pound, shell, strafe, torpedo. **2** (with questions) assail, attack, barrage, besiege, beset, bother, harass, hassle *inf*, hound, pester
bond *n* **1** affinity, attachment, connection, link, relation, relationship, tie, union. **2** binding, chain, cord, fastening, fetters, manacles, shackles, rope. **3** agreement, bargain, compact, commitment, contract, covenant, deal, guarantee, obligation, pledge, promise, treaty, word
bond *v* bind, cement, fasten, fix, fuse, glue, join, stick
bonus *n* benefit, boon, bounty, commission, dividend, extra, gift, gratuity, hand-out, perk *inf*, perquisite, plus, prize, reward, tip
book *n* leaflet, magazine, manual, publication, text, title, tome, tract, treatise, volume, work
book *v* arrange, charter, engage, line up, make a reservation, organize, reserve, schedule
boom *n* **1** bang, bellow, blast, clap, crash, explosion, reverberation, roar, roll, rumble, shout, thunder. **2** advance, burgeoning, development, expansion, gain, growth, increase, progress, success, spurt, upsurge, upturn
boom *v* **1** bang, bellow, blare, blast, crash, echo, explode, resound, reverberate, roar, roll, rumble, shout, thunder. **2** advance, burgeon, develop, expand, flourish, grow, increase, progress, prosper, succeed, thrive
boost *n* advance, assistance, augmentation, encouragement, help, improvement, increase, inspiration, plug *inf*, praise, promotion, stimulus, rise, support
boost *v* advance, amplify, assist, augment,

enlarge, encourage, facilitate, foster, further, heighten, help, improve, increase, inflate, inspire, plug *inf*, praise, promote, raise, stimulate, support, uplift

border *n* **1** boundary, brim, brink, edge, edging, fringe, hem, limit, margin, outskirts, perimeter, rim, skirt, verge. **2** (between countries) borderline, boundary, frontier

bore *v* be tedious, bother, exhaust, fatigue, pall, put sb to sleep, tire, vex, wear out, weary; ***opp*** inspire

bored *adj* apathetic, blasé, fatigued, fed up *inf*, indifferent, jaded, languorous, lukewarm, tired, unenthusiastic, unimpressed, uninspired, uninterested, unmoved, weary

boredom *n* apathy, dullness, monotony, sameness, tediousness, tedium, weariness; ***opp*** excitement

boring *adj* dead, dull, humdrum, insipid, monotonous, repetitious, routine, stale, tedious, tiresome, uneventful, unexciting, uninteresting

borrow *v* acquire, adopt, appropriate, cadge *inf*, commandeer, filch, help yourself to, pinch, pirate, plagiarize, scrounge *inf*, sponge *inf*, take, use; ***opp*** lend

boss *n* chief, employer, foreman, head, master, overseer, owner, supervisor

boss *v* bully, domineer, order about, order around, push around, ride roughshod over, throw your weight about

bossy *adj* assertive, bullying, dominating, domineering, high-handed, imperious, lordly, officious, overbearing, pushy *inf*, self-assertive

botch *v* bungle, fumble, make a hash *inf*, make a mess, mess up *inf*, mismanage, ruin, spoil

bother *n* annoyance, difficulty, effort, exertion, fuss, hassle *inf*, inconvenience, irritation, nuisance, strain, trouble, worry

bother *v* **1** (bother sb) annoy, disturb, exasperate, give sb a hard time *inf*, harass, hassle *inf*, irritate, molest, nag, pester, provoke, torment, vex, worry. **2** (needn't bother) be concerned, care, concern yourself, go to any trouble, inconvenience yourself, make the effort, mind, put yourself out, take the time, trouble yourself. **3** (sth bothers you) alarm, concern, dismay, distress, perturb, upset, trouble, worry

bottom *n* **1** base, bed, depth, floor, foot, foundation, underneath, underside. **2** backside, behind, bum *inf*, butt *inf*, buttocks, hindquarters, rear, rear end, seat, tail. **3** basis, cause, center, core, essence, heart, nitty-gritty, origin, root, source, substance

bounce *n* **1** elasticity, give, resilience, spring, springiness. **2** animation, dynamism, energy, go *inf*, life, liveliness, oomph *inf*, pep, spirit, vigor, vitality, vivacity, zip *inf*. **3** bound, leap, jump, skip, spring

bounce *v* bob, bound, jump, leap, rebound, recoil, ricochet, spring

bound *adj* **1** (bound to happen) certain, destined, doomed, fated, predestined, sure, very likely. **2** (bound with rope) fettered, lashed, roped, secured, strapped, tethered, tied, tied up, trussed. **3** (obliged to do sth) committed, compelled, constrained, duty-bound, forced, obligated, obliged, required

bound *v* bob, bounce, caper, frisk, frolic, gambol, hop, jump, leap, pounce, prance, skip, spring, vault

boundary *n* barrier, border, bounds, brink, demarcation, edge, end, extremity, fringe, frontier, limits, margin, perimeter, threshold

boundless *adj* endless, immeasurable, incalculable, infinite, never-ending, unbounded, unending, untold, vast

bounds *n* boundary, border, confines, edges, limitations, limits, periphery, perimeter

bouquet *n* **1** (flowers) arrangement, bunch, buttonhole, corsage, garland, posy, spray, wreath. **2** (wine) aroma, fragrance, odor, perfume, savor, scent, smell

bout *n* **1** (fighting) competition, contest, encounter, engagement, fight, match, set-to *inf*. **2** (of illness) attack, fit, spell. **3** (of activity) period, run, spell, stint, stretch, time, turn

bow *n* bob, curtsy, genuflexion, nod, obeisance

bow *v* **1** bend, bob, curtsy, genuflect, incline your head, kowtow, make obeisance, nod, prostrate yourself, salaam, stoop. **2 bow to** capitulate, give in, give way, submit, surrender, yield

bowels *n* **1** entrails, guts, innards *inf*, insides *inf*, intestines. **2** belly, core, depths, heart, inside, interior

bowl *n* basin, container, dish, tureen, vessel

box *n* carton, case, chest, container, crate, pack, package, trunk

boy *n* fellow, kid *inf*, lad, schoolboy, son, youngster, youth

boycott *n* ban, embargo, prohibition

boycott *v* ban, bar, blacklist, ostracize, place an embargo on, reject, spurn

boyfriend *n* date, lover, man, sweetheart, young man

brace *n* **1** buttress, clamp, prop, reinforcement, stanchion, stay, strut, support, truss. **2** couple, duo, pair, two

brace *v* bolster, buttress, fortify, hold up, prop up, reinforce, secure, shore up, steady, strengthen

braced *adj* prepared, ready, rigid, set, steady, tense

brain *n* **1** brainpower, gray matter *inf*, intellect, intelligence, mind, reason, sense, understanding, wit. **2** (clever person) genius, intellectual, mastermind, thinker

brainwash *v* condition, indoctrinate, influence, reeducate

brake *v* check, decelerate, reduce speed, slow, slow down, stop

branch *n* **1** (of a tree) arm, bough, limb, offshoot, prong, stem, twig. **2** (of an organization) department, division, office, part, section, subdivision, subsection, tributary, wing

brand *n* **1** class, grade, kind, line, make, quality, sort, species, trademark, trade name, type, variety. **2** hallmark, label, marker, sign, stamp, symbol, tag

brand *v* **1** (cattle) burn, mark, scar, sear, stamp. **2** (give sb a bad name) characterize, denounce, discredit, stigmatize, vilify. **3** (impress on sb's mind) engrave, fix, impress, imprint, print, stamp

brandish *v* flaunt, flourish, shake,

swing, wave, wield

brash *adj* arrogant, bold, brazen, cocky *inf*, forward, impertinent, insolent, pushy *inf*, rude

bravado *n* arrogance, audacity, bluster, boastfulness, boldness, bombast, bragging, machismo, swagger

brave *adj* bold, courageous, daring, dauntless, fearless, gutsy *inf*, heroic, intrepid, tough, unafraid, undaunted, unshrinking; ***opp*** cowardly

bravery *n* boldness, courage, daring, fearlessness, gallantry, guts *inf*, heroism, nerve *inf*, pluck, spirit, valor; ***opp*** cowardice

brazen *adj* barefaced, blatant, brash, flagrant, immodest, insolent, rude, saucy, shameless, unashamed

breach *n* **1** aperture, break, chasm, cleft, crack, fissure, fracture, gap, hole, opening, split. **2** breaking, contravention, infringement, transgression, violation

breach *v* **1** break through, burst through, open up, rupture. **2** break, contravene, defy, disobey, infringe, violate

breadth *n* **1** (distance across) broadness, latitude, span, spread, thickness, wideness, width. **2** (wide range) comprehensiveness, extensiveness, extent, range, scale, scope, sweep

break *n* **1** breach, breakage, cleft, crack, division, hole, fissure, fracture, gap, gash, hole, opening, rent, rift, rupture, split, tear. **2** (pause) breather *inf*, breathing-space, halt, hiatus, interlude, interval, lull, pause, respite, rest, stop, time out *inf*. **3** breach, disruption, estrangement, lapse, rift, schism, separation, split, suspension

break *v* **1** (break into parts) bust *inf*, chip, crack, crumple, damage, demolish, destroy, fracture, fragment, part, separate, sever, shatter, shiver, smash, smash to smithereens, snap, splinter, split, tear, wreck. **2** (break a rule) contravene, defy, disobey, disregard, flout, infringe, transgress, violate. **3** (break a person) bankrupt, bring sb to his knees, cow, cripple, crush, defeat, dispirit, make bankrupt, overwhelm, ruin, subdue, tame, weaken. **4** (stop) discontinue, interrupt, knock off *inf*, pause, rest, stop, take a break, take five *inf*. **5** (break a record) beat, cap *inf*, exceed, go beyond, outdo, outstrip, pass, shatter, smash, surpass. **6** (of news) announce, appear, become public, be revealed, disclose, divulge, emerge, make public, reveal, tell. **7** (of waves) crash, dash, hit. **8** (break a code) decipher, decode, unravel, solve. **9 break down** collapse, come to grief, conk out *inf*, crack up *inf*, fail, fall through, go to pieces, seize up, stop, stop working. **10 break in** barge in, break and enter, burgle, burst in, butt in, interfere, interrupt, intervene, intrude, invade, push your way in, rob, thrust your way in. **11 break off** detach, divide, pull off, separate, sever, splinter. **12 break off** bring to an end, call a halt, cease, discontinue, end, finish, stop, suspend, terminate. **13 break out** abscond, bolt, break loose, escape, flee, free yourself. **14 break out** (spots) appear, emerge, occur. **15 break up** adjourn, come to an end, dismantle, disrupt, dissolve, divorce, end, part, scatter, separate, split up, stop, terminate

breakdown *n* 1 collapse, destruction, disintegration, failure, malfunction, nervous breakdown, ruin, stoppage. 2 analysis, categorization, classification, diagnosis, dissection, rundown *inf*

breakthrough *n* advance, development, discovery, innovation, invention, leap forward, progress, revolution

breast *n* bosom, bust, chest, front

breath *n* 1 air, breathing, exhalation, gasp, gulp, pant, respiration, wheeze. 2 (suggestion) hint, murmur, suggestion, suspicion, touch, trace, undertone, whisper

breathe *v* 1 exhale, gasp, inhale, pant, puff, respire, wheeze. 2 murmur, say, sigh, tell, whisper

breathless *adj* 1 exhausted, choking, gasping, gulping, out of breath, panting, puffed *inf*, puffing, spent, tired out, wheezing, winded. 2 (with excitement) agog, all agog, avid, eager, excited, on tenterhooks, openmouthed, with bated breath

breed *n* class, family, kind, line, lineage, pedigree, race, stock, strain, type, variety

breed *v* bear, bring up, hatch, increase, multiply, nurture, procreate, produce, propagate, raise, rear, reproduce

breeze *n* draft, gentle wind, gust, light wind, puff of air, waft

brew *n* beer, beverage, blend, concoction, drink, infusion, liquor, mixture, potion, preparation, tea

brew *v* 1 boil, concoct, ferment, infuse, prepare, simmer, steep, stew. 2 (of trouble) contrive, cook up *inf*, devise, foment, hatch, plan, plot, scheme, stir up

bribe *n* backhander *sl*, bribery, carrot *inf*, enticement, hush money *sl*, inducement, kickback *inf*, pay-off *inf*, sweetener *inf*

bribe *v* buy off, corrupt, get at *inf*, give an inducement to, grease sb's palm *inf*, pay sb off, tempt

bridge *n* 1 aqueduct, arch, causeway, crossing, footbridge, overpass, span, viaduct. 2 bond, connection, link, stepping stone, tie

bridge *v* bind, connect, cross, join, link, span, straddle, traverse, unite

brief *adj* 1 compact, concise, condensed, crisp, incisive, pithy, short, succinct, terse, thumbnail, to the point; ***opp*** lengthy, long. 2 ephemeral, fleeting, impermanent, passing, quick, short, short-lived, swift, temporary, transient, transitory; ***opp*** lengthy, long

brief *n* advice, briefing, description, guidance, information, instructions, orders, outline, summary

brief *v* advise, fill sb in *inf*, give the facts to, instruct, prepare, prime, put sb in the picture *inf*

bright *adj* 1 (of light) beaming, blazing, brilliant, dazzling, flashing, gleaming, glittering, glowing, illuminated, incandescent, intense, luminous, radiant, scintillating, shining, shiny, sparkling, twinkling, vivid; ***opp*** dark, dull. 2 (clever) acute, astute, clever, intelligent, inventive, quick, sharp, smart; ***opp*** dull. 3 (of weather) clear, cloudless, fair, sunny; ***opp*** dull. 4 (of prospects) encouraging, favorable, good, hopeful, optimistic, promising, propitious, rosy; ***opp*** gloomy. **5** (of a person) cheerful, gay, happy, jolly, joyful, light-hearted, lively, merry; ***opp*** miserable. **6** (of color) bold, brilliant, colorful, fresh, gaudy, intense, rich, vivid; ***opp*** pale

brighten *v* **1** cheer up, enliven, gladden, illuminate, lighten, light up, liven up, make brighter, perk up, revitalize. **2** (of weather) clear, clear up; ***opp*** cloud over

brilliance *n* **1** (of light) brightness, dazzle, glare, intensity, luminosity, radiance, sheen, sparkle, vividness. **2** (of an occasion) glamour, glitter, grandeur, luster, magnificence, splendor. **3** (genius) braininess, cleverness, eminence, fame, genius, giftedness, talent

brilliant *adj* **1** (shining) bright, dazzling, glittering, intense, radiant, scintillating, shining, sparkling, vivid. **2** (good) excellent, fabulous, great, good, marvelous, superb, wonderful. **3** (clever) bright, celebrated, clever, exceptional, famous, gifted, intelligent, remarkable, smart, talented

bring *v* **1** (take somewhere) accompany, bear, carry, convey, deliver, escort, fetch, gather, guide, import, lead, take, transport. **2** (lead to sth happening) attract, cause, contribute to, create, draw, earn, effect, generate, give rise to, inflict, lead to, occasion, produce, prompt, provoke, result in, wreak. **3 bring about** accomplish, achieve, cause, create, effect, give rise to, lead to, make happen, occasion, produce, result in. **4 bring up** care for, educate, nurture, raise, rear, support. **5 bring up** (bring up a subject) allude to, broach, introduce, mention, refer to, touch on/upon

brink *n* border, brim, edge, fringe, limit, rim, threshold, verge

brisk *adj* **1** (a brisk walk) energetic, lively, quick, smart, spanking *inf*, speedy, vigorous; ***opp*** leisurely. **2** (of weather) bracing, crisp, exhilarating, fresh, invigorating, keen, nippy *inf*, refreshing. **3** (of business) active, bustling, busy, hectic; ***opp*** slow

brittle *adj* breakable, crisp, crumbling, delicate, easily broken, fragile, frail, hard, splintery, weak

broach *v* bring up, introduce, mention, propose, raise, speak about, suggest, talk about, touch on

broad *adj* **1** (wide) ample, boundless, capacious, extensive, large, open, spacious, sweeping, vast, wide, widespread; ***opp*** narrow. **2** (of knowledge) comprehensive, encyclopedic, far-reaching, general, wide, wide-ranging. **3** (of sb's mind) liberal, open, permissive, progressive, tolerant, unbiased, unprejudiced; ***opp*** narrow. **4** (of a description) general, imprecise, inexact, loose, sweeping, vague; ***opp*** detailed. **5** (of taste) all-embracing, catholic, eclectic, varied; ***opp*** narrow

broadcast *n* program, show, transmission

broadcast *v* advertise, air, announce, beam, circulate, disseminate, make known, make public, proclaim, publish, report, spread, televise, transmit

broaden *v* develop, enlarge, expand, make broader, make wider, open up, spread, stretch, swell, widen

broad-minded *adj* enlightened, flexible, liberal, open-minded, permissive, tolerant, unbiased, unprejudiced, unshockable; ***opp*** narrow-minded

brochure *n* booklet, catalog, circular, folder, hand-out, leaflet, pamphlet, prospectus

broken *adj* **1** burst, bust *inf*, cracked, demolished, destroyed, fractured, fragmented, punctured, severed, shattered, smashed, split, torn; ***opp*** whole. **2** (not working) broken down, bust *inf*, damaged, defective, faulty, kaput, out of order. **3** (not continuous) discontinuous, disrupted, disturbed, erratic, fragmentary, intermittent, interrupted, spasmodic. **4** (having lost the will to fight) beaten, crippled, crushed, defeated, demoralized, discouraged, dispirited, subdued, tamed, vanquished

brood *n* chicks, children, clutch, family, litter, offspring, progeny, young

brood *v* **1** agonize, dwell upon, fret, mope, mull over, muse, ponder, sulk, think, worry. **2** hatch, incubate, sit on

brown *adj* **1** beige, buff, chocolate, cocoa, copper, coppery, dun, ecru, fawn, hazel, khaki, mahogany, maroon, ochre, russet, rust, sepia, tan, tawny, terracotta, umber. **2** (of hair) auburn, chestnut, dark, ginger. **3** (of skin) bronze, bronzed, coffee-colored, dark, sunburnt, sun-tanned, tanned

browse *v* **1** dip into, flip through, leaf through, look through, scan, skim. **2** look round, window-shop. **3** crop, eat, feed, graze, nibble

bruise *n* black eye, blemish, bump, contusion, discoloration, mark, shiner *inf*, swelling, welt

bruise *v* blacken, blemish, crush, damage, discolor, knock, make black and blue, mark

brush *v* **1** buff, clean, comb, groom, polish, sweep, tidy, wash. **2** caress, contact, flick, glance, graze, kiss, scrape, stroke, sweep, touch. **3 brush up** go over, polish up, read up, refresh your memory, relearn, revise, study

brutal *adj* barbaric, barbarous, bloodthirsty, bloody, callous, cold-blooded, cruel, heartless, inhuman, merciless, murderous, pitiless, remorseless, ruthless, sadistic, savage, vicious, violent; ***opp*** gentle

brutality *n* atrocity, barbarism, barbarity, bloodiness, bloodthirstiness, cruelty, ferocity, savageness, savagery

brutalize *v* abuse, corrupt, dehumanize, harden, inure, make brutal, toughen

brute *n* **1** animal, beast, creature, dumb animal, wild animal. **2** barbarian, beast, bully, devil, fiend, monster, ruffian, sadist, savage, swine

bubble *v* **1** effervesce, fizz, fizzle, foam, froth, gurgle, sparkle. **2** boil, percolate, simmer

buckle *n* catch, clasp, clip, fastener, fastening, hasp

buckle *v* **1** bend, bulge, cave in, crumple, curve, dent, fold, kink, twist, warp. **2** clip, do up, fasten, hitch, hook up, secure

budding *adj* aspiring, burgeoning, fledgling, flowering, growing, potential, promising, would-be *inf*

budge *v* **1** dislodge, give way, go, move,

push, remove, roll, shift, slide. 2 acquiesce, change, change your mind, convince, give in, give way, persuade, sway, yield

budget *n* accounts, allowance, cost, finances, financial plan, funds, means, resources

budget *v* allocate, allow, apportion, cost, estimate, plan, provide, ration, save, set aside

buffer *n* bulwark, bumper, cushion, fender, guard, safeguard, screen, shield

bug *n* 1 creepy-crawly *inf*, flea, insect, mite. 2 bacterium, germ, infection, microorganism, virus. 3 (in a computer program) breakdown, defect, error, fault, flaw, gremlin *inf*, malfunction, mistake, virus

bug *v* 1 eavesdrop, listen to, phone-tap, spy on, tap, wiretap. 2 anger, annoy, get on sb's nerves *inf*, hassle *inf*, infuriate, irk, irritate, provoke

build *v* 1 assemble, construct, erect, form, make, manufacture, put together, put up, raise. 2 base, begin, establish, found, originate, set up, start

building *n* construction, edifice, premises, structure

build-up *n* accumulation, collection, gathering, heap, hoard, mass, stockpile, store

bulge *n* bump, hump, lump, projection, protuberance, rise, swelling

bulging *adj* ballooning, bloated, distended, full, lumpy, popping, protruding, sticking out, swelling, swollen

bulk *n* 1 bulkiness, extent, immensity, largeness, magnitude, mass, massiveness, quantity, size, weight. 2 best part *inf*, greater part, lion's share, main part, majority, mass, most, nearly all

bullet *n* missile, pellet, shot, slug

bulletin *n* announcement, communication, communiqué, message, news-flash, notification, report, statement

bully *n* abuser, oppressor, persecutor, ruffian, thug, tormentor, tyrant

bully *v* browbeat, coerce, domineer, frighten, intimidate, oppress, persecute, pick on *inf*, push around *inf*, ride roughshod over, terrorize, threaten, tyrannize

bump *n* 1 bang, blow, collision, crash, jolt, knock, smash, thud, thump. 2 (a bump on sth) bulge, hump, knob, lump, nodule, protrusion, protuberance, swelling, welt

bump *v* 1 (hit sth) bang, collide, crash, hit, hurt, injure, jar, knock, ram, slam *inf*, smash into, strike, thump. 2 (bump up and down) bounce, jerk, jolt, rattle, shake. 3 **bump into** chance upon, come across, encounter, happen on, meet, run into, see

bunch *n* 1 (of things) batch, bundle, cluster, collection, group, heap, load, mass, pack, quantity, set. 2 (of flowers) bouquet, clump, posy, sheaf, spray. 3 (of people) band, crowd, gang, group, knot, party

bunch *v* 1 assemble, bundle, cluster, collect, crowd, flock, gather, group, herd, huddle, mass, pack; ***opp*** separate. 2 bunch up, fold, gather, pleat; ***opp*** lie flat

bundle *n* 1 assortment, batch, bunch, collection, heap, pile. 2 bag, pack,

package, parcel, roll, sheaf
bundle *v* bind, fasten, muffle, pack, package, roll, swathe, tie, truss, wrap
bungle *n* blunder, botch, error, fiasco, mess, mistake, mix-up, muddle, pig's ear *sl*, slip-up *inf*
bungle *v* blunder, botch, fudge, make a hash *inf*, make a mess *inf*, mess up *inf*, mismanage, muck up *inf*, ruin, spoil
buoyant *adj* **1** able to float, floating, light. **2** blithe, bouncy, bright, cheerful, jaunty, light-hearted, upbeat *inf*; ***opp*** depressed, low
burden *n* **1** anxiety, care, difficulty, duty, obligation, problem, responsibility, sorrow, stress, trial, trouble, worry. **2** cargo, encumbrance, load, weight
burden *v* afflict, bother, encumber, hamper, impose, load, lumber *inf*, overload, saddle *inf*, strain, tax, trouble, weigh down, worry
bureaucracy *n* administration, civil service, government, ministry, officialdom, red tape *inf*, rules and regulations
burglar *n* cat burglar, housebreaker, intruder, robber, thief
burglary *n* break-in, breaking and entering, housebreaking, larceny, robbery, stealing, theft, thieving
burly *adj* beefy, brawny, bulky, hefty, hulking, muscular, powerful, stocky, strong, sturdy, well-built; ***opp*** thin, weedy
burn *v* **1** be ablaze, be on fire, blaze, consume, flame, flare, flicker, glow, go up in flames, ignite, incinerate, kindle, light, reduce to ashes, set alight, set on fire, smoke, smolder, spark. **2** (damage) blister, char, parch, scald, sear, shrivel, singe, toast, wither
burning *adj* **1** alight, blazing, fiery, flaming, flickering, glowing, hot, incandescent, lit up, raging, scorching, smoking, smoldering. **2** ardent, eager, fervent, impassioned, intense, passionate, vehement. **3** biting, irritating, painful, prickling, searing, smarting, stinging. **4** acrid, caustic, corrosive, harsh, pungent, reeking, scorching, smoky
burrow *n* den, earth, hole, lair, shelter, tunnel, warren
burst *n* bang, blast, crack, discharge, explosion, rupture
burst *v* blow up, break, crack, disintegrate, erupt, explode, fly open, force open, fragment, give way, pierce, pop, puncture, rupture, shatter, split, tear
bury *v* **1** conceal, cover, cover up, embed, enclose, engulf, enshroud, hide, immerse, plant, sink, submerge. **2** (a dead person) entomb, inter, lay to rest
business *n* **1** (a firm) company, concern, enterprise, establishment, firm, industry, organization, outfit *inf*, partnership, practice, set-up *inf*, venture. **2** (to be in business) buying and selling, commerce, dealings, marketing, merchandising, selling, trade, transactions. **3** (business to be dealt with) affair, case, issue, matter, problem, question, subject, topic. **4** (line of business) career, job, line of work, occupation, profession, trade, work
businesslike *adj* efficient, methodical, neat, organized, professional, systematic,

thorough, well-ordered

bustle *n* activity, ado, agitation, commotion, excitement, flurry, fuss, haste, hurry, movement, toing and froing *inf*, tumult

bustle *v* dash, fuss, hurry, scamper, scramble, scurry, scuttle, tear, whirl

busy *adj* **1** (to be busy) active, employed, engaged, engrossed, hard at it *inf*, hard at work, industrious, occupied, on the go *inf*, rushed off your feet, slaving, up to your eyes *inf*, working; ***opp*** unoccupied. **2** (a busy life) chaotic, energetic, frantic, full, hectic, strenuous, tiring; ***opp*** quiet

butcher *n* killer, murderer, slaughterer, slayer

butcher *v* **1** (meat) carve, cut, kill, prepare, slice. **2** (people) kill, murder, massacre, put to death, slaughter, slay

butt *n* **1** (cigarette butt) end, stub. **2** (butt of a joke) dupe, laughing-stock, object, subject, target, victim

buy *v* acquire, come by, get, invest in *inf*, obtain, pay for, procure, purchase, shop for

bypass *v* avoid, circumvent, detour around, evade, go around, sidestep, skirt

bystander *n* eyewitness, observer, onlooker, passerby, spectator, witness

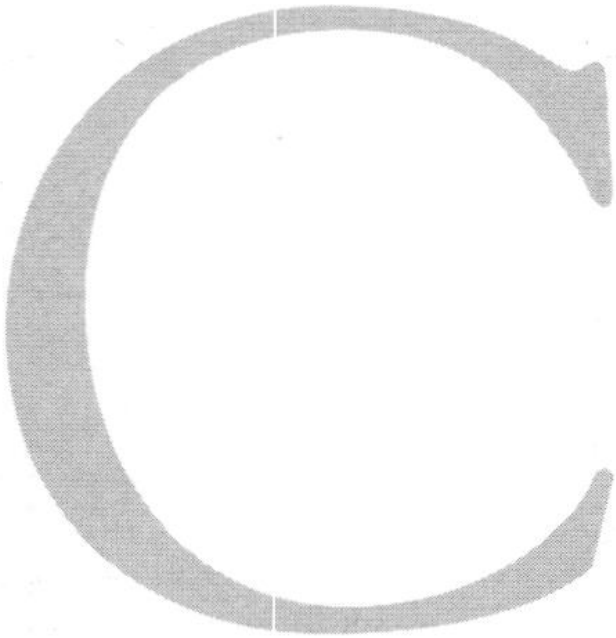

cabin *n* **1** chalet, hut, lodge, log cabin, shack, shed, shelter. **2** (on a ship) berth, compartment, quarters, room

café *n* cafeteria, coffee bar, coffee shop, diner, restaurant, snack bar, tearoom

cage *n* aviary, birdcage, corral, enclosure, hutch, pen, pound

cage *v* confine, coop up, corral, fence in, imprison, incarcerate, lock up, pen, restrain, shut up

calculate *v* **1** assess, consider, determine, evaluate, figure out, gauge, judge, rate, reckon, weigh up, work out. **2** (numbers) add, compute, count, estimate, find out, measure, reckon, total, weigh

calculated *adj* considered, deliberate, intended, intentional, on purpose, planned, premeditated

calculating *adj* canny, crafty, cunning, devious, manipulative, scheming, shrewd, sly; ***opp*** ingenuous

calculation *n* answer, computation, estimate, forecast, judgment, reckoning, result

call *n* **1** bellow, cry, exclamation, roar, shout, shriek, signal, song, whoop, yell. **2** appeal, command, demand, invitation, plea, request

call *v* **1** (call to sb) cry, cry out, exclaim, hail, shout, yell. **2** (using a telephone) call up, contact, give sb a buzz *inf*, give sb a ring, phone, ring, ring up *inf*, telephone. **3** (call somewhere) drop in *inf*, pay a call, pop in *inf*, stop by, visit. **4** (name sb or sth) christen, designate, dub, entitle, label, name, style, term, title. **5** (call a meeting) announce, convene, convoke, gather, order. **6** (call an ambulance) ask for, fetch, order, send for, summon. **7 call for** demand, entail, justify, necessitate, need, require

calling *n* business, career, job, occupation, profession, trade, vocation, work

callous *adj* cold, cool, dispassionate, hardened, hard-hearted, heartless, indifferent, insensitive, ruthless, soulless, stony-hearted, thick-skinned, uncaring, unemotional, unfeeling; ***opp*** sensitive

calm *adj* **1** airless, balmy, flat, mild, motionless, peaceful, placid, quiet, restful, serene, slow-moving, smooth, still, tranquil, windless. **2** (relaxed) collected, composed, controlled, cool, laid-back *inf*, level-headed, patient, relaxed, sensible, together *inf*, unexcited, unfazed *inf*, unflappable *inf*, unmoved, unruffled, untroubled; ***opp*** frantic

calm *n* **1** peace, peacefulness, quietness, restfulness, serenity, stillness, tranquillity. **2** composure, equanimity, impassivity, poise, sang-froid, self-control

calm *v* **1** (calm a situation) appease, compose, control, cool, mollify, smooth; ***opp*** inflame. **2** (calm a baby) hush, lull, pacify, placate, quieten, relax, settle, soothe, tranquilize; ***opp*** disturb

camouflage *n* blind, concealment, cover, disguise, facade, guise, markings, mask, mimicry, protective covering, veil

camouflage *v* cloak, conceal, cover, disguise, hide, mask, obscure, screen, veil

campaign *n* **1** action, crusade, drive, effort, fight, movement, promotion, struggle. **2** (military) attack, battle, expedition, offensive, push, war

campaign *v* agitate, battle, canvass, crusade, fight, push, struggle, work

cancel *v* **1** abandon, abolish, abort, annul, call off, declare void, invalidate, nullify, postpone, quash, repeal, rescind, revoke, scrap, scrub *inf*, wipe out, write off. **2** cross out, delete, erase, strike out

cancer *n* canker, carcinoma, growth, malignancy, melanoma, tumor

candid *adj* blunt, forthright, frank, honest, open, outspoken, plain, straightforward, truthful, upfront *inf*; ***opp*** cagey, deceitful

candidate *n* applicant, competitor, contender, contestant, entrant, nominee, possibility, runner *inf*

canvass *v* **1** (seek votes) campaign, drum up support *inf*, electioneer. **2** (investigate) analyze, examine, find out, inspect, investigate, scan, sift, study. **3** (seek opinions) ask for, discuss, poll, solicit

cap *v* **1** beat, better, eclipse, exceed, excel, outdo, outstrip, surpass, top, transcend. **2** coat, cover, crown, top

capability *n* ability, aptitude, capacity, competence, faculty, means, potential, power, skill, wherewithal

capable *adj* able, adept, clever, competent, efficient, experienced, gifted, handy *inf*, intelligent, masterly, practiced, proficient, qualified, skillful, skilled, talented, trained

capacity *n* **1** amplitude, dimensions, extent, magnitude, range, room, scope, size, space, volume. **2** ability, aptitude, cleverness, competence, intelligence, potential, power, skill, talent. **3** duty, function, job, office, position, post, responsibility, role

capital *adj* **1** (letters) big, block, initial, large, upper-case. **2** cardinal, central, chief, foremost, important, key, leading, main, major, paramount, primary, prime, principal

capital *n* **1** assets, cash, finance, funds, investments, liquid assets, money, principal, property, resources, savings, stock, wealth, wherewithal. **2** center of government, chief city, first city, seat of government

capitulate *v* acquiesce, admit defeat, back down, be defeated, concede, give in, give up, relent, submit, succumb, surrender, throw in the towel *inf*, yield

capsize *v* flip over, invert, keel over, knock over, overturn, tip over, turn over, turn upside down, upset

captain *n* boss, chief, commander, head, leader, master, officer, pilot, skipper

captive *adj* caged, captured, chained, confined, enslaved, fettered, imprisoned, in captivity, incarcerated, interned, jailed, locked up, taken prisoner, under lock and key *inf*; ***opp*** free

captive *n* convict, detainee, hostage, internee, prisoner, prisoner of war, slave

captivity *n* bondage, confinement, custody, detention, imprisonment, incarceration, internment, slavery; ***opp*** freedom

capture *n* apprehension, arrest, imprisonment, seizure

capture *v* apprehend, arrest, catch, collar *inf*, corner, ensnare, nab *inf*, nick *inf*, seize, take captive, take into custody, take prisoner, trap

car *n* automobile, vehicle, wheels *sl*

carcass *n* body, cadaver, corpse, dead body, meat, remains

care *n* **1** anxiety, burden, concern, difficulty, hardship, problem, sorrow, stress, trouble, woe, worry. **2** (do sth with care) attention, carefulness, caution, circumspection, concentration, consideration, diligence, forethought, heed, meticulousness, prudence, thought, vigilance, watchfulness. **3** (in sb's care) charge, control, custody, guardianship, keeping, management, protection, safekeeping, supervision

care *v* **1** be concerned, be interested, be troubled, bother, concern yourself with, give a hoot *inf*, mind, worry. **2 care for** (look after sb or sth) cherish, foster, look after, mind, minister to, mother, nurse, protect, provide for, take care of, tend, watch over. **3 care for** (like sb) be fond of, be in love with, cherish, hold dear, like, love. **4 care for** (want sth) desire, enjoy, fancy, want

career *n* business, calling, employment, livelihood, living, métier, occupation, profession, trade, vocation, work

carefree *adj* **1** blasé, casual, cheerful, contented, easygoing, happy, happy-go-lucky, insouciant, laid-back *inf*, light-hearted, nonchalant, relaxed, unworried; ***opp*** anxious. **2** (a carefree time) peaceful, quiet, relaxing, restful, trouble-free; ***opp*** stressful

careful *adj* **1** (careful in your work) accurate, conscientious, methodical, meticulous, neat, painstaking, particular, precise, rigorous, systematic, thorough, well-organized; ***opp*** careless. **2** (be careful) alert, attentive, cautious, circumspect, discreet, heedful, mindful, observant, on guard, solicitous, thoughtful, vigilant, wary, watchful; ***opp*** careless. **3** (careful with money) canny, cautious, economical, thrifty; ***opp*** wasteful

careless *adj* **1** absentminded, forgetful, hasty, inattentive, inconsiderate, indiscreet, irresponsible, negligent, rash, reckless, remiss, scatterbrained, thoughtless, unguarded, unthinking, unwary; ***opp*** careful. **2** (careless with your work) casual, disorganized, hasty, imprecise, inaccurate, messy, shoddy, slapdash, slipshod, sloppy *inf*, untidy; ***opp*** careful

caress *n* cuddle, embrace, hug, kiss, pat, touch

caress *v* cuddle, embrace, fondle, hug, kiss, nuzzle, pat, pet, stroke, touch

caretaker *n* curator, custodian, janitor,

keeper, porter, superintendent, warden, watchman

cargo *n* baggage, consignment, contents, freight, goods, haul, load, merchandise, shipment

caricature *n* cartoon, lampoon, parody, satire, send-up *inf*, spoof, take-off *inf*, travesty

caring *adj* altruistic, charitable, compassionate, concerned, considerate, helpful, humane, interested, kind, kind-hearted, kindly, loving, solicitous, sympathetic, thoughtful, understanding, unselfish, well-meaning; ***opp*** uncaring

carnage *n* bloodbath, bloodshed, butchery, massacre, murder, slaughter

carnival *n* celebration, fair, festival, fête, fiesta, gala, jamboree, holiday, merrymaking, parade, procession, revelry

carriage *n* **1** cab, car, coach, compartment. **2** bearing, comportment, demeanor, gait, manner, mien, posture, stance

carry *v* **1** (take sth somewhere) bear, bring, cart *inf*, conduct, convey, ferry, fetch, haul, lug *inf*, manhandle, move, remove, ship, shoulder, take, transfer, transmit, transport. **2** (support sth) bear, hold, support, sustain, underpin. **3** (carry a punishment) demand, entail, involve, lead to, occasion, require, result in. **4 carry on** continue, endure, go on, keep, keep going, last, maintain, persevere, persist. **5 carry out** accomplish, achieve, carry through, do, effect, fulfill, perform, realize

cartoon *n* animated film, animation, comic strip, drawing, sketch

carve *v* **1** cut, cut in, chisel, engrave, etch, form, hack, scratch, sculpture, shape. **2** (carve meat) cut up, do the honors, serve, slice, slice up

case *n* **1** box, carton, chest, container, crate, holder, pack. **2** bag, briefcase, hand luggage, luggage, suitcase, trunk. **3** casing, cover, covering, jacket, sheath, outer shell, wrapper. **4** (display case) cabinet, display cabinet, display case, glass case, showcase. **5** circumstances, example, illustration, instance, occasion, occurrence, position, situation. **6** (legal action) action, dispute, hearing, inquiry, investigation, lawsuit, legal action, proceedings, trial, tribunal

cash *n* change, coins, currency, dough *sl*, funds, money, notes, pennies *inf*, resources, small change

cast *n* **1** actors, cast list, characters, company, dramatis personae *tech*, performers, players, troupe. **2** casting, impression, mold, shape

cast *v* **1** chuck *inf*, fling, heave, hurl, lob, scatter, sling, throw, toss. **2** discard, get rid of, shed, slough off, throw off. **3** (cast a glow) direct, emit, give off, send out, shed

castle *n* citadel, chateau, fort, fortress, mansion, pile, stately home, stronghold

casual *adj* **1** blasé, carefree, careless, couldn't-care-less, cursory, easygoing, free and easy, happy-go-lucky, indifferent, informal, laid-back, nonchalant, offhand, relaxed, slap-happy, sloppy, unconcerned. **2** accidental, chance, impromptu, occasional, random, unexpected, unintentional, unplanned

casualty *n* fatality, injured, injured

person, hospital case, stretcher case, victim, wounded

catalog *n* **1** classification, directory, inventory, record, register. **2** booklet, brochure, guide, leaflet

catastrophe *n* blow, disaster, calamity, crisis, devastation, fiasco, mishap, tragedy

catch *n* **1** clasp, clip, fastener, fastening, hook, latch, lock. **2** (disadvantage) bad news, difficulty, disadvantage, downside, drawback, fly in the ointment, problem, snag. **3** bag, haul, prize, take

catch *v* **1** apprehend, arrest, capture, collar *inf*, grab, grab hold of, grasp, nab *inf*, seize, snatch; ***opp*** drop, let go. **2** catch sb red-handed, discover, expose, surprise, take sb by surprise. **3** (catch flu) be affected by, contract, get, develop, be down with. **4** (catch a train) get, get on, go by, take, travel by; ***opp*** miss. **5 catch on** be all the rage, be in demand, be popular. **6 catch on** get it, get the picture, realize, sth dawns on you, the penny drops, understand

catching *adj* contagious, communicable, infectious, transmissible, transmittable

categorical *adj* absolute, clear, complete, definite, explicit, express, out-and-out, total, unambiguous, unequivocal

category *n* class, classification, division, department, group, grouping, heading, kind, nature, section, sector, sort, type, variety

cater *v* look after, provide, satisfy, supply

catty *adj* bitchy, malicious, nasty, spiteful, vicious, vindictive

cause *n* **1** basis, grounds, incentive, motive, origin, reason, source; ***opp*** effect, result. **2** aim, campaign, end, movement, objective, purpose, struggle, undertaking

cause *v* be the cause of, bring about, bring on, create, end in, generate, give rise to, instigate, lead to, make, produce, provoke, result in, set off, spark off, trigger

caution *n* **1** care, carefulness, circumspection, discretion, prudence, vigilance, wariness; ***opp*** recklessness. **2** admonition, reprimand, talking-to, telling-off, warning

caution *v* **1** admonish, give sb a caution, reprimand, reprove, tell off, warn. **2** admonish, advise, counsel, urge

cautious *adj* alert, careful, chary, guarded, tentative, vigilant, wary; ***opp*** reckless

cave *n* cavern, chamber, grotto

cavernous *adj* deep, huge, massive, vast, yawning

cavity *n* aperture, gap, hole, hollow, opening, pit

cease *v* break off, bring sth to a halt, come to an end, die away, end, fizzle out, grind to a halt, finish, pack in *inf*, pack up *inf*, quit, stop; ***opp*** begin, start

celebrate *v* **1** commemorate, drink to, eulogize, honor, observe, toast. **2** enjoy yourself, have fun, let your hair down, live it up, paint the town red, party

celebrated *adj* acclaimed, distinguished, eminent, famed, famous, illustrious, legendary, renowned, revered, well-known

celebration *n* **1** commemoration, remembrance. **2** bash *inf*, do *inf*, event, festivity, party, shindig *inf*

celebrity *n* big name, bigwig *inf*,

dignitary, luminary, personality, star, VIP, worthy

celibate *adj* chaste, innocent, pure, virgin, virginal

cell *n* cubicle, dungeon, lock-up, prison, room

censor *v* ban, bowdlerize, blue-pencil, clean up, cut, edit, expurgate, prohibit, remove

censure *n* blame, castigation, criticism, condemnation, disapproval, rebuke, reproach

censure *v* berate, blame, castigate, condemn, criticize, denounce, lambast, rebuke, reprimand, reproach, take to task, upbraid

center *n* central point, core, crux, focal point, heart, hub, middle, mid-point, nucleus

central *adj* **1** mid, middle, inner, interior; ***opp*** outer, peripheral. **2** basic, chief, core, fundamental, important, key, main, pivotal, principal

centralize *v* amalgamate, center, concentrate, consolidate, converge, focus, rationalize; ***opp*** decentralize, devolve

ceremonial *adj* formal, official, ritual, ritualistic

ceremony *n* celebration, commemoration, formal occasion, function, rite, service

certain *adj* **1** (sure in your mind) confident, convinced, definite, positive, satisfied, sure. **2** beyond question, bound to happen, clear, definite, evident, inescapable, inevitable, irrevocable, in the bag *inf*, obvious, plain

certainty *n* **1** assurance, confidence, conviction, sureness. **2** dead cert *inf*, foregone conclusion, inevitability, open-and-shut case, safe bet

certificate *n* authorization, accreditation, award, degree, diploma, document, guarantee, license, pass, qualification, voucher, warrant

certify *v* accredit, authenticate, authorize, confirm, declare, guarantee, license, validate, verify

chain *n* progression, sequence, series, string, succession, train

chain *v* bind, fasten, fetter, fix, shackle, secure, tether, tie

chairman, chairwoman *n* chair, chairperson, convenor, moderator

challenge *n* **1** dare, invitation, taunt. **2** hard task, hurdle, job-and-a-half *inf*, obstacle, test, uphill struggle, venture

challenge *v* **1** (challenge sb to do sth) dare, defy, test, throw down the gauntlet. **2** (question sth) campaign against, contest, dispute, object to, query, question, raise an objection to, stand up to

champion *n* **1** gold-medalist, prize-winner, title-holder, victor, winner. **2** advocate, backer, campaigner, defender, promoter, supporter

chance *n* **1** (fate) accident, coincidence, destiny, fate, fluke, fortune, luck, providence. **2** risk, gamble. **3** likelihood, odds, probability, prospect. **4** (opportunity) opening, opportunity, possibility, prospect

change *n* about-turn, alteration, difference, innovation, metamorphosis, modification, mutation, reorganization, sea change, transformation, variation, volte-face

change *v* **1** alter, do an about-face *inf*, modify, rearrange, reform, reorganize, restyle, shift, transform, vary. **2** exchange, replace, substitute, swap

changeable *adj* changing, erratic, fickle, fluctuating, fluid, irregular, mercurial, shifting, uncertain, unpredictable, unstable, vacillating, variable, volatile

channel *n* canal, conduit, culvert, ditch, duct, groove, gutter, strait, waterway

channel *v* direct, force, guide, lead, move, send, steer

chant *v* intone, sing

chaos *n* bedlam, confusion, disorder, disarray, pandemonium, mayhem, shambles, tumult, turmoil

chaotic *adj* confused, disordered, disorganized, haywire, in a mess, in chaos, messy, muddled, topsy-turvy, untidy

character *n* **1** (nature) disposition, flavor, individuality, make-up, manner, nature, personality, quality, temperament. **2** (a person) case *inf*, eccentric, individual, oddball *inf*, oddity, person, sort

characteristic *adj* distinctive, distinguishing, individual, peculiar, typical

characteristic *n* attribute, feature, idiosyncrasy, mannerism, peculiarity, quality, quirk, trait

charade *n* absurdity, farce, fiasco, game, humbug, nonsense, pantomime, parody, pretense, put-up job *inf*, sham, show, travesty, whitewash

charge *n* **1** cost, fare, fee, levy, price, rate, rent, toll. **2** accusation, allegation, indictment. **3** care, custody, safe hands, safekeeping

charge *v* **1** ask, bill, debit, demand, invoice, set a price, want. **2** dash, hurtle, run, rush, stampede, storm, tear, zoom. **3** accuse, arraign, bring charges against, indict, put on trial

charitable *adj* **1** big-hearted, compassionate, forgiving, generous, indulgent, kind, magnanimous, sympathetic, tolerant, understanding; ***opp*** mean, uncharitable. **2** benevolent, humanitarian, philanthropic

charity *n* aid, alms, assistance, handouts, relief, welfare

charm *n* allure, appeal, attraction, charisma, fascination, lure, magic, magnetism, pull, seduction

charm *v* attract, beguile, bewitch, captivate, delight, enchant, fascinate, mesmerize

charming *adj* attractive, beautiful, captivating, delightful, enchanting, lovely, picturesque, pleasant, pretty, sweet; ***opp*** unattractive, horrid

chart *n* diagram, map, plan, table

chart *v* log, map out, mark, note, plot, record, show, sketch

charter *n* agreement, bill of rights, canon, code, constitution, contract, mission statement

chase *v* **1** follow, hound, pursue, run after, set off after, shadow, sit on sb's tail, tail, track. **2** drive away, see off, send packing

chaste *adj* celibate, innocent, pure, undefiled, unsullied, virgin, virginal; ***opp*** immoral, licentious

chastity *n* celibacy, innocence, purity,

virginity, virtue

chat *n* chit-chat, confab *inf*, discussion, gossip, heart-to-heart, one-to-one, small talk, talk

chat *v* chatter, chew the fat *inf*, cozy up to *inf*, discuss, gossip, have a chat, have a heart-to-heart *inf*, talk

chatter *v* chat, discuss, gossip, have a chat, talk

cheap *adj* 1 bargain-rate, budget, cut-price, dirt-cheap *inf*, discounted, economical, economy, marked-down, inexpensive, knock-down, low-cost, low-priced, reasonable, reduced, rock-bottom *inf*, sale; ***opp*** expensive, extortionate, over-priced, top-rate. 2 cheapo *inf*, second-rate, shoddy, tacky, tawdry, trashy

cheat *n* con man *inf*, fraud, racketeer, shark *inf*, swindler

cheat *v* con *inf*, deceive, defraud, do *inf*, double-cross, fleece *inf*, hoodwink, overcharge, pull a fast one *inf*, rip off *inf*, rob *inf*, sting *inf*, swindle, take sb for a ride *inf*, take sb to the cleaners *inf*, trick

check *n* 1 examination, inspection, test, once-over *inf*, spot-check. 2 brake, curb, delay, halt, slow-down, stoppage

check *v* 1 confirm, make sure, see, verify. 2 check out, check over, examine, give sth the once-over *inf*, inspect, look at, test. 3 curb, halt, inhibit, limit, obstruct, put the brakes on, restrain, slowdown, stem, stop

cheek *n* audacity, effrontery, gall, impudence, nerve, temerity

cheeky *adj* discourteous, impertinent, impudent, insolent, rude, sassy; ***opp*** polite

cheer *n* cheering, hooray, hurrah, shout, whoop

cheerful *adj* bright and breezy, bright-eyed and bushy-tailed, chipper, contented, full of beans, full of the joys of spring, enthusiastic, happy, in a good mood, in high spirits, optimistic, perky, sanguine, smiling, upbeat

cheer up *v* bring a smile to sb's face, buck up *inf*, buoy up, console, liven up, make sb happier, raise sb's spirits, perk up *inf*, uplift

cherish *v* 1 adore, care for, hold dear, love, revere, treasure, value. 2 (cherish a hope) foster, harbor, have, maintain, nurse, nurture

chest *n* 1 box, case, casket, coffer, crate, trunk. 2 chest of drawers, tallboy. 3 bosom, breast

chew *v* champ, chomp, crunch, gnaw, masticate, munch

chief *adj* central, first, foremost, key, leading, main, most important, paramount, premier, primary, principal, top, uppermost, vital

chief *n* bigwig *inf*, boss, controller, director, head, leader, manager, number one, person in charge, person at the top, principal, ringleader, ruler, superior, supremo, top dog *inf*

child *n* baby, boy, daughter, girl, infant, juvenile, kid, kiddie, little one, minor, mite, offspring, son, teenager, toddler, tot, youngster

childhood *n* adolescence, babyhood, boyhood, early days, formative years, girlhood, infancy, school days, teens, young days, youth

childish *adj* adolescent, babyish, boyish,

girlish, immature, infantile, juvenile, naive, puerile, silly

childlike *adj* artless, innocent, naive, simple, youthful

chill *adj* chilly, cold, cool, fresh, icy, raw

chill *v* cool, cool down, make cold, put on ice, refrigerate; ***opp*** warm

chip *n* **1** break, nick, notch. **2** fragment, bit, shaving, shard, flake, sliver, splinter

chivalrous *adj* courteous, courtly, gallant, gentlemanly, gracious, honorable, knightly, noble, polite, protective

choice *adj* best, desirable, exclusive, fine, first-class, first-rate, prime, quality, select, special, superior, top-quality; ***opp*** low-quality, poor, second-rate

choice *n* **1** alternative, decision, option, pick, possibility, preference, selection, vote. **2** array, assortment, range, selection, supply, variety

choke *v* **1** asphyxiate, smother, strangle, suffocate, throttle. **2** cough, gag, gasp for air, retch. **3** block, block up, clog, congest, jam, obstruct

choose *v* decide on, desire, fix on, name, opt for, pick, pick out, prefer, select, single out, vote for

chore *n* **1** job, daily grind, duty, hack work, housework, task, toil. **2** bore, burden, drag *inf*, drudgery

chorus *n* call, refrain, response, shout

chronic *adj* **1** appalling, awful, bad, boring, dire, dreadful, tedious, terrible. **2** confirmed, constant, habitual, incessant, incurable, lifelong, long-term, nonstop, persistent

chunk *n* bit, hunk, lump, part, piece, section, wedge

circle *n* **1** ball, band, disk, hoop, ring, round, sphere. **2** (of people) band, clique, crowd, gang, group, set

circle *v* **1** circumnavigate, draw a ring round, encircle, ring. **2** gyrate, revolve, rotate, spin, turn, wheel, whirl

circuit *n* course, journey, lap, loop, ring, round, tour, track

circuitous *adj* indirect, meandering, labyrinthine, roundabout, tortuous; ***opp*** direct

circular *adj* **1** ring-shaped, disk-shaped, round, spherical. **2** (circular argument) going nowhere, illogical, repetitive, tautologous

circulate *v* broadcast, disseminate, distribute, pass round, promulgate, send around, spread, transmit

circumstance *n* accident, event, factor, happenstance, occasion, position, situation

circumstances *n* how things stand, position, situation, state of affairs

citizen *n* civilian, man/woman in the street, member of society, person, resident, subject, taxpayer, voter

city *n* concrete jungle, conurbation, downtown, town, metropolis, metropolitan area, urban area

civil *adj* **1** cordial, courteous, pleasant, polite, well-mannered; ***opp*** rude. **2** civic, domestic, home, internal, municipal, public, state

civilization *n* country, culture, life, people, society, way of life

civilize *v* advance, cultivate, develop, educate, improve, refine

civilized *adj* **1** advanced, cultivated, developed, educated, refined, social. **2** comfortable, enjoyable, luxurious, pleasant

claim *n* **1** allegation, assertion, protestation, statement. **2** application, call, demand, request, right

claim *v* **1** allege, assert, declare, maintain, profess, say, state. **2** ask for, collect, demand, get, pick up, request, send off for

clamber *v* climb, scrabble, scramble, shin

clan *n* clique, faction, family, gang, group, set, tribe

clap *v* applaud, give sb a round of applause, put your hands together, show your appreciation in the usual way

clarify *v* disambiguate, elucidate, explain, make clear, put your cards on the table, simplify, spell out what you mean, resolve

clash *n* brush, confrontation, disagreement, dispute, fight, quarrel, row, showdown

clash *v* come into conflict, come to blows, confront, cross swords, fall out, fight, quarrel, squabble, wrangle

clasp *v* clutch, embrace, grasp, hold, hug

class *n* **1** category, classification, division, grade, group, league, rank, set, sort, status, type, variety. **2** lesson, period, seminar, study group, tutorial

class *v* arrange, categorize, classify, grade, group, order, rank, rate

classic *adj* **1** brilliant, definitive, excellent, fine, first-rate, great, superlative. **2** archetypal, copybook, model, prototypical, typical. **3** (a classic style) elegant, simple, timeless, traditional

classical *adj* **1** Greek, Latin, Roman. **2** elegant, harmonious, simple, traditional, well-proportioned

classification *n* **1** arrangement, cataloging, codification, grading, grouping, ordering, organization, taxonomy. **2** category, class, division, grade, group, rank

classify *v* arrange, categorize, catalog, class, grade, group, order, rank, rate

clause *n* condition, item, part, passage, point, proviso, section, statement, stipulation, subsection

clean *adj* **1** clean as a whistle, hygienic, immaculate, laundered, polished, pristine, scrubbed, shining, spick and span, spotless, sterile, sterilized, washed; ***opp*** dirty. **2** (clean water) clear, fresh, pure, uncontaminated, unpolluted; ***opp*** contaminated, polluted

clean *v* dust, polish, sanitize, scrub, spring-clean, sterilize, sweep, vacuum, wash, wipe

clear *adj* **1** apparent, beyond doubt, beyond question, coherent, distinct, evident, lucid, obvious, plain, unambiguous, understandable, unmistakable; ***opp*** unclear. **2** (clear glass, water) clean, colorless, see-through, transparent, unclouded. **3** (clear sky) bright, cloudless, fine, moonlit, sunny, starlit; ***opp*** cloudy, dull, overcast. **4** empty, free, open, unblocked, unobstructed; ***opp*** blocked

clear *v* **1** clean, clean out, empty, free, get rid of, remove, unblock, unclog, tidy, tidy up. **2** (clear sb) absolve, acquit, excuse, exonerate, vindicate. **3** (the sky clears) brighten, brighten up, lighten. **4 clear up** (solve a mystery) crack *inf*, explain, find an answer to, resolve,

solve, unravel. **5 clear up** (tidy things away) pack up, put sth in order, put things away, sort out, tidy up. **6 clear up** get better, improve

clearly *adv* distinctly, evidently, obviously, patently, plainly, visibly

clever *adj* astute, brainy *inf*, bright, brilliant, canny *inf*, competent, educated, intelligent, ingenious, knowledgable, quick, sharp, shrewd, smart, streetwise, talented

cliché *n* adage, hackneyed phrase, maxim, platitude, saying, stereotype, truism, well-worn expression

client *n* consumer, customer, patron, regular, user

climate *n* **1** (weather) atmospheric conditions, microclimate, temperature, weather. **2** atmosphere, conditions, feeling, mood, spirit, setting, situation

climax *n* apogee, crowning point, culmination, finale, height, peak, pinnacle, zenith

climax *v* **1** culminate, peak, come to a head, result, end. **2** have an orgasm

climb *v* **1** ascend, clamber, climb up, go up, move up, mount, rise, shin up, shoot up, soar. **2** (climb a mountain) ascend, conquer, reach the summit of, reach the top of, scale

cling *v* adhere, attach yourself, cling on, grip, hold, hold fast, hold on, stick

clip *n* **1** clasp, fastener, paper clip, pin. **2** clipping, cutting, excerpt, extract, passage, scene, snippet

clip *v* **1** attach, fasten, fix, pin, staple. **2** crop, cut, cut off, lop, prune, shear, shorten, snip, trim

cloak *n* cape, coat, overcoat, shawl, wrap

clog *v* block, block up, choke, clog up, congest, jam, jam up, obstruct, stop up

close *adj* **1** (in space) adjacent, adjoining, close by, convenient, handy, hard by, near, nearby, neighboring, at hand; ***opp*** distant. **2** (in time) approaching, at hand, imminent, impending, near, nigh; ***opp*** distant. **3** (of friends) dear, devoted, inseparable, intimate, loving. **4** (of weather) humid, muggy, oppressive, sultry, sweaty, sweltering

close *n* cessation, completion, conclusion, dénouement, end, ending, finish, termination

close *v* **1** bolt, fasten, lock, seal, shut, slam; ***opp*** open. **2** (close an investigation) bring to a close, bring to an end, cease, complete, conclude, end, finish, terminate, wind up; ***opp*** open. **3** (get nearer) approach, catch up, chase, near, pursue

closed *adj* **1** bolted, fastened, locked, sealed, shut, unopened; ***opp*** open. **2** completed, concluded, ended, finished, over, over and done with, resolved, settled

cloth *n* **1** fabric, material, textile. **2** (piece of cloth) cover, dishcloth, dishtowel, napkin, serviette, tablecloth, wipe

clothes *n* apparel, attire, clothing, costume, dress, garb, garments, gear *inf*, get-up *inf*, outfit, raiment, togs *inf*, wardrobe, wear

cloud *n* **1** cloud cover, fog, haze, mist, vapor, water vapor. **2** cirrus, cumulus, nimbus, stratus

cloudy *adj* **1** (of sky, weather) dull, foggy, hazy, misty, overcast. **2** (of liquid, glass) frosted, milky, misty, muddy, murky, opaque, smoky, steamed up

clown *n* **1** (performer) comedian, comic, fool, jester, pierrot. **2** buffoon, fool, idiot, joker

club *n* **1** association, brotherhood, circle, federation, fraternity, group, guild, league, organization, society, sorority, team, union. **2** bar, cabaret, disco *inf*, discothèque, nightclub, night spot. **3** baton, blackjack, bludgeon, cudgel, shillelagh, stave, stick, truncheon

clue *n* hint, idea, indication, inkling, key, lead, pointer, sign

clumsy *adj* awkward, blundering, bumbling, bungling, gawky, graceless, ham-fisted, lumbering, maladroit, uncoordinated, ungainly

cluster *n* accumulation, bunch, clump, collection, gathering, group, knot, mass

cluster *v* accumulate, bunch, coalesce, gather, group, mass, press

clutch *v* clasp, cling to, grasp, grip, hang on to, hold, hold on to

clutter *n* chaos, disorder, jumble, litter, mess, garbage, untidiness

clutter *v* encumber, fill, fill up, litter, pack, pile high, strew, stuff

coach *v* direct, drill, exercise, guide, instruct, manage, prepare, teach, train, tutor

coalition *n* alliance, allies, amalgamation, association, bloc, compact, confederacy, confederation, league, merger, pact, union

coarse *adj* **1** crude, rough, tough, uneven, unrefined. **2** (in manners) boorish, common, crude, gross, ill-mannered, uncouth, vulgar

coast *n* coastline, littoral, shore, seaboard, seaside, shoreline

coast *v* cruise, drift, freewheel, glide, relax, slide

coat *n* **1** anorak, cloak, duffel coat, fleece, jacket, mac *inf*, mackintosh, overcoat, parka, raincoat, topcoat. **2** (of an animal) fleece, fur, hair, pelt. **3** (of paint) coating, covering, film, finish, glaze, layer, patina

coat *v* cover, plaster, spread, smear

coax *v* cajole, encourage, entice, induce, inveigle, persuade, talk sb into/out of sth, sweet-talk *inf*, wheedle

code *n* **1** (system of rules, beliefs) canon, code of conduct, convention, custom, ethics, etiquette, manners, oath, rules. **2** (for writing and understanding messages) coding system, cipher, key, notation. **3** (sequence of letters or numbers) combination, password, PIN, user ID. **4** (types of code) Morse code, semaphore, sign language

coerce *v* compel, constrain, force, intimidate, make, persuade, twist sb's arm

coherent *adj* articulate, clear, cogent, cohesive, consistent, intelligible, logical, lucid, organized, reasoned, sound, systematic, well-ordered, well-structured; ***opp*** incoherent

coil *v* curl, entwine, loop, snake, spiral, twine, twist, wind

coincide *v* accord, agree, be the same, clash, combine, come together, concur, correspond, happen at the same time, line up, match, tally

coincidence *n* accident, chance, fluke, stroke of luck

cold *adj* **1** arctic, biting, bitter, chill, chilled, chilly, cool, drafty, freezing, fresh, frigid, frosty, frozen, glacial, ice-cold, icy, nippy *inf*, refrigerated, wintry; ***opp*** hot, warm. **2** (of a person, atmosphere) aloof, callous, chilly, cold-blooded, cold-hearted, cool, distant, forbidding, frigid, frosty, hard-hearted, heartless, indifferent, inhospitable, inhuman, insensitive, passionless, reserved, standoffish, stony, uncaring, unemotional, unfeeling, unfriendly, unsympathetic, unwelcoming; ***opp*** warm

cold *n* bug *inf*, chill, common cold, flu, influenza, sniffle *inf*, viral infection, virus

collaborate *v* assist, band together, collude, connive, conspire, cooperate, help, join forces, pool resources, pull together, team up, work together

collaborator *n* **1** accomplice, assistant, associate, co-author, confederate, colleague, fellow worker, helper, helpmate, partner. **2** (with an enemy) Judas, quisling, traitor, turncoat

collapse *n* breakdown, disintegration, failure, implosion

collapse *v* **1** (of an object) cave in, come apart, fall apart, fall down, fall in, fall over, fall to pieces, give way, implode, subside. **2** (of a person) be taken ill, crumple, faint, fall over, keel over, pass out. **3** (of an idea) break down, disintegrate, fail, fall apart, fall through, fall to pieces, fold, founder; ***opp*** succeed, thrive

colleague *n* associate, collaborator, comrade, fellow worker, partner, peer, workmate

collect *v* accumulate, assemble, bring together, gather, hoard, marshal, pile up, stock, stockpile, store

collected *adj* **1** accumulated, assembled, assorted, complete. **2** (of a person) calm, composed, cool, focused

collection *n* accumulation, anthology, array, assemblage, assembly, assortment, cluster, compilation, gathering, group, heap, hoard, pile, set, stack, stock, stockpile, store

collide *v* bang, bump into, crash into, come into collision with, meet head-on, smash into, strike, strike against

collision *n* bang, bump, crash, impact, smash

colloquial *adj* common, conversational, everyday, idiomatic, informal, popular, slang, spoken, vernacular

color *n* **1** coloration, coloring, hue, pigment, pigmentation, shade, tinge, tint, tone. **2** (attractive quality) excitement, interest, spice, variety, vividness

color *v* color in, dye, paint, stain, tinge, tint

colorful *adj* **1** bright, brilliant, gaudy, iridescent, multicolored, psychedelic, vibrant, vivid; ***opp*** drab, dull. **2** (of a story, event) exciting, exotic, graphic, interesting, lively, stimulating, striking, vivid; ***opp*** dull. **3** (of a person) dashing, eccentric, distinctive, extrovert, flamboyant, glamorous, larger-than-life, unusual; ***opp*** dull

column *n* **1** monument, pilaster, pile, pillar, pole, post, shaft, support, strut, upright. **2** (in a newspaper) article, diary, editorial, feature, leader, leading article, section. **3** (of people) file, line, procession, queue, trail, train

comb *v* examine, look in, rummage through, scour, search, turn inside out

combat *n* battle, battlefield, conflict, fighting, hand-to-hand combat, hostilities, struggle, war

combat *v* battle against, defeat, fight, oppose, resist, struggle against, wage war against

combination *n* alliance, amalgam, amalgamation, blend, conjunction, fusion, integration, merger, mix, mixing, union

combine *v* **1** (combine things, people) add together, ally, amalgamate, bind, blend, bring together, fuse, integrate, intertwine, interweave, join, join together, lump together, marry, merge, mingle, mix, pool, put together, synthesize, unite. **2** (people, things combine) ally, amalgamate, blend, club together, coalesce, coincide, come together, conspire, co-occur, cooperate, form an alliance, fuse, gang up, integrate, intertwine, interweave, join, join forces, join together, merge, mingle, mix, team up, unite

come *v* **1** (move toward) advance, appear, approach, come up, draw nearer, enter, move toward, reach. **2** (come to an event or place) arrive, attend, be present, get (to), show up, turn up, visit. **3 come about** come to pass, fall out, happen, occur, take place. **4 come across** encounter, find, meet, see. **5 come back** get back, retrace your steps, return. **6 come from** be derived from, be made from, have its origin(s) in, have its source in, originate from, originate in. **7 come from** (of a person) be a native of, be born in, be from, be originally from, hail from. **8 come around** (after being unconscious) recover, recover consciousness, regain consciousness, wake, wake up. **9 come around** (to sb's home) come over, drop in *inf*, pay a visit, pop in *inf*, pop over *inf*, visit. **10 come around to** (= agree with) accede to, acquiesce in, agree, be convinced of, be converted to, be persuaded of. **11 come up with** deliver, devise, discover, find, invent, offer, produce, propose, provide, put forward, submit, suggest, turn up

comeback *n* recovery, resurrection, return, revival

comedian *n* clown, comedienne, comic, entertainer, humorist

comedy *n* **1** clowning, humor, situation comedy, slapstick, stand-up comedy; ***opp*** tragedy. **2** (individual play or performance) sitcom, situation comedy, sketch, turn. **3** (of a situation) absurdity, amusement, funny side, humor, ridiculousness, silliness

comfort *n* ease, luxuriousness, luxury, opulence, warmth, well-being; ***opp*** discomfort

comfortable *adj* **1** (of furniture, surroundings) comfy *inf*, cozy, de luxe, easy, homey, luxurious, opulent, padded, plush, relaxing, snug, soft, upholstered, warm. **2** (of a person) at ease, comfy *inf*, cozy, relaxed, snug

comforting *adj* compassionate, considerate, consoling, fatherly, gentle, kind, paternal, reassuring, supportive, sympathetic

comic *adj* absurd, amusing, comical, droll, facetious, funny, hilarious, humorous, joking, light, rib-tickling, side-splitting, silly, waggish, whimsical, witty; ***opp*** tragic

comical *adj* absurd, amusing, comic, farcical, funny, laughable, ludicrous, rich, silly, ridiculous

coming *adj* approaching, at hand, future, imminent, impending, in store, next, upcoming

command *n* **1** (words to be obeyed) commandment, decree, directive, edict, injunction, instruction, order. **2** (power to command) ascendancy, authority, charge, control, direction, domination, dominion, government, leadership, mastery, power, superiority, supremacy

command *v* **1** (tell sb to do sth) ask, charge, decree, direct, instruct, order, tell. **2** (command an army) be in charge of, be in control of, control, dominate, have authority over, have dominion over, have power over, have superiority over, have supremacy over, have the ascendancy over, direct, govern, head, head up, lead, outrank

commander *n* **1** boss, chief, commandant, commanding officer, head, leader, superior, superior officer, supremo. **2** (military and police ranks) admiral, captain, commander-in-chief, field marshal, general

commemorate *v* celebrate, honor, pay homage to, pay your respects to, remember, salute

commendable *adj* admirable, creditable, estimable, exemplary, laudable, meritorious, praiseworthy, valiant, worthy

comment *n* **1** allusion, mention, observation, opinion, reaction, reference, remark, response. **2** (in writing) annotation, footnote, note

comment *v* **1** express an opinion, interpose, note, observe, opine, react, remark, respond, say, venture. **2 comment on** allude to, annotate, discuss, mention, refer to, talk about

commentary **1** (spoken) comments, narration, narrative, remarks, running commentary, voice-over. **2** criticism, discussion, exegesis, interpretation, review

commentator **1** announcer, broadcaster, DJ, narrator, presenter, pundit, reporter, speaker. **2** critic, expert, reviewer, specialist, writer

commerce *n* business, buying and selling, commercial activity, dealing, money-making, trade, trading

commercial *adj* business, capitalist, entrepreneurial, financial, mercenary, money-making, profit-making

commiserate *v* comfort, console, empathize, sympathize; ***opp*** congratulate

commission *n* **1** (sth to be done) brief, instruction, mandate, remit, task. **2** (official body) authority, board, committee, tribunal

commission *v* appoint, contract, employ, engage, hire, order, request

commit *v* **1** carry out, do, effect, execute, perform, perpetrate. **2** (commit sth to sb's care) assign, certify, consign, deliver, entrust, give, hand over, send. **3 commit yourself** bind yourself, engage, give an assurance, give an undertaking, make a decision, make up your mind, pledge, promise, swear, take the plunge

committed *adj* active, ardent, card-carrying, confirmed, dedicated, determined, devoted, diehard, earnest, engaged, fervent, firm, loyal, militant, passionate, persevering, resolute, resolved, single-minded, stalwart, staunch, sworn, unswerving, unwavering, wholehearted, zealous

commitment *n* **1** (dedication) ardor, dedication, determination, devotion, fervor, loyalty, passion, perseverance, resolution, single-mindedness, support, zeal. **2** (sth you have committed yourself to) engagement, oath, promise, undertaking

committee *n* board, executive, panel, steering group

common *adj* **1** (ordinary) common-or-garden, commonplace, customary, everyday, familiar, habitual, normal, ordinary, plain, regular, routine, run-of-the-mill, standard, stock, traditional, typical, unexceptional, usual. **2** (not rare) frequent, numerous, plentiful, popular, widespread; ***opp*** rare. **3** collective, communal, general, in common, joint, jointly owned, mutual, reciprocal, same, shared. **4** (of a person, manners) coarse, crude, earthy, ill-bred, lower-class, plebeian, uneducated, vulgar

common sense *n* intelligence, level-headedness, practicality, prudence, reason, sense

commotion *n* agitation, bedlam *inf*, chaos, confusion, din, disorder, disturbance, excitement, ferment, fray, furor, fuss, hubbub, hullabaloo *inf*, pandemonium, racket *inf*, rumpus, sensation, stir, to-do *inf*, trouble, tumult, turmoil, unrest, uproar

communal *adj* collective, common, community, general, in common, joint, jointly owned, public, same, shared

communicate *v* **1** (with sb) be in communication, be in contact, be in touch, commune, contact, get through to, interact, speak to, talk to. **2** (communicate an idea) convey, express, get across, get over, impart, transmit

communication *n* **1** broadcasting, contact, correspondence, exchange, interaction, intercourse, speech, telecommunications. **2** (letter, message) announcement, bulletin, cable, card, communiqué, conversation, dialogue, directive, dispatch, E-mail, fax, letter, memo, memorandum, message, note, notice, piece of news, report, signal, statement, telegram, telephone call, transmission, wire

communicative *adj* chatty, expressive, forthcoming, informative, open, outgoing, talkative

community *n* colony, commune, group, neighborhood, settlement, society

compact *adj* compressed, concise, condensed, dense, miniature, neat, small, tightly packed

companion *n* assistant, associate, chaperone, comrade, colleague, confidant, confidante, consort, escort, fellow traveler, friend, mate, partner, servant, sidekick

companionship *n* company, comradeship, friendship, partnership

company *n* **1** business, concern, corporation, enterprise, establishment, firm, organization. **2** (group of people) assembly, audience, band, crew, crowd, ensemble, gang, gathering, group, troop, troupe. **3** companionship, friends, friendship, guests, society, visitors

comparable *adj* alike, analogous, equal, equivalent, like, matching, parallel, related, similar

compare *v* **1** balance, contrast, differentiate, juxtapose, set against. **2** draw a parallel, draw/make a comparison, equate, liken, look like, match, resemble

comparison *n* **1** (make a comparison) analogy, contrast, difference, distinction, juxtaposition, parallel. **2** (there's no comparison) comparability, correlation, likeness, resemblance, similarity

compartment *n* area, berth, booth, carriage, cell, chamber, cubby-hole *inf*, cubicle, locker, pigeonhole, section, slot, space

compassion *n* benevolence, concern, consideration, heart, humanitarianism, humanity, kind-heartedness, kindness, leniency, mercy, pity, soft-heartedness, sorrow, sympathy, tenderness, understanding

compassionate *adj* benevolent, considerate, gentle, humane, humanitarian, kind, kind-hearted, lenient, merciful, soft-hearted, sympathetic, tender, understanding

compatible *adj* **1** (of people) in-tune, like-minded, similar, suitable, suited, well-matched; ***opp*** incompatible. **2** (of claims, ideas) consistent, in keeping, reconcilable; ***opp*** incompatible

compensate *v* **1** atone, expiate, indemnify, make amends, make good, pay back, pay compensation, recompense, refund, reimburse, repay. **2** (one thing compensates for another) balance, cancel, counteract, counterbalance, even up, make up for, neutralize, nullify, offset, redress

compensation *adj* atonement, damages, indemnity, recompense, refund, reimbursement, reparation, repayment, redress, restitution

compete *v* be a contestant, be in competition, challenge, contend, contest, fight, oppose, participate, pit yourself against, rival, take part, vie

competent *adj* able, accomplished, adept, capable, clever, effective, experienced, expert, fit, good, handy *inf*, proficient, qualified, skillful, skilled, trained; ***opp*** inept

competition *n* **1** championship, contest, game, heat, match, race, rally, tournament. **2** conflict, contention, opposition, rivalry, strife, struggle

competitive *adj* aggressive, ambitious, antagonistic, combative, cutthroat, dog-eat-dog

competitor *n* adversary, antagonist, candidate, challenger, contender, contestant, entrant, opponent, opposition, participant, rival

compile *v* accumulate, amass, arrange, assemble, collate, collect, compose, draw up, gather, organize, put together

complacent *adj* at ease, pleased, satisfied,

self-assured, self-satisfied, smug, unconcerned

complain *v* bellyache *inf*, bemoan, carp, criticize, find fault, fuss, go on about *inf*, gripe *inf*, grouch *inf*, grouse, grumble, moan, nag, object, protest, remonstrate, whine

complaint *n* **1** accusation, charge, condemnation, criticism, grievance, gripe *inf*, grouch *inf*, grouse, grumble, moan, objection, protest, remonstrance. **2** (medical) affliction, ailment, condition, disease, disorder, illness, infection, sickness, upset

complementary *adj* corresponding, interdependent, interrelating, matching, paired, reciprocal, twin

complete *adj* **1** comprehensive, entire, exhaustive, full, in its entirety, intact, total, unabbreviated, unabridged, unbroken, uncut, unedited, whole; ***opp*** partial. **2** (finished) accomplished, achieved, completed, concluded, done, ended, finished, over; ***opp*** incomplete. **3** (total) absolute, arrant, consummate, downright, out-and-out, outright, thorough, total, unmitigated, unqualified, utter

complete *v* accomplish, achieve, clinch, close, conclude, discharge, do, effect, end, execute, finalize, finish, fulfill, realize, round off, settle, terminate, wind up *inf*, wrap up; ***opp*** begin

completely *adv* absolutely, altogether, entirely, from beginning to end, fully, perfectly, thoroughly, totally, utterly, wholly

complex *adj* complicated, convoluted, difficult, elaborate, intricate, involved, knotty, problematic, sophisticated, tangled, tortuous; ***opp*** simple

complex *n* fixation, hang-up, mania, neurosis, obsession, phobia, preoccupation

complexion *n* cast, color, coloring, hue, skin, skin tone, tinge

complicate *v* compound, confound, confuse, entangle, jumble, mix up, muddle, snarl up; ***opp*** simplify

complicated *adj* complex, convoluted, difficult, elaborate, intricate, involved, knotty, problematic, sophisticated, tangled, tortuous; ***opp*** simple

complication *n* **1** difficulty, drawback, obstacle, problem, setback, snag. **2** complexity, confusion, convolution, difficulty, dilemma, intricacy, mix-up, muddle

compliment *n* accolade, commendation, endorsement, eulogy, flattery, honor, plaudits, praise, tribute; ***opp*** insult

complimentary *adj* **1** admiring, appreciative, approving, commendatory, favorable, flattering, generous, laudatory; ***opp*** critical. **2** free, free of charge, gratis, on the house

comply *v* abide by, accede, acquiesce, adhere to, agree, assent, conform, consent, fall in, fit in, follow, fulfill, heed, keep, meet, obey, observe, respect, satisfy, submit, yield; ***opp*** disobey

component *n* bit, constituent, element, ingredient, part, piece, section, segment

compose *v* **1** (music, poetry) arrange, concoct, create, devise, invent, make up, produce, think up, write. **2** (compose yourself) calm down, calm yourself, collect your thoughts, relax

composed *adj* at ease, calm, confident, cool, laidback, level-headed, poised, relaxed, sedate, self-controlled, self-possessed, serene, undisturbed, unfazed, unflappable, unperturbed, unruffled, together *inf*; ***opp*** disturbed, upset

composition *n* **1** arrangement, configuration, constitution, design, form, formation, layout, make-up, organization, structure. **2** creation, essay, literary work, opus, piece, study, work, work of art

compound *n* blend, combination, composite, fusion, mixture, synthesis

compound *v* **1** amalgamate, blend, combine, fuse, mix, put together, synthesize. **2** add to, aggravate, augment, complicate, exacerbate, heighten, intensify, magnify, make worse, worsen; ***opp*** alleviate

comprehend *v* appreciate, apprehend, catch on *inf*, conceive, discern, fathom, follow, get *inf*, grasp, know, make out, realize, see, take in, understand

comprehension *n* appreciation, grasp, knowledge, perception, realization, sense, understanding

comprehensive *adj* all-embracing, all-inclusive, blanket, broad, complete, exhaustive, extensive, far-reaching, full, inclusive, thorough, total, umbrella, universal, wide, wide-ranging; ***opp*** selective, partial

comprise *v* be composed of, consist of, contain, cover, embody, embrace, encompass, include, incorporate, involve

compromise *n* agreement, bargain, concession, deal, give-and-take, happy medium, middle course, settlement, trade-off, understanding

compromise *v* **1** (compromise on sth) come to an understanding, concede, make concessions, meet halfway, negotiate a settlement, settle, strike a balance. **2** (compromise sb's reputation) bring into disrepute, damage, discredit, endanger, imperil, jeopardize, prejudice, risk, undermine, weaken

compulsion *n* **1** desire, drive, fixation, necessity, need, obsession, preoccupation, urge. **2** coercion, constraint, duress, enforcement, force, oppression, pressure, requirement

compulsive *adj* **1** (compulsive drinker, gambler) addicted, habitual, incurable, obsessive, persistent. **2** (compulsive viewing) compelling, fascinating, gripping, irresistible

compulsory adj mandatory, necessary, obligatory, required, requisite, statutory; ***opp*** optional

computer *n* machine, mainframe, PC, personal computer, system, word-processor

comrade *n* ally, associate, colleague, confederate, co-worker, crony *inf*, fellow-worker, friend, mate *inf*, pal *inf*

conceal *v* **1** (from view) blot out, camouflage, cloak, cover, disguise, hide, keep out of sight, mask, obscure, screen, secrete, shelter. **2** (conceal a fact) cover up, gloss over, hush up, keep quiet, keep secret, keep the lid on, veil; ***opp*** reveal

concede *v* **1** accede, accept, acknowledge, admit, make a concession. **2** capitulate, cave in *inf*, cede, give in, give up, hand over, relinquish, resign, submit, surrender, yield

conceited *adj* arrogant, big-headed, boastful, cocky, egotistical, full of yourself, immodest, puffed up, self-important, smug, vain; ***opp*** modest

conceivable *adj* believable, not beyond the realms of possibility, credible, feasible, imaginable, likely, possible, thinkable; ***opp*** inconceivable

conceive *v* **1** (a plan, idea) conjure up, contrive, create, design, develop, devise, draw up, dream up *inf*, evolve, form, formulate, hatch, initiate, invent, make up, plan, think up. **2** (understand) apprehend, believe, comprehend, envisage, grasp, imagine, suppose, think, understand, visualize

concentrate *v* **1** apply yourself, be absorbed, be attentive, consider closely, engross yourself, give your attention to, pay attention, put your mind to, rack your brains, think, work hard. **2** (in a place) accumulate, center, cluster, collect, congregate, converge, gather, mass; ***opp*** scatter

concentrated *adj* **1** (concentrated effort) all-out *inf*, concerted, consolidated, intense, intensive, rigorous, vigorous; ***opp*** half-hearted . **2** rich, strong, thick, undiluted; ***opp*** diluted

concentration *n* **1** absorption, application, close attention, heed, single-mindedness. **2** (in a place) accumulation, cluster, collection, congregation, convergence, gathering, group, mass

concept *n* conception, hypothesis, idea, notion, theory, view

conception *n* **1** (biological) conceiving, fertilization, impregnation, insemination, pregnancy. **2** beginning, birth, creation, design, formation, inception, invention, origin, outset; ***opp*** completion. **3** plan, project, proposal. **4** (have no conception of) appreciation, clue, comprehension, concept, idea, inkling, notion, perception, understanding

concern *n* **1** anxiety, apprehension, disquiet, distress, disturbance, fear, malaise, solicitude, worry. **2** (that's my concern) affair, business, department, duty, field, interest, job, matter, problem, regard, responsibility, subject, task. **3** business, company, corporation, enterprise, establishment, firm, house, organization

concern *v* **1** affect, apply, be relevant to, have a bearing on, interest, involve, pertain, refer, regard, relate, touch. **2** bother, distress, disturb, perturb, preoccupy, trouble, worry

concerned *adj* **1** anxious, bothered, distressed, disturbed, fearful, perturbed, troubled, uneasy, unhappy, upset, worried; ***opp*** unconcerned. **2** (the people concerned) affected, connected, implicated, interested, involved, mixed up, privy to, relevant

concerted *adj* collaborative, collective, combined, cooperative, coordinated, joint, mutual, shared, unified, united

concession *n* **1** acknowledgment, acceptance, admission, allowance, ceding, giving in, recognition, relinquishment, settlement, surrender, yielding. **2** (make a concession) adjustment, allowance, compromise, exception, indulgence, modification, privilege

conciliatory *adj* accommodating, appeasing, mollifying, obliging, pacifying, peaceable, placatory; ***opp*** aggressive

concise *adj* brief, compact, compressed, condensed, pithy, pointed, short, small, succinct, summary, terse, to the point

conclude *v* **1** bring to an end, cease, close, come to an end, complete, end, finish, halt, round off, stop, terminate, wind up *inf*. **2** assume, come to the conclusion, conjecture, decide, deduce, gather, infer, judge, presume, reckon, suppose, surmise

conclusion *n* **1** close, completion, end, ending, finale, finish, rounding-off, termination; ***opp*** beginning. **2** consequence, culmination, issue, outcome, result, solution, upshot. **3** (belief) answer, belief, conviction, decision, deduction, inference, judgment, opinion, resolution, settlement, verdict

conclusive *adj* categorical, certain, clinching, convincing, decisive, definite, definitive, final, incontestable, irrefutable, persuasive, unambiguous, unanswerable, unequivocal, unquestionable; ***opp*** inconclusive

concoct *v* contrive, cook up *inf*, design, devise, formulate, hatch, invent, make up, manufacture, plan, plot, prepare, project, put together, think up

concrete *adj* actual, definite, existing, explicit, factual, firm, material, objective, palpable, physical, real, solid, specific, substantial, tangible, visible; ***opp*** abstract

condemn *v* **1** berate, blame, castigate, censure, chide, criticize, damn, decry, denounce, deprecate, disapprove, disparage, rebuke, reproach, reprove, upbraid; ***opp*** commend, praise. **2** convict, find guilty, judge, pass judgment, pass sentence, punish, sentence; ***opp*** acquit

condemnation *n* blame, censure, criticism, denunciation, deprecation, disapproval, disparagement, rebuke, reproach, reprobation, reproof, stricture; ***opp*** praise

condense *v* **1** (make shorter) compress, contract, curtail, cut, reduce, shorten, summarize; ***opp*** expand, lengthen. **2** (of liquid) concentrate, distill, reduce, thicken; ***opp*** dilute

condescend *v* **1** deign, descend, humble yourself, lower yourself, stoop, submit. **2** look down your nose at, patronize, talk down to

condescending *adj* disdainful, haughty, high-and-mighty, imperious, patronizing, pompous, snobbish, snooty *inf*, stuck-up *inf*, supercilious, superior

condition *n* **1** case, circumstances, plight, position, predicament, situation, state, state of affairs. **2** demand, essential, necessity, precondition, prerequisite, provision, proviso, qualification, requirement, requisite, restriction, stipulation, terms. **3** fettle, fitness, form, health, kilter, order, shape. **4** (medical) affliction, ailment, disease, disorder, illness, infection, sickness

condition *v* acclimatize, accustom, adapt, educate, equip, habituate, inure, make ready, prepare, train

conditional *adj* contingent, dependent, provisional, restricted, subject to, with conditions, with reservations, with restrictions, with strings attached *inf*; ***opp*** unconditional

condone *v* accept, allow, approve, endorse, excuse, forgive, ignore, let pass, look the other way, make allowances, overlook, pardon, put up with, tolerate, turn a blind eye

conduct *n* **1** actions, behavior, manners, mien, ways. **2** administration, control, command, direction, government, handling, leadership, management, organization, regulation, running, supervision

conduct *v* **1** administer, be in charge, be in control, chair, command, control, direct, govern, handle, head, lead, look after, manage, organize, oversee, preside, regulate, rule, run, steer, supervise. **2** accompany, escort, guide, lead, pilot, take, usher

confer *v* **1** compare notes, consult, converse, debate, discuss, exchange ideas, exchange views, have discussions, put your heads together *inf*, seek advice. **2** award, bestow, give, grant, invest, present

conference *n* colloquium, congress, convention, forum, meeting, seminar, symposium

confess *v* accept blame, acknowledge, admit, come clean, concede, confide, disclose, divulge, own up, plead guilty, reveal, tell all, unburden yourself

confession *n* admission, disclosure, divulgence, owning-up, revelation

confide *v* admit, confess, disclose, divulge, open your heart, reveal, spill the beans, unburden yourself

confidence *n* **1** assertiveness, assurance, boldness, composure, courage, nerve, poise, self-assurance, self-confidence, self-possession; ***opp*** shyness. **2** belief, certainty, credence, dependence, faith, reliance, trust; ***opp*** doubt

confident *adj* **1** assertive, bold, brave, cocksure, composed, courageous, fearless, outgoing, poised, self-assured, self-confident, self-possessed; ***opp*** shy. **2** certain, convinced, positive, satisfied, sure; ***opp*** doubtful

confidential *adj* classified, hush-hush *inf*, intimate, off the record, personal, private, secret

confine *v* bind, cage, coop up *inf*, detain, enclose, hem in, imprison, incarcerate, intern, jail, limit, lock up, repress, restrain, restrict, shut up; ***opp*** liberate

confirm *v* **1** authenticate, back up, bear out, corroborate, endorse, establish, give credence to, prove, show, substantiate, verify; ***opp*** disprove. **2** (confirm a deal) authorize, clinch, establish, formalize, fix, settle, ratify, sanction. **3** (confirm sb's doubts) add to, increase, strengthen, make firmer, reinforce, fortify; ***opp*** assuage

confirmation *n* **1** corroboration, endorsement, evidence, proof, substantiation, testimony, verification. **2** acceptance, agreement, approval, assent, authorization, endorsement, ratification

confirmed *adj* chronic, compulsive, established, habitual, hardened, ingrained, inveterate, long-established, seasoned, through-and-through

confiscate *v* commandeer, expropriate, impound, remove, seize, take, take possession of

conflict *n* **1** (violent) altercation, battle, brush *inf*, clash, combat, confrontation, encounter, engagement, fight, strife, war, warfare. **2** antagonism, antipathy, bad blood, difference of opinion, disagreement, discord, dissension, feud, friction, hostility, opposition

conflict *v* **1** clash, contradict, contrast, differ, disagree. **2** clash, contend, contest, cross swords, fight, struggle

conflicting *adj* at odds, at variance, clashing, contradictory, contrary, contrasting, differing, discordant, incompatible, inconsistent, mutually exclusive, opposed, opposing, paradoxical; ***opp*** similar

conform *v* be good, behave conventionally, blend in, do what you are told *inf*, comply, fall in with, fit in, follow the crowd, keep in step, obey, run with the pack, toe the line; ***opp*** rebel

confront *v* accost, brave, challenge, defy, encounter, face, face up to, meet head on, oppose, resist, stand up to, tackle, take on; ***opp*** avoid

confrontation *n* battle, clash, conflict, contest, crisis, encounter, head-to-head, set-to *inf*, showdown

confuse *v* **1** (confuse sb) baffle, befuddle, bemuse, bewilder, disconcert, disorient, flummox, fluster, mystify, perplex, puzzle. **2** jumble, mess up, mingle, mix up, muddle, snarl up, tangle, throw into disarray, upset

confused *adj* **1** at a loss, at sea, baffled, bamboozled, befuddled, bemused, bewildered, dazed, disorganized, flummoxed, muddled, mystified, nonplussed, perplexed, puzzled, taken aback, thrown *inf*; ***opp*** clear. **2** chaotic, disordered, disorderly, disorganized, in disarray, in disorder, jumbled, messy, misunderstood, mixed up, muddled, out of order, tangled, untidy; ***opp*** tidy

confusing *adj* ambiguous, baffling, bewildering, complex, complicated, contradictory, difficult, disorganized, disorientating, disorienting, incomprehensible, jumbled, misleading, mixed up, muddled, mystifying, perplexing, puzzling, unclear; ***opp*** clear

confusion *n* **1** bafflement, befuddlement, bemusement, bewilderment, mystification, perplexity, puzzlement. **2** chaos, commotion, disarray, disorder, hodge-podge, jumble, mess, mix-up, muddle, shambles *inf*, tangle, turmoil; ***opp*** order

congenital *adj* constitutional, hereditary, inborn, inbred, inherent, inherited, innate, natural; ***opp*** acquired

congested *adj* blocked, clogged, crammed, crowded, jammed, obstructed, overcrowded, overfilled, overflowing, packed, plugged, stuffed, teeming; ***opp*** clear

congratulate *v* applaud, compliment, offer your congratulations

congratulations *n* best wishes, compliments, felicitations, good wishes

congregate *v* assemble, collect, come together, convene, converge, convoke, crowd around, flock, gather, group together, mass, meet, muster, rally, rendezvous, swarm, throng; ***opp*** disperse

congregation *n* assembly, audience, brethren, convocation, crowd, fellowship, flock, gathering, group, host, laity, listeners, mass, meeting, multitude, parish, parishioners, rally, throng

congress *n* assembly, chamber, conclave, conference, convention, convocation, council, delegates, gathering, house, legislature, meeting, parliament, representatives, synod

conjugal *adj* bridal, connubial, marital, married, matrimonial, nuptial, wedded

conjure *v* 1 do magic, do tricks, juggle. **2 conjure up** bring forth, call up, create, evoke, produce, recall, recreate

connect *v* **1** affix, ally, attach, combine, couple, fasten, fix, join, link, relate, tie, unite; ***opp*** disconnect. **2** associate, bracket, equate, identify, link, relate

connection *n* **1** attachment, coupling, fastening, joint, junction, link, tie. **2** affinity, alliance, association, bond, correspondence, equivalence, link, relatedness, relation, relationship, relevance, tie. **3** acquaintance, ally, associate, contact, friend

connive *v* **1** collaborate, collude, conspire, intrigue, plot, scheme. **2 connive at** abet, aid, allow, be an accessory to, be party to, condone, let sth pass, overlook, pass over, shut your eyes to, tolerate, turn a blind eye to

connoisseur *n* aficionado, authority, buff *inf*, cognoscenti, devotee, epicure, expert, fan, gourmet, savant, specialist

conquer *v* annex, beat, capture, crush, defeat, get the better of, invade, lick *inf*, master, occupy, overcome, overpower, overrun, overthrow, prevail, quell, rout, seize, subdue, subjugate, surmount, take, thrash *inf*, triumph, trounce, vanquish, win

conqueror *n* champion, hero, lord, master, vanquisher, victor, winner

conquest *n* annexation, appropriation, capture, coup, crushing, defeat, invasion, licking *inf*, mastery, occupation, overpowering, overrunning, overthrow, quelling, rout, seizing, subjugation, taking, thrashing *inf*, triumph, trouncing, vanquishing, victory

conscience *n* better nature, better self, compunction, ethics, morals, moral sense, principles, qualms, scruples

conscientious *adj* careful, dedicated, diligent, dutiful, faithful, hard-working, meticulous, painstaking, particular, perfectionist, punctilious, responsible, rigorous, scrupulous, thorough

conscious *adj* **1** alert, alive to, awake, aware, cognizant, knowing, responsive, sensible, sensitive to, sentient, wise to; ***opp*** unconscious. **2** calculated, deliberate, intended, intentional, knowing, on purpose, premeditated, studied, voluntary, willful, willed; ***opp*** unconscious

consciousness *n* alertness, awareness, cognizance, knowledge, perception, realization, recognition, responsiveness, sense, sensibility, sentience; ***opp*** unconsciousness

consecrate *v* bless, dedicate, devote, make holy, make sacred, ordain, sanctify, set apart

consecutive *adj* continuous, following, in a row, in sequence, in turn, one after another, running, sequential, serial, succeeding, successive, unbroken, uninterrupted

consensus *n* agreement, common consent, common ground, concord, concurrence, general opinion, harmony, unanimity

consent *n* acceptance, acquiescence, agreement, approval, assent, compliance, concurrence, go-ahead *inf*, permission, say-so *inf*, sanction, seal of approval, support; ***opp*** refusal

consent *v* accept, acquiesce, agree, allow, approve, assent, comply, concede, concur, condone, go along with, permit, sanction, support, yield; ***opp*** refuse

consequence *n* **1** aftermath, by-product, effect, end, follow-up, issue, outcome, repercussion, result, reverberation, sequel, side-effect, upshot. **2** importance, moment, note, relevance, significance, value, weight

consequent *adj* ensuing, following, resultant, resulting, subsequent

conservation *n* care, charge, custody, husbandry, keeping, maintenance, preservation, preserving, protection, safeguarding, safekeeping, saving, upkeep

conservative *adj* careful, cautious, conventional, die-hard, guarded, hidebound, narrow-minded, old-fashioned, old-school, orthodox, reactionary, right-wing, stick-in-the-mud, straitlaced, traditional, traditionalist; ***opp*** progressive

conserve *v* be economical with, hoard, keep, maintain, preserve, protect, safeguard, save, store, take care of; ***opp*** waste

consider *v* **1** cogitate, contemplate, deliberate, examine, meditate, mull over, ponder, reflect, ruminate, study, think, weigh. **2** allow for, bear in mind, have regard for, make allowances for, reckon with, remember, respect, take into account, take into consideration. **3** believe, be of the opinion, deem, hold, judge, reckon, regard, think

considerable *adj* abundant, ample, appreciable, decent, enormous, goodly, great, huge, large, lavish, notable, not inconsiderable, respectable, significant, sizeable, substantial, tolerable; ***opp*** negligible

considerably *adv* a great deal, a lot, appreciably, enormously, greatly, hugely, markedly, notably, significantly, substantially, very much

considerate *adj* accommodating, attentive, aware, caring, compassionate, concerned, discreet, helpful, kind, mindful, obliging, sensitive, solicitous, tactful, thoughtful, unselfish; ***opp*** inconsiderate

consideration *n* **1** awareness, compassion, concern, discretion, kindness, sensitivity, solicitude, tact, thought, thoughtfulness, unselfishness. **2** attention, cogitation, contemplation, deliberation, discussion, examination, inspection, perusal, reflection, regard, review, scrutiny, study, thought

consignment *n* batch, cargo, delivery, goods, load, shipment

consist of *v* be composed of, be made up

of, comprise, contain, include, incorporate, involve

consistent *adj* constant, dependable, predictable, reliable, regular, stable, steady, true, unchanging, undeviating, uniform, unvarying; ***opp*** inconsistent

consolation *n* cheer, comfort, ease, encouragement, help, relief, solace, soothing, succor, support, sympathy

console *v* assuage, calm, cheer, comfort, ease, encourage, hearten, placate, relieve, solace, soothe, succor, support, sympathize

consolidate *v* cement, fortify, reinforce, secure, stabilize, strengthen; ***opp*** weaken

conspicuous *adj* apparent, blatant, clear, evident, flagrant, glaring, intrusive, loud, manifest, marked, noticeable, obtrusive, obvious, ostentatious, patent, prominent, striking, unconcealed, visible; ***opp*** inconspicuous

conspiracy *n* cabal, collusion, connivance, frame-up *inf*, intrigue, machination, plot, scheme, stratagem, treason

conspirator *n* collaborator, plotter, schemer, traitor

conspire *v* be in cahoots *inf*, be in league, collaborate, collude, connive, contrive, devise, hatch a plot, intrigue, maneuver, plot, scheme

constant *adj* **1** ceaseless, continual, continuous, endless, eternal, everlasting, incessant, interminable, never-ending, nonstop, perpetual, persistent, relentless, sustained, unbroken, unceasing, unending, unrelenting, unremitting. **2** dependable, even, faithful, firm, fixed, immutable, invariable, loyal, permanent, regular, reliable, steadfast, steady, staunch, true, trusty, unchanging, uniform, unvarying; ***opp*** changeable

constantly *adv* all the time, always, ceaselessly, continually, continuously, endlessly, eternally, incessantly, interminably, nonstop, perpetually, persistently, relentlessly, unceasingly, unrelentingly, unremittingly

constituent *n* component, element, factor, ingredient, member, part, principle, unit

constitute *v* **1** compose, comprise, form, make, make up. **2** create, establish, form, found, inaugurate, institute, make, set up

constitution *n* **1** charter, code, law, rules, principles, system. **2** condition, disposition, health, make-up, nature, temperament. **3** creation, establishment, formation, forming, foundation, founding, inauguration, organization, setting up

constitutional *adj* **1** chartered, constituted, legal, legitimate, statutory, vested. **2** congenital, inborn, inbred, inherent, innate, intrinsic, natural, organic

constrain *v* **1** compel, coerce, drive, force, impel, oblige, pressure, pressurize, push. **2** bind, check, curb, hinder, hold back, impede, limit, restrain, restrict, tie

constraint *n* **1** compulsion, coercion, force, impulsion, necessity, obligation, pressure. **2** check, curb, hindrance, limit, limitation, obstacle, restraint, restriction, tie

construct *v* assemble, build, compose, create, design, devise, erect, establish, fabricate, fashion, forge, form, formulate, found, frame, make, manufacture, organize, produce, put together, put up, raise, set up, shape

construction *n* assembly, building, composition, creation, design, edifice, erection, fabric, figure, form, formation, framework, shape, structure

constructive *v* cooperative, creative, helpful, positive, practical, productive, useful, valuable; ***opp*** destructive

consult *v* ask, call in, compare notes, confer, debate, deliberate, discuss, interrogate, question, refer to, seek advice, turn to

consultant *n* adviser, authority, expert, specialist

consultation *n* appointment, audience, conference, council, deliberation, dialogue, discussion, examination, hearing, interview, meeting, session, talk

consume *v* absorb, burn, deplete, devour, drain, eat up, exhaust, expend, finish off, guzzle *inf*, polish off *inf*, ingest, spend, use, use up, utilize, wear out

contact *n* **1** communication, connection, contiguity, correspondence, join, juxtaposition, proximity, touch, union. **2** (sb you know) acquaintance, ally, associate, connection, friend

contact *v* approach, call, communicate, correspond, get in touch, get hold of, notify, reach, ring, speak, talk, telephone, write

contagious *adj* catching, communicable, epidemic, infectious, passed on, pestilential, spreading, transmissible, transmittable

contain *v* **1** accommodate, carry, enclose, have capacity for, have room for, hold, seat. **2** be composed of, be made up of, comprise, consist of, include, incorporate, involve

container *n* holder, receptacle, vessel

contaminate *v* adulterate, corrupt, debase, dirty, foul, infect, poison, pollute, soil, stain, sully, taint, tarnish; ***opp*** purify

contemplate *v* **1** brood, cogitate, consider, deliberate, examine, gaze, look, meditate, mull over, muse, ponder, reflect, ruminate, study, view. **2** (contemplate doing sth) consider, envisage, expect, foresee, have in mind, imagine, intend, plan, propose, think

contemporary *adj* **1** coeval, coexistent, coexisting, concurrent, contemporaneous, simultaneous, synchronous. **2** à la mode, current, fashionable, in fashion, latest, modern, newfangled *inf*, present-day, recent, trendy *inf*, up-to-date, with it *inf*; ***opp*** old, outdated

contempt *n* abhorrence, derision, disdain, disregard, disrespect, distaste, loathing, mockery, ridicule, scorn, sneering; ***opp*** respect

contemptible *adj* abhorrent, abject, base, cheap, despicable, detestable, distasteful, hateful, ignominious, loathsome, low, mean, pathetic, ridiculous, shabby, shameful, vile, worthless

contemptuous *adj* cutting, derisive, disdainful, disrespectful, haughty, insulting, jeering, mocking, scathing, scornful, sneering, snide, snobbish, snotty *inf*, supercilious, superior, withering; ***opp*** respectful

contend *v* **1** affirm, allege, argue, assert, avow, claim, hold, maintain, put forward, say, state, testify. **2** battle, challenge, clash, compete, contest, fight, oppose, strive, struggle, vie, wrestle

content *adj* at ease, at peace, cheerful, comfortable, contented, fulfilled, gratified, happy, pleased, relaxed, replete, satisfied, tranquil, untroubled, unworried; ***opp*** dissatisfied, unhappy

content *n* cheer, comfort, contentment, ease, equanimity, fulfillment, gratification, happiness, peace of mind, pleasure, satisfaction, tranquillity; ***opp*** unhappiness

content *v* appease, cheer, comfort, fulfill, gladden, gratify, mollify, pacify, placate, please, put at ease, relax, satisfy, soothe; ***opp*** anger, annoy

contented *adj* at ease, at peace, cheerful, comfortable, content, fulfilled, gratified, happy, pleased, relaxed, replete, satisfied, tranquil, untroubled, unworried; ***opp*** dissatisfied, unhappy

contentious *adj* **1** arguable, controversial, debatable, disputable, dubious, tendentious; ***opp*** uncontroversial. **2** aggressive, argumentative, bickering, combative, competitive, cross, disputatious, factious, fractious, peevish, perverse, pugnacious, quarrelsome, querulous, wrangling; ***opp*** conciliatory

contentment *n* cheer, cheerfulness, comfort, content, ease, equanimity, fulfillment, gladness, gratification, happiness, peace, pleasure, repletion, satisfaction, serenity, tranquillity; ***opp*** dissatisfaction, unhappiness

contents *n* components, constituents, ingredients, material, matter, subject matter, substance, theme

contest *n* battle, competition, fight, game, head-to-head, match, rivalry, tournament, trial

contest *v* **1** battle, compete, contend, fight, fight over, strive, struggle, tussle, vie. **2** argue, call into question, challenge, debate, disagree with, dispute, doubt, object, oppose, question

contestant *n* adversary, candidate, competitor, contender, entrant, opponent, participant, player, rival

context *n* background, circumstances, conditions, environment, frame of reference, framework, milieu, setting, situation, surroundings

continual *adj* ceaseless, constant, continuous, endless, eternal, everlasting, incessant, interminable, never-ending, nonstop, ongoing, perpetual, persistent, recurrent, regular, relentless, repeated, sustained, unbroken, unceasing, unending, unrelenting, unremitting

continually *adv* all the time, always, ceaselessly, constantly, continuously, endlessly, eternally, incessantly, interminably, nonstop, perpetually, persistently, recurrently, regularly, relentlessly, repeatedly, unceasingly, unrelentingly, unremittingly

continue *v* abide, carry on, endure, go on, keep on, last, live on, maintain, persevere, persist, proceed, remain, rest, resume, stay, subsist, survive

continuous *adj* connected, consecutive, constant, continuing, endless, extended, never-ending, nonstop, prolonged, sustained, unbroken, unceasing, unending, uninterrupted

contract *n* agreement, arrangement, bargain, bond, commitment, compact, convention, covenant, deal, lease, pact, settlement, transaction, treaty, understanding

contract *v* **1** abridge, compress, condense, constrict, curtail, dwindle, lesson, narrow, reduce, shorten, shrink, shrivel, tighten, wither, wrinkle; ***opp*** expand. **2** (contract to do sth) agree, arrange, bargain, pledge, stipulate, undertake. **3** (contract an illness) be/become infected with, catch, develop, get, go down with

contradict *v* argue, be at odds, be at variance, belie, challenge, clash, conflict, counter, deny, disagree, dispute, dissent from, negate, oppose, rebut, refute; ***opp*** agree

contradiction *n* clash, conflict, counter, denial, disagreement, dissension, incompatibility, incongruity, inconsistency, negation, opposite, paradox, rebuttal, variance; ***opp*** agreement

contradictory *adj* antagonistic, at odds, at variance, clashing, conflicting, contrary, dissenting, incompatible, incongruous, inconsistent, irreconcilable, opposite, paradoxical

contrary *adj* **1** clashing, conflicting, contradictory, different, discordant, hostile, incompatible, incongruous, inconsistent, inimical, irreconcilable, opposed, opposite. **2** (of a person) awkward, headstrong, intractable, intransigent, obstinate, perverse, stubborn, uncooperative, wayward, willful; ***opp*** amenable, obliging

contrast *n* clash, comparison, difference, disparity, dissimilarity, distinction, divergence, foil, opposition

contrast *v* **1** compare, differentiate, discriminate, distinguish, juxtapose, oppose, put side by side. **2** be at variance, clash, differ, diverge, oppose, set off

contribute *v* add, bestow, chip in *inf*, donate, endow, furnish, give, grant, pitch in *inf*, provide, subscribe, supply

contribution *n* donation, gift, grant, hand-out *inf*, offering, payment, present, subscription

contrive *v* concoct, construct, design, devise, engineer, improvise, invent

contrived *adj* artificial, forced, labored, unnatural

control *n* **1** authority, charge, command, discipline, dominance, influence, leadership, management, mastery, power, rule, supervision, supremacy. **2** (lose control) direction, grip, hold, restraint, self-control

control *v* **1** administer, be at the helm *inf*, be in charge, direct, dominate, govern, handle, have control, lead, look after, manage, manipulate, oversee, preside, rule, run, supervise. **2** (control a vehicle) command, pilot, steer. **3** (control your temper) bridle, check, constrain, curb, hold back, master, restrain, subdue

controversial *adj* arguable, at issue, contentious, controvertible, debatable, disputable, disputed, doubtful, open to question, questionable

controversy *n* altercation, argument, debate, disagreement, discussion, dispute, dissension, quarrel, row, squabble, wrangle

convene *v* assemble, bring together, call, come together, congregate, convoke, gather, meet, summon

convenience *n* accessibility, appropriateness, availability, expedience, fitness, handiness, suitability, timeliness, usefulness

convenient *adj* **1** (easy to use) accessible, at hand, available, close at hand, handy, labor-saving, nearby, neat, useful; ***opp*** inconvenient. **2** (suitable) appropriate, favorable, helpful, opportune, suitable, timely; ***opp*** inconvenient

convention *n* **1** code, custom, etiquette, matter of form, practice, propriety, protocol, tradition. **2** conclave, conference, congress, convocation, meeting

conventional *adj* **1** accepted, commonplace, correct, customary, expected, formal, mainstream, normal, ordinary, orthodox, proper, received, standard, straight, traditional, usual; ***opp*** unconventional. **2** (of people) conformist, conservative, pedestrian, reactionary, stuffy *inf*, unadventurous; ***opp*** unconventional

conversation *n* chat, dialogue, discussion, exchange, gossip, heart-to-heart *inf*, talk, tête-à-tête

converse *v* chat, communicate, discuss, have a conversation, speak, talk

conversion *n* adaptation, alteration, change, exchange, metamorphosis, modification, rebuilding, reorganization, substitution, transfiguration, transformation

convert *v* **1** alter, change, modify, reconstruct, reshape, transform, transmute, transpose, turn, switch. **2** (convert sb) change sb's mind, convince, persuade, reeducate, reform, rehabilitate, save, win

convey *v* **1** (take sth) bear, bring, carry, cart, ferry, fetch, move, send, shift, ship, take, transfer, transport. **2** (convey meaning) communicate, disclose, impart, imply, mean, reveal, signify, transmit

convict *v* condemn, find guilty, sentence; ***opp*** acquit

conviction *n* **1** assurance, certainty, confidence, earnestness, firmness. **2** belief, creed, faith, persuasion, principle

convince *v* assure, persuade, prove to, reassure, satisfy, sway, talk round, win over

convinced *adj* assured, certain, confident, persuaded, positive, satisfied, sure; ***opp*** uncertain

convincing *adj* **1** (of a theory) believable, cogent, compelling, credible, likely, logical, plausible, probable, valid; ***opp*** unconvincing. **2** (of a result) conclusive, decisive, impressive, unambiguous

convoy *n* caravan, company, escort, group, line

cool *adj* **1** chilled, chilly, cold, fresh, iced, lukewarm, nippy; ***opp*** warm. **2** calm, collected, composed, dignified, laid-back *inf*, self-possessed, sensible, together *inf*, unflustered, unruffled; ***opp*** flustered. **3** aloof, distant, indifferent, offhand, reserved, standoffish *inf*, unfriendly, unwelcoming; ***opp*** friendly, warm. **4** bold, brazen, cheeky, impudent, shameless. **5** streetwise *inf*, urbane; ***opp*** uncool. **6** brilliant, excellent, good, great, marvelous, splendid, terrific, wonderful; ***opp*** bad

cool *n* **1** coolness, freshness, coldness. **2** calmness, composure, control, poise, self-control

cool *v* become cold, chill, cool off, freeze, refrigerate; ***opp*** heat. **2** assuage, calm, dampen, diminish, lessen, reduce; ***opp*** inflame

cooperate *v* assist, collaborate, combine, help, join forces, pitch in *inf*, unite, work together

cooperation *n* assistance, collaboration, contribution, give-and-take, help, helpfulness, participation, support, teamwork, unity

cooperative *adj* **1** accommodating, constructive, helpful, keen, obliging, supportive, willing; ***opp*** unhelpful. **2** collaborative, collective, combined, communal, joint, mutual, shared; ***opp*** individual

coordinate *v* arrange, integrate, match, organize, synchronize

cope *v* carry on, get by, get through, make do, make out *inf*, manage, muddle through, survive

copious *adj* abundant, ample, bountiful, extensive, extravagant, full, generous, lavish, luxuriant, overflowing, plentiful, profuse, rich, unstinting

copy *n* carbon copy, clone, counterfeit, double, duplicate, facsimile, fake, forgery, image, imitation, likeness, model, pattern, photocopy, print, replica, representation, reproduction, transcript, twin

copy *v* **1** (make a copy of) counterfeit, duplicate, forge, photocopy, reproduce, replicate, transcribe. **2** (copy sb's work) crib, plagiarize, steal. **3** ape, echo, imitate, mimic, mirror, parrot, repeat

cordon *n* barrier, chain, fence, line, ring

core *n* center, crux, essence, gist, heart, inside, kernel, middle, nitty-gritty *inf*, nub, nucleus

corner *n* **1** angle, bend, intersection, joint, junction, turn, turning. **2** cranny, hideaway, hole, niche, nook, recess

corporation *n* business, company, conglomerate, firm, organization, partnership, trust

corpse *n* body, cadaver, carcass, dead body, remains, skeleton, stiff *inf*

correct *adj* **1** (of behavior) appropriate, conventional, proper, seemly, suitable; ***opp*** improper. **2** (of work) accurate, exact, faultless, flawless, perfect, right; ***opp*** wrong

correct *v* **1** (correct sth) adjust, alter, amend, cure, fix, improve, mark, put right, rectify, redress, remedy, repair, right. **2** (correct sb) admonish, chastise, criticize, discipline, punish, rebuke, reprimand, scold, tell off *inf*

correction *n* adjustment, alteration, amendment, improvement, rectification, revision

correspond *v* **1** communicate, exchange letters, keep in touch, write. **2** agree, be analogous, be consistent, be equivalent, be similar, coincide, compare, correlate, fit, match, tally

correspondence *n* **1** communication, letters, e-mail, mail, memoranda, notes, post, writing. **2** analogy, accord, conformity, correlation, resemblance, similarity

corresponding *adj* analogous, comparable, equivalent, matching, parallel, reciprocal, similar

corroborate *v* attest, authenticate, back up, bear out, confirm, endorse, establish, support, verify

corrode *v* abrade, consume, eat away, erode, gnaw, oxidize, rot, rust, tarnish, wear away

corrosive *adj* abrasive, caustic, corroding, destructive, eroding, virulent, wearing

corrupt *adj* bent *inf*, crooked, degenerate, depraved, dirty *inf*, dishonest, evil, fraudulent, immoral, perverted, rotten, sinful, unethical, unprincipled, untrustworthy, wicked; ***opp*** honest

corrupt *v* **1** bribe, buy off, deprave, fix *inf*, influence, lead astray, pervert, seduce, subvert, tempt, warp. **2** contaminate, debase, infect, taint

corruption *n* **1** bribery, dishonesty, extortion, fraud, profiteering, villainy. **2** (corruption in society) decadence, degeneration, depravity, evil, immorality, iniquity, perversion, sinfulness, vice, wickedness

cosmopolitan *adj* **1** (of people) cultured, sophisticated, urbane, well-traveled, worldly, worldly-wise. **2** (of a place) international, multiracial

cost *n* **1** amount, charge, damage *inf*, expenditure, expense, fare, figure, outlay, payment, price, quotation, rate, tariff, value, worth. **2** damage, detriment, harm, hurt, loss, penalty, sacrifice, suffering

cost *v* be priced at, be valued at, be worth, come to, fetch, go for, realize, sell at, sell for, set you back

council *n* assembly, board, cabinet, chamber, committee, convocation, governing body, house, local authority, panel, parliament, synod

counsel *n* advice, direction, guidance, information, opinion, recommendation, suggestion, warning

counsel *v* advise, advocate, caution, discuss, exhort, give help, recommend, urge, warn

count *v* **1** add, add up, calculate, compute, enumerate, estimate, figure out, number, reckon, score, tally, tot up, work out. **2** be important, be of account, carry weight, have significance, matter, mean sth, signify. **3 count on** bank on, believe in, depend on, put your faith in, rely on, swear by, trust

counter *v* answer, combat, come back at *inf*, contradict, dispute, oppose, rebut, refute, reply, resist, respond, retaliate

counteract *v* be an antidote to, cancel out, check, counterbalance, cross, defeat, foil, frustrate, hinder, invalidate, negate, neutralize, offset, resist, thwart, work against

counterfeit *adj* artificial, bogus, copied, ersatz, faked, false, feigned, forged, fraudulent, imitation, phony *inf*, pretend *inf*, pseudo- *inf*, sham, simulated, spurious, synthetic; ***opp*** genuine

counterfeit *v* copy, fabricate, fake, falsify, forge, sham, simulate

countless *adj* endless, immeasurable,

incalculable, infinite, innumerable, myriad, numerous, untold, without end, without limit

country *n* **1** empire, kingdom, nation, principality, realm, state. **2** fatherland, homeland, land of your birth, motherland, native land. **3** (people) citizens, inhabitants, nation, people, populace, public, society, voters. **4** countryside, farmland, green belt, provinces, rural area, sticks, wilds. **5** (landscape) area, land, landscape, scenery, terrain, territory

coup *n* **1** accomplishment, achievement, deed, exploit, feat, maneuver, stratagem, stroke, stunt, tour de force. **2** coup d'etat, overthrow, revolt, revolution

couple *n* brace, duo, pair, twosome

courage *n* boldness, bravery, daring, determination, fearlessness, fortitude, gallantry, guts *inf*, heroism, intrepidity, nerve, pluck, resolution, spirit, valor; ***opp*** cowardice

courageous *adj* bold, brave, daring, fearless, gutsy *sl*, heroic, indomitable, intrepid, plucky, stout-hearted, tough, unafraid, undaunted, valiant; ***opp*** cowardly

course *n* **1** advance, continuity, development, flow, march, movement, progress, progression, sequence, succession, unfolding. **2** channel, circuit, direction, line, orbit, passage, path, road, route, tack, track, trail, trajectory, way. **3** circuit, lap, race, racecourse, round. **4** classes, curriculum, lectures, program, studies, syllabus

court *n* **1** cloister, courtyard, piazza, plaza, quad *inf*, quadrangle, square, yard. **2** assizes, bar, bench, court of justice, court of law, law court, tribunal. **3** castle, palace, royal residence. **4** attendants, entourage, followers, retinue, royal household

court *v* **1** (court sb) date, go out with, make advances to, run after, woo. **2** (court sth) ask for *inf*, attract, bring on yourself, crave, invite, provoke, risk, seek

courteous *adj* attentive, chivalrous, civil, considerate, gallant, gracious, polite, refined, respectful, well-mannered; ***opp*** rude

courtesy *n* **1** chivalry, civility, courteousness, good breeding, good manners, politeness, respect. **2** (as a courtesy) benefit, consideration, favor, indulgence, kindness, service

courtyard *n* area, court, enclosure, forecourt, patio, quad *inf*, quadrangle, square, yard

cover *n* **1** blanket, canopy, cap, case, coating, covering, lid, roof, top, wrapper. **2** (blow sb's cover) disguise, facade, front, pretense, smokescreen. **3** (seek cover) concealment, hiding place, protection, refuge, sanctuary. **4** (insurance) compensation, indemnity, insurance, protection

cover *v* **1** (cover sth) blanket, carpet, bury, cloak, clothe, coat, conceal, disguise, drape, encase, enclose, envelop, hide, house, mask, obscure, plaster, screen, shade, sheathe, shelter, shroud, veil, wrap. **2** (stand in for sb) fill in, relieve, replace, stand in, take over. **3** (cover a story) describe, investigate, recount, report, write up. **4** (cover a topic) contain, deal with, encompass, include, incorporate, involve, take in, treat. **5 cover up** conceal, hide, hush up, keep secret, repress, suppress

covering *n* blanket, canopy, casing, cladding, coat, coating, cover, film, layer, rind, sheet, skin, surface, veneer, wrapping

covet *v* crave, desire, hanker after, long for, lust after, set your heart on, thirst for, want, wish for, yearn for

coward *n* chicken *sl*, scaredy-cat *inf*, wimp *inf*

cowardly *adj* fainthearted, fearful, gutless *inf*, lily-livered, scared, soft, spineless, timorous, weak, wimpish *inf*, yellow *inf*; ***opp*** brave

cower *v* cringe, crouch, draw back, flinch, grovel, hide, quail, recoil, shrink, skulk, tremble

coy *adj* bashful, demure, diffident, evasive, flirtatious, modest, reticent, shy, self-conscious

cozy *adj* **1** (of a house) comfortable, comfy *inf*, homely, safe, secure, sheltered, snug, warm; ***opp*** drafty. **2** (a cozy chat) easy, friendly, intimate, reassuring; ***opp*** awkward

crack *n* (break in sth) break, chink, chip, cleft, crevice, fissure, flaw, fracture, gap, opening, rift, slit, split. **2** (sound) burst, clap, crash, explosion, pop. **3** (have a crack at sth) (*inf*) go *inf*, stab *inf*, try. **4** (funny remark) (*inf*) dig *inf*, gag *inf*, insult, jibe, joke, quip, wisecrack, witticism

crack *v* **1** (be broken) break, chip, craze, fracture, fragment, snap, splinter, split. **2** (of thunder) boom, crackle, go bang, resound, ring out. **3** (hit a part of your body) bang, bash, bump, clout, hit, knock, smack, strike, whack. **4** (of people) break down, collapse, give way, go to pieces, lose control, succumb, yield

cracked *adj* broken, chipped, crazed, damaged, faulty, flawed, imperfect, split

craft *n* **1** ability, art, artistry, craftsmanship, expertise, handiwork, knack, skill, technique, workmanship. **2** aircraft, boat, ship, spacecraft, vessel

crafty *adj* artful, calculating, canny, clever, conniving, cunning, deceitful, devious, dodgy *inf*, furtive, guileful, scheming, sharp, shifty, shrewd, sly, sneaky *inf*, wily

cram *v* compact, compress, crowd, crush, fill, force, jam, overcrowd, overfill, pack, press, squeeze, stuff

cramped *adj* awkward, close, closed in, confined, congested, crowded, hemmed in, narrow, overcrowded, packed, restricted, small, tight, uncomfortable; ***opp*** spacious

crash *n* **1** bang, boom, clang, clash, din, explosion, racket, thunder. **2** accident, bump, collision, disaster, pile-up *inf*, smash. **3** (financial) bankruptcy, collapse, depression, failure, fold, ruin

crash *v* **1** bang, batter, boom, clash, clatter, dash, shatter, smash, splinter. **2** dive, fall, give way, hurtle, lurch, overbalance, pitch, plummet, plunge, topple, tumble. **3** (of a vehicle) crash into, collide, hit, plough into, smash into. **4** (of a driver) bump, crash-land, drive into, wreck, write off. **5** (of a business) collapse, fail, fold, go bust *inf*, go to the wall *inf*, go under

crate *n* box, case, container, packing case, tea chest

crater *n* chasm, depression, dip, hole, hollow, pit

crave *v* be dying for, cry out for *inf*, desire, fancy *inf*, hanker after, hope for, hunger after, long for, lust after, need, pine for, require, thirst for, want, yearn for

craving *n* addiction, appetite, desire, hankering, hope, hunger, longing, lust, need, thirst, urge, yearning

crawl *v* **1** clamber, creep, drag yourself, edge, go on all fours, inch, move on hands and knees, pull yourself along, slither, worm your way, wriggle, writhe.
2 be obsequious, flatter, grovel, humble yourself, suck up *sl*

craze *n* enthusiasm, fad, fashion, infatuation, mania, novelty, obsession, passion, pastime, rage, thing *inf*, trend, vogue

crazy *adj* **1** berserk, cracked *sl*, crazed, delirious, demented, deranged, hysterical, idiotic, insane, loopy *inf*, lunatic, mad, maniacal, nuts *sl*, touched, unbalanced, unhinged; ***opp*** sane.
2 (of ideas) bizarre, confused, eccentric, fantastic, impractical, odd, outrageous, peculiar, ridiculous, silly, strange, wacko *sl*, weird, wild, zany; ***opp*** sensible.
3 crazy about sth enthusiastic, fanatical, fervent, keen, mad, nuts *inf*, passionate

creak *v* grate, grind, jar, rasp, scrape, scratch, screech, squeak, squeal

cream *n* liniment, lotion, ointment, paste, salve

crease *n* corrugation, crinkle, fold, furrow, groove, line, pleat, pucker, ridge, tuck, wrinkle

crease *v* crimp, crinkle, crumple, crush, fold, furrow, groove, pleat, pucker, ridge, rumple, wrinkle

create *v* bring into being, build, coin, compose, conceive, concoct, construct, design, develop, devise, dream up *inf*, establish, forge, formulate, found, generate, give life to, hatch, initiate, invent, make, originate, produce, shape, think up

creation *n* **1** beginning, birth, building, establishment, formation, foundation, generation, genesis, inception, making, origin, procreation, setting up.
2 (sth a person has made) achievement, brainchild, concoction, handiwork, invention, masterpiece, opus, pièce de résistance, work, work of art

creative *adj* artistic, fertile, imaginative, inspired, inventive, original, productive, visionary

creativity *n* imagination, ingenuity, inspiration, inventiveness, originality, productivity, talent

creator *n* architect, author, designer, inventor, maker, producer, writer

creature *n* animal, beast, being, brute, living thing, organism

credentials *n* authorization, certificate, diploma, documentation, documents, identity card, license, passport, permit, proof of identity, recommendation, reference, testimonial, warrant

credible *adj* believable, conceivable, convincing, imaginable, likely, persuasive, plausible, possible, reasonable; ***opp*** unbelievable

credit *n* acknowledgment, approval, commendation, distinction, esteem, fame, glory, honor, kudos, merit, praise, prestige, recognition, thanks, tribute

credit *v* **1** (accept that sth is true) accept, believe, buy *inf*, fall for *inf*, have faith in, swallow *inf*, trust; ***opp*** doubt. **2** (give sb credit for sth) accredit, ascribe to, assign to, attribute, chalk up to, impute to

credulity *n* blind faith, credulousness, greenness, gullibility, naiveté; ***opp*** skepticism

creed *n* articles of faith, belief, canon, catechism, credo, doctrine, dogma, principles, statement of beliefs, teaching, tenet

creep *v* **1** (of creatures) crawl, glide, slither, squirm, worm, wriggle, writhe. **2** (of people) crawl, dawdle, drag yourself, edge, go on all fours, inch, move on hands and knees, move quietly, move slowly, move stealthily, pussyfoot, skulk, slink, sneak, steal, tiptoe. **3** bow and scrape, butter up *inf*, curry favor, flatter, grovel, suck up *sl*

crest *n* **1** (of a hill) apex, brow, crown, peak, pinnacle, ridge, summit, top. **2** (feathers) comb, plume, tassel, mane, tuft. **3** (family crest) badge, bearing, coat of arms, device, emblem, heraldic device, insignia, regalia, seal, shield, symbol

crestfallen *adj* dejected, depressed, despondent, disappointed, disconsolate, disheartened, dispirited, downcast, downhearted; ***opp*** cheerful

crevice *n* chink, cleft, crack, cranny, fissure, rift, slit, split

crew *n* **1** band, company, corps, force, gang, party, posse, squad, team. **2** (on a ship) hands, sailors, ship's company

crime *n* **1** (a crime) felony, misdeed, misdemeanor, offense, outrage, transgression, unlawful act, violation, wrong. **2** (crime in general) delinquency, dishonesty, lawbreaking, lawlessness, wrongdoing

criminal *adj* **1** bent *inf*, corrupt, crooked *inf*, culpable, dishonest, evil, illegal, illicit, immoral, unlawful, villainous, wicked, wrong. **2** deplorable, immoral, reprehensible, scandalous, shameful, shocking, wrong

criminal *n* con *inf*, convict, crook *inf*, culprit, delinquent, desperado, felon, jailbird, lawbreaker, miscreant, offender, outlaw, sinner, villain, wrongdoer

cringe *v* cower, draw back, duck, flinch, quail, recoil, shrink, shy away, tremble, wince

cripple *v* **1** (cripple sb) disable, enfeeble, handicap, incapacitate, make sb lame, maim, paralyze, weaken. **2** (cripple sth) damage, mutilate, paralyze, put out of action, ruin, sabotage, spoil

crisis *n* **1** calamity, catastrophe, dilemma, dire straits, disaster, emergency, predicament, quandary, trouble. **2** climax, critical point, crunch *inf*, crux, height, moment of truth, turning point

crisp *adj* **1** (of food) breakable, crispy, crumbly, crunchy, dry, firm, fresh; ***opp*** soggy. **2** (of the wind) bracing, brisk, cool, fresh, invigorating, refreshing

criterion *n* benchmark, gauge, measure, norm, principle, rule, scale, standard, test, touchstone, yardstick

critic *n* **1** commentator, connoisseur, expert, judge, pundit, reviewer. **2** attacker, backbiter, detractor, faultfinder, nit-picker *inf*; ***opp*** supporter

critical *adj* **1** carping, censorious, criticizing, derogatory, disapproving, disparaging, fault-finding, hypercritical, judgmental, nagging, niggling, nit-picking *inf*, quibbling, uncomplimentary, unfavorable; ***opp*** complimentary. **2** (a critical moment) deciding, decisive, important, key, momentous, pivotal. **3** (a critical situation) crucial, dangerous, grave, perilous, risky, serious, touch-and-go, urgent

criticism *n* **1** (criticism in general) bad press, censure, character assassination, condemnation, disapproval, disparagement, fault-finding, outcry, stick *sl*; ***opp*** approval. **2** complaint, diatribe, rebuke, reprimand, reproach, tirade. **3** (a criticism) analysis, appraisal, appreciation, assessment, comment, critique, evaluation, judgment, review

criticize *v* blame, castigate, censure, complain, condemn, disapprove, disparage, find fault, give flak *inf*, knock *inf*, nag, nit-pick *inf*, pick holes, slam *inf*; ***opp*** praise

croak *v* caw, gasp, grunt, speak hoarsely, speak huskily, squawk, wheeze

crook *n* cheat, criminal, robber, rogue, swindler, thief, villain

crooked *adj* **1** (not straight) bent, bowed, contorted, curved, curving, deformed, distorted, gnarled, irregular, misshapen, twisted, twisting, warped, winding, zigzag; ***opp*** straight. **2** (not even) askew, aslant, asymmetric, at an angle, awry, lopsided, off-center, slanted, slanting, sloping, tilted, uneven, unsymmetrical. **3** (not honest) bent *sl*, corrupt, criminal, deceitful, dishonest, dubious, fraudulent, illegal, questionable, shady *inf*, shifty, underhand; ***opp*** honest

crop *n* fruits, gathering, harvest, produce, season's growth, sowing, vintage, yield

crop *v* **1** clip, cut, lop, mow, pare, prune, shear, shorten, snip, trim. **2 crop up** arise, come up, emerge, happen, occur, turn up

cross *adj* angry, annoyed, bad-tempered, disagreeable, fractious, fretful, grouchy, grumpy *inf*, ill-humored, in a bad mood, irritable, irritated, short, short-tempered, sullen, surly, testy, upset, vexed; ***opp*** cheerful

cross *n* **1** crucifix, rood. **2** amalgam, blend, combination, cross-breed, hybrid, hybridization, mix, mixture, mongrel

cross *v* **1** (cross a river) bridge, cut across, ford, pass over, span, traverse. **2** (of lines) crisscross, intersect, intertwine, meet, zigzag. **3** (of breeds) blend, cross-breed, cross-fertilize, cross-pollinate, interbreed, mix. **4 cross out** cancel, delete, obliterate, strike out

crossing *n* **1** crossroads, intersection, junction, pedestrian crossing. **2** (a rough crossing) journey, passage, ride, trip, voyage

crouch *v* bend down, bow, duck, kneel, squat, stoop

crowd *n* **1** (group of people) army, bevy, bunch, circle, clique, company, flock, gang, group, herd, horde, host, lot, mass, mob, multitude, pack, rabble, set, swarm, throng. **2** (people watching sth) audience, gate, house, spectators, turnout

crowd *v* assemble, cluster, concentrate,

congregate, cram, flock, gather, huddle, jam, pile *inf*, press, push, squeeze, stuff, surge, swarm, throng

crowded *adj* busy, congested, cramped, crushed, full, jam-packed *inf*, packed, swarming, teeming

crown *n* **1** circlet, coronet, diadem, tiara. **2** apex, brow, head, peak, ridge, summit, top

crown *v* **1** anoint, appoint, enthrone, inaugurate, invest, install. **2** be the climax of, be the culmination of, cap, complete, consummate, finish, fulfill, put the finishing touch to, round off, top

crucial *adj* central, critical, decisive, determining, essential, high-priority, important, major, momentous, pivotal, significant

crude *adj* **1** coarse, crass, dirty, gross, indecent, indelicate, lewd, obscene, raunchy *inf*, smutty, tasteless, uncouth, vulgar. **2** natural, unprocessed, unrefined. **3** awkward, clumsy, inelegant, makeshift, primitive, rough, rough-and-ready, rudimentary, sketchy, undeveloped, unfinished, unskillful; ***opp*** sophisticated

cruel *adj* **1** (of people) barbaric, barbarous, brutal, callous, cold-blooded, fiendish, hard-hearted, heartless, inhuman, malevolent, merciless, murderous, pitiless, ruthless, sadistic, savage, spiteful, stony-hearted, unfeeling, unkind, vengeful, vicious; ***opp*** kind. **2** (of conditions) atrocious, bitter, fierce, grim, hard, harsh, hellish, painful, raw, severe, unrelenting

cruise *v* coast, drift, move, sail, travel, voyage

crumb *n* bit, bite, grain, morsel, particle, scrap, shred, speck

crumble *v* **1** (of food) break into pieces, break up, crush, granulate, grind, pound, powder, pulverize. **2** (of materials) come to dust, decay, decompose, disintegrate, fall apart, fall to pieces, molder, perish, rot

crumple *v* crease, crinkle, crush, fold, pucker, rumple, wrinkle

crunch *v* bite, chew, chomp, crush, munch, scrunch *inf*, smash, squash

crusade *n* campaign, cause, drive, holy war, jihad, military campaign, movement, struggle

crush *v* **1** break, bruise, compress, crumble, crunch, grind, mangle, mash, pound, press, pulp, pulverize, shatter, smash, squeeze. **2** (of fabric) crease, crinkle, crumple, rumple, wrinkle. **3** conquer, defeat, overcome, overpower, put down, quash, quell, stamp out, subdue, thrash, vanquish. **4** (crush sb's spirit) chagrin, humiliate, mortify, shame

crust *n* coating, covering, outer layer, outside, rind, scab, shell, skin, surface, topping

crux *n* core, essence, gist, heart, nub, point

cry *n* **1** bellow, howl, scream, shriek, shout, whoop, yell, yelp. **2** blub *inf*, howl, keening, lamentation, sob, sobbing, wail, weep, weeping

cry *v* **1** bawl, blubber, grizzle, howl, lament, shed tears, snivel, sob, wail, weep, whimper, whine. **2** bawl, bellow, call, call out, exclaim, roar, scream, screech, shout, shriek, sing out, yell

cryptic *adj* coded, enigmatic, hidden, mysterious, mystical, obscure, puzzling, secret, unclear, veiled; ***opp*** clear, obvious

cuddle *v* **1** clasp, embrace, fondle, hold closely, hug, kiss, neck *inf*, pet, smooch *inf*. **2** curl up, nestle, snuggle

cue *n* hint, nod, prompt, reminder, sign, signal, suggestion

culminate *v* build up to, climax, close, come to a crescendo, come to a head, conclude, end, finish, peak, terminate

culprit *n* bad guy *inf*, delinquent, guilty party, miscreant, offender, person responsible, wrongdoer

cult *n* **1** church, denomination, faction, group, order, party, religion, sect

cultivate *v* **1** dig, farm, fertilize, grow, harvest, hoe, plant, plough, prepare, produce, raise, sow, take cuttings, tend, till, turn, work. **2** court, develop, devote yourself to, encourage, foster, improve, promote, pursue, support. **3** civilize, educate, enlighten, polish, refine, train

cultivation *n* **1** agriculture, farming, gardening, growing, horticulture. **2** advancement, development, encouragement, fostering, furtherance, promotion, support

cultural *adj* **1** (cultural experiences) artistic, broadening, civilizing, edifying, educational, elevating, enriching, highbrow, improving. **2** (cultural diversity) ethnic, racial

culture *n* **1** civilization, customs, lifestyle, mores, society, way of life. **2** (person of culture) education, enlightenment, erudition, good taste, refinement, sophistication

cultured *adj* accomplished, civilized, cultivated, educated, enlightened, erudite, genteel, intellectual, knowledgable, learned, refined, scholarly, versed, well-educated, well-read; ***opp*** ignorant

cunning *adj* artful, astute, canny, clever, crafty, devious, guileful, imaginative, ingenious, resourceful, sharp, shrewd, subtle, wily

cup *n* **1** beaker, chalice, glass, goblet, mug, tankard, tumbler. **2** prize, trophy

curb *v* bite back, bridle, check, constrain, contain, control, hinder, hold back, impede, inhibit, keep in check, limit, moderate, muzzle, put a brake on, repress, restrain, restrict, suppress

cure *n* **1** antidote, cure-all, medication, medicine, palliative, panacea, prescription, remedy, solution, therapy, treatment. **2** convalescence, healing, improvement, progress, recovery

cure *v* **1** (make sb better) heal, make better, make well, rehabilitate, restore to health, treat. **2** (put sth right) correct, fix, put right, rectify, remedy, repair, solve. **3** (preserve food) dry, preserve, salt, smoke

curiosity *n* **1** inquisitiveness, interest, interference, meddling, nosiness *inf*, prying, snooping. **2** (sth unusual) freak, novelty, oddity, phenomenon, rarity, spectacle

curious *adj* **1** (a curious mind) inquiring, inquisitive, interested, probing, puzzled, questioning. **2** (nosy) inquisitive, interfering, intrusive, meddlesome, meddling, nosy *inf*, prying, snooping. **3** (a curious object) bizarre, exotic, mysterious, novel, odd, puzzling, strange, unusual, wonderful

curl *v* 1 bend, coil, corkscrew, curve, entwine, loop, meander, ripple, snake, spiral, turn, twine, twirl, twist, wind, wreathe, writhe. 2 (of hair) corkscrew, crimp, crinkle, frizz, kink, perm, wave

curly *adj* curling, crimped, crinkly, frizzy, fuzzy, permed, wavy; ***opp*** straight

current *adj* 1 alive, contemporary, continuing, existing, fashionable, happening *inf*, in *inf*, in fashion, in vogue, living, modern, now *inf*, popular, present, present-day, prevailing, trendy *inf*, up-to-date; ***opp*** old, outdated

current *n* 1 (of water) course, drift, flow, river, stream, tide, undercurrent, undertow. 2 (of air) draft, movement, thermal, wind

curriculum *n* course, program, syllabus

curse *n* 1 bad language, blasphemy, expletive, oath, obscenity, profanity, swear word. 2 (put a curse on sb) evil eye, imprecation, jinx. 3 affliction, bane, evil, hardship, misfortune, plague, scourge, tribulation

curse *v* 1 be foul-mouthed, blaspheme, cuss *inf*, swear, take God's name in vain, use bad language. 2 damn, jinx, put a curse on, put a jinx on, put the evil eye on

cursory *adj* brief, careless, casual, desultory, fleeting, hasty, hurried, perfunctory, quick, superficial

curtail *v* abbreviate, break off, cut short, dock, pare down, reduce, restrict, shorten, stop, terminate, trim; ***opp*** extend

curve *n* arc, arch, bend, bow, bulge, camber, circle, crescent, curvature, half-moon, loop, spiral, twist, undulation

curve *v* arc, arch, bend, bow, coil, curl, loop, meander, snake, swerve, swirl, turn, twist, wind

curved *adj* arched, bent, bowed, concave, convex, crooked, curvilinear, curvy, humped, rounded, sinuous, twisted, undulating

custody *n* 1 (in custody) arrest, detention, imprisonment, incarceration. 2 (in sb's custody) care, charge, control, guardianship, keeping, possession, protection, safe-keeping, supervision, trusteeship

custom *n* convention, etiquette, form, formality, habit, manner, observance, practice, ritual, routine, tradition, usage, way, wont

customary *adj* accepted, common, conventional, established, everyday, familiar, general, habitual, normal, ordinary, regular, routine, traditional, typical, usual

customer *n* buyer, client, consumer, patron, purchaser, regular *inf*, shopper

cut *n* 1 gash, graze, groove, incision, laceration, nick, opening, rent, rip, slash, slit, snip, split, tear, wound. 2 cutback, economy, fall, lowering, reduction, saving

cut *v* 1 (injure sb) gash, gouge, graze, knife, lacerate, lance, nick, open, sever, slash, snick, stab, wound. 2 (cut sth) carve, chip, chisel, chop, cleave, clip, crop, dice, dissect, divide, engrave, grate, guillotine, hack, hew, lop, mow, notch, pare, pierce, prune, saw, score, sculpt, shave, shear, shred, slice, slit, whittle. 3 (reduce) abbreviate, abridge, condense, curtail, cut back, decrease, delete, economize, edit, excise, lessen, rationalize, reduce, retrench, shorten, slash, slim down, trim, truncate; ***opp*** increase. **4 cut down** bring down, chop down, fell, flatten, hew, level, lop, raze. **5 cut off** break off, disconnect, interrupt, isolate, remove, separate, sever, suspend. **6 cut out** delete, excise, extract, remove. **7 cut up** carve, chop, dice, divide, mince, slice

cutback *n* cut, decrease, economy, reduction

cutthroat *adj* **1** bloodthirsty, bloody, cruel, ferocious, fierce, homicidal, murderous, savage, violent. **2** competitive, dog-eat-dog, fierce, merciless, relentless, ruthless, unprincipled

cutting *adj* acerbic, acid, barbed, biting, hurtful, incisive, malicious, sarcastic, scathing, sharp, stinging, spiteful, trenchant, wounding

cycle *n* circle, revolution, rotation, round, sequence, series, succession

cynic *n* doubting Thomas, killjoy, pessimist, skeptic

cynical *adj* doubting, full of doom and gloom, negative, pessimistic, skeptical, scornful, sneering; ***opp*** optimistic

cynicism *n* doubt, pessimism, skepticism, scorn, suspicion

dagger *n* blade, knife, sheath knife
daily *adj, adv* common, day-to-day, everyday, regular, routine, usual
dainty *adj* delicate, elegant, fine, graceful, neat, petite, pretty
dam *n* **1** barrage, barricade, barrier, wall, weir. **2** artificial lake, lake, reservoir
dam *v* barricade, block, check, dam up, hold back, stop
damage *n* abuse, detriment, devastation, harm, havoc, hurt, injury, loss, sabotage, vandalism
damage *v* bend, break, bruise, bump, bust *inf*, chip, crack, crash, deface, dent, harm, hurt, impair, injure, rip, ruin, sabotage, scrape, scratch, spoil, tear, vandalize, warp, wreck
damaging *adj* critical, detrimental, discreditable, disparaging, harmful, hurtful, injurious, prejudicial
damp *adj* clammy, dank, humid, misty, moist, muggy, soggy, steamy, sticky, wet; ***opp*** dry
damp *n* clamminess, dampness, humidity, moisture, mist, mugginess, steaminess, wetness
dance *n* ball, ballet, bop *inf*, dancing, disco, hop, jig, square dance
dance *v* cavort, do a jig, jive, leap about, shake a leg *inf*, smooch, sway, take the floor, twirl, waltz
danger *n* hazard, jeopardy, menace, peril, pitfall, risk, threat
dangerous *adj* chancy, daredevil, foolhardy, hairy *inf*, hazardous, life-threatening, nasty, perilous, risky, ugly, unsafe; ***opp*** safe
dare *n* challenge, provocation, taunt
dare *v* **1** challenge, defy, goad, provoke, taunt, throw down the gauntlet. **2** brave, have the courage, have the guts *inf*, have the nerve, pluck up the courage, risk, take the plunge, take the risk, venture
daring *adj* adventurous, audacious, bold, brave, fearless, rash, wild; ***opp*** timid
dark *adj* **1** black, cloudy, dim, dingy, gloomy, inky, overcast, poorly lit, shadowy, unlit; ***opp*** bright, light. **2** (of complexion) black, brown, dark-skinned, olive, swarthy, tanned; ***opp*** pale. **3** (of colors) deep, dense, rich; ***opp*** light
dark *n* blackness, darkness, dusk, gloom, murkiness, night, nightfall, nighttime, shade, shadows, twilight
darken *v* blacken, cloud over, dim, get dark, grow dim, make dark, shade
darkness *n* blackness, dark, dusk, gloom, murkiness, night, nightfall, nighttime, shade, shadows, twilight
darling *n* dear, dearest, love, pet,

sweetheart, sweetie

dart *v* bolt, dash, fly, hop, hurtle, nip, race, run, rush, scuttle, shoot, sprint, tear

dash *v* **1** bolt, charge, chase, fly, hurry, hurtle, race, run, rush, speed, sprint, tear, zoom *inf*. **2** crash, fling, hurl, pitch, slam, smash, throw

data *n* details, facts, figures, information, statistics

date *n* **1** age, day, day and age, epoch, era, period, time, vintage, year. **2** appointment, assignation, engagement, meeting, rendezvous

dated *adj* ancient, antiquated, fuddy-duddy *inf*, fusty, obsolete, old, old-fashioned, old-hat, outmoded, passé, stale, unfashionable; ***opp*** latest, modern, up-to-date

daunting *adj* disconcerting, discouraging, frightening, intimidating, overwhelming, scary, terrifying, unnerving

dawdle *v* amble, dilly-dally, drag your feet, go slowly, hang about, lag behind, linger, loiter, saunter, shilly-shally, take your time, waste time; ***opp*** rush

dawn *n* **1** crack of dawn, daybreak, daylight, first light, start of the day, sunrise, sun-up; ***opp*** dusk, sunset. **2** advent, beginning, birth, genesis, onset, start; ***opp*** end

dawn *v* **1** begin, break, come into being, emerge, start. **2** (sth dawns on you) come to you, enter your mind, flash across your mind, hit, occur to you, register, strike

day *n* **1** daytime, daylight; ***opp*** night. **2** age, date, day and age, epoch, era, generation, period, point in time, time

daybreak *n* crack of dawn, dawn, daylight, first light, start of the day, sunrise, sun-up; ***opp*** dusk, sunset

daydream *n* castle in the air, dream, fantasy, pipe-dream, reverie

daydream *v* be in your own little world, be lost in thought, dream, fantasize, imagine, let your thoughts wander, stare into space

daze *v* bemuse, bewilder, confuse, floor *inf*, numb, shock, stagger, stun, stupefy

dazed *adj* bemused, bewildered, confused, dizzy, floored *inf*, fuddled, muddled, numbed, shocked, staggered, stunned, stupefied

dazzle *v* **1** blind, confuse, disorientate. **2** bedazzle, bowl over *inf*, impress, overwhelm, stagger, stun, take your breath away

dazzling *adj* amazing, brilliant, glittering, magnificent, sensational, sparkling, splendid, terrific, stunning

dead *adj* **1** deceased, departed, late, lifeless, no more, out of your misery, passed away, pushing up the daisies *inf*, six feet under *inf*, stillborn; ***opp*** alive. **2** (obsolete) extinct, obsolete; ***opp*** living. **3** (unresponsive) cold, emotionless, indifferent, inert, lifeless, numb, paralyzed, unresponsive, without feeling, wooden. **4** (not working) broken, defunct, had it, kaput, out of order, worn out; ***opp*** working. **5** boring, dreary, dull, flat, lifeless, uninteresting; ***opp*** lively

deaden *v* blunt, dull, muffle, numb, soothe, smother, stifle, suppress

deadlock *n* checkmate, dead end,

impasse, logjam, stalemate, standoff, standstill

deadly *adj* 1 fatal, lethal, malignant, noxious, poisonous, virulent. 2 (boring) awful, boring, dire, dull, tedious, terrible

deaf *adj* hard of hearing, stone deaf, with a hearing problem, with impaired hearing

deafen *v* make deaf, damage sb's hearing, hurt your ears

deafening *adj* at full blast, at full volume, blaring, ear-splitting, loud, roaring, thudding, thunderous

deal *n* agreement, arrangement, bargain, business deal, contract, pact, transaction, understanding, venture

deal *v* 1 (share out) allocate, allot, dish out, distribute, dole out, give, hand out, share out. 2 **deal in** buy and sell, do business, handle, trade, traffic. 3 **deal with** attend to, do, fix, handle, see to, sort *inf*, sort out, tackle, take care of, take on, take responsibility for

dealer *n* agent, broker, buyer, handler, retailer, seller, trader, vendor, wholesaler

dear *adj* 1 cost-a-fortune *inf*, costly, exorbitant, expensive, extortionate, high-priced, luxury, overpriced, pricey, steep *inf*, stiff *inf*, top-rate, up-market, upscale; ***opp*** cheap, inexpensive. 2 (much-loved) close, close to your heart, darling, intimate, loved, much-loved

dear *n* darling, dearest, love, pet, sweetheart, sweetie

death *n* 1 bloodshed, curtains *inf*, decease, demise, dying, end, fatality, killing, loss of life, massacre, slaughter. 2 (end) annihilation, destruction, downfall, end, eradication, extermination, finish, obliteration, ruin

debase *v* cheapen, degrade, demean, devalue, discredit, disgrace, lower, shame, spoil, sully

debatable *adj* arguable, borderline, controversial, doubtful, dubious, iffy *inf*, open to question, questionable

debate *n* argument, deliberation, disagreement, discussion, dispute

debate *v* argue, deliberate, disagree, discuss, talk about

debris *n* detritus, dross, garbage, litter, remains, rubbish, rubble, trash, waste

debt *n* arrears, credit, dues, liability, loan, money owing, mortgage, overdraft

debut *n* appearance, entrance, first appearance, inauguration, introduction, launch, première

decadent *adj* corrupt, debauched, decaying, declining, degenerate, depraved, dissipated, dissolute, immoral, licentious, permissive

decay *n* collapse, corrosion, crumbling, death, decline, decomposition, disintegration, going bad, rot, rotting, putrefaction, withering away

decay *v* corrode, crumble, decompose, die, disintegrate, go bad, mold, rot, perish, putrefy, shrivel, waste away, wither

deceased *adj* dead, departed, late, no more, passed away, passed on

deceit *n* cheating, deception, dishonesty, disloyalty, double-dealing, duplicity, false pretenses, fraud, lying, misrepresentation, pretense, subterfuge, treachery, trickery, untruthfulness

deceitful *adj* bogus, crooked, dishonest, disloyal, double-dealing, false, fraudulent, lying, sham, two-faced, underhand, untrustworthy, untruthful; ***opp*** honest

deceive *v* cheat, cheat on, con *inf*, double-cross, dupe, fool, lead sb on, mislead, hoodwink, pull a fast one, pull the wool over sb's eyes, swindle, take for a ride, take in, trick

decency *n* civility, courtesy, correctness, dignity, good manners, honesty, propriety, respectability

decent *adj* **1** courteous, dependable, dignified, good, honest, honorable, nice, proper, respectable, suitable, trustworthy, upright, worthy. **2** (adequate) acceptable, adequate, fair, good, reasonable, sufficient

deception *n* **1** cheating, deceit, dishonesty, double-dealing, duplicity, false pretenses, fraud, lying, misrepresentation, pretense, subterfuge, treachery, trickery, untruthfulness. **2** con *inf*, cover-up, dodge, fiddle *inf*, hoax, lie, pretense, ruse, sham, swindle, trick

deceptive *adj* deceiving, false, illusory, misleading, unreliable

decide *v* choose, come to a conclusion, conclude, determine, give your verdict, go for, make a decision, make up your mind, opt for, resolve, settle, settle for, settle on, take the plunge

decision *n* choice, conclusion, finding, judgment, outcome, pronouncement, resolution, result, ruling, verdict

decisive *adj* **1** definite, firm, forceful, positive, resolute, self-confident, strong-minded, sure of yourself, unfaltering, unwavering; ***opp*** hesitant, indecisive, tentative. **2** critical, crucial, deciding, definitive, determining, key, pivotal, significant

declaration *n* announcement, assertion, decree, disclosure, edict, notice, press release, proclamation, revelation, statement

declare *v* affirm, announce, assert, claim, contend, disclose, maintain, make known, proclaim, profess, reveal, say, state

decline *n* degeneration, deterioration, downturn, downward trend, drop, fall, reversal, slump

decline *v* **1** refuse, reject, say no, send your apologies, turn down; ***opp*** accept. **2** decrease, degenerate, deteriorate, diminish, dwindle, fade, fall, fall off, get worse, go down, go downhill, go to the dogs *inf*, peter out, sink, tail off, wane, weaken; ***opp*** get better, improve, increase

decorate *v* **1** do up *inf*, paint, paper, refurbish, smarten up, wallpaper. **2** deck, embellish, garnish, festoon, trim

decoration *n* **1** decor, color scheme. **2** bauble, embellishment, fancywork, flounce, frill, garnish, ornamentation, spangle, tinsel, trimmings

decorative *adj* nonfunctional, ornamental, ornate; ***opp*** functional

decoy *n* bait, distraction, inducement, lure, trap

decoy *v* attract, bait, entice, induce, inveigle, lure, tempt

decrease *n* cutback, decline, downsizing, downturn, drop, fall, let-up, reduction, shrinkage; ***opp*** increase

decrease *v* abate, cut, cut back on, decline, diminish, downsize, dwindle, drop, fall off, go down, lessen, lower, peter out, reduce, subside, taper off; ***opp*** increase

decree *n* announcement, command, dictum, directive, edict, injunction, judgment, law, order, policy statement, regulation, rule, ruling

decree *v* announce, dictate, direct, lay down, prescribe, ordain, order, proclaim, pronounce, rule, say, state

decrepit *adj* broken-down, derelict, dilapidated, doddering, incapacitated, on its last legs, ramshackle, rickety, run-down, tottering, worn-out, wrecked

dedicate *v* **1** assign, commit, devote, give over to, pledge. **2** bless, consecrate, sanctify

dedicated *adj* committed, devoted, enthusiastic, keen, loyal, single-minded, wholehearted, zealous

dedication *n* **1** commitment, determination, devotion, keenness, loyalty, single-mindedness, zeal. **2** address, inscription, message

deduce *v* come to a conclusion, conclude, infer, gather, realize, surmise, understand, work out

deduct *v* allow, cut, discount, knock off *inf*, subtract, take away, take off; ***opp*** add

deduction *n* **1** allowance, cut, discount, markdown, rebate, reduction, stoppage, subtraction. **2** assumption, conclusion, inference, presumption, reasoning

deed *n* **1** achievement, act, action, effort, enterprise, exercise, exploit, feat, job, operation, undertaking. **2** agreement, contract, deed of covenant, document, indenture, paper, policy, proof of ownership, record, title deed

deep *adj* **1** abyssal, bottomless, cavernous, yawning; ***opp*** shallow. **2** broad, large, wide. **3** (of a voice) bass, booming, low, low-pitched, rich; ***opp*** high. **4** (of a color) dark, intense, rich, strong, vivid; ***opp*** light, pale. **5** (of an emotion) deep-rooted, deep-seated, heartfelt, intense, passionate, profound, strong; ***opp*** superficial

deface *v* damage, disfigure, mutilate, spoil, vandalize

default *v* backslide, be negligent, dodge, evade, fail to fulfill, fail to pay, fall into arrears, get behind, let sb down, shirk, stop payment, withhold payment

defeat *n* **1** conquest, drubbing *inf*, overthrow, rout, thrashing, trouncing, victory, win. **2** collapse, disappointment, downfall, failure, frustration, reverse, ruin; ***opp*** victory

defeat *v* annihilate, beat, conquer, foil, get the better of, hammer *inf*, get the upper hand, knock the socks off *inf*, knock the stuffing out of *inf*, outclass, overthrow, rout, thrash, thwart, topple, trounce, vanquish, wipe the floor with *inf*

defect *n* blemish, bug *inf*, deficiency, error, failing, fault, flaw, mistake, shortcoming, weakness, weak spot

defect *v* change sides, desert, desert the cause, go over to the other side, join the opposition, turn traitor

defective *adj* broken, damaged, faulty, flawed, malfunctioning, not working, out of order

defend *v* **1** fortify, guard, protect, safeguard, secure; ***opp*** attack. **2** champion, espouse, justify, speak up for, stand by, stand up for, support, uphold; ***opp*** attack

defendant *n* accused, appellant, culprit, litigant, offender, prisoner, respondent, suspect

defense *n* 1 (protection) barricade, bastion, cover, deterrent, fortification, fortress, protection, shelter, shield. 2 (military matters) armaments, armed forces, the military, weapons. 3 (justification) case, excuse, explanation, justification, vindication

defenseless *adj* exposed, helpless, impotent, powerless, unarmed, vulnerable, weak; ***opp*** strong

defensive *adj* 1 feeling accused *inf*, sensitive, uptight *inf*, wary. 2 protective

defer *v* adjourn, delay, hold, hold over, postpone, put off, put on ice, put on the back burner, shelve, table

defiant *adj* belligerent, challenging, disobedient, noncompliant, intransigent, rebellious, recalcitrant, scornful, stubborn, uncooperative; ***opp*** compliant, submissive

deficiency *n* dearth, deficit, inadequacy, lack, scarcity, shortage

deficient *adj* inadequate, lacking, meager, scant, scarce, short, skimpy

deficit *n* arrears, deficiency, loss, shortage, shortfall

define *v* clarify, describe, elucidate, explain, give the meaning of, outline, set out, specify, spell out

definite *adj* 1 certain, confident, confirmed, guaranteed, positive, sure. 2 clear, clear-cut, explicit, marked, obvious, precise, unmistakable

definition *n* description, explanation, meaning

definitive *adj* 1 conclusive, decisive, final, unconditional. 2 authoritative, complete, exhaustive, reliable

deflect *v* bounce off, change course, divert, glance off, ricochet, shy, swerve, turn aside, veer

deformed *adj* contorted, damaged, disfigured, distorted, injured, maimed, malformed, misshapen, mutilated, twisted

defraud *v* cheat, con *inf*, embezzle, fleece, pull a fast one *inf*, rip off *inf*, rob, rook, sting *inf*, swindle, take sb for a ride

defunct *adj* deceased, dead, expired, extinct, gone, invalid, obsolete

defy *v* challenge, confront, disobey, disregard, flout, foil, frustrate, rebel against, resist, thumb your nose at *inf*, thwart, withstand

degenerate *adj* corrupt, decadent, degraded, depraved, dissolute, fallen, immoral, low, unacceptable

degenerate *v* decline, deteriorate, fall off, get worse, go downhill, go from bad to worse, go to rack and ruin, go to seed *inf*, go to the dogs *inf*, sink, slide

degrade *v* cheapen, debase, demean, devalue, discredit, disgrace, dishonor, downgrade, lower, shame

degrading *adj* demeaning, embarrassing, humiliating, mortifying, shameful, undignified

degree *n* amount, extent, intensity, level, limit, point, stage, standard

deign *v* bother, condescend, consent, lower yourself, stoop

deity *n* divinity, god, goddess, holy being, object of worship, spirit

dejected *adj* cut up *inf*, depressed, despairing, despondent, disappointed, discouraged, disgruntled, dispirited, down, downhearted, down in the dumps *inf*, gloomy, miserable, out of sorts, sad, with a long face

delay *n* break, hiatus, hitch, holdup, interruption, lull, postponement, setback, suspension, time-lag, wait

delay *v* 1 adjourn, defer, hold, hold over, postpone, put off, put on ice, put on the back burner, shelve, table. 2 detain, hold up, make late, slow down

delegate *n* agent, emissary, envoy, go-between, messenger, representative, spokesman, spokesperson, spokeswoman

delegate *v* 1 (a task) assign, devolve, hand over, pass on, transfer. 2 (a person) appoint, authorize, choose, empower, mandate

delegation *n* contingent, delegates, deputation, group, mission, representatives

delete *v* cancel, cut out, cross out, erase, get rid of, remove, rub out, strike out, take out, wipe out

deliberate *adj* 1 calculated, cold-blooded, conscious, intentional, knowing, preconceived, premeditated, willful; ***opp*** accidental, unintentional. 2 careful, determined, measured, methodical, painstaking, patient, ponderous, resolute, slow; ***opp*** hasty

deliberate *v* 1 (think about) consider, evaluate, mull over, ponder, reflect, review, ruminate, think over, think, weigh. 2 (discuss) consider, debate, discuss

deliberately *adj* 1 consciously, in cold-blood, intentionally, knowingly, on purpose, willfully, wittingly; ***opp*** accidentally, unintentionally. 2 carefully, determinedly, methodically, painstakingly, patiently, resolutely, slowly; ***opp*** hastily

delicacy *n* 1 daintiness, elegance, fineness, flimsiness, fragility, intricacy. 2 (sensitivity) care, diplomacy, discretion, sensitivity, tact. 3 (a luxury food) luxury, titbit, treat

delicate *adj* 1 dainty, elegant, fine, flimsy, fragile, graceful, intricate. 2 (pastel) muted, pale, pastel, soft, subtle, understated. 3 (sensitive) awkward, difficult, diplomatic, discreet, sensitive, tactful, tricky

delicious *adj* appetizing, gorgeous, mouth-watering, scrumptious, tasty, tempting, yummy *inf*

delight *n* amusement, ecstasy, elation, enjoyment, enthusiasm, excitement, happiness, joy, jubilation, pleasure, thrill

delight *v* amuse, captivate, cheer, enchant, entertain, excite, please, thrill, tickle

delighted *adj* captivated, ecstatic, enchanted, glad, happy, in raptures, jubilant, on cloud nine *inf*, on top of the world, overjoyed, pleased, thrilled, tickled pink *inf*

delightful *adj* agreeable, amusing, appealing, attractive, captivating, charming, cute, enchanting, engaging, enjoyable, entertaining, fascinating, lovely, nice, pleasant, pleasurable, thrilling, wonderful; ***opp*** unpleasant

delinquent *n* hoodlum, hooligan, rowdy, ruffian, thug, tough, troublemaker, vandal, young offender

delirious *adj* 1 demented, deranged, distracted, feverish, hallucinating, incoherent, lightheaded, rambling, raving. 2 carried away, ecstatic, euphoric, on a high *inf*

deliver *v* 1 (deliver goods) bring, dispatch, hand over, produce, send, supply, take, transfer, transport. 2 (deliver a speech or verdict) announce, declare, give, make, pronounce, read. 3 (deliver a ball or punch) administer, aim, deal, direct, hit, hurl, inflict, send, throw

delivery *n* 1 carriage, conveyance, dispatch, distribution, shipment, transfer, transport, transportation. 2 batch, consignment, load, shipment

deluge *n* 1 downpour, flash flood, flood, inundation, overflowing, rainstorm, torrent. 2 barrage, flood, rush, spate; ***opp*** trickle

delusion *n* dream, error, false impression, fancy, fantasy, hallucination, illusion, mirage, misapprehension, misbelief, misconception, mistake, misunderstanding; ***opp*** reality

demand *n* 1 appeal, claim, clamor, entreaty, insistence, pressure, request, requisition. 2 challenge, inquiry, interrogation, question. 3 (the demands of sth) exigency, necessity, need, requirement. **4 in demand** all the rage *inf*, fashionable, in vogue, popular, sought after, trendy *inf*

demand *v* 1 (ask for sth) appeal, ask, call for, claim, clamor for, cry out for, insist on, lay claim to, make a claim for, press for, request, urge. 2 (ask a question) ask, challenge, inquire, interrogate, question. 3 call for, entail, involve, necessitate, need, require, take, want

demanding *adj* arduous, challenging, daunting, difficult, exacting, exhausting, grueling, hard, taxing, tiring, tough, trying, wearing; ***opp*** undemanding

demeanor *n* air, appearance, bearing, behavior, carriage, conduct, deportment, manner, mien

democratic *adj* autonomous, classless, egalitarian, free, of the people, popular, populist, representative, republican, self-governing; ***opp*** totalitarian

demolish *v* bulldoze, destroy, dismantle, flatten, knock down, level, pull down, raze, ruin, tear down, trash *sl*, wreck; ***opp*** build

demon *n* devil, evil spirit, fiend, goblin, imp, monster

demonstrate *v* 1 (demonstrate that sth is true) confirm, establish, indicate, prove, show, testify, validate, verify; ***opp*** disprove. 2 (demonstrate how to do sth) describe, explain, give a demonstration, give an idea of, illustrate, make clear, show how, teach. 3 lobby, march, parade, picket, protest, rally, sit in

demonstration *n* 1 (of the truth of sth) confirmation, evidence, illustration, proof, testimony, validation, verification. 2 (how to do sth) description, explanation, exposition, illustration, lesson, presentation. 3 lobby, march, parade, picket, protest, rally, sit-in

demonstrative *adj* affectionate, effusive, emotional, expressive, gushing, lovey-dovey *inf*, loving, open, uninhibited, unreserved, unrestrained; ***opp*** reticent

demoralize *adj* break, crush, daunt, depress, discourage, dishearten, dispirit, unnerve, weaken; ***opp*** encourage

demure *adj* bashful, coy, diffident, modest, quiet, reserved, reticent, retiring, sedate, shy, sober, staid, unassuming; ***opp*** wild

den *n* **1** cave, cavern, haunt, hideaway, hideout, hiding place, hole, lair, shelter. **2** retreat, sanctum, sanctuary

denial *n* backpedaling, disavowal, disclaimer, retraction, taking back; ***opp*** admission, confession. **2** (not allowing sb to do sth) prohibition, rebuff, refusal, rejection, thumbs-down *inf*, veto; ***opp*** permission

denote *v* be the sign for, express, indicate, mark, mean, represent, show, signal, signify, stand for, symbolize

denounce *v* **1** attack, castigate, condemn, criticize, damn, decry, revile, stigmatize, vilify; ***opp*** praise. **2** accuse, betray, blame, incriminate, report

dense *adj* **1** close, compact, compressed, concentrated, condensed, heavy, impenetrable, lush, opaque, solid, substantial, thick; ***opp*** thin. **2** bird-brained, brainless, clueless, dim *inf*, dopey, dumb, ignorant, simple, slow, stupid, thick *inf*, unintelligent; ***opp*** clever

dent *n* chip, crater, depression, dimple, dip, hollow, indentation

dent *v* buckle, crumple, depress, knock in, press in, push in

deny *v* **1** refute, retract, take back; ***opp*** admit, confess. **2** (deny sb sth) give the thumbs down, prohibit, rebuff, refuse, reject, revoke, turn down, veto, withhold; ***opp*** allow

depart *v* abscond, be off *inf*, be on your way *inf*, clear off *inf*, disappear, emigrate, exit, go, go away, hit the road *inf*, leave, make tracks *inf*, migrate, move away, move off, quit, retire, retreat, split *inf*, take your leave, take yourself off, vanish, withdraw; ***opp*** arrive

department *n* **1** agency, branch, bureau, division, office, section, sector, subdivision, unit. **2** (sb's department) area, concern, domain, field, function, job, line, realm, responsibility, specialty, sphere. **3** canton, county, district, province, region, state, territory

departure *n* **1** disappearance, emigration, exit, exodus, going, leaving, migration, retreat, withdrawal; ***opp*** arrival. **2** (from the norm) deviation, difference, digression, divergence, shift, variation. **3** (a new departure) branching out, change, change of direction, innovation, novelty

depend *v* **1** bank on, be dependent on, cling to, count on, lean on, need, put your faith in, rely on, trust in, turn to. **2** be based on, be dependent on, be determined by, be subject to, hinge on, pivot on, rest on, revolve around

dependable *adj* consistent, faithful, reliable, reputable, responsible, sensible, stable, staunch, steadfast, trustworthy, trusty, unfailing; ***opp*** unreliable

dependent *adj* **1** conditional, contingent, controlled by, determined by, liable to, relative to, subject to. **2** (dependent children) defenseless, helpless, reliant, vulnerable, weak; ***opp*** independent

depict *v* describe, draw, illustrate, narrate, outline, paint, picture, portray, represent, reproduce, show, sketch

deplete *v* consume, cut, decrease, diminish, drain, empty, evacuate, exhaust, expend, impoverish, lessen, lower, reduce, use up

deplorable *adj* abominable, atrocious, awful, despicable, disgraceful, disreputable, dreadful, reprehensible, scandalous, shameful, shocking

deplore *v* abhor, censure, condemn, decry, denounce, deprecate, disapprove of, object to, regret; ***opp*** approve

deport *v* banish, exile, expatriate, expel, extradite, oust, remove, send abroad/overseas

depose *v* dethrone, dismiss, displace, get rid of, oust, overthrow, remove, topple, unseat

deposit *n* 1 advance payment, down-payment, initial payment, installment, part-payment, retainer, security, stake. 2 accumulation, layer, sediment, silt, sludge

depot *n* 1 arsenal, base, depository, repository, store, storehouse, warehouse. 2 bus station, terminal, terminus, train station

depraved *adj* base, corrupt, debased, debauched, degenerate, dissolute, evil, immoral, indecent, lewd, licentious, obscene, perverted, profligate, sinful, unprincipled, vicious, vile, wicked

depress *v* dampen your spirits, discourage, dishearten, dismay, dispirit, sadden, upset, weigh down; ***opp*** encourage

depressed *adj* blue, dejected, despondent, discouraged, disheartened, dismayed, dispirited, down, down in the dumps, downcast, fed up, gloomy, glum, low, melancholy, miserable, moody, morose, sad, saddened, unhappy, upset; ***opp*** cheerful

depressing *adj* black, bleak, discouraging, disheartening, dismal, dispiriting, distressing, dreary, gloomy, hopeless, melancholy, miserable, sad, somber; ***opp*** encouraging

depression *n* 1 dejection, desolation, despair, despondency, dolefulness, downheartedness, gloominess, hopelessness, low spirits, melancholy, misery, sadness, the blues, weariness; ***opp*** cheerfulness. 2 (economic) bad times, decline, hard times, recession, slump, stagnation; ***opp*** boom

deprive *v* deny, dispossess, rob, starve, strip, take away, withdraw

deprived *adj* bereft, destitute, disadvantaged, forlorn, in need, lacking, needy, poor; ***opp*** advantaged

depth *n* 1 deepness, drop, extent, measure, profundity. 2 (of forest) bowels, middle, midst; ***opp*** edge. 3 (of sea) bottom, deepest part; ***opp*** surface

deputy *adj* assistant, proxy, representative, second in command, sidekick, understudy, vice-chairman, vice-president

derelict *adj* abandoned, crumbling, decrepit, deserted, dilapidated, falling-down, neglected, ramshackle, ruined, rundown, tumbledown

derisory *adj* 1 (a derisory amount) contemptible, inadequate, insulting, laughable, ludicrous, outrageous, preposterous, ridiculous, tiny; ***opp*** fair. **2** (derisory remarks) contemptuous, derisive, jeering, mocking, scornful

derive *v* acquire, collect, draw, elicit, extract, gain, gather, get, glean, infer, lift, obtain, pick up, procure, receive

derogatory *adj* damaging, defamatory, disapproving, disparaging, injurious, insulting, offensive, uncomplimentary, unfavorable, unflattering; ***opp*** complimentary

descend *v* **1** come down, drop, fall, go down, move down, plummet, plunge, sink, tumble; ***opp*** rise. **2** (the path descends) go down, dip, incline, slant, slope; ***opp*** rise

descent *n* **1** dip, drop, fall, plunge, slump, swoop; ***opp*** rise. **2** (family background) ancestry, background, blood, extraction, genealogy, heredity, lineage, origin, parentage, stock

describe *v* define, depict, detail, explain, express, give a description, give an account, give details, illustrate, narrate, outline, portray, put into words, recount, relate, report, sketch, specify, tell

description *n* account, chronicle, depiction, explanation, illustration, narrative, outline, portrayal, report, representation, sketch

descriptive *adj* colorful, detailed, explanatory, expressive, graphic, illustrative, striking, vivid; ***opp*** bland

desecrate *v* abuse, contaminate, corrupt, debase, defile, degrade, dishonor, infect, pervert, pollute, profane, vandalize, violate; ***opp*** revere

desert *n* sand, waste, wasteland, wilderness, wilds

desert *v* abandon, forsake, give up, jilt, leave, leave high and dry, leave in the lurch, maroon, strand, turn your back on, walk out on

deserted *adj* abandoned, derelict, desolate, empty, forlorn, godforsaken, isolated, lonely, neglected, solitary, uninhabited, unoccupied, vacant; ***opp*** bustling

deserter *n* defector, escapee, fugitive, outlaw, renegade, runaway, traitor, truant

deserve *v* be entitled to, be worthy of, earn, gain, have a claim to, have a right to, justify, merit, rate, warrant, win

design *n* **1** (a design of a building) blueprint, draft, drawing, model, outline, plan, sketch. **2** (pattern) arrangement, motif, pattern, shape

design *v* **1** conceive, create, devise, draft, draw, draw up, hatch, invent, originate, outline, plan, sketch, think up. **2 designed for** aimed at, intended for, tailor-made for

designer *n* architect, creator, inventor, originator, stylist

desirable *adj* **1** advantageous, advisable, beneficial, in sb's interest, profitable, worthwhile; ***opp*** undesirable. **2** (of a person) alluring, attractive, beguiling, erotic, fetching, seductive, sexually attractive; ***opp*** undesirable

desire *n* ambition, appetite, ardor, aspiration, craving, hunger, inclination, longing, lust, need, passion, preference, urge, wish, yearning

desire *v* aspire to, covet, crave, dream of, fancy, hanker after, have a yen for, hope for, hunger for, itch for *inf*, long for, lust after, set your heart on, set your sights on, strive for, thirst for, want, wish for, yearn for

desolate *adj* **1** (of a place) bare, barren, bleak, cheerless, deserted, dreary, godforsaken, inhospitable, isolated, remote, solitary, uninhabited, waste, wild. **2** (of a person) abandoned, alone, dejected, depressed, despairing, despondent, downcast, forlorn, gloomy, grieving, inconsolable, lonely, melancholy, miserable, neglected, sad, unhappy, wretched; ***opp*** cheerful

despair *n* defeatism, dejection, depression, desperation, despondency, distress, gloom, hopelessness, misery, pessimism, wretchedness; ***opp*** enthusiasm, happiness, optimism

despair *v* give in, give up, lose heart, lose hope, quit, resign yourself, surrender, throw in the towel; ***opp*** hope

desperate *adj* **1** at your wits end, despairing, frantic, inconsolable, wretched. **2** (a desperate situation) acute, critical, dangerous, drastic, grave, hopeless, irretrievable, pressing, risky, serious, severe, urgent

despicable *adj* abominable, base, cheap, contemptible, detestable, disgraceful, disgusting, disreputable, hateful, ignominious, loathsome, low, mean, odious, reprehensible, shameful, sordid, vile, worthless, wretched

despise *v* abhor, be contemptuous of, can't bear, can't stand, detest, disdain, hate, loathe, revile

despondent *adj* blue, dejected, discouraged, disheartened, dismayed, dispirited, down, down in the dumps, downcast, fed up, gloomy, glum, low, melancholy, miserable, unhappy, upset; ***opp*** cheerful

despot *n* authoritarian, autocrat, dictator, tyrant; ***opp*** democrat

destination *n* end of the line, journey's end, landing-place, port of call, resting-place, stop, terminus; ***opp*** starting point

destined *adj* **1** bound for, en route to, heading for. **2** bound to, certain, doomed, fated, intended, meant, pre-ordained, unavoidable

destiny *n* chance, doom, fate, fortune, lot, providence

destitute *adj* badly off *inf*, bankrupt, bereft, broke *inf*, disadvantaged, hard up *inf*, impoverished, in need, lacking, needy, on the breadline, penniless, poor, poverty-stricken, without two pennies to rub together; ***opp*** rich

destroy *v* annihilate, break, break down, crush, decimate, demolish, devastate, dismantle, knock down, level, obliterate, ravage, raze, ruin, shatter, smash, spoil, trash *sl*, wipe out, wreck

destruction *n* annihilation, decimation, demolition, devastation, dismantling, downfall, end, extermination, havoc, obliteration, ruin, ruination, wrecking

destructive *adj* damaging, deadly, detrimental, devastating, fatal, harmful, hurtful, injurious, lethal, malignant, pernicious; ***opp*** beneficial

detach *v* cut loose, cut off, disconnect, disengage, disentangle, free, isolate, loosen, part, pull off, release, remove, sever, take off, tear off, uncouple, undo, unfasten; ***opp*** attach

detached *adj* 1 disconnected, disengaged, disentangled, free, isolated, loose, released, removed, separate, severed, uncoupled, undone, unfastened; ***opp*** connected. 2 aloof, cool, disinterested, dispassionate, distant, formal, remote, removed, reserved, standoffish, unapproachable; ***opp*** friendly. 3 fair, impartial, neutral, objective, unbiased, uncommitted, uninvolved, unprejudiced; ***opp*** biased

detail *n* aspect, component, element, fact, factor, feature, intricacy, item, part, particular, point, respect, technicality

detail *v* 1 (detail sb to a place/job) allocate, appoint, assign, charge, commission, delegate, detach, send. 2 (detail in a list) catalog, cite, enumerate, indicate, itemize, list, point out, set out, specify, spell out, relate

detailed *adj* all-inclusive, blow-by-blow, complete, comprehensive, elaborate, exact, exhaustive, full, intricate, in (minute) detail, specific, thorough; ***opp*** vague

detain *v* 1 (make sb late) delay, hinder, hold up, keep, slow down. 2 (in custody) arrest, confine, hold, impound, imprison, incarcerate, intern, lock up, restrain; ***opp*** release

detect *v* ascertain, catch, discern, discover, distinguish, find, find out, identify, note, notice, observe, recognize, scent, spot, uncover

detective *n* investigator, police officer, private eye, sleuth *inf*

detention *n* arrest, confinement, custody, imprisonment, incarceration, internment, quarantine, restraint

deter *v* daunt, discourage, dissuade, frighten, inhibit, intimidate, prevent, put off, scare, stop, talk sb out of, warn off; ***opp*** encourage

deteriorate *v* crumble, decay, decline, decompose, degenerate, depreciate, disintegrate, fade, fall apart, get worse, go downhill *inf*, go to pot *inf*, go to the dogs *inf*, spoil, weaken, worsen; ***opp*** improve

determination *n* backbone, commitment, conviction, dedication, doggedness, drive, fortitude, grit *inf*, guts *inf*, perseverance, persistence, resolution, resolve, single-mindedness, staying power, tenacity, willpower

determine *v* 1 (determine what will happen) agree on, arbitrate, decide, decree, judge, ordain, regulate, settle. 2 (learn) ascertain, calculate, detect, discover, establish, find out, learn, work out. 3 (determine to do sth) choose, decide, elect, make up your mind, resolve

determined *adj* 1 (determined to do sth) bent on, fixed on, intent on, resolved, set on. 2 (a determined person) dedicated, dogged, firm, focused, insistent, persistent, purposeful, resolute, resolved, singleminded, steadfast, strong-willed, tenacious, tough, unwavering; ***opp*** irresolute

deterrent *n* check, curb, discouragement, disincentive, restraint, turn-off *inf*; ***opp*** encouragement

detest *v* abhor, abominate, despise, disdain, dislike, hate, loathe, scorn; ***opp*** love

detract from *v* devalue, diminish, lessen,

lower, reduce, take away from; ***opp*** enhance

detrimental *adj* adverse, damaging, destructive, harmful, inimical, injurious, pernicious, prejudicial, unfavorable; ***opp*** advantageous, helpful

devastate *v* **1** demolish, destroy, flatten, lay waste, level, obliterate, ravage, raze, ruin, spoil, trash *sl*, wreck. **2** disappoint, horrify, overwhelm, shock, take aback, traumatize

devastating *adj* **1** deadly, destructive, ruinous, savage. **2** (devastating news) disappointing, horrifying, overwhelming, shocking, traumatic, upsetting

develop *v* **1** advance, enlarge, evolve, expand, flourish, grow, mature, progress, ripen, spread. **2** (develop an idea) amplify, augment, broaden, dilate on, elaborate, enlarge on, expand. **3** (develop a habit, illness) acquire, catch, contract, get, pick up

development *n* **1** advance, advancement, enlargement, evolution, expansion, flourishing, growth, increase, maturing, maturity, progress, progression, ripening, spreading. **2** change, circumstance, event, happening, incident, occurrence, outcome, result, situation, turn of events, upshot

deviate *v* branch off, deflect, depart, differ, digress, diverge, drift, err, part, stray, swerve, turn aside, vary, veer, wander

device *n* **1** apparatus, appliance, contraption, gadget, gizmo *inf*, implement, instrument, machine, tool, utensil, widget *inf*. **2** (a trick) artifice, con, expedient, fraud, gambit, machination, maneuver, plan, ploy, ruse, scheme, sleight, strategy, stunt, subterfuge, tactic, trick, wile

devil *n* **1** Beelzebub, demon, Evil One, evil spirit, fiend, Lucifer, Prince of Darkness, Satan. **2** beast, brute, fiend, monster, ogre, savage, terror, thug, villain

devious *adj* artful, calculating, crafty, crooked, cunning, deceitful, dishonest, evasive, guileful, indirect, insidious, insincere, misleading, scheming, sly, sneaky, surreptitious, treacherous, tricky, underhand, wily; ***opp*** direct, ingenuous

devise *v* arrange, come up with, conceive, concoct, construct, contrive, cook up *inf*, create, design, dream up, engineer, form, formulate, frame, imagine, invent, plan, plot, prepare, scheme, think up, work out

devoid *adj* barren, bereft, deficient, denuded, destitute, empty, free from, lacking, missing, vacant, void, wanting, without

devote *v* allocate, allot, apply, assign, commit, consign, dedicate, give, pledge, reserve, set aside

devoted *adj* adoring, ardent, attentive, besotted, caring, committed, concerned, conscientious, constant, dedicated, devout, dutiful, enthusiastic, faithful, fond, loving, loyal, passionate, staunch, steadfast, true, unswerving, zealous

devotion *n* adherence, adoration, allegiance, ardor, attentiveness, caring, commitment, concern, constancy, dedication, devotedness, enthusiasm, faithfulness, fervor, fidelity, fondness, love, loyalty, passion, staunchness, steadfastness, zeal

devout *adj* dutiful, God-fearing, godly, holy, orthodox, pious, prayerful, religious, reverent, righteous, zealous

dexterous *adj* adept, adroit, agile, clever, deft, expert, handy, neat, nimble, proficient, sharp, skilled, skillful; ***opp*** clumsy

diagnose *v* detect, determine, distinguish, identify, interpret, isolate, pinpoint, recognize

diagnosis *n* analysis, conclusion, explanation, interpretation, judgment, opinion, pronouncement, recommendation, verdict

diagram *n* chart, drawing, figure, illustration, outline, picture, representation, sketch, symbol, table

dialect *n* accent, argot, idiom, jargon, language, patois, regionalism, slang, speech, tongue, variety, vernacular

dialogue *n* **1** chat, communication, conference, conversation, discourse, discussion, exchange, interchange, talk. **2** (of a film) conversation, lines, script

diary *n* annals, appointment book, calendar, chronicle, engagement book, journal, log, memoir, personal organizer, record

dictate *n* **1** command, declare, decree, direct, enjoin, give orders, impose, lay down, ordain, order, prescribe. **2** read out, say, speak, recite, transmit, utter

dictator *n* absolute ruler, autocrat, despot, oppressor, tyrant

die *v* **1** be no more, bite the dust *inf*, cease to exist, croak *sl*, decease, depart, expire, kick the bucket *inf*, lose your life, meet your end, pass away, pass on, perish, snuff out *inf*. **2** come to an end, decay, decline, decrease, disappear, dwindle, ebb, end, fade, lapse, pass, sink, vanish, wane, wilt, wither. **3** (of a machine) break down, come to a halt, fail, fizzle out, halt, lose power, peter out, run down, stop

diet *n* alimentation, consumption, fare, food, intake, nourishment, nutrition, provisions, rations, regime, regimen, subsistence, viands, victuals

diet *v* abstain, cut down, fast, go on a diet, lose weight, reduce, slim

differ *v* **1** be different, be dissimilar, be distinct, be unlike, contrast, deviate, diverge, vary. **2** argue, be at odds, clash, conflict, contradict, debate, disagree, dispute, dissent, diverge, object, oppose, quarrel, quibble, take issue; ***opp*** agree

difference *n* **1** contrast, discrepancy, disparity, dissimilarity, distinction, divergence, incongruity, nonconformity, peculiarity, singularity, variation, variety; ***opp*** similarity. **2** altercation, argument, clash, conflict, controversy, debate, difference of opinion, disagreement, dispute, objection, quarrel, quibble, tiff, wrangle; ***opp*** agreement

different *adj* **1** assorted, clashing, contradictory, contrasting, contrastive, disparate, dissimilar, distinct, diverging, diverse, incongruous, inconsistent, miscellaneous, mixed, other, peculiar, separate, singular, various, varying, unlike; ***opp*** similar. **2** abnormal, bizarre, distinctive, eccentric, interesting, novel, odd, original, peculiar, singular, special, strange, striking, uncommon, unconventional, unique, unorthodox, unusual, weird; ***opp*** ordinary

differentiate *v* contrast, discern, discriminate, distinguish, identify, make a distinction, mark off, separate, sort, tell apart, tell the difference

difficult *adj* **1** arduous, burdensome, challenging, complex, complicated, demanding, daunting, exacting, formidable, grueling, hard, laborious, onerous, painful, problematic, strenuous, taxing, thorny, tough, tricky, wearisome; ***opp*** easy. **2** (of a person) argumentative, awkward, contrary, demanding, fastidious, fractious, fussy, intractable, obstreperous, perverse, quarrelsome, tiresome, troublesome, trying, uncooperative, unmanageable; ***opp*** cooperative

difficulty *n* **1** adversity, arduousness, awkwardness, challenge, hardship, laboriousness, labor, ordeal, pain, problem, strain, struggle, toughness, tribulation. **2** dilemma, distress, fix *inf*, jam *inf*, mess, pickle *inf*, plight, predicament, quandary, scrape *inf*, spot *inf*, straits

diffident *adj* apprehensive, backward, bashful, constrained, coy, doubtful, fearful, hesitant, humble, inhibited, insecure, introverted, meek, modest, nervous, shy, reluctant, reserved, retiring, self-conscious, self-effacing, sheepish, shrinking, tentative, timid, timorous, unassertive, unassuming, unconfident, unsure, withdrawn; ***opp*** brash

dig *v* **1** burrow, delve, excavate, fork, gouge, grub, harrow, hoe, hollow, mine, penetrate, pierce, plow, quarry, scoop, till, tunnel, turn over. **2** (dig for information) delve, go into, investigate, probe, research, search. **3** (dig sb in the ribs) jab, nudge, poke, prod, punch, push, shove

digest *v* **1** absorb, assimilate, break down, consume, dissolve, eat, incorporate, take in. **2** (digest information) absorb, assimilate, comprehend, consider, contemplate, grasp, master, mull over, ruminate, ponder, study, take in, understand

dignified *adj* ceremonious, decorous, distinguished, elegant, formal, graceful, gracious, grave, honorable, imposing, impressive, lofty, noble, proper, proud, regal, solemn, stately, tasteful; ***opp*** undignified

dignitary *n* celebrity, luminary, notability, notable, official, personage, public figure, VIP, worthy

dignity *n* ceremony, class, decorum, distinction, elegance, formality, grace, grandeur, gravitas, gravity, hauteur, honor, loftiness, majesty, nobility, pride, propriety, solemnity, stateliness, taste

digress *v* depart, deviate, diverge, drift, get off the subject, get sidetracked, go off at a tangent, lose your thread, meander, ramble, stray, veer, wander

digression *n* aside, departure, detour, deviation, divergence, diversion, drifting, footnote, meander, rambling, straying, wandering

dilapidated *adj* battered, broken-down, crumbling, decaying, decrepit, derelict, falling apart, falling down, in disrepair, in ruins, neglected, peeling, ramshackle, rickety, ruined, rundown, shabby, tumbledown, uncared-for, worn out

dilemma *n* catch-22, difficulty, fix *inf*, impasse, jam *inf*, perplexity, pickle *inf*, plight, predicament, problem, puzzle, quandary, scrape *inf*, spot *inf*, straits, vicious circle

diligent *adj* assiduous, attentive, busy, careful, conscientious, dutiful, earnest, hard-working, indefatigable, industrious, meticulous, painstaking, patient, persevering, persistent, punctilious, scrupulous, sedulous, studious, thorough, tireless; ***opp*** careless, slapdash

dilute *v* adulterate, cut *inf*, mix, thin, water down, weaken; ***opp*** concentrate

dim *adj* **1** bleary, blurred, blurry, cloudy, dark, dingy, dull, dusky, faint, foggy, fuzzy, gloomy, hazy, indistinct, misty, murky, muted, obscure, obscured, shadowy, unclear, vague; ***opp*** bright. **2** dense, dozy *inf*, dull, dull-witted, dumb *inf*, obtuse, slow, stupid, thick *inf*; ***opp*** bright

dim *v* blur, cloud, darken, dull, fade, fog, lower, mask, obscure, shade, shadow, shroud, turn down

dimensions *n* amplitude, area, bulk, capacity, extent, greatness, largeness, magnitude, measurements, proportions, range, scale, scope, size, volume

diminish *v* abate, contract, curtail, cut, decline, decrease, dwindle, ebb, lessen, lower, peter out, recede, reduce, shrink, subside, wane, weaken

dine *v* banquet, eat, feast, feed, have dinner, sup

dingy *adj* cheerless, dark, depressing, dim, dirty, dismal, drab, dreary, dull, faded, gloomy, grimy, murky, rundown, seedy, shabby, soiled, somber, threadbare, worn; ***opp*** bright

dinner *n* banquet, feast, meal, repast, spread *inf*, supper

dip *n* **1** bathe, ducking, dunking, immersion, plunge, rinse, soak, soaking, sousing, submersion, swim. **2** concavity, declivity, dent, depression, hole, hollow, incline, slope, valley. **3** (a dip in amount) decline, dive, drop, fall, lowering, plunge, slip, slump

dip *v* **1** bathe, douse, drench, duck, dunk, immerse, lower, plunge, rinse, soak, souse, steep, submerge. **2** decline, descend, dive, drop, fall, go down, lower, plunge, sag, slip, slump

diplomacy *n* adroitness, delicacy, discretion, finesse, sensitivity, skill, subtlety, tact

diplomat *n* ambassador, conciliator, emissary, envoy, go-between, intermediary, mediator, moderator, negotiator, peacemaker, politician, representative, statesman

diplomatic *adj* adept, adroit, careful, considerate, delicate, discreet, judicious, politic, prudent, sensitive, subtle, tactful

dire *adj* alarming, appalling, atrocious, awful, calamitous, catastrophic, chronic, disastrous, dreadful, frightful, ghastly, grievous, horrendous, horrible, horrifying, shocking, terrible, unspeakable, woeful

direct *adj* **1** immediate, non-stop, shortest, straight, through, unbroken, uninterrupted; ***opp*** indirect. **2** blunt, candid, categorical, clear, explicit, forthright, frank, honest, open, outspoken, plain, plainspoken, straight, straightforward, to the point, unambiguous, unequivocal, upfront; ***opp*** indirect. **3** (direct opposite) absolute, complete, diametrical, downright, exact, thorough, total, utter

direct *v* **1** administer, be in charge of, conduct, control, govern, guide, handle, head, manage, orchestrate, oversee, preside, regulate, run, superintend, supervise. **2** bid, command, dictate, enjoin, instruct, order, require, tell. **3** (direct sb to a place) conduct, escort, give directions, guide, indicate, lead, navigate, pilot, point, show the way, steer, usher

direction *n* 1 bearing, course, line, orientation, path, road, route, tack, track, way. **2** administration, command, control, government, guidance, handling, leadership, management, orchestration, order, overseeing, regulation, running, supervision. **3** bidding, command, decree, edict, injunction, instruction, order, ruling

directions *n* briefing, guidance, guide, guidelines, indications, instructions, map, plan, recommendations

director *n* administrator, boss, chair, chairman, chairwoman, chief, conductor, controller, executive, governor, head, manager, managing director, organizer, overseer, president, principal, regulator, supervisor

dirt *n* dust, earth, filth, gunge, gunk, impurity, mire, muck, mud, ordure, pollution, slime, smudge, spot, stain, soil, tarnish

dirty *adj* **1** contaminated, dusty, filthy, foul, grimy, grubby, grungy *inf*, impure, marked, messy, mucky *inf*, muddy, nasty, polluted, smudged, soiled, spotted, stained, sticky, sullied, tainted, tarnished, unclean; ***opp*** clean. **2** corrupt, crooked, deceitful, dishonest, dishonorable, fraudulent, illegal, treacherous, unfair, unscrupulous, unsporting; ***opp*** honest. **3** bawdy, blue, coarse, improper, indecent, lascivious, lewd, obscene, offensive, pornographic, ribald, risqué, rude, salacious, sleazy *inf*, smutty, suggestive, vulgar; ***opp*** clean

disability *n* affliction, ailment, defect, disadvantage, disorder, handicap, impairment, incapacity, infirmity, malady

disabled *adj* afflicted, crippled, debilitated, disadvantaged, handicapped, immobilized, impaired, incapacitated, infirm, lame, maimed, mutilated, paralyzed, weak, weakened; ***opp*** able-bodied

disadvantage *n* defect, disability, downside, drawback, fault, flaw, handicap, hindrance, hitch, impediment, inconvenience, minus, obstacle, problem, snag, weakness; ***opp*** advantage

disagree *v* argue, bicker, clash, conflict, contend, contest, contradict, counter, debate, differ, discuss, dispute, dissent, diverge, fall out, fight, object, oppose, quarrel, question, quibble, squabble, take issue, wrangle; ***opp*** agree

disagreeable *adj* bad-tempered, churlish, cross, crotchety, difficult, horrible, ill-natured, irritable, nasty, objectionable, obnoxious, peevish, rude, surly, unfriendly, ungracious, unpleasant; ***opp*** agreeable

disagreement *n* altercation, argument, clash, conflict, contention, contradiction, controversy, debate, difference, discord, discussion, dispute, dissent, divergence, division, falling out, fight, objection, opposition, quarrel, row, squabble, strife, tiff, wrangle; ***opp*** agreement

disallow *v* ban, bar, boycott, cancel, deny, dismiss, embargo, forbid, prohibit, proscribe, refuse, reject, repudiate, veto; ***opp*** allow

disappear *v* **1** become invisible, be lost to view, dematerialize, dissolve, evaporate, fade, flee, melt away, recede, vanish, vaporize, wane; ***opp*** appear. **2** become extinct, cease, come to an end, die, die out, end, evaporate, expire, go, pass away, perish, stop, vanish; ***opp*** appear

disappearance *n* dissolving, ebbing, ending, evaporation, fading, fleeing, going, invisibility, melting, passing, receding, vanishing; ***opp*** appearance

disappoint *v* depress, disenchant, dishearten, disillusion, dismay, dispirit, dissatisfy, fail, frustrate, let down, sadden, thwart, upset; ***opp*** satisfy

disappointed *adj* cast down, depressed, despondent, discouraged, disenchanted, disheartened, disillusioned, dismayed, dispirited, dissatisfied, downcast, frustrated, let down, sad, saddened, thwarted; ***opp*** satisfied

disappointing *adj* depressing, discouraging, disenchanting, disheartening, disillusioning, dismaying, dispiriting, dissatisfying, frustrating, inadequate, insufficient, paltry, pathetic, unsatisfactory, upsetting; ***opp*** encouraging, satisfying

disappointment *n* **1** depression, discouragement, disenchantment, disillusionment, dismay, dissatisfaction, frustration, regret, sadness; ***opp*** satisfaction. **2** blow, disaster, failure, fiasco, letdown, setback; ***opp*** success

disapprove *v* be against, censure, condemn, criticize, deplore, deprecate, dislike, frown on, look askance at, not take kindly to, object to, reject, take a dim view, take exception; ***opp*** approve

disaster *n* accident, act of God, adversity, blow, calamity, cataclysm, catastrophe, misadventure, mischance, misfortune, mishap, reverse, ruin, tragedy, trouble

disastrous *adj* adverse, appalling, awful, calamitous, cataclysmic, catastrophic, destructive, devastating, dire, dreadful, fatal, fateful, ill-fated, ill-starred, ruinous, terrible, tragic, unfortunate, unlucky

discard *v* abandon, cast aside, chuck out *inf*, dispense with, dispose of, ditch *inf*, drop, dump *inf*, get rid of, jettison, junk *inf*, reject, repudiate, scrap, shed, throw away, throw out

discharge *n* **1** emission, excretion, matter, pus, secretion. **2** dismissal, expulsion, firing, redundancy, removal, sacking. **3** acquittal, clearance, exoneration, freeing, liberation, pardon, release

discharge *v* **1** belch, eject, emit, excrete, exude, give off, produce, release, secrete, send out, spew. **2** dismiss, expel, fire, let go, make redundant, relieve, remove, sack. **3** absolve, acquit, clear, exonerate, free, let go, liberate, pardon, release, set free. **4** detonate, fire, let off, shoot

disciple *n* acolyte, adherent, apostle, believer, convert, devotee, follower, partisan, proselyte, pupil, supporter

discipline *n* **1** chastisement, control, correction, drilling, exercise, punishment, regime, regulation, rules, strictness, training. **2** control, organization, restraint, self-control, self-discipline, self-restraint, strength, will-power

discipline *v* chastise, control, correct, penalize, punish, rebuke, regulate, reprimand, train

disclose *v* admit, bring to light, confess, divulge, expose, impart, let slip, make known, make public, reveal, tell, unveil

discomfort *n* ache, disquiet, distress, hardship, hurt, inconvenience, irritation, nuisance, pain, pang, soreness, trouble, twinge, uneasiness, vexation; ***opp*** comfort

disconcerting *adj* alarming, baffling, bewildering, dismaying, distracting, disturbing, off-putting, perplexing, perturbing, puzzling, troubling, unnerving, unsettling, upsetting, worrying; ***opp*** reassuring

disconnect *v* break off, cut off, detach, disengage, divide, part, separate, sever, uncouple, undo, unplug

discontented *adj* annoyed, disaffected, disgruntled, displeased, dissatisfied, fed up, fretful, impatient, restless, troubled, unfulfilled, unhappy, unsatisfied, unsettled; ***opp*** contented

discontinue *v* abandon, ax *inf*, break off, cancel, cease, cut, drop, end, give up, halt, interrupt, put an end to, quit, stop, suspend, terminate; ***opp*** continue

discord *n* **1** arguing, argument, clashing, conflict, contention, controversy, difference, disagreement, disharmony, dispute, dissent, disunity, division, falling-out, friction, hostility, opposition, quarreling, rupture, strife, variance, wrangling; ***opp*** agreement. **2** cacophony, din, dissonance, harshness, jangle, jarring, racket; ***opp*** harmony

discount *v* **1** disbelieve, disregard, gloss over, ignore, overlook, pass over, pay no attention to, reject, take no notice of. **2** cut, lower, mark down, reduce, take off, slash

discourage *v* **1** abash, cast down, dampen, daunt, demoralize, depress, deter, dishearten, dismay, dissuade, intimidate, put off, unnerve; ***opp*** encourage. **2** advise against, caution against, disapprove, dissuade, deter, frown on, oppose, put off, repress, take a dim view, urge against; ***opp*** encourage

discouraged *adj* abashed, cast down, cowed, crestfallen, dashed, daunted, dejected, demoralized, depressed, despondent, deterred, disheartened, dismayed, dispirited, downhearted, intimidated, put off, unnerved; ***opp*** encouraged

discouragement *n* **1** dejection, demoralization, depression, despondency, dismay, downheartedness; ***opp*** encouragement. **2** barrier, check, constraint, curb, damper, deterrent, disincentive, hindrance, impediment, obstacle, restriction; ***opp*** encouragement

discouraging *adj* daunting, demoralizing, depressing, disheartening, dismaying, dispiriting, inauspicious, intimidating, off-putting, unnerving, worrying; ***opp*** encouraging

discourse *n* **1** chat, communication, conversation, dialogue, discussion, exchange, interchange, speech, talk. **2** address, dissertation, essay, lecture, oration, paper, speech, study, treatise

discourse *v* **1** chat, communicate, confer, converse, debate, discuss, have a conversation, speak, talk. **2** declaim, deliver a paper, expatiate, give a talk, hold forth, lecture, make a speech, orate, speak

discover *v* **1** come across, come upon, dig up, find, light on, locate, track down, turn up, uncover, unearth. **2** ascertain, come to know, detect, determine, disclose, expose, find out, identify, learn, perceive, realize, recognize, see, spot, uncover

discovery *n* **1** detection, digging up, disclosure, exposing, finding, identification, locating, location, recognition, spotting, tracking down, uncovering, unearthing. **2** breakthrough, coup, find, innovation, invention

discredit *v* blacken sb's name, cast doubt on, decry, denigrate, disparage, show up

discreet *adj* careful, circumspect, diplomatic, judicious, polite, politic, prudent, tactful, tasteful; ***opp*** indiscreet

discrepancy *n* anomaly, contradiction, difference, disparity, error, inconsistency, inequality, miscalculation, mismatch, mistake, shortfall

discretion *n* care, circumspection, diplomacy, politeness, prudence, tact, tactfulness

discriminate *v* **1 discriminate against** be biased against, be intolerant of, be prejudiced against, pick on, segregate, single out, treat unfairly, victimize. **2** choose, differentiate, distinguish, draw a distinction, judge, make a distinction, select

discriminating *adj* choosy, cultivated, discerning, fastidious, refined, selective, tasteful

discrimination *n* **1** ageism, apartheid, bias, bigotry, intolerance, male chauvinism, prejudice, racism, segregation, sexism, victimization. **2** culture, discernment, fastidiousness, judgment, refinement, sensitivity, taste

discuss *v* argue, confer, consider, converse, debate, deliberate, put your heads together, talk, talk about, talk over

discussion *n* argument, conference, conversation, debate, deliberation, dialogue, pow-wow *inf*, talk

disdainful *adj* aloof, contemptuous, disparaging, disrespectful, proud, scornful, sneering, superior

disease *n* ailment, bug *inf*, complaint, disorder, illness, infection, malady, sickness, syndrome, virus

diseased *adj* **1** ailing, festering, infected, ill, septic, sick, swollen, unhealthy; ***opp*** healthy. **2** (with a particular disease) arthritic, asthmatic, cancerous, gangrenous, leprous, rabid

disembark *v* alight, arrive, get off, get

out, go ashore, land; ***opp*** embark

disentangle *v* **1** disengage, extricate, loose, undo, unravel, untangle, untie, unwind; ***opp*** entangle. **2** ascertain, decipher, disembroil, resolve, solve, sort out, straighten out, understand

disgrace *n* abasement, abjection, discredit, dishonor, disrepute, embarrassment, humiliation, rejection, shame, stigma

disgrace *v* **1** discredit, drag through the mud, dishonor, embarrass, humiliate, shame, stigmatize. **2 disgrace yourself** abase yourself, degrade yourself, demean yourself, prostitute yourself, stoop to

disgraceful *v* **1** (morally) abject, contemptible, corrupt, degrading, disgusting, dishonorable, ignominious, outrageous, shameful. **2** (very bad) appalling, awful, dreadful, pathetic, shocking, terrible

disguise *n* **1** camouflage, concealment, costume, cover, false identity, fancy dress, mask. **2 in disguise** disguised, incognito, undercover

disguise *v* **1** camouflage, cloak, cover, cover up, conceal, dissemble, fake, falsify, hide, mask. **2 disguise yourself as** dress up as, impersonate, masquerade as

disgust *n* contempt, dislike, distaste, loathing, nausea, offense, outrage, repugnance, repulsion, revulsion

disgust *v* appal, make sick, nauseate, offend, outrage, put off, repel, revolt, sicken

disgusting *adj* appalling, awful, disgraceful, distasteful, gross, horrible, nauseating, obscene, offensive, off-putting, outrageous, repugnant, repellent, repulsive, revolting, sickening, ugly, unpleasant, unsavory

dish *n* **1** (container) bowl, plate, platter, serving dish, vessel. **2** (food) course, creation, delicacy, meal, recipe, specialty

dishearten *v* dampen sb's spirits, deflate, deject, depress, demoralize, deter, discourage, dismay, put off, sadden; ***opp*** hearten

disheveled *adj* bedraggled, messy, ruffled, slovenly, tousled, unkempt, untidy

dishonest *adj* cheating, criminal, crooked, deceitful, dishonorable, duplicitous, lying, unscrupulous, untrustworthy; ***opp*** honest

dishonesty *n* cheating, criminality, deceit, deception, duplicity, lies, unscrupulousness

disillusioned *adj* alienated, cynical, disabused, disaffected, disappointed, disenchanted, fed up

disinfect *v* bathe, clean, clean out, cleanse, sterilize

disintegrate *v* break down, collapse, decay, fall apart, fall to pieces, implode

disinterested *adj* above the fray, aloof, detached, dispassionate, impartial, objective, unbiased, unselfish, with no ax to grind

dislike *n* antipathy, aversion, detestation, distaste, hate, hatred, hostility; ***opp*** liking

dislike *v* be disgusted by, be hostile to, be put off by, detest, hate, have an aversion to; ***opp*** like

disloyal *adj* disobedient, false, mutinous, perfidious, traitorous, treacherous, seditious, unfaithful; ***opp*** faithful, loyal

dismal *adj* 1 bleak, cheerless, demoralizing, depressing, disheartening, dispiriting, gloomy, miserable, sad. 2 (of weather) appalling, awful, dark, dreadful, gloomy, murky, rainy, miserable, shocking, terrible, unpleasant, wet, wretched; ***opp*** lovely, wonderful

dismantle *v* disassemble, strip down, take apart, take down, take to pieces

dismay *n* annoyance, disappointment, consternation, displeasure, frustration, shock

dismay *v* annoy, disconcert, dishearten, disappoint, displease, frustrate, shatter, sadden, shock, upset

dismiss *v* 1 (from sb's presence) banish, cast out, chuck out *inf*, exclude, excuse, send away, send out, throw out. 2 (from a job) downsize, fire, get rid of, kick out *inf*, remove, sack. 3 (dismiss an idea) brush aside, brush off, discount, disregard, forget about, ignore, reject, ridicule

disobedient *adj* cheeky, defiant, disrespectful, dissenting, dissident, disloyal, insubordinate, mutinous, naughty, unruly; ***opp*** obedient

disobey *v* 1 (disobey a rule) break, contravene, defy, disregard, flout, infringe, transgress; ***opp*** obey. 2 (act disobediently) answer back, mutiny, rebel, refuse, resist, revolt, stand firm, stand up to; ***opp*** obey

disorder *n* 1 chaos, clutter, disarray, jumble, muddle, untidiness; ***opp*** order. 2 (violent) anarchy, chaos, civil disobedience, discontent, insurrection, rioting, trouble, turbulence, turmoil, unrest, unruliness, violence; ***opp*** order. 3 (medical) ailment, complaint, disease, dysfunction *tech*, illness, malady, sickness, syndrome

disorganized *adj* 1 anarchic, chaotic, disorderly, in disarray, jumbled, random, uncontrolled, unplanned, unstructured, unsystematic, untidy; ***opp*** organized. 2 (of a person) aimless, in disarray, illogical, muddled, undisciplined, unsystematic; ***opp*** organized

disown *v* deny, disclaim, dissociate yourself from, distance yourself from, reject, repudiate

disparaging *adj* belittling, contemptuous, critical, disapproving, disdainful, insulting, scornful

dispassionate *adj* calm, cool, detached, disinterested, distant, unbiased, unsentimental

dispatch *n* consignment, message, missive, package, parcel, report

dispatch *v* 1 distribute, forward, mail, post, send, send off, send out. 2 (dispatch a task) conclude, deal with, dispose of, expedite, finish off, make short work of, polish off *inf*

dispel *v* clear up, deny, put an end to, put a stop to, scotch

dispense *v* 1 distribute, disseminate, give, give out, hand out, impart, prescribe, provide, vend. 2 **dispense with** cancel, do without, eliminate, forget, forget about, get rid of, go without, not bother with, remove, scrap

disperse *v* 1 (of a crowd) break up, separate, scatter, leave, melt away, spread out. 2 banish, drive away, scatter

displace *v* 1 (move out of position) disturb, misplace, move, remove, shift, transpose. **2** (cause sb to lose position) dislodge, drive out, force out, oust, replace, supplant, take the place of

display *n* array, demonstration, exhibition, exposure, presentation, show

display *v* **1** (display goods) arrange, exhibit, present, put on view, show, show off. **2** (display an emotion) betray, reveal, show

displease *v* anger, annoy, disappoint, frustrate, irk, irritate, offend, upset; ***opp*** please

displeasure *n* anger, annoyance, disappointment, dissatisfaction, frustration, indignation, irritation, offense; ***opp*** pleasure

disposable *adj* **1** biodegradable, expendable, nonreturnable, paper, plastic, temporary, throwaway. **2** (disposable income) after tax, available, net, take-home, to spend

disposal *n* **1** clearance, destruction, dumping, elimination, removal, scrapping. **2 at your disposal** accessible, at your discretion, available, free, handy, obtainable, to hand

dispose of *v* chuck away *inf*, dispense with, dump, eliminate, finish off, get rid of, polish off *inf*, remove, scrap, throw away

disprove *v* demolish, explode, invalidate, prove wrong, refute; ***opp*** prove

dispute *n* **1** altercation, argument, battle, conflict, controversy, difference of opinion, differences, disagreement, feud, fight, friction, quarrel, row. **2** (between workers and management) go slow, grievance, industrial action, lock-out, strike. **3 beyond dispute** crystal clear, definite, incontrovertible, unarguable, undisputed

dispute *v* **1** contest, deny, reject, oppose, question, wrangle over. **2** (dispute the leadership) battle for, challenge for, compete for, contend for, contest, fight over, vie for

disqualify *v* ban, bar, debar, disallow, exclude, make ineligible, rule out

disregard *v* brush aside, discount, dismiss, ignore, reject, take no notice of

disreputable *adj* crooked, dishonest, dishonorable, dubious, of ill repute, shady, unscrupulous

disrespect *n* cheek, contempt, disdain, disobedience, impertinence, impudence, insolence, insults, irreverence, insubordination, scorn; ***opp*** respect

disrespectful *adj* cheeky, contemptuous, disdainful, disobedient, impertinent, impolite, impudent, insolent, insubordinate, insulting, irreverent, scornful; ***opp*** respectful

disrupt *v* disturb, impede, interfere with, interrupt, sabotage, throw into disarray, upset

disruptive *adj* badly behaved, distracting, ill-behaved, interfering, naughty, troublesome, unruly

dissatisfied *adj* angry, annoyed, displeased, frustrated, irked, irritated, unfulfilled, unsatisfied; ***opp*** satisfied

dissent *n* argument, defiance, disagreement, discontent, disobedience, dissension, dissidence, nonconformism, opposition; ***opp*** agreement

dissent *v* break ranks, contest, defy, disagree with, disobey, dissociate yourself from, distance yourself from, oppose, reject, speak out against

dissident *n* critic, dissenter, nonconformist, opponent, political prisoner, prisoner of conscience

dissipate *v* **1** blow away, break up, disappear, disperse, evaporate, melt away, scatter, vanish. **2** (use wastefully) consume, expend, fritter, misspend, spend, squander, use up, waste

dissociate *v* **dissociate yourself from** break away from, break ranks with, deny, disclaim, dissent from, disown, distance yourself from, repudiate, reject, say no to, sever your connections with

dissolve *v* **1** (add to liquid) dilute, melt, mix, mix in, stir in. **2** (of feelings) crumble, disappear, dissipate, evaporate, fade, fade away, melt away, vanish. **3** (dissolve a partnership, an organization) annul, break up, disband, end, terminate, wind up

dissuade *v* deter, discourage, persuade against, prevent, put off, stop, talk sb out of

distance *n* **1** interval, length, long way, remoteness, space, way. **2 in the distance** a long way away, distantly, far away, far off, just in sight, just in view, on the horizon, yonder

distant *adj* **1** faint, far, faraway, far-off, remote, yonder. **2** (of a person) aloof, cold, day-dreaming, detached, haughty, other-worldly, preoccupied, private, superior, unfriendly

distaste *n* antipathy, aversion, disgust, disapproval, dislike, displeasure, repugnance

distasteful *adj* disgusting, gross, in bad taste, in poor taste, obscene, repugnant, repellent, unpleasant, unsavory

distinct *adj* **1** (that can be noticed) audible, clear, clear as a bell, definite, discernible, noticeable, perceptible, tangible, unmistakable, visible; ***opp*** indistinct. **2** (distinct from each other) contrasting, different, discrete, independent, individual, separate, unconnected

distinction *n* **1** contrast, difference, differentiation, dissimilarity, dividing line, division, separation. **2** (personal quality) eminence, excellence, prestige, refinement, standing. **3** award, commendation, credit, decoration, honor

distinctive *adj* characteristic, distinguishing, own, peculiar, specific, tell-tale

distinguish *v* **1** discern, hear, make out, notice, perceive, see. **2** (distinguish between two things) differentiate, discriminate, draw a distinction, make a distinction, tell apart, tell the difference

distinguished *adj* award-winning, celebrated, eminent, experienced, favored, honored, respected

distort *v* bend out of shape, change, deform, falsify, misrepresent, pervert, twist, warp

distract *v* beguile, confuse, disturb, disturb sb's concentration, divert sb's attention, put off, sidetrack

distracted *adj* confused, day-dreaming, inattentive, other-worldly, preoccupied, wandering

distraction *n* **1** confusion, day-dreaming, inattention, lack of concentration, other-worldliness. **2** (sth which distracts) amusement, digression, disturbance, diversion, interruption, irruption, sideshow. **3 to distraction** bonkers *inf*, crazy, frantic, insane, mad, nuts *inf*, off the wall *inf*

distress *n* agony, anguish, anxiety, grief, misery, pain, sadness, suffering, torment, trauma, trouble, worry

distress *v* afflict, aggrieve, grieve, perturb, traumatize, trouble, upset, worry

distressed *adj* anguished, anxious, distraught, grieving, in distress, in pain, jumpy, nervous, panicky, suffering, traumatized, troubled, upset, worried

distressing *adj* difficult, disturbing, painful, sad, stressful, traumatic, troubling, trying, upsetting, worrisome, worrying

distribute *v* allocate, allot, deal, deal out, deliver, dispense, dispatch, disseminate, divide up, give out, hand out, issue, send out, share out

distribution *n* allocation, delivery, dispatch, dissemination, division, transport

district *n* area, borough, constituency, division, locality, neighborhood, part of town, postal district, quarter, ward

distrust *v* be skeptical of, be suspicious of, be wary of, disbelieve, doubt, have doubts about, have no confidence in, have no faith in, mistrust, suspect; ***opp*** trust

disturb *v* **1** bother, butt in, distract, hassle *inf*, harass, hinder, interrupt, intrude, pester; ***opp*** leave alone. **2** (upset) agitate, alarm, concern, distress, fluster, perturb, shake, trouble, unnerve, unsettle, upset, worry; ***opp*** reassure. **3** (disturb sth) interfere with, mess about *inf*, mix up, move, muddle, rearrange, throw into confusion, touch; ***opp*** leave alone

disturbance *n* agitation, confusion, disorder, fracas, interruption, intrusion, riot, upheaval, uproar

disturbed *adj* **1** (a disturbed child) neurotic, psychotic, troubled, unbalanced, upset. **2** (feeling disturbed) alarmed, concerned, distracted, distraught, troubled, uneasy, worried

disturbing *adj* alarming, distressing, frightening, harrowing, troubling, unsettling, upsetting, worrying; ***opp*** reassuring

disused *adj* abandoned, dead, discarded, idle, neglected, unused

ditch *n* channel, drain, dike, gully, gutter, moat, trench

ditch *v* abandon, chuck *inf*, discard, dispose of, drop, dump *inf*, get rid of, junk *inf*, scrap, throw out

dive *v* **1** (dive into water) go under, jump, leap, plunge. **2** (dive behind a hedge) dart, disappear, dodge, drop, duck. **3** (dive through the air) fall, nosedive, plummet, swoop

diverse *adj* assorted, different, differing, dissimilar, distinct, miscellaneous, mixed, separate, several, sundry, varied, various

diversify *v* branch out, broaden, change, develop, expand, mix, spread out, vary

diversion *n* amusement, entertainment, fun, game, hobby, interest, play, recreation, relaxation, sport

diversity *n* difference, diverseness, mixture, range, variety

divert *v* **1** alter, change the course of, deflect, redirect, reroute, switch, turn aside. **2** deflect, distract, sidetrack. **3** amuse, delight, enchant, entertain, keep happy, occupy

diverting *adj* amusing, enjoyable, entertaining, fun, interesting

divide *v* **1** cut, detach, disconnect, halve, part, partition, quarter, segregate, separate, sever, shear, split, subdivide. **2** (share) allocate, deal out, dole out, measure out, parcel out, share. **3** (of a road) branch, diverge, fork, split. **4** (divide into categories) arrange, classify, group, organize, separate, sort

divine *adj* **1** angelic, celestial, godlike, heavenly, holy, saintly. **2** (to do with God) holy, religious, sacred. **3** beautiful *inf*, glorious, lovely, marvelous, perfect, splendid, super *inf*, wonderful

divinity *n* **1** deity, god, goddess, spirit. **2** divine nature, holiness, sanctity

division *n* **1** category, class, compartment, department, group, part, piece, portion, section, sector, segment, share, slice. **2** border, boundary, frontier, line, partition, wall. **3** arm, branch, department, unit

divorce *n* annulment, break-up *inf*, separation, split *inf*

divorce *v* (get divorced) annul the marriage, dissolve the marriage, part, separate, split up

divulge *v* betray, disclose, impart, leak, let slip, make known, reveal, tell

dizzy *adj* dazed, faint, giddy, light-headed, muddled, reeling, shaky, staggering, swimming, unsteady, weak at the knees, wobbly, woozy *inf*

do *v* **1** accomplish, achieve, carry out, cause, complete, finish, perform, undertake. **2** (make sth) arrange, create, design, get ready, look after, make, manufacture, organize, prepare, produce, provide, see to. **3** (do a crossword) complete, figure out, solve, understand, work out. **4** (do a play) act, perform, present, put on. **5** (this will do) be adequate, be enough, be sufficient, satisfy, serve, suffice

docile *adj* compliant, cooperative, obedient, passive, submissive

dock *n* boatyard, harbor, jetty, landing stage, marina, pier, waterfront, wharf

doctor *n* consultant, general practitioner, GP, medic *inf*, physician, quack *inf*, surgeon

doctrine *n* belief, canon, conviction, creed, dogma, principle, teaching, theory

document *n* certificate, diploma, documentation, manuscript, paper, record, report

document *v* authenticate, back up, certify, chart, corroborate, prove, record, report, support, validate, verify

dodge *v* **1** (dodge sb) elude, escape, evade, give sb the slip. **2** (move) dart, dive, sidestep, swerve, veer, weave. **3** (dodge doing sth) avoid, get out of, shirk, steer clear of, wriggle out of

dog *n* bitch, canine, cur, hound, mongrel, mutt *inf*, pooch *inf*, puppy

dogma *n* article, belief, creed, doctrine, orthodoxy, principle, tenet, truth

dogmatic *adj* arrogant, assertive, authoritarian, dictatorial, hard-line *inf*, imperious, insistent, overbearing

dole *n* benefit, income support, welfare
dole out *v* administer, allocate, deal out, dispense, distribute, divide, give out, hand out, share
domestic *adj* **1** (domestic problems) family, home, personal, private. **2** (domestic animal) domesticated, house-trained, pet, tame; ***opp*** wild. **3** (domestic affairs) home, internal, national; ***opp*** foreign
domesticated *adj* **1** (of an animal) broken-in, house-trained, tame, tamed, trained; ***opp*** wild. **2** (of a person) domestic, home-loving, house-trained *inf*
dominant *adj* **1** assertive, controlling, domineering, leading, most influential, ruling, superior; ***opp*** self-effacing, passive. **2** (of a feature) biggest, conspicuous, eye-catching, highest, imposing, largest, main, major, tallest
dominate *v* **1** (of a person) be in the driver's seat, boss *inf*, command, control, direct, govern, have the upper hand, influence, lead, monopolize, outnumber, prevail, rule, take control, tyrannize, wear the pants. **2** (of a feature) dwarf, loom over, overlook, overshadow, stand over, tower above
domineering *adj* bossy *inf*, bullying, forceful, high-handed, menacing, overbearing, strict, threatening, tyrannical; ***opp*** passive
donate *v* chip in *inf*, contribute, give, kick in *inf*, make a gift of, present, supply
donation *n* contribution, gift, grant, offering, present
donor *n* backer, benefactor, contributor, giver, sponsor, supporter
doom *n* **1** destiny, end, fate, kismet. **2** annihilation, catastrophe, death, destruction, downfall, extinction, ruin. **3** doomsday, end of the world, Judgment Day, Last Judgment
doomed *adj* condemned, fated, hopeless, ill-fated, ruined, star-crossed, unlucky
door *n* barrier, doorway, entrance, entry, exit, gate, opening
dormant *adj* asleep, hibernating, inactive, motionless, quiet, resting, sleeping, sluggish, slumbering; ***opp*** active
dose *n* amount, measure, portion, prescribed amount, quantity
dot *n* **1** circle, dab, fleck, jot, mark, point, speck, speckle, spot. **2** decimal point, full stop
dote on *v* admire, adore, idolize, love, prize, treasure, worship
doting *adj* adoring, devoted, fond, indulgent, loving
double *adj* coupled, doubled, dual, duplicate, in pairs, paired, twice, twin, twofold, two-ply
double *v* enlarge, grow, increase, magnify, multiply by two, rise; ***opp*** halve
doubt *n* apprehension, cynicism, disbelief, fear, hesitation, incredulity, lack of confidence, lack of conviction, lack of faith, misgivings, mistrust, qualms, reservations, skepticism, suspicion, uncertainty, uneasiness, worries
doubt *v* be dubious, be undecided, be skeptical, be suspicious, distrust, fear, have doubts, have misgivings, have reservations, have scruples, hesitate, question, suspect

doubtful *adj* **1** (not likely to happen) iffy *inf*, improbable, in doubt, uncertain, unconfirmed, unlikely, unsettled, vague; ***opp*** certain. **2** (feeling doubt) distrustful, hesitating, incredulous, mistrustful, skeptical, suspicious, tentative, unconvinced, unsure, wavering; ***opp*** certain. **3** (open to doubt) ambiguous, debatable, dodgy *inf*, dubious, equivocal, inconclusive, obscure, open to question, problematic, questionable

downfall *n* collapse, defeat, disgrace, fall, overthrow, ruin, undoing

downpour *n* cloudburst, deluge, flood, rainstorm, torrents of rain

downward *adj* descending, downhill, earthbound, earthward, going down

drab *adj* colorless, dingy, dismal, dowdy, dreary, dull, flat, gray, lackluster, mousy, somber; ***opp*** bright

draft *n* **1** first version, outline, plan, rough version, sketch. **2** breeze, current, flow, movement, wind

draft *v* compose, design, draw, draw up, formulate, outline, plan, put together, sketch, work out

drag *v* **1** haul, lug, pull, tow, trail, tug, yank. **2** (the afternoon dragged) be tedious, crawl, creep, go on too long, go slowly, move slowly, stretch out

drain *n* channel, conduit, culvert, ditch, drainpipe, gutter, outlet, pipe, sewer, sink, trench

drain *v* **1** (get liquid out) bleed, draw off, dry, empty, filter, milk, pump, remove, tap, withdraw. **2** (of liquid) drip, ebb, flow, leak, ooze, seep, trickle. **3** (use up resources) consume, deplete, expend, exhaust, spend, strain, use up. **4** (make sb tired) enervate, exhaust, sap, tax, weary

drama *n* **1** (a play) comedy, dramatization, melodrama, play, production, show, tragedy. **2** (studying drama) acting, dramatic art, improvisation, stagecraft, theater. **3** crisis, excitement, histrionics, scene, spectacle

dramatic *adj* **1** breathtaking, electrifying, exciting, impressive, melodramatic, powerful, sensational, startling, tense, thrilling, unexpected, vivid. **2** (a dramatic gesture) artificial, exaggerated, flamboyant, large, overdone, showy, stagy. **3** stage, theatrical

drastic *adj* desperate, dire, extreme, radical, severe, strong

draw *n* **1** allure, attraction, enticement, lure, pull *inf*. **2** (in a game) dead heat, stalemate, tie. **3** lottery, raffle, sweepstake

draw *v* **1** color, depict, design, make a drawing, make a picture, paint, pencil, sketch, trace. **2** (draw the crowds) attract, coax, entice, lure, persuade, pull. **3** (draw a caravan) haul, pull, tow. **4** (draw a weapon) bring out, produce, pull out, remove, take out, unsheathe. **5** (draw in a game) be equal, be neck and neck, tie. **6 draw up** compose, draft, frame, put in writing, put together, write out

drawback *n* catch, disadvantage, downside, flaw, fly in the ointment *inf*, hitch, hurdle, obstacle, problem, snag, stumbling-block; ***opp*** advantage

drawing *n* cartoon, depiction, diagram,

illustration, outline, picture, portrait, portrayal, representation, sketch, study

dread *n* alarm, apprehension, cold feet *inf*, dismay, fear, foreboding, fright, horror, terror, trepidation, uneasiness, worry

dread *v* be afraid of, be terrified of, fear, shrink from, worry about

dreadful *adj* appalling, awful, dire, disgusting, distressing, fearful, frightful, ghastly, grim, gruesome, harrowing, hideous, horrible, horrifying, monstrous, nasty, repugnant, revolting, shocking, terrible, very bad

dream *n* **1** daydream, delusion, fantasy, hallucination, illusion, imagination, mirage, nightmare, reverie, stupor, trance, vision. **2** aim, ambition, aspiration, desire, fantasy, goal, hope, pipedream, wish

dream *v* daydream, fantasize, hallucinate, have dreams, have nightmares, have visions, imagine, muse, think

dreary *adj* **1** boring, colorless, comfortless, depressing, drab, dull, flat, funereal, gloomy, joyless, melancholy, miserable, monotonous, mournful, sad, somber, sorrowful, uninteresting, wretched. **2** (dreary weather) bleak, dark, dismal, downcast, gloomy, overcast; ***opp*** bright

dregs *n* deposit, dross, grounds, remains, residue, scum, sediment

drench *v* douse, drown, flood, saturate, soak, wet

dress *n* **1** frock, gown, robe, shift. **2** (in strange dress) attire, clothes, clothing, costume, garb, gear *inf*, get-up *inf*

dress *v* **1** (put clothes on) don, get changed, get dressed, put on, slip on. **2** (decorate) adorn, decorate, trim. **3** (dress a wound) attend to, bandage, bind, cover, put a plaster on, tend, treat. **4 dress up** dress smartly, get dolled up *inf*. **5 dress up** (dress up as sb) disguise yourself, put fancy dress on, wear a disguise. **6 dress up** (make sth look better) beautify, decorate, embellish, improve, ornament, trim

dribble *v* **1** drip, drop, leak, ooze, run, seep, trickle. **2** drool, slaver, slobber

drift *v* be carried, coast, float, ramble, roam, stray, waft, wander

drill *n* discipline, exercise, instruction, practice, training

drill *v* **1** bore, make a hole, pierce, puncture. **2** coach, discipline, exercise, instruct, practice, put sb through his paces, rehearse, teach, train

drink *n* **1** alcohol, beverage, booze *inf*, grog, hard stuff *inf*, liquid refreshment, liquor, spirits. **2** cup, dram *inf*, glass, gulp, nip *inf*, sip, slug *inf*, swig *inf*, tot

drink *v* **1** gulp, guzzle, knock back *inf*, lap, sip, suck, swallow, swig *inf*. **2** (drink alcohol) booze *inf*, carouse, get drunk, have a few, hit the bottle *inf*, indulge, take a drop *inf*

drip *n* **1** bead, dribble, drop, leak, plop, splash, spot, tear, trickle. **2** coward, weakling, weak person, wimp *inf*

drip *v* dribble, drizzle, drop, filter, plop, splash, sprinkle, trickle

drive *n* **1** excursion, jaunt, journey, outing, ride, run, spin *inf*, trip. **2** (determination) ambition, determination, energy, enterprise, enthusiasm, get-up-and-go *inf*, initiative, motivation, vigor. **3** (sales drive) campaign, effort, push

drive *v* **1** (make sth or sb go) direct, guide, herd, move, propel, push, send, steer, urge. **2** (go in a car) chauffeur, give sb a lift, go by car, ride, run. **3** (drive a machine) operate, push, work. **4** (make sb do sth) coerce, compel, force, goad, impel, oblige, prod, put pressure on, spur. **5** (push sth in) bang, hammer, hit, knock, ram, thrust

droop *v* bend, dangle, drop, fall, flop, hang, sag, sink, slump, stoop, wilt

drop *n* **1** (drop of liquid) bead, blob, drip, droplet, globule, pearl, tear. **2** (amount) dab, dash, mouthful, sip, smidgen *inf*, splash, spot, taste, trace, trickle. **3** (a drop in unemployment) cut, decline, decrease, dip, downturn, fall-off, reduction; ***opp*** rise. **4** (a steep drop) cliff, descent, precipice, slope

drop *v* **1** (go downwards) descend, dip, dive, fall, fall away, go downhill, plummet, plunge, sink, subside, tumble; ***opp*** rise. **2** (of liquid) dribble, drip, fall, plop. **3** (of prices) collapse, decrease, dip, fall, lessen, plummet; ***opp*** rise. **4** (drop sth) let fall, let go; ***opp*** hold. **5** (lose interest in) abandon, chuck *inf*, desert, discontinue, ditch *inf*, finish with, give up, kick *inf*, stop; ***opp*** take up. **6 drop off** decline, decrease, diminish, drop, dwindle, fall off, lessen; ***opp*** increase. **7 drop off** doze off, fall asleep, nod off *inf*. **8 drop out** abandon, back out, cop out *sl*, give up, leave, quit, resign, stop

drought *n* dry spell, lack of rain

drown *v* **1** deluge, drench, engulf, flood, immerse, inundate, submerge, swamp. **2** (of people) go under, sink. **3** (of noise) deaden, drown out, muffle, overpower, swallow up

drudge *n* hack, menial, servant, slave, worker

drudgery *n* chores, grind *inf*, hard work, labor, slavery, slog, toil

drug *n* **1** medication, medicine, remedy, treatment. **2** barbiturate, illegal substance, narcotic, opiate

drug *v* **1** anesthetize, knock out, sedate, tranquillize. **2** dope *inf*, dose, give drugs to, medicate, poison, treat

drum *v* beat, pulsate, rap, reverberate, tap, throb, thrum

drunk *adj* blind drunk, inebriated, intoxicated, loaded *sl*, out of it *inf*, plastered *inf*, sloshed *inf*, smashed *inf*, tight *inf*, tipsy, under the influence; ***opp*** sober

drunk *n* alcoholic, boozer *inf*, drunkard, heavy drinker, wino *inf*

dry *adj* **1** arid, baked, barren, dead, dehydrated, dried up, moistureless, parched, shriveled, waterless, wilted, withered, wizened. **2** (of food) desiccated, dried, hard, stale; ***opp*** fresh. **3** (of humor) deadpan, droll, ironic, laconic, sarcastic. **4** (of a text) boring, dreary, dull, monotonous, tedious, uninteresting; ***opp*** exciting

dry *v* dehydrate, desiccate, drain, dry off, dry out, dry up, make dry, parch, sear, shrivel, wither, wilt

dual *adj* binary, double, duplicate, linked, matched, paired, twin, twofold

dubious *adj* **1** (dubious about sth) doubtful, hesitant, skeptical, suspicious, uncertain, unconvinced, undecided, unsure, wavering; ***opp*** sure. **2** ambiguous, debatable, dodgy *inf*, doubtful, equivocal, fishy *inf*, iffy *inf*, indefinite, obscure, problematic, unclear, unresolved, unsettled, up in the air, vague

duck *v* **1** bend, bob, bow, crouch, drop, lower yourself, squat, stoop. **2** (duck sb) dunk, immerse, plunge, push under, submerge

due *adj* **1** (the money due) in arrears, outstanding, owed, owing, payable, unpaid. **2** (with the respect that was due) appropriate, decent, deserved, fit, fitting, merited, proper, right. **3** (train is due) awaited, expected, scheduled

duel *n* battle, clash, competition, contest, engagement, fight

dull *adj* **1** (of a person) dense, dim, dim-witted, obtuse, slow, stupid, unintelligent; ***opp*** bright. **2** boring, dreary, mind-numbing, tame, tedious, unexciting, unimaginative, uninteresting; ***opp*** exciting. **3** (of colors) dark, dingy, drab, dreary, faded, flat, lackluster, matt, muted, somber, toned down, washed-out; ***opp*** bright. **4** (of weather) cloudy, dark, dismal, gloomy, gray, murky, overcast; ***opp*** bright, sunny. **5** (a dull expression) apathetic, blank, dead, empty, expressionless, lifeless, unresponsive. **6** (feeling dull) depressed, drowsy, idle, inactive, lethargic, listless, sleepy, slow, sluggish, stagnant. **7** (a dull blade) blunt, blunted, dulled, unsharpened; ***opp*** sharp. **8** (a dull thud) deadened, indistinct, muffled, muted

dumb *adj* **1** at a loss for words, inarticulate, mute, silent, soundless, speechless, tongue-tied, unable to speak, wordless. **2** (stupid) dense, dim, slow, stupid, unintelligent; ***opp*** clever

dump *n* garbage heap, junkyard, refuse heap, tip

dump *v* **1** (put) deposit, drop, fling down, park *inf*, put, throw. **2** (dump garbage) dispose of, ditch *inf*, empty out, get rid of, jettison, scrap, throw away, throw out, unload. **3** (dump sb) (*inf*) chuck *inf*, ditch *inf*, finish with, leave, stop going out with

dungeon *n* cage, pit, prison

duplicate *adj* alternative, copied, corresponding, identical, matched, matching, second, twin

duplicate *n* carbon copy, clone, copy, double, exact match, facsimile, imitation, photocopy, replica, spitting image *inf*, twin

duplicate *v* clone, copy, do again, double, echo, photocopy, print, repeat, replicate, reproduce

dusk *n* dark, evening, gloaming, nightfall, sundown, sunset, twilight

dust *n* dirt, earth, grime, grit, powder, smut, soil, soot

dusty *adj* **1** dirty, dust-covered, filthy, grimy, sooty, undusted, unswept. **2** chalky, crumbly, dry, fine, gritty, powdery, sandy

dutiful *adj* attentive, conscientious, devoted, faithful, hard-working, obedient, obliging, reliable, respectful, submissive, willing

duty *n* **1** (sth you have to do) assignment, chore, job, mission, obligation, responsibility, task. **2** (a sense of duty) allegiance, deference, loyalty, obligation, respect, responsibility. **3** (pay duty on sth) charge, customs, dues, levy, tariff, tax, toll

dwarf *adj* baby, miniature, pocket, small, tiny, undersized

dwarf *n* midget, pygmy

dwarf *v* dominate, overshadow, tower above, tower over

dwell *v* hang out *inf*, inhabit, live, lodge, remain, reside, rest, settle, stay, stop

dwelling *n* abode, home, house, residence

dye *n* color, coloring, pigment, stain, tint

dye *v* color, stain, tint

dynamic *adj* active, energetic, enterprising, enthusiastic, forceful, go-ahead *inf*, go-getting, high-powered, lively, motivated, powerful, spirited, vigorous

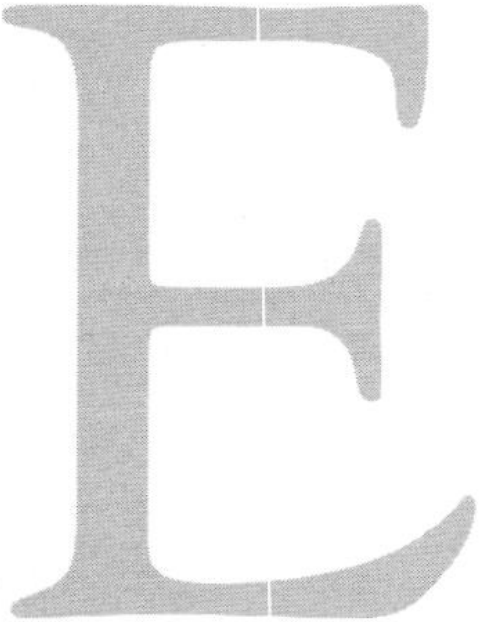

eager *adj* agog, anxious, ardent, bursting, committed, enthusiastic, excited, greedy, hungry, impatient, intent, itching *inf*, keen, longing, passionate, raring, thirsty; ***opp*** unenthusiastic

early *adj* **1** advanced, ahead of time, before time, forward, precocious, premature, untimely. **2** (early people) ancient, first, prehistoric, primitive

earn *v* **1** (earn money) bring in *inf*, clear *inf*, gain, get, gross, make, net, pocket, pull in, realize, receive, take home *inf*. **2** (earn points) accumulate, collect, gain, qualify for, receive, win. **3** (earn respect) be entitled to, be worthy of, deserve, gain, have a right to, merit, rate, secure, win

earnest *adj* **1** (of people) committed, conscientious, dedicated, determined, grave, hard-working, intense, purposeful, resolved, serious, solemn, studious, zealous. **2** (an earnest plea) heartfelt, impassioned, passionate, sincere, wholehearted

earnings *n* fee, income, pay, remuneration, return, reward, salary, wages

earth *n* **1** globe, planet, sphere, world. **2** clay, dirt, ground, land, loam, soil, turf

earthly *adj* human, material, mortal, terrestrial, worldly

ease *n* **1** calmness, comfort, composure, contentment, enjoyment, happiness, leisure, peace, relaxation, serenity, tranquillity. **2** (do sth with ease) casualness, dexterity, easiness, effortlessness, nonchalance

easy *adj* **1** (easy work) cushy *inf*, light, simple, soft, straightforward, undemanding; ***opp*** demanding, difficult. **2** (easy to do) child's play, clear, foolproof, idiot-proof *inf*, not difficult, simple, uncomplicated, user-friendly; ***opp*** complicated. **3** (an easy climb) gentle, leisurely, smooth, undemanding, unhurried; ***opp*** hard. **4** (an easy life) carefree, comfortable, cozy, peaceful, pleasant, quiet, troublefree, uncomplicated; ***opp*** hard

easygoing *adj* calm, carefree, casual, even-tempered, flexible, informal, laid-back *inf*, lenient, liberal, mellow, permissive, patient, placid, relaxed, tolerant, understanding

eat *v* **1** (eat food) bolt, chew, consume, devour, digest, gobble, graze *inf*, munch, nibble, put away *inf*, stuff yourself *inf*, swallow, wolf. **2** (time to eat) dine, feast, have a meal, lunch, snack *inf*

eavesdrop *v* bug *inf*, listen, listen in, monitor, overhear, snoop, spy, tap

ebb *v* **1** (of the tide) fall away, flow back,

go out, recede, retreat, subside, withdraw. **2** (of sb's confidence) decline, decrease, die, diminish, drop, dwindle, fade, flag, lessen, peter out, sink, wane, weaken

eccentric *adj* abnormal, bizarre, cranky, dotty *inf*, erratic, freakish, idiosyncratic, irregular, nutty *inf*, odd, outlandish, peculiar, queer, strange, uncommon, unconventional, unusual, wacky *sl*, way-out *inf*, weird, zany

echo *n* **1** answer, repetition, resounding, reverberation, ringing. **2** (echoes of another occasion) hint, memory, overtones, reminder, suggestion, trace

echo *v* **1** (of a sound) repeat, resound, reverberate, ring, sound again. **2** (echo sb) copy, imitate, mimic, mirror, parrot, reflect

eclipse *n* **1** blocking, blotting out, dimming, shading, veiling. **2** decline, deterioration, failure, fall, weakening; ***opp*** rise

eclipse *v* **1** block, blot out, cloud, darken, dim, obscure, overshadow, shroud, veil. **2** dwarf, exceed, excel, outdo, outshine, outstrip, put in the shade, surpass, transcend

economic *adj* **1** (for economic reasons) business, commercial, financial, industrial, trade. **2** (not economic) cost-effective, money-making, productive, profitable, profit-making, solvent, viable. **3** (economic policy) budgetary, financial, fiscal, monetary

economical *adj* **1** cheap, cost-effective, efficient, inexpensive, money-saving, time-saving; ***opp*** uneconomical. **2** (of a person) careful, economizing, frugal, mean, miserly, parsimonious, prudent, scrimping, sparing, thrifty; ***opp*** wasteful

economics *n* budgeting, finance, money

economize *v* be economical, be frugal, be sparing, cut back, cut corners, save, scrimp, tighten your belt; ***opp*** splash out

economy *n* **1** carefulness, meanness, miserliness, prudence, restraint, saving, stinginess, thrift. **2** (a country's economy) budget, economic affairs, financial management, wealth

edge *n* **1** border, boundary, brim, brink, circumference, fringe, limit, line, lip, margin, outline, perimeter, periphery, rim, side, threshold, verge. **2** (have the edge) advantage, dominance, head start, lead, superiority, upper hand

edible *adj* digestible, eatable, fit to eat, good to eat, palatable, safe to eat, wholesome; ***opp*** inedible

edit *v* adapt, amend, annotate, arrange, assemble, censor, check, compile, correct, polish, prepare, put together, rephrase, revise, rewrite

edition *n* copy, impression, issue, number, printing, publication, version, volume

educate *v* **1** (educate sb at school) coach, discipline, drill, indoctrinate, inform, instruct, lecture, nurture, prepare, school, teach, train, tutor. **2** (travel educates you) civilize, cultivate, develop, edify, enlighten, inform

educated *adj* civilized, cultivated, cultured, enlightened, experienced, informed, knowledgable, learned, literate, well-informed, well-read; ***opp*** ignorant

education *n* instruction, knowledge, scholarship, schooling, teaching,

training, tuition
educational *adj* edifying, enlightening, improving, informative, instructive
eerie *adj* awesome, creepy *inf*, fearful, frightening, ghostly, mysterious, scary *inf*, spine-chilling, spooky *inf*, strange, uncanny, unearthly, unnatural, weird
effect *n* **1** (the effect of sth) aftermath, conclusion, consequence, outcome, repercussion, result, upshot. **2** (create an effect) feeling, illusion, impression, sensation, sense
effect *v* (effect a change) accomplish, achieve, bring about, carry out, cause, complete, create, execute, fulfill, give rise to, implement, initiate, make, perform, produce, put into effect
effective *adj* **1** (effective argument, lighting) compelling, convincing, impressive, moving, noticeable, persuasive, powerful, striking, strong. **2** (working well) capable, competent, efficacious, efficient, powerful, productive, serviceable, strong, successful, useful. **3** (in force) active, current, in force, in operation, valid
effeminate *adj* feminine, girlish, unmanly, weak, wimpish *inf*, womanly; ***opp*** manly
effervescent *adj* **1** (of liquid) bubbling, bubbly, carbonated, fizzing, fizzy, foaming, foamy, frothing, gassy, sparkling. **2** (of personality) animated, bubbly, exuberant, irrepressible, lively, vivacious
efficiency *n* ability, capability, competence, economy, effectiveness, organization, power, skill
efficient *adj* **1** (an efficient worker) able, businesslike, capable, competent, effective, organized, productive, proficient. **2** (an efficient use of time) cost-effective, economic, effective, productive, profitable, sensible; ***opp*** inefficient
effort *n* **1** application, challenge, diligence, elbow grease *inf*, endeavor, energy, exertion, force, labor, muscle, power, strain, stress, struggle, trouble, work. **2** (a good effort) attempt, crack *inf*, shot *inf*, stab *inf*, try. **3** accomplishment, achievement, attainment, exploit, feat, outcome, result
effortless *adj* easy, painless, simple, uncomplicated, undemanding; ***opp*** difficult
egotism *n* egocentricity, egoism, narcissism, pride, self-absorption, self-centeredness, self-importance, selfishness, vanity
egotist *n* bighead *inf*, egomaniac
egotistic(al) *adj* boastful, conceited, egocentric, egoistic, full of yourself, narcissistic, proud, self-centered, self-important, selfish, vain
eject *v* **1** (get rid of sb) banish, boot out *inf*, cast out, chuck out *inf*, deport, discharge, dismiss, evict, exile, expel, get rid of, kick out *inf*, oust, remove, sack, throw out, turn out. **2** (get rid of sth) disgorge, emit, excrete, expel, exude, release, send out, shoot out, spew, spout, throw out, vomit. **3** (remove) dislodge, extract, remove, take out; ***opp*** insert
elaborate *adj* **1** (worked out carefully) careful, detailed, exact, exhaustive, painstaking, precise, thorough;

opp vague. **2** (complicated) complex, complicated, fancy, fussy, intricate, involved, ornate, showy; ***opp*** simple

elaborate *v* add detail, add to, amplify, develop, embellish, embroider, enlarge, expand, fill out, flesh out, improve, polish, refine

elapse *v* go by, lapse, pass, roll, slip away, slip by

elastic *adj* bendy, bouncy, flexible, plastic, pliable, resilient, rubbery, springy, stretchy, supple, yielding

elect *v* adopt, appoint, cast your vote, choose, decide upon, nominate, opt for, pick, plump for, prefer, select, settle on, vote

election *n* ballot, hustings, poll, referendum, vote, voting

elector *n* constituent, voter

electric *adj* **1** (of a speech) charged, dynamic, electrifying, galvanizing, rousing, stimulating, stirring, tense, thrilling. **2** (of an appliance) battery-operated, electrical

elegant *adj* **1** (elegant clothes) beautiful, chic, fashionable, stylish, tasteful. **2** (of sb's body) delicate, fine, handsome. **3** (elegant manners) charming, debonair, genteel, graceful, nice, polished, refined, sophisticated, suave. **4** (an elegant apartment) beautiful, luxurious, posh *inf*, smart, stylish, sumptuous, tasteful

element *n* component, constituent, factor, feature, ingredient, part, piece, unit

elementary *adj* **1** easy, plain, rudimentary, simple, straightforward, understandable. **2** basic, early, first, fundamental, initial, primary, introductory

elements *n* **1** basics, essentials, first principles, foundations, principles, rudiments. **2** atmosphere, climate, environment, weather

elevate *v* **1** hoist, lift, make higher, raise; ***opp*** lower. **2** advance, promote, upgrade

eligible *adj* acceptable, allowed, authorized, equipped, fit, qualified, suitable, suited, worthy

eliminate *v* cut out, exclude, get rid of, leave out, reject, remove, take out

elite *n* **1** best, cream *inf*, flower, pick, top. **2** aristocracy, nobility, upper class

elope *v* abscond, run away, run off, slip away, steal away

eloquent *adj* articulate, fluent, graceful, moving, persuasive, plausible, powerful, well-expressed

elude *v* avoid, dodge, escape, evade, get away, give the slip to, lose, shake off, slip away from, throw sb off the scent

elusive *adj* evasive, hard to find, hard to pin down, indefinable, intangible, shifting, shifty, slippery, subtle

emanate *v* arise, come forth, derive, emerge, flow, issue, originate, proceed, spring, stem

emancipate *v* **1** deliver, free, let go, liberate, release, set free, unchain, unshackle; ***opp*** enslave. **2** enfranchise, give rights to, give the vote to

embargo *n* ban, bar, boycott, prohibition, restriction, seizure, stoppage

embark *v* **1** (board a ship) board, go on board, go aboard. **2** (embark on a venture) begin, enter into, go into, have a go at, launch, set about, set out, take on, take the plunge, take up, undertake, venture into

embarrass *v* fluster, humiliate, make sb blush, make sb feel awkward, make sb go red, mortify, shame, show up

embarrassed *adj* ashamed, awkward, blushing, flustered, humiliated, mortified, red, red-faced, self-conscious, shamefaced, sheepish

embarrassing *adj* awkward, humiliating, mortifying, tricky, uncomfortable

embarrassment *n* awkwardness, bashfulness, humiliation, mortification, self-consciousness, shame

emblem *n* badge, crest, insignia, logo, symbol, sign

embody *v* **1** (include) comprise, constitute, embrace, encompass, include, incorporate, take in. **2** (represent) personify, represent, stand for, symbolize, typify

embrace *v* **1** (hug) clasp, cuddle, fold sb in your arms, hold, hug. **2** (include) comprise, embody, encompass, include, incorporate, take in, subsume. **3** (welcome) adopt, espouse, support, take up, take on board, welcome

emerge *v* **1** appear, come into view, come out, emanate, materialize, surface. **2** arise, become apparent, become known, crop up, come out, come to light, develop, get around, transpire, turn out

emergency *n* accident, crisis, critical situation, danger, dire straits, disaster, fix, hole, pickle *inf*, predicament

emigrate *v* go to live abroad, migrate, move, relocate

eminent *adj* celebrated, distinguished, esteemed, important, notable, prominent, renowned, respected

emission *n* discharge, leakage, outflow, output, radiation, release

emit *v* belch, discharge, disgorge, exude, give off, leak, let out, pour out, radiate, release, send out, spew out, spout

emotion *n* excitement, feeling, fervor, passion, sensation, sentiment, sentimentality

emotional *adj* ardent, demonstrative, excitable, fervent, fiery, heated, hot-blooded, impassioned, moved, moving, passionate, poignant, sensitive, sentimental, warm

emotive *adj* **1** controversial, delicate, sensitive. **2** emotional, heart-rending, moving, touching

emphasis *n* accent, attention, force, importance, priority, significance, stress, weight

emphasize *v* accentuate, bring out, feature, focus on, give prominence to, heighten, highlight, point up, press home, spotlight, stress, underline, underscore

emphatic *adj* absolute, categorical, decided, definite, determined, firm, forceful, positive, powerful, pronounced, strong, unequivocal, unmistakable; ***opp*** hesitant, tentative

empire *n* colonies, commonwealth, domain, dominion, jurisdiction, kingdom, protectorate, realm, territory

employ *v* **1** (hire) commission, engage, hire, put on the payroll, recruit, sign up, take on. **2** (use) exercise, make use of, use

employed *adj* earning, in a job, in

employment, in work, working, waged; ***opp*** unemployed

employee *n* member of staff, worker, workforce

employer *n* boss, management, manager, owner

employment *n* business, job, livelihood, living, occupation, profession, trade, vocation, work

emptiness *n* **1** bareness, barrenness, blank, vacuum, void. **2** futility, hollowness, meaninglessness, senselessness, triviality, worthlessness

empty *adj* **1** bare, barren, blank, clear, deserted, unfilled, vacant, with nothing inside. **2** futile, hollow, meaningless, purposeless, senseless, trivial, worthless

enable *v* allow, authorize, empower, entitle, equip, facilitate, make sth possible, open the way for, prepare, qualify; ***opp*** prevent

enamored *adj* besotted, captivated, crazy about *inf*, infatuated, in love, keen on, nuts about *inf*, smitten *inf*, sweet on

enchant *v* allure, bewitch, captivate, cast a spell on, charm, delight, entrance, fascinate

enchanted *adj* **1** bewitched, captivated, charmed, delighted, entranced, fascinated, spellbound. **2** charmed, magic, magical, under a spell

enchanting *adj* alluring, attractive, bewitching, captivating, charming, delightful, fascinating, spellbinding

enclose *v* **1** cocoon, encase, encircle, fence off, ring, shut in, surround, wall in, wrap. **2** (enclose sth with a letter) include, insert, put in with, send with

enclosure *n* arena, compound, corral, paddock, pen, pound, ring, run, stockade, yard

encounter *n* confrontation, meeting

encounter *v* be faced with, bump into, come across, come up against, confront, meet, run into

encourage *v* be conducive to, bolster, buoy up, cheer on, egg on *inf*, foster, give courage to, give hope to, hearten, inspire, reassure, root for, spur on, stimulate, strengthen, support, urge; ***opp*** discourage

encouragement *n* boost, incentive, inspiration, pep talk, reassurance, shot in the arm, support; ***opp*** discouragement

encouraging *adj* heartening, hopeful, inspiring, optimistic, promising, reassuring, supportive, uplifting; ***opp*** discouraging

encroach *v* barge in *inf*, get in on *inf*, impinge, interfere, intrude, invade, make inroads, muscle in, obtrude, poke your nose in *inf*, tread on sb's toes, trespass

end *n* **1** cessation, climax, close, completion, conclusion, culmination, finale, finish. **2** boundary, edge, extent, limit, margin, terminus, tip. **3** (remnant) butt, leftover, remnant, stub. **4** (death) curtains *inf*, death, demise, destruction, downfall, extermination, extinction, ruin. **5** (objective) aim, goal, intention, motive, object, objective, purpose

end *v* **1** abolish, conclude, finish, halt, phase out, put an end to, put a stop to, stop, terminate, wind up; ***opp*** begin, start. **2** break off, cease, close, come to an end, conclude, culminate, finish, peter out, stop, terminate; ***opp*** begin, start. **3 end up** become, come to, come to rest, finish up, reach, turn out, wind up

endanger *v* expose, jeopardize, put at risk, risk, threaten

endearing *adj* adorable, captivating, charming, cute, engaging, lovable, sweet; ***opp*** repulsive

endless *adj* continual, continuous, everlasting, incessant, interminable, limitless, never-ending, nonstop, perpetual, unbroken, unending, uninterrupted, unremitting

endorse *v* **1** advocate, approve, authorize, back, champion, give approval to, give sth the go-ahead, give sth the red light, okay, sanction, second, support, vote for. **2** countersign, initial, sign

endure *v* bear, cope with, face, go through, put up with, stand, stick *inf*, stomach, tolerate, withstand. **2** carry on, continue, exist, last, live, persist, prevail, survive

enemy *n* adversary, foe, opponent, rival, them *inf*, the opposition, the other side; ***opp*** ally, friend, one of us

energetic *adj* active, animated, brisk, dynamic, forceful, hard-working, lively, spirited, tireless, vigorous; ***opp*** lethargic, sluggish

energy *n* animation, drive, dynamism, enthusiasm, get-up-and-go *inf*, life, liveliness, potency, stamina, strength, vigor, vitality, vivacity; ***opp*** lethargy, weakness

enforce *v* administer, carry out, implement, impose, insist on, put into force

engage *v* **1** (engage sb's interest) attract, allure, captivate, capture, catch, draw, engross, gain, grip, hold, occupy. **2** (engage gear) interconnect, interlock, lock on. **3** (employ) appoint, commission, employ, hire, put on the payroll, take on. **4 engage in** be/get involved in, join in, participate in, practice, tackle, take part in

engaged *adj* **1** busy, occupied, tied up, unavailable. **2** betrothed, spoken for

engagement *n* **1** appointment, commitment, date, meeting. **2** betrothal

engine *n* generator, locomotive, machine, motor, turbine

engineer *n* architect, designer, mechanic, planner, technician

engineer *v* bring about, create, devise, effect, manage, mastermind, orchestrate, plan

engrave *v* carve, chisel, cut, etch, gouge, inscribe, scratch

engraving *n* block, carving, etching, inscription, plate, print

engrossed *adj* absorbed, fascinated, immersed, intent, involved, preoccupied, rapt, riveted, wrapped up

enhance *v* add to, augment, boost, emphasize, enrich, improve, increase, intensify, reinforce, strengthen, upgrade

enigma *n* conundrum, mystery, paradox, puzzle, riddle

enigmatic *adj* baffling, curious, inexplicable, mysterious, obscure, puzzling, strange, weird

enjoy *v* **1** adore, get a buzz from *inf*, get a kick out of *inf*, get pleasure from, go in for *inf*, like, love, luxuriate in, relish, revel in; ***opp*** dislike, hate. **2 enjoy**

yourself celebrate, have a field day, have a good time, have fun, have the time of your life, let your hair down, party, treat yourself

enjoyable *adj* brilliant, entertaining, fun, good, good fun, great, lovely, nice, pleasant, super, superb, wonderful; ***opp*** awful, dreadful

enjoyment *n* amusement, delight, entertainment, fun, gratification, joy, pleasure, relish, satisfaction

enlarge *v* add to, blow up, broaden, deepen, expand, extend, increase, inflate, lengthen, let out, magnify, make bigger, stretch, widen; ***opp*** contract, reduce, shrink

enlighten *v* advise, edify, educate, fill sb in on, inform, instruct, make aware, make sb understand, put sb in the picture, put sb right, teach, tell sb about

enlightened *adj* **1** aware, educated, informed, knowledgable, learned, well-informed, wise; ***opp*** ignorant. **2** broad-minded, fair-minded, liberal, open-minded, tolerant; ***opp*** bigoted, prejudiced

enlist *v* employ, engage, enroll, hire, join up, recruit, register, sign up, take on, volunteer for

enormous *adj* astronomic, big, colossal, excessive, giant, gigantic, huge, immense, jumbo, mammoth, massive, vast; ***opp*** minuscule, small, tiny

enough *adj* adequate, ample, as much as you need, plenty, sufficient

enrich *v* augment, embellish, enhance, improve, make richer, supplement; ***opp*** impoverish

enroll *v* admit, enlist, join, recruit, register, sign on, sign up, take on

ensue *v* come after, derive, flow, follow, happen afterwards, occur as a result, result, stem from, turn out

ensure *v* certify, confirm, guarantee, make certain, make sure, secure

entail *v* call for, give rise to, involve, lead to, necessitate, require, result in

enter *v* **1** (go inside) board, come in, come inside, get into, get onto, go in, go inside, penetrate. **2** (enter information) add, document, log, note, put down, register, take down, write down, write in. **3** (enroll) become a member, enlist, enroll, go in for, join, participate in, put your name down for, sign up for, take part in

enterprise *n* **1** business, effort, endeavor, operation, project, scheme, undertaking, venture. **2** ambition, drive, enthusiasm, get-up-and-go *inf*, gumption, imagination, initiative

enterprising *adj* adventurous, ambitious, entrepreneurial, go-ahead, imaginative, resourceful; ***opp*** staid, stick-in-the-mud, unimaginative

entertain *v* amuse, divert, keep sb amused, keep sb happy, keep sb's attention, occupy

entertainer *n* artist, artiste, performer

entertaining *adj* amusing, diverting, funny, hilarious, interesting, witty; ***opp*** boring, dull

entertainment *n* **1** amusement, distraction, diversion, enjoyment, fun, pleasure, treat. **2** performance, presentation, production, show, spectacle

enthralled *adj* captivated, engrossed,

fascinated, gripped, intrigued, hypnotized, riveted, spellbound, taken up with

enthusiasm *n* commitment, eagerness, excitement, exuberance, fervor, gusto, keenness, passion, relish; ***opp*** apathy

enthusiast *n* addict, buff *inf*, devotee, fan, fanatic, fiend *inf*, follower, freak *inf*, lover, supporter

enthusiastic *adj* avid, crazy *inf*, dead keen *inf*, eager, keen, excited, fanatical, mad about *inf*, passionate, raring to go, vehement, wholehearted; ***opp*** apathetic, half-hearted

entice *v* allure, encourage, induce, lead on, lure, seduce, tempt

entire *adj* complete, full, total, whole

entitle *v* authorize, empower, enable, give sb the right, license, make sb eligible, permit, qualify

entourage *n* attendants, band, escort, followers, groupies *inf*, retinue

entrails *n* bowels, guts *inf*, innards, insides, intestines

entrance *n* **1** (way in) access point, door, doorway, entry, foyer, gate, gateway, lobby, mouth, opening, portal, threshold, way in. **2** (admission) access, admission, admittance, entry, right of entry

entrant *n* applicant, candidate, competitor, contestant, participant, player

entrenched *adj* deep-rooted, deep-seated, established, firmly held, fixed, ingrained, well-established

entry *n* **1** (way in) access point, door, doorway, entrance, foyer, gate, gateway, lobby, opening, threshold, way in. **2** (admission) access, admission, admittance, entrance, right of entry. **3** (in a diary) account, description, item, note, record

envelop *v* blanket, cover, encase, enclose, enfold, engulf, shroud, surround, swathe, veil, wrap

envelope *n* bubble bag, case, casing, cover, covering, folder, mailing bag, sheathe, skin, wrapper

enviable *adj* desirable, favored, fine, fortunate, privileged, plum *inf*, sought-after, worth having

envious *adj* green-eyed, green with envy, jealous, resentful

environment *n* conditions, context, environs, habitat, locale, locality, milieu, setting, situation, surroundings

envisage *v* anticipate, conceive of, contemplate, expect, imagine, picture, see, suppose, visualize

envoy *n* agent, ambassador, consul, delegate, emissary, go-between, intermediary, messenger, representative

envy *n* enviousness, jealousy, resentfulness, resentment

ephemeral *adj* brief, evanescent, fleeting, momentary, passing, short-lived, temporary, throwaway, transient

epidemic *n* outbreak, plague, rash, scourge, wave

epidemic *adj* global, pandemic, prevalent, rampant, rife, spreading, sweeping, universal, widespread

episode *n* **1** affair, chapter, escapade, event, experience, incident, interlude, matter, occasion, occurrence. **2** edition, installment, part, scene, section

epitome *n* embodiment, essence, model,

personification, prototype
epoch *n* age, date, day, era, generation, period, time
equal *adj* **1** alike, comparable, identical, equivalent, on a par, similar, the same, uniform. **2** even, evenly matched, fifty-fifty, level, neck-and-neck. **3** egalitarian, even-handed, fair, impartial, just, unbiased
equal *n* clone, counterpart, equivalent, match, twin
equality *n* egalitarianism, equal opportunity, fairness, impartiality, justice; ***opp*** discrimination, inequality
equalize *v* balance, compensate, equate, even up, level, level the score, make equal, match, standardize
equate *v* associate, be equivalent, compare, correspond to, draw a parallel between, group together, liken, link, pair, regard as the same, talk of in the same breath
equation *n* calculation, sum
equilibrium *n* balance, evenness, stability, symmetry
equip *v* arm, fit out, furnish, prepare, provide, supply
equipment *n* apparatus, gear, instruments, kit *inf*, machinery, materials, rig, stuff, supplies, tackle, things, tools, trappings, utensils
equivalent *adj* alike, analogous, comparable, corresponding, equal, identical, interchangeable, matching, on a par, similar, the same, twin; ***opp*** dissimilar
equivocal *adj* ambiguous, ambivalent, doubtful, dubious, evasive, hesitant, qualified, questionable, uncertain, vague; ***opp*** categorical, definite, unequivocal
era *n* age, date, day, epoch, generation, period, stage, time
eradicate *v* abolish, annihilate, destroy, eliminate, expunge, exterminate, get rid of, obliterate, remove, root out, stamp out, take out, weed out, wipe out
erase *v* blot out, cancel, cross out, delete, remove, rub out, scratch out, scrub out, wipe out
erect *adj* perpendicular, rigid, standing, stiff, straight, straight as a ramrod, upright, vertical
erect *v* assemble, build, construct, pitch, put together, put up, set up; ***opp*** demolish, dismantle, take down
erode *v* abrade, corrode, eat away, rub away, wash away, wear away, weather
erotic *adj* amorous, aphrodisiac, pornographic, raunchy, sensual, sexual, sexy, steamy, suggestive
err *v* be mistaken, be wrong, blunder, do wrong, get it wrong, get the wrong end of the stick, go wrong, make a mistake, make an error, miscalculate, slip up
errand *n* assignment, chore, job, message, task
erratic *adj* changeable, chaotic, fickle, inconsistent, irregular, meandering, sporadic, unpredictable, unreliable; ***opp*** constant, regular
error *n* blunder, boo-boo *inf*, bug, fault, gaffe, miscalculation, misprint, mistake, oversight, slip-up *inf*
erupt *v* blow up, burst out, explode, flare up, go off, gush, spew out, spout
escalate *v* accelerate, climb, get worse, grow, heighten, increase, intensify,

mount, rise, spiral, step up

escapade *n* adventure, affair, episode, exploit, incident, prank, stunt

escape *n* **1** breakout, flight, flit, getaway, jailbreak. **2** discharge, emission, leak, leakage, seepage

escape *v* **1** abscond, bolt, break loose, break out, get away, get free, get out, run away, run off, flit *inf*. **2** (escape doing sth) avoid, dodge, duck, evade. **3** (leak) bleed, discharge, drain, leak, ooze, seep

escort *n* attendant, bodyguard, chaperon, companion, date, entourage, guard, outrider, partner, retinue

escort *v* accompany, conduct, go with, guide, lead, partner, shepherd, take

essay *n* article, assignment, comment, composition, critique, paper, piece, treatise, review, writings

essence *n* **1** core, crux, essential part, fundamental principle, heart, innermost being, marrow, nature, spirit, substance. **2** concentrate, essential oil, extract, flavoring, tincture

essential *adj* critical, crucial, important, indispensable, key, necessary, vital. **2** basic, cardinal, fundamental, inherent, intrinsic, principal

establish *v* **1** create, form, found, install, put in place, set up, start. **2** confirm, demonstrate, prove, show, verify

established *adj* accepted, deep-rooted, entrenched, ingrained, long-standing, orthodox, official, settled, traditional, tried-and-tested

establishment *n* **1** creation, formation, foundation, inauguration, inception, setting up. **2** business, company, concern, firm, household, office, organization, outfit *inf*, residence, shop, store. **3 the Establishment** big brother *inf*, bureaucracy, the authorities, the government, the powers that be, the ruling classes, the system

estate *n* **1** domain, holding, land, park, property. **2** assets, belongings, fortune, inheritance, possessions, property

esteem *n* acclaim, admiration, approbation, favor, good opinion, honor, kudos, prestige, regard, respect, reverence

estimate *n* approximation, assessment, ballpark figure, calculation, evaluation, guess, guesstimate *inf*, judgment, reckoning, rough figure

estimate *v* **1** (cost) assess, calculate, evaluate, gauge, judge, reckon, value, work out. **2** (believe) appraise, assess, believe, consider, judge, rate, reckon, surmise, think, view

estimation *n* **1** (opinion) appraisal, assessment, belief, consideration, considered opinion, evaluation, judgment, opinion, view, way of thinking. **2** (esteem) admiration, approval, esteem, good opinion, regard, respect

estranged *adj* alienated, antagonized, apart, at odds, divided, going their separate ways, separated

eternal *adj* **1** abiding, everlasting, deathless, immortal, infinite, permanent, perpetual, timeless, unceasing, undying, without end. **2** ceaseless, constant, continual, continuous, endless, everlasting, incessant, interminable, never-ending, nonstop, perpetual, unending

eternity *n* 1 ages, an age, endlessness, forever, infinity, long time, timelessness. 2 afterlife, heaven, paradise, the hereafter, the next world, world without end

ethical *adj* correct, decent, fair, good, honest, honorable, just, moral, principled, proper, right, upright, virtuous

ethics *n* moral code, morality, morals, principles, standards, values

ethnic *adj* 1 cultural, national, native, racial, tribal. 2 folk, traditional

etiquette *n* 1 (politeness) civility, courtesy, decorum, good manners, politeness, propriety. 2 (convention) accepted behavior, code of behavior, code of conduct, code of practice, convention, custom, manners, propriety, protocol, the proprieties

evacuate *v* abandon, desert, flee, go away from, leave, move out of, pull out of *inf*, quit, retreat from, vacate, withdraw from

evade *v* 1 avoid, dodge, duck *inf*, elude, escape, give sb the slip, keep out of the way of, shake off, sidestep, steer clear of; ***opp*** confront. 2 (evade a question or issue) avoid, beat about the bush, dodge, equivocate, fudge, hedge, not give a straight answer to, quibble about, prevaricate. 3 (evade work) avoid, dodge, shirk, skive *inf*

evaluate *v* appraise, assess, estimate, gauge, judge, put a value on, rate, reckon, size up, value, weigh up

evaporate *v* 1 dry, dry up, vaporize. 2 disappear, disperse, dissipate, dissolve, fade away, melt away, vanish

evasive *adj* 1 (of a person, tactic) artful, cagey *inf*, cunning, devious, disingenuous, elusive, shifty. 2 (of a reply) ambiguous, disingenuous, equivocal, indirect, misleading, oblique, prevaricating; ***opp*** direct

even *adj* 1 (level) flat, flush, horizontal, level, plane, smooth, uniform. 2 (steady, constant) consistent, constant, regular, stable, steady, unbroken, unchanging, uniform, unvarying. 3 (equal) alike, all square, balanced, equal, identical, level, much the same, on an equal footing, similar, the same, tied. 4 (fair) balanced, disinterested, equitable, evenhanded, fair, impartial, just, unbiased. 5 **get even** be revenged, get your own back, get your revenge, give as good as you get, pay sb back, reciprocate, revenge yourself, settle the score

event *n* 1 episode, experience, happening, occasion, occurrence, phenomenon. 2 (sporting event) competition, contest, fixture, game, match, race, round, tournament

even-tempered *adj* calm, cool, easy-going, equable, laid back *inf*, imperturbable, peaceable, placid, relaxed, serene, unflappable, unruffled

eventful *adj* action-packed, active, busy, exciting, full, lively, never a dull moment

eventual *adj* concluding, consequent, ensuing, final, future, later, resulting, ultimate

eventually *adv* after all, at last, at the end of the day, finally, in the end, in the long run, in time, sooner or later, one day, one fine day *inf*, some day, sooner or later, when all is said and done

everlasting *adj* **1** deathless, enduring, eternal, immortal, imperishable, indestructible, infinite, lasting, never-ending, perpetual, timeless, undying, unending. **2** ceaseless, constant, continual, continuous, eternal, incessant, interminable, never-ending, nonstop, perpetual, tiresome, without let-up

everyday *adj* common, commonplace, customary, familiar, habitual, mundane, nothing special, ordinary, regular, routine, run-of-the-mill, standard, usual, workaday

evict *v* bounce *inf*, chuck out *inf*, dislodge, dispossess, drive out, eject, expel, give notice to quit, kick out *inf*, oust, put out, remove, show sb the door, throw out, throw sb out on his ear, turn out

evidence *n* **1** confirmation, corroboration, data, facts, indication, information, mark, proof, sign, substantiation, support, verification. **2** affidavit, declaration, deposition, statement, testimony. **3 give evidence** swear on oath, testify, witness. **4 in evidence** conspicuous, evident, having a high profile, noticeable, obvious, on display, on view

evident *adj* (easy to see or understand) apparent, clear, easy to see, incontestable, incontrovertible, indisputable, manifest, noticeable, obvious, palpable, perceptible, plain, plain as the nose on your face *inf*, self-explanatory, tangible, transparent, undeniable, undoubted, unmistakable, visible

evidently *adv* **1** apparently, as far as you can tell, from all appearances, it appears, it seems, ostensibly, outwardly, seemingly. **2** clearly, obviously, surely, undoubtedly, without question

evil *adj* atrocious, bad, base, corrupt, cruel, demonic, diabolic, depraved, fiendish, foul, heinous, immoral, iniquitous, malicious, malevolent, shameful, sinful, vicious, vile, villainous, wicked; ***opp*** good

evil *n* **1** atrocity, badness, corruption, cruelty, depravity, immorality, vice, villainy, wickedness, wrong, wrong-doing. **2** affliction, calamity, curse, disaster, hardship, harm, misery, misfortune, pain, suffering, wrong

evocative *adj* bringing to mind, redolent, reminiscent, suggestive

evoke *v* **1** (a response or emotion) arouse, awaken, cause, elicit, excite, give rise to, induce, inspire, kindle, provoke, stimulate, stir up. **2** (an image or memory) call to mind, call up, conjure up, invoke, inspire, recall, summon up

evolution *n* **1** advance, development, emergence, growth, maturing, progress, progression, unfolding. **2** natural selection

evolve *v* change, develop, grow, expand, improve, mature, open out, progress, unfold

exact *adj* **1** (an exact copy) accurate, careful, correct, explicit, faithful, literal, precise, strict, true, word for word. **2** (of a person) accurate, careful, conscientious, meticulous, painstaking, precise, punctilious

exact *v* call for, compel, demand, enforce, extort, extract, impose, insist on, require

exactly *adv* **1** (quite right) absolutely, certainly, definitely, indeed, precisely, quite, quite right, quite so. **2** accurately, carefully, correctly, faithfully, precisely, strictly, to the letter, word for word. **3 not exactly** by no means, not at all, not really

exaggerate *v* amplify, embellish, embroider, magnify, make a drama out of, make a mountain out of a molehill, make too much of, overemphasize, overestimate, overrate, overstate, stretch the truth, talk up *inf*

exaggeration *n* embellishment, embroidery, hyperbole, inflation, overestimation, overstatement

examination *n* **1** (the examination of sth) appraisal, analysis, consideration, exploration, inspection, investigation, observation, perusal, probe, review, scrutiny. **2** (undergo an examination) check-up, inspection, the once-over *inf*. **3** (of a witness) cross-examination, interrogation, questioning. **4** assessment, exam, test

examine *v* **1** analyze, appraise, assess, check out, consider, explore, look into, scrutinize, study, weigh, weigh up. **2** check, give the once-over *inf*, go over, inspect, look at, look over, observe, peruse, scan, take a look at. **3** (examine a witness) cross-examine, grill *inf*, interrogate, question, test

example *n* **1** case, case in point, illustration, instance, sample, specimen. **2** ideal, model, paragon, pattern, standard. **3 for example** as an illustration, e.g., for instance, such as

exasperate *v* anger, annoy, drive crazy *inf*, enrage, get on your nerves, incense, infuriate, irk, irritate, madden, make your blood boil, needle *inf*, provoke, rouse, try the patience of, vex, wind up *inf*

excavate *v* burrow, dig, dig out, dig up, hollow out, mine, tunnel, uncover, unearth

exceed *v* **1** (be better than) beat, be better than, be greater than, better, do more than, excel, outdo, outshine, outstrip, surpass. **2** (be more than) be greater than, be more than, go beyond, pass, top. **3** (go beyond a limit) do more than, go beyond, go over, go over the top, overstep

excel *v* **1** (be better than) beat, be better than, be superior to, do better than, eclipse, outdo, outclass, outshine, outstrip, overshadow, surpass. **2** (be very good) be excellent, be outstanding, be very good, do well, shine, stand out

excellence *n* distinction, eminence, greatness, high quality, merit, quality, perfection, superiority, value, worth

excellent *adj* **1** (very good) ace *inf*, brilliant *inf*, exceptional, fabulous *inf*, fantastic *inf*, great, marvelous, outstanding, perfect, superb, superior, wonderful; ***opp*** awful, dreadful. **2** (of good quality) A1, choice, exquisite, fine, first-class, first rate, good quality, of high quality, prime, select. **3** (admirable) admirable, exemplary, superior, supreme, worthy

exception *n* **1** anomaly, departure, deviation, freak, irregularity, oddity, special case. **2** exclusion, omission. **3 with the exception of** apart from, bar, but for, except, except for, excepting. **4 take exception** be offended, object to, resent, take offense, take umbrage

exceptional *adj* **1** (unusually good) excellent, outstanding, phenomenal, prodigious, remarkable, special. **2** (unusual) abnormal, atypical, odd, out of the ordinary, peculiar, rare, unusual; ***opp*** normal, usual

excerpt *n* clip, extract, part, passage, quotation, quote, selection

excess *n* **1** abundance, glut, more than enough, overdose, overkill *inf*, surfeit, surplus, too much, too many. **2** leftovers, overflow, remainder, residue. **3** debauchery, dissipation, intemperance, overindulgence

excessive *adj* exaggerated, extravagant, immoderate, inordinate, lavish, needless, overdone, over the top *inf*, superfluous, uncalled-for, undue, unnecessary, unreasonable, unwarranted

exchange *n* barter, dealing, give and take, interchange, substitution, swap *inf*, switch, trade, trade-off

exchange *v* **1** barter, do a swap *inf*, reciprocate, swap *inf*, trade. **2** change, interchange, replace, substitute, swap *inf*, switch, trade in

excitable *adj* **1** edgy, emotional, highly strung, jumpy, lively, nervous, restive, volatile. **2** hasty, hot-headed, quick-tempered, temperamental, testy, touchy; ***opp*** calm

excite *v* **1** (make sb excited) agitate, arouse, disturb, get sb going *inf*, inflame, provoke, rouse, set off *inf*, stimulate, stir up, thrill, titillate, turn on *inf*, upset, wind up *inf*, work up *inf*. **2** (arouse feelings) arouse, awaken, cause, evoke, incite, inspire, kindle, stir up

excited *adj* **1** agog, animated, aroused, boisterous, enthusiastic, exhilarated, exuberant, high *inf*, in high spirits, intoxicated, thrilled, turned on *inf*. **2** agitated, at fever pitch, frantic, frenzied, hysterical, in a frenzy, overwrought, wound up

excitement *n* **1** agitation, animation, anticipation, elation, exhilaration, enthusiasm, ferment, tumult. **2** adventure, kick *inf*, thrill

exciting *adj* **1** (of an experience) dramatic, electrifying, exhilarating, heady, stimulating, stirring, thrilling; ***opp*** dull, boring. **2** (of a story, film) action-packed, dramatic, fast-moving, gripping, riveting, spectacular, spine-tingling; ***opp*** dull, boring

exclaim *v* blurt out, call, call out, come out with, cry, cry out, shout, utter, yell

exclude *v* **1** (keep out) ban, bar, blacklist, debar, forbid, ignore, keep out, leave out, ostracize, pass over, prohibit, proscribe, refuse, reject, repudiate, shut out. **2** (be exclusive of) be apart from, be exclusive of, except; ***opp*** include

exclusive *adj* **1** closed, limited, posh *inf*, private, restricted, select, selective, smart, snobbish. **2** only, single, sole, unique. **3 exclusive of** apart from, excluding, not including

excursion *n* day trip, expedition, jaunt, outing, pleasure trip, tour, trip

excuse *n* **1** apology, defense, explanation, justification, mitigation, mitigating circumstances, plea, pretext, reason. **2** cop-out *inf*, ostensible reason, pretense, pretext, rationalization

excuse *v* **1** (a person) absolve, allow sb to get away with sth, exonerate, forgive, let off, make allowances for, pardon. **2** (excuse bad behavior) condone, defend, explain, explain away, forgive, ignore, justify, mitigate, pardon. **3** (excuse sb from doing sth) exempt, free sb from, let sb off, liberate sb from, release sb from, relieve, spare

execute *v* **1** carry out the death sentence, kill, lynch, put to death. **2** (execute a plan) accomplish, achieve, carry out, discharge, do, effect, enact, fulfill, implement, perform, put into practice, realize

execution *n* **1** capital punishment, death sentence, killing, putting to death. **2** (the execution of a plan) accomplishment, achievement, carrying out, discharge, effecting, fulfillment, implementation, performance, realization

executioner *n* hit-man *inf*, killer

executive *adj* administrative, controlling, decision-making, directing, governing, managerial

executive *n* **1** administrator, boss *inf*, chief *inf*, director, manager, officer, official. **2** administration, government, leadership, management, top brass *inf*

exemplify *v* **1** (give an example of) demonstrate, give an example, illustrate, show. **2** (be an example) be an example of, be typical of, epitomize, represent, symbolize, typify

exempt *adj* excepted, excused, free from, immune, let off, not liable to, released from, spare

exempt *v* except, exclude, excuse, free sb from, grant immunity from, let sb off, make an exception for, release sb from, spare

exercise *n* **1** (physical exercise) activity, effort, exertion, games, gym, gymnastics, keep fit, movement, sport, training, workout. **2** (use) application, employment, practice, use, utilization

exercise *v* **1** (take exercise) do exercises, drill, exert yourself, take exercise, train, work out. **2** (use) apply, employ, exert, make use of, practice, use, utilize

exert *v* **1** apply, bring to bear, employ, make use of, use, utilize, wield. **2** (exert yourself) apply yourself, do your best, do your utmost, drive yourself hard, give your all, go all out, make an effort, push yourself, put yourself out, strain, strive, struggle, toil, work hard

exertion *n* activity, action, effort, endeavor, exercise, hard work, strain, toil, work

exhaust *v* **1** (tire) burn out *inf*, debilitate, do in *inf*, drain, enervate, fatigue, knock out *inf*, overtax, sap your strength, take it out of you, tire, tire out, wear out, weary. **2** (use up) consume, deplete, dissipate, drain, empty, finish off, finish up, run out of, run through, spend, squander, use up, waste

exhausted *adj* **1** (tired) all in, burnt out, bushed, dead beat *inf*, dead on your feet *inf*, debilitated, dog-tired *inf*, drained, enervated, faint, fatigued, prostrate, ready to drop, shattered *inf*, spent, tired out, worn out. **2** (used up) all gone, at an end, depleted, finished, spent, used up

exhausting *adj* arduous, back-breaking, debilitating, enervating, fatiguing, grueling, laborious, punishing, tiring, taxing, wearing, wearying; ***opp*** easy

exhaustive *adj* all-embracing, careful, complete, comprehensive, full, in-depth, intensive, thorough

exhibit *v* **1** (exhibit things) demonstrate, display, flaunt, parade, present, put on display, put on a show, put on view, show, show off, unveil. **2** (exhibit a quality, feeling) betray, disclose, display, express, give away, flaunt, indicate, reveal, show, show off

exhibition *n* **1** (of things) demonstration, display, exposition, fair, presentation, show. **2** (of feelings) demonstration, display, expression, indication, revelation

exhilarating *adj* breathtaking, exciting, thrilling

exile *n* **1** banishment, deportation, expulsion, transportation. **2** (a person) deportee, displaced person, outcast, refugee

exile *v* banish, bar, deport, drive out, eject, evict, expel, send into exile, uproot

exist *v* **1** be, be extant, be found, be in existence, be real, happen, live, occur. **2** (survive) continue, endure, last, live, persist, remain, stay alive, stay in existence, subsist, survive

existence *n* **1** actuality, being, existing, fact, living, reality. **2** (survival) duration, endurance, persistence, subsistence, survival. **3** (way of life) life, lifestyle, way of life

exit *n* **1** escape, outlet, passage, vent, way out. **2** departure, escape, exodus, going, leaving, retreat, withdrawal

exodus *n* emigration, escape, exit, flight, leaving, migration, retreat; ***opp*** arrival

exorbitant *adj* excessive, extortionate, extreme, high, inordinate, outrageous, preposterous, ridiculous, steep, unreasonable; ***opp*** modest

exotic *adj* **1** (foreign) alien, foreign, imported, introduced, non-native. **2** (different and exciting) bizarre, colorful, curious, extraordinary, fascinating, glamorous, mysterious, novel, odd, outlandish, peculiar, sensational, striking, unusual

expand *v* **1** (make sth bigger) amplify, augment, broaden, build up, develop, dilate, distend, diversify, elaborate, enlarge, extend, fill out, increase, inflate, make bigger, make larger, open up, widen. **2** (become bigger) become bigger, become larger, get bigger, grow, increase in size, open out, stretch, swell, widen; ***opp*** contract

expanse *n* **1** (size) area, breadth, extent, range, spread, vastness. **2** (expanse of land, sea) area, plain, stretch, sweep, tract

expect *v* **1** assume, believe, calculate, guess, imagine, presume, reckon, suppose, surmise, suspect, think, think likely, trust. **2** anticipate, await, be prepared for, envisage, foresee, hope for, look forward to, plan for, predict, wait for. **3** call for, consider necessary, demand, insist on, look for, require, want

expectant *adj* **1** anxious, eager, expecting, hopeful, in suspense, keyed up, looking forward to, on tenterhooks, ready, ready and waiting. **2** (expecting a baby) expecting, having a baby, in the family way *inf*, pregnant

expectation *n* **1** assumption, belief, calculation, conjecture, forecast, likelihood, presumption, probability, reckoning, surmise, supposition, trust. **2** anticipation, expectancy, hope, readiness

expectations *n* hopes, outlook, prospects

expedition *n* enterprise, excursion, exploration, journey, mission, outing, pilgrimage, quest, safari, tour, trek, trip, voyage

expel *v* **1** (send sb away) ban, banish, cast out, chuck out *inf*, deport, drive out, eject, evict, exile, kick out *inf*, oust, remove, send away, send packing *inf*, throw out, turn out. **2** (send sth out) belch, discharge, eject, emit, force out, give off, push out, send out, spew out

expend *v* **1** (time, money) disburse, dish out *inf*, fork out *inf*, fritter, fritter away, lavish, lay out, pay out, shell out *inf*, spend, squander, waste. **2** (use up) consume, deplete, drain, exhaust, finish off, use, use up

expendable *adj* dispensable, disposable, inessential, nonessential, replaceable, unimportant, unnecessary

expenditure *n* costs, disbursements, expenses, outgoings, overheads, payments, spending; ***opp*** income, revenue

expense *n* **1** cost, expenditure, investment, money, outlay, price, spending. **2 at the expense of** in place of, instead of, rather than, to the detriment of, to the disadvantage of

expensive *adj* beyond sb's means, costly, dear, exorbitant, extortionate, overpriced, pricey, prohibitive; ***opp*** cheap, inexpensive

experience *n* **1** (sth that happens to you) encounter, episode, event, incident, occurrence, perception, sensation. **2** competence, expertise, familiarity, grounding, knowledge, maturity, record, track record, wisdom; ***opp*** inexperience

experienced *adj* competent, expert, familiar, knowledgable, mature, versed, well-versed, wise; ***opp*** inexperienced

experiment *n* **1** attempt, pilot study, test, trial, try-out, venture. **2** (the practice of experimenting) experimentation, innovation, research, testing, trial and error

experiment *v* **1** carry out experiments, conduct experiments, explore, improvise, innovate, play around. **2 experiment with** explore, investigate, pilot, research, test, try, try out

experimental *adj* avant-garde, exploratory, innovative, new, pilot, probationary

expert *adj* adept, advanced, brainy *inf*, capable, competent, experienced, practiced, proficient, qualified, skillful, skilled, specialist, technical

expert *n* academic, authority, brain, brains, connoisseur, egghead *inf*, maestro, mastermind, professional, pundit, sage, specialist

expertise *n* command, competence, dexterity, experience, proficiency, skillfulness, skill, mastery, professionalism, proficiency, specialism

expire *v* 1 breathe your last, depart this world, die, kick the bucket *inf*, pass away, pass on, perish, snuff it *inf*. 2 (of a document) become invalid, cease, come to an end, end, finish, go out of date, lapse, run out

explain *v* account for, answer, clarify, clear up, describe, give a reason for, interpret, make clear/plain, solve, spell out, throw light on

explanation *n* account, answer, clarification, defense, description, elucidation, excuse, explication, hypothesis, interpretation, justification, reason, reply

explanatory *adj* descriptive, illuminating, illustrative, informative, revealing, theoretical

explicit *adj* categorical, clear, crystal clear, definite, detailed, direct, distinct, exact, express, obvious, overt, patent, plain, precise, specific, straightforward, unambiguous, unequivocal; ***opp*** implicit

explode *v* 1 (sth explodes) blow up, burst, erupt, fly apart, go bang, go off, go up, implode. 2 (explode sth) blast, blow up, detonate, drop, let off, set off, trigger

exploit *n* accomplishment, achievement, adventure, deed, feat, stunt, triumph

exploit *v* 1 (use sth) capitalize on, develop, employ, make use of, press into service, put to good use, take advantage of, use, utilize, work. 2 (use sb unfairly) abuse, impose on, manipulate, overwork, take advantage of, use, walk all over

exploration *n* 1 discovery, expedition, journey, travel, visit, voyage. 2 (of an issue, problem) analysis, consideration, discussion, examination, inquiry, investigation, research, study, survey

explore *v* 1 discover, journey, look around, travel, visit, voyage. 2 analyze, consider, discuss, examine, go into, inquire into, investigate, look into, probe, research, survey

explosion *n* 1 bang, blast, boom, burst, detonation, eruption, gunshot, mushroom cloud, report. 2 (of new developments, ideas) escalation, expansion, flowering, growth, increase, outbreak, mushrooming

explosive *adj* 1 combustible, exploding, flammable, incendiary, inflammable, unstable, volatile. 2 (likely to cause trouble) controversial, highly charged, sensational, tense, unstable, volatile

explosive *n* charge, dynamite, gunpowder, plastic explosive, TNT

exponent *n* advocate, apologist, backer, champion, practitioner, propagandist, promoter, proponent, supporter

expose *v* 1 bare, denude, display, exhibit, flash, lay bare, reveal, show, uncover, unveil. 2 (expose dishonesty) bring to light, draw attention to, highlight, reveal, uncover, unmask

exposed *adj* bare, for all to see, in full view, naked, on display, open, public, unprotected, vulnerable

exposure *n* 1 (publicity) advertising, coverage, publicity. 2 (revealing of sth) baring, disclosure, display, revelation, showing, uncovering, unmasking, unveiling

express *adj* 1 clear, conscious, deliberate, distinct, explicit, expressed, intentional, manifest, plain, willful. 2 fast, first-class, nonstop, prompt, quick, rapid, special, speedy, swift

express *v* announce, articulate, communicate, convey, declare, describe, display, give vent to, indicate, make known, manifest, put into words, say, show, speak, state, utter, verbalize, voice

expression *n* **1** announcement, articulation, communication, declaration, demonstration, description, display, exhibition, indication, manifestation, reflection, statement, voicing. **2** (group of words) figure of speech, idiom, phrase, proverb, saying, utterance. **3** (on sb's face) air, appearance, countenance, face, look, mien

expressive *adj* articulate, colorful, demonstrative, descriptive, eloquent, emotional, explicit, lyrical, moving, poetic, poignant, suggestive, vivid

exquisite *adj* artistic, beautiful, delicate, excellent, fine, high-quality, lovely, ornate, perfect, refined, superb, sublime, tasteful

extend *v* **1** (make bigger) add to, augment, elongate, enlarge, expand, increase, lengthen, prolong, spread, stretch, stretch out. **2** (extend to full size) pay out, pull out, put up, stretch out, uncoil, unfold, unroll. **3** (extend over an area) cover, range, reach, span, spread, stretch. **4** (extend a deadline) postpone, protract, put back, put off, relax, reschedule. **5** (give) advance, give, grant, hold out, impart, offer, make available, proffer

extension *n* **1** accessory, addition, adjunct, add-on, appendage, enlargement, expansion. **2** (to a house) annex, conservatory, lean-to, outbuilding, outhouse, wing

extensive *adj* comprehensive, considerable, enormous, great, large, lengthy, long, prolonged, sizeable, vast, wide, wide-ranging, widespread

extent *n* area, breadth, dimensions, expanse, length, magnitude, range, scope, size, spread

extenuating *adj* exceptional, exonerating, justifying, mitigating, qualifying

exterior *adj* external, outer, outermost, outside, outward, surface

exterior *n* facade, face, outside, outward appearance, shell, surface

exterminate *v* annihilate, destroy, eliminate, eradicate, extirpate, kill, massacre, slaughter, wipe out

external *adj* exterior, outer, outermost, outside, outward, surface

extinct *adj* dead, defunct, died out, exhausted, extinguished, gone, lost, vanished, wiped out

extinguish *v* **1** destroy, end, eradicate, kill, quench, snuff out, stifle, suppress. **2** (extinguish a fire, light) blow out, put off, put out, smother, snuff out, switch off, turn off, turn out

extortionate *adj* dear, excessive, exorbitant, expensive, outrageous, overpriced

extra *adj* added, additional, bonus, further, more, supplementary, surplus

extra *n* **1** accessory, addition, additive, add-on, bonus, supplement, surplus. **2** (in a film) bit part, chorus girl, non-speaking part, walk-on part

extract *n* **1** concentrate, derivative,

essence. **2** (piece of writing) cutting, excerpt, highlight, part, quotation, quote, selection

extract *v* abstract, derive, distill, draw, draw out, obtain, pull out, remove, select, take out

extraordinary *adj* amazing, astonishing, exceptional, incredible, marvelous, out of the ordinary, outstanding, rare, remarkable, singular, striking, unique, unusual, wonderful; ***opp*** ordinary

extravagant *adj* excessive, immoderate, overgenerous, spendthrift, squandering, wasteful

extreme *adj* **1** (great) absolute, acute, drastic, great, high, intense, severe, utmost. **2** furthest, furthest away, most distant, outer, remotest. **3** (extreme views, measures) drastic, exaggerated, excessive, fanatical, harsh, radical, uncompromising, unreasonable, over-the-top

extreme *n* absolute, boundary, edge, end, extremity, height, limit, maximum, ultimate

extremist *n* diehard, fanatic, militant, radical, ultra, zealot; ***opp*** moderate

extremity *n* boundary, edge, end, extreme, limit, tip

extricate *v* disembroil, disentangle, free, loose, rescue, unravel, untangle

extroverted *adj* boisterous, extrovert, friendly, fun-loving, gregarious, lively, loud, outgoing, outward-looking, sociable, talkative; ***opp*** introverted

exuberant *adj* celebrating, cheerful, effervescent, elated, enthusiastic, irrepressible, joyful, joyous, jubilant, rejoicing, sparkling, vivacious

eye *v* gaze at, glance at, inspect, keep an eye on, look at, peer at, regard, scrutinize, stare at, study, survey, watch

eyesight *n* eyes, perception, powers of observation, range of vision, sight, vision

eyesore *n* blemish, blight, blot on the landscape, disfigurement, monstrosity, scar

eyewitness *n* bystander, observer, onlooker, spectator, witness

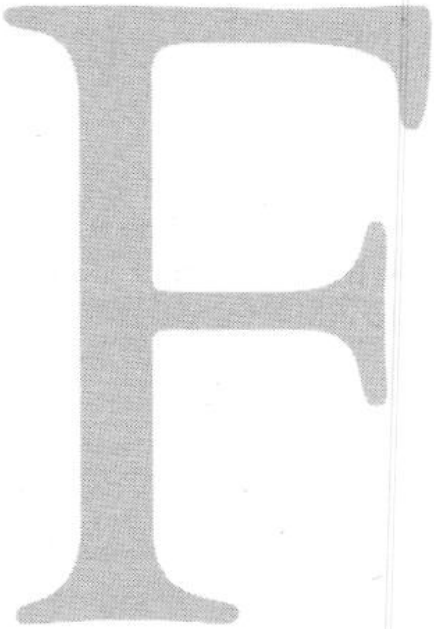

fabric *n* **1** cloth, material, textile. **2** (the fabric of society) constitution, essence, framework, make-up, nature, structure

fabricate *v* **1** (falsely) concoct, fake, forge, invent, make up. **2** assemble, construct, make, make up, manufacture, produce, put together

fabulous *adj* **1** (good) ace *inf*, brilliant, fantastic, good, great, super, superb, wonderful. **2** (imaginary) fantastic, imaginary, invented, legendary, make-believe, mythical

face *n* **1** complexion, countenance, expression, head, mug *inf*, physiognomy, visage. **2** (outward appearance) appearance, aspect, facet, side, surface

face *v* **1** (of a person) gaze at, look sb in the face, look towards, stare at, turn to, turn towards. **2** (of a building) be opposite, front onto, give onto, have a view of, look out on, overlook. **3** (in a contest) be opposed to, confront, meet, play, play against. **4** (face a problem) accept, come to terms with, confront, deal with, face up to; ***opp*** avoid. **5** (a problem that faces sb) be before sb, be in store, confront, lie ahead, present itself

facetious *adj* flippant, frivolous, humorous, ironic, jocular, jokey, joking, sarcastic, silly, teasing, tongue-in-cheek

facile *adj* banal, glib, oversimplified, shallow, silly, trite; ***opp*** profound

facilitate *v* aid, allow, assist, enable, encourage, help, make easier, permit, simplify, speed up

facility *n* **1 facilities** amenities, comforts, equipment, resources, service. **2** dexterity, ease, effortlessness, elegance, fluency, simplicity

fact *n* **1** actuality, certainty, reality, truth. **2 in fact** actually, as a matter of fact, as it happens, in actual fact, indeed, in point of fact, in reality, in truth, really

faction *n* band, camp, caucus, clique, group, lobby, party, pressure group, ring, section, set, splinter group

factor *n* aspect, component, consideration, detail, element, facet, influence, ingredient, part

factory *n* foundry, industrial unit, mill, plant, works, workshop

factual *adj* accurate, authentic, exact, faithful, informative, objective, real, real-life, true, true to life, truthful, unbiased; ***opp*** fictional

faculty *n* **1** (in a university) department, division, section, school. **2** ability, aptitude, capability, capacity, sense. **3 faculties** awareness, cognition, consciousness, perception, reason, understanding

fade *v* **1** (of colors) become pale, dim, dull, grow pale. **2** (become less) decline, die away, disappear, dwindle, grow faint, vanish, wane

fail *v* **1** be defeated, break down, collapse, come to grief, crash, draw a blank, fall down, fall flat, fall short, fall through, founder, go bankrupt, go under, lose, malfunction, miscarry, misfire, miss, stumble; ***opp*** succeed. **2 fail to do sth** avoid, decline, neglect, omit, refuse. **3** (fail a person) abandon, desert, disappoint, forsake, let down. **4** (fail an exam) be unsuccessful, drop out, flunk; ***opp*** pass

failing *n* defect, drawback, failure, fault, imperfection, inadequacy, shortcoming, weakness

failure *n* **1** bankruptcy, breakdown, collapse, defeat, malfunction; ***opp*** success. **2** (failure to do sth) dereliction of duty, inability, omission, oversight, refusal. **3** (sb who has failed) incompetent, loser. **4** (sth that has failed) disaster, dud, flop, washout; ***opp*** success

faint *adj* **1** barely audible, barely perceptible, barely visible, blurred, dim, feeble, indistinct, quiet, soft, unclear, weak; ***opp*** bright, loud. **2** (feel faint) dizzy, giddy, light-headed, weak, woozy *inf*

faint *v* black out, collapse, lose consciousness, pass out, swoon; ***opp*** come round, come to

fair *adj* **1** balanced, equitable, even-handed, honest, impartial, just, legitimate, objective, reasonable, right, sporting, unbiased, unprejudiced. **2** (of hair) blond, blonde, flaxen, yellow. **3** (of skin) light, pale, white

faith *n* **1** commitment, confidence, conviction, expectation, hope, loyalty, sincerity, trust. **2** (religious belief) belief, communion, confession, congregation, creed, denomination, religion

faithful *adj* **1** committed, loyal, reliable, true, trusting, trusty. **2 be faithful to** believe in, have confidence in, keep faith with, stand by, stick to, trust in

fake *adj* artificial, counterfeit, fabricated, false, forged, fraudulent, imitation, sham; ***opp*** genuine

fake *v* copy, counterfeit, fabricate, falsify, forge, pretend, simulate

fall *n* **1** collapse, descent, slip, stumble, trip, tumble. **2** collapse, decline, decrease, dip, drop, falling-off; ***opp*** rise. **3** (the fall of sb in power) defeat, demise, dismissal, downfall, end, fall from grace, impeachment, removal, resignation; ***opp*** rise

fall *v* **1** (move downwards) be dropped, collapse, come crashing down, descend, drop, plop, plummet, sink, stumble, tip over, topple over, trip, tumble. **2** (of a person) collapse, fall down, fall over, keel over, lose your balance, slip, stumble, trip, tumble. **3** (of a price, amount) be marked down, collapse, come down, decline, decrease, drop, fall off, go down, plummet, slump, tumble; ***opp*** rise. **4** (of sb in power) be defeated, be dismissed, be impeached, be kicked out *inf*, be ousted, be voted out, fall from grace, lose office, lose power, resign, stand down. **5 fall out** argue, disagree, have a difference of opinion, quarrel, row

fallacy *n* error, misconception, mistake, paradox

fallible *adj* erring, error-prone, flawed, human, imperfect, sinful, unreliable, weak; ***opp*** infallible

false *adj* **1** erroneous, fallacious, incorrect, invalid, mistaken, spurious, unfounded, untrue, wrong; ***opp*** true. **2** (of a person) deceitful, dishonest, disloyal, insincere, unfaithful. **3** artificial, counterfeit, fake, forged, imitation, mock, synthetic; ***opp*** real

falsify *v* alter, counterfeit, doctor, fabricate, fake, forge, lie about, manipulate, misrepresent, retouch, tamper with, touch up

falter *v* bumble, go wrong, hesitate, stammer, stutter

fame *n* celebrity, distinction, eminence, esteem, greatness, importance, infamy, note, notoriety, pre-eminence, renown, reputation, stardom

familiar *adj* **1** common, commonplace, conventional, customary, everyday, frequent, habitual, household, mundane, normal, ordinary, predictable, recognizable, regular, routine, run-of-the mill, stock, usual, well-known; ***opp*** unusual. **2** (of people) amiable, casual, close, confidential, cordial, easy, free, friendly, informal, intimate, open, relaxed, sociable, unceremonious, unreserved; ***opp*** formal. **3 familiar with** acquainted with, at home with, aware of, conscious of, conversant with, expert in, informed about, no stranger to, trained in, versed in, well up in

familiarize *v* accustom, acquaint, get to know, habituate, make familiar with, make conversant with

family *n* brood, flesh and blood, household, issue, kin, nearest and dearest *inf*, relations, relatives, tribe

famine *n* food shortage, hunger, lack of food, starvation

famished *adj* dying of hunger, dying of starvation, hungry, ravenous, starved, starving, undernourished; ***opp*** full

famous *adj* acclaimed, big, celebrated, eminent, famed, illustrious, legendary, much-publicized, notorious, prominent, renowned, well-known, world-famous; ***opp*** unknown

fan *n* adherent, admirer, aficionado, buff *inf*, devotee, enthusiast, fanatic, follower, lover, nut *inf*, supporter, zealot

fanatic *n* **1** (sports fanatic) enthusiast, fan, follower, lover, nut *inf*, supporter. **2** (religious fanatic) activist, extremist, maniac, militant, radical, zealot

fanatical *adj* enthusiastic, excessive, extreme, fervent, fervid, frenzied, mad, obsessive, overenthusiastic, passionate, rabid, wild, zealous; ***opp*** moderate

fanciful *adj* **1** (of a design) extravagant, fabulous, fairy-tale, fancy; ***opp*** simple. **2** (of an idea) fabulous, fantastic, ideal, imaginary, legendary, mythical, poetic, romantic, unreal, wild; ***opp*** realistic. **3** (of a person) capricious, imaginative, inventive, whimsical

fancy *adj* decorated, decorative, elaborate, elegant, embellished, embroidered, glitzy *inf*, intricate, jazzy *inf*, lavish, ornamental, ornamented, ornate, posh *inf*, showy, snazzy *inf*; ***opp*** plain

fancy *v* **1** (fancy that sth will happen) believe, conceive, conjecture, guess, imagine, infer, reckon, suppose, surmise, think. **2** (fancy a drink) crave, feel like, long for, want, would like, wish for, yearn for. **3** (fancy sb) be attracted to, be infatuated by, be mad on, desire, fall for, have a crush on, lust after, take a shine to, take to

fantastic *adj* **1** ace *inf*, brilliant, excellent, fabulous, first-class, first-rate, great, magnificent, marvelous, outstanding, phenomenal, sensational, splendid, super, superb, terrific, tremendous, wonderful; ***opp*** terrible. **2** (fantastic notions) absurd, amazing, eccentric, exaggerated, exotic, fanciful, far-fetched, freakish, grotesque, incredible, odd, peculiar, quaint, queer, strange, weird, whimsical, wild; ***opp*** ordinary

fantasy *n* daydream, delusion, fancy, illusion, imagination, invention, make-believe, reverie; ***opp*** reality

far *adv* **1** afar, a good way, a great distance, a long way, deep. **2** (far better) considerably, decidedly, greatly, incomparably, much; ***opp*** slightly. **3 so far** thus far, to date, until now, up to now, up to the present, up to this point

farce *n* **1** (type of humor) buffoonery, comedy, parody, satire, slapstick. **2** joke, mockery, nonsense, sham, travesty

farcical *adj* **1** (of a type of humor) amusing, comic, droll, funny, satirical, slapstick. **2** (not good) absurd, derisory, foolish, laughable, ludicrous, nonsensical, preposterous, ridiculous, risible, silly; ***opp*** reasonable

far-fetched *adj* doubtful, dubious, improbable, ridiculous, unbelievable, unconvincing, unlikely, unnatural, unrealistic; ***opp*** realistic

farm *n* holding, homestead, land, plantation, ranch

farm *v* cultivate, operate, plant, plow, work

farming *n* agriculture,cultivation, food-production, husbandry

far-reaching *adj* broad, comprehensive, extensive, important, significant, sweeping, widespread

fascinate *v* absorb, beguile, bewitch, captivate, charm, delight, enchant, engross, enrapture, enthrall, entrance, hypnotize, intrigue, mesmerize, rivet, transfix; ***opp*** bore

fascinated *adj* absorbed, captivated, enchanted, engrossed, enraptured, enthralled, entranced, hypnotized, intrigued, mesmerized, riveted, spellbound, transfixed; ***opp*** uninterested

fascinating *adj* absorbing, captivating, compelling, enchanting, engaging, engrossing, enrapturing, enthralling, entrancing, gripping, hypnotizing, interesting, intriguing, irresistible, mesmerizing, riveting; ***opp*** dull

fashion *n* **1** (the latest fashion) convention, craze, custom, fad, the latest thing, trend, vogue. **2** (in such a fashion) manner, method, mode, style, system, way

fashionable *adj* à la mode, chic, current, in *inf*, in fashion, in vogue, latest, modern, trendy *inf*, up-to-date, up-to-the-minute, with it *inf*; ***opp*** unfashionable

fast *adj* breakneck, brisk, hasty, high-speed, hurried, quick, rapid, speedy, supersonic, swift; ***opp*** slow

fast *n* abstinence, fasting, hunger strike

fast *v* abstain, go hungry, go on hunger strike, go without food

fasten *v* affix, anchor, attach, bind, bolt, buckle, chain, clamp, connect, couple, do up, fix, hitch, join, link, seal, secure, tether, tie; ***opp*** unfasten

fastener *n* anchor, binding, bolt, buckle, chain, clamp, connection, coupling, link, seal

fat *adj* beefy, chubby, corpulent, flabby, heavy, large, obese, overweight, plump, portly, pudgy, rotund, solid, squat, stocky, stout, tubby, weighty; ***opp*** thin

fat *n* blubber, bulk, corpulence, extra weight, flab, paunch

fatal *adj* **1** (resulting in sb's death) deadly, final, incurable, killing, lethal, malignant, mortal, pernicious, terminal; ***opp*** harmless. **2** (resulting in sth unpleasant) calamitous, catastrophic, dire, disastrous, lethal, ruinous; ***opp*** harmless

fatality *n* casualty, death, loss, victim; ***opp*** survivor

fate *n* **1** chance, destiny, doom, fortune, lot, predestination, providence. **2** (the fate of sth) end, future, issue, outcome, result, upshot

fateful *adj* catastrophic, disastrous, lethal, fated, ruinous

father *n* **1** dad, daddy, male parent, old man *inf*, pa *inf*, papa, pop *inf*. **2** (the father of sth) architect, creator, discoverer, founder, initiator, maker, originator

fatigue *n* exhaustion, heaviness, languor, lethargy, listlessness, overtiredness, tiredness, weariness; ***opp*** liveliness

fault *n* **1** blemish, defect, deficiency, drawback, failing, flaw, imperfection, shortcoming, snag, weakness, weak point. **2** blunder, boob *inf*, error, faux pas, gaffe *inf*, howler *inf*, inaccuracy, miscalculation, misspelling, mistake, omission, oversight, slip, slip-up

faulty *adj* bad, broken, damaged, defective, deficient, flawed, erroneous, impaired, imperfect, malfunctioning, on the blink *inf*, out of order, unusable, weak, wrong; ***opp*** faultless

favor *n* **1** (win sb's favor) acceptance, approbation, approval, backing, benevolence, esteem, good opinion, good will, liking, partiality, support. **2** (do sb a favor) courtesy, good turn, kindness, service

favor *v* **1** (favor doing sth) advocate, approve, back, be in sympathy with, endorse, promote, recommend, sanction, support; ***opp*** disapprove. **2** (favor sb) indulge, pamper, reward, show favoritism towards, spoil. **3** (favor sth) be partial to, go for *inf*, go in for *inf*, incline towards, like best, prefer; ***opp*** dislike

favorable *adj* **1** advantageous, appropriate, auspicious, beneficial, conducive, convenient, fair, fit, good, helpful, hopeful, in your favor, on your side, opportune, positive, promising, suitable, timely; ***opp*** unfavorable. **2** (favorable comments) approving, complimentary, congratulatory, encouraging, enthusiastic, good, laudatory, praising, well-disposed; ***opp*** unfavorable

favorite *adj* best, best-loved, choice, chosen, dearest, favored, ideal, most-liked, preferred, selected

favorite *n* **1** choice, first choice, pick, preference. **2** (a child) apple of your eye, darling, idol, pet, teacher's pet

fear *n* **1** alarm, anxiety, apprehension, butterflies, cowardice, dread, fearfulness, faintheartedness, foreboding, fright, horror, nervousness, panic, qualms, shivers, terror, timidity, trepidation, uneasiness; ***opp*** courage. **2** (a fear of sth) aversion, hang-up, horror, neurosis, nightmare, phobia; ***opp*** love

fear *v* be afraid of, be scared of, dare not, dread, live in fear/terror of, shrink from, shudder at, take fright, tremble at, worry about

fearful *adj* **1** (fearful of sth) afraid, alarmed, anxious, apprehensive, frightened, intimidated, nervous, panic-stricken, scared, scared stiff, terrified, timid, uneasy. **2** (a fearful noise) appalling, awful, dire, dreadful, frightful, ghastly, horrible, terrible

fearless *adj* bold, brave, confident, courageous, daring, gallant, gutsy *inf*, hard *inf*, heroic, intrepid, plucky, unafraid, undaunted, valiant; ***opp*** cowardly

fearsome *adj* alarming, awesome, daunting, formidable, frightening, hair-raising, horrifying, intimidating, menacing, terrifying, unnerving

feasible *adj* achievable, attainable, doable, likely, possible, practicable, realizable, reasonable, viable, workable; ***opp*** impossible

feast *n* banquet, blow out *sl*, dinner, spread *inf*, treat

feat *n* accomplishment, achievement, act, action, attainment, deed, exploit, performance

feature *n* **1** aspect, attribute, characteristic, detail, facet, factor, mark, peculiarity, point, property, quality, side, trait. **2** (in a newspaper) article, column, item, piece, report, story

feature *v* **1** accentuate, emphasize, focus on, give prominence to, highlight, play up, present, promote, spotlight, stress. **2** (in a film) act, appear, figure, participate, perform, play a role, star

features *n* appearance, countenance, face, look

fed up *adj* annoyed, bored, depressed, discontented, dissatisfied, down, gloomy, glum, miserable, sad, weary; ***opp*** happy

fee *n* bill, charge, cost, dues, fare, payment, price, rate, remuneration, subscription, tariff, toll

feeble *adj* **1** decrepit, debilitated, delicate, doddering, exhausted, failing, faint, fragile, frail, infirm, languid, listless, poorly, puny, sickly, weak; ***opp*** strong. **2** (not determined) inadequate, incompetent, indecisive, ineffectual, irresolute, spineless, wimpy, wishy-washy *inf*; ***opp*** tough. **3** (a feeble excuse) flimsy, futile, inadequate, ineffective, insubstantial, lame, paltry, poor, unconvincing; ***opp*** good

feed *v* **1** cater for, give food to, nourish, nurture, provide for, provision, suckle, support, supply, sustain. **2** (feed on sth) devour, dine, eat, graze, live on, subsist

feel *n* 1 (a leathery feel) finish, surface, texture. 2 (the feel of a place) ambience, atmosphere, aura, impression, mood

feel *v* 1 (with your fingers) caress, finger, fondle, handle, manipulate, maul, paw, stroke, thumb, touch. 2 (in your mind) be aware of, be conscious of, detect, discern, endure, enjoy, experience, go through, have, know, notice, observe, perceive, suffer, undergo. 3 (feel your way) explore, fumble, grope, test, try. 4 (have an opinion) be convinced, believe, be of the opinion that, consider, have a (funny) feeling, intuit, judge, sense, think. 5 **feel like** desire, fancy, want, wish for, would like, yearn for

feeling *n* 1 sensation, sense of touch, sensitivity. 2 (have a feeling) funny feeling, hunch, idea, impression, inkling, notion, suspicion. 3 (sb's feeling about sth) attitude, belief, inclination, instinct, opinion, thought, view

feelings *n* ego, emotions, self-esteem, sensitivities, sentiments, susceptibilities

fell *v* chop down, cut down, demolish, flatten, floor, hew, knock down, level

feminine *adj* delicate, elegant, gentle, girlish, girly *inf*, graceful, ladylike, soft, tender, womanly; ***opp*** masculine

fen *n* bog, lowland, marsh, quagmire, swamp

fence *n* barricade, barrier, defense, fencing, hedge, hurdle, paling, palisade, railings, rampart, stockade, wall, wire

fence *v* bound, circumscribe, confine, coop, encircle, enclose, hedge, pen, surround

ferment *v* 1 boil, brew, bubble, fizz, foam, froth, heat, leaven, rise. 2 agitate, excite, incite, inflame, instigate, provoke, rouse, stir up; ***opp*** calm

ferocious *adj* barbaric, bloodthirsty, brutal, fierce, predatory, ruthless, savage, vicious, violent, wild; ***opp*** harmless

ferry *v* bring, carry, chauffeur, convey, fetch, shift, ship, shuttle, take, taxi, transport

fertile *adj* fecund, fruitful, lush, productive, prolific, rich, yielding; ***opp*** infertile

fertilize *v* 1 impregnate, inseminate, make pregnant, pollinate. 2 (fertilize soil) compost, dress, enrich, feed, make fertile, manure, mulch, nourish

fervent *adj* ardent, avid, devout, eager, earnest, emotional, enthusiastic, excited, fanatical, fiery, heartfelt, heated, impassioned, intense, keen, passionate, vehement, wholehearted, zealous; ***opp*** lukewarm

fester *v* 1 become infected, become inflamed, become poisoned, discharge, go septic, ooze, putrefy, ulcerate. 2 decay, decompose, disintegrate, go bad, go off, rot

festival *n* 1 (a public festival) anniversary, bank holiday, commemoration, day of observance, feast, holiday, holy day, saint's day. 2 carnival, celebration, festivities, gala, jubilee

festive *adj* celebratory, cheerful, convivial, gay, happy, holiday, jolly, jovial, joyful, joyous, merry

festivity *n* amusement, celebration, conviviality, entertainment, fun, fun and games, gaiety, joviality, joyfulness, merriment, merrymaking, mirth, pleasure, revelry

fetch *v* **1** bring, carry, conduct, convey, deliver, escort, get, go and get, import, obtain, retrieve, transport. **2** (fetch a price) bring in, earn, go for, make, raise, realize, sell for, yield

fete *n* bazaar, fair, festival, gala, garden party, sale of work, show

feud *n* **1** argument, conflict, disagreement, dispute, falling-out, quarrel, running battle. **2** (a state of feud) animosity, antagonism, argument, bad blood, conflict, disagreement, discord, dispute, dissension, estrangement, grudge, hostility, rivalry, strife, unfriendliness; ***opp*** harmony

fever *n* delirium, feverishness, high temperature, temperature

feverish *adj* **1** (of a person) burning up *inf*, delirious, flushed, hot. **2** (of activity) agitated, desperate, excited, distracted, excited, frantic, frenetic, frenzied, hectic, passionate; ***opp*** calm

fiasco *n* catastrophe, debacle, disaster, failure, farce, flop *inf*, mess, rout, washout; ***opp*** success

fiber *n* filament, hair, strand, thread

fickle *adj* capricious, changeable, changing, disloyal, erratic, fitful, flighty, inconstant, unpredictable, up and down *inf*, vacillating, volatile; ***opp*** constant

fiction *n* **1** fable, fantasy, legend, make-believe, myth, romance, story, tale; ***opp*** real life. **2** (sth not true) cock and bull story *inf*, deception, fabrication, falsehood, fancy, fantasy, fib, imagination, invention, lie, tall story, untruth, whopper *inf*; ***opp*** truth

fictional *adj* fictitious, imaginary, invented, made-up, make-believe, pretend, nonexistent, unreal; ***opp*** real

fictitious *adj* assumed, bogus, counterfeit, fabricated, fake, false, feigned, imaginary, imagined, invented, made-up, mythical, sham, spurious, unreal, untrue; ***opp*** genuine

fiddle *v* **1** fidget, finger, fuss, interfere, meddle, mess about, mess around, play, tamper, tinker, toy, trifle. **2** cheat, falsify, fix, maneuver, racketeer, swindle, wangle

fidelity *n* **1** allegiance, commitment, constancy, dependability, devotion, faithfulness, integrity, loyalty, reliability, staunchness, trustworthiness; ***opp*** disloyalty. **2** accuracy, adherence, authenticity, closeness, correspondence, exactness, faithfulness, precision; ***opp*** inaccuracy

fidget *v* fiddle, fuss, have ants in your pants, mess about, mess around, play about, shuffle, squirm, twitch, wriggle

fidgety *adj* agitated, frisky, impatient, jerky, jittery, jumpy, nervous, on edge, restless, twitchy, uneasy; ***opp*** still

field *n* **1** clearing, enclosure, grassland, green, meadow, paddock, pasture. **2** (a sports field) arena, court, ground, pitch, playing field, recreation ground, stadium, turf. **3** (a field of activity) area, discipline, domain, line, province, specialty, sphere, subject, territory

fiend *n* **1** demon, devil, evil spirit, goblin, imp, Satan, spirit. **2** addict, devotee, enthusiast, fan, fanatic, follower, freak *inf*, lover, maniac, nut *inf*, supporter, zealot

fiendish *adj* accursed, atrocious, barbaric,

bloodthirsty, brutal, cruel, demonic, devilish, diabolical, hellish, implacable, infernal, inhuman, malevolent, malicious, malignant, merciless, monstrous, pitiless, ruthless, satanic, savage, ungodly, unspeakable, vicious, wicked; ***opp*** godly, good

fierce *adj* barbaric, brutal, cold-blooded, cruel, dangerous, fearsome, ferocious, menacing, murderous, passionate, ruthless, savage, threatening, uncontrollable, untamed, vicious, violent, wild; ***opp*** gentle

fight *n* **1** action, affray, attack, battle, bout, brawl, clash, conflict, contest, engagement, fracas, fray, joust, scrap *inf*, skirmish, struggle, tussle, war, wrestle. **2** altercation, argument, brush, disagreement, dispute, falling out, feud, quarrel, squabble, wrangle

fight *v* **1** attack, battle, box, brawl, clash, come to blows, contend, engage, grapple, have a fight, joust, scrap *inf*, skirmish, spar, struggle, tussle, war, wrestle. **2** challenge, contest, defy, dispute, oppose, resist, struggle against, take a stand against, withstand. **3** argue, be at odds, bicker, clash, dispute, fall out, feud, quarrel, squabble, wrangle. **4 fight back** counterattack, defend yourself, hit back, put up a fight, reply, resist, retaliate, stand up for yourself. **5 fight off** beat off, fend off, hold at bay, repel, repulse, stave off, ward off

fighter *n* boxer, combatant, contender, pugilist, soldier, warrior, wrestler

figure *n* **1** amount, cipher, digit, integer, number, numeral, sum, value. **2** body, build, form, frame, outline, physique, shape, silhouette. **3** chart, diagram, graph, illustration, symbol, table

figure *v* **1** comprehend, decipher, fathom, make out, see, realize, understand, work out. **2 figure out** assess, calculate, compute, reckon, solve, work out

file *n* **1** data, document, dossier, folder, portfolio, record. **2** column, line, procession, queue, row, stream, string, train

file *v* **1** categorize, classify, document, enter, organize, put on record, record, register. **2** march, parade, troop. **3** abrade, rasp, rub, scrape, shape, smooth

fill *v* block, cram, crowd, gorge, jam, load, pack, refill, replenish, satisfy, stock, stuff

filling *n* contents, insides, middle, padding, stuffing, wadding

film *n* **1** flick *inf*, motion picture, movie, picture, video. **2** coat, coating, covering, haze, layer, membrane, scum, skin, tissue, veil, veneer

filter *v* clarify, filtrate, purify, refine, screen, sieve, sift, strain

filth *n* **1** contamination, dirt, dung, effluent, excrement, feces, filthiness, foulness, grime, muck, ordure, pollution, refuse, sewage, sludge, squalor. **2** impurity, indecency, obscenity, pornography, smut, vulgarity

filthy *adj* **1** begrimed, contaminated, defiled, dirty, foul, grimy, grubby, mucky, polluted, squalid; ***opp*** clean. **2** bawdy, blue *inf*, coarse, impure, indecent, lewd, licentious, obscene, pornographic, raunchy, rude, smutty, sordid, vulgar

final *adj* closing, concluding, conclusive, dying, end, eventual, finishing, last, parting, terminating, ultimate; ***opp*** first

finale *n* climax, close, conclusion, culmination, denouement, end, epilogue, finish, last act

finalize *v* agree, arrange, clinch, complete, conclude, confirm, decide, settle, tie up, wrap up

finance *n* **1** (dealing with money) accounting, banking, business, commerce, economics, investment, stock market. **2** (money) accounts, assets, capital, cash, funds, money, resources, revenue, wealth, wherewithal

finance *v* back, fund, guarantee, invest in, pay for, subsidize, support, underwrite

financial *adj* budgetary, commercial, economic, fiscal, monetary, money, pecuniary

find *n* acquisition, asset, bargain, discovery, good buy, innovation, invention

find *v* **1** (find sth new) chance upon, come across, discover, encounter, espy, happen on, hit on, light on, spot, turn up, uncover, unearth. **2** (find sth lost) get back, locate, recoup, recover, rediscover, regain, retrieve, trace, track down; ***opp*** lose. **3** become aware, conclude, discover, note, notice, observe, perceive, realize. **4 find out** become aware, bring sth to light, detect, discover, expose, learn, observe, realize, reveal, see

fine *adj* **1** admirable, beautiful, choice, classic, consummate, elegant, excellent, exceptional, exquisite, first-class, first-rate, good, great, high-class, high-quality, magnificent, outstanding, quality, rare, refined, select, splendid, superb, superior, supreme, top-notch *inf*, world-class. **2** acceptable, agreeable, all right, OK *inf*, satisfactory, suitable. **3** (a fine day) balmy, bright, clear, cloudless, dry, fair, pleasant, sunny; ***opp*** wet. **4** (fine porcelain) dainty, delicate, flimsy, fragile, light, minute, narrow, slender, slim, small, thin, translucent; ***opp*** coarse. **5** (a fine distinction) abstruse, discriminating, exact, fastidious, fine-drawn, hair-splitting, minute, nice, precise, subtle; ***opp*** clear, obvious

fine *n* charge, forfeit, penalty, punishment

finesse *n* adroitness, artfulness, cleverness, craft, delicacy, expertise, grace, polish, refinement, savoir-faire, skill, subtlety

finish *n* **1** cessation, close, closing, completion, conclusion, culmination, denouement, end, ending, finale, termination; ***opp*** start. **2** coating, gloss, lacquer, luster, patina, polish, sheen, shine, smoothness, surface, veneer

finish *v* **1** accomplish, achieve, bring to an end, clinch, close, complete, conclude, culminate, discharge, end, execute, finalize, fulfill, get done, perfect, settle, wrap up. **2** break off, cease, desist, discontinue, halt, interrupt, pack up, phase out, stop, suspend, terminate, wind up. **3** annihilate, beat, be too much for, bring down, conquer, destroy, dispose of, exterminate, get rid of, get the better of, kill, overcome, overpower, ruin. **4** consume, devour, dispatch, dispose of, drink up, eat up, get through, polish off *inf*

finished *adj* 1 clinched, closed, complete, completed, done, ended, final, finalized, over, perfect, settled, through, tied up, wrapped up. 2 beaten, defeated, done for *inf*, doomed, overcome, past it *inf*, ruined, through, undone, washed up *inf*, wrecked

finite *adj* calculable, certain, countable, definable, defined, determinable, fixed, limited, measurable, numbered, restricted; ***opp*** infinite

fire *n* 1 blaze, burning, combustion, conflagration, flame, inferno, pyre. 2 barrage, bombardment, gunfire, salvo, shelling, shooting, shot, sniping. 3 ardor, energy, fervor, intensity, life, passion, spark, spirit, vehemence, vigor, vivacity, zeal

fire *v* 1 (set fire to sth) burn, ignite, kindle, put a match to, set sth alight, set fire to, set sth on fire, torch. 2 (fire a gun) detonate, discharge, launch, let off, pull the trigger, set off, shoot. 3 (fire sb) discharge, dismiss, down-size, get rid of, give sb the boot *inf*, let sb go, make sb redundant, sack, throw sb out

firm *adj* 1 compact, compressed, condensed, dense, hard, inflexible, resilient, resistant, rigid, set, solid, solidified, strong, taut, tight, stiff, unyielding; ***opp*** soft. 2 anchored, braced, embedded, fast, fixed, immovable, motionless, rooted, secured, solid, stable, steady, strong, sturdy, tight, unmoving; ***opp*** loose. 3 adamant, certain, constant, definite, determined, fixed, immovable, inflexible, intransigent, obdurate, resolute, resolved, set, settled, staunch, stalwart, steadfast, strict, stubborn, sure, unalterable, unbending, unmoving, unshakable, unswerving, unwavering, unyielding

firm *n* association, business, company, concern, corporation, enterprise, establishment, house, group, organization, partnership

first *adj* 1 earliest, initial, maiden, opening, original, preliminary, primeval, primitive, primordial. 2 chief, dominant, foremost, head, highest, leading, pre-eminent, premier, prime, principal, ruling, superior, supreme, uppermost. 3 axiomatic, basic, cardinal, elementary, essential, fundamental, key, primary, rudimentary

first-rate *adj* admirable, choice, classic, consummate, excellent, exceptional, first class, high-class, high-quality, magnificent, outstanding, quality, rare, refined, select, splendid, superb, superior, superlative, top-notch *inf*, world class

fit *adj* 1 energetic, healthy, in shape, robust, strapping, strong, toned, trim, vigorous, well; ***opp*** unfit. 2 able, adequate, appropriate, capable, competent, correct, decent, eligible, equipped, fitting, good enough, qualified, proper, right, suitable, up to the job *inf*, worthy; ***opp*** unfit

fit *n* attack, bout, convulsion, eruption, explosion, outbreak, outburst, paroxysm, seizure, spasm, spell, turn

fit *v* 1 accord, agree, be right, belong, concur, dovetail, interlock, match, meet, suit, tally. 2 arrange, assemble, build, construct, install, interlock, join, match, put in, put together. 3 adapt, adjust, alter, cut, modify, shape, tailor

fitting *adj* adequate, appropriate, becoming, correct, decent, decorous, good enough, proper, right, seemly, suitable, worthy

fix *n* bind *inf*, corner, difficulty, dilemma, jam *inf*, mess, pickle *inf*, plight, predicament, problem, quandary, scrape *inf*, spot *inf*

fix *v* **1** anchor, attach, connect, embed, fasten, fit, install, join, secure, stick, tie. **2** agree, appoint, arrange, arrive at, conclude, decide, define, determine, establish, finalize, limit, name, resolve, set, settle, specify. **3** mend, patch up, put right, remedy, repair, restore, sort out

fixed *adj* **1** attached, immobile, permanent, rigid, secured; ***opp*** movable. **2** agreed, arranged, definite, established, planned, prearranged, predetermined, set, settled

fixture *n* arrangement, date, engagement, event, game, match, meeting

fizzy *adj* bubbling, bubbly, carbonated, effervescent, gassy, sparkling; ***opp*** still

flag *n* banner, bunting, colors, ensign, pennant, standard, streamer

flag *v* **1** fade, fail, decline, decrease, diminish, ebb, taper off, tire, wane, weaken, weary. **2** indicate, label, mark, pick out, signal

flagrant *adj* barefaced, blatant, bold, brazen, glaring, gross, obvious, open, ostentatious, outrageous, overt, scandalous, shameless, shocking, unashamed, unconcealed, undisguised

flair *n* **1** ability, aptitude, facility, feel, genius, gift, knack, skill, talent. **2** chic, dash, elegance, panache, style, taste

flamboyant *adj* bold, colorful, dashing, dazzling, extravagant, fancy, flashy, gaudy, glamorous, ostentatious, outrageous, shocking, showy, splendid, swashbuckling, theatrical

flame *n* **1** blaze, conflagration, fire, tongue. **2** ardor, fervor, fire, intensity, passion, warmth

flame *v* be ablaze, blaze, burn, flare, flash, glare, glow, shine

flap *v* **1** agitate, beat, flail, flutter, oscillate, shake, swing, swish, thrash, wag, waggle, wave. **2** be agitated, be in a state, fuss, get flustered, panic

flare *v* blaze, burn, dazzle, flash, flicker, glare, gleam, glint, shine

flash *n* **1** beam, blaze, bolt, burst, flare, flicker, glare, gleam, glimmer, glint, ray, shaft, shimmer, shine, spark, sparkle, twinkle. **2** instant, jiffy *inf*, minute, moment, second, split second, twinkling of an eye

flash *v* beam, blaze, dazzle, flare, flicker, glare, gleam, glimmer, glint, glisten, glitter, light up, reflect, shimmer, shine, sparkle, twinkle

flashy *adj* bold, brash, bright, extravagant, fancy, flamboyant, garish, gaudy, glitzy, loud, ostentatious, showy, tacky *inf*, tasteless, tawdry, vulgar; ***opp*** understated

flat *adj* **1** even, horizontal, level, leveled, plane, smooth, unbroken. **2** lying down, outstretched, prone, prostrate, reclining, recumbent, sprawling, spread-eagled, stretched out, supine. **3** bland, boring, dead, dry, dull, insipid, lackluster, lifeless, monotonous, prosaic, stale, tedious, uninteresting, unvarying, vapid; ***opp*** interesting

flatten *v* **1** compact, compress, even out, iron out, level out, plane, press down, smooth out. **2** crush, demolish, destroy, knock down, level, raze, squash, trample

flatter *v* blandish, butter up, cajole, compliment, court, eulogize, fawn, get round *inf*, gush, humor, kiss up to *inf*, lay it on thick *inf*, lick sb's boots *inf*, pander to, pay court to, play up to *inf*, praise, soft-soap *inf*, suck up to *sl*, sweet-talk *inf*, wheedle

flattery *n* adulation, blandishments, blarney, boot-licking *inf*, buttering-up, cajoling, compliments, eulogy, fawning, gushing, kissing up *inf*, obsequiousness, pandering, praise, soft soap *inf*, sucking-up *sl*, sweet talk *inf*, wheedling

flavor *n* **1** aroma, essence, extract, odor, piquancy, relish, savor, seasoning, smack, tang, taste, tastiness, zest. **2** ambience, atmosphere, aura, character, essence, feel, feeling, nature, quality, soul, spirit, tone

flavor *v* add flavor to, add piquancy to, imbue, infuse, lace, season, spice

flaw *n* blemish, defect, failing, fault, foible, imperfection, shortcoming, weakness

flawed *adj* blemished, broken, chipped, cracked, damaged, defective, faulty, imperfect, marred, spoilt, unsound; ***opp*** perfect

flee *v* abscond, beat a retreat, beat it *inf*, bolt, decamp, disappear, escape, fly, make off, run away, run off, take flight, take off, vanish

fleet *n* armada, convoy, flotilla, naval force, navy, task force, warships

fleeting *adj* brief, ephemeral, momentary, passing, quick, rapid, short, short-lived, swift, transient, transitory

flesh *n* **1** brawn, carrion, fat, meat, muscle, tissue. **2** body, carnality, physicality, sensuality

flexible *adj* **1** bendable, ductile, giving, elastic, malleable, plastic, pliable, springy, stretchy, supple, yielding; ***opp*** rigid. **2** adaptable, amenable, biddable, compliant, fluid, malleable, open, responsive, tractable, yielding; ***opp*** inflexible

flicker *v* blink, flash, flutter, glimmer, glint, glitter, oscillate, quiver, tremble, twinkle, vibrate, waver, wink, wobble

flicker *n* blink, flash, flutter, glimmer, glint, glitter, twinkle, spark, wink

flight *n* **1** journey, trajectory, trip. **2** aviation, flying, soaring, winging. **3** absconding, decamping, departure, disappearance, escape, exit, exodus, fleeing, getaway, retreat, vanishing

flimsy *adj* **1** breakable, brittle, delicate, fine, fragile, frail, insubstantial, lightweight, makeshift, ramshackle, rickety, shaky, slight, thin, weak; ***opp*** strong. **2** (a flimsy excuse) feeble, implausible, inadequate, pathetic, poor, thin, transparent, trifling, trivial, unconvincing, unsatisfactory, weak; ***opp*** sound

flinch *v* balk, blench, cower, cringe, dodge, duck, flee, jump, quail, recoil, retreat, shirk, shrink, shy away, start, swerve, wince, withdraw

fling *v* cast, chuck *inf*, heave, hurl, launch, lob *inf*, pitch, propel, send, shy, sling, throw, toss

flippant *adj* casual, cheeky, disrespectful, facetious, flip, frivolous, glib, light-hearted, impertinent, impudent, irreverent, jokey, offhand, pert, shallow, superficial, thoughtless

flirt *n* coquette, heartbreaker, philanderer, tease

flirt *v* lead sb on, make advances, ogle, philander, tease, toy with, trifle with

flirtatious *adj* coquettish, coy, flirty, philandering, playful, provocative, teasing

float *v* be buoyant, bob, drift, glide, hang, hover, poise, sail, slide, slip, stay afloat; ***opp*** sink

floating *adj* 1 afloat, bobbing, buoyant, drifting, gliding, hanging, hovering, poised, sailing, suspended. 2 changeable, fluctuating, unattached, uncommitted, undecided, variable, wandering

flock *n* 1 (of animals) drove, flight, gaggle, herd. 2 (of people) assembly, company, congregation, crowd, gathering, group, horde, host, mass, multitude, throng

flock *v* amass, assemble, congregate, converge, crowd, gather, group, herd, huddle, mass, swarm, throng, troop

flog *v* beat, cane, chastise, flagellate, flay, lash, scourge, thrash, whip

flood *n* 1 deluge, downpour, flash flood, inundation, overflow, spate, tidal wave, tide, torrent. 2 abundance, excess, flow, glut, plethora, profusion, rush, stream, surfeit, surge

flood *v* 1 (to flood an area) cover, deluge, drown, engulf, fill, immerse, inundate, submerge, sweep. 2 (of a river) break its banks, brim over, overflow, pour, stream, surge, swell

floor *n* deck, level, stage, story, tier

flop *n* debacle, disaster, dud *inf*, failure, fiasco, loser, no-hoper *inf*, nonstarter, washout *inf*; ***opp*** success

flop *v* 1 collapse, dangle, droop, drop, fall, flag, hang, sag, slump, topple, tumble, wilt. 2 bomb *inf*, close, fail, fall flat, founder

flounder *v* blunder, flail, fumble, grope, muddle, struggle, stumble, thrash, wallow

flourish *n* brandishing, display, gesture, shaking, show, swing, swish, twirl, wave

flourish *v* 1 be fruitful, be successful, bloom, blossom, burgeon, grow, prosper, succeed, thrive; ***opp*** fail. 2 brandish, hold up, shake, swing, swish, twirl, wave, wield

flourishing *adj* blooming, blossoming, booming, burgeoning, fruitful, growing, prosperous, successful, thriving; ***opp*** ailing, failing

flout *v* defy, disobey, disregard, ignore, insult, jeer at, laugh at, make a mockery of, mock, ridicule, scorn, show contempt for, sneer at, spurn, treat sth with disdain

flow *v* cascade, circulate, course, dribble, drip, ebb, glide, gush, leak, move, ooze, pour, roll, run, rush, seep, slide, slip, spill, spout, squirt, stream, surge, sweep, swirl, trickle, well, whirl

flower *n* 1 bloom, blossom, bud, floret. 2 best, choice, cream, elite, height, pick

flower *v* bloom, blossom, bud, burgeon, flourish, open, unfold

fluctuate *v* alternate, be unsteady, change, hesitate, oscillate, move, seesaw, shift, swing, vacillate, vary, veer, waver, yo-yo

fluent *adj* articulate, easy, effortless, eloquent, flowing, fluid, mellifluous, natural, ready, smooth, voluble

fluid *adj* **1** flowing, liquefied, liquid, melted, molten, running, runny, sloppy, watery; ***opp*** solid. **2** adaptable, adjustable, changeable, flexible, floating, indefinite, mobile, mutable, open, shifting, variable; ***opp*** fixed

flurry *n* bustle, commotion, excitement, flap, fluster, flutter, hubbub, stir, tumult, whirl

flush *n* bloom, blush, color, glow, radiance, redness, rosiness

flush *v* **1** (of a face) blush, burn, color, flame, glow, go red, redden. **2** clean out, cleanse, flood, hose down, rinse, wash down, wash out

fly *v* **1** flit, flutter, glide, hover, sail, soar, swoop, take flight, take to the air, take wing. **2** (of a pilot) control, maneuver, operate, pilot, take off. **3** (of a flag) display, flap, flutter, hoist, raise, show, wave. **4** (of time) elapse, pass, race, roll on, slip away, slip past. **5** dart, dash, hurry, race, rush, shoot, sprint, tear, zoom

foam *n* bubbles, froth, head, lather, scum, spray, spume, suds

foam *v* boil, bubble, effervesce, fizz, froth, lather

focus *n* center, core, focal point, heart, hub, pivot, target

focus *v* **1** aim, concentrate, direct attention, fix, home in, pinpoint, spotlight. **2** (of a lens) bring into focus, turn, zoom in

fog *n* cloud, gloom, haze, mist, mistiness, murk, murkiness, smog

foggy *adj* blurred, blurry, clouded, cloudy, dim, gray, hazy, indistinct, misty, murky, obscure, smoggy; ***opp*** clear

foil *v* baffle, defeat, frustrate, outwit, prevent, stop, thwart

fold *n* bend, corrugation, crease, crinkle, furrow, gather, layer, line, overlap, pleat, pucker, turn, wrinkle

fold *v* **1** bend, crease, crimp, crinkle, crumple, double, gather, jackknife, overlap, pleat, pucker, tuck, turn. **2** (fold sth in your arms) embrace, enclose, enfold, entwine, envelop, hold, wrap. **3** (of a business) close, collapse, crash, fail, go bankrupt, go bust *inf*, go under *inf*

follow *v* **1** (go behind sb or sth) chase, dog, hound, hunt, pursue, shadow, stalk, tag along *inf*, tail *inf*, track, trail. **2** (follow a rule) abide by, comply with, conform, honor, obey, observe, stick to. **3** (come after sb or sth) replace, step into sb's shoes, succeed, supersede, supplant, take sb's place

follower *n* admirer, apostle, believer, convert, devotee, disciple, enthusiast, fan, groupie *inf*, pupil, supporter, worshiper

folly *n* foolishness, idiocy, insanity, lunacy, madness, nonsense, silliness, stupidity

fond *adj* **1** adoring, affectionate, amorous, caring, devoted, loving, warm. **2 fond of** addicted to, attached to, enamored of, hooked on, in love with, keen on, mad about, partial to

fondle *v* caress, cuddle, pat, pet,

stroke, touch

food *n* 1 cooking, cuisine, diet, eats *inf*, fare, foodstuffs, grub *inf*, meals, nosh *sl*, nourishment, provisions, refreshments, sustenance. 2 fodder, feed

fool *n* 1 blockhead, clot *inf*, dope *inf*, fathead *inf*, half-wit, idiot, jerk *sl*, moron, nerd *sl*, nincompoop, nit, nitwit, twerp *inf*, twit *inf*. 2 buffoon, clown, comedian, comic, jester

fool *v* 1 bamboozle, beguile, bluff, cheat, con *inf*, deceive, delude, dupe, hoax, hoodwink, kid *inf*, make a fool of, mislead, play a trick on, string sb along *inf*, take sb in, trick. 2 **fool around** act the fool, clown around, joke, mess about *inf*, play tricks, tease

foolish *adj* brainless, crazy, daft, dumb *inf*, hare-brained, idiotic, ill-advised, inane, ludicrous, mad, ridiculous, senseless, silly, simple, stupid, thoughtless, unintelligent, unwise; ***opp*** sensible

foolproof *adj* certain, guaranteed, infallible, safe, sure

foot *n* 1 base, bottom, end, foundation. 2 claw, hoof, paw, trotter

forbid *v* ban, bar, deny, exclude, inhibit, make illegal, prevent, prohibit, refuse, rule out, say no to, stop, veto; ***opp*** allow

forbidden *adj* against the law, banned, outlawed, out of bounds, prohibited, restricted, secret, taboo, wrong

force *n* 1 effort, energy, exertion, impact, might, muscle, power, pressure, stamina, strength, stress. 2 (making sb do sth) aggression, arm-twisting *inf*, coercion, compulsion, duress, pressure, violence. 3 (force of an argument) effect, effectiveness, influence, persuasiveness, power, strength, validity, weight. 4 (spoke with force) drive, emphasis, feeling, fierceness, intensity, passion, persistence, vehemence, vividness. 5 army, battalion, body, corps, division, group, squad, squadron, troops, unit

force *v* 1 (make sb do sth) bulldoze *inf*, coerce, compel, constrain, dragoon, impose, make, oblige, press-gang, pressurize, railroad *inf* , twist sb's arm. 2 (force sth open) blast, break open, thrust, use force, wrench. 3 (force sth out) drag, exact, extort, wring. 4 (force sth along) drive, press, propel, push, urge

forced *adj* (a forced smile) affected, artificial, false, insincere, self-conscious, stiff, strained, unnatural, wooden; ***opp*** natural

forceful *adj* assertive, compelling, convincing, dynamic, effective, powerful, strong; ***opp*** weak

foreboding *n* anxiety, apprehension, chill, dread, fear, feeling, forewarning, intuition, misgiving, omen, premonition, presentiment, suspicion, warning, worry

forecast *n* guess, outlook, prediction, prognosis, projection, prophecy, speculation

forecast *v* divine, estimate, foresee, foretell, forewarn, predict, prophesy

foreign *adj* 1 (foreign lands) alien, distant, exotic, faraway, outlandish, remote, strange, unfamiliar, unknown. 2 (foreign affairs) external, international, outside, overseas; ***opp*** domestic

foreigner *n* alien, immigrant, newcomer, outsider, stranger, visitor
forerunner *n* 1 ancestor, forebear, forefather, predecessor. 2 harbinger, herald, precursor
foresee *v* anticipate, divine, envisage, expect, forebode, forecast, foretell, predict, prophesy
foresight *n* anticipation, care, farsightedness, forethought, looking ahead, precaution, prescience, vision
forest *n* coppice, copse, jungle, plantation, trees, wood, woodland
foretell *v* forecast, foresee, foreshadow, forewarn, herald, predict, prophesy
forfeit *n* damages, fee, fine, loss, penalty
forfeit *v* be deprived of, give up, hand over, lose, relinquish, renounce, surrender
forge *v* 1 (forge metal) beat, cast, form, hammer, make, mold, shape, work. 2 (forge an object) coin, copy, counterfeit, fake, falsify, imitate, make illegally, reproduce
forgery *n* copy, counterfeit, fake, imitation, replica, reproduction
forget *v* disregard, fail to remember, ignore, lose sight of, neglect, omit, overlook, put out of your mind; ***opp*** remember
forgetful *adj* absentminded, careless, distracted, dreamy, inattentive, neglectful, oblivious, preoccupied, vague
forgive *v* absolve, acquit, condone, excuse, exonerate, ignore, let off, overlook, pardon, spare
forgiveness *n* absolution, amnesty, clemency, compassion, exoneration, leniency, mercy, pardon, reprieve
forgiving *adj* compassionate, lenient, magnanimous, merciful, mild, soft-hearted, tolerant, understanding
forgo *v* do without, give up, go without, relinquish, renounce, sacrifice, surrender
forgotten *adj* blotted out, buried, dead, gone, left behind, lost, obliterated, out of mind, past
forlorn *adj* 1 alone, desolate, lonely, miserable, pathetic, pitiable, pitiful, unhappy, wretched. 2 abandoned, deserted, forgotten, forsaken, neglected. 3 (a forlorn hope) desperate, hopeless
form *n* 1 (the shape of sth) arrangement, configuration, design, formation, pattern, shape, structure. 2 (type) kind, sort, type, variety. 3 (form to fill in) application, document, paper, sheet. 4 (a slim form) anatomy, body, build, figure, frame, outline, physique, shape, silhouette
form *v* 1 build, cast, concoct, construct, create, fashion, forge, make, model, mold, produce, shape, stamp. 2 appear, arise, become visible, come into existence, develop, grow, materialize, take shape. 3 devise, draw up, dream up *inf*, formulate, plan, think up. 4 assemble, bring about, establish, found, organize, set up. 5 comprise, constitute, make up
formal *adj* 1 (of an occasion) ceremonial, dignified, elaborate, official, posh *inf*, ritualistic, sophisticated; ***opp*** informal. 2 (of people) aloof, conventional, correct, prim, reserved, rigid, stuffy, unbending, unfriendly; ***opp*** relaxed. 3 (of an agreement) binding, contractual, legal, official, proper;

opp informal

formality *n* 1 (a formality) ceremony, convention, custom, form, gesture, rite, ritual, rule. 2 ceremoniousness, correctness, decorum, etiquette, procedure, protocol, red tape

formative *adj* developing, forming, growing, impressionable, shaping, susceptible

former *adj* 1 (his former wife) ex-, last, late, one-time, previous. 2 (former times) ancient, bygone, earlier, long gone, old, past

formidable *adj* 1 (of a person) alarming, daunting, frightening, intimidating, scary *inf*. 2 (of a sight) awe-inspiring, awesome, daunting, fearful, frightful, horrible, menacing, petrifying, terrifying. 3 (of a task) arduous, challenging, daunting, difficult, onerous, overwhelming; ***opp*** simple. 4 (of an enemy) mighty, invincible, powerful, strong

formula *n* blueprint, method, prescription, procedure, recipe, technique

formulate *v* 1 articulate, define, express, frame, give form to, set out, specify. 2 create, devise, draw up, evolve, map out, plan, work out

fort *n* camp, castle, citadel, fortification, fortress, garrison, stronghold, tower

forthcoming *adj* 1 (the forthcoming exam) approaching, coming, imminent, impending, prospective, upcoming. 2 (of a person) chatty, communicative, talkative, voluble

fortification *n* barricade, battlement, bulwark, castle, defense, fort, fortress, parapet, rampart, stronghold

fortify *v* 1 (make sth stronger) brace, buttress, defend, guard, protect, reinforce, secure, shore up, stiffen, strengthen. 2 (encourage yourself) boost, buoy up, cheer, embolden, encourage, hearten, invigorate, reassure, revive, sustain; ***opp*** discourage

fortress *n* castle, citadel, fort, stronghold

fortunate *adj* 1 blessed, favored, happy, lucky, prosperous, successful; ***opp*** unfortunate. 2 auspicious, favorable, felicitous, opportune, propitious, timely

fortune *n* 1 affluence, assets, inheritance, millions *inf*, money, prosperity, riches, treasure, wealth. 2 accident, chance, destiny, fate, kismet, luck, providence

fortune-teller *n* astrologer, clairvoyant, crystal-gazer, oracle, palmist, prophet, seer, soothsayer, stargazer *inf*

forward *adj* 1 advanced, early, precocious, premature, well-developed; ***opp*** backward. 2 bold, brash, brazen, impudent, insolent, overfamiliar, presumptuous, shameless; ***opp*** shy

forward *v* 1 dispatch, readdress, send, send on, transmit. 2 advance, encourage, further, hasten, help, promote, speed up

foster *v* 1 adopt, bring up, care for, look after, raise, rear, take care of. 2 (foster links) cultivate, encourage, promote, support. 3 (foster hopes) cherish, entertain, harbor, sustain

foul *adj* 1 bad, contaminated, dirty, disgusting, fetid, filthy, impure, infected, polluted, putrid, rank, repugnant, repulsive, revolting, rotten, smelly, squalid, stinking, unclean; ***opp*** clean.

2 atrocious, contemptible, cruel, disgraceful, evil, horrible, scandalous, sordid, vicious, violent, wicked. 3 (foul language) blasphemous, coarse, filthy, obscene, offensive, rude, vulgar. 4 (a foul day) blustery, foggy, rainy, rough, stormy, wet, wild, windy; ***opp*** beautiful, lovely

foul *v* blacken, contaminate, defile, dirty, pollute, smear, stain, taint

found *v* begin, bring about, create, endow, establish, organize, set up, start

foundation *n* 1 base, basis, bottom, cornerstone, footing, substructure. 2 basis, fundamentals, origin, principles, rudiments

founder *n* beginner, benefactor, builder, designer, inventor, maker, organizer, originator

founder *v* 1 be lost, be wrecked, capsize, go down, run aground, sink. 2 come to grief, fail, fall through, go wrong

fountain *n* fount, jet, spout, spray, spring, well

fraction *n* division, part, portion, small part, subdivision

fracture *n* break, crack, fissure, opening, rift, rupture, split

fracture *v* break, crack, rupture, split, suffer a fracture

fragile *adj* breakable, brittle, delicate, feeble, flimsy, frail, insubstantial, thin, weak; ***opp*** robust

fragment *n* bit, chip, crumb, fraction, morsel, part, particle, piece, portion, remnant, scrap, shard, shred, sliver

fragment *v* break, chip, crack, disintegrate, fall apart, fracture, shatter, shiver, smash, splinter

fragrance *n* 1 aroma, bouquet, perfume, scent, smell. 2 cologne, perfume, scent

fragrant *adj* aromatic, perfumed, sweet-scented, sweet-smelling

frail *adj* 1 (of a person) decrepit, delicate, feeble, fragile, ill, infirm, puny, sickly, slight, unwell, unsteady, vulnerable, weak; ***opp*** strong. 2 (of an object) breakable, dainty, easily damaged, flimsy, fragile, insubstantial, rickety, thin; ***opp*** strong

frame *n* 1 body, casing, chassis, framework, scaffolding, shell, skeleton, structure, substructure. 2 border, edge, mount, mounting, setting

frame *v* 1 compose, devise, draft, draw up, formulate, sketch. 2 box in, encase, enclose, mount, put in a frame, set off, surround. 3 (frame sb) accuse, implicate, incriminate, point the finger at, set up

framework *n* bare bones, core, fabric, foundation, groundwork, outline, plan, shell, skeleton, structure, support

frank *adj* blunt, candid, direct, forthright, free, honest, no-nonsense *inf*, open, outspoken, plain, sincere, straight, straightforward, truthful, unconcealed, undisguised, upfront *inf*

frantic *adj* agitated, berserk, beside yourself, crazy, desperate, distracted, distraught, excitable, frenetic, frenzied, furious, hectic, hysterical, mad, overwrought, panic-stricken, raving, wild

fraternize *v* associate, consort, go around with, hang around with *inf*, keep company with, mingle, mix, socialize

fraud *n* 1 (accused of fraud) cheating, deceit, deception, dishonesty, double-dealing, fraudulence, sharp practice, skulduggery, treachery, trickery. **2** (a trick) con *inf*, deception, hoax, put-up job *inf*, ruse, scam *sl*, trick. **3** (a person) cheat, confidence trickster, con man *inf*, fake, hoaxer, imposter, phony *inf*, pretender, quack, scoundrel, swindler. **4** (sth not genuine) counterfeit, fake, forgery, phony *inf*

fraudulent *adj* bent *inf*, bogus, corrupt, criminal, crooked *inf*, deceitful, deceptive, dishonest, false, forged, illegal, phony *inf*, spurious, unscrupulous; ***opp*** honest

freak *adj* abnormal, atypical, bizarre, exceptional, extraordinary, freakish, odd, peculiar, queer, rare, unexpected, unpredictable, unusual, weird; ***opp*** normal, usual

freak *n* **1** aberration, abnormality, anomaly, curiosity, monster, monstrosity, mutant, quirk, rarity. **2** addict, buff *inf*, enthusiast, fan, fanatic

free *adj* **1** (free tickets) at no cost, complimentary, for nothing, free of charge, on the house *inf*. **2** (free to move) able, allowed, at large, at liberty, clear, liberated, loose, unchained, unhindered, unblocked, unobstructed, unrestrained. **3** easygoing, footloose, independent, liberated, relaxed, unconstrained, uninhibited; ***opp*** tied down. **4** (a free country) autonomous, democratic, independent, self-governing. **5** (available for use) available, empty, extra, spare, unoccupied, unused, vacant. **6 free with** generous, hospitable, lavish, open-handed, unsparing

free *v* cut loose, discharge, emancipate, extricate, let go, let out, liberate, loose, release, rescue, save, turn loose, unchain, undo, unleash, untie

freedom *n* **1** (freedom to do what you want) carte blanche, flexibility, free hand, free rein, latitude, leeway, license, opportunity, range, scope. **2** (fighting for freedom) autonomy, deliverance, emancipation, home rule, independence, liberty, sovereignty

freely *adv* **1** (go freely) of your own accord, of your own free will, voluntarily, willingly. **2** (speak freely) bluntly, candidly, frankly, honestly, openly

freeze *v* **1** become frozen, chill, harden, ice over, ice up, solidify; ***opp*** thaw. **2** be cold, chill, cool, go numb, make cold, numb. **3** be immobilized, go rigid, stand still, stop dead, stop in your tracks; ***opp*** move

freezing *adj* arctic, biting, bitter, cutting, frosty, ice-cold, icy, raw, snowy, wintry; ***opp*** boiling

freight *n* cargo, consignment, goods, load, merchandise, shipment

frenzied *adj* agitated, excited, frantic, frenetic, furious, hysterical, maniacal, rabid, uncontrolled, wild; ***opp*** calm

frenzy *n* **1** agitation, delirium, excitement, fury, hysteria, insanity, lunacy, madness, mania, paroxysm, passion, rage, seizure. **2** bout, fit, outburst

frequent *adj* common, constant, continual, customary, everyday, familiar, habitual, incessant, innumerable, many, numerous, persistent, recurrent, repeated; ***opp*** rare

frequent *v* go to, hang out at *inf*, haunt, spend time at, visit

fresh *adj* **1** (fresh colors) bright, clean, crisp, unfaded, vivid. **2** (fresh food) crisp, healthy, natural, raw, unprocessed, untreated; ***opp*** processed. **3** (fresh water) clean, clear, drinkable, pure, refreshing, sweet, uncontaminated; ***opp*** stale. **4** (fresh ideas) different, innovative, modern, new, novel, original, up-to-date; ***opp*** old. **5** (fresh-faced) bright, clear, fair, healthy, pink, rosy, wholesome. **6** (feel fresh after a shower) alive, awake, bright, energetic, full of beans *inf*, invigorated, lively, perky *inf*, refreshed, restored, revived, tingling; ***opp*** tired. **7** (a fresh wind) bracing, brisk, chilly, cool, invigorating, strong; ***opp*** gentle. **8** (fresh supplies) additional, extra, further, more, other. **9** (fresh bedding) clean, crisp, laundered, starched, unused, washed; ***opp*** dirty

freshen *v* **1** liven up, refresh, restore, revitalize, revive, rouse. **2** air, purify, ventilate

fret *v* agonize, be distressed, brood, complain, feel unhappy, grumble, lose sleep, whine, worry

friction *n* **1** abrasion, chafing, erosion, grating, irritation, resistance, rubbing, scraping. **2** (friction between people) antagonism, arguing, bad feeling, conflict, disagreement, dissension, hostility, resentment

friend *n* boyfriend, buddy *inf*, chum, companion, comrade, girlfriend, mate *inf*, pal *inf*, partner, pen pal, playmate

friendliness *n* amiability, helpfulness, hospitality, kindliness, kindness, neighborliness, sociability, warmth

friendly *adj* affectionate, agreeable, amicable, approachable, civil, companionable, helpful, hospitable, intimate, kind, kindhearted, kindly, neighborly, sociable, sympathetic, warm, welcoming; ***opp*** unfriendly

friendship *n* affection, closeness, companionship, harmony, intimacy, rapport, relationship

fright *n* **1** (fear) alarm, apprehension, dismay, dread, fear, horror, panic, terror, trepidation. **2** (have a fright) scare, shock, surprise

frighten *v* **1** alarm, intimidate, make you afraid, make your blood run cold, make your hair stand on end, petrify, scare, spook *inf*, startle, terrify, unnerve, upset. **2** browbeat, bully, menace, persecute, terrorize, threaten, tyrannize

frightened *adj* afraid, alarmed, anxious, apprehensive, cowardly, fearful, horrified, horror-struck, panicky, panic-stricken, petrified, scared, shocked, startled, terrified, trembling, unnerved, upset

frightening *adj* alarming, blood-curdling, creepy *inf*, daunting, dreadful, eerie, fearful, fearsome, ghostly, hair-raising, horrifying, intimidating, menacing, scary, shocking, sinister, spine-chilling, terrifying, weird

frigid *adj* **1** aloof, forbidding, formal, icy, remote, rigid, stiff, unfeeling, unfriendly, unresponsive; ***opp*** warm. **2** arctic, bitter, cold, cool, frosty, frozen, glacial, icy, wintry

fringe *n* **1** border, boundary, edge, limits,

margin, outskirts, perimeter, periphery. 2 edging, flounce, frill, ruffle, tassel, trimming

frisk *v* 1 caper, cavort, dance, frolic, gambol, jump, play, romp, skip. 2 inspect, search

frisky *adj* active, bouncy, full of beans *inf*, high *inf*, high-spirited, lively, playful, sprightly

frivolous *adj* empty-headed, facetious, flighty, flip *inf*, flippant, foolish, giddy, idle, inconsequential, juvenile, pointless, puerile, shallow, silly, superficial, trivial, unimportant; ***opp*** serious

frolic *v* caper, cavort, dance, frisk, gambol, have fun, play, prance, romp, skip

front *adj* first, foremost, head, lead, leading

front *n* 1 exterior, facade, face, foreground, forepart, frontage. 2 beginning, front line, head, top, vanguard. 3 (just a front) blind, cover, disguise, facade, pretext, show

frontier *n* border, boundary, confines, edge, limit

froth *n* bubbles, foam, head, lather, scum, suds

froth *v* bubble over, bubble up, effervesce, fizz, foam, lather

frothy *adj* 1 bubbly, foaming, foamy, lathery. 2 frivolous, insignificant, insubstantial, light, slight, trivial, worthless

frown *v* glare, glower, knit your brows, look sullen, scowl

frozen *adj* 1 (frozen wastes) arctic, chilled, frosted, glacial, hard, icebound, icy, polar, Siberian. 2 (without feeling) anesthetized, asleep *inf*, deadened, frigid, numb. 3 (not able to move) petrified, rooted to the spot, stock-still, suspended

fruit *n* 1 crop, harvest, produce, yield. 2 effect, outcome, profit, result, return, reward

fruitful *adj* 1 beneficial, productive, profitable, rewarding, successful, useful, well-spent, worthwhile; ***opp*** fruitless. 2 abundant, copious, fertile, flourishing, lush, luxurious, plentiful, potent, prolific, rich

frustrate *v* annoy, defeat, disappoint, discourage, dishearten, embitter, foil, hinder, prevent, spoil, stymie, thwart, vex

frustrated *adj* annoyed, disappointed, discontented, discouraged, disheartened, embittered, resentful, unfulfilled, unsatisfied

frustration *n* anger, annoyance, dissatisfaction, disappointment, exasperation, irritation, resentment, vexation

fudge *v* 1 avoid, dodge, equivocate, hedge, waffle. 2 botch, fake

fuel *n* 1 coal, diesel, electricity, gas, kerosene, oil, paraffin. 2 ammunition, encouragement, fodder, incentive, provocation, stimulus

fugitive *n* deserter, escapee, refugee, runaway

fulfill *v* 1 (do sth) accomplish, achieve, bring about, carry out, complete, do, execute, finish, implement, make sth come true, realize. 2 (satisfy sth) answer, comply with, conform to, fill, meet, obey, satisfy

full *adj* 1 (full of sth) brimful, brimming,

bursting, filled, gorged, loaded, overflowing, replete, sated, satisfied, saturated, stuffed, well-stocked; ***opp*** empty. **2** (detailed) complete, comprehensive, copious, detailed, entire, exhaustive, thorough, unabridged, whole. **3** (full lips) ample, broad, curvaceous, fat, generous, large, plump, rounded; ***opp*** thin. **4** (a full bus) chock-full *inf*, crammed, crowded, jammed, jam-packed *inf*, packed; ***opp*** empty

full-grown *adj* adult, developed, fully grown, grown-up, mature, ripe

full-scale *adj* all-out, comprehensive, extensive, in-depth, major, proper, thorough, wide-ranging

fumble *v* **1** botch, bungle, drop, flounder, make a mess of *inf*, mess up, mishandle, miss, muff, spoil, stumble. **2** (fumble in your pocket) feel around, grope, scrabble

fume *v* **1** emit fumes, smoke, smolder. **2** be angry, be enraged, be incensed, be livid, blow your top *inf*, boil, flip your lid *inf*, fly off the handle *inf*, rage, rant, rave, see red *inf*, seethe, storm

fumes *n* exhaust, gases, pollution, smog, smoke, vapor

fun *n* amusement, distraction, diversion, enjoyment, entertainment, games, jokes, joking, joy, laughter, merriment, pleasure, recreation, relaxation, sport

function *n* **1** aim, purpose, raison d'être, use. **2** capacity, duty, job, responsibility, role. **3** affair, do *inf*, event, occasion, party, reception, social occasion

function *v* act, behave, go, operate, perform, run, serve, work

functional *adj* hard-wearing, practical, serviceable, useful, utilitarian, working

fund *n* hoard, kitty, mine, pool, repository, reserve, reservoir, stock, store, storehouse, supply, treasury

fund *v* finance, pay for, subsidize, support, underwrite

fundamental *adj* basic, central, crucial, elementary, essential, first, important, inherent, intrinsic, key, necessary, principal, quintessential, underlying, vital

funds *n* assets, capital, cash, endowments, finance, investments, means, money, resources, riches, savings, wealth

funeral *n* burial, cremation, entombment, interment

funny *adj* **1** amusing, comic, comical, daft *inf*, droll, entertaining, hilarious, humorous, ironic, ludicrous, mad, nonsensical, preposterous, ridiculous, riotous, satirical, side-splitting, uproarious, witty. **2** (strange) curious, mysterious, odd, peculiar, puzzling, strange, suspicious, unusual; ***opp*** normal. **3** (feel funny) (*inf*) dizzy, ill, off-color *inf*, queasy, sick

fur *n* bristles, coat, down, fleece, hair, wool

furious *adj* **1** angry, beside yourself, enraged, foaming at the mouth *inf*, fuming, hot under the collar *inf*, incensed, infuriated, irate, livid *inf*, mad. **2** fierce, frantic, frenetic, intense, stormy, turbulent, violent, wild

furnish *v* **1** decorate, equip, fit out. **2** give, offer, present, provide, supply

furniture *n* equipment, fittings, furnishings, household goods, possessions

furtive *adj* clandestine, conspiratorial,

covert, disguised, hidden, secret, secretive, shifty, skulking, slinking, sly, sneaking, sneaky, stealthy, surreptitious, underhand

fury *n* **1** anger, frenzy, madness, passion, rage, wrath. **2** ferocity, force, intensity, power, savagery, tempestuousness, violence

fuss *n* **1** bother, bustle, confusion, excitement, flurry, tumult, uproar. **2** (make a fuss) argument, dispute, furor, objection, protest, row, squabble, trouble, upset

fuss *v* bustle about, complain, fidget, flap, fret, get in a stew *inf*, get worked up *inf*, gripe *inf*, grumble, kick up a fuss, make a fuss, take on *inf*, worry

fussy *adj* choosy, difficult, finicky, hard to please, nit-picking *inf*, particular, picky *inf*

futile *adj* fruitless, ineffectual, in vain, pointless, to no avail, unproductive, unsuccessful, useless, wasted, worthless; ***opp*** useful

future *n* **1** (in the future) hereafter, time ahead, time to come, tomorrow. **2** (no future) expectations, outlook, prospects

future *adj* **1** (a future time) approaching, awaited, coming, forthcoming, impending, prospective, subsequent, to come. **2** (his future wife) destined, eventual, expected, intended, planned, prospective

gadget *n* appliance, contraption, contrivance, device, instrument, invention, novelty, tool, utensil

gag *n* crack *inf*, funny remark, jest, joke, one-liner *inf*, quip, wisecrack *inf*, witticism

gag *v* **1** keep sb quiet, muffle, muzzle, quiet, silence, smother, stifle, suppress. **2** choke, gasp, heave, retch

gain *n* acquisition, advantage, attainment, benefit, earnings, improvement, income, increase, profit, return, rise, winnings, yield; ***opp*** loss

gain *v* achieve, acquire, attain, build up, capture, collect, earn, get, make, net, obtain, pick up, reach, secure, win, yield

gale *n* blast, cyclone, hurricane, squall, storm, tempest, tornado, typhoon, wind

gallant *adj* attentive, bold, brave, chivalrous, courageous, courteous, courtly, daring, dashing, fearless, heroic, honorable, intrepid, manly, noble, polite, valiant, valorous

gallop *v* canter, go at full speed, hurry, hurtle, race, run, rush, sprint, tear

galvanize *v* arouse, awaken, electrify, excite, inspire, jolt, shock, spur, stimulate, stir, urge

gamble *v* **1** (bet money) bet, lay bets, stake money, wager. **2** (take a chance) speculate, stick your neck out *inf*, take a chance, take a risk, trust, venture

game *adj* **1** brave, courageous, daring, plucky, unafraid. **2** agreeable, eager, happy, interested, ready, willing

game *n* **1** amusement, entertainment, pastime, recreation, sport, toy. **2** (just a game) fun, joke, laugh, prank, trick. **3** (a game you play) competition, contest, match, round, tournament

gang *n* band, clique, club, crew *inf*, crowd, group, herd, horde, lot, mob, pack, posse, team

gangster *n* bandit, brigand, desperado, gunman, robber, thug, tough

gap *n* **1** (gap between two things) aperture, blank, breach, break, cavity, chink, crack, crevice, divide, gulf, hole, opening, rift, space, void. **2** (gap in time) break, breathing-space, interlude, interruption, interval, lull, pause, respite, rest, suspension, wait. **3** (gap between people) difference, distance, division, divergence, gulf, incompatibility

gape *v* **1** gawk, gaze, goggle, ogle, stare. **2** crack, open, part, split, yawn

garbled *adj* confused, distorted, jumbled, misquoted, mixed up, twisted; ***opp*** clear

garish *adj* brassy, bright, crude, flash *inf*, flashy, gaudy, loud, lurid, showy, tacky *inf*, tasteless, vulgar

garland *n* crown, loop, wreath
garment *n* article of clothing, attire, clothing, costume, dress, garb, item of clothing, outfit
garnish *v* adorn, beautify, decorate, embellish, enhance, grace, ornament, set off, trim
gash *n* cut, incision, laceration, slash, slit, tear, wound
gash *v* cut, gouge, lacerate, nick, score, slash, slit, split, tear, wound
gate *n* barrier, door, doorway, entrance, exit, gateway, portal, portcullis, turnstile
gather *v* **1** (collect) accumulate, amass, collect, heap, hoard, pile up, stockpile. **2** (of people) assemble, congregate, convene, crowd, get together, flock, group, herd, marshal, mass, mobilize, round up, summon, swarm, throng. **3** (understand) assume, believe, deduce, draw the conclusion, guess, hear, infer, learn, understand. **4** (gather flowers) harvest, pick, pluck, reap
gathering *n* assembly, congregation, convention, crowd, get-together *inf*, group, horde, meeting, mob, party, rally
gaudy *adj* bright, brilliant, flash *inf*, flashy, garish, glaring, harsh, loud, ostentatious, showy, tasteless, tawdry, vivid, vulgar
gauge *n* **1** (size) bore, caliber, capacity, depth, dimensions, height, measure, size, thickness, width. **2** (instrument) dial, indicator, instrument, meter. **3** (yardstick) benchmark, guide, guideline, indication, indicator, model, standard, yardstick
gauge *v* **1** (gauge an amount) ascertain, calculate, check, count, determine, measure, value, weigh, work out. **2** (gauge sb's response) assess, discern, estimate, evaluate, guess, judge, reckon
gaunt *adj* angular, bony, drawn, emaciated, haggard, hollow-cheeked, lanky, pinched, scrawny, skinny, starving, thin, wasted; ***opp*** fat, plump, well-rounded
gay *adj* **1** (of colors) bright, colorful, rich, showy, vivid; ***opp*** dull. **2** (happy) cheerful, happy, jolly, merry, vivacious; ***opp*** sad. **3** homosexual, lesbian; ***opp*** straight
gaze *n* look, stare
gaze *v* eye, gape, look, stare, watch
gear *n* **1** belongings, bits and pieces, equipment, kit, paraphernalia, possessions, stuff, things, tools, trappings. **2** cog, cogwheel, gearwheel, machinery, mechanism. **3** clothes, clothing, dress, get-up *inf*, outfit, rig, togs *inf*
gem *n* **1** gemstone, jewel, precious stone, stone. **2** pearl, prize, star, treasure
general *adj* **1** across-the-board, all-encompassing, blanket, broad, comprehensive, global, inclusive, overall, universal; ***opp*** specific. **2** accepted, common, customary, normal, regular, typical, usual. **3** approximate, ballpark, broad, loose, outline, rough, vague; ***opp*** precise
generally *adv* **1** (on the whole) as a rule, broadly speaking, by and large, commonly, mostly, normally, on the whole, typically, usually. **2** (widely) commonly, popularly, universally, widely
generate *v* arouse, bring about, cause, engender, give rise to, lead to, produce, stir up

generation *n* **1** age group, contemporaries, day, era, period, time. **2** arousal, creation, production, stirring up

generic *adj* across-the-board, broad, typical, universal

generosity *n* benevolence, kindness, lavishness, magnanimity, munificence, philanthropy; ***opp*** meanness

generous *adj* **1** benevolent, big-hearted, charitable, kind, magnanimous, philanthropic; ***opp*** mean. **2** abundant, huge, large, lavish, plentiful

genius *n* **1** expert, know-all *inf*, mastermind, prodigy, boy wonder, girl wonder, master, virtuoso, whiz-kid *inf*, whiz *inf*. **2** ability, aptitude, brains, brilliance, flair, gift, talent

genteel *adj* cultured, elegant, ladylike, polished, polite, posh *inf*, refined, well-mannered

gentle *adj* **1** (of a person) amiable, easy-going, kind, kindly, mild, placid, soft-hearted, soft, tender. **2** delicate, easy, light, mild, muted, peaceful, quiet, soft, soothing. **3** (of a slope) easy, gradual, moderate, slight, smooth, steady; ***opp*** steep

genuine *adj* **1** authentic, bona fide, guaranteed, kosher, legitimate, original, pukka *inf*, real, solid, true. **2** candid, honest, open, sincere, straight, unaffected

germ *n* bacteria, bug *inf*, infection, micro-organism, virus

germinate *v* develop, grow, shoot, sprout, start growing, start, take root

gesticulate *v* gesture, indicate, motion, sign, signal, wave

gesture *n* gesticulation, hand movement, indication, motion, sign, signal, wave

gesture *v* gesticulate, indicate, motion, sign, signal, wave

get *v* **1** (obtain) achieve, acquire, attain, come by, come into possession of, earn, gain, inherit, land *inf*, lay your hands on, make, obtain, procure, receive, secure, win. **2** (get old) become, go, grow, turn. **3** collect, fetch, pick up. **4** arrest, capture, collar, grab, nail, seize, trap. **5** (get sb to do sth) encourage, make, persuade, prevail on. **6** (get flu) be infected by, catch, come down with, contract, develop, fall ill with, go down with, pick up. **7** (get to a place) arrive, come, reach. **8 get along** (be friendly) be friendly, be on good terms, get on, hit it off. **9 get at** (criticize) attack, blame, carp, criticize, make fun of, nag, pick on, taunt, tease. **10 get at** (imply) hint, imply, insinuate, mean, suggest. **11 get away** (escape) abscond, break free, break out, depart, disappear, escape, get out, leave, run away. **12 get on** (get on a bus, ship, bike) board, catch, climb on, embark, get, go on board, mount. **13 get on** (manage) cope, do, get along, make out, manage, progress. **14 get on** (carry on working) carry on, continue, get cracking *inf*, press on. **15 get around** avoid, bypass, circumvent, evade, skirt

ghastly *adj* appalling, awful, bad, dreadful, foul, grim, gruesome, hideous, horrendous, horrible, horrid, nasty, terrible

ghost *n* apparition, ghoul, phantom, poltergeist, shade, specter, spirit, spook *inf*, wraith

ghostly *adj* creepy, eerie, ghostlike, phantom, spectral, spooky *inf*, supernatural, unearthly

giant *n* behemoth, colossus, Goliath, leviathan, monster, titan, whopper *inf*

giddy *adj* dizzy, faint, light-headed, reeling, spinning, unsteady

gift *n* **1** bequest, contribution, donation, endowment, freebie *inf*, gratuity, handout, honorarium, legacy, offering, present, tip. **2** ability, flair, genius, knack, power, talent

gifted *adj* accomplished, brainy *inf*, bright, brilliant, clever, expert, skillful, talented

gigantic *adj* colossal, enormous, giant, huge, immense, jumbo *inf*, king-size, mammoth, massive, monstrous, towering, vast

giggle *v* chortle, chuckle, laugh, snigger, titter

gimmick *n* dodge, gizmo, publicity stunt, stunt, trick

girdle *n* **1** band, cummerbund, sash, waistband. **2** corset, pantie-girdle

girl *n* daughter, female, kid, lass, schoolgirl, woman, young woman, youngster

girlfriend *n* date, lover, sweetheart, young lady, woman

girth *n* circumference, perimeter

gist *n* drift, essence, idea, meaning, nub, point, sense, significance, substance

give *v* **1** allocate, award, contribute, deliver, dish out, dole out, donate, grant, hand over, let sb have, present, provide, share out, supply. **2** (give a speech, information) announce, communicate, deliver, make, reveal, tell, utter. **3** (give sb medicine, a punishment) administer, dish out, dispense, impose, inflict, prescribe. **4** (give a party) arrange, have, organize, put on. **5** (yield) buckle, fall, give way, sink, yield. **6 give in** capitulate, comply, concede defeat, give up, quit, submit, succumb, surrender, throw in the towel. **7 give out** (share out) deal, distribute, dole out *inf*, hand out. **8 give out** (emit) discharge, emit, exude, give off, produce, release. **9 give out** (announce) advertise, announce, broadcast, make known, make public, notify, publish. **10 give up** (give up an attempt) abandon the attempt, capitulate, comply, concede defeat, give in, lose heart, quit, submit, succumb, surrender, throw in the towel. **11 give up** (give up smoking) abandon, cut out, leave off, quit, stop

glad *adj* **1** (happy) cheerful, delighted, elated, happy, joyful, pleased, satisfied, thrilled, well-pleased; ***opp*** disappointed. **2** (willing) delighted, eager, happy, keen, more than willing, pleased, ready, willing; ***opp*** unwilling

glamorous *adj* appealing, attractive, beautiful, beguiling, dazzling, exciting, flashy, glittering, glitzy *inf*, glossy, prestigious, smart

glamour *n* appeal, attraction, beauty, glitter, magic, prestige

glance *n* glimpse, look, peek, peep, quick look

glance *v* cast an eye over, dip into, flick through, have a quick look at, leaf through, look, peek, peep, scan

glare *n* **1** black look, frown, look, scowl, stare. **2** blaze, brightness, brilliance, dazzle

glare *v* frown, give sb a black look, glower, look daggers at, scowl, stare
glaring *adj* 1 blatant, conspicuous, obvious. 2 blazing, bright, dazzling
glass *n* beaker, crystal, flute, glassware, goblet, tumbler, wineglass
glaze *v* coat, enamel, lacquer, varnish
gleam *v* flash, glimmer, glint, glisten, glow, shine, sparkle, twinkle
glee *n* delight, excitement, happiness, joy, pleasure, triumph; ***opp*** misery
glide *v* coast, drift, sail, skate, skim, slide, slip, soar
glimmer *n* flash, flicker, gleam, glow, shimmer, sparkle, twinkle
glimmer *v* blink, flicker, gleam, glint, glow, shimmer, shine, sparkle, twinkle
glimpse *v* catch sight of, notice, see, spot
glint *v* flash, gleam, glisten, glitter, shimmer, shine, sparkle, twinkle
glisten *v* gleam, glint, glitter, shimmer, shine, sparkle
glitter *v* flash, glint, glisten, shine, sparkle, twinkle
gloat *v* boast, brag, crow about, revel in, rub it in, show off, wallow in
global *adj* 1 international, universal, worldwide; ***opp*** local, parochial. 2 across-the-board, all-encompassing, all-inclusive, general, universal, wide-ranging
globe *n* 1 ball, orb, sphere. 2 earth, planet, planet earth, world
gloom *n* 1 dejection, depression, despair, despondency, low spirits, misery, pessimism, sadness, unhappiness; ***opp*** happiness. 2 dark, darkness, dimness, dusk, murkiness, shadow; ***opp*** brightness
gloomy *adj* 1 dejected, depressed, dismal, down in the dumps *inf*, down, low, miserable, pessimistic, sad; ***opp*** cheerful. 2 dark, dim, dull, murky, overcast; ***opp*** bright
glorious *adj* beautiful, brilliant, fine, gorgeous, lovely, magnificent, splendid, superb, terrific, wonderful; ***opp*** awful, dreadful, terrible
glory *n* 1 credit, distinction, fame, honor, kudos, prestige, triumph. 2 brilliance, grandeur, magnificence, radiance, splendor, wonder
glory *v* exult in, revel in, take pride in
gloss *n* 1 gleam, luster, polish, sheen, shine, varnish. 2 (outward appearance) appearance, outward appearance, semblance, veneer. 3 (explanation) comment, definition, explanation, note, paraphrase, translation
glossy *adj* gleaming, lustrous, polished, shining, shiny, sleek; ***opp*** dull, matt
glow *n* brightness, flush, gleam, light, luster, radiance, redness, rosiness, shine
glow *v* burn, gleam, light up, redden, shine, smolder
glower *v* give sb a black look, glare, look daggers at sb, scowl
glowing *adj* 1 bright, flushed, radiant, red, rich, rosy, vivid. 2 complimentary, enthusiastic, favorable, full of praise, warm
glue *n* adhesive, cement, paste
glue *v* bond, cement, fasten, fix, paste, stick
glut *n* excess, overabundance, oversupply, surplus; ***opp*** scarcity
glutton *n* gourmand, overeater, pig *inf*
gnarled *adj* arthritic, contorted,

knotted, twisted

gnaw *v* bite, chew, chomp, eat, eat away, munch, nibble, wear away

go *v* **1** (leave) beat it *inf*, buzz off *inf*, depart, disappear, get away, get going, get moving, leave, retreat, set off, set out, shove off *inf*, vanish. **2** (move) make for, move, pass, proceed, progress, travel. **3** (work) be working, function, operate, run, work. **4** (this road goes to Boston, our land goes as far as the river) continue, extend, lead to, reach, spread, stretch. **5** (time goes quickly) elapse, fly, pass, slip by. **6** (go gray) become, get, grow, turn. **7** (the interview went well, how is the project going?) develop, end up, fare, happen, pan out, proceed, turn out, work out. **8 go by** (time goes by) elapse, fly, pass. **9 go by** (use as a guide) be guided by, follow, obey, observe, use as a guide. **10 go for** (fetch) collect, fetch, go and get, go to pick up. **11 go for** (attack) assault, attack, launch yourself at, lunge at. **12 go for** (like) choose, like, prefer. **13 go off** (explode) detonate, explode, go bang. **14 go over** check, examine, inspect, look through, rehearse, review, run through, scan, study. **15 go through** (look through) check, examine, hunt through, inspect, look through, run through, scan, study. **16 go through** (endure) brave, endure, experience, have to put up with, suffer, undergo. **17 go without** abstain from, deny yourself, do without, forego, go short, manage without

goad *v* egg on *inf*, prod, prompt, provoke, push, spur, stimulate, urge

goal *n* aim, ambition, aspiration, end, objective, target

godforsaken *adj* desolate, dismal, dreary, gloomy, miserable, wretched

godsend *n* bit of luck, blessing, boon, miracle, unexpected bonus

golden *adj* **1** (gold) fair, gilded, gilt, gold, yellow. **2** (golden opportunity) excellent, fortuitous, ideal, opportune, perfect, wonderful

good *adj* **1** brilliant, delicious, enjoyable, excellent, first-class, great, hunky-dory *inf*, interesting, lovely, nice, pleasant, satisfactory, suitable, super; ***opp*** awful, bad, terrible. **2** (good at a job) accomplished, capable, clever, competent, conscientious, efficient, professional, proficient, skillful, skilled, talented. **3** (a good person) caring, considerate, decent, generous, honest, honorable, kind, kindhearted, trustworthy, virtuous; ***opp*** bad, evil, wicked. **4** (well-behaved) obedient, well-behaved; ***opp*** naughty

good-bye *interj* adieu, au revoir, bye, bye-bye, cheerio, ciao *inf*, farewell, see you, so long

good-looking *adj* attractive, beautiful, gorgeous, handsome, pretty; ***opp*** ugly

goods *n* **1** freight, merchandise, products, stock. **2** belongings, effects, possessions, property, stuff, things

gorge *n* canyon, chasm, gully, ravine

gorge *v* be greedy, cram, devour, eat as much as you can, eat ravenously, fill yourself up, gobble, gulp down, make a pig of yourself *inf*, overeat, shovel, stuff, wolf

gorgeous *adj* beautiful, brilliant, glorious, good-looking, handsome, impressive, lovely, magnificent, stunning, superb, terrific, wonderful

gory *adj* blood-and-guts *inf*, blood-stained, bloody, brutal, grisly, gruesome, savage, violent

gospel *n* creed, doctrine, message, teaching, word

gossip *n* **1** hearsay, report, rumor, scandal. **2** (a person) busybody, scandalmonger

gossip *v* blab, chat, chatter, spread rumors, talk

gourmet *n* connoisseur, epicure

govern *v* **1** administer, be in power, control, look after, manage, oversee, reign, rule, run. **2** affect, control, decide, determine, influence

government *n* **1** administration, authorities, executive, parliament, regime, ruling party, state, the powers that be. **2** control, leadership, management, regulation, rule

governor *n* administrator, commissioner, director, executive, head, leader, manager, ruler

grab *v* catch hold of, collar *inf*, get hold of, grasp, seize, snap up, snatch, take hold of

grace *n* charm, elegance, finesse, gracefulness, poise, polish

grace *v* adorn, decorate, dignify, enhance, favor, honor

graceful *adj* attractive, charming, deft, elegant, natural, polished, tasteful

grade *n* category, class, level, position, rank, rung, stage

grade *v* categorize, classify, group, order, rank, size, sort

gradient *n* hill, incline, rise, slope

gradual *adj* **1** continuous, even, progressive, regular, steady, step-by-step; ***opp*** abrupt, sudden. **2** easy, gentle, moderate; ***opp*** steep

gradually *adv* bit by bit, evenly, gently, little by little, progressively, slowly, steadily, step by step; ***opp*** abruptly, suddenly

graduate *v* **1** become a graduate, get your degree, pass, qualify. **2** calibrate, classify, grade, group, mark off, order, rank, sort

grain *n* **1** cereal, corn, seed. **2** atom, bit, crumb, granule, iota, jot, piece, scrap, speck

grand *adj* elegant, imposing, impressive, luxurious, magnificent, majestic, palatial, regal, stately

grandeur *n* elegance, luxury, magnificence, opulence, pomp, splendor

grandiose *adj* ambitious, extravagant, grand, imposing, majestic, ostentatious, over-the-top *inf*, pretentious, splendid

grant *n* allowance, award, bursary, donation, endowment, scholarship

grant *v* **1** allocate, allot, assign, award, bestow, confer, donate, give. **2** (allow) accept, acknowledge, admit, allow, concede, go along with, permit

graph *n* bar chart, chart, diagram, pie chart

graphic *adj* blow-by-blow, clear, descriptive, detailed, explicit, realistic, striking, vivid

grapple *v* clash, fight, struggle, tackle, tussle, wrestle

grasp *n* **1** clutches, grip, hold. **2** (understanding) awareness, comprehension, knowledge, mastery, understanding. **3** (ability to achieve sth) capabilities, capacity, limitations, limits, reach. **4** (power) clutches, control, domination, dominion, possession, power

grasp *v* **1** grab, catch, clutch, grip, hold, seize, take hold of. **2** comprehend, follow, get your mind around, get, realize, see, understand

grasping *adj* avaricious, grabbing, greedy, mean, mercenary, miserly, selfish, stingy, tight-fisted

grateful *adj* appreciative, full of gratitude, indebted, pleased, thankful; ***opp*** ungrateful

gratitude *n* appreciation, gratefulness, thankfulness, thanks; ***opp*** ingratitude

gratuitous *adj* needless, uncalled-for, undeserved, unjustifiable, unjustified, unnecessary, unprovoked, unwarranted, without reason

grave *adj* **1** grim, serious, sober, solemn, somber, stony-faced. **2** (a grave situation) critical, crucial, serious, severe, worrying

grave *n* burial chamber, crypt, mausoleum, sepulcher, tomb, vault

graveyard *n* burial ground, cemetery, churchyard

gravity *n* consequence, importance, magnitude, seriousness, solemnity, urgency, weightiness

gray *adj* **1** (of sb's face) ashen, pale, white. **2** (of weather) cloudy, dull, foggy, gloomy, leaden, misty, murky, overcast

graze *n* abrasion, cut, scrape, scratch

graze *v* cut, scrape, scratch

grease *n* fat, lubrication, oil, tallow

greasy *adj* fatty, oily, slimy, slippery, smeary, waxy

great *adj* **1** (excellent) brilliant, classic, excellent, marvelous, outstanding, superb, terrific, wonderful; ***opp*** awful, dreadful, terrible. **2** (large) big, enormous, huge, immense, large, massive, vast. **3** (considerable) acute, considerable, extreme, intense, severe. **4** (important) celebrated, chief, distinguished, eminent, famous, important, leading, main, prominent, renowned. **5** (very skillful) ace *inf*, expert, gifted, good, skillful, talented

greed *n* **1** gluttony, greediness, piggishness *inf*, voraciousness. **2** avarice, miserliness, selfishness, tight-fistedness

greedy *adj* **1** gluttonous, piggish *inf*, voracious. **2** avaricious, grasping, miserly, money-grabbing, selfish, tight-fisted

green *adj* **1** grassy, leafy, lush, verdant. **2** callow, gullible, inexperienced, naive, new, raw, wet behind the ears. **3** ecological, environmental, environmentally friendly, environmentally sound

greet *v* meet, receive, say hello to, welcome

greeting *n* good wishes, hello, message, nod, reception, regards, tidings, wave, welcome

grief *n* anguish, bereavement, despair, heartache, misery, mourning, sadness, unhappiness

grievance *n* allegation, charge, complaint, dispute, gripe *inf*, grouse *inf*, injustice

grieve *v* be distressed, be in mourning, be sad, despair, fret, lament, mourn, suffer; ***opp*** rejoice

grim *adj* **1** (gruesome) appalling, dreadful,

ghastly, grisly, gruesome, harrowing, shocking, terrible. **2** (unpleasant) awful, dire, dreadful, horrendous, horrid, unattractive, unpleasant. **3** (stern) gloomy, morose, serious, somber, sour, stern, sullen. **4** (stubbornly determined) determined, obdurate, obstinate, resolute, unrelenting

grimace *n* expression, face, frown, scowl, wry expression

grind *v* **1** crush, granulate, mill, powder, pulverize. **2** file, polish, sharpen, smooth

grip *n* **1** grasp, hold. **2** clutches, control, influence, power

grip *v* **1** clasp, grab, grasp, hold, seize, take hold of. **2** capture, enthrall, fascinate, hold spellbound, mesmerize

gripping *adj* absorbing, compulsive, exciting, fascinating, heady, interesting, riveting, sensational, thrilling; ***opp*** boring

grisly *adj* appalling, dreadful, ghastly, gory, grim, gruesome, horrifying, macabre, shocking, sickening

groan *v* cry out, moan, object, protest, sigh, wail

groom *v* **1** arrange, brush, clean, comb, fix, make tidy, smarten up, spruce up, tidy, titivate. **2** coach, drill, get ready, instruct, prepare, prime, school, teach, train

groove *n* channel, cutting, furrow, gouge, gutter, hollow, indentation, rut, slot, track

grope *v* **1** feel, finger, touch. **2** (seek by touch) feel about for, feel for, fish for, fumble for, search blindly, seek

gross *adj* **1** (fat) bloated, bulky, fat, heavy, huge, massive, obese, overweight; ***opp*** skinny, thin. **2** coarse, crude, disgusting, offensive, rude, vulgar. **3** (a gross error) blatant, flagrant, glaring, outrageous, serious, shameful, shocking

grotesque *adj* **1** absurd, bizarre, curious, fantastic, outlandish, peculiar, strange, surreal, unnatural, weird. **2** deformed, distorted, gnarled, misshapen, twisted, ugly

ground *n* **1** (soil) dirt, earth, mud, soil. **2** (under your feet) deck *inf*, earth, floor, terra firma. **3** (for sports) arena, field, pitch, playing field, stadium

groundless *adj* baseless, false, irrational, unfounded, unjustified, unreasonable, unwarranted, without cause, without foundation; ***opp*** true

grounds *n pl* **1** (around a building) area, estate, gardens, land, park, surroundings. **2** (reason) basis, cause, excuse, foundation, justification, motive, pretext, rationale, reason, reasons

groundwork *n* elements, essentials, fundamentals, preparation, preparations, spadework

group *n* **1** (small group of people) band, bunch *inf*, cluster, company, congregation, crew, gaggle *inf*, gang, party, team. **2** (large group of people) assembly, crowd, flock, gathering, horde, host, mob, multitude, rabble, swarm, throng. **3** (exclusive group of people) association, cadre, circle, clique, club, faction, ring, school, sect, set. **4** (of animals) flock, herd, swarm. **5** (of things) assortment, batch, bunch, bundle, category, class, cluster, collection, lot, set

group *v* **1** (make a group) arrange,

assemble, bring together, categorize, classify, collect, gather, marshal, organize, put together, set out. **2** (become a group) associate, cluster, come together, congregate, flock, gather, get together, swarm, team up, throng

grovel *v* abase yourself, bow and scrape, crawl, creep, fawn, humble yourself, ingratiate yourself with, kowtow, lick sb's boots *inf*, prostrate yourself, suck up to

grow *v* **1** (get bigger) develop, enlarge, expand, extend, fill out, get bigger, get taller, heighten, increase, lengthen, multiply, spread, swell, thicken, widen. **2** (come from) arise, issue, originate, spring, stem. **3** (grow old) become, come to be, get, turn. **4** (of a business) develop, expand, flourish, make headway, make progress, progress, prosper, thrive. **5** (of plants) come up, flourish, shot up, spring up, sprout. **6** cultivate, farm, plant, produce, propagate, raise

growth *n* **1** development, enlargement, evolution, expansion, extension, increase, multiplication. **2** advance, expansion, improvement, progress, proliferation, rise, success. **3** (of plants) crop, harvest, produce, yield. **4** (on the body) cancer, cyst, lump, swelling, tumor

grub *n* **1** caterpillar, larva, maggot. **2** (food) a bite *inf*, a bite to eat *inf*, fast food *inf*, junk food *inf*, meal, nosh *inf*, refreshments, snacks, something to eat

grudge *n* bitterness, grievance, hard feelings, pique, rancor, resentment

grudge *v* **1** begrudge, give unwillingly. **2** begrudge, be jealous of, envy, mind, resent

grudging *adj* envious, guarded, half-hearted, hesitant, jealous, reluctant, resentful, unenthusiastic, ungracious; ***opp*** enthusiastic

grueling *adj* arduous, backbreaking, demanding, exhausting, laborious, punishing, strenuous, taxing, tiring, tough, wearying; ***opp*** easy

gruesome *adj* awful, disgusting, dreadful, ghastly, grim, grisly, horrendous, horrible, horrific, horrifying, macabre, repulsive, shocking, sickening

gruff *adj* **1** (of a voice) hoarse, husky, rasping, rough, throaty. **2** (of a person) abrupt, bad-tempered, brusque, crabby *inf*, crotchety, crusty, curt, grouchy *inf*, grumpy, impolite, rough, rude, surly, uncivil

grumble *v* bellyache *inf*, bitch *inf*, carp, complain, find fault with, go on about *inf*, groan, gripe *inf*, grouch *inf*, grouse *inf*, moan, object, protest, whine

guarantee *n* **1** (of good quality) warranty. **2** assurance, bond, oath, pledge, promise, word, word of honor. **3** (financial) bond, collateral, security, surety

guarantee *v* **1** assure, certify, give a guarantee, give an assurance, give your word, pledge, promise, vouch for, swear, vow, warrant. **2** (guarantee a loan) back, be a guarantor for, provide collateral for, provide security for, underwrite

guard *n* **1** (of a person) bodyguard, escort, guardian, protector. **2** (of a place) bouncer *inf*, custodian, defender, lookout, night watchman, patrol, security guard, sentry, watch, watchman.

3 (prison guard) jailer, prison officer, warden. **4 off (your) guard** unprepared, unready, with your defenses down. **5 on your guard** alert, careful, cautious, on the lookout, prepared, ready, vigilant, wary

guard *v* 1 (people or animals) escort, keep, keep under guard, keep watch over, mind, protect, save, secure, shelter, shield, tend, watch, watch over. 2 (a place) cover, defend, patrol, police, secure, watch over. 3 **guard against** be alert, be on the lookout for, beware of, be wary of, keep an eye out for, keep your eyes open, take care

guardian *n* 1 caretaker, curator, custodian, keeper, steward, warden. 2 champion, defender, protector, preserver, trustee

guerrilla *n* freedom fighter, member of the resistance, partisan, terrorist

guess *n* assumption, conjecture, estimate, feeling, guesstimate, hypothesis, prediction, speculation, suspicion, surmise

guess *v* conjecture, estimate, have a feeling, have a hunch, have an idea, hazard a guess, make a guess, postulate, predict, speculate, surmise, suppose, think likely

guest *n* 1 caller, house guest, visitor. 2 (in a hotel) customer, patron, resident

guidance *n* advice, brief, counsel, counseling, direction, guidelines, hint, instruction, leadership, management, supervision, teaching, tip

guide *n* 1 attendant, courier, director, escort, leader, usher. 2 advisor, counselor, guru, mentor, teacher, tutor. 3 beacon, clue, guiding light, key, landmark, sign. 4 directory, guidebook, guidelines, handbook, instructions, manual, tourist guide

guide *v* 1 (to a place) accompany, conduct, direct, escort, lead, lead the way, pilot, shepherd, show, show the way, steer, usher. 2 advise, brief, counsel, give counseling to, give advice, give a hint, give a pointer, give a tip, give guidance, influence, inform, instruct, make suggestions, take sb by the hand *inf*. 3 command, control, govern, handle, manage, preside over, regulate, steer, supervise

guilt *n* 1 blame, culpability, fault, liability, responsibility; ***opp*** innocence. 2 bad conscience, contrition, disgrace, dishonor, penitence, regret, remorse, repentance, self-reproach, shame

guilty *adj* 1 at fault, blameworthy, convicted, criminal, culpable, responsible, to blame; ***opp*** innocent. 2 (feel guilty) ashamed, conscience-stricken, contrite, penitent, remorseful, repentant, shamefaced, sheepish

gulf *n* 1 bay, bight, inlet. 2 abyss, breach, canyon, chasm, cleft, gap, gorge, ravine, rent, rift, split. 3 (between people) difference, division, rift, split

gullible *adj* credulous, easily taken in, foolish, green, innocent, naive, silly, simple, trusting, unsuspecting; ***opp*** shrewd

gulp *v* bolt, devour, gobble, guzzle, knock off *inf*, swallow, swig *inf*, toss off, wolf, wolf down

gumption *n* ability, acumen, common-sense, enterprise, get-up-and-go, horse sense *inf*, initiative, judgment, resourcefulness, savvy *inf*, sense, shrewdness

gun *n* firearm, machine-gun, musket, pistol, revolver, rifle, shotgun

gunman *n* armed robber, bandit, gangster, gunfighter, gunslinger *inf*, hired gun, hit man *inf*, hold-up man, terrorist

gurgle *v* **1** (of water) babble, bubble, murmur, splash, tinkle. **2** (of a baby) babble, burble, chuckle, crow

gush *n* burst, cascade, flood, jet, spate, spurt, stream, surge, torrent

gush *v* **1** burst out, cascade, flood, flow, pour, rush, spout, spurt, stream, surge; ***opp*** trickle. **2** (of a person) babble, be effusive, be overenthusiastic, bubble over, get carried away *inf*, make too much of sth, prattle, speak effusively, wax lyrical

gust *n* blast, flurry, puff, rush, squall

gusto *n* appetite, delight, enjoyment, enthusiasm, excitement, pleasure, relish, verve, zest

guts *n* **1** alimentary canal, entrails, innards *inf*, intestines, viscera. **2** boldness, bravery, courage, daring, grit, mettle, nerve, pluck, spirit

gutter *n* channel, conduit, culvert, ditch, drain, open sewer, sluice, trench, trough

guzzle *v* bolt, cram yourself, devour, gobble, gulp down, knock off *inf*, swallow, swig *inf*, swill, toss off *inf*, stuff yourself *inf*, wolf down

H

habit *n* 1 convention, custom, practice, procedure, routine, rule, second nature, tradition, way, wont. 2 bent, inclination, leaning, predisposition, propensity, tendency. 3 addiction, compulsion, craving, dependence

habitation *n* abode, accommodation, domicile, dwelling, home, housing, lodging, pad *inf*, place *inf*, quarters, residence

habitual *adj* 1 accustomed, common, customary, established, familiar, fixed, natural, normal, ordinary, regular, routine, standard, traditional, usual. 2 (having a habit) addicted, chronic, confirmed, hardened, inveterate

hack *v* carve, chop, cut, cut down, gash, hew, lacerate, mutilate, slash

hackneyed *adj* banal, clichéd, commonplace, conventional, corny *inf*, overworked, platitudinous, predictable, stale, stereotyped, stock, trite, unoriginal, worn-out; ***opp*** new, original

haggard *adj* drawn, emaciated, gaunt, pinched, scraggy, thin, tired, wan, wasted, worn out

haggle *v* 1 bargain, beat sb down, drive a hard bargain. 2 argue, bicker, dispute, quarrel, squabble, wrangle

hail *v* 1 acknowledge, greet, salute, say hello to, welcome. 2 accost, call out to, flag down, signal to, shout to, wave to. 3 acclaim, applaud, extol, glorify, honor, praise, sing the praises of

hair *n* 1 head of hair, locks, mop, shock, tresses. 2 coiffure, cut, haircut, hairdo, hairstyle, style. 3 (of an animal) bristles, coat, fleece, fur, mane, pelt, wool

hairy *adj* bearded, bristly, fleecy, furry, hirsute, long-haired, shaggy, unshaven, woolly

half *n* division, equal part, equal share, fifty percent, percentage

half-hearted *adj* apathetic, cool, cursory, indifferent, lackluster, lukewarm, perfunctory, superficial, unenthusiastic; ***opp*** enthusiastic

hall *n* 1 assembly room, auditorium, meeting room. 2 entrance hall, entry, foyer, lobby, vestibule

hallmark *n* 1 authentication, endorsement, mark, seal, sign, stamp, symbol. 2 badge, indicator, mark, sign, stamp, sure sign, trademark

hallucination *n* apparition, delusion, dream, fantasy, figment of the imagination, illusion, mirage, vision

halt *n* 1 (temporary) break, breather *inf*, breathing space, hiatus, interruption, interval, pause, stoppage, time out *inf*. 2 (permanent) cessation, end, standstill, stop, termination; ***opp*** start

halt *v* 1 break off, cease, come to a standstill, come to a stop, draw up, pull up, stand still, stop, wait. 2 (stop sth happening) arrest, block, check, crush, end, nip in the bud, put an end to, put a stop to, stop, terminate

halve *v* bisect, cut in half, cut in two, divide equally, reduce by fifty percent, share equally, split in half, split in two

hamper *v* block, delay, encumber, foil, frustrate, hinder, hold back, hold up, impede, inhibit, interfere with, obstruct, restrain, slow down, stymie, thwart; ***opp*** help

hand *n* 1 fist, mitt *inf*, palm, paw *inf*. 2 (of a dial) indicator, needle, pointer. 3 (helping hand) aid, assistance, help, helping hand, support. 4 (worker) artisan, employee, laborer, worker. 5 calligraphy, handwriting, penmanship, script. 6 **a big hand** applause, ovation, round of applause. 7 **at hand** about to happen, approaching, imminent, impending. 8 **to hand** accessible, available, handy, ready, within reach. 9 **try your hand** attempt, have a go, have a shot *inf*, make an attempt, try your skill

hand *v* 1 convey, deliver, give, offer, pass, present. 2 **hand down** bequeath, hand on, leave, pass down, pass on, will. 3 **hand out** deal out, disburse, dish out *inf*, dispense, distribute, dole out *inf*, give out, share out. 4 **hand over** deliver, donate, give, present, surrender, turn over

handicap *n* 1 disability, impairment. 2 disadvantage, hindrance, impediment, limitation, obstacle, problem, stumbling block

handiwork *n* 1 artifacts, craft, craftsmanship, handicraft. 2 achievement, creation, design, doing, product, production, work

handle *n* grip, haft, hand-grip, hilt, knob, shaft, stock

handle *v* 1 feel, finger, grasp, hold, maul, paw *inf*, stroke, turn over in your hands. 2 administer, be in charge of, control, cope with, deal with, direct, manage, take care of. 3 (handle goods) deal in, market, sell, stock, trade in, traffic in

handsome *adj* 1 (of a man) attractive, good-looking, gorgeous. 2 (of a woman) elegant, fine, fine-looking, good-looking, striking. 3 (of a gift) big, bountiful, generous, large, lavish, liberal, magnanimous, sizable, valuable

handy *adj* 1 accessible, at your fingertips, available, close at hand, convenient, nearby, on tap *inf*, ready, to hand, within reach. 2 convenient, easy to use, functional, helpful, practical, serviceable, useful. 3 (handy with sth) adept, capable, clever, competent, deft, dexterous, good with your hands, nimble-fingered, proficient, skillful

hang *v* 1 be suspended, dangle, droop, flap, swing. 2 attach, drape, fix, pin up, put up, suspend. 3 (in the air) be poised, drift, float, hover. 4 (hang sb) execute, lynch, put the noose around sb's neck, send sb to the gallows. 5 **hang on** (hold on to sth) cling, cling on to, clutch, grasp, grip, hold, hold on to. 6 **hang on** (wait) hold on, hold the line, stop, wait, wait a minute. 7 **hang on sb's words** be all ears, be rapt, be very attentive, concentrate on, give sb your undivided attention, listen closely

haphazard *adj* **1** accidental, chance, random, unplanned. **2** aimless, careless, casual, disorganized, hit-or-miss, indiscriminate, slapdash, slipshod, unmethodical, unplanned, unsystematic

happen *v* **1** arise, come about, come to pass, crop up, occur, take place, transpire. **2** (happen to sb) become of, befall. **3** (happen by chance) chance, fall out, pan out *inf*, turn out *inf*

happening *n* accident, adventure, affair, event, incident, occurrence

happiness *n* **1** bliss, good fortune, heaven *inf*, prosperity, well-being; ***opp*** misery. **2** (happy feeling) cheerfulness, cheeriness, contentment, delight, ecstasy, elation, enjoyment, euphoria, gaiety, gladness, high spirits, joy, merriment, pleasure; ***opp*** misery

happy *adj* **1** carefree, cheerful, cheery, contented, glad, in a good mood, in good spirits, jolly, jovial, light-hearted, merry, pleased, satisfied, smiling, untroubled; ***opp*** miserable, sad, unhappy. **2** (very happy) blithe, delighted, ecstatic, euphoric, in high spirits, in seventh heaven *inf*, joyful, joyous, on cloud nine *inf*, on top of the world *inf*, overjoyed, radiant, rapt, starry-eyed *inf*, thrilled, thrilled to bits *inf*. **3** (fortunate) advantageous, auspicious, beneficial, convenient, fortunate, lucky, opportune, welcome

harass *v* annoy, badger, be on sb's back *inf*, bother, exasperate, give sb a hard time *inf*, harry, hassle *inf*, hound, persecute, pester, plague, tease, torment, trouble, vex

harassed *adj* agitated, careworn, distraught, hassled *inf*, strained, stressed, under pressure, vexed

harbor *n* **1** anchorage, dock, haven, marina, port. **2** asylum, haven, place of safety, refuge, safe house, sanctuary, shelter

harbor *v* **1** (a person) conceal, give shelter to, grant asylum to, hide, protect, shelter, shield. **2** (a feeling) brood over, cherish, cling on to, hold on to, nurse, maintain, retain

hard *adj* **1** (of a substance) close-packed, compact, dense, firm, inflexible, rigid, rocklike, solid, solidified, stiff, stony, tough, unyielding; ***opp*** soft. **2** (of work) arduous, backbreaking, daunting, difficult, exhausting, grueling, heavy, Herculean, laborious, no easy task, onerous, strenuous, taxing, tiring; ***opp*** easy. **3** (of a problem) baffling, complex, complicated, daunting, difficult, perplexing, puzzling, thorny *inf*, tough; ***opp*** easy. **4** (of a person) callous, cold, cruel, hard-hearted, harsh, heartless, implacable, inflexible, merciless, pitiless, ruthless, severe, stern, strict, unbending, unfeeling, unkind. **5** (of conditions) austere, bad, difficult, distressing, grim, harsh, intolerable, unbearable, unpleasant; ***opp*** good. **6** (of a worker) assiduous, conscientious, diligent, dogged, enthusiastic, indefatigable, industrious, keen, steady, untiring, zealous. **7** (of a blow) forceful, heavy, powerful, strong, violent; ***opp*** light, soft

hard and fast *adj* binding, immutable,

inflexible, invariable, rigorous, strict, stringent, unalterable

harden *v* 1 bake, cake, clot, coagulate, congeal, freeze, jell, ossify, petrify, set, solidify, stiffen; ***opp*** soften. 2 (a person) brutalize, deaden, make callous, make tough, numb, toughen

hardened *adj* 1 (a hardened criminal) experienced, habitual, incorrigible, inveterate, irredeemable, reprobate, shameless. 2 (hardened to sth) accustomed, habituated, inured, seasoned, toughened, used to

hardheaded *adj* astute, practical, pragmatic, rational, realistic, sensible, shrewd, tough, unsentimental

hard-hearted *adj* callous, cold, cruel, hard, heartless, insensitive, merciless, pitiless, stony-hearted, uncaring, unfeeling, unkind, unmoved, unsympathetic

hardly *adv* barely, faintly, just, only just, scarcely, with difficulty

hardship *n* adversity, affliction, austerity, deprivation, destitution, difficulty, misery, misfortune, need, poverty, privation, tribulation, trouble, want

hard-working *adj* assiduous, busy, conscientious, diligent, energetic, indefatigable, industrious, zealous; ***opp*** lazy

hardy *adj* fit, hale, healthy, hearty, robust, rugged, sound, stalwart, stout, strong, sturdy, tough, vigorous; ***opp*** delicate, weak

harm *n* abuse, damage, detriment, disservice, hurt, impairment, injury, loss, misfortune, ruin

harm *v* abuse, be harmful to, damage, hurt, ill-treat, impair, injure, maltreat, spoil, wound

harmful *adj* damaging, destructive, detrimental, evil, hurtful, injurious, noxious, pernicious, poisonous, prejudicial, toxic, unhealthy, unwholesome

harmless *adj* benign, innocent, innocuous, inoffensive, nonviolent, safe, tame; ***opp*** dangerous

harmony *n* accord, agreement, concord, conformity, cooperation, peace, peacefulness, unison, unity; ***opp*** discord

harness *n* bridle, gear, lead, reins, straps, tack, tackle, yoke

harness *v* 1 attach, bind, couple, fasten, hitch, hitch up, join, tether, tie, yoke. 2 appropriate, channel, control, employ, exploit, put to use, use, utilize

harrowing *adj* distressing, excruciating, frightening, heartbreaking, heartrending, horrifying, painful, terrifying, traumatic

harsh *adj* 1 (of a voice) croaking, grating, gravelly, guttural, rasping, raucous, rough. 2 (harsh conditions) austere, bleak, difficult, grim, hard, spartan. 3 (of a person, a punishment) brutal, cruel, despotic, domineering, draconian, excessive, hard, heavy-handed, severe, stern, strict, unfair, unjust, unkind; ***opp*** lenient

harvest *n* 1 crops, flowers, fruit, grain, produce, vintage, yield. 2 (things won or gained) fruits, gains, haul, prize, return, reward, spoils, winnings

harvest *v* 1 (harvest crops) bring in, dig up, gather in, pick, pluck, pull up, reap, uproot. 2 be rewarded with, collect, gain, obtain, reap, secure, win

hassle *n* annoyance, aggravation, argument, bother, difficulty, grief *inf*, harassment, irritation, pain *inf*, problem, trouble, upset

hassle *v* annoy, argue with, bother, get on sb's back *inf*, harass, harry, irritate, pester, plague, trouble

haste *n* hurry, impetuosity, recklessness, rush, speed, urgency

hasten *v* bring forward, bring on, encourage, speed, speed up, urge on

hasty *adj* hurried, impetuous, premature, rash, rushed, urgent

hatch *v* **1** be born, break open, breed, emerge, incubate. **2** (hatch a plot) conceive, concoct, cook up *inf*, design, devise, formulate, instigate, think up

hate *n* abhorrence, antipathy, aversion, contempt, detestation, dislike, enmity, hatred, hostility, ill-will, loathing, odium, spite; ***opp*** love

hate *v* **1** abhor, be contemptuous of, be unable to bear, be unable to stand, despise, detest, dislike, loathe; ***opp*** love. **2** (hate doing sth) be averse to, be reluctant to, be unwilling to, shy away from, shrink from

hateful *adj* **1** abominable, abhorrent, atrocious, contemptible, despicable, detestable, foul, hated, heinous, obnoxious, odious, ugly, unpleasant. **2** (feeling hate) angry, bitter, contemptuous, hostile, jealous, resentful, spiteful

hatred *n* abhorrence, antipathy, aversion, contempt, detestation, dislike, enmity, hate, hostility, ill-will, loathing, odium, spite

haughty *adj* aloof, arrogant, condescending, disdainful, proud, snooty *inf*, superior

haul *n* bag, booty, catch, gains, harvest, loot, spoils, winnings

haul *v* drag, draw, heave, lug, pull, tow, tug

haunt *v* **1** (go to a place frequently) frequent, hang around *inf*, inhabit, patronize, visit. **2** (haunt a person) beset, hang over, nag at, obsess, preoccupy, worry

haunted *adj* **1** cursed, possessed, scary, spooky *inf*. **2** (haunted look) haggard, hagridden, troubled, tormented, tortured, worried

haunting *adj* eerie, evocative, fascinating, nagging, poignant, spine-tingling, unforgettable

have *v* **1** be blessed with, enjoy, hold, keep, own, possess, retain. **2** (have a walk, bath, meal) enjoy, go for, indulge in, manage, partake of, take. **3** (have an illness, accident, operation) be affected by, experience, get, meet with, suffer, sustain, undergo. **4** (have a baby) bear, beget, bring into the world, give birth to, produce. **5** (have sb do sth) ask, command, commission, compel, direct, force, instruct, make, order, request, tell. **6 have to** be bound to, be compelled to, be forced to, be made to, be obliged to, be ordered to, be required to, be to, be told to, must, need to

haven *n* hideaway, hideout, love nest, oasis, refuge, retreat, safe haven, sanctuary, shelter

havoc *n* anarchy, chaos, destruction, mayhem, trouble, violence

hazard *n* danger, difficulty, obstacle, pitfall, problem, risk

hazardous *adj* dangerous, difficult, poisonous, risky, toxic, tricky

haze *n* fog, heat haze, mist, pollution, smog, smoke, steam, vapor

hazy *adj* **1** foggy, misty, polluted, smoky, steamy, vaporous. **2** (a hazy memory) blurred, confused, distant, faint, indistinct, obscure, unclear, vague

head *adj* chief, commanding, first, foremost, highest, leading, principal, senior, supreme, top

head *n* **1** brain, cranium, face, mind, skull. **2** boss, chairman, chief, chief executive, director, headmaster, headmistress, head teacher, leader, manager, principal. **3** (highest part) apex, beginning, start, summit, tip, top, vertex; ***opp*** foot

head *v* **1** be in charge of, control, direct, head up, lead, manage, run. **2** (head a list) be at the head of, be at the top of, begin, lead, lead off, start, start off, top. **3** (go in a particular direction) aim, go, make a beeline *inf*, move, set off, set out, travel. **4 head off** block, counter, deflect, forestall, obstruct, preempt, prevent, stop

heading *n* **1** caption, headline, name, rubric, subheading, title. **2** category, class, classification, division, head, section

headlong *adj* direct, fast, nonstop, onrushing, straight, wild

headstrong *adj* determined, driven, overconfident, rash, reckless, self-willed, uncontrollable, willful

heal *v* cure, make better, mend, remedy, restore to health, soothe, treat

health *n* **1** (good health) fitness, healthiness, strength, vigor, vitality, well-being; ***opp*** illness, sickness. **2** (state of your body) condition, constitution, medical history, shape, state of health. **3** (public health) health care, health service, hygiene, medical science, medicine, public health, sanitation

healthy *adj* **1** fit, fit as a fiddle *inf*, hale and hearty, in fine fettle, in good health, in good shape, in tiptop condition *inf*, sound, strong, vigorous, well; ***opp*** ill, sick, unhealthy. **2** good for you, health-giving, hygienic, invigorating, nourishing, nutritious, restorative, wholesome; ***opp*** unhealthy

heap *n* **1** accumulation, collection, hoard, lot, mass, mound, mountain, pile, quantity, stack. **2 heaps** a lot, a great deal, loads, lots, masses, plenty, stacks, tons

heap *v* amass, heap up, pile, pile up, stack, stack up

hear *v* catch, detect, hark, heed, listen, notice, overhear, perceive

hearing *n* **1** ears, earshot, hailing distance, sound. **2** audience, case, court martial, inquest, proceedings, session, trial

heart *n* **1** center, core, hub, kernel, middle, nerve center, nucleus. **2** affection, courage, emotions, feelings, love, mercy, pity, soul, sympathy, tenderness, warmth. **3 by heart** by rote, from memory, without looking, without notes, word for word

heartbreaking *adj* agonizing, crushing, devastating, distressing, heart-rending, painful, shattering, upsetting

heartbroken *adj* anguished, crushed, devastated, grief-stricken, sad, shattered

heartfelt *adj* deep, earnest, emotional, from the heart, genuine, honest, sincere, warm

heartless *adj* cold, cruel, harsh, merciless, pitiless, ruthless, uncaring, unfeeling, unsympathetic

heart-to-heart *adj* confessional, frank, intimate, man-to-man, personal, sincere, woman-to-woman

hearty *adj* **1** cordial, expansive, extrovert, hail-fellow-well-met, jolly, jovial, loud, welcoming. **2** (a hearty meal) big, filling, large, nourishing, square, substantial, sumptuous

heat *n* **1** energy, fire, heating, sun, temperature, warmth. **2** (emotional) anger, emotion, energy, excitement, pressure, urgency, vehemence

heat *v* boil, heat up, microwave, raise the temperature of, reheat, warm, warm up

heated *adj* angry, emotional, energetic, excited, fierce, frenzied, furious, passionate, vehement, vigorous, violent, worked up

heathen *n* barbarian, idolater, infidel, pagan, savage

heave *v* cart *inf*, drag, lift, lug, pull, push, raise, shove, struggle with, tow, tug

heaven *n* **1** Elysian Fields, Elysium, heavens, Olympus, paradise, sky, Valhalla; ***opp*** hell. **2** (happiness) bliss, dream come true, heaven on earth, Nirvana, paradise, perfection; ***opp*** hell

heavy *adj* **1** big, cumbersome, dense, fat, heavyweight, large, overweight, weighty; ***opp*** light. **2** (heavy pressure, rainfall) abundant, considerable, great, hard, high, intense, severe, strong; ***opp*** light. **3** (of a discussion) deep, dense, difficult, profound, serious, solemn, weighty; ***opp*** light

heckle *v* answer back, argue, catcall, interrupt, jeer, mock, shout, take issue with

hectic *adj* busy, chaotic, exciting, fevered, feverish, frantic, frenetic, frenzied, rushed

hedge *n* border, boundary, bushes, fence, hedgerow, hurdle, privet, shrubs, topiary

hedge *v* dither, dodge, duck, equivocate, evade, hesitate, prevaricate, play for time, sidestep

heed *v* acknowledge, bear in mind, consider, follow, hearken, listen to, notice, obey, pay attention to, pay heed to, pay regard to, respect, take account of, take heed of, take notice of; ***opp*** ignore

hefty *adj* big, cumbersome, enormous, great, heavy, huge, large, strong, weighty, whopping *inf*

height *n* **1** altitude, depth, elevation, size, stature. **2** (high place) apex, cliff, crest, hill, mountain, peak, pinnacle, summit. **3** (the height of bad manners) acme, apogee, culmination, embodiment, essence, pinnacle, ultimate

heighten *v* add to, augment, boost, enhance, improve, increase, intensify, pile on, sharpen, stimulate, wind up

heir *n* beneficiary, daughter, heiress, inheritor, next in line, son, successor

hell *n* **1** Hades, inferno, nether world, other place, purgatory, underworld; ***opp*** heaven. **2** (unhappiness) agony, hell on earth, misery, murder *inf*, nightmare, suffering, torture; ***opp*** heaven

help *n* aid, assistance, contribution, donation, hand, helping hand, hint, service, succour

help *v* **1** advise, aid, assist, come to the rescue, contribute, give sb a hand, help out, lend sb a hand, rescue, serve, succor, volunteer. **2** (can't help doing sth) avoid, prevent, resist, stop

helper *n* aide, adviser, assistant, collaborator, contributor, helpmate, partner, volunteer

helpful *adj* **1** (of a person) accommodating, amenable, benevolent, cooperative, friendly, kind, generous, obliging, supportive. **2** beneficial, constructive, convenient, handy, positive, practical, productive, profitable, serviceable, useful, valuable

helping *n* dollop *inf*, plate, plateful, portion, ration, serving, share

helpless *adj* **1** (not knowing what to do) at a loss, bewildered, floundering, forlorn, hapless, incapable, incompetent, struggling, uncomprehending, useless. **2** (unable to defend yourself) defenseless, exposed, impotent, powerless, unprotected, vulnerable, weak

herd *n* crowd, flock, group, mob, rabble, troop

herd *v* assemble, bring together, collect, drive, flock, gather, rally, muster, shepherd

hereditary *adj* **1** (in biology) congenital, family, genetic, inborn, inherited, innate. **2** (hereditary wealth) ancestral, by divine right, family, genealogical, handed down, inherited

heresy *n* blasphemy, dissent, idolatry, nonconformism, sacrilege

heretic *n* agnostic, atheist, blasphemer, dissenter, free thinker, idolater, infidel, nonconformist, pagan, renegade, skeptic, unbeliever

heretical *adj* agnostic, atheistic, blasphemous, dissenting, idolatrous, nonconformist, pagan, renegade, sacrilegious, skeptical

heritage *n* birthright, culture, endowment, inheritance, legacy, patrimony, tradition

hermit *n* anchorite, loner, recluse, solitary

hero *n* **1** (brave person) celebrity, champion, conqueror, daredevil, star, superhero, superman, superstar, victor. **2** (of a story) lead, leading man, main character, protagonist, star. **3** (person who is looked up to) example, exemplar, ideal, idol, inspiration, role model

heroic *adj* **1** bold, brave, courageous, daring, gallant, fearless, intrepid, valiant. **2** (a heroic achievement) enormous, epic, huge, monumental, painstaking, tremendous

heroine *n* **1** celebrity, champion, daredevil, star, superstar, superwoman *inf*, victor. **2** (of a story) lead, leading lady, main character, protagonist, star. **3** (woman who is looked up to) example, exemplar, ideal, idol, inspiration, role model

heroism *n* bravery, courage, daring, fearlessness, gallantry, valor; ***opp*** cowardice

hesitant *adj* dithering, doubting,

equivocal, evasive, hesitating, indecisive, reluctant, reticent, uncertain, undecided, unsure

hesitate *v* delay, dither, equivocate, falter, hang back, have doubts, have second thoughts, hedge, pause, stall, think carefully, think twice, wait

hesitation *n* delay, dithering, doubt, equivocation, evasion, hedging, indecision, pause, reluctance, reticence, thought, uncertainty, wait

hidden *adj* concealed, in disguise, in hiding, invisible, lurking, secret, undetectable, undercover

hide *v* **1** conceal, cover, cover up, disguise, hide away, keep secret, mask, obscure, put away, secrete; ***opp*** reveal. **2** go into hiding, hole up, lie low, lurk, take cover, take refuge

hideous *adj* disfigured, disgusting, ghastly, gruesome, horrible, horrific, nightmarish, repulsive, ugly, unsightly

hiding *n* **1 in hiding** hidden, incommunicado, on the run, under cover. **2** (a good hiding) beating, corporal punishment, drubbing, flogging, smack, spanking, thrashing

high *adj* **1** elevated, lofty, high up, raised, tall, top, upper; ***opp*** low. **2** (high in an organization) chief, commanding, elevated, high-ranking, high up, influential, leading, powerful, senior, superior, supreme, top; ***opp*** lowly. **3** (high in amount) abundant, buoyant, considerable, elevated, excessive, expensive, extreme, great, heavy, hot, intense, loud, severe; ***opp*** low. **4** (a high voice) alto, falsetto, fluting, high-pitched, soprano, squeaky, treble; ***opp*** deep

high-class *adj* aristocratic, choice, classy *inf*, de luxe, elite, first-class, five-star, high-quality, luxurious, pedigree, posh *inf*, quality, select, superior, top, up-market, upper-class

highlight *n* climax, excerpt, extract, good point, strong point

highly *adv* abundantly, considerably, extremely, greatly, intensely, really, seriously, severely, very

highly strung *adj* delicate, edgy *inf*, emotional, irritable, nervous, nervy, neurotic, temperamental, tense, unstable

hijack *v* appropriate, car-jack, commandeer, expropriate, seize, skyjack, take control of, take over, steal

hike *n* march, ramble, tramp, trek, trudge, walk, wander

hike *v* backpack, march, ramble, tramp, trek, trudge, walk, wander

hilarious *adj* a great laugh, amusing, comic, comical, funny, humorous, hysterical *inf*, side-splitting, uproarious, witty, zany

hill *n* elevation, fell, foothill, height, high land, hillock, hillside, hilltop, knoll, mound, mount, mountain, peak, pike, prominence, ridge, summit

hinder *v* arrest, bar, block, check, curb, delay, deter, encumber, frustrate, get in the way, hamper, handicap, hold back, hold up, impede, inhibit, interrupt, keep back, limit, obstruct, oppose, prevent, restrain, restrict, retard, sabotage, slow down, slow up, stand in the way, stop, thwart; ***opp*** aid, help

hindrance *n* bar, barrier, block, check,

curb, deterrent, difficulty, disadvantage, drawback, encumbrance, handicap, hitch, hold-up, impediment, inconvenience, limitation, obstacle, obstruction, restraint, restriction, snag, stumbling block; ***opp*** aid, help

hinge *v* center, depend, hang, pivot, rest, revolve, turn

hint *n* **1** allusion, clue, idea, implication, indication, inkling, innuendo, insinuation, intimation, mention, reminder, sign, suggestion, tipoff. **2** (give sb a hint) advice, help, pointer, suggestion, tip. **3** (a hint of sth) breath, dash, scent, soupçon, speck, sprinkling, suggestion, suspicion, taste, tinge, touch, trace, undertone, whiff, whisper

hint *v* allude, imply, indicate, insinuate, intimate, mention, signal, suggest, tip off

hire *n* charge, cost, fee, lease, price, rent, rental

hire *v* appoint, book, contract, employ, engage, enlist, sign on, sign up, take on

hiss *n* **1** buzz, fizz, purr, rasp, rustle, shrill, sizzle, wheeze, whir, whistle, whizz. **2** boo, catcall, condemnation, damnation, derision, hoot, jeer, mocking, ridiculing, scoff, taunt; ***opp*** applause

hiss *v* **1** buzz, fizz, purr, rasp, rustle, shrill, sizzle, wheeze, whir, whistle, whizz. **2** boo, catcall, condemn, damn, decry, deride, hoot, jeer, mock, ridicule, scoff, scorn, taunt; ***opp*** applaud

historic *adj* celebrated, extraordinary, famous, important, memorable, momentous, notable, outstanding, remarkable, significant; ***opp*** ordinary

historical *adj* **1** (historical reasons) ancient, bygone, former, old, past, prior; ***opp*** current. **2** (a historical figure) actual, attested, authentic, chronicled, confirmed, documented, factual, real, real-life, recorded, true, verifiable; ***opp*** fictional

history *n* **1** antiquity, before, bygone days, former times, the good old days, the old days, the past, time gone by, yesterday, yesteryear; ***opp*** today. **2** (a history) account, biography, chronicle, diary, memoirs, narration, narrative, recital, record, relation, report, saga, story, study, tale

hit *n* **1** bang, bash, blow, bump, clash, clout *sl*, clip, collision, crash, cuff, impact, knock, punch, slap, smack, smash, spank, strike, swat, thump, wallop, whack. **2** sellout, sensation, success, triumph, winner *inf*; ***opp*** flop

hit *v* **1** (deliberately) bang, bash, batter, beat, belt *sl*, clout *sl*, clobber *sl*, cuff, deck *sl*, knock, lay one on *sl*, punch, slap, smack, sock *sl*, spank, strike, swat, thump, wallop, whack. **2** (accidentally) bang into, bump, clip, collide, crash, run into, smash into

hitch *n* catch, check, delay, difficulty, drawback, encumbrance, hindrance, hold-up, impediment, inconvenience, mishap, obstacle, obstruction, problem, restraint, snag, stumbling block, trouble

hitch *v* attach, bind, connect, couple, fasten, harness, join, tether, tie, yoke; ***opp*** unhitch

hoard *n* accumulation, cache, collection, fund, heap, mass, pile, reserve, reservoir, stash *inf*, stock, stockpile, store, supply

hoard *v* accumulate, amass, assemble, buy

up, collect, deposit, gather, put by, save, stash *inf*, stockpile, stock up, store

hoarse *adj* croaky, grating, gravely, growling, gruff, guttural, harsh, husky, rasping, rough, throaty; ***opp*** smooth

hoax *n* cheat, con *inf*, deception, fake, fast one *inf*, fraud, jest, joke, practical joke, prank, ruse, scam, spoof, swindle, trick

hobby *n* diversion, interest, leisure activity, pastime, pursuit, recreation, relaxation, sideline

hoist *n* crane, elevator, jack, lift, pulley, tackle, winch

hoist *v* elevate, erect, heave, jack up, lift, pull up, raise, rear, winch

hold *n* **1** clasp, clutch, grasp, grip. **2** anchorage, foothold, footing, leverage, prop, purchase, stay, support, vantage

hold *v* **1** (hold sth in your hand) bear, carry, clasp, clinch, cling to, clutch, grasp, grip, hang on to, hug. **2** (hold sb in your arms) cradle, cuddle, embrace, enfold, hug . **3** (hold a passport) have, keep, maintain, own, possess, retain. **4** (hold sb in custody) arrest, bind, check, confine, detain, impound, imprison, incarcerate, keep in custody, lock up, put behind bars, restrain; ***opp*** release. **5** (hold a view) assume, believe, consider, deem, esteem, judge, maintain, presume, reckon, regard, think. **6** (hold a meeting) assemble, call, conduct, convene, have, organize, run. **7** (a theater holding 500 people) accommodate, comprise, contain, have a capacity of, seat, take. **8** (hold the weight of sth) bear, brace, buttress, carry, keep up, prop, shoulder, support, sustain, take. **9** (my offer still holds) be unaltered, carry on, continue, endure, go on, persist, remain, stay. **10 hold out** carry on, continue, endure, hang on *inf*, keep going, last, persevere, persist, remain, resist, stand fast, stand firm, stick at it, withstand; ***opp*** give in. **11 hold up** delay, detain, hinder, impede, obstruct, retard, set back, slow, slow down, stop; ***opp*** speed up

holder *n* bearer, custodian, incumbent, keeper, owner, possessor, proprietor, purchaser

holdup *n* bottleneck, delay, difficulty, hindrance, hitch, impediment, inconvenience, obstacle, obstruction, restraint, setback, snag, stoppage, trouble, wait

hole *n* **1** aperture, breach, break, chink, crack, fissure, gap, opening, orifice, perforation, puncture, rift, rip, slit, slot, space, split, tear, vent. **2** (in the ground) abyss, cavity, chasm, crater, dent, depression, dip, excavation, hollow, indentation, pit, pocket, pothole, shaft. **3** (in sb's argument) crack, defect, discrepancy, error, fault, flaw, inconsistency

holiday *n* **1** break, day/week off, leave, recess, respite, rest, sabbatical, semester break, time off, vacation. **2** (public holiday) celebration, day of observance, feast, federal holiday, festival, gala, holy day, saint's day

hollow *adj* **1** cavernous, concave, deep-set, depressed, dimpled, indented, sunken; ***opp*** convex. **2** empty, hollowed-out, unfilled, vacant, void; ***opp*** solid. **3** (a hollow sound) deep, dull, flat, low, muffled, muted, rumbling, toneless;

opp clear. **4** (a hollow promise) artificial, empty, false, hypocritical, insincere, two-faced; ***opp*** sincere. **5** (a hollow victory) fruitless, futile, insignificant, meaningless, pointless, useless, vain, worthless; ***opp*** meaningful

hollow *n* cavity, crater, dent, depression, dimple, dint, dip, excavation, hole, indentation, pit, trough

holocaust *n* annihilation, bloodbath, butchery, carnage, destruction, devastation, ethnic cleansing, extermination, genocide, massacre, mass murder, ravaging, slaughter

holy *adj* **1** (of an object) blessed, consecrated, divine, hallowed, revered, sacred, sacrosanct. **2** (of a person) devout, faithful, God-fearing, godly, pious, pure, religious, reverent, righteous, saintly, spiritual, virtuous; ***opp*** atheistic

home *n* **1** abode, base, domicile, dwelling, dwelling-place, habitation, house, lodging, pad *inf*, quarters, residence. **2** birthplace, country of origin, fatherland, homeland, home town, motherland, native land. **3** (the home of the cheetah) environment, habitat, haunt, home ground, range, territory. **4 at home** at ease, comfortable, familiar, relaxed; ***opp*** uncomfortable

homeless *adj* abandoned, destitute, displaced, dispossessed, down-and-out, evicted, exiled, itinerant, nomadic, of no fixed abode, rootless, vagrant, wandering, without a roof over your head

homicidal *adj* dangerous, deadly, lethal, maniacal, mortal, murderous, violent

homicide *n* assassination, bloodshed, killing, manslaughter, murder, slaughter, slaying

honest *adj* **1** (of a person) aboveboard, decent, ethical, genuine, high-minded, honorable, law-abiding, reliable, reputable, scrupulous, straight *inf*, trustworthy, trusty, truthful, upright, upstanding, virtuous; ***opp*** dishonest. **2** (an honest answer) blunt, candid, direct, forthright, frank, open, outright, plain, sincere, upfront

honesty *n* ethics, honor, incorruptibility, integrity, morality, morals, reliability, reputability, scrupulousness, straightness, trustworthiness, truthfulness, uprightness, veracity, virtue; ***opp*** dishonesty

honor *n* **1** (a sense of honor) decency, fairness, goodness, honesty, integrity, loyalty, morality, principle, rectitude, righteousness, uprightness, virtue. **2** (it would be an honor) compliment, credit, pleasure, privilege. **3** (the honor of representing your country) credit, dignity, distinction, eminence, esteem, fame, glory, good name, prestige, rank, renown, reputation, repute. **4** (treat sb with honor) acclaim, accolade, commendation, deference, homage, kudos, prestige, recognition, regard, respect, reverence, tribute; ***opp*** disrespect

honor *v* acclaim, admire, applaud, appreciate, celebrate, commemorate, commend, dignify, esteem, exalt, glorify, hallow, praise, prize, respect, revere, value, venerate, worship

honorable *adj* admirable, chivalrous,

creditable, decent, dependable, ethical, fair, faithful, good, honest, irreproachable, just, law-abiding, moral, principled, proper, reliable, righteous, straight *inf*, true, truthful, trustworthy, trusty, upright, upstanding, virtuous, worthy; ***opp*** dishonorable

honorary *adj* complimentary, ex-officio, formal, nominal, titular, unofficial, unpaid

honors *n* awards, decorations, dignities, distinctions, prizes, rewards, titles

hook *n* **1** (on clothing) catch, clasp, clip, fastener, hasp, link, lock. **2** (coat hook) holder, nail, peg

hook *v* catch, clasp, fasten, fix, secure

hooligan *n* bully, delinquent, hoodlum, lout, ruffian, tearaway, thug *inf*, troublemaker, vandal

hoop *n* band, circle, girdle, loop, ring, wheel

hoot *n* **1** (of an owl) call, cry, screech, toot, whoop. **2** (of people) boo, catcall, hiss, jeer, scoff, taunt. **3** (it was a hoot) laugh, scream

hoot *v* **1** (of an owl) call, cry, screech, toot, whoop. **2** (of people) boo, catcall, condemn, damn, decry, deride, hiss, jeer, mock, ridicule, scoff, scorn, taunt; ***opp*** applaud

hop *v* bounce, bound, caper, dance, jump, leap, prance, skip, spring, vault, trip

hope *n* **1** ambition, aspiration, craving, desire, dream, longing, wish, yearning. **2** anticipation, assumption, assurance, belief, conviction, expectation

hope *v* **1** aspire, crave, desire, dream, long, wish, yearn. **2** anticipate, assume, await, be hopeful, believe, contemplate, expect, foresee, look forward to, trust

hopeful *adj* **1** (of a person) buoyant, confident, expectant, optimistic, positive, sanguine; ***opp*** pessimistic. **2** (of news) auspicious, cheerful, cheering, encouraging, favorable, heartening, promising, propitious, reassuring, rosy; ***opp*** gloomy

hopefully *adv* **1** (full of hope) confidently, expectantly, full of hope, optimistically, positively, with anticipation, with assurance, with hope; ***opp*** pessimistically. **2** all being well, if everything goes according to plan, most likely, probably, with any luck

hopeless *adj* **1** (feel hopeless) defeated, dejected, demoralized, despairing, desperate, despondent, disconsolate, downhearted, forlorn, in despair, negative, pessimistic, resigned, without hope; ***opp*** hopeful. **2** (a hopeless case) beyond (all) hope, helpless, incurable, irremediable, irreparable, irretrievable, irreversible, lost. **3** (a hopeless task) forlorn, futile, impossible, impracticable, no-win, pointless, unattainable, useless, vain

horde *n* army, band, crew, crowd, drove, flock, gang, group, host, mass, mob, multitude, pack, press, swarm, throng, tribe, troop

horizontal *adj* even, facedown, flat, level, lying down, prone, prostrate, supine; ***opp*** vertical

horrible *adj* abominable, appalling, awful, cruel, disagreeable, disgusting, dreadful, fearful, frightful, ghastly, grim, grisly, gruesome, hateful, heinous, hideous, horrendous, horrid, loathsome, macabre, mean, nasty, objectionable, obnoxious, repulsive, revolting, shameful, shocking, terrible, unkind, unpleasant, vile; ***opp*** pleasant

horrid *adj* abominable, appalling, awful, cruel, disagreeable, disgusting, dreadful, fearful, frightful, ghastly, hateful, heinous, hideous, horrendous, horrible, loathsome, mean, nasty, objectionable, obnoxious, repulsive, revolting, shameful, shocking, terrible, unkind, unpleasant, vile; ***opp*** pleasant

horrific *adj* appalling, atrocious, blood-curdling, disgusting, dreadful, frightening, grisly, gruesome, hair-raising, harrowing, horrendous, horrifying, nauseating, shocking, sickening, unthinkable

horrified *adj* 1 alarmed, frightened, petrified, scared, scared out of your wits, scared stiff, scared to death, terrified. 2 appalled, disgusted, dismayed, outraged, revolted, scandalized, shocked, sickened

horrify *v* 1 alarm, frighten, petrify, scare, scare sb out of his wits, scare sb stiff, scare sb to death, terrify. 2 appal, disgust, dismay, outrage, revolt, scandalize, shock, sicken

horrifying *adj* 1 alarming, frightening, petrifying, scary, terrifying. 2 appalling, disgusting, dismaying, outrageous, revolting, shocking, sickening

horror *n* 1 alarm, apprehension, consternation, dismay, dread, fear, fearfulness, fright, panic, terror, trepidation, uneasiness; ***opp*** delight. 2 (have a horror of sth) abhorrence, antipathy, aversion, disgust, dislike, distaste, hatred, loathing, repugnance, revulsion; ***opp*** love

horse *n* colt, filly, foal, gelding, hack, mare, mount, mule, mustang, nag *inf*, packhorse, pony, racehorse, stallion, steed

hospitable *adj* amicable, convivial, cordial, courteous, friendly, generous, genial, gracious, kind, neighborly, sociable, warm, warmhearted, welcoming; ***opp*** unwelcoming

hospital *n* clinic, health center, hospice, infirmary, medical center, nursing home, sanatorium, sick bay

hospitality *n* cheer, conviviality, cordiality, courtesy, friendliness, generosity, geniality, graciousness, kindness, neighborliness, sociability, warmheartedness, warmth, welcome; ***opp*** unfriendliness

host *n* 1 anchor man, announcer, entertainer, interviewer, master of ceremonies, MC, presenter. 2 hostess, landlord, owner, proprietor. 3 army, band, crew, crowd, drove, flock, gang, group, hoard, mass, mob, multitude, pack, press, swarm, throng, tribe, troop

host *v* introduce, officiate, present, preside

hostage *n* captive, pawn, prisoner, security, surety

hostile *adj* 1 aggressive, antagonistic, anti *inf*, belligerent, combative, confrontational, contrary, inimical, malevolent, opposed, unfriendly, unkind, unsympathetic, unwelcoming; ***opp*** friendly. 2 (hostile conditions) adverse, inauspicious, unfavorable, unhelpful; ***opp*** favorable

hostilities *n* conflict, confrontation, fighting, military action, strife, war, warfare

hostility *n* aggression, anger, animosity, antagonism, antipathy, aversion, bad feeling, belligerence, enmity, friction, hatred, ill will, malevolence, malice, opposition, rancor, resentment, spite, unfriendliness, unkindness, wrath; ***opp*** friendliness

hot *adj* **1** baking, blistering, boiling, burning, fiery, flaming, heated, piping, red-hot, roasting, scalding, scorching, searing, steaming, sultry, sweltering, thermal, torrid, tropical, warm; ***opp*** cold. **2** (spicy) peppery, piquant, pungent, sharp, spicy, strong; ***opp*** mild

hound *v* **1** annoy, badger, browbeat, bully, harass, harry, nag, persecute, pester. **2** chase, drive, follow, hunt, pursue, shadow, stalk, trail

house *n* **1** abode, building, domicile, dwelling, edifice, habitation, home, pad *inf*, place *inf*, residence. **2** (a publishing house) business, company, concern, corporation, enterprise, establishment, firm, organization, outfit *inf*

house *v* accommodate, board, harbor, keep, lodge, place, put up, shelter, sleep, take in

hovel *n* cabin, den, dump *inf*, hole *inf*, hut, shack, shanty, shed

hover *v* **1** be suspended, drift, float, flutter, fly, hang, poise. **2** hang about, hang around, linger, loiter, wait about

howl *v* **1** bay, bellow, cry, holler, roar, scream, shout, shriek, yell, yelp. **2** bawl, cry, sob, wail, weep

huddle *n* band, bevy, bunch, cluster, crowd, gang, gathering, group, knot, mass, pack, posse, throng, troupe

huddle *v* **1** bunch, cluster, converge, cram, crowd, flock, gather, group, herd, jam, pile, squeeze, swarm, throng; ***opp*** spread out. **2** crouch, cuddle, curl up, hug, hunch, nestle, snuggle; ***opp*** stretch

hug *n* bearhug, clinch *inf*, cuddle, embrace, squeeze

hug *v* **1** (hug a person) cuddle, embrace, enfold, hold, squeeze. **2** (hug sth) clasp, cling, crush, nurse, squeeze

huge *adj* colossal, elephantine, enormous, extra-large, gargantuan, giant, gigantic, great, hulking, immense, jumbo *inf*, large, mammoth, massive, mighty, monster *inf*, mountainous, outsize, vast, whopping *inf*; ***opp*** tiny

hulk *n* body, carcass, frame, hull, shell, skeleton, wreck

hull *n* body, casing, covering, frame, framework, skeleton, structure

hum *v* **1** buzz, drone, murmur, purr, sing, throb, thrum, vibrate, whir. **2** (be humming with activity) be active, be busy, bustle, buzz, pulsate, pulse, stir, vibrate

human *adj* **1** anthropoid, hominid, mortal. **2** compassionate, considerate, humane, kind, rational, reasonable, sensible, sensitive, sympathetic, thoughtful, understanding; ***opp*** inhuman. **3** (only human) fallible, frail, mortal, natural, normal, vulnerable, weak

humane *adj* altruistic, benevolent, benign, charitable, compassionate, feeling, forgiving, gentle, good, humanitarian, kind, kindhearted, lenient, magnanimous, merciful, mild, sympathetic, tender, understanding, unselfish, warmhearted; ***opp*** inhumane

humanitarian *adj* altruistic, beneficent, benevolent, charitable, compassionate, gentle, good, humane, kind, lenient, merciful, philanthropic, public-spirited, sympathetic

humanity *n* humankind, man, mankind, men, mortals, people, the human race

humanize *v* civilize, cultivate, educate, polish, refine, soften, tame

humble *adj* 1 deferential, docile, meek, modest, submissive, unostentatious, unpretentious; ***opp*** brash. 2 (a humble cottage) common, commonplace, ignoble, insignificant, low, lowly, modest, ordinary, poor, simple, undistinguished, unimportant; ***opp*** great

humdrum *adj* banal, boring, dreary, dull, everyday, mind-numbing, monotonous, mundane, ordinary, repetitious, routine, run-of-the-mill, tedious, tiresome, uninteresting; ***opp*** exciting

humid *adj* clammy, close, damp, dank, moist, muggy, steamy, sticky, sultry, wet

humiliate *v* abase, chasten, crush, deflate, debase, degrade, demean, disgrace, embarrass, humble, make sb feel small, mortify, put down, put sb in his place, shame, show sb up *inf*, take sb down a peg *inf*

humiliating *adj* chastening, crushing, deflating, degrading, demeaning, embarrassing, humbling, ignominious, mortifying, shameful, shaming

humiliation *n* abasement, crushing, debasement, degradation, disgrace, dishonor, embarrassment, humbling, ignominy, indignity, loss of face, mortification, shame

humility *n* deference, diffidence, humbleness, lack of pride, lowliness, meekness, modesty, self-effacement, servility, submissiveness, unpretentiousness; ***opp*** arrogance

humor *n* 1 banter, comedy, drollness, farce, fun, hilarity, jesting, jocularity, jokes, joking, laughter, ludicrousness, merriment, quips, repartee, ridiculousness, satire, wisecracks, wit, witticisms. 2 (mood) disposition, frame of mind, mood, state of mind, spirits, temper, temperament

humorist *n* caricaturist, comedian, comic, jester, joker, satirist, sketch-writer

humorous *adj* amusing, comic, comical, droll, entertaining, facetious, farcical, funny, hilarious, laughable, ludicrous, ridiculous, satirical, witty

hump *n* bulge, bump, growth, hunch, lump, mound, projection, protrusion, protuberance, swelling

hunch *n* 1 feeling, guess, idea, impression, inkling, intuition, premonition, presentiment, sixth sense, suspicion. 2 bulge, bump, growth, hump, lump, swelling

hunger *n* 1 appetite, emptiness, famine, hungriness, ravenousness, starvation. 2 (have a hunger for sth) appetite, craving, desire, eagerness, greed, hankering, itch, keenness, longing, lust, pining, yearning

hunger *v* crave, desire, hanker, have a hankering, have an appetite for, itch, long, lust, pine, yearn

hungry *adj* 1 empty, famished, hollow, malnourished, ravenous, starved, starving, underfed, undernourished, voracious. 2 (hungry for sth) aching, craving, desperate, eager, greedy, hankering, itching, keen, longing, lusting, pining, yearning

hunk *n* block, chunk, lump, mass, piece, slab, wedge

hunt *n* chase, course, pursuit, quest, search, trail

hunt *v* 1 chase, course, hound, pursue, stalk, track, trail. 2 ferret out, forage, look for, search, seek, scour, trace, track down

hurdle *n* barrier, block, handicap, hindrance, impediment, obstacle, obstruction, stumbling block

hurl *v* cast, chuck *inf*, fire, fling, heave, launch, lob *inf*, pitch, propel, send, shy, sling, throw, toss

hurricane *n* cyclone, gale, storm, tempest, tornado, typhoon, whirlwind, windstorm

hurry *n* acceleration, bustle, dispatch, expeditiousness, flurry, haste, rush, rushing, speed, urgency

hurry *v* 1 belt, dash, fly, hasten, get a move on *inf*, make haste, run, rush, scurry, speed, step on it *inf*. 2 (hurry sth) accelerate, expedite, hasten, press, push through, quicken, speed up, urge; ***opp*** slow down

hurt *n* 1 (emotional) affliction, distress, grief, offense, pain, sadness, upset. 2 (physical) burning, discomfort, pain, smarting, soreness, stinging, throbbing

hurt *v* 1 bruise, cut, damage, disable, harm, impair, injure, mar, spoil, wound. 2 (sth hurts) ache, be painful, be sore, burn, smart, sting, throb. 3 affect, afflict, aggrieve, be hurtful, cut, distress, grieve, insult, offend, pain, sadden, sting, upset, wound

husky *adj* croaking, croaky, deep, gravely, gruff, harsh, hoarse, low, rasping, rough, throaty

hut *n* cabin, hovel, lean-to, refuge, shack, shanty, shed, shelter

hybrid *adj* amalgam, blend, composite, compound, cross, crossbreed, half-blood, half-breed, mix, mixture, mongrel

hygiene *n* cleanliness, health, purity, sanitation

hygienic *adj* aseptic, clean, disinfected, healthy, germ-free, pure, salubrious, sanitary, sterile, sterilized, uncontaminated, unpolluted; ***opp*** unhygienic

hype *n* advertising, build-up, exaggeration, plugging *inf*, PR, promotion, propaganda, publicity

hypnotic *adj* fascinating, magnetic, mesmeric, mesmerizing, narcotic, soporific, spellbinding, stupefying

hypnotize *v* entrance, fascinate, magnetize, mesmerize, put a spell on, put sb in a trance, spellbind, stupefy

hypocrisy *n* cant, deceit, deception, dishonesty, dissembling, double standards, duplicity, falsity, humbug, insincerity, pretense, sham, two-facedness *inf*

hypocrite *n* charlatan, deceiver, dissembler, fake, fraud, imposter, liar, phony *inf*, pretender

hypocritical *adj* deceitful, dishonest, dissembling, duplicitous, fake, false, fraudulent, hollow, inconsistent, insincere, phony *inf*, pretended, sanctimonious, sham, spurious, two-faced *inf*

hypothesis *n* assumption, axiom, conjecture, guess, idea, postulate, premise, proposition, speculation, theorem, theory, thesis

hypothetical *adj* academic, assumed, conjectured, imaginary, notional, possible, presumed, proposed, putative, speculative, suggested, theoretical

hysteria *n* delirium, frenzy, hysterics, madness, mania, panic

hysterical *adj* berserk, beside yourself, crazed, delirious, distracted, distraught, frantic, frenzied, in hysterics, irrational, manic, out of control, raving, uncontrollable

icy *adj* **1** arctic, biting, bitter, chill, chilly, freezing, frosty, frozen, glacial, ice-cold, polar, raw; ***opp*** hot. **2** aloof, cold, cool, chilly, distant, frigid, frosty, glacial, steely, stony, unfriendly; ***opp*** warm

idea *n* **1** abstraction, belief, concept, conception, construct, hypothesis, image, impression, notion, opinion, perception, principle, tenet, thought, theory, understanding, view. **2** (a new idea) brainwave, creation, design, inspiration, plan, proposal, scheme, suggestion. **3** (give an idea of sth) approximation, clue, estimate, estimation, guess, guidelines, impression, inkling, intimation

ideal *adj* archetypal, classic, complete, consummate, exemplary, faultless, flawless, model, optimum, perfect, quintessential, supreme

idealist *n* dreamer, optimist, romantic, Utopian, visionary

idealistic *adj* impracticable, impractical, optimistic, quixotic, romantic, starry-eyed, unrealistic, Utopian, visionary; ***opp*** realistic

identical *adj* alike, duplicate, equal, indistinguishable, interchangeable, like, matching, the same, twin; ***opp*** different

identify *v* **1** discern, distinguish, label, name, pick out, pinpoint, recognize, single out, specify, spot. **2** (identify a problem) ascertain, detect, diagnose, discover, establish, find, find out, uncover

identity *n* **1** ID *inf*, name. **2** character, distinctiveness, ego, existence, individuality, nature, personality, self, selfhood, uniqueness

ideology *n* belief, convictions, credo, creed, doctrine, dogma, philosophy, politics, principles, teaching, tenets, theory, thesis

idiom *n* **1** colloquialism, expression, manner of speaking, phrase, turn of phrase. **2** argot, dialect, jargon, language, parlance, patois, speech, usage, vernacular

idiosyncrasy *n* characteristic, eccentricity, feature, habit, mannerism, oddity, peculiarity, quirk, trait, trick, way

idiosyncratic *adj* characteristic, distinctive, eccentric, individual, odd, particular, peculiar, personal, quirky, singular, unique, unusual

idiot *n* blockhead, bonehead *inf*, dimwit, dummy *inf*, dunce, fool, halfwit, ignoramus, imbecile, moron, nitwit, numbskull, simpleton, twit *inf*

idiotic *adj* asinine, crazy, daft *inf*, dense, dimwitted, dumb *inf*, fatuous, foolish, half-witted, inane, moronic, senseless, stupid

idle *adj* **1** apathetic, indolent, lazy, loafing, shiftless, slothful, sluggish, torpid; ***opp*** hard-working, industrious. **2** (not working) inactive, inoperative, jobless, not working, out of action, out of use, redundant, unemployed, unoccupied, unproductive, unused. **3** (idle gossip) fatuous, frivolous, fruitless, futile, inane, insignificant, irrelevant, pointless, superficial, trivial, useless, worthless; ***opp*** serious

idle *v* coast, drift, hang around *inf*, laze around, lie around, loaf, loll, lounge, mess around *inf*, shirk, sit around, slack, take it easy *inf*, vegetate, waste time

idol *n* deity, god, guru, hero, heroine

idolize *v* adore, adulate, deify, glorify, hero-worship, look up to, love, revere, venerate, worship

idyllic *adj* Arcadian, blissful, ideal, heavenly, lovely, perfect, picturesque, wonderful; ***opp*** awful, terrible

ignite *v* burn, catch fire, fire, inflame, kindle, light, set alight, set fire to, set on fire, spark off

ignorant *adj* benighted, blind, ill-informed, inexperienced, innocent, naive, oblivious, stupid, unaware, unconscious, uneducated, unenlightened, unknowing, unwitting; ***opp*** knowledgable

ignore *v* brush aside, discount, disregard, neglect, omit, overlook, pass over, pay no attention, reject, shut your eyes, take no notice, turn a blind eye

ill *adj* **1** ailing, groggy *inf*, indisposed, infected, infirm, invalid, not well, off-color, out of sorts, poorly, sick, sickly, under the weather, unhealthy, unwell; ***opp*** well. **2** bad, damaging, detrimental, evil, foul, harmful, injurious, ruinous, unfavorable, unfortunate, unlucky, vile, wicked; ***opp*** good

ill-bred *adj* badly brought up, bad-mannered, boorish, coarse, crass, discourteous, ill-mannered, impolite, indelicate, loutish, rude, uncivil, uncouth, ungentlemanly, unladylike, unmannerly, vulgar

illegal *adj* against the law, banned, barred, black-market, criminal, felonious, forbidden, illegitimate, illicit, lawless, outlawed, prohibited, proscribed, unauthorized, unlawful, unlicensed, unofficial, wrongful; ***opp*** legal

illegible *adj* incomprehensible, indecipherable, indistinct, obscure, scrawled, scribbled, unintelligible, unreadable; ***opp*** legible

illegitimate *adj* **1** illegal, illicit, improper, incorrect, invalid, irregular, unauthorized, unlawful, unwarranted, wrongful; ***opp*** legitimate. **2** (of a person) bastard, born out of wedlock, fatherless; ***opp*** legitimate

illicit *adj* banned, forbidden, furtive, illegal, illegitimate, immoral, improper, irregular, prohibited, proscribed, unauthorized, unlawful, unlicensed, wrong, wrongful

illiterate *adj* unable to read, uncultured, uneducated, unlettered, unschooled, untaught; ***opp*** educated, literate

illness *n* affliction, ailment, attack, bug *inf*, complaint, condition, disease, disorder, ill-health, indisposition, infection, infirmity, invalidity, malady, malaise, sickness

illogical *adj* absurd, fallacious, faulty, inconsistent, incorrect, invalid, irrational, meaningless, senseless, specious, spurious, unreasonable, unscientific, unsound, untenable; ***opp*** logical

ill-treat *v* abuse, be cruel, damage, harm, hurt, injure, maltreat, mistreat, misuse, oppress, treat sb badly, wrong

illusion *n* **1** apparition, daydream, fantasy, figment, hallucination, mirage, phantasm, phantom. **2** delusion, error, fallacy, false impression, misapprehension, misconception, mistake

illustrate *v* **1** bring home, clarify, demonstrate, elucidate, emphasize, exemplify, exhibit, explain, interpret, prove, show. **2** adorn, decorate, embellish, illuminate

illustrated *adj* decorated, embellished, graphic, illuminated, pictorial, with pictures

illustration *n* **1** decoration, diagram, drawing, embellishment, figure, graphic, picture, plate, sketch. **2** analogy, case, clarification, demonstration, elucidation, example, explanation, instance, sample, specimen

image *n* **1** depiction, figure, likeness, photograph, picture, portrayal, projection, reflection, representation, semblance. **2** conception, idea, mental picture, notion, perception. **3** (improve your image) impression, name, perception, reputation, repute, standing, status

imaginable *adj* conceivable, credible, feasible, likely, plausible, possible, thinkable; ***opp*** unimaginable

imaginary *adj* dreamed-up, fabulous, fanciful, fantastic, fictional, ideal, illusory, imagined, invented, legendary, made-up, mythical, mythological, non-existent, shadowy, supposed, unreal, visionary; ***opp*** real

imagination *n* creativity, fancy, ingenuity, insight, inspiration, inventiveness, originality, vision

imaginative *adj* clever, creative, fanciful, ingenious, innovative, inspired, inventive, novel, original, unique, visionary; ***opp*** unimaginative

imagine *v* **1** conceive, conjure up, create, devise, dream up, envisage, fantasize, invent, make believe, picture, pretend, project, think of, think up, visualize. **2** assume, believe, conjecture, deduce, gather, guess, infer, judge, presume, reckon, suppose, surmise, suspect, think

imitate *v* **1** ape, caricature, counterfeit, do an impression of, duplicate, echo, impersonate, mimic, mirror, mock, parody, repeat, simulate. **2** copy, emulate, follow, follow sb's example, model yourself on

imitation *n* **1** aping, copying, impersonation, impression, mimicry, parody. **2** clone, copy, counterfeit, dummy, duplication, fake, forgery, look-alike, mock-up, model, replica, reproduction, sham, simulation

imitative *adj* copied, derivative, mock, parrot-like, plagiarized, unoriginal; ***opp*** original

immaculate *adj* **1** clean, impeccable,

neat, spick and span, spotless, spruce, squeaky-clean. **2** faultless, flawless, guiltless, impeccable, innocent, irreproachable, perfect, pure, sinless, spotless, squeaky-clean, unpolluted, unstained, unsullied, untainted, untarnished, virtuous

immature *adj* **1** (not fully developed) crude, green, half-formed, raw, undeveloped, unformed, unripe, young; ***opp*** mature. **2** (of a person) adolescent, babyish, backward, callow, childish, infantile, juvenile, puerile; ***opp*** mature

immediate *adj* **1** instant, instantaneous, on the spot, prompt, quick, rapid, speedy, sudden, swift, unhesitating. **2** adjacent, close, direct, near, next

immense *adj* colossal, elephantine, enormous, extensive, gargantuan, giant, gigantic, great, huge, infinite, mammoth, massive, mighty, monumental, prodigious, stupendous, titanic, tremendous, vast; ***opp*** tiny

immerse *v* **1** bathe, cover, dip, douse, drench, duck, dunk, lower, plunge, sink, soak, submerge. **2** absorb, engage, engross, lose yourself, occupy, preoccupy

immigrant *n* alien, expatriate, migrant, newcomer, settler

imminent *adj* approaching, at hand, close, coming, forthcoming, gathering, impending, looming, near, on the horizon, on the way

immobilize *v* bring to a standstill, cripple, disable, freeze, halt, paralyze, put out of action, stop, transfix

immoral *adj* bad, base, corrupt, debauched, degenerate, depraved, dishonest, dissolute, evil, impure, indecent, lewd, licentious, obscene, sinful, unethical, unprincipled, unscrupulous, vicious, vile, villainous, wicked, wrong; ***opp*** moral

immortal *adj* abiding, ageless, constant, deathless, endless, enduring, eternal, evergreen, everlasting, imperishable, indestructible, infinite, lasting, never-ending, perennial, perpetual, timeless, undying, unfading

immortalize *v* celebrate, commemorate, enshrine, exalt, glorify, keep alive, memorialize, perpetuate, preserve

immovable *adj* **1** anchored, fast, firm, fixed, immobile, jammed, riveted, rooted, secure, set, stable, stationary, stuck. **2** adamant, constant, determined, dogged, immutable, inflexible, obdurate, resolute, staunch, steadfast, stubborn, unbending, unchanging, unshakable, unswerving, unwavering

immune *adj* exempt, free, immunized, invulnerable, proof against, protected, resistant, safe, unaffected

immunize *v* inoculate, protect, safeguard, vaccinate

impact *n* **1** bang, blow, bump, collision, contact, crash, force, impetus, jolt, knock, shock, smash, stroke, thump. **2** bearing, consequence, effect, force, impression, influence, repercussions, result

impair *v* blunt, damage, debilitate, deteriorate, diminish, disable, enfeeble, harm, hinder, hurt, impede, injure, lessen, mar, reduce, spoil, undermine, weaken, worsen

impart *v* **1** communicate, convey, disclose, make known, pass on, relate, reveal, tell, transmit. **2** accord, bestow, confer, contribute, give, grant, lend

impartial *adj* balanced, detached, disinterested, dispassionate, equal, equitable, evenhanded, fair, fair-minded, just, neutral, objective, open-minded, unbiased, unprejudiced; ***opp*** biased

impassable *adj* blocked, closed, impenetrable, insurmountable, obstructed, unconquerable

impasse *n* dead end, deadlock, full stop, stalemate, standoff, standstill, stop

impatience *n* abruptness, agitation, eagerness, edginess, impetuosity, intolerance, irritability, restiveness, restlessness, shortness; ***opp*** patience

impatient *adj* **1** (waiting for sth) agitated, edgy, fidgety, intolerant, irritable, restive, testy; ***opp*** patient. **2** (eager to do sth) anxious, eager, keen, longing, raring *inf*. **3** (impatient with sb) abrupt, brusque, hasty, irritable, peevish, quick-tempered, short-tempered, snappish, terse; ***opp*** patient

impeccable *adj* **1** exact, exquisite, faultless, flawless, perfect, precise. **2** innocent, irreproachable, pure, virtuous

impediment *n* bar, block, defect, deterrent, difficulty, disadvantage, handicap, obstacle, problem, snag, stumbling block

impending *adj* approaching, at hand, brewing, close, coming, gathering, imminent, looming, menacing, near, on the horizon, threatening

imperative *adj* critical, crucial, essential, important, necessary, vital

imperceptible *adj* faint, fine, inaudible, indistinct, insignificant, invisible, microscopic, negligible, shadowy, slight, subtle, tiny, undetectable, unnoticeable, unobtrusive, vague; ***opp*** obvious

imperfect *adj* blemished, broken, chipped, cracked, damaged, defective, faulty, flawed, incomplete, limited, partial, spoilt, unfinished; ***opp*** perfect

imperfection *n* blemish, defect, deficiency, failing, fault, flaw, inadequacy, shortcoming, spot, stain, weakness, weak point

imperial *adj* **1** kingly, majestic, princely, queenly, regal, royal, sovereign. **2** grand, great, high, imposing, magnificent, majestic, noble, stately, superior

impersonal *adj* businesslike, cold, cool, detached, disinterested, dispassionate, distant, formal, mechanical, remote, stiff, unfriendly, without emotion; ***opp*** friendly, warm

impersonate *v* do *inf*, do an impression of, imitate, masquerade as, mimic, parody, pose as, pretend to be, take off *inf*

impertinent *adj* brazen, cheeky, cocky *inf*, disrespectful, forward, fresh *inf*, impolite, impudent, insolent, irreverent, rude, saucy; ***opp*** respectful

impervious *adj* **1** (not letting sth in) impenetrable, impermeable, nonporous, resistant, sealed, waterproof, watertight. **2** (impervious to her charms) immune, resistant, unaffected, unmoved, unreceptive, untouched

impetuous *adj* ardent, careless, eager, hasty, hot-headed, impromptu, impulsive, quick, rash, reckless, spontaneous, spur-of-the-moment, thoughtless, unplanned, unthinking

impetus *n* 1 encouragement, impulse, incentive, inducement, motivation, push, spur, stimulus. 2 force, momentum, power, propulsion, thrust

implement *v* achieve, bring about, carry out, enforce, execute, fulfill, perform, put into effect, put into practice

implicate *v* 1 connect, concern, embroil, entangle, imply, include, involve. 2 (implicate sb in the crime) accuse, blame, compromise, incriminate, involve

implication *n* assumption, hint, inference, innuendo, meaning, overtone, significance, suggestion

implicit *adj* 1 (implicit in sth) contained, hinted at, implied, indirect, inherent, tacit, understood, unspoken; ***opp*** explicit. 2 (implicit obedience) absolute, complete, total, unconditional, unquestioning, utter

implied *adj* implicit, indirect, inherent, insinuated, suggested, tacit, unspoken

imply *v* hint, indicate, insinuate, intimate, mean, point to, signify, suggest

impolite *adj* bad-mannered, discourteous, disrespectful, ill-mannered, impertinent, insolent, rough, rude, uncivil, uncouth, vulgar; ***opp*** polite

import *v* bring in, introduce, ship in; ***opp*** export

importance *n* 1 gravity, momentousness, newsworthiness, prestige, rarity, seriousness, significance, status. 2 (of no importance) consequence, interest, relevance, usefulness, value, worth

important *adj* 1 (of things, issues) basic, big, cardinal, central, chief, far-reaching, grave, historic, key, main, major, momentous, principal, salient, serious, significant, urgent, weighty; ***opp*** unimportant. 2 (of a person) celebrated, distinguished, eminent, famous, high-ranking, influential, leading, powerful, prominent, well-known; ***opp*** ordinary. 3 (it's important that you do this) critical, crucial, essential, necessary, pivotal, pressing, vital

impose *v* 1 (impose sth on sb) apply, dictate, enforce, exact, foist, force, inflict, introduce, levy, prescribe, put, saddle *inf*, set. 2 (don't want to impose) abuse, be a burden, butt in *inf*, crash *inf*, exploit, force yourself, intrude, take advantage

imposing *adj* commanding, effective, grand, impressive, lofty, majestic, striking

impossible *adj* 1 (not possible) difficult, hopeless, impracticable, impractical, inconceivable, insoluble, insuperable, out of the question, unattainable, unimaginable, unthinkable, unworkable; ***opp*** possible. 2 (not true) absurd, incredible, outrageous, preposterous, unbelievable. 3 (of people) (*inf*) insufferable, unbearable, unmanageable

impostor *n* charlatan, cheat, con man *inf*, fake, fraud, hypocrite, phony *inf*, swindler, trickster

impotent *adj* feeble, helpless, inadequate, incapable, incapacitated, ineffective, ineffectual, paralyzed, powerless, unable, weak

impoverished *adj* 1 bankrupt, needy, penniless, poor, poverty-stricken, ruined; ***opp*** rich, wealthy. 2 barren, bare, depleted, desolate, empty, exhausted, spent, weakened

impracticable *adj* awkward, impossible, inconvenient, not feasible, unattainable, unsuitable, useless

impractical *adj* abstract, academic, idealistic, impossible, ineffective, romantic, theoretical, unbusinesslike, unrealistic, visionary; ***opp*** practical

imprecise *adj* ambiguous, approximate, estimated, hazy, inaccurate, indefinite, inexact, loose, rough, sloppy *inf*, unscientific, vague; ***opp*** precise

impregnable *adj* impenetrable, invincible, invulnerable, safe, secure, strong, unassailable

impress *v* **1** (impress sb) affect, be memorable, excite, influence, inspire, leave your mark, make an impression, make an impact, persuade, stick in sb's mind *inf*, stir, sway, touch. **2** (impress sth on sb) emphasize, instill, stress. **3** emboss, engrave, print, stamp

impression *n* **1** (do an impression of sb) imitation, impersonation, parody, take-off *inf*. **2** (I had the impression that she was lying) feeling, hunch, idea, inkling, sensation, sense, suspicion. **3** (made a good impression) effect, impact, mark, response. **4** (your impression of sth) idea, memory, opinion, recollection, view. **5** (an impression on the grass) dent, hollow, imprint, indentation, mark

impressionable *adj* easily influenced, gullible, inexperienced, open, receptive, sensitive, susceptible, vulnerable

impressive *adj* awe-inspiring, awesome, exciting, formidable, grand, inspiring, magnificent, memorable, moving, powerful, stirring, striking, touching; ***opp*** unimpressive

imprison *v* confine, detain, incarcerate, jail, lock up, put away, put in prison, remand, send down *inf*, send to prison, shut up; ***opp*** free

improbable *adj* doubtful, dubious, fanciful, far-fetched, hard to believe, highly unlikely, implausible, incredible, questionable, unbelievable, unconvincing, unlikely; ***opp*** likely

impromptu *adj* ad-lib, improvised, off the cuff *inf*, off the top of your head *inf*, spontaneous, unplanned, unpremeditated, unrehearsed, unscripted

improve *v* **1** (make sth better) correct, enhance, enrich, help, mend, modernize, put right, rectify, refine, reform, repair, revise, touch up, update, upgrade. **2** (get better) advance, develop, gain strength, get better, get well, increase, look up *inf*, make headway, pick up *inf*, progress, rally, recover; ***opp*** worsen

improvement *n* advance, amendment, correction, development, enhancement, gain, growth, increase, progress, recovery, rise, upswing, upturn

improvise *v* **1** ad-lib, make it up as you go along, play it by ear. **2** concoct, devise, invent, make do, throw together

imprudent *adj* careless, foolish, ill-advised, ill-judged, indiscreet, irresponsible, rash, reckless, thoughtless, unwise; ***opp*** prudent, wise

impudent *adj* bad-mannered, bold, brazen, cheeky *inf*, disrespectful, forward, fresh *inf*, immodest, impertinent, insolent, presumptuous, rude, saucy

impulse *n* **1** force, impetus, momentum, movement, pressure, push, stimulus. **2** desire, drive, instinct, urge, whim

impulsive *adj* **1** (of an action) automatic, hasty, impetuous, instinctive, quick, rash, spontaneous, sudden, unplanned; ***opp*** planned. **2** (of a person) demonstrative, emotional, hot-headed, intuitive, passionate, spontaneous; ***opp*** cautious

impurity *n* contamination, dirt, dirtiness, filth, foreign body, infection, pollution

inability *n* impotence, incapability, incompetence, powerlessness, uselessness

inaccessible *adj* cut off, god-forsaken, impassable, inconvenient, isolated, off the beaten track *inf*, out of reach, remote, unattainable, unobtainable

inaccuracy *n* error, falsehood, fault, imprecision, inconsistency, miscalculation, misprint, mistake, slip, slip-up *inf*, unreliability

inaccurate *adj* **1** careless, erroneous, false, faulty, flawed, imprecise, incorrect, inexact, misleading, mistaken, out, unfaithful, untrue, wrong; ***opp*** accurate. **2** (an inaccurate shot) off-target, out, wide, wild; ***opp*** accurate

inactive *adj* asleep, dormant, hibernating, idle, immobile, inert, lazy, lethargic, out of action, passive, quiet, sedentary, sleepy, slothful, sluggish, unoccupied, unused, vegetating; ***opp*** active

inadequate *adj* **1** deficient, disappointing, incapable, incompetent, incomplete, unacceptable, unqualified, unsatisfactory, unsuitable; ***opp*** adequate. **2** (inadequate rainfall) insubstantial, insufficient, limited, meager, not enough, scanty, scarce

inadvisable *adj* foolish, ill-advised, ill-judged, imprudent, misguided, unwise; ***opp*** advisable, wise

inane *adj* fatuous, foolish, frivolous, idiotic, mindless, senseless, silly, stupid

inanimate *adj* cold, dead, defunct, extinct, inert, lifeless, unconscious; ***opp*** living

inarticulate *adj* dumb, faltering, halting, hesitant, incoherent, incomprehensible, indistinct, muffled, mute, shy, silent, speechless, stammering, stuttering, tongue-tied, unclear, unintelligible, wordless; ***opp*** articulate

inaudible *adj* faint, hard to hear, indistinct, low, muted, quiet, soft, unheard, whispered; ***opp*** audible

inaugural *adj* first, initial, introductory, maiden, opening

inaugurate *v* begin, commence, get off the ground, initiate, institute, introduce, launch, originate, set up, start

inauspicious *adj* bad, black, discouraging, ill-fated, ill-starred, ominous, unfortunate, unlucky, unpromising, untimely; ***opp*** auspicious

incapable *adj* feeble, helpless, inadequate, incompetent, ineffective, inept, powerless, unfit, unqualified, useless, weak; ***opp*** capable

incapacitated *adj* disabled, disqualified, immobilized, indisposed, laid up *inf*, out of action *inf*, unfit

incarnation *n* bodily form, embodiment, life, manifestation

incentive *n* bait, carrot *inf*, encouragement, impetus, impulse, inducement, lure, motivation, motive, reward, spur, stimulus, sweetener *inf*

incessant *adj* ceaseless, constant, continual, endless, interminable, never-ending, nonstop, persistent, relentless, unbroken, unrelenting

incident *n* **1** adventure, affair, episode, event, experience, happening, matter, occasion, occurrence. **2** brush, clash, confrontation, disturbance, fight, row, scene, skirmish

incidental *adj* accidental, chance, fortuitous, odd, random, unplanned

incisive *adj* acute, biting, clear, clever, cutting, decisive, direct, keen, penetrating, piercing, precise, sarcastic, sharp, shrewd, telling

incite *v* drive, egg on, encourage, excite, goad, inflame, provoke, rouse, whip up, work up

inclement *adj* bitter, blustery, foul, rough, severe, squally, stormy

inclination *n* **1** aptitude, bent, bias, habit, leaning, tendency. **2** desire, fancy, fondness, liking, partiality, penchant, preference, wish. **3** ascent, descent, gradient, slant, slope

incline *n* ascent, descent, drop, gradient, hill, ramp, rise, slope

incline *v* bank, bend, bow, drop, lean, rise, slant, slope, tilt, tip, veer

inclined *adj* apt, disposed, given to, having a tendency to, in the habit of, liable to, likely to, prone to, willing

include *v* comprise, contain, cover, embrace, encompass, hold, incorporate, involve, take in; ***opp*** exclude

inclusion *n* incorporation, insertion, introduction; ***opp*** exclusion

inclusive *adj* **1** all-embracing, all in, comprehensive, full, general, overall. **2** including, taking into account

incoherent *adj* confused, disjointed, garbled, illogical, inarticulate, incomprehensible, muddled, rambling, unintelligible; ***opp*** coherent

income *n* earnings, interest, pay, profit, revenue, salary, takings, wages

incoming *adj* approaching, arriving, coming in, entering, landing, new, next

incompatible *adj* clashing, conflicting, contradictory, contrasting, different, incongruous, inconsistent, jarring, mismatched, unsuitable; ***opp*** compatible

incompetent *adj* clumsy, hopeless *inf*, incapable, ineffectual, inept, inexpert, unable, unqualified, unskillful, untrained, useless; ***opp*** competent

incomplete *adj* fragmentary, imperfect, insufficient, lacking, partial, short, undeveloped, undone, unfinished

incomprehensible *adj* baffling, beyond comprehension, complicated, deep, illegible, impenetrable, inexplicable, inscrutable, meaningless, mysterious, obscure, opaque, puzzling, strange, unfathomable, unintelligible, unreadable

inconceivable *adj* impossible, incredible, mind-boggling *inf*, out of the question, unbelievable, unheard-of, unimaginable, unthinkable; ***opp*** conceivable

inconclusive *adj* ambiguous, indecisive, open, open-ended, uncertain, undecided, unresolved, unsettled, up in the air *inf*, vague; ***opp*** conclusive

incongruous *adj* conflicting, contradictory, inappropriate, incompatible, inconsistent, odd, out of keeping, out of place, surprising

inconsiderate *adj* careless, insensitive, intolerant, rude, self-centered, selfish, tactless, thoughtless, uncaring, unhelpful, unkind, unsympathetic; ***opp*** considerate

inconsolable *adj* brokenhearted, desolate, despairing, grief-stricken, heartbroken, miserable, sick at heart, unhappy

inconspicuous *adj* camouflaged, discreet, hidden, insignificant, in the background, invisible, low-key *inf*, modest, muted, ordinary, plain, quiet, small, unassuming, unobtrusive, unremarkable; ***opp*** conspicuous

inconvenient *adj* annoying, awkward, difficult, disrupting, embarrassing, inappropriate, irritating, tiresome, troublesome, unmanageable, unsuitable; ***opp*** convenient

incorporate *v* absorb, amalgamate, assimilate, blend, combine, comprise, consist of, contain, fuse, include, integrate, meld, merge, mix, take in, unify, unite

incorrect *adj* erroneous, false, faulty, flawed, inaccurate, misleading, mistaken, out, untrue, wide of the mark, wrong; ***opp*** correct

incorrigible *adj* beyond redemption, confirmed, dyed-in-the-wool *inf*, habitual, hardened, hopeless *inf*, incurable, inveterate, shameless, unrepentant

incorruptible *adj* honest, honorable, moral, straight, trustworthy, upright, virtuous

increase *n* addition, boost, development, enlargement, escalation, expansion, extension, gain, growth, rise, upturn; ***opp*** decrease

increase *v* **1** (of size) add to, augment, broaden, build up, dilate, enlarge, expand, extend, gain, get bigger, grow, inflate, lengthen, magnify, make bigger, maximize, multiply, mushroom, proliferate, prolong, snowball, spread, strengthen, stretch, swell, widen; ***opp*** decrease. **2** (of sound) amplify, boost, intensify, swell, turn up; ***opp*** decrease. **3** (of quality) advance, broaden, develop, enhance, improve, step up *inf*. **4** (of seriousness, tension) build, escalate, grow, heighten, intensify, mount, raise

increasing *adj* developing, escalating, greater than ever, growing, on the increase, spreading; ***opp*** decreasing

incredible *adj* **1** absurd, beyond belief, far-fetched, highly unlikely, implausible, impossible, improbable, inconceivable, miraculous, preposterous, surprising, unbelievable, unconvincing, unimaginable. **2** (good) amazing, extraordinary, fantastic *inf*, great, wonderful; ***opp*** dreadful, terrible

incriminate *v* accuse, blame, charge, implicate, involve, point your finger at *inf*, put the blame on

incur *v* **1** (incur sb's anger) arouse, bring upon yourself, draw, provoke. **2** (incur a fine) be liable to, earn, get, lay yourself open to, run up, suffer

incurable *adj* fatal, hopeless, inoperable,

terminal, untreatable; ***opp*** curable

indebted *adj* grateful, in sb's debt, obliged, thankful, under an obligation

indecent *adj* **1** blue, crude, dirty, filthy, impure, lewd, naughty, obscene, pornographic, risqué, sexy *inf*, smutty, suggestive, vulgar. **2** improper, in bad taste, offensive, outrageous, unbecoming, unseemly, unsuitable

indecipherable *adj* illegible, unclear, unintelligible, unreadable

indecisive *adj* dithering, faltering, hesitating, of two minds *inf*, shilly-shallying, sitting on the fence, tentative, uncertain, undecided, unsettled, up in the air *inf*, wavering; ***opp*** decisive

indefensible *adj* inexcusable, unforgivable, unjustifiable, unpardonable, wrong

indefinite *adj* **1** (not decided) ambiguous, doubtful, inconclusive, open, uncertain, undecided, undetermined. **2** (not clear) blurred, confused, dim, fuzzy, hazy, indistinct, unclear, vague

indelible *adj* enduring, fast, fixed, indestructible, ingrained, lasting, permanent, unfading

independence *n* **1** (of countries) freedom, home rule, liberty, self-determination, self-government, self-rule, sovereignty. **2** (of people) freedom, individualism, liberty, self-confidence, self-sufficiency

independent *adj* **1** (of countries) free, liberated, neutral, self-governing. **2** (of things) distinct, free-standing, individual, private, self-contained, separate, unconnected, unrelated. **3** (of people) carefree, footloose, free, free-thinking, individualistic, liberated, open-minded, self-reliant, self-sufficient, self-supporting, unbiased

indescribable *adj* beyond words, indefinable, unspeakable, unutterable

indestructible *adj* durable, enduring, eternal, everlasting, immortal, indelible, lasting, permanent, solid, strong, tough, unbreakable; ***opp*** breakable, delicate

index *n* catalog, directory, guide, key, table of contents

indicate *v* be a sign of, communicate, convey, denote, imply, manifest, mean, point to, reveal, say, show, signal, signify, stand for, suggest, symbolize

indication *n* clue, evidence, explanation, hint, sign, signal, symptom, token, warning

indicator *n* display, gauge, guide, index, marker, meter, needle, pointer, sign, signal, signpost, symbol

indictment *n* accusation, allegation, charge, prosecution, summons

indifferent *adj* **1** (indifferent to sth) aloof, apathetic, blasé, callous, cold, cool, detached, distant, uncaring, unconcerned, unfeeling, uninterested, unmoved, unresponsive. **2** (not very good) average, fair, mediocre, ordinary, undistinguished, uninspired

indigestion *n* acidity, dyspepsia, heartburn

indignant *adj* angry, annoyed, disgruntled, exasperated, furious, in a huff, incensed, infuriated, irate, miffed *inf*, peeved *inf*, put out *inf*, resentful, vexed; ***opp*** pleased

indirect *adj* **1** (not straight) circuitous, crooked, meandering, rambling, roundabout, tortuous, wandering, winding, zigzag; ***opp*** direct. **2** (not intended) accidental, incidental, secondary, unintended. **3** (not open) devious, disguised, euphemistic, implicit, implied, oblique, sneaky *inf*, surreptitious; ***opp*** open

indiscreet *adj* careless, foolish, ill-considered, imprudent, insensitive, tactless, undiplomatic; ***opp*** discreet

indiscretion *n* **1** blunder, error, faux pas, gaffe, mistake, slip, slip of the tongue. **2** carelessness, foolishness, lack of diplomacy, tactlessness, thoughtlessness

indiscriminate *adj* **1** (indiscriminate bombing) careless, general, haphazard, random, sweeping, unsystematic, wholesale. **2** (not choosing carefully) aimless, casual, desultory, promiscuous, uncritical, undiscerning, unsystematic; ***opp*** selective

indispensable *adj* basic, crucial, essential, imperative, important, necessary, needed, required, vital; ***opp*** dispensable

indistinct *adj* **1** bleary, blurred, dim, faint, fuzzy, hazy, misty, out of focus, shadowy, vague; ***opp*** clear, distinct. **2** ambiguous, confused, doubtful, indefinite, muffled, slurred, unclear, weak; ***opp*** clear, distinct

indistinguishable *adj* alike, identical, interchangeable, the same

individual *adj* **1** characteristic, distinct, distinctive, exclusive, idiosyncratic, original, own, particular, personal, specific, unique. **2** (for one person) for one, private, separate, single

individual *n* character, human being, person, type

individualist *n* free spirit, individual, loner, maverick, nonconformist, original

indoctrinate *v* brainwash, drill, instill, reeducate, school, teach, train

induce *v* coax, convince, encourage, get, impel, incite, motivate, persuade, prompt, talk into, tempt, urge

inducement *n* attraction, bait, encouragement, incentive, lure, motive, provocation, reward, stimulus, sweetener *inf*

indulge *v* **1** (indulge sb's wishes) cater to, fulfill, give in to, give way to, gratify, pander to, satisfy, yield to. **2** (indulge in sth) bask, give yourself up to, luxuriate, revel, wallow. **3** (indulge sb) baby, be indulgent to, cosset, mollycoddle, pamper, spoil, treat

indulgence *n* **1** fulfillment, gratification, satisfaction. **2** excess, extravagance, luxury, self-gratification. **3** compassion, fondness, forgiveness, kindness, tolerance, understanding

indulgent *adj* compassionate, doting, easygoing, fond, humane, kind, lenient, liberal, permissive, sympathetic, tolerant, understanding

industrious *adj* active, busy, conscientious, diligent, energetic, hardworking, keen, productive, tireless, unflagging; ***opp*** lazy

industry *n* **1** business, commerce, manufacturing, production, trade. **2** activity, application, busyness, diligence, effort, energy, industriousness, labor, perseverance, steadiness, tirelessness, toil, zeal

inedible *adj* bad, harmful, indigestible,

not fit to eat, off *inf*, poisonous, rotten, uneatable, unpalatable; ***opp*** edible

ineffective *adj* **1** (not having any effect) fruitless, futile, ineffectual, unavailing, unsuccessful, vain; ***opp*** effective. **2** (an ineffective leader) hopeless *inf*, inadequate, incapable, incompetent, inefficient, inept, powerless, unproductive, useless, weak, worthless; ***opp*** effective

inefficient *adj* **1** extravagant, uneconomical, wasteful; ***opp*** efficient. **2** (of a person) disorganized, incapable, ineffectual, inept; ***opp*** efficient

ineligible *adj* disqualified, inappropriate, out of the running *inf*, ruled out, unacceptable, undesirable, unfit, unqualified, unsuitable, unworthy; ***opp*** eligible

inept *adj* **1** (inept handling of the crisis) awkward, bungling, clumsy, gauche, heavy-handed, incompetent, ineffectual, unskillful. **2** (an inept remark) ill-timed, inappropriate, out of place, tactless, tasteless, unsuitable

inequality *n* bias, discrepancy, discrimination, lack of balance, imbalance, prejudice, unevenness, variation; ***opp*** equality

inert *adj* comatose, dead, dormant, immobile, inactive, inanimate, lifeless, motionless, passive, stationary, still, torpid, unresponsive; ***opp*** active

inertia *n* apathy, drowsiness, idleness, inactivity, laziness, lethargy, listlessness, passivity, sloth, stillness, torpor

inevitable *adj* assured, bound to happen, certain, destined, fixed, inescapable, inexorable, ordained, sure, unavoidable

inexcusable *adj* indefensible, outrageous, reprehensible, unforgivable, unjustifiable, unpardonable

inexpensive *adj* bargain, budget, cheap, dirt-cheap *inf*, economical, low-cost, low-priced, modest, reasonable; ***opp*** expensive

inexperienced *adj* amateur, immature, innocent, naive, new, raw, unpracticed, unqualified, unskilled, unsophisticated, untrained, wet behind the ears *inf*, young; ***opp*** experienced

inexplicable *adj* baffling, bewildering, incomprehensible, mysterious, mystifying, puzzling, strange, unaccountable, unfathomable, weird

infallible *adj* **1** (of a method) certain, dependable, foolproof, reliable, sound, sure, sure-fire *inf*, trustworthy, unfailing. **2** (of a person) faultless, flawless, perfect, without fault

infamous *adj* **1** (well-known) ill-famed, notorious, renowned, well-known. **2** (bad) disgraceful, dishonorable, disreputable, monstrous, outrageous, scandalous, shameful, shocking, villainous, wicked

infant *n* babe, baby, child, little child, toddler, tot

infatuated *adj* besotted, bewitched, captivated, enamored, enchanted, fascinated, in love, obsessed, smitten *inf*, spellbound, swept off your feet, under sb's spell

infatuation *n* crush *inf*, fixation, mania, obsession, passion, thing *inf*

infect *v* **1** blight, contaminate, corrupt, poison, pollute, spoil, taint, touch. **2** pass on, spread, transmit

infection *n* **1** bacteria, bug *inf*, disease, epidemic, germs, septicemia, virus. **2** contamination, poison, pollution
infectious *adj* catching, contagious, spreading, transmissible, transmittable
infer *v* conclude, deduce, draw a conclusion, gather, presume, read between the lines, understand
inference *n* assumption, conclusion, conjecture, deduction, presumption
inferior *adj* **1** (in rank) humble, junior, lesser, lower, lowly, minor, secondary, second-class, subordinate, unimportant; ***opp*** superior. **2** (in quality) cheap, defective, faulty, imperfect, poor, second-rate, shoddy, substandard; ***opp*** good, superior
infertile *adj* arid, barren, childless, sterile, unfruitful, unproductive; ***opp*** fertile
infest *v* crawl over, flood, invade, overrun, plague, ravage, swarm
infested *adj* alive, crawling, overrun, plagued, ridden, swarming, teeming
infiltrate *v* creep in, enter secretly, filter through, insinuate into, intrude, penetrate, pervade, seep in, soak into, spy on, worm into
infinite *adj* bottomless, boundless, enormous, eternal, huge, immense, incalculable, inexhaustible, limitless, measureless, never-ending, numberless, unbounded, uncounted, unending, untold, vast, wide, without end, without number
infinity *n* endlessness, eternity, space, vastness
infirm *adj* decrepit, doddering, doddery, feeble, frail, weak; ***opp*** healthy, strong
infirmity *n* ailment, disability, disease, disorder, illness, impairment, sickness, weakness
inflame *v* anger, arouse, enrage, exasperate, excite, ignite, incense, infuriate, kindle, madden, provoke, rile, stir up, whip up
inflamed *adj* angry-looking, festering, fevered, hot, infected, red, septic, sore, swollen
inflammable *adj* combustible, flammable, incendiary, likely to burn, volatile
inflammation *n* abscess, boil, burning, heat, infection, irritation, painfulness, rash, redness, sore, soreness, swelling, tenderness
inflate *v* balloon, blow up, boost, dilate, enlarge, expand, increase, puff out, puff up, pump up, swell
inflexible *adj* **1** (of a person) adamant, firm, obstinate, pig-headed *inf*, strict, stubborn, unbending, uncompromising, unhelpful; ***opp*** flexible. **2** (of a material) firm, fixed, hard, inelastic, rigid, stiff, unyielding; ***opp*** flexible
inflict *v* apply, deal out, deliver, exact, impose, levy, wreak
influence *n* ascendancy, authority, clout *inf*, control, dominance, hold, importance, power, prestige, standing
influence *v* affect, bias, change, determine, have an effect, manipulate, persuade, prejudice, pull strings *inf*, put pressure on, sway
influential *adj* authoritative, important, instrumental, momentous, persuasive, potent, powerful, prestigious, significant, strong
influx *n* arrival, flood, flow, inflow,

inrush, invasion, rush, stream

inform *v* **1** advise, announce, enlighten, fill sb in *inf*, give information, give sb the lowdown *inf*, leak, let sb know, notify, put sb in the picture *inf*, teach, tell. **2** (inform on sb) blab, blow the whistle *inf*, rat *sl*, sneak *inf*, split *inf*, squeal *inf*, tell *inf*, tell tales *inf*, tip off *inf*

informal *adj* **1** (of an event) casual, cozy, friendly, relaxed, simple, unceremonious, unofficial; ***opp*** formal. **2** (of a person) approachable, easygoing, free and easy, friendly, unpretentious. **3** (of language) chatty, colloquial, everyday, slangy *inf*; ***opp*** formal

information *n* advice, data, evidence, facts, info *inf*, intelligence, knowledge, news, statistics

informative *adj* chatty, educational, enlightening, factual, gossipy, helpful, illuminating, instructive, newsy, revealing; ***opp*** uninformative

informed *adj* **1** (keep sb informed) posted, primed, up-to-date, well-briefed. **2** (knowing a lot) clued in, enlightened, intelligent, knowledgable, well-informed, well-read

informer *n* betrayer, informant, sneak, spy, stool pigeon *inf*, tattletale *inf*, traitor

infrequent *adj* few and far between, irregular, occasional, once in a blue moon *inf*, rare, sporadic, uncommon, unusual; ***opp*** frequent

infringe *v* break, defy, disobey, disregard, flout, ignore, overstep

infuriate *v* aggravate *inf*, anger, bug *inf*, drive sb mad *inf*, enrage, exasperate, incense, irritate, madden, make sb's blood boil, make sb see red, outrage, provoke, rile

infuriating *adj* aggravating *inf*, annoying, exasperating, galling, irritating, maddening, provoking

ingenious *adj* brilliant, clever, crafty, cunning, imaginative, inventive, neat, original, smart

ingenuous *adj* guileless, honest, inexperienced, innocent, naive, simple, sincere, trusting, unsophisticated; ***opp*** crafty

ingredient *n* component, constituent, contents, element, factor, part

inhabit *v* colonize, dwell, live, make your home, occupy, populate, rent, reside, set up home, settle, stay, take up residence in

inhabitable *adj* habitable, in reasonable condition, livable in, livable, weatherproof; ***opp*** uninhabitable

inhabitant *n* dweller, tenant, occupant, householder, citizen, resident, inmate, lodger, native, townsperson

inhale *v* breathe in, draw in, suck in, take down into your lungs; ***opp*** exhale

inherent *adj* basic, built-in, congenital, essential, fundamental, hereditary, inbred, inbuilt, ingrained, inherited, innate, intrinsic, natural

inherit *v* accede to, be heir to, be left, be willed, come into, succeed to, take over

inheritance *n* bequest, birthright, endowment, estate, heritage, legacy

inhibit *v* check, constrain, curb, hold back, interfere with, prevent, repress, restrict, stem, straitjacket, suppress

inhibited *adj* constrained, embarrassed, guarded, reserved, self-conscious, shy, uptight *inf*; ***opp*** uninhibited

inhibition *n* angst, constraint, embarrassment, reserve, reticence, self-consciousness, shyness

inhospitable *adj* 1 (of a person) aloof, antisocial, cold, cool, hostile, unfriendly, unsociable, unwelcoming. 2 (of a landscape) barren, bleak, desolate, forbidding, godforsaken, hostile, uninviting

inhuman *adj* barbaric, barbarous, cruel, heartless, inhumane, merciless, pitiless, savage, unfeeling, unnatural

inhumane *adj* brutal, callous, cold-blooded, cruel, hard-hearted, heartless, inhuman, pitiless, unfeeling; ***opp*** humane

iniquitous *adj* corrupt, criminal, evil, immoral, infamous, outrageous, scandalous, unfair, unjust, wicked, wrong; ***opp*** fair, right

initial *adj* early, first, inaugural, introductory, opening; ***opp*** final

initiate *v* begin, commence, get under way, instigate, launch, originate, pioneer, prompt, set up, start, stimulate, trigger; ***opp*** terminate

initiation *n* admission, baptism, debut, enrollment, induction, initiation rite, introduction, investment, ordination, rite of passage

initiative *n* 1 ambition, creativity, drive, dynamism, enterprise, resourcefulness, self-motivation. 2 plan, program, project, proposal, scheme, suggestion. 3 advantage, first move, first step, lead, opening gambit

inject *v* 1 inoculate, mainline *inf*, shoot *inf*, shoot up *inf*, squirt in, vaccinate. 2 (inject cash into sth) add, bring in, infuse, insert, instill, introduce, put

injection *n* 1 booster, fix *inf*, immunization, inoculation, jab *inf*, shot *inf*, vaccination. 2 (an injection of cash) addition, introduction

injure *v* 1 (wound) cut, damage, disable, disfigure, fracture, harm, hurt, mutilate, wound. 2 (spoil) damage, harm, ruin, spoil, undermine, weaken

injured *adj* 1 (wounded) disabled, fractured, hurt, sore, wounded. 2 (spoiled) damaged, harmed, spoiled, undermined, weakened. 3 (an injured look) aggrieved, hurt, put out, reproachful, wounded

injury *n* bruise, cut, fracture, gash, laceration, sore, wound

injustice *n* bias, discrimination, favoritism, inequity, offense, one-sidedness, prejudice, unfairness, wrong; ***opp*** justice

inn *n* bed-and-breakfast, guesthouse, motel

innate *adj* built-in, inborn, inbuilt, inherent, inherited, instinctive, intrinsic, natural

inner *adj* 1 central, innermost, inside, interior, internal, middle; ***opp*** external, outer. 2 intimate, personal, private, secret; ***opp*** external, outer, public

innocence *n* 1 honesty, probity, purity, virtue; ***opp*** guilt. 2 gullibility, inexperience, naivety, simplicity

innocent *adj* 1 blameless, in the clear, not guilty; ***opp*** guilty. 2 childlike, credulous, gullible, inexperienced, naive; ***opp*** experienced

innovation *n* change, creativity, introduction, invention, new method, novelty, reform

innuendo *n* allusion, hint, implication, insinuation, rumor, suggestion, whisper

inquest *n* hearing, inquiry, investigation, probe, study

inquire *v* ask, explore, investigate, look into, make inquiries, query

inquiry *n* **1** examination, exploration, investigation, review, study, survey. **2** query, question, request

inquisitive *adj* curious, interested, interfering, meddlesome, nosy, prying

insane *adj* **1** crazy, deranged, disturbed, mad, mental, mentally disturbed, mentally ill, not all there, off your rocker *inf*, out of you mind, senile, unbalanced, unhinged; ***opp*** sane. **2** (an insane idea) crackpot *inf*, crazy, daft *inf*, foolish, harebrained, mad, ridiculous, stupid; ***opp*** sensible

insanity *n* **1** dementia, madness, mental disability, mental disorder, mental illness, senility. **2** (stupidity) folly, foolhardiness, lunacy, madness, stupidity

insatiable *adj* avid, greedy, inordinate, irrepressible, never satisfied, voracious

inscribe *v* carve, cut, engrave, etch, mark, sign, write

inscription *n* dedication, engraving, legend, lettering, message, signature, words

inscrutable *adj* blank, cryptic, deadpan, enigmatic, impenetrable, mysterious, poker-faced

insect *n* beetle, bug *inf*, creepy-crawly *inf*, fly

insecure *adj* anxious, exposed, lacking confidence, nervous, uncertain, unsafe, vulnerable; ***opp*** secure

insecurity *n* anxiety, lack of confidence, nervousness, uncertainty, vulnerability; ***opp*** security

insensitive *adj* crass, heartless, impervious, indifferent, oblivious, tactless, thoughtless, unaffected, uncaring, unfeeling, unmoved, unsympathetic, unthinking; ***opp*** sensitive

inseparable *adj* close, devoted, indivisible, inextricable, integral, intimate

insert *v* add, enclose, enter, implant, interject, introduce, pop in, put in, set in, slide in, stick in

inside *adj* **1** indoor, inner, innermost, interior, internal; ***opp*** outside. **2** (inside information) classified, confidential, secret

insidious *adj* furtive, pervasive, sneaking, sneaky, stealthy, subtle, surreptitious

insight *n* acumen, awareness, grasp, intuition, perception, perceptiveness, understanding, vision

insignificant *adj* inconsequential, irrelevant, minor, negligible, paltry, petty, trivial, unimportant; ***opp*** significant

insincere *adj* deceitful, dishonest, disloyal, evasive, false, feigned, hypocritical, lying, phony *inf*, put on *inf*, shifty, two-faced, underhand, untruthful; ***opp*** honest, open, sincere

insinuate *v* give the impression, hint, imply, intimate, suggest

insinuation *n* hint, implication, innuendo, intimation, slur, suggestion

insipid *adj* **1** anemic, bland, colorless, pale, washed-out, watery, weak, wishy-washy *inf*. **2** boring, dead, dull, flat, humdrum, lifeless, stale, unimaginative, uninteresting

insist *v* assert, be firm, demand, emphasize, persist, put your foot down *inf*, stand firm, stick to your guns *inf*, stress

insistent *adj* demanding, determined, dogged, forceful, incessant, urgent, persistent, unrelenting

insolence *n* cheek, disrespect, impertinence, impudence, insubordination, nerve, rudeness

insolent *adj* bad-mannered, cheeky, disrespectful, impertinent, impudent, offensive, rude

insoluble *adj* impenetrable, incomprehensible, inexplicable, mystifying, obscure, perplexing, puzzling, unanswerable, unsolvable; ***opp*** simple, straightforward

insolvent *adj* bankrupt, broke, failed, finished, gone bust *inf*, in debt, in the hands of the receivers, in the red, penniless, ruined

insomnia *n* sleeplessness

inspect *v* audit, check out, examine, give sth the once-over *inf*, go over, go through, look at, look over, scrutinize, study

inspection *n* audit, check, examination, once-over *inf*, scrutiny

inspector *n* auditor, checker, examiner, investigator

inspiration *n* **1** brainstorm, brainwave, bright idea, brilliant idea, idea, insight, revelation, thought. **2** creativity, encouragement, imagination, motivation, muse, stimulus

inspire *v* encourage, enthuse, fire sb's imagination, galvanize, motivate, prompt, spur, stimulate, trigger

inspired *adj* brilliant, dazzling, excellent, exciting, impressive, stunning, supreme, thrilling, wonderful

instability *n* **1** precariousness, shakiness, unsteadiness, wobbliness. **2** insecurity, precariousness, uncertainty, unpredictability, variability, volatility

install *v* ensconce, fit, fit in, inaugurate, instate, load, locate, position, put in place, put in, set up

installment *n* chapter, edition, episode, part, section

instance *n* case, example, occasion, occurrence, time

instant *adj* direct, fast, immediate, instantaneous, on-the-spot, quick, rapid, snap

instigate *v* bring about, encourage, incite, prompt, put into action, set in motion, set up, start, stir up, whip up

instill *v* implant, inculcate, infuse, ingrain, inject, teach

instinct *n* aptitude, feel, feeling, gut feeling, hunch, impulse, intuition, natural ability, predisposition, sixth sense

instinctive *adj* automatic, inborn, inbred, innate, intuitive, involuntary, natural, reflex

institute *n* academy, association, establishment, foundation, institution, organization, society

institute *v* bring about, develop, establish, found, initiate, introduce, launch, organize, originate, set in motion, set up, start

institution *n* **1** (organization) academy, association, establishment, foundation, home, hospital, institute, organization, society. **2** (custom) convention, custom, practice, tradition. **3** (the process of instituting) creation, establishment, formation, foundation, initiation, introduction

institutional *adj* bureaucratic, clinical, conventional, drab, formal, impersonal, orderly, regimented, unimaginative, unvarying

instruct *v* **1** (teach) coach, drill, educate, inform, teach, train. **2** (order) brief, direct, order, tell

instruction *n* **1** (order) brief, command, direction, injunction, order, requirement. **2** (education) classes, coaching, drilling, education, grounding, guidance, lessons, preparation, training, tuition

instructions *n* **1** brief, directions, orders. **2** directions, instruction booklet, manual, rule book

instructive *adj* edifying, educational, enlightening, helpful, illuminating, informative, revealing, useful

instructor *n* coach, guru, lecturer, mentor, teacher, trainer, tutor

instrument *n* **1** apparatus, appliance, contraption, device, gadget, implement, machine, musical instrument, tool, utensil. **2** dial, meter, gauge

instrumental *adj* a prime mover in, contributory, helpful, influential, involved, significant

insubordinate *adj* defiant, disobedient, disorderly, mutinous, rebellious, recalcitrant, undisciplined, unruly; ***opp*** obedient

insufficient *adj* inadequate, meager, not enough, pathetic *inf*, scant, scanty, skimpy; ***opp*** ample, plentiful

insular *adj* closed, cut off, independent, isolated, limited, narrow, parochial, remote, self-contained, self-sufficient, solitary

insulate *v* **1** cover, encase, lag, protect, put insulation in, soundproof. **2** cushion, cut off, protect, shelter, shield

insult *n* abuse, affront, insolence, libel, rudeness, slander, slight, slur; ***opp*** compliment

insult *v* abuse, affront, be rude to, call names, hurt sb's feelings, libel, offend, slander, snub; ***opp*** compliment, praise

insulting *adj* abusive, disparaging, insolent, offensive, rude, scurrilous

insurance *n* assurance, cover, indemnity, protection, provision, safeguard, surety

insure *v* cover, indemnify, protect, take out insurance, underwrite

insurgent *n* freedom fighter, guerrilla, rebel, revolutionary, terrorist

insurrection *n* coup, insurgency, mutiny, rebellion, revolt, uprising

intact *adj* in one piece, perfect, sound, unbroken, undamaged, unharmed, unscathed, whole

integral *adj* basic, constituent, essential, fundamental, indispensable, inherent, intrinsic, necessary, requisite

integrate *v* amalgamate, assimilate, combine, fuse, incorporate, interweave, knit, merge, mesh, unite

integrity *n* decency, honesty, honor, morality, principle, probity, rectitude, virtue

intellect *n* brain, intelligence, mind, reason, understanding
intellectual *adj* academic, bookish, cerebral, mental, scholarly, studious
intellectual *n* academic, don, egghead *inf*, member of the intelligentsia, scholar, thinker
intelligence *n* aptitude, brains, brilliance, cleverness, gumption *inf*, intellect, IQ, mental capacity, wit
intelligent *adj* brainy *inf*, bright, brilliant, clever, educated, gifted, knowledgable, learned, quick, sensible, sharp, smart, well-informed; ***opp*** slow, unintelligent
intelligible *adj* clear, comprehensible, lucid, meaningful, straightforward, unambiguous, understandable; ***opp*** incomprehensible, unintelligible
intend *v* aim, be determined, expect, have in mind, mean, plan
intense *adj* acute, deep, extreme, fierce, forceful, heavy, keen, passionate, powerful, severe, strong, vehement
intensify *v* add to, boost, deepen, emphasize, escalate, exacerbate, fuel, increase, inflame, magnify, reinforce, step up, strengthen
intensity *n* degree, depth, fierceness, force, power, severity, strength
intensive *adj* all-out, concentrated, detailed, exhaustive, in-depth, total
intent *adj* absorbed, attentive, concentrated, concentrating, engrossed, fixed, focused, rapt
intention *n* aim, ambition, goal, idea, objective, plan, purpose, wish
intentional *adj* calculated, conscious, deliberate, done on purpose, intended, meant, planned, premeditated, willful; ***opp*** accidental, unintentional
intercept *v* block, catch, cut off, head off, stop
interchangeable *adj* equivalent, exchangeable, identical, standard
intercourse *n* **1** (sexual) copulation, love-making, sex, sexual intercourse, sexual relations. **2** (social) association, connection, conversation, dealings, interaction
interest *n* **1** (attention) absorption, attention, curiosity, notice. **2** (be of interest) concern, consequence, note, relevance, significance. **3** (a leisure activity) hobby, leisure activity, pastime, pursuit. **4** (an appealing quality) appeal, attraction, charm, fascination. **5** (in sb's interest) advantage, benefit. **6** (on a loan or investment) charge, dividend, profit, rate, return
interest *v* amuse, appeal to, arouse sb's curiosity, attract, captivate, divert, fascinate, hold sb's attention, intrigue; ***opp*** bore
interested *adj* **1** absorbed, attracted, captivated, curious, engrossed, enthusiastic, fascinated, intent, into *inf*, keen; ***opp*** bored. **2** (an interested party) concerned, involved, partial
interesting *adj* absorbing, appealing, compelling, curious, entertaining, fascinating, intriguing, thought-provoking; ***opp*** dull, boring
interfere *v* **1** butt in, fiddle with, intrude, meddle, poke your nose in *inf*, pry. **2 interfere with** frustrate, get in the way of, hamper, hinder, hold up, impede, inhibit, prevent
interference *n* intervention, intrusion,

meddling, nosiness *inf*, prying
interim *adj* acting, makeshift, pro tem, provisional, stopgap, temporary
interior *adj* central, core, inland, inner, inside, internal; ***opp*** exterior, outside
interlude *n* break, breather *inf*, breathing space, delay, intermission, interval, pause, recess, respite
intermediary *n* arbitrator, broker, go-between, mediator, negotiator
intermediate *adj* halfway, in-between, mid, midway, transitional
interminable *adj* constant, continual, endless, incessant, innumerable, long-winded, never-ending, perpetual, rambling, tedious, unending
intermission *n* break, interlude, interval, letup, lull, pause, respite
intermittent *adj* erratic, fitful, irregular, occasional, on-and-off, periodic, spasmodic, sporadic; ***opp*** regular
internal *adj* **1** central, core, inland, inner, inside, interior; ***opp*** external. **2** civil, domestic, home, in-house, national
international *adj* cosmopolitan, global, intercontinental, worldwide
interpret *v* clarify, crack, decipher, decode, elucidate, explain, expound, gloss, make sense of, read, translate, understand
interpretation *n* analysis, explanation, meaning, reading, sense, translation, understanding, version
interpreter *n* commentator, exponent, translator
interrogate *v* cross-examine, debrief, give sb the third degree, grill, put sb through the mill, question, quiz
interrogation *n* cross-examination, debriefing, grilling, inquisition, investigation, probing, questioning, third degree
interrupt *v* **1** barge in *inf*, break in, butt in *inf*, chime in *inf*, disturb, heckle, interject, intervene, muscle in *inf*. **2** block, break off, break, bring to a standstill, cut off, obstruct, postpone, punctuate, suspend
interruption *n* break, delay, disruption, disturbance, gap, hitch, interval, intrusion, pause, postponement, stoppage, suspension
interval *n* **1** break, delay, gap, intermission, interlude, lull, pause, recess. **2** interim, intervening, time, meantime, period, space, spell, time
intervene *v* **1** (intervene in sth) butt in *inf*, get in the way, get involved, intercede, step in. **2** (sth intervenes) come between, happen, occur
interview *n* **1** (for a job or award) assessment, evaluation procedure, oral examination. **2** (discussion with sb) audience, consultation, dialogue, discussion, exchange, face-to-face, one-to-one, press conference, question and answer session
interview *v* cross-examine, grill, interrogate, put questions to, question, see, talk to, vet
interviewer *n* **1** assessor, examiner, interrogator, questioner. **2** (in the media) reporter, talk-show host
intimate *adj* **1** affectionate, close, familiar, informal, loving, sexual, warm. **2** confidential, personal, private, secret
intimate *v* communicate, hint, impart, imply, indicate, insinuate, let it be

known, signal, suggest

intimidate *v* browbeat, bulldoze, bully, coerce, cow, frighten, lean on *inf*, menace, overawe, pressur, push around, put pressure on, scare, subdue, terrify, terrorize, threaten, twist sb's arm *inf*, tyrannize

intimidation *n* arm-twisting *inf*, browbeating, bullying, coercion, pressure, terror, threatening behavior

intolerable *adj* 1 impossible to bear, more than you can stand, unbearable, unendurable. 2 (of behavior) insupportable, offensive, unacceptable

intolerant *adj* bigoted, chauvinistic, dogmatic, narrow-minded, one-sided, prejudiced, racist, sexist, small-minded, uncharitable, xenophobic; ***opp*** tolerant

intransigent *adj* die-hard, hard-line, immovable, implacable, inflexible, intractable, obdurate, obstinate, stubborn, tough, uncompromising

intrepid *adj* adventurous, bold, brave, courageous, daring, fearless, game, plucky, resolute, stalwart

intricate *adj* complex, complicated, convoluted, detailed, elaborate, entangled, involved, tangled; ***opp*** simple

intrigue *n* 1 collusion, conspiracy, double-dealing, plot, scheme. 2 affair, liaison, love affair, romance

intrigue *v* 1 appeal to, arouse sb's curiosity, attract, beguile, captivate, capture sb's interest, charm, fascinate, interest, rivet. 2 connive, conspire, plot, scheme

intriguing *adj* appealing, captivating, exciting, fascinating, interesting, riveting, tantalizing

intrinsic *adj* basic, built-in, central, congenital, essential, fundamental, inborn, inherent, native, natural, real

introduce *v* 1 acquaint, bring together, familiarize, make acquainted, make known, present. 2 begin, bring in, establish, found, inaugurate, initiate, introduce, institute, launch, organize, originate, pioneer, set in motion, set up, start, usher in. 3 announce, begin, lead into, lead up to, preface

introduction *n* 1 foreword, lead-in, opening, preamble, preface, preliminaries, prelude, prologue. 2 (first experience of sth) baptism, debut, inauguration, induction, initiation, launch, presentation. 3 (the start of sth) beginning, establishment, inauguration, institution, launch, start

introductory *adj* 1 first, inaugural, initial, opening, prefatory, preliminary. 2 basic, fundamental, preparatory, rudimentary

introspective *adj* brooding, contemplative, introverted, inward-looking, meditative, pensive

introverted *adj* introspective, inward-looking, reserved, self-absorbed, shy, withdrawn; ***opp*** extroverted

intrude *v* barge in, break in, butt in, crash, encroach, enter uninvited, interfere, interrupt, invade sb's privacy, invade sb's space, poke your nose in, stick your nose in, trespass

intruder *n* 1 burglar, housebreaker, invader, prowler, stalker, trespasser. 2 crasher, infiltrator, interloper, uninvited guest, unwelcome visitor

intrusion *n* encroachment, infringement, interference, interruption, invasion, trespass, violation

intrusive *adj* impertinent, interfering, meddlesome, nosy, officious, pushy *inf*, uncalled-for, unwanted

intuition *n* feeling, hunch, insight, instinct, perception, presentiment, sixth sense

invade *v* **1** (a place) assail, assault, attack, march into, occupy, overrun, penetrate, raid, storm, take over. **2** (sb's privacy) encroach, infringe, interfere, intrude, trespass on, violate

invader *n* aggressor, assailant, attacker, occupying force, raider, trespasser

invalid *adj* **1** ailing, bedridden, chronically sick, disabled, feeble, frail, ill, infirm, sick, weak. **2** (of an agreement) null and void, unusable, void, worthless; ***opp*** valid. **3** (of criticism) baseless, false, spurious, unfounded, unreasonable, wrong; ***opp*** valid

invalid *n* chronic patient, convalescent, patient, sick person, sufferer, valetudinarian

invalidate *v* annul, cancel, negate, nullify, overrule, overthrow, quash, repeal, rescind, revoke, terminate

invaluable *adj* beyond price, indispensable, irreplaceable, precious, priceless, worth its weight in gold

invasion *n* **1** (of a place) assault, attack, foray, incursion, inroad, offensive, onslaught, raid. **2** (of sb's privacy) breach, infringement, interference, intrusion, trespass, violation

invent *v* **1** coin, come up with, conceive, contrive, create, design, devise, formulate, frame, improvise, originate, think up. **2** (a story) come up with, concoct, cook up *inf*, dream up, fabricate, make up, think up

invention *n* **1** (the act of inventing) coinage, contrivance, creation, design, devising, innovation, origination. **2** (sb's invention) brainchild, coinage, contraption, contrivance, construction, design, device. **3** (the ability to invent) creativeness, creativity, genius, imagination, ingenuity, inventiveness, resourcefulness. **4** (sth made-up) cock-and-bull story, fabrication, falsehood, fiction, figment of sb's imagination, lie, story, tall tale

inventive *adj* creative, imaginative, ingenious, innovative, original, resourceful

inventor *n* architect, author, creator, designer, initiator, innovator, maker, originator, prime mover, producer

inventory *n* account, catalog, checklist, description, list, record, register, schedule, statement

inverse *adj* **1** opposite, reverse, transposed. **2** flip side *inf*, obverse, opposite side, other side, reverse

invert *v* capsize, overturn, reverse, transpose, turn upside down, upset, upturn

invest *v* **1** (in a business) buy shares, endow, fund, provide capital for, put money into, sink money into. **2** (money) expend, lay out, play the market, put in, put to work, speculate, spend, use profitably, venture

investigate *v* analyze, conduct an

inquiry, conduct a survey, consider, inquire into, examine, explore, go into *inf*, hold an inquiry, inspect, look into, make inquiries, probe, research, search, study, weigh up

investigation *n* analysis, inquiry, examination, exploration, inquest, inquiry, inspection, probe, research, review, scrutiny, search, study, survey

investigator *n* 1 examiner, inquirer, researcher. 2 detective, private detective, private eye, sleuth *inf*

investment *n* 1 risk, speculation, venture. 2 capital, finance, funding, stake money

invigorate *v* brace, energize, enliven, quicken, pep up, perk up, put new strength into, refresh, rejuvenate, stimulate, strengthen

invigorating *adj* bracing, enlivening, exhilarating, refreshing, rejuvenating, revitalizing, strengthening, tonic

invincible *adj* impregnable, indestructible, indomitable, insuperable, invulnerable, unassailable, unbeatable, unconquerable, unstoppable; ***opp*** vulnerable

invisible *adj* camouflaged, concealed, disguised, hidden, indiscernible, obscured, out of sight, unseen; ***opp*** visible

invitation *n* 1 asking, call, invite *inf*, request, summons. 2 encouragement, enticement, incitement, overture, provocation, temptation, welcome

invite *v* 1 ask, request sb's company, summon. 2 appeal for, ask for, request, seek, solicit. 3 (invite disaster) bring sth on yourself, make sth liable to happen, provoke

inviting *adj* alluring, attractive, captivating, delightful, engaging, enticing, pleasing, seductive, tempting, warm, welcoming, winning

invoice *n* account, bill, statement of charges

invoke *v* 1 appeal to, beg, call for, call upon, entreat, implore, pray, solicit, supplicate. 2 (invoke a law) apply, implement, put into effect, resort to, use

involuntary *adj* 1 automatic, knee-jerk *inf*, instinctive, mechanical, spontaneous, unintentional, unthinking. 2 against sb's will, compulsory, obligatory, reluctant, unwilling

involve *v* 1 entail, imply, mean, necessitate, require. 2 comprise, bring in, draw in, hold, include, incorporate, take in. 3 affect, concern, interest, touch

involved *adj* 1 complex, complicated, confused, confusing, convoluted, intricate, knotty, mixed up, tangled; ***opp*** simple. 2 (involved in sth) busy, concerned, interested, participating, taking part. 3 (involved in a crime) associated, implicated, incriminated

involvement *n* association, commitment, concern, connection, interest, participation

ironic *adj* 1 derisive, double-edged, mocking, sarcastic, sardonic, satirical, wry. 2 paradoxical

irony *n* 1 double meaning, mockery, sarcasm, satire. 2 paradox

irrational *adj* 1 (of an idea) absurd, crackpot *inf*, groundless, illogical, implausible, ridiculous, senseless, unreasonable, unsound, wild, without foundation; ***opp*** sensible. **2** (of a person) confused, crazy, demented, illogical, insane, mad, muddled, muddle-headed, unintelligent, unstable, unthinking

irreconcilable *adj* **1** (of ideas) at odds, clashing, conflicting, contrary, diametrically opposed, incompatible. **2** (of enemies) hard-line, implacable, inflexible, intransigent, uncompromising

irrefutable *adj* beyond doubt, certain, conclusive, incontestable, incontrovertible, indisputable, indubitable, sure, unanswerable, undeniable

irregular *adj* **1** abnormal, eccentric, extraordinary, odd, peculiar, quirky, unusual. **2** (in shape) asymmetric, bumpy, crooked, craggy, jagged, lumpy, ragged, rough, uneven; ***opp*** regular. **3** erratic, fitful, fluctuating, haphazard, intermittent, occasional, patchy, random, shaky, spasmodic, sporadic, uneven, unsteady, varying; ***opp*** regular. **4** (not honest) against the rules, illegal, improper, out of order, unconventional, unofficial, unorthodox. **5** (of troops) guerrilla, mercenary, partisan, resistance, underground

irregularity *n* **1** aberrance, abnormality, deviation, eccentricity, oddity, peculiarity. **2** (an irregularity on a surface) asymmetry, bump, bumpiness, hole, lump, pothole, roughness, unevenness. **3** fluctuation, inconsistency, inconstancy, patchiness, shakiness, unevenness, unsteadiness, variability; ***opp*** regularity. **4** (dishonest behavior) breach, malpractice, unconventionality, unorthodoxy

irrelevant *adj* beside the point, extraneous, immaterial, inapplicable, inappropriate, neither here not there, nothing to do with it, out of place, unconnected, unrelated; ***opp*** relevant

irreparable *adj* beyond repair, incurable, irremediable, irreversible, irretrievable, past mending, unalterable

irresistible *adj* **1** compelling, imperative, inevitable, inexorable, overpowering, overwhelming, powerful, unavoidable. **2** alluring, enticing, fascinating, seductive, tempting

irresponsible *adj* careless, feckless, flighty, immature, negligent, reckless, shiftless, thoughtless, unreliable, untrustworthy, wild; ***opp*** responsible

irreverent *adj* **1** blasphemous, heretical, impious, irreligious, profane, sacrilegious, ungodly. **2** cheeky, derisive, disrespectful, flippant, impertinent, impudent, rude; ***opp*** respectful

irrigate *v* flood, spray, sprinkle, water, wet

irritable *adj* bad-tempered, cantankerous, crabby *inf*, cross, crotchety, fractious, grumpy, impatient, irascible, peevish, petulant, querulous, short-tempered, tetchy, touchy

irritate *v* **1** anger, annoy, bother, drive sb mad, drive sb up the wall *inf*, exasperate, get on sb's nerves, get sb's back up, nettle, pester, provoke, ruffle, try sb's patience, vex. **2** (irritate the skin) chafe, cause irritation, itch, rub, tickle

irritated *adj* **1** annoyed, cross, exasperated, nettled, ruffled, vexed. **2** (of skin) inflamed, itchy

irritating *adj* annoying, irksome,

maddening, nagging, provoking, troublesome, trying, upsetting

irritation *n* **1** anger, annoyance, exasperation, impatience, irritability, vexation. **2** (on the skin) inflammation, itch, rash

island *n* isle, islet

isolate *v* cloister, cordon off, cut off, detach, disconnect, exclude, insulate, keep apart, quarantine, segregate, separate, sequester, shut out, single out

isolated *adj* **1** (of a person) alone, excluded, forlorn, lonely, segregated, separated, solitary. **2** (of a place) cut off, hidden, lonely, off the beaten track, out of the way, remote, secluded. **3** (of an incident, example) abnormal, anomalous, exceptional, freak, single, solitary, unique

issue *n* **1** affair, argument, bone of contention, controversy, matter, point, problem, question, subject, topic. **2** edition, impression, installment, number, printing, version. **3** conclusion, consequence, effect, end, outcome, result, upshot *inf*. **4** children, descendants, offspring

issue *v* **1** circulate, distribute, emit, give out, publish, put out, release. **2** come out, emanate, emit, exude, flow, gush, ooze, pour out, seep. **3** appear, come out, emerge, leave

itch *n* **1** irritation, itchiness, prickling, tickling, tingle. **2** craving, desire, hankering, hunger, longing, thirst, yearning, yen

itch *v* **1** be itchy, irritate, prickle, tickle, tingle. **2** (be itching to do sthg) ache, burn, crave, hanker, hunger, long, wish, yearn

item *n* **1** account, article, bit, feature, piece, report, story. **2** aspect, component, consideration, detail, element, ingredient, matter,. **3** (on a list) entry, record. **4** (for sale) article, lot, object, thing

itinerary *n* journey, plan, program, schedule, timetable, travel arrangements, travel plan

J

jab *n* 1 dig, nudge, poke, prod, punch, stab. 2 injection, inoculation, vaccination

jab *v* dig, elbow, nudge, poke, prod, punch, stab, thrust

jacket *n* 1 (garment) anorak, blazer, cardigan, sports jacket. 2 case, casing, covering, envelope, folder, sheath, wrapper

jagged *adj* angular, barbed, chipped, craggy, indented, irregular, notched, ragged, rough, serrated, sharp, spiky, toothed, uneven, zigzag

jail *n* can, cooler *inf*, inside, jailhouse, lockup, pen *inf*, penitentiary, prison, slammer *inf*

jail *v* confine, detain, immure, imprison, incarcerate, intern, lock up, send down, send to jail, send to prison

jailer *n* guard, keeper, prison officer, warden

jam *n* 1 conserve, jelly, marmalade, preserve. 2 blockage, bottleneck, congestion, gridlock, hold-up, obstruction, stoppage, traffic jam. 3 crowd, crush, press, squeeze, swarm, throng. 4 (be in a jam) dilemma, fix, hole, hot water, plight, predicament, quandary, straits, tight spot, trouble

jam *v* 1 block, clog, congest, cram, fill, obstruct, overcrowd, pack, stop up, stuff. 2 (people jam into a place) cram, crowd, crush, force, pack, ram, squash, squeeze. 3 (jam sth in) force, press, ram, thrust, wedge. 4 become stuck, stall, stick, stop

jangle *v* 1 clang, clank, clash, clatter, clink, jingle, rattle, vibrate. 2 (on sb's nerves) disturb, grate on, irritate, jar

jar *n* bottle, container, crock, pot, tub, urn

jar *v* 1 jerk, jog, jolt, rattle, shake, shock, vibrate. 2 be at odds with, clash, conflict, oppose. 3 annoy, disturb, grate, grate on, irritate, jangle, offend, upset

jargon *n* 1 argot, cant, dialect, idiom, language, patois, slang, vernacular. 2 (of a profession) buzz words, language, slang, specialized language, technical terms, usage

jaundiced *adj* bitter, cynical, distrustful, envious, pessimistic, resentful, skeptical, suspicious

jaunt *n* airing, excursion, expedition, outing, ramble, stroll, trip

jealous *adj* 1 bitter, covetous, envious, green with envy, grudging, jaundiced, resentful. 2 distrustful, possessive. 3 careful, on guard, protective, vigilant, watchful, wary

jeer *v* boo, deride, gibe, heckle, hiss, laugh, make fun of, mock, ridicule, scoff, scorn, sneer, taunt

jeopardize *v* chance, endanger, gamble with, imperil, put at risk, put in jeopardy, risk, take a chance with, threaten

jeopardy *n* **in jeopardy** at risk, compromised, endangered, imperiled, in danger, in peril, jeopardized, threatened, under threat

jerk *v* 1 pull, shake, snatch, tug, wag, waggle, wrench, yank. 2 (move unevenly) jolt, jump, lurch, rattle, shake, twitch

jerky *adj* disjointed, fitful, irregular, jumpy, lurching, spasmodic, staccato, twitchy

jest *n* gag, joke, lampoon, laugh *inf*, prank, practical joke

jest *v* banter, clown, crack a joke, joke, kid *inf*, pull sb's leg, quip, tease

jester *n* buffoon, clown, comedian, comedienne, comic, entertainer, fool, funny man, joker

jet *n* cascade, flow, fountain, rush, spurt, stream

jetty *n* breakwater, landing stage, marina, mole, mooring, pier, wharf

jewel *n* 1 gem, gemstone, item of jewelry, ornament, piece of jewelry, precious stone, semi-precious stone, stone. 2 (types of jewel) diamond, emerald, lapis lazuli, onyx, pearl, ruby

jewelry *n* 1 adornments, costume jewelry, jewels, regalia, trinkets, valuables. 2 (item of jewelry) anklet, bracelet, brooch, earring, medallion, necklace, pendant, ring, tiara

jingle *v* chime, chink, clink, jangle, ping, ring, sound, tinkle

jinx *n* bad luck, curse, evil eye, gremlin, malediction, spell

job *n* 1 (paid employment) appointment, employment, opening, position, post, situation, vacancy, work. 2 (type of work) career, duties, occupation, business, line, profession, trade, vocation. 3 (thing to be done) chore, commission, errand, matter, mission, odd job, piece of work, project, task, undertaking

jobless *adj* at a loose end, between jobs, idle, on the dole *inf*, out of a job, out of work, redundant, seeking employment, unemployed, unoccupied, workless

jog *v* 1 canter, run, run-walk, shuffle, toddle, trot, waddle, warm up. 2 (hit sth lightly) agitate, brush, bump, jar, jolt, jostle, knock, nudge, prod, push, set in motion, shake, tap

join *n* boundary, connection, dividing line, edge, joint, junction, meeting point, seam

join *v* 1 (join two things) attach, bind, bring together, connect, join up, merge, put together, tie, unify, unite; ***opp*** separate. 2 (two things join) come together, connect, converge, join up, meet, merge, unite; ***opp*** separate.

3 (join a club, the army) become a member of, enlist, enroll, join up, register, subscribe; ***opp*** leave

joint *adj* collective, common, communal, concerted, cooperative, mutual, shared

joint *n* **1** angle, articulation, binding, connection, join, junction. **2** (in the body) ankle, elbow, hip, knee, knuckle, shoulder, wrist

joke *n* crack *inf*, funny story, gag, jape, jest, laugh *inf*, one-liner, practical joke, prank, punch line, quip, riddle, shaggy-dog story, sketch, spoof, story, wisecrack, witticism

joke *v* banter, clown, crack a joke, jest, josh, kid *inf*, laugh, pull sb's leg, quip, tease, wisecrack

joker *n* clown, comedian, comedienne, comic, funny man, jester, satirist, wit

jolly *adj* bright, cheerful, cheery, happy, hearty, jovial, joyful, laughing, merry, pleasant

jolt *v* agitate, bump, jar, jerk, jog, knock, nudge, push, shake, shock, shove

jostle *v* brush, crowd, elbow, manhandle, push, push out of the way, shove

journal *n* bulletin, diary, newsletter, newspaper, magazine, periodical, record, review

journalist *n* broadcaster, columnist, critic, correspondent, cub reporter, editor, feature writer, hack *slang*, newshound, press man, reporter, reviewer, writer

journey *n* crossing, drive, excursion, expedition, flight, hike, holiday, odyssey, passage, pilgrimage, ride, trek, trip, voyage, walk

joy *n* bliss, delight, ecstasy, elation, euphoria, happiness, joie de vivre, jubilation, pleasure, rapture, rejoicing; ***opp*** dismay

joyful *adj* blissful, cheerful, delighted, ecstatic, elated, euphoric, glad, happy, in seventh heaven, jolly, jovial, joyous, jubilant, merry, on cloud nine *inf*, on top of the world, rapturous; ***opp*** miserable

jubilee *n* anniversary, celebration, centenary, centennial, festival, festivities, royal occasion

judge *n* **1** circuit judge, jurist, justice, magistrate, your Honor. **2** (in a competition) adjudicator, arbiter, assessor, official, referee, umpire

judge *v* **1** appraise, assess, calculate, consider, decide, estimate, evaluate, form an opinion, gauge, guess, weigh, weigh up. **2** (judge a competition) adjudge, adjudicate, arbitrate, decide, referee, umpire. **3** (in law) find, hear, pass sentence, preside, pronounce, rule, sentence, sit in judgment, try

judgment *n* **1** (official) adjudication, arbitration, award, decision, finding, ruling, sentence, verdict. **2** (sb's judgment of sth) appreciation, appraisal, assessment, calculation, consideration, estimate, estimation, evaluation, guess, opinion, view. **3** (ability to make the right decision) common sense, discretion, discrimination, good sense, level-headedness, maturity, objectivity, sense of proportion, sensitivity, sobriety, tact. **4** (mental ability) awareness, balance of your mind, clear head, control, co-ordination, faculties, mind, perception, self-control, senses, sobriety

judicial *adj* constitutional, institutional, juridical, legal, official, statutory

jug *n* carafe, ewer, pitcher, pot, urn, vase, vessel

juggle *v* (juggle your responsibilities) combine, keep all your balls in the air, manipulate, play off, prioritize, reorder, shuffle, swap, switch

juice *n* cordial, crush, essence, gravy, liquid, mineral, sap, squash

juicy *adj* dripping, moist, ripe, sappy, squashy, squelchy *inf*, succulent, watery

jumble *n* chaos, confusion, heap, mixture, muddle, randomness

jumble *v* confuse, entangle, mix, mix up, muddle, shuffle, tangle

jump *n* **1** bounce, bound, dive, hop, leap, skip, spring, takeoff, vault. **2** high jump, long jump, pike, pole vault, ski-jump, straddle, triple jump, parachute jump. **3** (thing jumped over) bar, barrier, ditch, fence, hurdle, obstacle, wall

jump *v* **1** bounce, bound, dive, hop, leap, prance, rise, skip, soar, spring, take off, vault. **2** (over an obstacle) clear, cross, jump over, leap, leapfrog, straddle, traverse. **3** (with fright) flinch, jump out of your skin *inf*, recoil, shiver, start, twitch

jumpy *adj* agitated, edgy *inf*, fidgety, jittery, nervy *inf*, nervous, on edge, on tenterhooks, restless, twitchy *inf*

junction *n* crossroads, fork, intersection

juncture *n* moment, moment in time, occasion, point, position, present time, situation, stage

jungle *n* bush, forest, rain forest, tropical forest, vegetation

junior *adj* inferior, lowly, low-ranking, second, subordinate, young, younger; ***opp*** senior

junk *n* antiques, bric-a-brac, odds and ends, refuse, rubbish, scrap, trash

jurisdiction *n* authority, brief, command, competence, control, department, orbit, power, remit

just *adj* **1** (of a decision) equitable, fair, justifiable, justified, legitimate, right; ***opp*** unjust. **2** (of a person) equitable, evenhanded, fair, fair-minded, honest, honorable, impartial, objective, respectful, righteous, unbiased, upright; ***opp*** unjust

justice *n* **1** (legal concept) constitutionality, jurisprudence, law, lawfulness, legality, legitimacy, right. **2** (quality of being just) decency, equity, fairness, fair play, impartiality, plain dealing, rectitude, respect; ***opp*** injustice. **3** (after being wronged) amends, compensation, expiation, redress, reparation, retribution, revenge

justifiable *adj* defensible, fair, just, justified, legitimate; ***opp*** unjustifiable

justify *v* account for, defend, excuse, exonerate, explain, legitimize, vindicate

jut *v* jut out, overhang, poke out, project, protrude, stick out

juvenile *adj* **1** adolescent, immature, underage, young, youthful.

2 (juvenile attitude) adolescent, childish, immature, infantile, puerile, silly

juvenile *n* adolescent, child, minor, young person, youngster, youth

juxtapose *v* compare, contrast, draw parallels, place side by side

keen *adj* **1** ardent, avid, crazy about *inf*, desirous, eager, earnest, enthusiastic, fervent, mad *inf*, passionate. **2** (a keen sense of smell) acute, astute, penetrating, sensitive, sharp, shrewd, strong

keep *n* **1** castle, fort, inner sanctum, stronghold, tower. **2** (pay for your keep) bed and board, living, maintenance, means, survival

keep *v* **1** conserve, detain, guard, have, hold, own, possess, preserve, retain. **2** (keep a person) care for, feed, look after, maintain, pay for, nurture, provide for, subsidize, sustain, take care of. **3** (keep doing sth) carry on, continue, go on, keep on, persevere, persist. **4** (keep a promise) abide by, adhere to, fulfill, honor, observe, realize, respect. **5 keep up** conserve, hold, maintain, look after, persevere with, preserve

keeper *n* caretaker, curator, guard, guardian, jailer, warden

key *adj* crucial, essential, important, indispensable, major, vital

key *n* acid test, answer, clue, criterion, explanation, solution

kick *v* **1** boot *inf*, drive, pass, shoot, strike. **2** (kick a habit) beat *inf*, forswear, give up, quit, renounce. **3 kick out** banish, chuck out *inf*, dismiss, eject, exclude, exile, expel, send out, throw out, vote out

kidnap *v* abduct, capture, hold to ransom, seize, snatch, take hostage

kill *v* assassinate, butcher, cut down, destroy, do sb in, electrocute, eliminate, execute, exterminate, gas, gun down, hang, massacre, murder, poison, slaughter, put down, put out of its misery, put to death, put to sleep, shoot, slay, smother, stone, strangle, suffocate

killer *n* assassin, butcher, executioner, gunman, hangman, murderer, murderess, poisoner, strangler

killing *n* **1** assassination, atrocity, butchery, capital punishment, death, death penalty, electrocution, elimination, euthanasia, execution, extermination, hanging, homicide, manslaughter, massacre, mercy killing, murder, shooting, slaying, strangulation, suffocation. **2** (make a killing) bonanza, fortune, gain, profit, success, windfall

kin *n* blood, family, kindred, kinsfolk, kinsmen, kinswomen, kith, relations, relatives, you and yours

kind *adj* benevolent, compassionate, considerate, fair, friendly, generous, helpful, kindhearted, kindly, obliging, sympathetic, understanding, warm, welcoming, well-meaning; ***opp*** cruel, unkind

kind *n* category, class, sort, species, type

kindle *v* **1** (kindle a fire) get going, ignite, light, set fire to, set light to, start. **2** (kindle emotions) excite, inspire, rouse, stimulate, stir, stir up

kindness *n* benevolence, compassion, consideration, fairness, friendliness, generosity, kindheartedness, sympathy, warmth; ***opp*** cruelty, unkindness

king *n* crown, head of state, His Majesty, liege, lord, monarch, ruler, sire

kingdom *n* country, domain, fiefdom, land, monarchy, realm, territory

kiosk *n* booth, box, office, pavilion, stall, window

kiss *v* neck *inf*, peck, smooch *inf*

kit *n* **1** (items for making or doing sth) apparatus, implements, outfit, set, tools, utensils. **2** (items carried or worn) belongings, clothes, equipment, gear *inf*, stuff *inf*, tackle, things

knack *n* ability, aptitude, gift, habit, instinct, talent, trick

knead *v* manipulate, massage, press, pummel, roll, squeeze, work

kneel *v* be on your knees, fall to your knees, genuflect, get down on your knees, kneel down

knife *n* blade, carving knife, cutter, dagger, penknife, sheath knife, stiletto

knit *v* bind, intertwine, make, purl, sew, stitch, weave

knob *n* **1** button, doorknob, handle, lever, switch. **2** boss, bulge, bump, lump, nub, protuberance, protrusion

knock *v* **1** bump, collide, hit, jog, push, strike, tap. **2 knock down** cut down, demolish, fell, floor, pull down, push over, raze, run over. **3 knock out** (make sb lose consciousness) anesthetize, chloroform, floor, knock unconscious, KO *inf*, put to sleep. **4 knock out** (from a competition) beat, defeat, eliminate, overcome, put out, vanquish

knot *n* **1** bow, granny knot, loop, nexus, reef knot, tangle. **2** (knot of people) bunch, circle, cluster, gaggle, gathering, group, huddle, ring

knot *v* bind, entangle, tangle, tie, tie up

know *v* **1** (know a fact) be aware, be certain, be conscious, be familiar with, be informed, be sure, comprehend, understand. **2** (know a person, place) be a friend of, be acquainted with, be familiar with, be friends with, get to know, have been introduced to, have met

knowing *adj* **1** (a knowing grin, remark) conspiratorial, meaningful, sardonic, self-satisfied, sly, superior, worldly-wise, wry. **2** calculated, conscious, deliberate, intended, intentional, purposeful, willful

knowledgable *adj* aware, brainy *inf*, clever,informed, learned, intelligent, scholarly, well-informed; ***opp*** ignorant

knowledge *n* **1** awareness, certainty, cognition, comprehension, consciousness, erudition, intelligence, learning, understanding. **2** (things that are known) data, facts, findings, information, learning, lore, observations, scholarship, science

label *n* **1** brand, flag, marker, stamp, sticker, tab, tag, ticket. **2** category, classification, designation, epithet, heading, name, pigeonhole, stigma, term

label *v* **1** brand, flag, mark, stamp, tag. **2** brand, categorize, classify, designate, name, pigeonhole, stigmatize, term

labor *n* **1** (work) chores, drudgery, effort, grind *inf*, hard labor, hard work, manual work, strain, toil, work. **2** (workers) hands, laborers, manpower, workers, workforce, workmen. **3** (giving birth) birth pangs, childbirth, contractions, delivery

labor *v* **1** exert yourself, slave, strain, strive, sweat, toil, work, work your fingers to the bone, work your socks off *inf* . **2** (labor a point) behavior, dwell on, elaborate, emphasize, get bogged down on, get stuck on, overdo, overelaborate, overemphasize, repeat, stress

laborer *n* blue-collar worker, hand, manual worker, unskilled worker, worker, workman

laborious *adj* difficult, hard, labored, painstaking, tedious, wearisome; ***opp*** easy

lace *n* crochet, embroidery, filigree, net, string

lace *v* **1** (lace a shoe) attach, bind, close, do up, fasten, secure, strap, string, thread, tie. **2** (lace a drink) add to, blend, fortify, mix, spike

lack *n* absence, dearth, deficiency, insufficiency, need, scarceness, scarcity, shortage, want; ***opp*** abundance

lack *v* be lacking in, be short of, be without, have need of, miss, need, require, want

lacking *adj* **1** (the system is sadly lacking) defective, flawed, impaired, inadequate, unsatisfactory, weak; ***opp*** satisfactory. **2** (be lacking in social skills) missing, needing, wanting, without

laden *adj* burdened, charged, encumbered, hampered, heavily laden, loaded, piled high, weighed down, weighted

lady *n* **1** female, girl, lass *inf*, wife *inf*, woman; ***opp*** gentleman. **2** baroness, countess, dame, duchess, marchioness, noblewoman, peeress, viscountess; ***opp*** lord

ladylike *adj* courtly, cultivated, dainty, decorous, elegant, genteel, gracious, modest, polished, polite, proper, refined, respectable, well-bred, well-mannered; ***opp*** coarse

lag *v* bring up the rear, dawdle, delay, dilly dally *inf*, drag your feet, drop behind, fall behind, go slow, hang about, hang back, idle, linger, loiter, saunter, straggle, trail; ***opp*** lead

laid-back *adj* at ease, calm, casual, easy-going, nonchalant, relaxed, unflappable, unhurried; ***opp*** anxious

lair *n* burrow, covert, den, earth, hideout, hole, nest, refuge, resting place, retreat, shelter

lake *n* lagoon, lido, loch, pool, pond, reservoir, sea, tarn, water

lame *adj* **1** crippled, disabled, handicapped, hobbling, limping. **2** (a lame excuse) feeble, flimsy, inadequate, pathetic, poor, tame, thin, unconvincing, weak; ***opp*** convincing

lament *v* **1** (lament sth) bemoan, bewail, complain, deplore, regret; ***opp*** praise. **2** (lament sb's death) beat your breast, cry, grieve, mourn, shed tears, sorrow, wail, weep; ***opp*** rejoice

lamp *n* lantern, light, nightlight, streetlight, table lamp, torch

land *n* **1** (back on land) coast, dry land, earth, ground, shore, solid ground, terra firma; ***opp*** sea, space. **2** (fertile land) dirt, earth, ground, loam, soil. **3** (own a lot of land) acres, estate, grounds, property, realty. **4** (a distant land) country, district, nation, province, region, state, territory, tract

land *v* alight, arrive, berth, come ashore, come in to land, debark, disembark, dismount, dock, touch down; ***opp*** set off

landlord *n* **1** host, hostess, hotelier, innkeeper, landlady, restaurateur; ***opp*** customer. **2** landowner, manager, manageress, owner, proprietor; ***opp*** tenant

landmark *n* **1** feature, guidepost, identification, monument. **2** (landmark in sth's history) critical point, milestone, new era, turning point, watershed

landscape *n* aspect, countryside, outlook, panorama, prospect, rural scene, scene, scenery, view, vista

landslide *n* avalanche, landslip, rockfall

language *n* **1** communication, conversation, discourse, expression, parlance, speaking, speech, talk, talking, verbal expression, vocalization, words. **2** (a particular language) argot, dialect, idiom, jargon, lingo *inf*, patois, tongue, vernacular, vocabulary. **3** (the language of a novel) expression, phraseology, phrasing, style, terminology, vocabulary, wording

languish *v* decline, droop, fade, fail, faint, flag, go downhill *inf*, stagnate, suffer, waste, weaken, wilt, wither; ***opp*** flourish

lank *adj* **1** (of hair) drooping, dull, lifeless, limp, long, lusterless, straggling, straight; ***opp*** bouncy. **2** (of a person) bony, emaciated, gangling, gaunt, lanky, lean, scraggy, scrawny, skinny, slender, slim, tall, thin; ***opp*** chubby

lanky *adj* awkward, gangling, lank, lean, scrawny, skinny, tall, thin, ungraceful; ***opp*** chubby

lap *n* **1** circle, circuit, coarse, loop, orbit, revolution, round, tour. **2** (sit on sb's lap) knee

lap *v* **1** (waves lapping the shore) ripple, slap, slosh, splash, swish, wash. **2** (a cat lapping milk) drink, gulp, guzzle, lick, sip, sup

lapse *v* **1** decline, deteriorate, diminish, drop, fail, fall, go downhill *inf*, go to pot *inf*, sink, slide, slip; ***opp*** improve. **2** (a passport lapses) become invalid, become void, end, expire, finish, run out, stop, terminate

lapse *n* blunder, error, failing, fault, indiscretion, mistake, omission, oversight, slip, slip-up *inf*

large *adj* ample, big, broad, bulky, colossal, considerable, elephantine, enormous, extensive, generous, giant, gigantic, grand, great, huge, immense, jumbo *inf*, king-size, liberal, lofty, massive, mighty, monumental, roomy, sizable, spacious, sweeping, substantial, vast, wide; ***opp*** small

lash *n* blow, hit, strike, stripe, stroke, thwack *inf*, wallop *inf*, whack *inf*, whip

lash *v* **1** (lash one thing to another) bind, fasten, hitch, join, leash, rope, secure, strap, tether, tie. **2** (rain lashing the windows) batter, beat, buffet, dash, drum, hammer, hit, knock, pound, smack, strike. **3** (lash sb) beat, birch, flog, horsewhip, strike, thrash, wallop *inf*, whack *inf*, whip

last *adj* **1** closing, concluding, final, terminal, ultimate; ***opp*** first. **2** latest, most recent; ***opp*** first. **3** (last in a line) back, end, final, hindmost, rearmost; ***opp*** front

last *v* abide, carry on, continue, endure, go on, hold, keep, linger, live, persist, remain, survive; ***opp*** end

lasting *adj* abiding, ceaseless, constant, continuing, durable, enduring, eternal, long-lasting, long-term, ongoing, permanent, perpetual, unceasing, undying, unending; ***opp*** temporary

late *adj* **1** behind, behind schedule, behind time, belated, delayed, overdue, slow, tardy; ***opp*** early. **2** (the late Mr. Smith) dead, deceased, defunct, departed

lately *adv* latterly, of late, recently; ***opp*** previously

latitude *n* carte blanche, elbow-room *inf*, freedom, free play, indulgence, leeway, liberty, license; ***opp*** restriction

latter *adj* **1** last-mentioned, later, second; ***opp*** former. **2** (the latter part) closing, concluding, end, final, last; ***opp*** opening

laugh *n* **1** belly laugh *inf*, chortle, chuckle, giggle, guffaw, roar of laughter, snigger, titter. **2** (sb is a laugh) card *inf*, case *inf*, hoot, scream. **3** (sth is a laugh) fun, lark, scream

laugh *v* **1** be in stitches, burst out laughing, chortle, chuckle, crack up *inf*, giggle, guffaw, roll about, snigger, split your sides, titter. **2 laugh at** deride, jeer, lampoon, make fun of, mock, ridicule, scoff, send up, taunt, tease

laughable *adj* absurd, derisory, derisive, ludicrous, outrageous, preposterous, ridiculous, risible; ***opp*** reasonable

laughing stock *n* butt, dupe, everybody's fool, fair game, fall guy *inf*, figure of fun, target, victim

laughter *n* **1** chortling, chuckling, giggling, guffawing, laughing, laughs, sniggering, tittering. **2** amusement, entertainment, glee, hilarity, hysterics, light-heartedness, merriment, mirth

launch *v* **1** (launch a new business) begin, commence, embark, establish, get going, inaugurate, initiate, instigate, introduce, open, set up, start. **2** (launch a rocket) cast, catapult, discharge, dispatch, fire, hurl, let fly, project, propel, send off, set off, shoot, throw

lavatory *n* bathroom, convenience,

john *inf*, latrine, little boy's room *inf*, little girl's room *inf*, powder room, the gents, the ladies, toilet, urinal, washroom

lavish *adj* exuberant, lush, luxuriant, luxurious, opulent, sumptuous; ***opp*** simple. **2** (lavish with sth) bountiful, extravagant, free, generous, liberal, munificent, open-handed, unselfish, unstinting; ***opp*** mean

law *n* act, bill, bylaw, code, commandment, covenant, decree, directive, edict, enactment, injunction, mandate, order, ordinance, regulation, rule, statute

law-abiding *adj* compliant, decent, dutiful, good, honest, lawful, obedient, peaceable, respectable, upright, well-behaved; ***opp*** criminal, trouble-making

lawful *adj* allowable, allowed, authorized, constitutional, just, legal, legalized, legitimate, permissible, permitted, prescribed, proper, rightful, sanctioned, valid; ***opp*** unlawful

lawsuit *n* action, case, dispute, indictment, industrial tribunal, litigation, proceedings, prosecution, suit, trial

lawyer *n* advocate, attorney, counsel, legal advisor, legal practitioner, member of the bar

lax *adj* careless, casual, neglectful, negligent, remiss, slack, slipshod, unreliable, vague

lay *adj* **1** (lay preacher) nonclerical, non-ordained, part-time, secular; ***opp*** ordained. **2** (lay person) amateur, inexpert, nonprofessional; ***opp*** professional

lay *v* **1** (lay sth somewhere) deposit, leave, place, plant, put, rest, set, settle. **2** (lay sth out) arrange, dispose, organize, position, set out. **3** (lay eggs) bear, deposit, produce. **4** (lay blame) allot, ascribe, assign, attribute, charge, impose, impute. **5** (lay plans) arrange, concoct, contrive, create, design, devise, make, plan, plot, prepare, set up, work out. **6 lay down** (a law) command, formulate, ordain, order, prescribe, proclaim, set down, stipulate. **7 lay on** furnish, give, provide, supply

layabout *n* good-for-nothing, idler, laggard, loafer, shirker

layer *n* **1** (of rock) bed, row, seam, stratum, thickness, tier. **2** (of paint) coat, coating, covering, film, skin

layman *n* amateur, lay person, nonprofessional, nonspecialist; ***opp*** professional

layout *n* **1** (of a place) arrangement, design, geography, plan. **2** (of a page) arrangement, design, format, outline

laze *v* do nothing, idle, lie around, loaf, lounge, relax, sit around, unwind

laziness *n* idleness, inactivity, indolence, lax, slackness *inf*, sloth

lazy *adj* idle, inactive, indolent, laxity, slack *inf*, slothful; ***opp*** hard-working

lead *n* **1** (the lead) advantage, edge, first place, precedence, priority, supremacy, vanguard. **2** (follow sb's lead) direction, example, guidance, leadership. **3** (get a lead) clue, guide, hint, indication, line, suggestion, tip-off . **4** (lead role) hero, heroine, leading role, pointer, principal, protagonist, starring role, title role. **5** (extension lead) cable, wire

lead *v* **1** (lead sb somewhere) conduct, draw, escort, guide, pilot, show the way, steer, usher. **2** (lead sb to think sth) cause, dispose, draw, incline, induce, influence, move, persuade, prevail, prompt. **3** (lead an army) be in charge of, captain, command, direct, govern, head, manage, rule, supervise. **4** (be in the lead) be ahead, be first, be in the lead, exceed, excel, head, leave behind, outdo, outstrip, surpass; ***opp*** trail. **5** (lead an exciting life) experience, have, live, pass, spend. **6 lead on** deceive, delude, dupe, hoodwink, mislead, string along *inf*, trick

leader *n* boss, captain, chief, commander, conductor, director, foreman, guide, head, number one *inf*, principal, ruler, skipper *inf*, supremo *inf*

leading *adj* best, chief, first, foremost, greatest, highest, major, main, number one *inf*, premier, principal, ruling, senior, top; ***opp*** minor

leaf *n* **1** blade, foliage, frond, greenery, needle. **2** (in a book) folio, flyleaf, page, sheet

leaflet *n* booklet, circular, flyer, handout, notice, pamphlet

league *n* alliance, association, band, coalition, compact, confederacy, confederation, consortium, corporation, fellowship, fraternity, group, guild, order, partnership, society, syndicate, union

leak *n* **1** discharge, drip, emission, leakage, seepage, trickle. **2** (of information) disclosure, divulgence, revelation

leak *v* **1** discharge, drip, escape, exude, issue, ooze, seep, spill, trickle. **2** (leak information) disclose, divulge, give away, let out, let slip, let the cat out of the bag, make known, reveal, spill the beans

lean *adj* bony, emaciated, gaunt, lanky, scrawny, skinny, slender, slim, thin, wiry; ***opp*** fat

lean *v* **1** be propped, be supported, recline, repose, rest. **2** be at an angle, bend, incline, slant, slope, tilt, tip

leaning *n* aptitude, bend, bias, fondness, inclination, instinct, liking, partiality, penchant, predilection, preference, propensity, taste, tendency

leap *v* bounce, bound, caper, cavort, frisk, gambol, hop, jump, skip, spring

learn *v* **1** acquire, assimilate, attain, grasp, imbibe, master, pick up. **2** (learn your lines) commit sth to memory, get off pat, learn by heart, memorize. **3** (learn that sth is true) ascertain, discover, find out, gather, hear, understand

learned *adj* academic, cultured, erudite, expert, intellectual, knowledgable, scholarly, skilled, versed, well-educated, well-read; ***opp*** uneducated

learner *n* apprentice, beginner, cadet, novice, pupil, student, trainee

learning *n* education, knowledge, letters, scholarship, schooling, study, tuition, wisdom

lease *v* charter, hire, let, loan, rent

leave *n* **1** (leave to do sth) authorization, consent, dispensation, freedom, liberty, permission, sanction. **2** (on leave) break, holiday, sabbatical, time off, vacation

leave *v* **1** (leave a place) be off *inf*, check out, depart, disappear, exit, go, move, quit, retire, split *inf*, withdraw; ***opp*** arrive. **2** (leave your wife) abandon, break up with, desert, dump *inf*, finish with, split with. **3** (leave your job) cease, chuck it, desist, drop out, give up, pull out, relinquish, resign, stop, walk out. **4** (leave sth to sb) bequeath, endow, hand down, transmit, will. **5 leave out** disregard, exclude, ignore, miss out, neglect, omit, overlook, reject, skip; ***opp*** include

lecture *n* **1** (a history lecture) address, class, lesson, paper, seminar, speech, talk. **2** (telling off) chiding, rebuke, remonstration, reprimand, reproof, scolding, sermon, talking to, telling-off

lecture *v* **1** (lecture in history) address, expound, hold forth, instruct, speak, talk, teach. **2** (lecture a child) admonish, castigate, censure, chide, read the riot act, reprimand, reprove, scold, tear into, tell off

ledge *n* mantle, overhang, projection, protrusion, ridge, shelf, sill, step

left *adj* communist, leftist, left-wing, liberal, progressive, radical, red, socialist

leftover *adj* excess, extra, remaining, surplus, uneaten, unused, unwanted

leftovers *n* excess, extra, remainder, remains, remnants, scraps, surplus

leg *n* **1** (of a person) limb, member, peg *inf*, pin *inf*. **2** (of a piece of furniture) column, pillar, prop, support, upright. **3** (leg of a journey) bit, lap, part, portion, section, segment, stage, stretch

legacy *n* bequest, endowment, estate, gift, heirloom, inheritance

legal *adj* aboveboard, allowed, approved, authorized, decriminalized, lawful, legalized, legitimate, licensed, permissible, proper, sanctioned, valid; ***opp*** illegal

legalize *v* allow, approve, authorize, decriminalize, legitimize, license, make legal, permit, sanction, validate; ***opp*** ban

legend *n* epic, fable, fairy tale, fiction, folk tale, myth, narrative, saga, story, tale

legendary *adj* acclaimed, celebrated, famed, famous, glorious, great, immortal, proverbial, world-famous; ***opp*** unknown

legible *adj* clear, decipherable, distinct, easy to read, intelligible, neat, plain, readable; ***opp*** illegible

legislate *v* authorize, decree, enact, establish, ordain, order, prescribe

legislation *n* **1** authorization, codification, enactment, law-making, prescription. **2** (a piece of legislation) act, bill, charter, code, constitution, law, measure, regulation, rule, statute

legitimate *adj* aboveboard, allowed, approved, authorized, decriminalized, lawful, legal, legalized, licensed, permissible, sanctioned, valid; ***opp*** illegal

legitimize *v* allow, approve, authorize, legalize, license, make legal, permit, sanction, validate; ***opp*** ban

leisure *n* holiday, recreation, relaxation, relief, rest, spare time, time off, vacation; ***opp*** work

leisurely *adj* comfortable, easy, gentle, laidback, lazy, relaxed, relaxing, restful, slow, unhurried; ***opp*** frantic

lend *v* **1** advance, give sb the loan of, loan; ***opp*** borrow. **2** add, afford, bestow, contribute, endow, furnish, give, grant, impart, provide, supply

length *n* **1** distance, extent, footage, measure, mileage, reach, span. **2** duration, period, span, stretch, time

lengthen *v* continue, drag out, draw out, elongate, expand, extend, increase, prolong, protract, stretch; ***opp*** shorten

lengthy *adj* extended, interminable, long, long-drawn-out, long-winded, protracted

lenient *adj* charitable, clement, forbearing, forgiving, gentle, humane, indulgent, kind, lax, magnanimous, merciful, mild, soft, sparing, tolerant

lessen *v* **1** assuage, curtail, decrease, diminish, ease, lighten, lower, mitigate, reduce, relieve, tone down; ***opp*** intensify. **2** abate, decline, decrease, die down, diminish, ease off, ebb, let up, moderate, slacken, subside, tail off, weaken; ***opp*** intensify

lesson *n* **1** class, coaching, drill, instruction, period, schooling, seminar, session, teaching, tutoring. **2** admonition, deterrent, example, exemplar, message, model, moral, warning

let *v* **1** agree to, allow, authorize, consent, give leave, give permission, give the go-ahead, grant, permit, sanction, tolerate. **2** contract out, hire, lease, rent, sublet. **3 let down** disappoint, disillusion, fail, fall short. **4 let off** detonate, discharge, explode, fire, launch, set off, trigger. **5 let off** (forgive) absolve, acquit, discharge, excuse, exempt, forgive, let sb go, pardon, release, reprieve, spare. **6 let out** (information) betray, disclose, leak, let slip, make known, reveal, tell. **7 let out** (a person) free, discharge, let sb go, liberate, release, set sb free

letdown *n* anticlimax, disappointment, disillusionment, failure, flop *inf*, washout *inf*

lethal *adj* deadly, devastating, fatal, mortal, murderous, virulent

lethargic *adj* apathetic, drowsy, dull, enervated, fatigued, heavy, inactive, indolent, inert, languid, languorous, lazy, listless, passive, sleepy, slothful, slow, sluggish, somnolent, torpid, weary; ***opp*** energetic

lethargy *n* apathy, drowsiness, dullness, fatigue, heaviness, indolence, inertia, lack of energy, languor, lassitude, laziness, listlessness, passivity, sleepiness, sloth, slowness, sluggishness, somnolence, torpor, weariness; ***opp*** energy

letter *n* **1** card, communication, dispatch, epistle, line, missive, note. **2** character, consonant, initial, sign, symbol, vowel

level *adj* **1** even, flat, flush, horizontal, smooth, straight, true, uniform; ***opp*** uneven. **2** aligned, balanced, comparable, equal, equivalent, identical, in line, matching, on a par, proportionate, the same

level *n* **1** degree, echelon, grade, plane, position, rank, rung, stage, standing, status. **2** altitude, depth, elevation, height. **3** floor, layer, story, stratum

level *v* **1** even out, flatten, plane, smooth. **2** bulldoze, demolish, destroy, flatten, knock down, lay low, pull down, raze, tear down

lever *n* crowbar, jimmy, handle, grip

lever *v* crowbar, force, jimmy, raise, wrench

levy *n* charge, dues, duty, excise, imposition, tariff, tax, toll

levy *v* charge, collect, demand, exact, gather, impose, tax

liability *n* **1** accountability, blame, culpability, duty, obligation, onus, responsibility. **2** (sth is a liability) burden, disadvantage, drag, drawback, encumbrance, handicap, hindrance, impediment, millstone, nuisance

liable *adj* **1** (liable for sth) accountable, answerable, bound, culpable, obligated, responsible. **2** (liable to do sth) apt, disposed, inclined, in the habit of, likely, predisposed, prone, susceptible, tending, vulnerable

liaison *n* **1** communication, connection, cooperation, contact, interchange, linkage, link-up, tie. **2** affair, amour, entanglement, intrigue, relationship, romance

liar *n* deceiver, false witness, fibber *inf*, perjurer

libel *n* aspersion, calumny, defamation, denigration, lie, obloquy, slander, slur, smear, vilification

libel *v* blacken sb's name, calumniate, cast aspersions, defame, denigrate, malign, misrepresent, slander, smear, traduce, vilify

libelous *adj* calumnious, damaging, defamatory, false, injurious, malicious, scurrilous, slanderous, untrue

liberal *adj* **1** broad-minded, easygoing, enlightened, lenient, libertarian, moderate, openminded, permissive, progressive, reformist, tolerant, unprejudiced. **2** (a liberal amount) abundant, ample, bountiful, copious, generous, lavish, magnanimous, munificent, plentiful, profuse, unstinting

liberalize *v* broaden, ease, expand, extend, free up, loosen, moderate, open up, relax, slacken, soften, stretch; ***opp*** tighten

liberate *v* deliver, discharge, emancipate, free, let go, let out, redeem, release, rescue, set free, unchain, untie

liberation *n* deliverance, discharge, emancipation, freedom, liberty, release, unchaining

liberty *n* autonomy, emancipation, freedom, independence, release, self-determination, sovereignty

license *n* **1** (permission) authorization, authority, dispensation, entitlement, leave, liberty, permission, privilege, right. **2** (document giving permission) certificate, charter, credentials, permit, warrant. **3** (in behavior) abandon, anarchy, decadence, disorder, dissipation, dissoluteness, excess, immorality, indulgence, laxity, licentiousness, unruliness

license *v* accredit, allow, authorize, certify, empower, entitle, grant a license to, permit, sanction, warrant

lick *v* brush, flick, lap, taste, tongue

lid *n* cap, cover, covering, stopper, top

lie *n* bluff, deceit, deception, equivocation, fabrication, falsehood, fib *inf*, fiction, invention, mendacity, misrepresentation, perjury, pretense, story, untruth, whopper *inf*; ***opp*** truth

lie *v* **1** bear false witness, bluff, deceive, dissemble, equivocate, fabricate, falsify, fib *inf*, invent, make up, misrepresent, perjure, pretend, tell a falsehood, tell a lie. **2** be horizontal, be lying, be prone, be prostrate, be recumbent, be supine, lean back, lounge, recline, repose, rest, sprawl, stretch out

life *n* **1** animation, being, breath, entity, existence, living; ***opp*** death. **2** activity, animation, dynamism, energy, enthusiasm, exuberance, liveliness, oomph *inf*, spark, sparkle, spirit, sprightliness, verve, vigor, vitality, vivacity, zest; ***opp*** dullness. **3** (sb's life) career, days, lifespan, lifetime, time on earth. **4** autobiography, biography, history, life story, memoir

lifeless *adj* **1** cold, dead, deceased, defunct, extinct, inanimate, inert, insensate; ***opp*** living. **2** colorless, dull, flat, heavy, lackluster, unexciting, uninspired, wooden; ***opp*** lively

lifelike *adj* authentic, convincing, exact, faithful, graphic, natural, real, realistic, true-to-life, vivid

lifelong *adj* abiding, constant, enduring, lasting, long-standing, long-term, perennial, permanent, persistent

lift *n* **1** amelioration, boost, enhancement, fillip, improvement, promotion, shot in the arm *inf*. **2** (give sb a lift) drive, ride, run, transport, transportation

lift *v* **1** carry, elevate, hoist, pick up, raise. **2** ameliorate, boost, buoy up, cheer, enhance, improve, promote

light *adj* **1** airy, delicate, flimsy, gossamer, lightweight, portable, slight; ***opp*** heavy. **2** bright, full of light, glowing, illuminated, lit-up, sunny, well-lit; ***opp*** dark. **3** (of a knock, touch) delicate, faint, gentle, indistinct, mild, soft, weak; ***opp*** heavy. **4** amusing, easy, entertaining, diverting, fun, frivolous, lighthearted, simple, superficial, trivial, undemanding; ***opp*** serious

light *n* **1** beam, blaze, brightness, brilliance, flare, flash, glare, gleam, glint, glitter, glow, illumination, incandescence, luminescence, luminosity, luster, phosphorescence, radiance, ray, scintillation, shaft, shine, sparkle, twinkle. **2** beacon, bulb, candle, lamp, lantern, taper, torch

light *v* fire, flame, ignite, kindle, put a match to, set alight

lighten *v* **1** brighten, cast light on, illuminate, irradiate, light up, make sth bright, shed light on, shine on. **2** allay, alleviate, assuage, ease, lessen, mitigate, reduce, relieve

likable *adj* agreeable, amiable, appealing, charming, congenial, endearing, engaging, friendly, genial, lovable, nice, personable, pleasant, pleasing, sympathetic, winning

like *adj/prep* akin, alike, allied, analogous, corresponding, equal, equivalent, identical, matching, parallel, relating, resembling, same, similar

like *v* admire, appreciate, approve of, be fond of, be keen on, be partial to, cherish, delight in, enjoy, esteem, have a soft spot for *inf*, love, prize, relish, revel in, take pleasure in; ***opp*** dislike, hate

likelihood *n* chance, hope, liability, possibility, probability, prospect

likely *adj* **1** anticipated, expected, feasible, in the cards, plausible, probable. **2** (likely to do sth) apt, disposed, inclined, liable, prone, tending

liken *v* compare, draw an analogy between, equate, link, match, relate

likeness *n* **1** affinity, congruity, correspondence, link, match, resemblance, similarity. **2** depiction, drawing, effigy, image, model, painting, picture, portrait, representation, sketch, statue, study

liking *n* admiration, affinity, appreciation, approval, bent, esteem, fondness, keenness, love, partiality, penchant, predilection, preference, soft spot *inf*, taste, weakness

limb *n* appendage, arm, extension, extremity, leg, member, offshoot, projection, wing

limelight *n* attention, celebrity, fame, prominence, public eye, publicity, recognition, spotlight, stardom

limit *n* **1** border, bound, boundary, brim, brink, confines, edge, end, extent, frontier, perimeter, periphery. **2** cap, ceiling, check, curb, cutoff, deadline, limitation, maximum, restraint, restriction

limit *v* cap, check, circumscribe, confine, control, curb, delineate, demarcate, fix, put a limit on, ration, restrain, restrict

limitation *n* **1** cap, ceiling, check, curb, cutoff, deadline, limit, maximum, restraint, restriction. **2** defect, deficiency, fault, inadequacy, shortcoming, weakness

limited *adj* **1** capped, checked, circumscribed, confined, controlled, curbed, delineated, demarcated, fixed, rationed, restrained, restricted. **2** basic, inadequate, insufficient, minimal, restricted, scanty, sparse; ***opp*** unlimited

limitless *adj* boundless, countless, endless, everlasting, immeasurable, incalculable, inexhaustible, infinite, innumerable, never-ending, numberless, unbounded, unconfined, unending, unlimited

limp *adj* drooping, flabby, flaccid, floppy, loose, relaxed, sagging, slack, soft, wilting; ***opp*** firm, stiff

limp *v* be lame, falter, hobble, shamble, shuffle, totter

line *n* **1** band, bar, border, boundary, contour, dash, hyphen, mark, rule, streak, striation, strip, stripe, stroke, trail, underscore. **2** channel, corrugation, crease, fold, furrow, groove, wrinkle. **3** cable, cord, filament, lead, rope, strand, string, thread, wire. **4** (of people) chain, column, cordon, crocodile, file, parade, procession, queue, rank, row, series. **5** approach, avenue, course, direction, drift, method, tack, track, way

line *v* **1** crease, furrow, inscribe, mark, rule, score, wrinkle. **2** border, edge, fringe, hem, rim. **3 line up** (form a line) get in line, form a line, form a queue, queue up. **4 line up** (put into a line) align, arrange in a line, marshal, place in line, straighten up

lines *n* **1** configuration, contour, delineation, figure, form, outline, shape. **2** part, script, speech, words

linger *v* **1** dally, dawdle, hang around, hover, lag, loiter, pause, remain, stay, stop, take your time, tarry, wait; ***opp*** hurry. **2** abide, continue, endure, persist, remain

lingering *adj* abiding, continuing,

enduring, long, long-drawn-out, persistent, protracted, remaining

link *n* **1** affiliation, association, attachment, bond, connection, relationship, tie. **2** (joining two things together) connection, connector, coupling, join, joint, loop, ring

link *v* **1** attach, bind, connect, couple, fasten, join, tie, yoke. **2** associate, attach, bracket, connect, join, put together, relate, tie up

lip *n* brim, brink, edge, margin, rim, verge

liquid *adj* flowing, fluid, liquefied, melted, molten, running, runny, sloppy

liquid *n* fluid, juice, liquor, solution

liquidate *v* annihilate, bump off *inf*, destroy, dispatch, do away with *inf*, eliminate, exterminate, get rid of *inf*, kill, murder, obliterate, remove, silence, wipe out

list *n* catalog, directory, file, index, inventory, listing, record, register, roll, schedule, table, tally

list *v* catalog, enter, enumerate, file, index, itemize, make a list, make an inventory, note, record, register, tabulate, write down

listen *v* attend, concentrate, hark, hear, heed, mind, note, observe, pay attention, take notice

listless *adj* apathetic, enervated, feeble, heavy, inactive, indolent, inert, languid, lethargic, limp, passive, sluggish, supine, torpid, weary; ***opp*** energetic

literal *adj* **1** actual, authentic, genuine, real, true, unexaggerated. **2** (a literal translation) accurate, close, exact, faithful, strict, verbatim, word-for-word

literary *adj* bookish, cultivated, cultured, educated, erudite, highbrow, learned, literate, scholarly, well-read, widely read

literate *adj* able to read, cultivated, educated, informed, lettered, schooled, well-read; ***opp*** illiterate

literature *n* **1** books, fiction, letters, writing. **2** booklet, brochure, circular, handout, information, leaflet, pamphlet

litigation *n* action, case, dispute, lawsuit, legal proceedings, suit

litter *n* clutter, debris, detritus, garbage, jetsam, junk, mess, refuse, rubbish, trash, waste

litter *v* clutter, make untidy, mess up, scatter, strew

little *adj* **1** baby, compact, diminutive, dinky *inf*, dwarf, infinitesimal, Lilliputian, microscopic, midget, mini *inf*, miniature, minuscule, minute, petite, short, small, teeny *inf*, tiny, wee *inf*; ***opp*** big. **2** (a little child) infant, junior, small, young; ***opp*** big. **3** (not much) inadequate, insufficient, meager, mean, measly *inf*, miserly, negligible, paltry, piddling *inf*, scant, skimpy, sparse

live *adj* **1** active, actual, alive, animate, breathing, existing, living, sentient, vital; ***opp*** dead. **2** (a live issue) burning, current, hot, important, pertinent, pressing, relevant, topical, vital. **3** (a live broadcast) as it happens, in real time, unedited; ***opp*** prerecorded

live *v* **1** be, be alive, breathe, draw breath, exist, have life. **2** abide, dwell, have your home, inhabit, lodge, occupy, reside, settle. **3** (of a custom) abide, continue, endure, last, persist, prevail, remain, stay alive, survive. **4** exist, get by *inf*, make a living, make ends meet, subsist, support oneself, survive

livelihood *n* daily bread, job, keep, living, means of support, occupation, subsistence, sustenance, trade, work

lively *adj* active, alert, animated, bouncy, bubbly *inf*, buoyant, bustling, cheerful, chirpy *inf*, energetic, enthusiastic, exuberant, frisky, high-spirited, irrepressible, jolly, nimble, perky *inf*, quick, spirited, sprightly, spry, vigorous, vital, vivacious; ***opp*** dull, lethargic

livid *adj* **1** angry, boiling *inf*, enraged, fuming, furious, hopping mad *inf*, incensed, infuriated, mad *inf*, outraged, seething. **2** (of a bruise) black-and-blue, bluish, bruised, discolored, purplish. **3** (of sb's face) ashen, deathly, ghastly, ghostly, gray, pale, pallid, white

living *adj* active, actual, alive, animate, breathing, existing, live, sentient, vital; ***opp*** dead

living *n* daily bread, employment, income, job, keep, livelihood, means of support, occupation, subsistence, sustenance, wage, work

load *n* **1** bale, cargo, charge, consignment, freight, shipment. **2** burden, cross, duty, encumbrance, millstone, pressure, responsibility, strain, trouble, weight, worry

load *v* **1** cram, fill, heap, pack, pile, stack, stuff. **2** burden, charge, oppress, pressure, saddle, trouble, weigh down, worry

loan *n* advance, credit, mortgage

loath, loth *adj* averse to, disinclined, opposed, reluctant, resistant, shy, unenthusiastic, unwilling; ***opp*** eager

loathe *v* abhor, abominate, despise, detest, execrate, hate, have an aversion to, recoil from, revile, shrink from, shudder at; ***opp*** love

lobby *n* **1** anteroom, entrance hall, foyer, hall, hallway, reception, waiting room. **2** (pressure group) campaign, campaigners, interest group, lobbyists, pressure group

lobby *v* campaign for, petition, pressurize, promote, push for, try to influence

local *adj* **1** community, neighborhood, parish, provincial, regional, district; ***opp*** central, national. **2** adjoining, nearby, neighboring

local *n* native, neighbor, resident, villager

locality *n* area, community, district, locale, neighborhood, vicinity

localize *v* confine, contain, limit, restrain, restrict

locate *v* **1** discover, find, pin down, pinpoint, put your hands on, track down, unearth. **2** establish, place, put, set up, site, situate

location *n* place, position, setting, site, situation, spot, venue, whereabouts

lock *n* bolt, catch, clasp, fastening, latch, padlock

lock *v* **1** bolt, fasten, padlock, secure, shut. **2** entangle, entwine, fix, jam, join, mesh. **3 lock up** detain, imprison, incarcerate, put behind bars, remand, take away sb's freedom, throw sb in jail

lodge *n* cabin, chalet, cottage, gatehouse, house, hut

lodge *v* **1** (lodge an appeal) enter, file, make, put in, register, submit. **2** (get stuck) become embedded, embed, get caught, get stuck, jam, stick. **3** (live) have digs, have lodgings, have rooms, live, stay

lodger *n* boarder, paying guest, resident, tenant

lodgings *n* accommodation, apartment, a roof over your head, boarding house, digs *inf*,, pad *inf*, rooms, somewhere to live

log *n* **1** block of wood, branch, chunk of wood, fuel, timber, trunk, twig, wood. **2** account, diary, journal, logbook, record, register

logic *n* argument, deduction, rationale, reasoning, sense

logical *adj* cogent, coherent, consistent, plausible, rational, reasonable, sensible, sound, structured, valid, well-organized; ***opp*** illogical

loiter *v* hang about, hang around, linger, loaf about, stand about, wait around

loll *v* flop, languish, lean, lie, lounge, slouch, slump, sprawl

lone *adj* isolated, single, solitary, unaccompanied

lonely *adj* abandoned, alone, deserted, desolate, forlorn, forsaken, isolated, lonesome, solitary

long *adj* **1** drawn out, elongated, endless, extended, interminable, lengthy, long-winded, never-ending, prolonged, protracted. **2** (four miles long) in length, lengthways

long *v* covet, crave, dream of, hanker after, have a craving for, want, yearn for

longing *n* ambition, craving, desire, hunger, urge, wish

look *n* **1** examination, gaze, glance, glare, glimpse, glower, inspection, peek, scan, stare. **2** appearance, expression, face, impression

look *v* **1** browse through, cast your eye over, examine, eye, eyeball *inf*, gaze, glance, have a look, peep, peer, scan, see, stare, study, watch. **2** (seem) appear, give the appearance of being, seem, strike you as being. **3** (look everywhere for sth) hunt, search, scour. **4 look after** care for, keep an eye on, mind, nurse, nurture, take care of, tend, watch. **5 look forward to** anticipate, count the days until, long for. **6 look into** check out, inquire about, examine, explore, go into, investigate, make some inquiries, research, study. **7 look out** be careful, be on the watch for, beware, keep an eye out, mind yourself, watch out. **8 look up** (look up sth in a reference book) consult, locate, refer to, search for, track down. **9 look up** (visit sb) call on, drop in on, go and see, visit. **10 look up** (improve) get better, improve, look rosy, pick up, shape up

lookout *n* guard, sentry, watch

loom *v* appear, dominate, hang over, materialize, overshadow, take shape, threaten, tower over

loop *n* circle, coil, curl, curve, hoop, noose, ring, spiral, turn, twist, whorl

loop *v* bend, coil, curl, spiral, twist, wind

loophole *n* excuse, flaw, pretext, way of avoiding sth, way out

loose *adj* **1** baggy, floppy, free, hanging, slack, straggling, trailing, unattached, wobbly. **2** at large, escaped, free, out, untethered. **3** approximate, ballpark *inf*, general, rough, vague

loose *v* free, let out, liberate, release, set free, let go, set loose, slacken, turn loose, undo, untether, untie

loosen *v* ease off, relax, release, slacken, undo, unfasten, untie; ***opp*** tighten
loot *n* bounty, goodies *inf*, haul, plunder, spoils
lopsided *adj* awry, crooked, skewed, tilting, uneven; ***opp*** straight
lord *n* **1** aristocrat, baron, count, duke, earl, noble. **2** chief, leader, master, ruler
lordly *adj* **1** arrogant, condescending, disdainful, haughty, imperious, patronizing. **2** aristocratic, noble
lose *v* **1** be unable to find, mislay, misplace; ***opp*** find. **2** be defeated, get beaten, get hammered *inf*, get thrashed *inf*; ***opp*** win
loser *n* also-ran, failure, runner-up
loss *n* bereavement, cost, damage, defeat, deficit, deprivation, disappearance, failure, harm, hurt, impairment, privation
lost *adj* **1** (sth is lost) disappeared, misplaced, missing, vanished. **2** (sb is lost) adrift, disoriented, off course. **3** (feel lost) baffled, bewildered, confused, mystified, puzzled. **4** (from the past) dead, extinct, forgotten, past, vanished, wiped out
lot *n* **1 a lot** a good deal, loads *inf*, lots, many, masses, piles *inf*, plenty, scores, stacks *inf*, tons *inf*. **2 a lot** a good deal, frequently, often, regularly. **3** batch, bunch, bundle, crowd, group
lotion *n* cream, liquid, milk, ointment
lottery *n* **1** draw, raffle, sweepstake. **2** gamble, game, the luck of the draw
loud *adj* **1** blaring, booming, deafening, ear-splitting, noisy, raucous, rowdy, shrill, thudding, thundering, tumultuous; ***opp*** quiet. **2** (of a color) flashy *inf*, garish, gaudy, lurid, ostentatious, showy; ***opp*** subdued, subtle
lounge *v* flop, laze, lie about, lie back, loll, relax, sprawl
lout *n* hoodlum, hooligan, oaf, slob, thug
lovable *adj* adorable, appealing, attractive, cuddly, cute, endearing, gorgeous, lovely, sweet
love *n* **1** adoration, affection, devotion, fondness, infatuation, liking, partiality, passion, soft spot, tenderness, weakness. **2** darling, dear, sweetheart, sweetie
love *v* **1** (be in love with) adore, be devoted to, be fond of, be in love with, be infatuated with, be keen about, be soft on *inf*, dote on, fancy *inf*, have a crush on, have a thing about *inf*, idolize, think the world of, worship. **2** (love strawberries, a song, dancing) adore, be keen about, be partial to, enjoy, get a kick out of, go for, have a weakness for, really like
lovely *adj* **1** (a lovely holiday) fabulous, gorgeous, great, marvelous, superb, terrific, wonderful. **2** (good-looking) attractive, beautiful, cute, good-looking, handsome, pretty, sweet
lover *n* another man, another woman, bit on the side *inf*, boyfriend, fiancé, fiancée, girlfriend, mistress, old flame, partner
loving *adj* adoring, affectionate, amorous, ardent, caring, close, devoted, passionate, tender, warm; ***opp*** cold
low *adj* **1** (short) dwarf, low-growing, low-lying, shallow, short, small, squat, stunted, sunken; ***opp*** tall. **2** (stocks are low) cut, deficient, depleted, inadequate, insufficient, meager, modest,

poor, reduced, scant, scarce; ***opp*** high. **3** (low volume, light) gentle, hushed, muffled, muted, pianissimo, quiet, soft, subdued; ***opp*** bright, loud, strong. **4** (bass) bass, deep; ***opp*** high-pitched, soprano. **5** (unhappy) depressed, despondent, dispirited, down, down in the dumps *inf*, downhearted, fed up *inf*, gloomy, miserable, sad, unhappy; ***opp*** happy, on a high *inf*

lower *adj* **1** inferior, junior, lesser, secondary, subordinate; ***opp*** higher. **2** (lower prices) cut, decreased, reduced, slashed; ***opp*** higher, increased

lower *v* **1** drop, let down, take down. **2** (lower prices) bring down, cut, decrease, discount, mark down, reduce, slash; ***opp*** put up. **3** (lower the volume) reduce, turn down; ***opp*** turn up

low-key *adj* casual, downbeat, laid-back, muted, played down, restrained, understated

loyal *adj* committed, dependable, devoted, dutiful, faithful, reliable, staunch, true, trusted, trustworthy; ***opp*** disloyal

loyalty *n* allegiance, dedication, dependability, devotion, faithfulness, fidelity, reliability, trustworthiness; ***opp*** disloyalty

lubricate *v* grease, moisturize, oil

lucid *adj* **1** (a lucid explanation) clear, comprehensible, distinct, explicit, logical, plain, simple, straightforward, understandable. **2** (clearheaded) all there *inf*, clearheaded, compos mentis, in your right mind, rational, sane, thinking straight

luck *n* **1** chance, destiny, fate, fluke, fortune, serendipity, the stars. **2** (good luck) best of luck, break *inf*, good luck, prosperity, stroke of luck, success, windfall

lucky *adj* auspicious, charmed, fortuitous, fortunate, handy, opportune, timely; ***opp*** unlucky

lucrative *adj* beneficial, fruitful, high-income, juicy *inf*, profitable, well-paid, worthwhile

ludicrous *adj* absurd, comic, crazy, daft *inf*, farcical, incongruous, preposterous, ridiculous, silly, stupid; ***opp*** sensible

luggage *n* baggage, bags, belongings, cases, gear *inf*, possessions, things

lukewarm *adj* **1** at room temperature, tepid. **2** half-hearted, indifferent, unenthusiastic, uninterested; ***opp*** enthusiastic

lull *n* calm, hush, letup, pause, quiet, quiet period, stillness, tranquillity

lull *v* calm down, die down, dwindle, let up, pacify, quiet down, soothe

luminous *adj* bright, fluorescent, glowing, lustrous, phosphorescent, radiant, shining, vivid; ***opp*** dull

lump *n* **1** (swelling) bulge, bump, growth, swelling, tumor. **2** (piece) blob, chunk, clump, hunk, piece, wad, wedge

lump *v* bunch, clump, combine, consolidate, fuse, group, merge, mix, pool, put

lunatic *adj* absurd, crackpot *inf*, crazy, daft *inf*, foolish, idiotic, insane, mad, stupid; ***opp*** sensible

lunatic *n* insane person, madman, maniac, nut case *inf*, psychopath

lunge *v* dive, fall on, jump, leap, lurch, plunge, pounce, thrust

lurch *v* list, lunge, pitch, reel, roll, stagger, stumble, sway, weave
lure *n* attraction, carrot, decoy, inducement, invitation, magnet, temptation
lure *v* attract, beckon, draw, ensnare, entice, invite, lead on, seduce, tempt
lurid *adj* 1 bright, garish, gaudy, glaring, loud, vivid. 2 disgusting, gory, grisly, gruesome, nasty, repulsive, revolting, shocking, unpleasant
lurk *v* hide, lie in wait, linger, skulk, sneak, snoop
luscious *adj* appetizing, delicious, juicy, mouth-watering, succulent, yummy *inf*
lush *adj* dense, flourishing, green, luxuriant, prolific, rich, thick
lust *n* craving, desire, lechery, longing, passion
lust after *v* crave, desire, fancy *inf*, need, want
luxurious *adj* affluent, comfortable, deluxe, expensive, extravagant, grand, lavish, opulent, plush, rich, ritzy *inf*, sumptuous, swanky *inf*; ***opp*** poor, spartan
luxury *n* 1 comfort, extravagance, grandeur, indulgence, opulence, richness, splendor, sumptuousness. 2 (a luxury) extra, extravagance, optional extra, treat, trimmings
lyrical *adj* emotional, expressive, impassioned, poetic, romantic
lyrics *n* libretto, text, words

macabre *adj* eerie, frightening, grisly, gruesome, horrible, morbid, sick *inf*

machine *n* apparatus, appliance, contraption, device, gadget, mechanism, robot, tool

machinery *n* **1** apparatus, equipment, gear, plant, tools. **2** channels, organization, procedure, set-up *inf*, structure, system, workings

mad *adj* **1** crazy *inf*, demented, insane, mentally handicapped, mentally ill, mentally unstable, nuts *inf*, out of your mind, senile, unbalanced, unhinged; ***opp*** sane. **2** (idiotic) crackpot *inf*, crazy, daft *inf*, foolish, idiotic, insane, lunatic, ridiculous, silly, stupid; ***opp*** sensible

madden *v* anger, annoy, enrage, exasperate, gall, get sb's back up *inf*, infuriate, irritate, make angry, make sb's blood boil, upset; ***opp*** please

made-up *adj* **1** fabricated, false, fictional, imaginary, invented, spurious; ***opp*** true. **2** prebuilt, readymade

madman *n* head case *inf*, loony *inf*, madwoman, mentally handicapped person, nut case *inf*, psychopath

madness *n* **1** dementia, insanity, mania, mental illness, psychosis. **2** absurdity, craziness, folly, foolishness, stupidity

magazine *n* journal, monthly, periodical, weekly

magic *adj* **1** brilliant, excellent, marvelous, terrific, wonderful. **2** charmed, enchanted, magical

magic *n* **1** black magic, conjuring, enchantment, illusion, sleight of hand, sorcery, the occult, the supernatural, voodoo, witchcraft. **2** charm, fascination, magnetism, spell

magician *n* conjuror, illusionist, sorcerer, warlock, witch, wizard

magnanimous *adj* benevolent, big-hearted, big, charitable, generous, kind

magnetic *adj* appealing, attractive, captivating, charismatic, enchanting, fascinating, gripping, inviting, irresistible, mesmerizing, seductive, tantalizing, tempting

magnetism *n* appeal, attraction, charm, draw, fascination, lure, magic, pull, spell, temptation

magnificent *adj* brilliant, excellent, fine, glorious, gorgeous, grand, magic, marvelous, out of this world, splendid, sumptuous, superb, tremendous, wonderful

magnify *v* amplify, blow up, boost, build up, enhance, enlarge, exaggerate, expand, heighten, increase, inflate, make bigger; ***opp*** reduce

magnitude *n* degree, enormity, extent, greatness, immensity, importance, significance, size, vastness

maid *n* **1** domestic servant, domestic, girl, housemaid, lady-in-waiting, lady's maid, servant. **2** girl, lass, young woman

mail *n* collection, delivery, letters, parcels, post, postal service

mail *v* e-mail, send, send off, transfer

maim *v* disable, handicap, damage permanently, injure, mutilate, wound

main *adj* basic, central, chief, critical, crucial, essential, first, foremost, key, major, most important, number one, paramount, predominant, primary, prime, principal, top, vital

main *n* cable, channel, conduit, line, pipe, water main

maintain *v* **1** (keep up) continue, keep up, keep, retain, sustain. **2** (maintain a building) carry out repairs, keep in good order, look after, preserve, repair, take care of. **3** (say that sth is true) allege, argue, assert, believe, claim, contend, profess, state

majestic *adj* grand, imperial, imposing, impressive, magnificent, noble, regal, splendid, stately

majesty *n* grandeur, magnificence, nobility, pomp, royalty, splendor, stateliness

major *adj* chief, considerable, crucial, extensive, great, important, key, leading, main, outstanding, principal, significant; ***opp*** minor

majority *n* best part, bulk, greater part, largest part, lion's share, main body, more than half, most; ***opp*** minority

make *n* brand, sort, type, variety

make *v* **1** (produce) assemble, bake, build, cook, create, draw up, fashion, fix *inf*, form, manufacture, prepare, produce, put together, synthesize. **2** (cause) bring about, cause, generate, give rise to. **3** (compel) coerce, compel, force, oblige, push sb into, require. **4** (earn) bring home, bring in, clear, earn, gain, net. **5** (one and one makes two) add up to, come to, constitute, equal, total. **6** (make a statement, speech) deliver, give, say, utter. **7 make off** bolt, clear off *inf*, decamp, escape, get away, run off. **8 make out** (be able to see or hear) detect, discern, distinguish, hear, pick out, recognize, see. **9 make out** (understand) decipher, figure out, follow, get *inf*, grasp, see, understand, work out. **10 make out** (make out a receipt) complete, fill in, fill out, write out. **11 make up** compose, concoct, create, dream up, fabricate, hatch, invent. **12 make up** comprise, constitute, form

make-believe *n* dream, fantasy, fiction, imagination, invention, play-acting, pretense, role-play; ***opp*** reality

make do *v* cope, get by, improvise, manage, put up with, survive

maker *n* architect, author, builder, composer, creator, manufacturer, originator, producer, writer

makeshift *adj* emergency, improvised, make-do, provisional, rough-and-ready, stopgap, temporary; ***opp*** permanent

makeup *n* cosmetics, face-paint, grease-paint, war paint

makings *n* beginnings, capability, ingredients, potential, promise, qualities, talent

maladjusted *adj* disturbed, neurotic,

unbalanced, unstable, with behavioral problems; ***opp*** well-adjusted

male *adj* boyish, manlike, manly, masculine; ***opp*** female

malevolent *adj* cruel, evil, fierce, hostile, malicious, malign, spiteful, unfriendly, venomous, vindictive; ***opp*** good

malice *n* animosity, bitchiness *inf*, bitterness, enmity, hatred, hostility, ill will, rancor, spite, venom, vindictiveness

malicious *adj* bitchy *inf*, bitter, hostile, hurtful, malignant, pernicious, spiteful, venomous, vicious, vindictive

malignant *adj* **1** hostile, malicious, pernicious, spiteful, venomous, vicious. **2** dangerous, destructive, life-threatening; ***opp*** benign

man *n* **1** chap *inf*, gentleman, guy *inf*, human being, individual, lad, male, young man. **2** Homo sapiens, human race, humankind, humans, men and women, people

man *v* crew, operate, staff, work

manacle *n* chain, fetter, handcuffs, irons, shackle

manage *v* **1** accomplish, bring off, cope, crack it *inf*, deal with, get by, handle, succeed, survive. **2** administer, be in charge of, control, direct, head, lead, organize, oversee, pilot, run, supervise

manageable *adj* **1** attainable, doable, feasible, possible, viable. **2** accommodating, amenable, compliant, controllable, docile, submissive

management *n* **1** administration, board, bosses, directors, employers, executive, managers, owners, top brass *inf*. **2** administration, command, control, direction, handling, organization, overseeing, running, supervision

manager *n* administrator, boss, controller, director, employer, executive, foreman, governor, head of department, head, owner, person in charge, proprietor, superintendent, supervisor

mandate *n* approval, authority, authorization, command, decree, direction, edict, order, power, ruling, sanction, support

maneuver *n* action, dodge, intrigue, machination, plan, plot, ploy, ruse, scheme, subterfuge, tactic, trick

maneuver *v* **1** contrive, engineer, intrigue, manage, manipulate, plan, plot, pull strings, scheme. **2** direct, drive, guide, move, steer

maneuvers *n* deployment, exercise, military exercise, movement, training

mangle *v* crush, destroy, distort, hack, maul, twist, wreck

mangy *adj* moth-eaten, scruffy, shabby, threadbare, wretched

manhandle *v* haul, heave, hump, push, shove

mania *n* **1** derangement, insanity, madness, mental illness. **2** addiction, craving, craze, obsession, passion

maniac *n* deranged person, idiot, loony *inf*, lunatic, madman, madwoman, nut case *inf*, psychopath

manifest *adj* clear, conspicuous, glaring, obvious, patent, plain, unmistakable

manifestation *n* demonstration, display, embodiment, evidence, expression, indication, sign, symbol, testimony

manipulate *v* **1** handle, maneuver,

operate, use, work. **2** (people) exploit, influence, misuse, take advantage of, use

mankind *n* Homo sapiens, human race, humanity, humans, men and women, people

manly *adj* **1** macho, male, masculine, virile; ***opp*** effeminate. **2** brave, chivalrous, gallant, strong, vigorous

man-made *adj* artificial, imitation, manufactured, simulated, synthetic, synthesized; ***opp*** natural

manner *adj* **1** approach, means, method, procedure, process, style, technique, way. **2** air, appearance, attitude, bearing, behavior, demeanor, look, mien, way. **3 all manner of** all kinds of, a mixture of, an assortment of, assorted, different, various, varying

mannerism *n* characteristic, gesture, foible, habit, idiosyncrasy, peculiarity, quirk

manners *n* **1** bearing, behavior, conduct, deportment. **2** civility, correct behavior, courtesy, decorum, etiquette, good form, politeness, protocol, propriety, social graces

manual *adj* **1** by hand, hand-operated. **2** (manual work) laboring, physical, with your hands

manufacture *v* **1** build, construct, create, fabricate, forge, form, make, mass-produce, process, produce, shape, turn out. **2** (a story) concoct, cook up *inf*, dream up, invent, think up

manure *n* compost, droppings, dung, fertilizer, guano, muck

many *adj* abundant, a lot of, copious, countless, frequent, heaps of *inf*, innumerable, loads of *inf*, lots of, myriad, numerous, oodles of *inf*, plenty of, profuse, tons of *inf*, umpteen *inf*

map *n* chart, guide, plan, street guide, road map, town plan

march *n* **1** parade, tramp, trek, walk. **2** demonstration, parade, procession, protest

march *v* file, parade, stride, tramp

margin **1** border, boundary, brink, edge, perimeter, periphery, rim, side, verge. **2** allowance, latitude, leeway, room, room for maneuver, scope, space

marginal *adj* **1** borderline, peripheral. **2** doubtful, insignificant, low, minimal, negligible, slight, small, unimportant

marginalize *v* decrease the influence of, exclude, make marginal, make unimportant, push out, push to the margins

marital *adj* conjugal, married, matrimonial, nuptial, wedded

mark *n* **1** blemish, blot, blotch, dent, dot, impression, pockmark, scar, scratch, smear, smudge, smut, speck, spot, stain, streak. **2** badge, brand, device, emblem, hallmark, seal, signature, symbol, trademark. **3** evidence, indication, proof, sign, symbol, token. **4** aim, goal, intention, objective, purpose, target. **5 below the mark** below par, below the norm, below the standard, inadequate, inferior, not up to scratch, substandard. **6 leave its mark** affect, have an effect, have an impact, impress, influence, make an impression. **7 wide of the mark** erroneous, fallacious, inaccurate, incorrect, wrong

mark *v* **1** blemish, blot, damage, deface, disfigure, dent, dirty, draw on, make a mark on, scar, scrawl on, scribble on, smudge, spot, stain, streak, write on. **2** brand, label, put a mark on, tag. **3** (mark sb's work) appraise, assess, correct, evaluate, grade. **4** (mark sb's words) attend to, heed, listen to, mind, note, notice, observe, pay attention to, see, take notice of, take seriously, take to heart, watch. **5** (mark an occasion) celebrate, commemorate, honor, observe

marked *adj* apparent, blatant, clear, conspicuous, decided, distinct, evident, notable, obvious, patent, pronounced, remarkable, striking

market *n* **1** bazaar, fair, marketplace, mart. **2** call, demand, desire. **3** business, buying and selling, commerce, dealing

market *v* advertise, peddle, promote, push *inf*, put on the market, retail, sell, trade in, vend

marketable *adj* desirable, in demand, salable, sought after, wanted

marksman *n* crack shot *inf*, good shot, markswoman, sharpshooter

maroon *v* abandon, desert, forsake, leave, leave behind, leave stranded, put ashore, strand

marriage *n* **1** matrimony, union, wedlock. **2** marriage ceremony, nuptials, wedding. **3** alliance, association, combination, link, merger, union

married **1** (of people) hitched *inf*, joined, united, wed, wedded. **2** conjugal, connubial, marital, matrimonial, wedded

marry *v* **1** become man and wife, be married, get hitched *inf*, get married, join in matrimony, tie the knot *inf*, unite, walk down the aisle *inf*, wed. **2** ally, combine, join, link, merge, unite

marsh *n* bog, fen, marshland, mire, morass, quagmire, quicksand, swamp, wetland

marshy *adj* boggy, miry, muddy, quaggy, soft, squelchy, swampy

marvel *v* admire, applaud, be amazed by, be astonished by, be surprised by, praise, wonder at

marvelous *adj* amazing, astounding, breathtaking, brilliant, extraordinary, fantastic, out of this world *inf*, remarkable, sensational, stupendous, superb, terrific, wonderful

masculine *adj* **1** macho, male, manly, virile; ***opp*** feminine. **2** (of a woman) butch *inf*, manly, unfeminine, unwomanly; ***opp*** feminine

mash *v* crush, mangle, pound, pulp, pulverize, purée, smash, squash

mask *n* camouflage, cover, disguise, facade, false colors, front, guise, pretense, screen, shield, smokescreen, veil

mask *v* cloak, conceal, cover up, disguise, hide, obscure, screen, veil

mass *adj* extensive, general, indiscriminate, large-scale, popular, universal, wholesale, widespread

mass *n* **1** accumulation, collection, concentration. **2** body, crowd, horde, host, lot, mob, multitude, throng. **3** body, bulk, greater part, lion's share, main body, majority, preponderance. **4** bulk, magnitude, size

mass *v* **1** accumulate, amass, assemble, bring together, collect, gather. **2** assemble, collect, flock together, gather, gather together, meet, marshal, rally, swarm, throng

massacre *n* annihilation, blood bath, butchery, carnage, genocide, mass execution, mass murder, slaughter

massacre *v* annihilate, butcher, kill, kill off, mow down, slaughter, slay, wipe out

massage *v* knead, manipulate, rub, rub down

masses *n* **1** an abundance, bags *inf*, heaps *inf*, hundreds, loads, lots, millions, oodles *inf*, thousands. **2 the masses** the common people, the mob, the hoi polloi, the proletariat, the rabble

massive *adj* colossal, enormous, gigantic, huge, immense, large, mammoth, vast, whopping *inf*; ***opp*** tiny

master *adj* chief, main, most important, predominant, principal

master *n* **1** boss, chief, controller, director, employer, governor, head, lord, lord and master, ruler, top dog *inf*. **2** (of a ship) captain, commander, skipper. **3** head, headmaster, head teacher, instructor, schoolmaster, schoolteacher, teacher, tutor. **4** (a master at sth) ace *inf*, authority, expert, genius, maestro, virtuoso, wizard

master *v* **1** become expert in, become proficient in, get the hang of *inf*, grasp, know, learn, learn thoroughly. **2** control, dominate, govern, overcome, overpower, quell, subdue, subjugate, tame

masterly *adj* accomplished, ace *inf*, adept, consummate, deft, dexterous, excellent, expert, first-rate, masterful, proficient, skillful, skilled

mastermind *n* **1** brains, expert, genius, intellect, intellectual. **2** architect, author, brains behind sth, creator, director, initiator, organizer, originator, planner

mastermind *v* be the brains behind *inf*, conceive, devise, direct, initiate, manage, organize, plan, think up

masterpiece *n* best work, chef d'oeuvre, magnum opus, masterwork, pièce de résistance, tour de force

match *n* **1** bout, competition, contest, game, tournament. **2** counterpart, equal, equivalent, peer, rival. **3** copy, double, duplicate, look-alike, spitting image *inf*, twin. **4** complement, counterpart, mate, pair, twin. **5** affiliation, alliance, marriage, pairing, partnership, union

match *v* **1** agree with, be a pair, be compatible with, be similar to, be the same as, blend with, complement, coordinate with, correspond to, fit, go with, harmonize, make a set, suit; ***opp*** contrast. **2** be a match for, be equal to, be in the same category as, be on a level with, compare with, compete with, keep pace with, keep up with, measure up to, rival. **3** bring together, combine, link, marry, pair off, pair up, put together, team up

matching *adj* **1** alike, identical, just like, the same, twin. **2** blending, complementing, coordinating, equivalent, harmonizing, identical, like, parallel, similar, twin

mate *n* **1** better half *inf*, husband, other half *inf*, partner, spouse, wife. **2** colleague, co-worker, fellow-worker, workmate. **3** buddy *inf*, chum *inf*, companion, comrade, friend, pal *inf*

mate *v* **1** breed, couple, copulate. **2** bring together, marry, match, join, pair, wed

material *adj* 1 concrete, palpable, physical, solid, substantial, tangible. 2 essential, grave, important, key, meaningful, pertinent, relevant, serious, significant, weighty

material *n* 1 element, matter, medium, stuff, substance. 2 cloth, fabric, stuff, textiles. 3 data, details, evidence, facts, info *inf*, information, notes

materialize *v* 1 come about, come into being, happen, occur, take place. 2 appear, become visible, come to light, emerge, present itself, show itself, turn up *inf*

maternal *adj* 1 motherly. 2 (maternal relations) on the distaff side, on your mother's side

matter *n* 1 material, medium, stuff, substance. 2 affair, business, episode, event, incident, issue, occurrence, question, situation, subject, topic. 3 consequence, import, importance, note, significance, weight

matter *v* be important, be relevant, be significant, carry weight, count, make a difference, make any difference, signify

matter-of-fact *adj* deadpan, down-to-earth, dull, factual, flat, literal, mundane, plain, prosaic, straightforward, unvarnished

mature *adj* 1 adult, full-grown, fully developed, fully grown, grown-up, of age, well-developed. 2 experienced, responsible, sensible, wise. 3 mellow, ready, ripe, ripened, seasoned

mature *v* 1 become adult, come of age, develop, grow up, reach adulthood. 2 become responsible, become sensible, become wise. 3 become ripe, grow ripe, mellow, ripen

maturity *n* 1 adulthood, coming-of-age, majority, manhood, womanhood. 2 sense, sense of responsibility, wisdom. 3 mellowness, ripeness

maul *v* 1 claw, lacerate, mangle, mutilate, savage, tear to pieces. 2 abuse, handle roughly, manhandle, molest, paw

maxim *n* adage, aphorism, axiom, motto, proverb, rule, saying

maximum *adj* biggest, extreme, full, fullest, greatest, highest, largest, most, supreme, top, topmost, utmost; ***opp*** minimum

maximum *n* acme, apex, ceiling, crest, height, highest point, peak, summit, top, upper limit, utmost, zenith; ***opp*** minimum

maybe *adv* conceivably, could be *inf*, perhaps, possibly, who knows? *inf*, you never know *inf*; ***opp*** certainly, definitely

maze *n* confusion, jungle, labyrinth, mesh, network, puzzle, tangle, web

meadow *n* field, grassland, paddock, pasture

meager *adj* deficient, inadequate, measly, paltry, poor, scanty, short, skimpy, sparse, stingy; ***opp*** generous

mean *adj* 1 close-fisted, illiberal, mingy *inf*, miserly, niggardly, parsimonious, stingy, tight, tight-fisted, ungenerous; ***opp*** generous. 2 bad-tempered, callous, disagreeable, hard-hearted, obnoxious, spiteful, surly, uncharitable, unfriendly, unkind, unpleasant. 3 (of an action) base, contemptible, despicable, ignoble, nasty, odious, shameful, vile. 4 (of a place) humble, miserable, poor, seedy, shabby, squalid, wretched

mean *n* average, balance, median, middle, midpoint, norm

mean *v* **1** convey, denote, drive at *inf*, express, imply, indicate, insinuate, represent, say, signify, spell, stand for, suggest, symbolize. **2** aim, have in mind, intend, plan, propose, set out. **3** bring about, cause, engender, entail, give rise to, involve, lead to, necessitate, produce

meander *v* **1** bend, curve, loop, snake, twist and turn, wind, zigzag. **2** ramble, stray, stroll aimlessly, wander, wander about

meaning *n* **1** drift, essence, explanation, gist, implication, import, message, sense, significance, substance, thrust, upshot. **2** consequence, effect, point, purpose, significance, value, worth. **3** aim, design, end, goal, intention, object, plan

meaningful *adj* **1** important, material, relevant, serious, significant, valid, worthwhile; ***opp*** meaningless. **2** eloquent, expressive, pointed, significant

meaningless *adj* **1** aimless, empty, futile, hollow, insignificant, pointless, trifling, trivial, useless, vain, worthless; ***opp*** important. **2** inane, incoherent, incomprehensible, nonsensical, senseless, unintelligible

means *n* **1** avenue, course, expedient, method, process, way. **2** affluence, capital, finance, fortune, funds, money, property, resources, riches, wealth

measure *n* **1** amount, capacity, degree, expanse, extent, proportion, quantity, range, reach, scope, size. **2** allotment, allowance, division, part, percentage, portion, quota, ration, share. **3** scale, standard, unit. **4** gauge, measuring spoon, measuring cup, meter, ruler, scale, tape measure. **5** benchmark, criterion, litmus test, test, yardstick. **6** action, course, course of action, expedient, procedure, proceeding, step. **7** act, bill, law, resolution, statute

measure *v* **1** assess, calculate, calibrate, compute, count, determine, evaluate, judge, mark out, meter, quantify, rate, reckon, size, survey, take measurements, value, weigh. **2 measure out** allocate, allot, deal out, distribute, divide, dole out, share out. **3 measure up** be adequate, be as good as, be equal to, be good enough, be on a level with, be suitable, come up to, come up to scratch *inf*, fit the bill, fulfill expectations, make the grade, match, meet, pass muster

measurement *n* **1** amount, capacity, depth, dimensions, extent, height, length, proportions, quantity, range, size, weight, width. **2** assessment, calculation, evaluation, judgment, quantification, quantifying, sizing, weighing

meat *n* **1** animal flesh, flesh, offal. **2** (meat and drink) food, grub *inf*, nosh *inf*, nourishment, provisions, rations, sustenance, victuals

mechanical *adj* **1** automated, automatic, machine-driven, motor-driven, technological. **2** automatic, cursory, habitual, instinctive, involuntary, knee-jerk *inf*, machinelike, perfunctory, reflex, routine, soulless, unconscious, unthinking

mechanism *n* **1** apparatus, appliance, contraption, contrivance, device, gadget, machine, system, tool. **2** components, innards *inf*, machinery, workings, works. **3** agency, channel, means, method, operation, procedure, proceeding, system

mechanize *v* automate, bring up to date, equip with machines, make automatic, modernize

medal *n* award, decoration, honor, medallion, prize, reward, trophy

meddle *v* be a busybody, butt in, interfere, intervene, intrude, poke your nose in *inf*, pry, stick your nose in *inf*, tamper

mediate *v* act as go-between, act as mediator, act as middleman, act as peacemaker, arbitrate, conciliate, intercede, intervene, liaise, make peace, negotiate, reconcile, referee, umpire

medicinal *adj* curative, healing, remedial, restorative, therapeutic

medicine *n* **1** cure, drug, medication, medicament, remedy, panacea. **2** healing, medical science, therapy, treatment

mediocre *adj* average, fair, indifferent, middling, no great shakes *inf*, nothing to write home about *inf*, ordinary, passable, pedestrian, run-of-the-mill, second-rate, so-so, undistinguished, uninspired

meditate *n* **1** be lost in thought, cogitate, deliberate, muse, ponder, reflect, study, think. **2** brood over, chew over *inf*, contemplate, consider, mull over, ponder, reflect on, think over

medium *adj* **1** average, fair, intermediate, mean, median, mediocre, middle, middling, moderate,

medium *n* **1** average, center, compromise, mean, median, middle, middle way. **2** agency, approach, channel, form, means, means of communication, means of expression, method, vehicle, way. **3** conditions, element, environment, habitat, milieu, setting. **4** clairvoyant, seer, spiritualist

medley *n* assortment, hotchpotch, jumble, miscellany, mishmash, mixed bag, mixture

meek *adj* **1** docile, forbearing, gentle, humble, long-suffering, mild, modest, patient, peaceable, resigned, self-effacing, unassuming, unpretentious. **2** acquiescent, compliant, deferential, docile, soft, spineless, submissive, timid, tractable, weak, weak-kneed *inf*, wimpish *inf*; ***opp*** aggressive

meet *v* **1** (meet sb) bump into, chance upon, come across, come face to face with, come upon, encounter, happen upon, join, make contact with, meet with, rendezvous with, run into. **2** (people meet) assemble, come together, congregate, gather, mingle, rendezvous. **3** (lines, roads meet) come together, connect, converge, intersect, join, link up, touch. **4** (one line, road meets another) abut, adjoin, reach. **5** (meet certain conditions) answer, comply with, correspond to, fulfill, measure up to, observe, satisfy

meeting *n* **1** (to discuss business) assembly, conclave, conference, convention, discussion, gathering, get-together *inf*, session. **2** (between two people) appointment, assignation, confrontation, contact, encounter, rendezvous. **3** (of roads, lines, rivers) confluence, convergence, crossroads, intersection, junction

melancholy *adj* dejected, depressed, disconsolate, doleful, down *inf*, down in the dumps *inf*, down in the mouth, gloomy, glum, inconsolable, melancholic, miserable, nostalgic, sad, somber, sorry for yourself, tearful, unhappy, wistful

mellow *adj* **1** (of food, taste) fruity, full-bodied, juicy, matured, rich, ripe, smooth, soft, tender. **2** (of a voice, sound) baritone, contralto, deep, mellifluous, resonant, rich, smooth, sweet. **3** (of colors) autumnal, golden, rich, soft, warm. **4** (of a person) calm, gentle, mature, indulgent, relaxed, serene, warm

mellow *v* **1** age, improve with age, mature, ripen, soften. **2** (of a person) chill out *inf*, lighten up *inf*, relax, relent, warm to sth

melodramatic *adj* dramatic, exaggerated, histrionic, sensational, sentimental, theatrical

melody *n* air, descant, music, song, strain, theme, tune

melt *v* **1** defrost, dissolve, liquefy, soften, thaw, unfreeze; ***opp*** freeze, solidify. **2** (of fears, anger) abate, die down, disappear, disperse, evaporate, fade, fade away, vanish

member *n* **1** adherent, associate, fellow, initiate, subscriber. **2** (of a set) component, constituent, element, part

memoirs *n* autobiography, diary, journal, life story, memories, recollections, reminiscences

memorable *adj* extraordinary, distinctive, historic, impressive, momentous, not to be forgotten, notable, noteworthy, remarkable, striking, unforgettable; ***opp*** unmemorable

memorial *adj* celebratory, commemorative, in celebration of sb/sth, in commemoration of sb/sth, in honor of sb/sth, in memory of sb/sth, monumental, in remembrance of sb/sth

memorial *n* cairn, cenotaph, homage, monument, plaque, shrine, statue, time capsule, tribute

memorize *v* absorb, commit to memory, learn, learn by heart, learn by rote, make a mental note of, remember, take in

memory *n* **1** (ability to remember) attention span, mind, powers of recall, recall, remembrance, retention. **2** (sth remembered) impression, recollection, reminiscence. **3** (in computing) bits, bytes, cache, capacity, data bank, data storage, gigabytes, hard disk, kilobytes, megabytes, RAM, random access memory, read-only memory, ROM

menace *n* **1** (dangerous thing, person) bane, danger, evil, hazard, nuisance, peril, risk, sword of Damocles, thorn in sb's side, threat. **2** (an atmosphere of menace) danger, evil, fear, foreboding, intimidation, peril, threat. **3** (naughty child) devil, hooligan, imp, mischief-maker, pest, rapscallion, rascal, scamp *inf*, terror *inf*, troublemaker

menace *v* **1** alarm, browbeat, bully, cow, frighten, intimidate, scare, terrify, terrorize, threaten. **2** (the dangers that menace our society) beset, endanger, hang over, imperil, threaten

menacing *adj* **1** frightening, glowering,

intimidating, lowering, ominous, terrifying, threatening. **2** (of future threats) dangerous, forbidding, impending, looming, ominous, threatening

mend *v* darn, fix, patch up *inf*, rebuild, reconstruct, renew, repair, restore, sew up

menial *adj* demeaning, dirty, domestic, humble, laboring, low-grade, lowly, low-status, routine, unglamorous, unskilled

mental *adj* cerebral, cognitive, emotional, in the mind, intellectual, psychological; ***opp*** physical

mentality *n* attitude, cast of mind, character, make-up, mind, mode of thought, personality, psyche, psychology

mentally *adv* cognitively, emotionally, in your mind, in your mind's eye, intellectually, psychologically, silently; ***opp*** physically

mention *n* acknowledgment, allusion, citation, comment, disclosure, indication, notice, quotation, reference, remark, report, statement

mention *v* acknowledge, allude to, cite, comment on, declare, disclose, divulge, indicate, quote, refer to, remark on, report, say, speak of, state, talk about, talk of

mercenary *adj* acquisitive, avaricious, covetous, grasping, greedy, in it for the money *inf*, materialistic, money-grubbing *inf*, selfish, venal

merchandise *n* articles, commodities, goods, items, products, wares

merchant *n* businessman, capitalist, entrepreneur, exporter, importer, seller, supplier, trader, tradesman, tradesperson, vendor

merciful *adj* compassionate, forgiving, indulgent, kind, lenient, pitying, soft-hearted, tender-hearted; ***opp*** merciless

merciless *adj* cruel, hard, pitiless, remorseless, ruthless, severe, without pity; ***opp*** merciful

mercy *n* **1** charity, clemency, compassion, forgiveness, indulgence, kindness, lenience, pity. **2 at the mercy of** exposed to, in the clutches of, in the power of, threatened by, under the control of, vulnerable to

merge *v* **1** (of companies, organizations) ally, amalgamate, be absorbed, be incorporated, be taken over, combine, form a coalition, form an alliance, join forces, join together, team up, unite. **2** (of substances, colors, feelings) be absorbed, be assimilated, be submerged, be swallowed up, blend, converge, fade into, fuse, intermingle, mingle, mix, seep into

merger *n* absorption, alliance, amalgamation, coalition, combination, conglomeration, incorporation, takeover

merit *n* **1** advantage, bonus, credit, good point, pro, quality; ***opp*** demerit. **2** ability, excellence, praiseworthiness, skill, talent, value, worth

merry *adj* **1** celebrating, cheerful, festive, happy, jolly, joyful, joyous, laughing, lively, rejoicing, reveling. **2** drunk, inebriated, intoxicated, tipsy

mesh *n* lattice, net, netting, network, tangle, web

mesh *v* agree, be in harmony, be on the same wave length, coincide, combine, connect, dovetail, fit, fit in, fit together, go together, harmonize, interlock, match, tally

mess *n* **1** chaos, confusion, debris, dirt, disorder, filth, jumble, muddle, pigsty *inf*, rubbish, untidiness. **2** (unsatisfactory situation) calamity, crisis, debacle, disarray, disaster, foul-up *inf*, hole, pickle *inf*, trouble. **3** (place where soldiers eat) bar, cafeteria, canteen, club, dining hall, mess hall

mess *v* **1 mess about** act up, have a laugh *inf*, joke, fool about, fool around, misbehave, tease. **2 mess with sth** fiddle with, fuss, meddle, play with, tinker with, trifle with. **3 mess up** botch, bungle, get sth wrong, make a mess of, make a pig's ear of *inf*

message *n* **1** cable, communication, E-mail, fax, letter, memo, memorandum, missive, note, telegram, telephone call, signal, transmission, wire. **2** (of a literary work) idea, import, interpretation, meaning, moral, purport, significance, theme

messenger *n* bearer, carrier, courier, emissary, envoy, errand-boy, go-between, harbinger, herald, runner

messy *adj* chaotic, complicated, confused, dirty, filthy, jumbled, untidy

metaphorical *adj* allegorical, emblematic, figurative, nonliteral, proverbial, symbolic

meteoric *adj* brilliant, dazzling, fast, irresistible, overnight, quick, rapid, spectacular, speedy, sudden, swift

method *n* approach, arrangement, manner, means, methodology, mode, modus operandi, plan, practice, procedure, process, rule, style, system, technique, way

methodical *adj* careful, deliberate, logical, meticulous, orderly, precise, step-by-step, systematic

meticulous *adj* accurate, careful, conscientious, correct, detailed, exact, methodical, painstaking, punctilious; ***opp*** sloppy

microbe *n* amoeba, bacillus, bacterium, bug *inf*, germ, microorganism, virus

middle *adj* **1** central, halfway, intermediate, mean, medial, median, mid-. **2** (between two extreme qualities) average, medium, middling

middle *n* center, core, halfway mark, heart, kernel, midpoint, midst, nucleus

might *n* energy, force, forcefulness, power, strength, sturdiness, vigor

mighty *adj* **1** (of person) all-powerful, almighty, forceful, great, powerful, strong, sturdy. **2** (of sound, force) extreme, great, heavy, intense, powerful, severe, strong, vigorous, violent

migrant *adj* globe-trotting, itinerant, migrating, migratory, traveling, wandering

migrant *n* asylum seeker, emigrant, exile, globe-trotter, guest worker, gypsy, immigrant, itinerant, nomad, refugee, traveler, voyager, wanderer

migrate *v* emigrate, flee, fly away, go away, journey, move, relocate, travel, trek, voyage, wander

migration *n* emigration, flight, immigration, journey, relocation, travel, trek, voyage, wandering

mild *adj* **1** (of taste, smell) bland, gentle, insipid, inoffensive, soft, subtle, sweet, unobtrusive, weak; ***opp*** harsh, strong.

2 (of a person) docile, gentle, inoffensive, kind, meek, mild-mannered, placid, unassertive; ***opp*** aggressive. 3 (of weather) balmy, clement, moderate, temperate, warm, warmish

milieu *n* background, environment, location, setting, social circle, surroundings

militant *adj* aggressive, campaigning, combative, committed, extreme, extremist, hardline, radical, strident, uncompromising; ***opp*** moderate

military *adj* armed, martial, naval, service, soldierly, warlike

military *n* armed forces, army, forces, militia, services

milk *v* (milk sb) bleed, drain, exploit, extort, extract, siphon, soak, squeeze, suck dry

mill about *v* circulate, hang about, hang around, loiter, mill around, move about, move around, saunter, stroll, walk, wander

mimic *n* chameleon, copycat *inf*, impersonator, impressionist, mime, mime artist

mimic *v* ape, caricature, copy, do an impression of, imitate, impersonate, mime, parody, resemble

mind *n* brain, head, imagination, intellect, intelligence, memory, mental capacity, mental health, mentality, opinion, psyche, psychology, sanity, soul, thinking, thought, will

mind *v* 1 guard, keep, keep an eye on, look after, protect, take care of, watch, watch over. 2 (mind the step) avoid, be aware, be careful, be mindful, beware, look out, pay attention, take care, watch, watch out. 3 (not mind sth) be bothered, be offended, be upset, care, disapprove, give a damn *inf*, object, take offense

mindful *adj* 1 attentive, aware, careful, conscious, thoughtful, wary, watchful. 2 **be mindful of** be alert to, be alive to, beware of, make allowances for, heed, pay attention to, take account of, take into account, take into consideration, think about

mindless *adj* brainless *inf*, cretinous, daft, hare-brained, idiotic, moronic, stupid, thoughtless, vacuous

mine *n* 1 colliery, deep mine, excavation, pit, quarry, shaft, supply, tunnel, working. 2 bomb, booby trap, detonator, explosive charge, landmine

mine *v* 1 bore, dig, drill, excavate, extract, hew, quarry, tunnel, work. 2 booby-trap, lay mines, plant mines

mingle *v* 1 blend, combine, confuse, fold, intermingle, melt, merge, mix. 2 (talk to people) associate, chat, circulate, fraternize, hobnob *inf*, join in, move around, socialize

minimal *adj* 1 basic, essential, indispensable, minimum. 2 little, nominal, low, meager, slight, small, tiny, token

minimize *v* 1 curtail, cut back, cut down, decrease, keep down, keep to a minimum, prune, reduce, shrink; ***opp*** maximize. 2 (think sth is unimportant) dismiss, downgrade, laugh off, play down, shrug off, underestimate, underplay, understate

minimum *adj* barest, least, lowest, minimal, smallest, slightest

minimum *n* least, low point, lowest level, nadir, smallest amount, trough; ***opp*** maximum

minion *n* aide, assistant, attendant, bodyguard, flunky, helper, henchman, hireling, lackey, menial, servant, sidekick, subordinate, underling

minister *n* **1** ambassador, consul delegate, diplomat, emissary, envoy. **2** clergyman, man of the cloth, moderator, parson, pastor, preacher, priest, rector, vicar

minor *adj* inconsequential, inferior, insignificant, lesser, negligible, slight, small, trivial, unimportant; ***opp*** major

mint *adj* new, perfect, pristine, unblemished, unsullied, untarnished, unused, virgin

mint *v* cast, coin, issue, press, print, produce, stamp, strike

minute *adj* diminutive, microscopic, mini-, miniature, miniaturized, minuscule, small, tiny; ***opp*** enormous, huge

minute *n* instant, jiffy *inf*, moment, second, short time, tick *inf*

minutes *n* notes, proceedings, record, transactions, transcript

miracle *n* marvel, mystery, phenomenon, prodigy, wonder

miraculous *adj* **1** inexplicable, magical, mysterious, paranormal, supernatural. **2** (extremely impressive) fantastic, incredible, marvelous, phenomenal, prodigious, stunning, superb, unbelievable, wonderful, wondrous

mirage *n* chimera, delusion, hallucination, illusion, image, optical illusion, trick of the light, vision

mirror *n* glass, looking-glass, reflector

mirth *n* comedy, fun, hilarity, joking, laughing, laughter, merriment

misapprehension *n* aberration, error, false impression, misreading, mistake, mistaken impression, misconception, misinterpretation, misjudgment, misunderstanding

misbehave *v* act up, be cheeky, be impolite, be naughty, be rude, be unruly, behave badly, break the rules, bully, fool about, fool around, make a scene, make mischief, mess about, mess around, play up, show off; ***opp*** behave

misbehavior *n* bad behavior, bullying, cheek, delinquency, disobedience, fooling about, fooling around, hooliganism, impoliteness, messing about, messing around, mischief, misconduct, naughtiness, rudeness, showing off, tantrum, tomfoolery, trouble, unruliness

miscalculate *v* err, get sth wrong, go wrong, make a mistake, misjudge, slip up

miscarriage *n* **1** abortion, stillbirth. **2** (miscarriage of justice) failure, injustice, mistake, travesty, unsafe conviction, wrongful conviction

miscarry *v* **1** abort, have a miscarriage, lose a baby. **2** (of a plan) come to nothing, fail, fall through, fall flat, flop, founder, go amiss, go awry, go up in smoke, go wrong, misfire

miscellaneous *adj* assorted, different, disparate, diverse, jumbled, mixed, motley, odd, sundry, various

mischief *n* **1** delinquency, misbehavior, misconduct, monkey business *inf*, naughtiness, pranks, shenanigans, trickery, unruliness. **2** damage, deception, dishonesty, evil, harm, hurt, lies, malice, scheming, trouble, vindictiveness, wickedness

mischievous *adj* **1** bad, badly behaved, cheeky, disobedient, impish, misbehaving, naughty, playful, unruly. **2** deceitful, dishonest, evil, injurious, libelous, malicious, slanderous, spiteful, untrue, vindictive, vicious, wicked

misconception *n* error, fallacy, false impression, misapprehension, misinterpretation, mistaken impression, misunderstanding

miser *n* cheapskate *inf*, hoarder, money-grubber *inf*, penny-pincher, scrooge, skinflint *inf*

miserable *adj* **1** blue *inf*, brokenhearted, crestfallen, cut-up *inf*, dejected, depressed, despondent, down *inf*, down in the dumps *inf*, downcast, downhearted, forlorn, gloomy, glum, low, melancholy, mournful, sad, sorrowful, unhappy, wretched; ***opp*** cheerful. **2** churlish, contemptible, cross, despicable, disagreeable, grumpy, ill-natured, low, mean, sour, sulky, sullen, surly, taciturn, unfriendly, unhelpful, unsociable; ***opp*** pleasant. **3** (of a place) awful, dilapidated, filthy, foul, seedy, shabby, sordid, sorry, squalid, uncomfortable, wretched; ***opp*** luxurious

misery *n* **1** anguish, depression, desolation, despair, despondency, distress, gloom, grief, hardship, heartache, hell *inf*, hopelessness, melancholy, pain, sadness, sorrow, suffering, torment, torture, unhappiness, woe; ***opp*** happiness. **2** (an unfortunate event) adversity, blow, hardship, load, misfortune, ordeal, trial, tribulation, trouble, woe; ***opp*** fortune

misfire *v* fail, fall through, flop, founder, go amiss, go awry, go up in smoke, go wrong

misfit *n* eccentric, fish out of water, maverick, nonconformist, oddball *inf*, square peg in a round hole, weirdo *inf*

misfortune *n* accident, adversity, bad luck, blow, calamity, catastrophe, disaster, hardship, harm, loss, misadventure, mishap, setback, tragedy, trial, tribulation, trouble, woe

misguided *adj* deluded, erroneous, foolish, ill-advised, imprudent, inappropriate, misled, misplaced, mistaken, unreasonable, unsound, unwise, wrong; ***opp*** well-advised

misjudge *v* be wrong about, get the wrong end of the stick, get the wrong idea, jump to the wrong conclusion, make a mistake, miscalculate, misconstrue, misinterpret, misread, overestimate, overrate, underestimate, underrate, undervalue

mislay *v* be unable to find, lose, lose track of, misplace, miss; ***opp*** find

mislead *v* beguile, bluff, confuse, deceive, delude, fool, give sb the wrong idea, give sb the wrong impression, hoodwink, lead sb up the garden path, misdirect, misguide, misinform, take sb for a ride, take sb in, throw sb off the scent, trick

misleading *adj* ambiguous, confusing, deceitful, deceptive, false, spurious, unreliable; ***opp*** clear

miss *n* blunder, botch, bungle, error, failure, fault, loss, mistake, omission, oversight, slip, slip-up

miss *v* **1** (miss a lesson) be too late for, forego, omit, play truant, skip *inf*. **2** (not include) fail to include, fail to mention, omit, overlook. **3** (narrowly miss being hit) avoid, dodge, escape, evade, sidestep, steer clear of. **4** (miss a target) blunder, botch, bungle, err, fail, fall short, lose, slip up. **5** (miss a person) grieve for, lament, long for, need, pine for, want, yearn for

misshapen *adj* bent, contorted, crooked, crumpled, deformed, disfigured, distorted, gnarled, grotesque, knotted, malformed, out of shape, screwed up, tangled, twisted, warped

missile *n* bomb, grenade, projectile, rocket, shell, torpedo, weapon

missing *adj* absent, astray, gone, lost, mislaid, misplaced, nowhere to be found, unaccounted for; ***opp*** present

mission *n* **1** aim, assignment, charge, duty, function, goal, job, objective, purpose, task, undertaking, work. **2** delegation, deputation, task force

missionary *n* crusader, evangelist, minister, preacher, priest

misspent *adj* dissipated, misapplied, squandered, thrown away, wasted

mist *n* cloud, condensation, fog, haze, smog, spray, steam, vapor

mistake *n* blunder, boob *inf*, botch, error, fault, faux pas, gaffe, inaccuracy, miscalculation, misjudgment, misprint, misspelling, misunderstanding, omission, oversight, slip, slip-up

mistake *v* **1** (mistake one thing for another) confuse, mix up, take sth for sth else. **2** (understand sth wrongly) get the wrong end of the stick, get wrong, misapprehend, misconstrue, misinterpret, misjudge, misread, misunderstand; ***opp*** understand

mistaken *adj* erroneous, false, inaccurate, incorrect, inexact, misguided, misinformed, wide of the mark, wrong; ***opp*** correct

mistress *n* concubine, girlfriend, kept woman, lover, paramour

mistrust *v* be skeptical, be suspicious, be unsure, be wary, disbelieve, doubt, fear, have doubts, have misgivings, have suspicions, question, suspect; ***opp*** trust

misty *adj* **1** (of weather) cloudy, foggy, hazy, murky; ***opp*** clear. **2** (of an image) bleary, blurred, dim, faint, fuzzy, indistinct, obscure, smoky, steamy, vague; ***opp*** distinct

misunderstand *v* be barking up the wrong tree *inf*, get the wrong end of the stick, get the wrong idea, get wrong, misapprehend, misconceive, misconstrue, mishear, misinterpret, misjudge, miss the point, mistake; ***opp*** understand

misunderstanding *n* error, misapprehension, misconception, misjudgment, misreading, mistake, mix-up

misuse *n* abuse, corruption, misapplication, squandering, waste

mitigate *v* allay, alleviate, appease, assuage, calm, check, decrease, diminish, dull, ease, extenuate, lessen, lighten, moderate, mollify, pacify, placate, quiet, reduce, relieve, soothe, subdue, take the edge off *inf*, temper, weaken; ***opp*** worsen

mitigating *adj* exonerating, extenuating,

justifying, qualifying, vindicating

mix *n* amalgam, assortment, blend, combination, compound, mixture, range, union, variety

mix *v* 1 amalgamate, blend, coalesce, combine, cross, fuse, incorporate, intermingle, interweave, join, jumble up, merge, mingle, muddle, unite; ***opp*** separate. 2 (mix with people) associate, fraternize, go out with, hobnob, keep company, mingle, socialize. 3 **mix up** confuse, mistake, muddle up

mixed *adj* 1 (a mixed bunch) assorted, diverse, heterogeneous, miscellaneous, motley, varied; ***opp*** similar. 2 (mixed feelings) ambiguous, ambivalent, confused, muddled, uncertain, unsure; ***opp*** clear-cut

mixed-up *adj* 1 at sea, bewildered, confused, muddled, perplexed, puzzled. 2 (a crazy mixed-up kid) disturbed, ill-adjusted, maladjusted, screwed-up *inf*; ***opp*** together

mixture *n* amalgam, amalgamation, association, blend, brew, collection, compound, cross, fusion, hotchpotch *inf*, medley, mishmash *inf*, mix, union, variety

mix-up *n* confusion, disorder, mistake, misunderstanding, muddle

moan *n* 1 (complaint) beef *inf*, complaint, grouch *inf*, grouse, grumble, whine; ***opp*** praise. 2 (a moan of pain) cry, groan, sigh, wail, whimper, whine

moan *v* 1 (complain) beef *inf*, carp, complain, grouch *inf*, grouse, grumble, whine. 2 (moan in pain) cry, groan, sigh, wail, whimper, whine

mob *n* body, bunch, collection, crowd, drove, flock, gang, gathering, herd, hoard, host, mass, pack, press, rabble, swarm, throng

mob *v* besiege, crowd, hem in, jostle, overrun, surround, swarm

mobile *adj* 1 (of an object) movable, portable, transportable; ***opp*** fixed. 2 (of people) itinerant, migrant, nomadic, peripatetic, traveling, wandering. 3 (of a face) animated, changeable, ever-changing, expressive, flexible; ***opp*** inexpressive

mobilize *v* activate, assemble, call up, gather, get together, marshal, muster, organize, prepare, rally, ready

mock *adj* artificial, bogus, counterfeit, dummy, fake, false, feigned, forged, imitation, pretend *inf*, sham, simulated, spurious; ***opp*** real

mock *v* deride, insult, jeer, laugh at, make fun of, parody, poke fun at, rib *inf*, ridicule, satirize, scoff, scorn, send up *inf*, sneer, taunt, tease

mockery *n* contempt, derision, disdain, jeering, laughter, parody, ribbing *inf*, ridicule, satire, scoffing, scorn, sending up *inf*, sneering, taunting, teasing

model *n* 1 copy, facsimile, image, imitation, miniature, mock-up, replica, representation. 2 (a model of excellence) archetype, byword, epitome, example, ideal, paradigm, paragon, standard

model *adj* 1 imitation, miniature, mock-up, replica. 2 (a model student) exemplary, ideal, perfect; ***opp*** terrible

model *v* 1 carve, cast, design, fashion, form, mold, sculpt, shape. 2 (model clothes) display, show off, wear

moderate *adj* 1 average, light, limited, medium, middle, mild, steady, temperate; ***opp*** extreme. 2 (of a person) balanced, calm, cautious, cool, fair, gentle, middle-of-the-road, peaceable, reasonable, sober; ***opp*** extreme

moderate *v* 1 (become less) abate, calm, decrease, diminish, ease, lessen, lighten, reduce, weaken. 2 (make sth less) alleviate, appease, assuage, calm, check, pacify, placate, quiet, soothe, subdue, take the edge off *inf*

moderation *n* calmness, composure, control, coolness, fairness, justice, mildness, reasonableness, restraint, temperance

modern *adj* 1 avant-garde, contemporary, current, fresh, new, newfangled, novel, present, recent. 2 fashionable, in *inf*, in vogue, latest, modish, progressive, stylish, trendy *inf*, up to date, up to the minute, with it *inf*; ***opp*** old-fashioned

modernize *v* bring up to date, do up *inf*, refurbish, regenerate, rejuvenate, remake, renew, renovate, revamp, update

modest *adj* 1 bashful, coy, demure, diffident, discreet, humble, meek, quiet, reserved, restrained, reticent, retiring, self-effacing, shy, unassuming, unpretentious; ***opp*** brash. 2 (a modest amount) limited, medium, moderate, normal, ordinary, small; ***opp*** huge

modesty *n* bashfulness, coyness, demureness, diffidence, discretion, humility, meekness, quietness, reticence, self-effacement, shyness, unpretentiousness; ***opp*** brashness

modification *n* adaptation, adjustment, alteration, change, conversion, refinement, reorganization, revision, transformation, variation

modify *v* adapt, adjust, alter, change, convert, recast, refine, reorganize, revise, transform, vary

moist *adj* clammy, damp, dank, dewy, humid, runny, steamy, watery, wet; ***opp*** dry

moisten *v* damp, dampen, soak, sponge, spray, water, wet; ***opp*** dry

moisture *n* damp, dew, humidity, liquid, spray, water, wet, wetness; ***opp*** dryness

mold *n* 1 (for making sth) cast, die, form, model, pattern, shape, stamp, template. 2 blight, fungus, growth, mildew, rot

mold *v* carve, cast, construct, fashion, forge, form, model, sculpt, shape, stamp, work

moldy *adj* blighted, decayed, decaying, fusty, mildewed, moldering, musty, rotten, rotting

molest *v* 1 abuse, accost, assault, attack, ill-treat, interfere with, mistreat, rape. 2 annoy, badger, bother, bug *inf*, disturb, harass, harry, hassle, hector, interfere with, irk, irritate, persecute, pester, torment, upset, vex, worry

moment *n* 1 (in a moment) flash, instant, jiffy *inf*, minute, second, ttwinkling of an eye *inf*. 2 (at that moment) instant, juncture, point, stage, time

momentary *adj* brief, ephemeral, fleeting, hasty, passing, quick, short, short-lived, transient, transitory; ***opp*** drawn-out

momentum *n* drive, energy, force,

impulse, power, propulsion, push, thrust
monarch *n* emperor, empress, king, potentate, prince, princess, queen, ruler, sovereign
monetary *adj* budgetary, capital, cash, financial, fiscal
money *n* bread *inf*, capital, cash, coin, currency, dough *inf*, finance, funds, income, means, resources, revenue, savings
mongrel *n* cross, cross-breed, hybrid, mixed breed; ***opp*** purebred
monitor *n* **1** (person) examiner, observer, overseer, prefect, supervisor, watchdog. **2** (device) detector, recorder, scanner, security camera
monitor *v* check, examine, follow, keep an eye on, keep track of, observe, oversee, record, supervise, survey, trace, track, watch
monk *n* abbot, brother, friar, hermit
monkey *n* **1** ape, primate, simian. **2** (you little monkey) devil, imp, rascal, rogue, scamp, terror
monopolize *v* control, corner, dominate, hog *inf*, take over
monotonous *adj* boring, colorless, dreary, droning, dull, flat, humdrum, mindnumbing, plodding, repetitive, soporific, tedious, tiresome, toneless, unchanging, unexciting, uninteresting; ***opp*** exciting
monster *n* barbarian, beast, bogey-man, brute, demon, devil, fiend, ghoul, ogre, savage, troll, villain
monstrosity *n* eyesore, horror
monstrous *adj* **1** (a monstrous act) abhorrent, abominable, atrocious, awful, brutal, cruel, diabolical, disgraceful, evil, foul, heinous, horrific, horrifying, inhuman, intolerable, loathsome, odious, outrageous, repulsive, scandalous, shocking, vicious, vile, villainous. **2** (a monstrous building) colossal, enormous, giant, gigantic, great, huge, hulking, immense, mammoth, massive, mighty, prodigious, tremendous, vast; ***opp*** tiny
monument *n* cenotaph, gravestone, mausoleum, memorial, obelisk, relic, shrine, statue, tombstone
monumental *adj* **1** awe-inspiring, awesome, classic, enduring, exceptional, extraordinary, great, historic, immortal, important, impressive, lasting, memorable, outstanding, significant, unforgettable
mood *n* disposition, frame of mind, humor, inclination, spirit, temper
moody *adj* abrupt, bad-tempered, cantankerous, crabby, cross, crotchety, curt, doleful, dour, frowning, grumpy, huffy *inf*, ill-tempered, irritable, miserable, morose, petulant, sulky, sullen, temperamental, testy, touchy, unpredictable; ***opp*** cheerful
moor *v* anchor, berth, dock, fasten, fix, lash, secure, tie up
moot *adj* arguable, contestable, controversial, debatable, disputable, questionable; ***opp*** uncontroversial
mope *v* brood, despair, fret, grieve, languish, pine, sulk
moral *adj* decent, ethical, fair, good, honest, irreproachable, just, law-abiding, noble, principled, proper, pure, respectable, responsible, righteous, upright, upstanding,

virtuous; ***opp*** immoral

morale *n* cheerfulness, confidence, determination, heart, hope, hopefulness, mettle, self-confidence, self-esteem, spirit, zeal

morality *n* decency, fairness, goodness, honesty, integrity, justice, principle, righteousness, uprightness, virtue; ***opp*** immorality

moralize *v* lecture, pontificate, preach

morals *n* ethics, ideals, manners, mores, principles, scruples, standards

morbid *adj* brooding, ghastly, ghoulish, gloomy, grim, grisly, gruesome, hideous, horrid, macabre, sick *inf*, somber, unhealthy, unwholesome

more *adj* added, additional, extra, fresh, further, increased, new, other, renewed, spare, supplementary; ***opp*** less

morose *adj* bad-tempered, churlish, depressed, dour, gloomy, glum, grim, humorless, melancholy, moody, mournful, pessimistic, somber, sour, sulky, sullen, taciturn; ***opp*** cheerful

morsel *n* bit, bite, crumb, fragment, grain, mouthful, nibble, piece, scrap, segment, slice, titbit

mortal *adj* **1** earthly, ephemeral, fleshly, human, temporal, transient, worldly; ***opp*** immortal. **2** (a mortal injury) deadly, fatal, killing, lethal, terminal; ***opp*** minor

mortality *n* **1** earthliness, humanity, impermanence, transience, worldliness; ***opp*** immortality. **2** (infant mortality) deaths, dying, fatalities, loss of life

mortified *adj* ashamed, crushed, deflated, embarrassed, filled with shame, humiliated, shamed; ***opp*** proud

mortify *v* crush, deflate, embarrass, fill with shame, humiliate, put down, shame

mostly *adv* as a (general) rule, chiefly, commonly, customarily, for the most part, generally, in general, in the main, largely, mainly, normally, on the whole, ordinarily, particularly, predominantly, primarily, principally, typically, usually

mother *n* female parent, ma *inf*, mama, mom *inf*, mommy *inf*, old lady *inf*

mother *v* care for, cherish, fuss over, indulge, look after, nourish, nurse, nurture, pamper, protect, raise, rear, spoil, take care of

motherly *adj* affectionate, caring, fond, kind, loving, maternal, nurturing, protective, tender, warm

motion *n* **1** action, activity, agitation, flow, move, movement, progress, shift, stirring, travel. **2** gesticulation, gesture, movement, signal, wave

motion *v* beckon, direct, gesticulate, gesture, nod, signal, sign, wave

motionless *adj* at rest, frozen, halted, immobile, inert, lifeless, paralyzed, static, stationary, still, stopped, unmoving; ***opp*** moving

motivate *v* activate, arouse, cause, drive, egg on, encourage, galvanize, goad, impel, incite, induce, influence, inspire, instigate, lead, move, persuade, prod, prompt, provoke, push, set, spur, stimulate, stir, urge

motivated *adj* ambitious, ardent, committed, dedicated, driven, eager, enthusiastic, fervent, galvanized, industrious, inspired, intent, keen

motivation *n* **1** (desire to do sth) ambition, desire, drive, eagerness, enthusiasm, fervor, hunger, inspiration, keenness. **2** (the thing that motivates sth) cause, encouragement, goading, incitement, inducement, inspiration, persuasion, prodding, prompting, pushing, spur

motive *n* basis, cause, grounds, incentive, inducement, influence, inspiration, intention, lure, motivation, occasion, prompting, provocation, purpose, push, rationale, reason, spur, stimulus

motley *adj* assorted, diverse, heterogeneous, ill-matched, mingled, miscellaneous, mixed, rag-bag, varied, various

mottled *adj* blotched, blotchy, dappled, flecked, freckled, marbled, marked, patchy, piebald, speckled, splotchy, spotted, stippled, streaked, variegated

motto *n* adage, catch-phrase, dictum, epigram, maxim, precept, proverb, rule, saying, slogan, watchword

mound *n* bank, dune, heap, hill, hillock, hummock, knoll, pile, rise, stack

mount *n* **1** backing, base, fixture, frame, setting, stand, support. **2** elevation, hill, mound, mountain, peak, summit

mount *v* **1** ascend, climb, go up, rise, scale. **2** climb on, get astride, get on, jump on. **3** (tension mounts) accumulate, build, escalate, expand, grow, increase, intensify, multiply, pile up, swell. **4** (mount an exhibition) display, exhibit, prepare, produce, put on, stage

mountain *n* alp, crest, elevation, height, mount, peak, pinnacle, range, sierra, summit

mountainous *adj* alpine, craggy, high, highland, rocky, rugged, soaring, steep, towering, upland

mourn *v* bemoan, bewail, cry for, feel the loss of, grieve, lament, miss, pine for, regret, sorrow, wail, weep

mournful *adj* depressing, dismal, distressing, doleful, gloomy, heart-breaking, heartrending, melancholy, miserable, painful, piteous, pitiful, plaintive, sad, sorrowful, tragic, unhappy, woeful

mouth *n* **1** jaws, lips, muzzle. **2** aperture, door, entrance, gateway, inlet, opening, orifice, portal, way in

mouthful *n* bit, bite, drop, forkful, gulp, morsel, sample, sip, spoonful, swallow, taste

movable *adj* bendable, detachable, flexible, mobile, moving, plastic, portable, transportable; ***opp*** immovable

move *n* **1** action, agitation, change, motion, movement, shift, stirring. **2** act, action, deed, gambit, maneuver, measure, play, step, stratagem, stroke, tactic, turn. **3** change, relocation, shift, transfer

move *v* **1** (sth or sb moves) budge, change places, change position, go, shift, stir. **2** (move sth) carry, transport, shift, take. **3** (move forward) advance, go, head, journey, make headway, make progress, pass, proceed, travel. **4** (move house) go away, leave, migrate, move away, move house, relocate. **5** (make sb feel moved) affect, arouse, fire, impassion, incite, induce, inspire, lead, motivate, persuade, prompt, provoke, push, rouse, spur, stimulate, stir, touch

movement *n* **1** action, activity, advance, agitation, change, gesture, motion, move, progress, shift, stirring. **2** carrying, moving, shifting, transfer, transferral, transport, transportation. **3** campaign, coalition, crusade, drive, faction, front, group, lobby, organization, party, pressure group

moving *adj* **1** affecting, emotional, emotive, heartrending, heartwarming, inspiring, pathetic, poignant, powerful, rousing, stirring, touching. **2** active, dynamic, in motion, mobile, movable

mow *v* **1** clip, crop, cut, scythe, shear, trim. **2 mow down** butcher, cut down, massacre, slaughter, slay

mud *n* clay, dirt, mire, ooze, silt, slime, sludge, soil

muddle *n* chaos, clutter, confusion, disarray, disorder, jumble, mess, mix-up, shambles *inf*, tangle

muddle *v* **1** clutter, disarrange, disorder, disorganize, get sth mixed up, jumble, mess up, mix up, scramble, tangle. **2** bemuse, bewilder, confound, confuse, daze, disorient, disorientate, perplex, puzzle

muddy *adj* **1** caked, dirty, filthy, messy, mucky. **2** boggy, marshy, slimy, sludgy, soft, spongy, waterlogged

muffle *v* **1** cloak, cover, enfold, hood, shroud, swathe, wrap up. **2** (muffle a sound) dampen, deaden, disguise, dull, hush, mask, mute, quieten, silence, smother, soften, stifle, suppress

muffled *adj* dampened, deadened, dull, faint, hushed, indistinct, muted, smothered, stifled, suppressed, unclear

mug *n* beaker, cup, flagon, jug, pot, tankard

mugger *n* assailant, attacker, bag-snatcher, robber, thief, thug

muggy *adj* clammy, close, damp, humid, oppressive, steamy, sticky, stuffy, sultry

multiple *adj* collective, many, numerous, several, sundry, various

multiply *v* accumulate, breed, expand, extend, increase, proliferate, propagate, reproduce, spread

multitude *n* army, assembly, congregation, crowd, horde, host, legion, mass, mob, sea, swarm, throng

mumble *v* grumble, murmur, mutter, speak indistinctly

munch *v* champ, chew, chomp, crunch, eat, gnaw, masticate

mundane *adj* banal, commonplace, dull, everyday, humdrum, ordinary, pedestrian, prosaic, quotidian, routine, unexciting, uninteresting, workaday; ***opp*** extraordinary

municipal *adj* borough, city, civic, civil, community, district, local, metropolitan, public, town, urban

murder *n* assassination, bloodshed, butchery, carnage, homicide, killing, manslaughter, massacre, slaughter, slaying

murder *v* assassinate, bump off *inf*, butcher, destroy, dispatch, do away with *inf*, do in *inf*, kill, massacre, put to death, slaughter, slay

murderer *n* assassin, butcher, cutthroat, gunman, killer, slaughterer, slayer

murderous *adj* barbaric, barbarous, bloodthirsty, bloody, butchering, death-dealing, homicidal, massacring, psychopathic, savage, slaughtering

murmur *n* 1 (sound) buzz, drone, hum, rumble, rumbling. 2 (way of speaking) grumble, mumble, mumbling, mutter, muttering, undertone, whisper

murmur *v* breathe, grumble, mumble, mutter, purr, rumble, speak in an undertone, whisper

muscle *n* 1 biceps, ligament, sinew, tendon. 2 brawn, clout *inf*, force, might, potency, power, strength

muscular *adj* athletic, beefy *inf*, brawny, burly, hefty, hunky *inf*, lusty, mighty, powerful, robust, sinewy, stalwart, strapping, strong, sturdy, tough, vigorous, well-built

muse *v* brood, cogitate, consider, contemplate, daydream, deliberate, dream, meditate, mull over, ponder, reflect, ruminate, speculate, think, weigh, wonder

musical *adj* dulcet, harmonious, lilting, melodic, melodious, sweet-sounding, tuneful

muster *v* assemble, call up, collect, congregate, convene, gather, group, marshal, mobilize, rally, round up, summon

musty *adj* airless, damp, dank, decaying, fusty, mildewed, moldy, smelly, stale, stuffy, unused

mutation *n* alteration, change, evolution, metamorphosis, modification, transformation, transmutation, variation

mute *adj* dumb, silent, speechless, unspoken, voiceless, wordless

mutilate *v* butcher, cripple, damage, deface, disable, disfigure, dismember, hack, lame, maim, mangle

mutinous *adj* defiant, disobedient, insubordinate, rebellious, restive, revolutionary, riotous, seditious, subversive, uncontrollable, ungovernable, unmanageable, unruly

mutiny *n* defiance, disobedience, insubordination, insurgence, insurrection, rebellion, resistance, revolt, revolution, riot, rising, sedition, subversion, uprising

mutiny *v* defy, disobey, rebel, resist, revolt, riot, rise up

mutter *v* complain, grumble, mumble, murmur, rumble, talk under your breath

mutual *adj* common, joint, reciprocal, reciprocated, requited, returned, shared

muzzle *v* censor, curb, gag, restrain, silence, stifle, suppress

mysterious *adj* abstruse, arcane, baffling, bizarre, cryptic, curious, dark, enigmatic, furtive, hidden, impenetrable, inexplicable, inscrutable, mystifying, obscure, perplexing, puzzling, secret, strange, uncanny, unexplained, unfathomable, unknown, weird

mystery *n* conundrum, enigma, paradox, problem, puzzle, riddle, secret

mystical *adj* arcane, hidden, metaphysical, mysterious, occult, otherworldly, paranormal, preternatural, spiritual, supernatural, transcendental

mystify *v* baffle, bemuse, bewilder, confound, confuse, elude, escape, flummox, nonplus, perplex, puzzle, stump *inf*

myth *n* **1** allegory, fable, fairy-tale, legend, parable, saga, story, tale. **2** delusion, fabrication, falsehood, fiction, figment of sb's imagination, invention, misconception, untruth

mythical *adj* **1** allegorical, fabled, fabulous, fairy-tale, fantastical, legendary, mythic, mythological. **2** fabricated, false, fantasy, imaginary, invented, made-up, nonexistent, pretended, unreal, untrue

nadir *n* bottom, depths, low point, rock bottom

nag *n* harpy, pest, scold, shrew, virago

nag *v* annoy, badger, be on sb's back *inf*, carp, goad, go on at *inf*, harass, harp on, hassle *inf*, hector, henpeck, pester, plague, worry

nagging *adj* continuous, ever-present, irritating, painful, persistent, worrying

nail *v* attach, fasten, fix, hammer, join, pin, secure, tack

naive *adj* artless, childlike, credulous, green *inf*, guileless, gullible, inexperienced, ingenuous, innocent, open, simple, trusting, unsophisticated, unsuspicious, unwary, unworldly; ***opp*** knowing

naked *adj* bare, exposed, in your birthday suit *inf*, in the altogether *inf*, in the buff *inf*, in the nude, in the raw *inf*, nude, stark-naked, stripped, unclothed, uncovered, undressed; ***opp*** clothed, dressed

name *n* **1** appellation, epithet, label, nickname, tag, term, title. **2** (make your name in sth) distinction, eminence, esteem, fame, honor, note, prestige, prominence, reputation, repute, renown

name *v* **1** baptize, call, christen, designate, dub, entitle, label, nickname, style, tag, term. **2** (name a new chairman) appoint, choose, commission, delegate, designate, elect, identify, nominate, pick, select, specify

nameless *adj* **1** anonymous, incognito, obscure, unidentified, unknown, unsung. **2** abominable, appalling, dreadful, horrible, indescribable, unmentionable, unspeakable, unutterable

nap *n* doze, forty winks *inf*, rest, siesta, sleep, snooze *inf*

nap *v* doze, drowse, have a nap, nod off *inf*, rest, sleep, snooze *inf*

narrate *v* chronicle, describe, detail, recite, recount, rehearse, relate, repeat, report, tell, unfold

narration *n* commentary, description, explanation, reading, recital, relation, reporting, storytelling, telling

narrative *n* account, chronicle, description, history, report, statement, story, tale

narrator *n* author, chronicler, commentator, reporter, storyteller, writer

narrow *adj* close, confined, cramped, fine, limited, meager, pinched, restricted, scanty, slender, slim, squeezed, straitened, thin, tight; ***opp*** wide

narrow *v* diminish, limit, reduce, shrink, straiten, tighten; ***opp*** widen

narrow-minded *adj* biased, bigoted, conservative, hidebound, inflexible, insular, intolerant, mean-spirited, old-fashioned, parochial, petty, prejudiced, reactionary, rigid, small-minded, strait-laced; ***opp*** broad-minded

nasty *adj* **1** awful, disgusting, filthy, foul, horrible, horrid, nauseating, odious, repellent, repugnant, repulsive, revolting, sickening, unpleasant, vile, yucky *inf*; ***opp*** nice. **2** (be nasty to sb) bitchy *sl*, catty, cruel, disagreeable, horrible, horrid, malicious, mean, spiteful, unkind, unpleasant, vicious; ***opp*** nice

nation *n* country, domain, kingdom, land, people, population, power, realm, republic, society, state

national *adj* **1** (not local) countrywide, federal, general, nationwide. **2** (not international) domestic, internal, patriotic, popular

nationalism *n* chauvinism, jingoism, loyalty, patriotism, xenophobia

native *adj* **1** (native to a place) aboriginal, domestic, indigenous, local, original. **2** (native intelligence) congenital, hereditary, inborn, inbred, inherited, innate, instinctive, intuitive, natural

native *n* citizen, countryman, dweller, inhabitant, local, resident

natural *adj* **1** authentic, genuine, real, sincere, spontaneous, unaffected, unfeigned; ***opp*** artificial. **2** (normal) common, logical, ordinary, normal, predictable, regular, routine, standard, typical, understandable, unsurprising, usual; ***opp*** unnatural. **3** (a natural ability) characteristic, congenital, god-given, hereditary, inborn, inbred, inherited, innate, instinctive, intuitive, native; ***opp*** learned

naturally *adv* **1** (behave naturally) candidly, ingenuously, unpretentiously. **2** as you would expect, certainly, of course

nature *n* **1** ecology, landscape, Mother Nature, natural history, scenery, the countryside, the earth, the environment, the universe, the world, wildlife. **2** (sth of that nature) description, kind, sort, species, style, type, variety. **3** (sb's nature) character, disposition, make-up, mood, outlook, personality, temperament, traits. **4** (the nature of a thing) character, essence, features, properties, quality

naught *n* nil, nothing, zero

naughty *adj* bad, badly behaved, defiant, delinquent, disobedient, disruptive, impolite, mischievous, rascally, rude, stubborn, undisciplined, unmanageable, unruly, wicked, willful

nausea *n* **1** biliousness, faintness, queasiness, seasickness, sickness, vomiting. **2** disgust, loathing, repugnance, revulsion

nauseate *v* disgust, horrify, make sb sick, make sb want to throw up *inf*, offend, repel, repulse, revolt, sicken, turn sb's stomach

nautical *adj* boating, marine, maritime, naval, sailing, seafaring, seagoing, yachting

navigate *v* **1** cross, cruise, journey, sail, sail across, voyage. **2** (navigate a ship) captain, drive, handle, maneuver, pilot, skipper, steer. 3 (find the way) direct, find the way, guide, plan the route

navigation *n* 1 directing, maneuvering, steering. 2 (the skills of navigation) sailing, seamanship

navigator *n* helmsman, mariner, pilot, seaman

navy *n* armada, convoy, fleet, flotilla

near *adj* 1 (near in space) accessible, adjacent, adjoining, at close quarters, beside, bordering, close, close by, connected, handy, nearby, neighboring, next-door, touching, within reach. 2 (near in time) approaching, coming, forthcoming, imminent, impending, in the offing, looming, next, round the corner *inf*

nearly *adv* about, all but, almost, approaching, approximately, around, as good as, just about, not quite, practically, roughly, virtually

neat *adj* 1 accurate, clean, dapper, fastidious, methodical, meticulous, orderly, organized, precise, shipshape, smart, spick and span, spruce, straight, systematic, tidy, trim, uncluttered, well-groomed, well-kept, well-turned-out; ***opp*** untidy. 2 (neat movements) agile, dainty, deft, dexterous, elegant, graceful, nimble, practiced, precise, skillful, stylish; ***opp*** clumsy. 3 (neat whisky) pure, straight, undiluted

necessary *adj* compulsory, essential, imperative, important, indispensable, mandatory, needed, obligatory, required, vital

necessitate *v* call for, demand, entail, involve, make necessary, require

necessity *n* (sth is a necessity) essential, must *inf*, need, prerequisite, requirement

need *n* 1 (need for affection) desire, lack, longing, shortage, wish, yearning. 2 (children in need) deprivation, destitution, distress, poverty. 3 (the need to do sth) call, necessity, obligation. 4 (a basic human need) demand, essential, requirement, want

need *v* 1 (need sth) be short of, be without, call for, demand, lack, require, want. 2 (need sb) depend on, desire, miss, rely on, want. 3 (need to do sth) be compelled, be obliged, have to

needless *adj* excessive, gratuitous, groundless, pointless, redundant, superfluous, uncalled for, unnecessary, unwanted

needy *adj* badly off, deprived, destitute, disadvantaged, hard up *inf*, penniless, poor, poverty-stricken, underprivileged

negate *v* cancel, contradict, deny, disprove, invalidate, neutralize, oppose, repeal, reverse, revoke, wipe out

negative *adj* 1 (negative outlook) complaining, cynical, gloomy, jaundiced, pessimistic, unenthusiastic, unhelpful; ***opp*** positive. 2 (saying no) anti *inf*, contradicting, contradictory, contrary, denying, disagreeing, opposing, refusing, resisting

neglect *n* carelessness, forgetfulness, inattention, indifference, lack of concern, negligence

neglect *v* 1 (leave sb or sth) abandon, forget, forsake, ignore, leave alone, pay no attention to. 2 (neglect to do sth) fail, forget, not remember, omit, overlook, shirk, skimp, skip

neglected *adj* 1 (of a place) abandoned,

derelict, forgotten, overgrown, run-down. 2 (of a child) abandoned, ignored, left alone, mistreated, uncared for

negligent *adj* careless, forgetful, irresponsible, neglectful, reckless, remiss, slack, slapdash, sloppy, thoughtless, unthinking; ***opp*** careful

negligible *adj* inconsequential, insignificant, minor, petty, slight, small, tiny, trifling, trivial, unimportant

negotiate *v* agree, bargain, deal, discuss, haggle, hold talks, settle, work out

negotiation *n* arbitration, bargaining, diplomacy, discussion, mediation, talks

neighborhood *n* area, community, district, locality, part, place, region, vicinity, zone

neighboring *adj* adjacent, adjoining, bordering, close, closest, near, nearby, nearest, next, next-door, surrounding

neighborly *adj* amiable, friendly, helpful, hospitable, kind, obliging, sociable

nerve *n* 1 (bravery) bravery, coolness, courage, daring, determination, fearlessness, guts *inf*, resolve, spirit, willpower. 2 (cheek) audacity, brazenness, cheek, impertinence, impudence, insolence, presumptuousness, rudeness

nerve-racking *adj* anxious, difficult, distressing, frightening, harrowing, nail-biting *inf*, stressful, tense, worrying

nerves *n* anxiety, butterflies in your stomach *inf*, jitters *inf*, nervousness, strain, stress, tension

nervous *adj* afraid, agitated, anxious, apprehensive, edgy, fearful, highly strung, impatient, insecure, jumpy, on edge, on tenterhooks *inf*, restless, shaky, strained, tense, timid, trembling, uneasy, unnerved, uptight *inf*, worried; ***opp*** calm

nestle *v* cuddle, curl up, huddle, nuzzle, snuggle

net *n* lattice, mesh, netting, web

net *v* capture, catch, enmesh, entangle, snare, trap

network *n* 1 crisscross *inf*, grid, labyrinth, lattice, maze, mesh, net, tangle, web. 2 arrangement, interconnection, organization, structure, system

neurosis *n* anxiety, depression, fixation, obsession, phobia

neurotic *adj* anxious, compulsive, disturbed, mentally ill, nervous, obsessive, overwrought, unstable

neuter *v* castrate, geld, spay, sterilize

neutral *adj* 1 (neutral in an argument) disinterested, fair, impartial, objective, open-minded, unbiased, uncommitted, undecided, uninvolved, unprejudiced. 2 (neutral colors) colorless, dull, indeterminate, pale, vague

neutralize *v* cancel, cancel out, compensate for, counteract, make ineffective, negate, undo, wipe out

never-ending *adj* boundless, constant, continual, endless, eternal, everlasting, incessant, infinite, limitless, nonstop, perpetual, relentless, unbroken, uninterrupted, without end

new *adj* advanced, brand-new, contemporary, current, different, fashionable, fresh, futuristic, latest, modern, newfangled, novel, original, recent, revolutionary, state-of-the-art, topical, trendy *inf*, unfamiliar, unknown, unused, unusual, up-to-date; ***opp*** old

newcomer *n* immigrant, new arrival, outsider, settler, stranger

newfangled *adj* gimmicky, modern, new, novel, state-of-the-art, ultra-modern

news *n* **1** (a news report) announcement, bulletin, dispatch, exposé, facts, headlines, leak, release, report, statement, story. **2** (catching up on the news) gossip, information, rumor, scandal, talk, the latest *inf*, word

newspaper *n* daily *inf*, gazette, journal, paper, rag *inf*, tabloid, weekly

next *adv* after, afterwards, later, subsequently, then

nibble *v* bite, eat, gnaw, munch, nip, peck at, pick at, snack on *inf*

nibble *n* bite, crumb, morsel, piece, snack, taste

nice *adj* **1** (of a person) agreeable, amiable, charming, courteous, friendly, kind, likeable, pleasant, polite, understanding; ***opp*** horrible, nasty. **2** (of the weather) dry, fine, pleasant, sunny, warm; ***opp*** awful, dreadful. **3** (a nice time) enjoyable, exciting, good, interesting, marvelous, pleasant, pleasurable; ***opp*** awful, horrible. **4** (of behavior) appropriate, cultivated, polite, proper, refined, respectable, seemly; ***opp*** bad

niche *n* alcove, corner, cranny, hollow, nook, opening, recess

nick *n* chip, cut, dent, mark, notch, scratch

nick *v* **1** (nick the edge of sth) chip, cut, mark, notch, scratch. **2** (steal) filch, lift, pilfer, pinch, pocket, shoplift, steal, swipe, take, walk off with

nickname *n* alias, family name, pet name

niggle *n* complaint, concern, misgiving, objection, worry

niggle *v* **1** criticize, find fault, fuss, nag, nitpick *inf*. **2** (sth niggles you) annoy, irritate, rankle, trouble, worry

niggling *adj* **1** finicky, fussy, nit-picking *inf*, picky *inf*. **2** insignificant, minor, petty, trifling, unimportant. **3** (niggling doubts) gnawing, irritating, persistent, troubling, worrying

night *n* dark, darkness, nighttime

nightfall *n* dusk, evening, sundown, sunset, twilight

nimble *adj* acrobatic, active, agile, deft, graceful, lithe, lively, quick, skillful, sprightly, spry

nip *n* **1** bite, nibble, pinch, tweak. **2** (nip of whisky) dram, drop, sip, taste

nip *v* **1** catch, clip, grip, hurt, pinch, snag, squeeze, tweak, twitch. **2** bite, sink your teeth into, snap at

nobility *n* aristocracy, elite, gentry, high society, l upper class

noble *adj* **1** (of noble birth) aristocratic, blue-blooded, born with a silver spoon in your mouth, distinguished, highborn, princely, titled, upper-class. **2** (a noble gesture) brave, gallant, generous, heroic, honorable, magnanimous, self-sacrificing, virtuous, worthy. **3** (a noble oak tree) awesome, great, imposing, impressive, splendid

noble *n* aristocrat, lady, lord, nobleman, noblewoman, peer

nocturnal *adj* night, nightly, nighttime

nod *v* **1** bob your head, bow your head, incline your head. **2** (as a signal) gesture, indicate, motion, sign, signal. **3 nod off** doze, drop off, drowse, fall asleep, nap, nod off, slumber

noise *n* babble, blare, cacophony, clamor, clatter, commotion, din, hubbub, hullabaloo *inf*, racket, row, screaming, shouting, sound, talk, uproar

noiseless *adj* hushed, inaudible, mute, muted, quiet, silent, soft, soundless, still; ***opp*** noisy

noisy *adj* blaring, blasting, boisterous, deafening, ear-splitting, loud, piercing, raucous, riotous, rowdy; ***opp*** quiet, silent

nomad *n* migrant, rambler, roamer, rover, traveler, wanderer

nomadic *adj* migrant, roaming, roving, traveling, wandering

nominal *adj* **1** (the nominal leader of the country) formal, in name only, ostensible, puppet, self-styled, so-called, supposed. **2** (a nominal fee) minimal, minor, small, symbolic, token; ***opp*** large

nominate *v* appoint, assign, choose, designate, elect, name, propose, put forward, put up *inf*, recommend, select, submit

nonchalant *adj* blasé, calm, casual, composed, cool, indifferent, laid-back *inf*, offhand, self-possessed, unconcerned, unemotional; ***opp*** tense, uptight

noncommittal *adj* careful, cautious, discreet, evasive, giving nothing away, guarded, neutral, tactful, unrevealing, vague, wary

non compos mentis *adj* crazy, insane, mad, mentally ill, mentally unbalanced, of unsound mind

nondescript *adj* characterless, dull, featureless, indeterminate, ordinary, undistinguished, uninteresting, unmemorable, unremarkable; ***opp*** special

nonentity *n* lightweight *inf*, nobody, nothing *inf*, person of no account

nonexistent *adj* fantasy, fictional, fictitious, hypothetical, illusory, imaginary, imagined, legendary, made-up, mythical, unreal; ***opp*** real

nonplussed *adj* astonished, astounded, amazed, baffled, disconcerted, dumbfounded, flummoxed, mystified, speechless, stunned, taken aback

nonsense *n* **1** balderdash, baloney *inf*, drivel, gibberish, gobbledegook *inf*, hogwash *inf*, rubbish, stuff and nonsense, twaddle. **2** clowning, foolishness, idiocy, joking, madness, silliness, stupidity

nonstop *adj* ceaseless, constant, continuous, endless, incessant, never-ending, steady, unbroken, unending, uninterrupted

norm *n* average, benchmark, mean, measure, par, pattern, rule, scale, standard, type, yardstick

normal *adj* accepted, average, common, customary, established, everyday, familiar, general, natural, ordinary, predictable, regular, routine, run-of-the mill *inf*, standard, typical, usual; ***opp*** abnormal

normality *n* naturalness, ordinariness, regularity, routine, usualness

normally *adv* as a rule, as usual, commonly, in general, mostly, naturally, ordinarily, regularly, routinely, typically, usually

nose *v* **1** detect, scent, smell out, sniff out. **2** interfere, look around, meddle, poke your nose in *inf*, pry, search, snoop *inf*

nostalgia *n* homesickness, longing, memory, pining, regret, reminiscence, sentiment, sentimentality, wistfulness, yearning

nostalgic *adj* emotional, homesick, longing, pining, regretful, remembering, romantic, sentimental, wistful, yearning

nosy *adj* curious, eavesdropping, inquisitive, interfering, intrusive, meddlesome, prying, snooping *inf*

notable *adj* **1** extraordinary, famous, impressive, memorable, noteworthy, noticeable, obvious, outstanding, rare, remarkable, singular, uncommon, unforgettable, unusual. **2** celebrated, distinguished, eminent, famous, great, noted, prominent, renowned, well-known

notation *n* characters, code, script, signs, symbols, system

note *n* **1** comment, correspondence, explanation, footnote, inscription, jotting, letter, memo *inf*, memorandum, message, minute, record, reference, reminder. **2** (a note of sarcasm in his voice) element, feeling, hint, intonation, quality, tone

note *v* detect, enter, indicate, jot down, make a note, mark, mention, notice, observe, record, register, remark, see, take note, take notice, write down

noted *adj* acclaimed, celebrated, distinguished, eminent, famous, great, illustrious, notable, of note, prominent, recognized, renowned, well-known

noteworthy *adj* exceptional, extraordinary, important, rare, remarkable, significant, striking, unique, unusual; ***opp*** ordinary

nothing *n* **1** nil, zero. **2** vacuum, void, blankness, naught, not anything, not a thing, nothingness, zilch *inf*

notice *n* **1** (a notice on the bulletin board) advertisement, announcement, bulletin, handout, leaflet, message, note, poster, sign, warning. **2** (come to sb's notice) attention, awareness, consciousness, observation, regard. **3** (receive notice of sth) advice, information, news, notification, warning. **4** (be given your notice) dismissal, marching orders *inf*, redundancy, the boot *inf*, the sack *inf*

notice *v* be aware, detect, discern, discover, distinguish, feel, find, make out, note, observe, pay attention, perceive, register, see, spot, take note

noticeable *adj* apparent, clear, conspicuous, discernible, distinct, evident, marked, obvious, plain, prominent, pronounced, salient, striking, unmistakable, visible

notify *v* advise, declare, inform, let sb know, make known, proclaim, publish, report, tell, warn

notion *n* assumption, belief, concept, idea, impression, opinion, theory, thought, understanding, view

notional *adj* abstract, conceptual, hypothetical, illusory, imaginary, theoretical, unreal

notoriety *n* bad reputation, dishonor, disrepute, ill repute, infamy, scandal

notorious *adj* disgraceful, dishonorable, disreputable, ill-famed, infamous, of ill repute, outrageous,

scandalous, well-known
nourish *v* care for, feed, maintain, nurture, provide for, strengthen, support, sustain
nourishing *adj* good for you, healthy, nutritious, sustaining, wholesome
nourishment *n* diet, food, goodness, nutrition, sustenance
novel *adj* different, fresh, ground-breaking, imaginative, innovative, new, original, trail-blazing, uncommon, unconventional, unfamiliar, unique, unusual; ***opp*** old
novel *n* best-seller, book, fiction, narrative, romance, story, work of fiction
novelty *n* **1** (the novelty of his plan) difference, freshness, newness, originality, strangeness, unusualness. **2** (cheap novelties) curiosity, gadget, gimmick, knickknack, memento, souvenir, trinket
novice *n* amateur, apprentice, beginner, learner, newcomer, new recruit, probationer, pupil, rookie *inf*, student, trainee
now *adv* at once, at present, at the moment, for the time being, immediately, instantly, just now, nowadays, promptly, right away, right now, straightaway; ***opp*** later
nowadays *adv* at present, at the moment, in this day and age, now, these days, today
noxious *adj* corrosive, foul, harmful, nasty, poisonous, polluting, toxic, unhealthy, unwholesome; ***opp*** harmless
nucleus *n* center, core, heart, kernel, middle, nub
nude *adj* bare, exposed, in your birthday suit *inf*, in the altogether *inf*, in the buff *inf*, naked, in the raw *inf*, stark-naked, stripped, unclothed, uncovered, undressed; ***opp*** clothed, dressed
nudge *v* bump, dig, dig sb in the ribs, elbow, jog, poke, prod, push, shove, touch
nuisance *n* annoyance, bore, bother, drag *inf*, hassle *inf*, inconvenience, irritation, pain *inf*, problem, trouble, worry
nullify *v* abolish, annul, cancel, declare null and void, do away with, invalidate, negate, neutralize, quash, repeal, revoke, set aside
numb *adj* anesthetized, asleep *inf*, cold, dead, deadened, frozen, paralyzed, stunned, stupefied, without feeling
numb *v* anesthetize, deaden, desensitize, dull, freeze, immobilize, make numb, paralyze
number *n* **1** digit, figure, integer, numeral, unit. **2** (of a magazine) copy, edition, imprint, issue, printing
number *v* add up, calculate, compute, count, reckon, total, work out
numberless *adj* countless, endless, infinite, innumerable, many, more than you can count, myriad, numerous, untold
numeral *n* Arabic numeral, character, digit, figure, integer, number, Roman numeral, symbol
numerous *adj* abundant, copious, countless, lots *inf*, many, multitudinous, myriad, plentiful, several, untold, various; ***opp*** few
nurse *v* care for, look after, minister to, take care of, tend, treat
nurture *v* bring up, cultivate, educate,

feed, nourish, nurse, provide for, rear, sustain, tend, train

nut *n* **1** kernel, pip, seed, stone. **2** crackpot *inf*, crank *inf*, eccentric, loony *inf*, lunatic, madman, maniac, nut case *inf*, psycho *sl*, psychopath, weirdo *inf*

nutritious *adj* good for you, health-giving, healthy, nourishing, wholesome

oasis *n* **1** spring, watering-hole, well. **2** haven, hiding-place, island, refuge, retreat, sanctuary

oath *n* **1** (oath of allegiance) affirmation, avowal, bond, pledge, promise, sworn statement, undertaking, vow, word of honor. **2** blasphemy, curse, expletive, obscenity, profanity, swear word

obedient *adj* acquiescent, amenable, compliant, docile, dutiful, law-abiding, manageable, respectful, submissive, well-behaved, well-trained; ***opp*** disobedient

obese *adj* corpulent, fat, fleshy, heavy, overweight, podgy, portly, stout, tubby; ***opp*** thin

obey *v* **1** (obey a rule) abide by, accept, adhere to, agree to, comply with, follow, keep, observe, respect, stick to *inf*. **2** (obey sb) be obedient to, be ruled by, bow to, defer to, heed, honor, submit to, take orders from, yield to. **3** (you must obey) be dutiful, be obedient, do what you are told, follow orders. **4** (obey the instructions) act upon, carry out, fulfill, perform

object *n* **1** (a useful object) article, item, thing. **2** (the object of the game) aim, goal, idea, intention, motive, objective, point, purpose, reason. **3** (the object of abuse/frustration) butt, focus, recipient, target, victim

object *v* argue, beg to differ, be opposed, complain, grumble, mind *inf*, oppose, protest, raise objections, take a stand against, take exception to

objection *n* argument, challenge, complaint, disapproval, dissatisfaction, doubt, grievance, opposition, protest, query, quibble

objectionable *adj* abhorrent, deplorable, disgusting, distasteful, foul, horrible, insufferable, intolerable, nasty, obnoxious, offensive, repugnant, revolting, unacceptable, undesirable, unpleasant, vile

objective *n* aim, ambition, aspiration, design, desire, end, goal, hope, intent, intention, object, plan, point, purpose, target

objective *adj* detached, disinterested, dispassionate, evenhanded, fair, impartial, just, neutral, open-minded, rational, unbiased, unemotional, uninvolved, unprejudiced; ***opp*** biased

obligation *n* commitment, compulsion, constraint, demand, duty, liability, necessity, need, requirement, responsibility

obligatory *adj* binding, compulsory, essential, imperative, mandatory, necessary, required, unavoidable; ***opp*** optional, voluntary

oblige *v* 1 (make sb do sth) bind, coerce, compel, constrain, force, leave sb no choice, make, put sb under an obligation, require. 2 (do sb a favor) accommodate, help, indulge, please, serve

obliged *adj* 1 (feel obliged to sb) appreciative, grateful, indebted, thankful. 2 (obliged to do sth) bound, compelled, constrained, duty-bound, forced, made, required

obliging *adj* agreeable, amiable, considerate, cooperative, courteous, eager to please, friendly, generous, good-natured, helpful, kind, polite, willing; ***opp*** difficult, unhelpful

oblique *adj* 1 (oblique line) angled, aslant, at an angle, diagonal, inclined, slanted, slanting, sloped, sloping. 2 (oblique mention) back-handed, implicit, implied, indirect, roundabout; ***opp*** direct

obliterate *v* blot out, cancel, delete, demolish, destroy, efface, eradicate, erase, leave no trace, remove, rub out, wipe out

oblivion *n* 1 absent-mindedness, abstraction, amnesia, forgetfulness, unawareness, unconsciousness. 2 (consigned to oblivion) anonymity, disuse, extinction, neglect, obscurity. 3 blackness, darkness, senselessness, stupor, unconsciousness

oblivious *adj* absent-minded, absorbed, blind, careless, deaf, forgetful, heedless, ignorant, neglectful, regardless, unaware, unconcerned, unheeding; ***opp*** aware

obnoxious *adj* disgusting, foul, horrid, insufferable, loathsome, nasty, nauseating, objectionable, odious, offensive, repellent, repugnant, repulsive, revolting, unpleasant; ***opp*** nice, pleasant

obscene *adj* blue, coarse, crude, depraved, dirty, disgusting, filthy, foul, foul-mouthed, immoral, indecent, lewd, offensive, perverted, pornographic, rude, shocking, sick *inf*, suggestive, vulgar

obscenity *n* 1 (shout an obscenity) curse, dirty word, expletive, four-letter word, naughty word, swear word. 2 (prosecuted for obscenity) blasphemy, evil, filth, immorality, indecency, lewdness, offensiveness, perversion, pornography, vulgarity

obscure *adj* 1 (not obvious) ambiguous, concealed, confusing, cryptic, deep, enigmatic, hidden, mysterious, puzzling, secret, unclear; ***opp*** obvious. 2 (not clear) blurred, cloudy, dark, dim, faint, fuzzy, gloomy, hazy, indistinct, masked, misty, murky, shadowy, shady, shrouded, unlit, vague; ***opp*** clear, distinct. 3 (not known about) forgotten, hidden, insignificant, remote, undistinguished, unheard-of, unknown

obscure *v* block, blur, cloak, cloud, conceal, cover, darken, dim, disguise, eclipse, hide, mask, overshadow, screen, shade, shroud, veil

observant *adj* alert, attentive, aware, eagle-eyed, having your eyes peeled, on the ball *inf*, on the lookout, perceptive, sharp, sharp-eyed, vigilant, watchful; ***opp*** unobservant

observation *n* 1 (watching sth or sb) attention, examination, inspection, monitoring, review, scrutiny, study, surveillance, watch, watching. **2** (sth that you notice) conclusion, finding, information, result. **3** (sth that you say or write) comment, opinion, reflection, remark, statement, thought

observe *v* **1** (notice) detect, discern, discover, note, notice, perceive, see, spot, witness. **2** (observe sth or sb) check out *inf*, keep an eye on *inf*, keep tabs on *inf*, keep under observation, keep under surveillance, monitor, scrutinize, spy on, stare at, study, view, watch. **3** (observe a religious custom) celebrate, follow, honor, keep, mark, obey, remember. **4** (make an observation) announce, comment, mention, remark, say

observer *n* bystander, commentator, eyewitness, onlooker, spectator, viewer, watcher, witness

obsess *v* become an obsession, be on your mind, consume, control, dominate, grip, haunt, plague, possess, preoccupy, prey on, take hold of, torment

obsessed *adj* gripped, haunted, hung up on *inf*, in the grip of, preoccupied

obsession *n* addiction, bee in your bonnet *inf*, complex, compulsion, fetish, fixation, hang-up *inf*, infatuation, mania, phobia, preoccupation, thing *inf*

obsessive *adj* addictive, compulsive, consuming, gripping, passionate

obsolete *adj* antiquated, antique, archaic, bygone, dated, discarded, extinct, old, old-fashioned, outmoded, out of date, passé, unfashionable

obstacle *n* bar, barrier, block, blockage, check, difficulty, hindrance, hitch, hurdle, interruption, obstruction, problem, snag, stumbling block

obstinate *adj* defiant, determined, dogged, firm, headstrong, inflexible, persistent, pigheaded, self-willed, single-minded, stubborn, tenacious, unbending, unreasonable, willful

obstreperous *adj* boisterous, disorderly, loud, naughty, noisy, out of control, out of hand, rampaging, rough, rowdy, uncontrolled, undisciplined, unruly, wild

obstruct *v* block, bring to a standstill, check, choke, clog, curb, cut off, delay, frustrate, halt, hamper, hinder, hold up, impede, interrupt, prevent, restrict, shut off, slow, stop, thwart

obstruction *n* bar, barrier, block, blockage, deterrent, hurdle, obstacle, restriction, snag, stumbling block

obstructive *adj* awkward, difficult, uncooperative, unhelpful, unwilling; ***opp*** cooperative, helpful

obtain *v* achieve, acquire, buy, come by, earn, find, gain, get, get hold of, get your hands on, pick up *inf*, secure, win

obtrusive *adj* blatant, conspicuous, intrusive, noticeable, obvious, out of place, prominent; ***opp*** unobtrusive

obvious *adj* apparent, blatant, clear, conspicuous, evident, glaring, manifest, noticeable, open, overt, patent, plain, pronounced, self-evident, straightforward, transparent, unmistakable, visible

occasion *n* **1** (special occasion) affair, celebration, do *inf*, event, function, party. **2** (happy occasion) episode, event, experience, happening, incident, occurrence. **3** (a different occasion) circumstance, instance, situation, time

occasional *adj* casual, incidental, infrequent, intermittent, irregular, odd, rare, sporadic; ***opp*** regular

occupant *n* householder, inhabitant, inmate, occupier, renter, resident, tenant

occupation *n* **1** business, employment, job, profession, trade, work. **2** activity, craft, diversion, hobby, interest, pursuit, recreation. **3** (occupation of a country) capture, colonization, conquest, invasion, overthrow, possession, seizure, takeover

occupied *adj* **1** (doing sth) active, at work, busy, employed, hard at it *inf*, tied up *inf*, working; ***opp*** idle. **2** (being used) engaged, full, in use, taken, unavailable; ***opp*** free

occupy *v* **1** (occupy sb) amuse, divert, engage, engross, entertain, interest, keep busy. **2** (occupy a country) capture, colonize, conquer, invade, overrun, seize, take over. **3** (occupy a house) inhabit, live in, move into, reside in, take up residence in. **4** (occupy your time) fill, fill up, preoccupy, take up, use up

occur *v* **1** appear, arise, come about, crop up, develop, happen, materialize, result, take place, turn up. **2 occur to sb** come to mind, cross your mind, dawn on you, enter your head, strike you

occurrence *n* affair, circumstance, development, episode, event, happening, incident, matter, occasion, phenomenon

odd *adj* **1** abnormal, bizarre, curious, different, eccentric, extraordinary, freak, funny, idiosyncratic, incongruous, irregular, outlandish, peculiar, puzzling, rare, remarkable, strange, uncommon, unconventional, unexpected, unusual, weird; ***opp*** normal. **2** extra, leftover, lone, remaining, single, solitary, spare, surplus, uneven, unmatched, unpaired, unused

oddity *n* aberration, abnormality, anomaly, curiosity, freak, irregularity, peculiarity, phenomenon, quirk, rarity, strangeness, uniqueness

odds *n* (the odds of sth happening) chance, likelihood, probability, prospect

odious *adj* disgusting, foul, hateful, horrible, loathsome, offensive, repellent, repugnant, repulsive, revolting, unpleasant; ***opp*** lovely, nice, pleasant

odor *n* aroma, bouquet, fragrance, perfume, pong *inf*, scent, smell, stench, stink

offend *v* **1** (offend sb) anger, annoy, displease, embarrass, give offense, humiliate, hurt sb's feelings, insult, irritate, outrage, pain, provoke, repel, revolt, sicken, slight, snub, upset, wound. **2** (commit a crime) break the law, commit a crime, do wrong, sin

offended *adj* affronted, annoyed, disgusted, embarrassed, hurt, insulted, miffed *inf*, outraged, put out, resentful, revolted, sickened, stung, upset, wounded

offender *n* criminal, culprit, delinquent, felon, lawbreaker, outlaw, villain, wrongdoer

offense *n* **1** (commit an offense) breach, crime, felony, illegal act, misdemeanor, sin, transgression, wrong. **2** (cause offense) anger, annoyance, disapproval, disgust, displeasure, hurt, irritation, outrage, resentment, upset *inf*

offensive *adj* **1** (of behavior) abusive, annoying, antisocial, disgusting, embarrassing, hurtful, indecent, insolent, insulting, irritating, provocative, objectionable, outrageous, rude, tasteless, uncivil, unpleasant, vulgar, wounding; ***opp*** inoffensive. **2** (of a smell) disgusting, distasteful, nasty, nauseating, obnoxious, odious, repellent, revolting, sickening, unsavory, vile, yucky *sl*; ***opp*** pleasant. **3** (invading a country) aggressive, attacking, belligerent, hostile, invading, on the warpath *inf*, threatening, warlike; ***opp*** defensive

offensive *n* assault, attack, drive, incursion, onslaught, push, raid, strike

offer *n* approach, bid, chance, incentive, invitation, opportunity, proposal, proposition, suggestion, tender

offer *v* bid, give, make an offer, make available, propose, provide, put forward, submit, suggest, tender, volunteer

offering *n* contribution, donation, gift, hand-out

offhand *adj* abrupt, brusque, casual, cavalier, cool, curt

office *n* **1** base, place of work, study, workplace. **2** (have the office of chairman) appointment, business, duty, job, place, position, post, responsibility, role, situation, work

officer *n* **1** administrator, agent, bureaucrat, committee member, dignitary, officeholder, official. **2** (police officer) police officer

official *adj* accredited, approved, authorized, bona fide, certified, formal, kosher *inf*, legitimate, licensed, recognized, sanctioned, valid, validated; ***opp*** unofficial

official *n* administrator, agent, authorized person, bureaucrat, civil servant, committee-member, dignitary, officeholder, officer, public servant

officiate *v* be in charge, be responsible, conduct, lead, preside, referee, run, take charge, take the chair, umpire

officious *adj* bossy, bumptious, dictatorial, domineering, interfering, obtrusive, opinionated, overbearing, pushy *inf*, self-important

off-putting *adj* daunting, demoralizing, disconcerting, discouraging, formidable, intimidating, unnerving, unsettling, upsetting; ***opp*** encouraging

offset *v* balance out, cancel out, compensate for, counteract, counterbalance, make up for, neutralize, set off

offshoot *n* arm, branch, by-product, derivative, limb, spin-off, splinter group

offspring *n* brood, children, descendants, family, heirs, issue, kids *inf*, litter, progeny, successors, young

often *adv* again and again, all the time, constantly, frequently, generally, many times, much, regularly, repeatedly, time after time, time and again; ***opp*** seldom

oil *v* anoint, grease, lubricate, wax

ointment *n* cream, liniment, lotion

okay *adj* acceptable, adequate, all right, convenient, fine, good, not bad, O.K., passable, reasonable

okay *v* agree, approve, authorize, consent to, endorse, give sth the go-ahead, give sth the green light, give sth the thumbs up, O.K., pass, rubber-stamp, sanction;

opp block, prevent

old *adj* **1** (of a person) aged, aging, ancient, doddery, elderly, geriatric, getting on, gray, in your dotage, mature. **2** (of objects) aged, ancient, antiquated, antique, early, prehistoric, veteran, vintage. **3** (dilapidated) crumbling, decrepit, dilapidated, past it, threadbare, worn-out, worn. **4** (old-fashioned) antiquated, dated, obsolete, old-fashioned, out of the ark, outdated, passé, stale, time-worn. **5** (traditional) age-old, original, time-honored, traditional. **6** erstwhile, former, previous

old-fashioned *adj* antiquated, dated, obsolescent, obsolete, old-hat *inf*, outdated, outmoded, out of fashion, passé, stale, time-worn, unfashionable

omen *n* bad sign, foreboding, harbinger, portent, sign, warning, writing on the wall

ominous *adj* bad, black, dark, dire, gloomy, inauspicious, menacing, sinister, unfavorable, unpromising; ***opp*** auspicious

omission *n* error, exclusion, gap, neglect, oversight

omit *v* drop, exclude, forget, leave out, miss, miss out, neglect, overlook

omnipotent *adj* all-powerful, almighty, supreme

onerous *adj* burdensome, difficult, exacting, hard, heavy, taxing, troublesome, unpleasant; ***opp*** easy, simple

one-sided *adj* biased, partial, partisan, unbalanced, unequal, uneven, unfair; ***opp*** balanced, impartial; ***opp*** balanced, fair, unbiased

onlooker *n* bystander, observer, passerby, spectator, viewer, witness

onslaught *n* assault, attack, bombardment, offensive, raid, thrust

onus *n* burden, duty, obligation, responsibility

ooze *v* bleed, drain, dribble, emit, escape, flow, leak, percolate, secrete, seep, trickle, weep

opaque *adj* **1** cloudy, dirty, filmy, hazy, muddy, murky; ***opp*** clear, transparent. **2** difficult, impenetrable, incomprehensible, obscure; ***opp*** clear, obvious, straightforward, understandable

open *adj* **1** ajar, uncovered, undone, unfastened, unlocked. **2** spread out, unfolded. **3** (of countryside) broad, clear, exposed, free, rolling, spacious, sweeping, treeless, unenclosed, unrestricted. **4** (of information) available, free, public, unrestricted; ***opp*** classified, secret. **5** (open aggression) blatant, clear, evident, flagrant, manifest, obvious, overt, plain, undisguised. **6** (the matter is still open) undecided, unresolved, unsettled, up for grabs *inf*

open *v* **1** unbolt, uncork, uncover, undo, unfasten, unlock, untie, unwrap; ***opp*** close, do up, fasten, shut, wrap up. **2** spread out, unfold, unfurl, unroll; ***opp*** close, fold up. **3** (open a meeting) begin, commence, get going, initiate, kick off *inf*, launch, set in motion, set up, start; ***opp*** close

opening *adj* first, inaugural, initial, introductory, preliminary; ***opp*** closing

opening *n* **1** aperture, chink, crack, doorway, gap, hatch, hole, orifice, slot, split, way in. 2 beginning, birth, dawn, launch, outset, start. 3 break *inf*, chance, opportunity

open-minded *adj* detached, dispassionate, enlightened, impartial, liberal, objective, open to suggestions, receptive, unbiased; ***opp*** narrow-minded

operate *v* 1 function, go, run, work. 2 (operate a machine) control, drive, handle, use, work. 3 (operate on sb) cut sb open *inf*, do an operation, perform surgery, put sb under the knife *inf*

operation *n* 1 control, management, performance, use, working. 2 (undertaking) business, campaign, effort, enterprise, process, project, task, undertaking, venture. 3 (surgery) biopsy, laparoscopy, surgery, transplant

operational *adj* functioning, going, in operation, in use, in working order, ready, up and running, viable, working

opinion *n* assessment, belief, estimation, feeling, idea, impression, judgment, stance, view, viewpoint, way of thinking

opinionated *adj* arrogant, dictatorial, doctrinaire, dogmatic, inflexible, pigheaded *inf*, pompous, single-minded, uncompromising

opponent *n* adversary, antagonist, competitor, contender, contestant, enemy, player, rival

opportune *adj* advantageous, appropriate, apt, favorable, good, right, suitable, timely, well-timed

opportunity *n* break *inf*, chance, moment, opening, possibility, time

oppose *v* attack, be hostile to, campaign against, combat, counter, defy, fight, obstruct, stand up to, take a stand against, take issue with, take on; ***opp*** support

opposed *adj* 1 against, antagonistic, anti, hostile, in opposition, on the other side. 2 conflicting, incompatible, opposing, opposite

opposite *adj* 1 facing, on the other side, overlooking. 2 conflicting, contradictory, converse, different, hostile, irreconcilable, opposed, rival, unlike; ***opp*** similar

opposite *n* antithesis, converse, inverse, reverse, the other side of the coin

opposition *n* 1 enemy, opponent, other side, rival. 2 antagonism, competition, defiance, disapproval, hostility, objection, resistance; ***opp*** support

oppress *v* 1 crush, intimidate, persecute, put down, subjugate, suppress, terrorize, tyrannize. 2 (make sb unhappy) afflict, depress, torment, weigh down

oppressed *adj* 1 browbeaten, crushed, downtrodden, enslaved, persecuted, subjugated, tyrannized. 2 (unhappy) depressed, desolate, despondent, downhearted, weighed down

oppressive *adj* 1 harsh, repressive, tyrannical, unjust. 2 burdensome, onerous. 3 airless, close, humid, muggy, stifling, stuffy, suffocating

oppressor *n* autocrat, bully, despot, dictator, tormentor, tyrant

opt for *v* choose, decide on, go for *inf*, pick, prefer, settle on

optimistic *adj* buoyant, cheerful, confident, hopeful, looking on the bright side, looking through rose-tinted spectacles, positive, sanguine; ***opp*** pessimistic

optimum *adj* best, ideal, maximum, optimal, peak, prime, top; ***opp*** worst
option *n* alternative, choice, possibility, route
optional *adj* discretionary, extra, up to you, voluntary; ***opp*** compulsory
oral *adj* by mouth, spoken, verbal, vocal
orator *n* lecturer, public speaker, speaker, speechmaker
orbit *n* circuit, course, path, revolution, track
orbit *v* circle, go round
orchestrate *v* arrange, organize, plan, put together, set up, stage-manage
ordeal *n* distress, hardship, misery, nightmare, suffering, tribulation, trouble
order *n* **1** command, court order, directive, injunction, instruction, regulation, requirement. **2** (sth you have ordered) booking, choice, commission, request, requirement, requisition, selection. **3** (way things are arranged) arrangement, categorization, grouping, method, pattern, plan, sequence, structure. **4** (restore order) calm, control, discipline, harmony, law and order, peace, symmetry; ***opp*** chaos, disorder, disruption
order *v* **1** (tell sb to do sth) decree, direct, give orders to, instruct, require, tell. **2** (put things in order) arrange, categorize, classify, organize, put in order, sort out. **3** (order goods) ask for, book, choose, commission, put in an order for, request, reserve, send off for
orderly *adj* **1** businesslike, efficient, methodical, neat, organized, systematic, tidy; ***opp*** chaotic, disorganized. **2** controlled, disciplined, quiet, well-behaved; ***opp*** rebellious, undisciplined
ordinary *adj* common, common-or-garden, customary, everyday, familiar, humdrum, normal, plain, regular, run-of-the-mill, standard, unexceptional, unremarkable
organic *adj* **1** chemical-free, natural, organically grown. **2** animate, biological, living
organism *n* animal, being, creature, living thing, plant, structure
organization *n* **1** (group) association, body, business, club, combine, company, confederation, consortium, corporation, federation, firm, group, institution, league, society. **2** (structure) arrangement, composition, configuration, construction, design, make-up, order, pattern, structure. **3** (the organizing of sth) logistics, management, operation, planning, regulation, running, setting up
organize *v* **1** (put in order) arrange, categorize, classify, configure, order, put in order, structure. **2** (organize a campaign) arrange, coordinate, design, establish, form, look after, manage, orchestrate, plan, run, see to, set up, sort out, take care of
orgy *n* **1** (wild party) binge *inf*, revel, wild party. **2** (an orgy of sth) binge, bout, fling, splurge, spree
orient *v* **1** design for, direct at, intend for, orientate, make sth suitable for. **2** align, get your bearings, locate, orientate, position, turn
origin *n* **1** basis, derivation, provenance, root, source, starting point. **2** ancestry, background, extraction, family, heritage,

lineage, parentage, pedigree, stock

original *adj* **1** fresh, ground-breaking, imaginative, innovative, new, novel, unusual, untried. **2** earliest, first, initial, primary

originality *n* creativity, freshness, imagination, individuality, innovation, invention, new ideas, novelty

originate *v* **1** (create) bring about, coin, create, develop, establish, give birth to, institute, introduce, invent, launch, pioneer, set up, start. **2** (come from) arise, begin, come from, derive from, flow from, spring from, start, stem from

ornament *n* bauble, decoration, knick-knack, trimming, trinket

ornamental *adj* attractive, decorative, elaborate, fancy, intricate, nonessential, showy

ornate *adj* busy, elaborate, fancy, flashy *inf*, flowery, fussy, grandiose, ornamental, pretentious, rococo, showy; ***opp*** plain

orthodox *adj* accepted, authorized, conformist, conservative, conventional, established, mainstream, official, standard, traditional; ***opp*** nonconformist, revolutionary, unconventional, unorthodox

orthodoxy *n* conformity, conservatism, conventionality, propriety, traditionalism

ostensible *adj* outward, pretended, professed, purported, seeming, so-called, stated, superficial, supposed

ostentatious *adj* affected, flamboyant, flashy *inf*, garish, gaudy, loud, overdone, pretentious, showy; ***opp*** quiet, restrained

ostracize *v* cold-shoulder *inf*, exclude, isolate, reject, shun, shut out, snub

oust *v* depose, dislodge, displace, drive out, expel, force out, kick out *inf*, overthrow, push out, replace, throw out, topple, unseat

outbreak *n* epidemic, eruption, explosion, flare-up, occurrence, rash, upsurge

outburst *n* burst, eruption, explosion, fit, flare-up, flood, outbreak, outpouring, storm, surge

outcast *n* exile, outsider, pariah, persona non grata, refugee, reject

outcome *n* consequence, effect, result, upshot

outcry *n* clamor, complaints, cries of indignation, fuss, howls of protest, hue and cry, hullaballoo, objections, opposition, row, uproar

outdated *adj* antiquated, dated, dead, fuddy-duddy *inf*, obsolete, old-fashioned, out, out of date, outmoded, out of fashion, passé, unfashionable

outdo *v* beat, eclipse, excel, get the better of, go one better than, outclass, outshine, outsmart, overshadow, run rings around *inf*, show up, surpass

outdoor *adj* alfresco, exterior, external, open-air, out of doors, outside; ***opp*** indoor

outer *adj* **1** exposed, exterior, external, outermost, outside, outward, surface, top; ***opp*** inner. **2** distant, far, fringe, outlying, peripheral, remote; ***opp*** inner

outfit *n* **1** clothes, costume, gear *inf*, get-up *inf*, rig *inf*, togs *inf*. **2** (organization) crew, enterprise, group, organization, set-up, team, unit

outgoing *adj* **1** (the outgoing president) departing, ex, former, leaving, old, previous, retiring; ***opp*** incoming. 2 (friendly) approachable, bubbly, extrovert, friendly, genial, gregarious, lively, sociable

outing *n* day-trip, excursion, expedition, jaunt, tour, trip, visit

outlaw *n* bandit, criminal, fugitive, highwayman, robber

outlaw *v* ban, bar, criminalize, forbid, make illegal, prohibit, proscribe

outlay *n* charge, cost, disbursement, expenditure, expense, investment, outgoings, spending

outlet *n* 1 market, retail outlet, retailer, shop, store. 2 channel, discharge, duct, escape valve, mouth, opening, release, vent; ***opp*** inlet

outline *n* 1 abstract, bare bones, draft, resume, rough idea, sketch, summary, synopsis. 2 contour, framework, perimeter, profile, shape, sketch, skeleton, tracing

outline *v* 1 draft, give a rough idea of, rough out, sketch out, sketch, summarize. 2 sketch, trace

outlook *n* 1 (outlook on life) attitude, opinion, perspective, position, standpoint, view. 2 (forecast) expectations, forecast, future, prognosis, prospect. 3 (a building with a pleasant outlook) aspect, panorama, view, vista

out of date *adj* antiquated, dated, dead, fuddy-duddy *inf*, obsolete, old-fashioned, out, outdated, outmoded, out of fashion, passé, unfashionable; ***opp*** modern, new

output *n* crop, efficiency, manufacture, performance, product, production figures, production, productivity, result, yield

outrage *n* 1 anger, disgust, fury, horror, indignation, rage, revulsion, shock. 2 affront, atrocity, crime, disgrace, evil, insult, offense, scandal

outrage *v* anger, disgust, horrify, incense, infuriate, offend, shock, upset

outrageous *adj* 1 disgraceful, disgusting, heinous, horrifying, infuriating, offensive, scandalous, shocking, terrible, upsetting. 2 crazy, excessive, mad, preposterous, unreasonable, wild

outright *adj* absolute, categorical, complete, definite, downright, out-and-out, thorough, total, unmitigated, unqualified, utter

outright *adv* 1 (frankly) candidly, explicitly, frankly, openly, plainly, straight. 2 (in one go) at once, directly, immediately, in one fell swoop, in one go, instantaneously, there and then. 3 (completely) categorically, completely, entirely, lock, stock, and barrel, totally

outset *n* beginning, birth, dawn, inception, kick-off *inf*, launch, start

outside *adj* 1 exterior, external, open-air, out of doors, outdoor, outer, outermost, outward, surface, top; ***opp*** inside. 2 (an outside possibility) faint, improbable, marginal, remote, slight, slim, unlikely

outsider *n* alien, exile, foreigner, incomer, misfit, odd one out, oddball, stranger

outskirts *n* edge, fringe, margin, outlying areas, periphery, suburbs

outspoken *adj* blunt, direct, explicit, forthright, frank, mouthy *inf*, tactless, undiplomatic; ***opp*** quiet, reserved

outstanding *adj* 1 excellent, exceptional, great, impressive, magnificent, memorable, notable, remarkable, special, stunning, superb, supreme, world-class. 2 (unresolved) ongoing, pending, remaining, to be dealt with, unpaid, unresolved, unsettled

outward *adj* 1 exterior, external, outer, outside, surface. 2 (visible) apparent, discernible, external, noticeable, visible; ***opp*** inward. 3 (ostensible) apparent, ostensible, professed, superficial, supposed

outweigh *v* be more important than, cancel out, have the edge on, override, prevail, take precedence over

outwit *v* beat, deceive, dupe, get the better of, outmaneuver, outsmart, pull the wool over sb's eyes, put one over on *inf*

ovation *n* acclaim, accolade, applause, clapping, standing ovation, tribute

overall *adj* all-embracing, blanket, broad, complete, comprehensive, general, global, inclusive, total, umbrella

overcast *adj* cloudy, dark, dull, gray, leaden, murky; ***opp*** clear

overcome *v* conquer, defeat, get the better of, master, quash, rise above, subdue, surmount, triumph over

overcritical *adj* carping, fussy, hard to please, hypercritical, pernickety, quibbling

overcrowded *adj* chock-a-block *inf*, congested, crammed full, full, heaving, jam-packed, overloaded, overrun, packed, swarming, teeming

overdue *adj* behind schedule, delayed, in arrears, late, outstanding, unpaid, unsettled

overeat *v* be greedy, binge, eat like a horse, eat too much, gorge, make a pig of yourself *inf*, overindulge, pig out *inf*, stuff your face *inf*, stuff yourself *inf*; ***opp*** diet, starve yourself

overflow *v* brim over, flood, pour over, run over, spill over

overgrown *adj* overrun, tangled, thick with weeds, unkempt, untidy, weedy, wild

overhang *v* droop over, jut out, loom over, project, protrude, stick out

overhaul *v* check over, fix, inspect, maintain, mend, recondition, refurbish, renovate, repair, restore, service

overheads *n* everyday expenditure, expenditure, expenses, operating costs, running costs

overjoyed *adj* delighted, ecstatic, euphoric, in raptures, jubilant, on cloud nine *inf*, on top of the world *inf*, thrilled; ***opp*** depressed, miserable

overlook *v* 1 forget, leave out, miss, not notice, omit. 2 excuse, ignore, let sth pass, let sth ride, turn a blind eye to *inf*, write off. 3 be opposite, face, front onto, have a view of, look out onto

overpower *v* crush, defeat, get the upper hand, get under control, immobilize, overwhelm, pin down, restrain, trounce

overpowering *adj* intolerable, oppressive, overwhelming, powerful, strong, suffocating, unbearable

overrule *v* cancel, countermand, disallow, invalidate, override, overturn, reject, reverse, revoke, set aside, veto

oversee *v* administer, control, keep an eye on, look after, preside over, supervise

overshadow *v* cloud, dwarf, eclipse, obscure, outshine, put in the shade, spoil

oversight *n* blunder, error, gaffe, mistake, omission, slip-up

overt *adj* blatant, evident, explicit, obvious, open, patent, plain, unconcealed, undisguised, visible; ***opp*** covert, secret

overtake *v* **1** go past, leave behind, outdistance, outstrip, pass, pull ahead of. **2** (events overtake you) befall, catch up with, engulf, hit, overwhelm

overthrow *v* beat, defeat, depose, displace, oust, remove from office, throw out, topple, unseat

overtone *n* connotation, feeling, hint, intimation, sense, suggestion, undercurrent

overturn *v* **1** capsize, keel over, knock over, tip over, topple over, upset, upturn. **2** (overturn a decision) annul, countermand, overrule, quash, reject, repeal, reverse, revoke, set aside, veto

overweight *adj* chubby, corpulent, fat, gross, heavy, massive, obese, outsize, plump, portly, pudgy, roly-poly, stout, tubby, well-padded *inf*; ***opp*** thin

overwhelm *v* **1** engulf, flood, inundate, snow under, swamp. **2** conquer, crush, defeat, overcome, overpower, quell, subjugate, vanquish. **3** bowl over *inf*, daze, devastate, leave speechless, move deeply, shake, prostrate, stagger, stun

overwhelming *adj* **1** (of an emotion) crushing, devastating, overpowering, shattering, staggering, stunning, uncontrollable. **2** (too many or too much) enormous, huge, immense, inordinate, mind-boggling *inf*, staggering, stupendous

overwrought *adj* agitated, beside yourself, distracted, frantic, frenzied, hysterical, in a state *inf*, tense, uptight *inf*

owe *v* **1** (owe money) be in arrears, be in debt, be in the red, be overdrawn. **2** (owe a favor) be indebted to, be obliged to, be under an obligation to

owing *adj* **1** due, in arrears, outstanding, overdue, owed, payable, unpaid. **2 owing to** as a result of, because of, due to, thanks to

own *v* **1** be the owner of, have, have in your possession, hold, keep, retain, possess. **2 own up** admit, come clean, confess, make a clean breast of it, put your hand up to *inf*

owner *n* **1** holder, keeper, possessor. **2** (of land or a business) homeowner, landlady, landlord, proprietor. **3** (of an animal) keeper, master, mistress

pace *n* **1** step, stride. **2** (way of walking) gait, tread, walk. **3** (speed) lick *inf*, rate, speed, tempo, velocity

pace *v* **1** pad, patrol, pound, stride, tread, walk. **2** give a lead to, set the pace for

pacifist *n* conscientious objector, dove, passive resistor, peace-lover, peacemaker; ***opp*** warmonger

pacify *v* calm, calm down, conciliate, placate, quieten, soothe, tranquilize

pack *n* **1** bale, bundle, package, parcel, truss. **2** backpack, haversack, knapsack, rucksack. **3** box, carton, container, package, packet, parcel. **4** (of animals) drove, flock, herd, troop. **5** (of people) band, gang, group, horde, mob, set, troop

pack *v* **1** (pack things) bale, box, bundle up, package, parcel up, place, put, store, stow, wrap, wrap up. **2** (pack a suitcase) cram, fill, fill up, load, stuff. **3** (pack people in) cram, crowd, fill, jam, press into, squeeze into. **4 pack down** compact, compress, press down, press together. **5 pack off** dismiss, dispatch, send away, send off, send packing *inf*. **6 pack up** (put things away) clear up, put away, tidy away, tidy up. **7 pack up** (give up) call it a day *inf*, cease, finish, give up, leave off, pack it in *inf* stop. **8 pack up** (stop working) break down, come to a halt, conk out *inf*, fail, stop working

package *n* **1** box, carton, container, packet, parcel. **2** combination, lot, package deal, package holiday, whole, whole shebang *inf*

package *v* box, pack, pack up, parcel up, wrap, wrap up

packed *adj* chock-a-block, congested, crowded, filled, filled to capacity, full, full up, jammed, jam-packed, overflowing; ***opp*** empty

packet *n* box, carton, container, pack, package

pact *n* agreement, alliance, arrangement, bargain, contract, deal, settlement, treaty, understanding

pad *n* **1** cushion, padding, wadding, wad. **2** jotter, notebook, notepad, writing pad. **3** foot, paw, sole

pad *v* **1** cushion, line, pack, protect, stuff, upholster. **2** amplify, augment, eke, elaborate, fill out, flesh out, protract, spin out, stretch

padding *n* **1** filling, packing, protection, stuffing, wadding. **2** verbiage, verbosity, waffle *inf*, wordiness

paddle *n* oar, scull

paddle *v* **1** propel, pull, row, scull. **2** dabble, splash, splash about, wade

pagan *adj* atheistic, godless, heathen,

idolatrous, infidel, polytheistic

page *n* 1 folio, leaf, sheet, side. 2 attendant, bellboy, pageboy, servant

pageant *n* parade, procession, show, spectacle, tableau

pageantry *n* ceremony, grandeur, magnificence, pomp, ritual, show, spectacle, splendor

pain *n* 1 ache, cramp, discomfort, hurt, irritation, pang, smart, soreness, spasm, sting, tenderness, twinge. 2 agony, anguish, suffering, torment, torture. 3 (mental) anguish, distress, grief, heartache, misery, suffering, torment, torture, unhappiness, woe

pain *v* 1 (hurt) ache, be painful, be sore, cause pain, chafe, hurt, smart, sting, throb. 2 (make sb unhappy) afflict, aggrieve, distress, grieve, hurt, make miserable, sadden, torment, torture

painful *adj* 1 aching, excrutiating, hurting, inflamed, smarting, sore, stinging, tender, throbbing. 2 disagreeable, distressing, harrowing, hurtful, nasty, traumatic, trying, unpleasant, upsetting. 3 arduous, difficult, hard, laborious, strenuous, tough; ***opp*** painless

painkiller *n* anesthetic, analgesic, anodyne, palliative

painless *adj* 1 pain-free, without pain; ***opp*** painful. 2 easy, effortless, simple, trouble-free; ***opp*** difficult

painstaking *adj* assiduous, careful, conscientious, diligent, meticulous, punctilious, thorough

paint *n* color, coloring, dye, pigment, stain, tint

paint *v* 1 apply paint to, color, cover, daub, decorate, dye, spray, stain, tint, touch up, varnish, whitewash. 2 (show sth) delineate, depict, describe, picture, portray, represent

painter *n* artist, decorator, illustrator

pair *n* brace, couple, duo, match, twins, twosome

pair *v* 1 **pair up** (put things together) arrange in pairs, couple, join up, link up, match, match up, put together, twin, yoke. 2 **pair off, pair up** (of people) double up, find a partner, get together, join up, make a twosome, marry, team up, wed

palatable *adj* appetizing, delicious, mouthwatering, savory, scrumptious, tasty, yummy *inf*; ***opp*** disgusting

palatial *adj* grand, imposing, luxurious, magnificent, majestic, opulent, posh *inf*, plush *inf*, spacious, splendid, stately, sumptuous; ***opp*** miserable, tiny

pale *adj* 1 anemic, ashen, as white as a sheet, colorless, deathly pale, drained, like death, like death warmed up *inf*, pallid, pasty, peaky *inf*, wan, washed-out *inf*, white, white-faced. 2 (of colors) bleached, faded, light, pastel, washed-out, wishy-washy *inf*. 3 (of light) dim, faint, inadequate, weak

pall *v* become boring, become tedious, become tiresome, cloy, lose its attraction, lose its interest, get boring, get/grow tedious, get/grow tiresome

palpable *adj* 1 apparent, blatant, clear, conspicuous, evident, glaring, manifest, obvious, patent, plain, unmistakable.

2 concrete, solid, tangible

palpitate *v* beat rapidly, flutter, pound, pulsate, throb, thud, thump

paltry *adj* 1 (too small) derisory, insignificant, meagrer, miserly, piddling *inf*, small, trifling, unimportant, worthless; ***opp*** generous. 2 contemptible, despicable, low, mean, miserable, sorry

pamper *v* cosset, humor, indulge, make a fuss of, mollycoddle, overindulge, pet, spoil, wait on hand and foot

pamphlet *n* booklet, brochure, circular, leaflet, tract

pan *n* 1 casserole, pot, saucepan. 2 container, receptacle, vessel

panacea *n* cure-all, cure for all ills, elixir, nostrum, universal remedy

panache *n* dash, élan, flair, flamboyance, pizzazz *inf*, style, verve

pandemonium *n* Babel, bedlam, chaos, commotion, hullabaloo, tumult, turmoil, uproar

panel *n* 1 insert, pane. 2 board, committee, jury

pang *n* 1 ache, pain, sharp pain, sting, twinge. 2 (pang of conscience) misgiving, qualm, remorse, scruple

panic *n* alarm, dismay, fear, horror, hysteria, terror

panic-stricken *adj* aghast, frightened, frightened to death *inf*, hysterical, panicky, petrified, scared out of your wits *inf*, scared stiff, scared to death *inf*, terrified; ***opp*** calm

panorama *n* aerial view, bird's-eye view, landscape, scene, view, vista

panoramic *adj* commanding, extensive, scenic, sweeping, wide

pant *v* blow, breathe heavily, gasp, gasp for breath, huff and puff, puff, wheeze

pants *n* jeans, slacks, trousers

paper *n* 1 (newspaper) broadsheet, daily, newspaper, rag *inf*, tabloid. 2 (give a paper) dissertation, monograph, record, study, treatise

papers *n* 1 contract, deed, deeds, document, documents, form, forms, legal papers. 2 ID, identification documents, identification papers, identity card, passport. 3 correspondence, diaries, files, letters, personal papers, records

parable *n* allegory, fable, moral tale, story with a moral

parade *n* 1 cavalcade, cortège, demonstration, march, motorcade, pageant, procession. 2 display, exhibition, show, spectacle

parade *v* 1 file past, march, march past. 2 (show sth off) air, display, exhibit, flaunt, make a show of, show, show off, vaunt. 3 show off, strut, swagger, swank *inf*

paradise *n* 1 Eden, Elysian Fields, Elysium, fairyland, Garden of Eden, heaven, heavenly kingdom, kingdom of heaven, Shangri-La, utopia, Valhalla. 2 bliss, delight, ecstasy, joy, seventh heaven

paradox *n* anomaly, contradiction, inconsistency, oxymoron, self-contradiction

paradoxical *adj* anomalous, contradictory, inconsistent

paragon *n* archetype, exemplar, example, ideal, model, model of excellence, pattern, perfect example, standard

parallel *adj* **1** equidistant, side by side. **2** analogous, comparable, corresponding, equivalent, like, matching, resembling, similar

parallel *n* **1** corollary, counterpart, duplicate, equal, equivalent, match, twin. **2** analogy, comparison, correspondence, likeness, resemblance, similarity

paralyze *v* **1** cripple, disable, immobilize, incapacitate, make powerless. **2** bring to a halt, bring to a standstill, bring to a stop, freeze, halt, immobilize, put out of action, put out of commission, stop. **3** deaden, desensitize, freeze, numb. **4** (with fear) freeze, petrify, stagger, stop, stun, transfix

paralyzed *adj* **1** crippled, disabled, immobilized, paraplegic, unable to move. **2** at a standstill, frozen, halted, immobile, immobilized, rigid, unable to move, unusable. **3** dead, deadened, frozen, numb. **4** (with fear) petrified, stunned, stupefied, transfixed

paramount *adj* cardinal, chief, foremost, main, most important, pre-eminent, primary, principle, supreme, uppermost

paraphernalia *n* **1** baggage, belongings, bits and pieces, effects, impedimenta, luggage, odds and ends, personal belongings, possessions, stuff, things. **2** (things needed for sth) accessories, apparatus, equipment, gear, kit, material, tackle, tools

paraphrase *v* explain, gloss, interpret, put into other words, rephrase, reword

parasite *n* bloodsucker, cadger, drone, freeloader *inf*, hanger-on, leech, scrounger, sponger

parcel *n* **1** bale, box, bundle, carton, pack, package. **2** (of land) lot, patch, piece, plot

parcel *v* **1** box, bundle up, do up, pack, package, pack up, parcel up, tie up, wrap, wrap up. **2 parcel out** allocate, allot, carve up, deal out, distribute, divide, share out

parch *v* bake, burn, dehydrate, dessicate, dry, dry up, scorch, shrivel, wither

parched *adj* **1** arid, baked, burned, dessicated, dehydrated, dried out, dried up, dry, scorched, shriveled, waterless, withered. **2** dry *inf*, dehydrated, thirsty

pardon *n* **1** forgiveness, indulgence, mercy. **2** (an official pardon) amnesty, exoneration, free pardon, release, reprieve

pardon *v* **1** condone, excuse, forgive, forgive and forget, let off, overlook. **2** (pardon sb officially) absolve, exonerate, grant a pardon to, release, reprieve

pardonable *adj* allowable, excusable, forgivable, minor, slight, understandable; ***opp*** unpardonable

parent *n* dad *inf*, father, mom *inf*, mother, old dear *inf*, old man *inf* old lady *inf*, old woman *inf*, procreator, progenitor, sire

parentage *n* ancestry, birth, descent, extraction, family, lineage, origin, pedigree, race, stock

park *n* **1** green, playground, public garden, public park, recreation ground. **2** estate, gardens, grounds, parkland

parliament *n* assembly, congress,

convocation, council, legislative assembly, legislature, senate

parody *n* burlesque, caricature, imitation, lampoon, satire, send-up *inf*, spoof *inf*, take off *inf*

parody *v* caricature, imitate, lampoon, mimic, satirize, send up *inf*, take off *inf*

parry *v* **1** (parry blows) avert, block, deflect, fend off, rebuff, repel, stave off, turn aside, ward off. **2** (parry awkward questions) avoid, dodge, duck *inf*, evade, elude, sidestep *inf*

part *n* **1** bit, fraction, fragment, percentage, piece, portion, scrap, section, segment, share, slice. **2** component, constituent, element, ingredient. **3** (part of an organization) branch, department, division, section, unit. **4** (theatrical) character, lines, role, words. **5** (your part in an undertaking) capacity, duty, function, job, responsibility, role, task. **6** (part of a town) area, district, neighborhood, quarter, region, sector, zone. **7 for the most part** all in all, by and large, generally, mostly, to all intents and purposes, usually. **8 take part** be involved, contribute, do your share, engage in, have a hand in, have something to do with, join in, participate, play a part

part *v* **1** (part things that are joined) break, break up, cleave, divide, separate, sever, split, tear. **2** (people part) break up, divorce, get a divorce, get a separation, get divorced, go their separate ways, part company, separate, split up. **3 part from** go away from, leave, say farewell to, say good-bye to, say your good-byes, separate, split *inf*, take your leave. **4 part with** cede, give away, give up, let go, let go of, relinquish, sacrifice, sell, yield

partake *v* **1** contribute to, engage in, have a hand in, have sth to do with, participate in, play a part in, share in, take part in. **2** (partake of food, drink) consume, drink, eat, share in

partial *adj* **1** imperfect, incomplete, in part, limited, part, unfinished. **2** biased, discriminatory, having an interest, inequitable, one-sided, partisan, prejudiced, unfair, unjust; ***opp*** impartial, unbiased. **3 be partial to** be fond of, be keen on, care for, have a liking for, have a taste for, have a weakness for, like

partially *adv* fractionally, half, in part, moderately, not completely, not fully, not wholly, partly, slightly, to a certain extent, to a limited extent, to some degree, to some extent

participant *n* competitor, contributor, member, party, shareholder

participate *v* be involved in, contribute to, engage in, join in, have a hand in, have sth to do with, play a part in, take part in

particle *n* **1** bit, crumb, fragment, grain, morsel, scrap, smidgen *inf*, speck, spot, tiny bit, tiny piece. **2** atom, molecule

particular *adj* **1** distinct, individual, precise, individual, specific, unique; ***opp*** general. **2** exceptional, outstanding, remarkable, singular, special, unusual. **3** choosy *inf*, discriminating, exacting, fastidious, finicky, fussy, pernickety *inf*, selective. **4 in particular** especially, particularly, specifically

parting *n* **1** adieu, departure, farewell, good-bye, leave-taking, leaving. **2** breaking up, divorce, separation, splitting up. **3** breaking up, detachment, dividing, division, partition, separating, separation, severance, splitting up

partisan *adj* biased, bigoted, doctrinaire, factional, one-sided, partial, prejudiced, sectarian, unbalanced, unfair; ***opp*** impartial

partisan *n* **1** adherent, backer, devotee, disciple, follower, supporter, sympathizer, upholder. **2** freedom fighter, guerrilla, insurgent, member of the resistance, terrorist

partition *n* **1** barrier, room divider, screen, wall. **2** (act of separating) division, partitioning, segregation, separation, split; ***opp*** unification

partition *v* divide, section off, segregate, separate, split, split up, wall off

partner *n* **1** (in business, sport) accomplice, ally, associate, collaborator, colleague, comrade, companion, co-worker, fellow worker, sleeping partner, teammate. **2** (in a couple) boyfriend, common-law husband, common-law wife, companion, girlfriend, husband, live-in lover *inf*, mate, significant other *inf*, spouse, wife

partnership *n* **1** alliance, association, brotherhood, collaboration, fellowship, fraternity, joint effort, union. **2** (in business) cartel, company, confederation, conglomerate, coop *inf*, cooperative, joint venture, syndicate

party *n* **1** bash *inf*, do *inf*, get-together *inf*, orgy, reception, social, social gathering, soirée. **2** (political) bloc, faction, fraction, grouping. **3** (the parties involved) individual, person. **4** (to a dispute, conspiracy) accomplice, litigant, participant, third party. **5 be a party to** approve of, condone, get involved in, participate in, support, take part in

pass *n* **1** (make a pass at sb) advance, approach, assault, fumble, lunge, proposition, harassment. **2** (between mountains) canyon, channel, cutting, gap, gorge, gully, opening, passage, path, ravine, valley. **3** (an official pass) authorization, identification, identity card, license, passbook, passport, permit, proof of identity, safe conduct, swipe card, ticket, warrant, visa

pass *v* **1** drive by, drive past, go by, go past, move past, overtake, pass by, run by, run past, walk by, walk past. **2** (pass a level, amount) break, exceed, go above, go beyond, outstrip, surpass, transcend. **3** (pass an exam) be successful, get through, graduate, qualify; ***opp*** fail. **4** (pass a law) accept, agree, approve, confirm, enact, establish, promulgate, ratify, validate, vote through; ***opp*** reject. **5** (pass sth to sb) circulate, deal, deliver, give, hand, hand over, pass on, present, proffer, transfer. **6** (in a quiz) fail to answer, give in, make no bid, miss a turn, opt out, say nothing. **7** (pass the time) fill, occupy, spend, while away. **8** (time passes) advance, continue, elapse, flow, fly, go on, tick by. **9 pass away** breathe your last, depart this world, die, expire, go to meet your Maker, kick the bucket *inf*, pass on, perish. **10 pass out** black out, collapse, faint, lose consciousness, swoon

passable *adj* adequate, average, fair, satisfactory, tolerable

passage *n* **1** (from a book) excerpt, extract, paragraph, part, quotation, reading, section, text, verse. **2** (narrow lane) alley, arcade, catwalk, channel, corridor, covered way, hall, hallway, lane, tunnel, passageway, walkway. **3** (on a ship) crossing, journey, transit, voyage

passenger *n* commuter, customer, tourist, traveler

passerby *n* bystander, passing motorist, pedestrian

passing *adj* brief, fleeting, incidental, momentary, short, short-lived, temporary, transient, transitory

passion *n* **1** (strong feeling) animation, ardor, devotion, emotion, enthusiasm, excitement, fervor, fire, heat, keenness, vehemence, zeal. **2** (strong sexual feeling) arousal, desire, craving, fondness, infatuation, love, lust

passionate *adj* **1** animated, ardent, burning, devoted, eager, emotional, enthusiastic, excitable, excited, fervent, fiery, heartfelt, hot, hot-headed, impassioned, intense, tempestuous, vehement, wild, zealous. **2** (sexually) amorous, aroused, hot, loving, lustful, randy *inf*, sensual, sexy, turned-on *inf*

passive *adj* inactive, inert, patient, quiescent, unassertive, unresisting, submissive; ***opp*** active

past *adj* **1** ancient, bygone, earlier, erstwhile, ex-, former, historical, old, onetime, preceding, previous, prior, yesterday's; ***opp*** future. **2** done, finished, forgotten, gone, in the past, over, over and done with; ***opp*** continuing, present, ongoing

past *n* **1** antiquity, bygone days, bygones, days gone by, former times, old times, olden days, history, mists of time, yesterday, yesteryear, yore; ***opp*** future. **2** (sb's past) background, experiences, former life, life history, origins, record; ***opp*** future

paste *n* adhesive, cement, glue, gum, putty

paste *v* affix, cement, fasten, fix, glue, gum, stick

pastiche *n* burlesque, copy, imitation, parody, satire, take-off *inf*

pastime *n* amusement, distraction, diversion, entertainment, hobby, interest, leisure activity, pursuit, recreation, sport

pastoral *adj* **1** agrarian, agricultural, Arcadian, bucolic, country, farming, rural, rustic. **2** (pastoral care) fatherly, in loco parentis, nurturing, parental, paternal

pasture *n* field, grass, grassland, grazing land, meadow, pastureland

pat *v* dab, hit, slap, tap, touch

patch *n* **1** area, blotch, mark, marking, shape, spot, stain. **2** (patch of land) area, lot, parcel, piece, plot, strip, tract

patch *v* **1** darn, mend, repair. **2 patch up** (patch up a quarrel) reconcile, repair, resolve, restore, settle

patchy *adj* erratic, good in parts,

inconsistent, intermittent, irregular, sketchy, uneven, variable, varying

patent *adj* apparent, blatant, clear, conspicuous, definite, evident, flagrant, glaring, manifest, obvious, palpable, plain, unmistakable

path *n* **1** alley, avenue, bridle path, bridleway, footpath, lane, pathway, pavement, road, route, track, trail, walkway, way. **2** (of a moving object) arc, course, curve, direction, orbit, trajectory

pathetic *adj* **1** abject, abysmal, bad, dismal, feeble, hapless, hopeless, ineffectual, miserable, pitiable, pitiful, poor, sad, sorry, weak, wretched. **2** (upsetting) affecting, heartbreaking, moving, piteous, pitiful, plaintive, poignant, sad, sentimental, sorry, tear-jerking, touching, upsetting

pathos *n* emotion, poignancy, sadness, sentimentality

patience *n* calm, calmness, endurance, forbearance, fortitude, passivity, resignation, stoicism, tolerance; ***opp*** impatience

patient *adj* **1** calm, long-suffering, passive, resigned, stoical, tolerant, waiting; ***opp*** impatient. **2** (of a piece of work) assiduous, diligent, indefatigable, meticulous, painstaking, persevering, persistent, thorough, unhurried, untiring; ***opp*** hurried

patient *n* case, client, inmate, invalid, resident, subject, sufferer, victim

patriot *n* chauvinist, loyalist, nationalist

patriotic *adj* chauvinistic, flag-waving, gung-ho *inf*, jingoistic, loyal, loyalist, my-country-right-or-wrong, nationalistic

patrol *n* garrison, guard, guards, posse, rangers, scouts, squad, vigilantes, watch

patrol *v* be on the beat, cruise, do the rounds, guard, inspect, keep vigil, monitor, police, watch

patron *n* **1** backer, benefactor, contributor, donor, friend, protector, sponsor, supporter. **2** client, customer, habitué, regular, visitor

patronage *n* **1** assistance, backing, endorsement, protection, sponsorship, support. **2** (of an unfair, illegal kind) back-scratching, jobs for the boys, nepotism, old school tie

patronize *v* **1** be condescending, look down on, look down your nose at, sneer at, talk down to. **2** (patronize a shop, restaurant) buy from, do business with, drink at, eat at, frequent, shop at, visit

patronizing *adj* condescending, disdainful, haughty, high-handed, overbearing, scornful, sneering, snobbish, snooty *inf*; ***opp*** respectful

pattern *n* **1** arrangement, decoration, design, device, figure, marking, motif, ornamentation, shape. **2** (for making sth) blueprint, guide, instructions, model, plan, sample, specimen, stencil, template. **3** (events following a pattern) order, plan, shape, structure, system

paunch *n* abdomen, beer belly *inf*, beer gut *inf*, belly, gut, middle-aged spread, pot *inf*, potbelly *inf*, stomach, spare tire *inf*, tummy *inf*

pause *n* abeyance, break, cessation, delay, gap, halt, hesitation, interlude, interruption, interval, rest, silence

pause *v* break off, cease, delay, hesitate, interrupt, rest, stop, wait

pave *v* **pave the way for** allow, enable, foreshadow, make possible, permit, precede, prepare

pay *n* allowance, commission, earnings, emoluments, honorarium, income, payment, take-home pay, remittance, remuneration, reward, salary, stipend, wage, wages

pay *v* **1** buy, cough up *inf*, fork out *inf*, foot the bill, hand over, lay out, part with, shell out *inf*, pay out, pay up, remit, settle up, spend. **2** (produce a profit, benefit) be advantageous, be profitable, be rewarding, be worthwhile, make a profit, make money, pay off. **3** (pay sb to do sth) employ, engage, hire, remunerate, reward, take on. **4** (pay sb for damage, expenses) compensate, defray, indemnify, pay back, recompense, refund, reimburse. **5 pay for** (suffer as a result of) atone for, be penalized for, be punished for, compensate for, do penance for, expiate, make amends for, make good, make reparations for, make up for, suffer for. **6 pay off** cancel, clear, close, discharge, liquidate, meet, repay, settle, square

payable *adj* due, outstanding, owed, owing, to be paid, unpaid

payment *n* amount, award, compensation, deposit, installment, premium, refund, reimbursement, repayment, reward, sum

peace *n* **1** armistice, concord, harmony, pacification, peacetime, reconciliation, truce; ***opp*** war. **2** calm, calmness, peacefulness, quiet, repose, rest, serenity, tranquillity

peaceable *adj* amicable, conciliatory, peaceful, peace-loving

peaceful *adj* **1** (wanting, seeking peace) amicable, conciliatory, peaceable, peace-loving; ***opp*** warlike. **2** (free of conflict) at peace, calm, harmonious, untroubled. **3** (without noise, movement) at peace, at rest, calm, placid, quiet, restful, serene, still, tranquil

peak *n* **1** brow, crest, hilltop, mountain top, pinnacle, point, summit, tip, top. **2** acme, apex, climax, height, high, high point, high-water mark, maximum, pinnacle, top, zenith; ***opp*** trough

peak *v* **1** climax, culminate, reach a crescendo, reach a peak. **2 have peaked** be in decline, be on the downward slide, be on the way down, be past your best, decline, fall off

peal *n* carillon, chime, clang, ring, ringing, toll, tolling

peal *v* chime, clang, resound, ring, ring out, toll

peasant *n* country dweller, countryman, country cousin *inf*, farm laborer, farm worker, farmer, farmhand, rustic, serf, smallholder, yokel *inf*

peck *v* bite, nibble, nip

peculiar *adj* **1** bizarre, eccentric, extraordinary, funny, odd, out of the ordinary, queer, singular, strange, unusual, weird; ***opp*** normal. **2** (peculiar to sth) characteristic, distinctive, distinguishing, exclusive, individual, own, particular, proper, special, specific, unique

peculiarity *n* **1** eccentricity, foible,

idiosyncrasy, oddity. **2** attribute, characteristic, feature, hallmark, property

pedantic *adj* academic, bookish, didactic, doctrinaire, dogmatic, donnish, nit-picking, over-literal, scholarly, scholastic

pedestrian *adj* boring, commonplace, dull, mediocre, plodding, prosaic, run-of-the-mill, unimaginative, uninspired, unoriginal

pedestrian *n* foot passenger, hiker, passerby, rambler, walker

pedigree *n* ancestry, background, descent, family, family tree, genealogy, heritage, lineage

peel *v* pare, skin, strip, uncover

peep *v* glance, glimpse, look, peek, sneak a look, snoop, take a butcher's *inf*

peer *n* **1** aristocrat, baron, baroness, count, duke, earl, lady, lord, marquis, noble, nobleman, viscount. **2** associate, colleague, companion, equal

peer *v* gaze, look, look closely, squint *inf*, stare

peevish *adj* bad-tempered, cantankerous, churlish, complaining, crabby *inf*, cross, crotchety *inf*, crusty *inf*, disagreeable, discontented, fractious, fretful, grouchy *inf*, grumbling, grumpy, ill-natured, irritable, petulant, querulous, rude, sulky, sullen, surly, testy

peg *v* fix, keep, maintain, pin, secure, stabilize

pelt *v* batter, beat, bombard, riddle, shower, sprinkle, stone

pen *n* **1** ballpoint, ballpoint pen, cartridge pen, felt-tip, felt-tip pen, fountain pen, quill. **2** cage, coop, corral, enclosure, fold, pound, sheep fold, pigsty, stall, stockade, sty

pen *v* **1** author, compose, draft, draw up, write. **2 pen in** box in, corral, enclose, enfold, fence in, hem in, imprison, pin down, restrict

penal *adj* corrective, criminal, disciplinary, prison, punitive

penalize *v* **1** book, caution, discipline, fine, punish. **2** (a situation which penalizes sb) disadvantage, place at a disadvantage, handicap

penalty *n* caution, endorsement, fine, forfeit, punishment, sentence

penance *n* amends, atonement, expiation, penitence, punishment, repentance

pending *adj* **1** on the table, outstanding, undecided, unfinished. **2** approaching, coming, imminent, impending, in store, in the offing, on the cards, on the way

penetrate *v* bore, enter, go in, go into, go through, perforate, permeate, pervade, pierce, stab

penitent *adj* apologetic, contrite, guilty, remorseful, repentant, sheepish, sorry

pen name *n* alias, assumed name, nom de guerre, nom de plume, pseudonym, stage name

penniless *adj* bankrupt, broke *inf*, cleaned out *inf*, destitute, impecunious, impoverished, indigent, poor, poverty-stricken, without a penny, without a penny to your name

pension *n* allowance, annuity, benefit, income support, private income

pensioner *n* old age pensioner, retired person, senior citizen, veteran

pensive *adj* contemplative, day-dreaming, deep in thought, meditative, reflective, ruminating, thinking, thoughtful, withdrawn, wistful

pent-up *adj* accumulated, built-up, frustrated, repressed

people *n* 1 folk, folks *inf*, human beings, human race, humanity, humankind, man, mankind, men, mortals, individuals. 2 (the people) citizenry, citizens, common people, commoners, electorate, hoi polloi, lower orders, masses, ordinary people, plebs *inf*, populace, population, proletariat, public, society, subjects, voters. 3 clan, community, ethnic group, nation, race, tribe

people *v* colonize, inhabit, live in, occupy, populate, settle, stock

perceive *v* apprehend, appreciate, be aware of, be conscious of, detect, discern, distinguish, experience, hear, note, notice, observe, recognize, register, see, sense

perceptible *adj* apparent, appreciable, audible, detectable, discernible, observable, noticeable, palpable, perceivable, recognizable, visible; ***opp*** imperceptible

perception *n* awareness, consciousness, discernment, experience, knowledge, grasp, insight, perceptiveness, recognition, understanding

perceptive *adj* acute, alert, astute, attentive, aware, bright, clever, discerning, intelligent, keen-eyed, observant, on the ball *inf*, penetrating, perspicacious, quick, sensitive, sharp, sharp-eyed, smart

perch *n* position, roost, seat, station, vantage point

perch *v* alight, balance, land, poise, position yourself, rest, roost, settle, sit, station yourself

percussion *n* bass drum, bongos, drum, kettledrum, glockenspiel, maracas, tambourine, snare drum, timpani, tom-tom, triangle, xylophone

perennial *adj* 1 constant, continuing, durable, enduring, eternal, everlasting, lasting, permanent, unceasing. 2 continual, cyclical, recurrent, recurring, regular, seasonal

perfect *adj* 1 consummate, faultless, flawless, ideal, immaculate, impeccable, incomparable, irreproachable, matchless, pure, spotless, sublime, unbeatable, unblemished, unmarred, untarnished; ***opp*** imperfect. 2 (a perfect circle) entire, finished, full, whole; ***opp*** imperfect. 3 (perfect nonsense) absolute, complete, downright, out-and-out, sheer, total, unadulterated, unmitigated, utter

perfect *v* accomplish, achieve, bring to fruition, carry out, complete, consummate, effect, execute, finish, fulfill, perform, realize, see through

perfection *n* 1 completeness, faultlessness, flawlessness, incomparability, integrity, precision, purity, spotlessness, wholeness; ***opp*** imperfection. 2 (the perfection of a technique) accomplishment, achievement, completion, consummation, end, execution, finishing, fruition, fulfillment, realization

perforate *v* bore, drill, penetrate, pierce, prick, punch, puncture, stab

perform *v* **1** (perform a task) accomplish, achieve, carry out, complete, discharge, do, effect, execute, finish, fulfill, pull off *inf*, satisfy, transact, work. **2** (perform a play) act, depict, enact, play, present, produce, put on, render, represent, stage

performance *n* **1** (a gala performance) act, appearance, entertainment, exhibition, gig *inf*, play, portrayal, presentation, production, show. **2** (the performance of a task) accomplishment, achievement, completion, conduct, discharge, effect, execution, finishing, fulfilment, satisfaction, transaction

performer *n* actor, actress, artist, artiste, dancer, entertainer, musician, player, singer, thespian

perfume *n* **1** after-shave, cologne, eau de cologne, fragrance, scent, toilet water. **2** (the perfume of flowers) aroma, bouquet, fragrance, odor, scent, smell

perhaps *adv* conceivably, feasibly, it could be, maybe, possibly; ***opp*** definitely

peril *n* danger, hazard, insecurity, jeopardy, menace, risk, susceptibility, uncertainty, vulnerability; ***opp*** safety

perilous *adj* dangerous, hazardous, insecure, precarious, risky, threatening, uncertain, unsafe; ***opp*** safe

perimeter *n* border, boundary, bounds, circumference, confines, edge, fringe, frontier, limit, margin, periphery, verge

period *n* interval, phase, season, session, space, span, spell, stage, stint, stretch, term, time, while

periodical *adj* cyclical, every once in a while, every so often, intermittent, occasional, periodic, recurrent, recurring, regular, repeated, spasmodic, sporadic

perish *v* **1** be killed, bite the dust *inf*, die, expire, fall, kick the bucket *inf*, lose, your life, pass away, snuff it *sl*; ***opp*** live. **2** collapse, crumble, decline, disappear, fall, vanish; ***opp*** survive. **3** decay, decompose, disintegrate, go bad, go off, go sour, rot, waste, wither

perishable *adj* biodegradable, decaying, destructible, unstable

perjure *v* bear false witness, commit perjury, give false testimony, lie under oath

perjury *n* false testimony, false witness, lying under oath, oath breaking, violation of oath

permanent *adj* abiding, constant, continual, continuous, durable, endless, enduring, eternal, everlasting, fixed, immutable, indestructible, invariable, irreparable, lasting, life-long, never-ending, nonstop, perpetual, persistent, steadfast, unchanging; ***opp*** temporary

permeate *v* diffuse, filter through, imbue, infiltrate, impregnate, penetrate, percolate, pervade, saturate, soak

permissible *adj* acceptable, allowable, authorized, lawful, legal, legitimate, permitted, sanctioned, within the law, within the rules; ***opp*** forbidden

permission *n* agreement, allowance, approval, assent, authorization, consent, dispensation, franchise, freedom, go-ahead *inf*, green light, leave, liberty, license, sanction, thumbs-up *inf*

permissive *adj* broad-minded, easygoing, indulgent, lenient, liberal, tolerant; ***opp*** strict

permit *n* authority, authorization, license, pass, passport, permission, sanction, ticket, visa, warrant

permit *v* agree, allow, approve, assent, authorize, consent, countenance, enable, endorse, entitle, grant, legalize, let, license, sanction, tolerate; ***opp*** forbid

perpendicular *adj* at 90 degrees, at right angles, erect, plumb, straight, upright, vertical

perpetrate *v* bring about, carry out, commit, do, effect, execute, inflict, perform, pull off *inf*

perpetual *adj* abiding, constant, continual, continuous, durable, endless, enduring, eternal, everlasting, fixed, immutable, indestructible, invariable, irreparable, lasting, life-long, never-ending, nonstop, permanent, persistent, steadfast, unchanging; ***opp*** temporary

perpetuate *v* continue, eternalize, immortalize, keep going, maintain, preserve, sustain; ***opp*** end

perplex *v* baffle, bamboozle *inf*, bewilder, dumbfound, confound, confuse, flummox, mystify, nonplus, puzzle, stump, throw *inf*

perplexing *adj* **1** baffling, bewildering, confounding, confusing, enigmatic, inexplicable, mysterious, mystifying, puzzling, strange, weird; ***opp*** normal. **2** complex, complicated, difficult, hard, intricate, involved, knotty; ***opp*** simple

perquisite *n* advantage, benefit, bonus, dividend, extra, freebie *inf*, gratuity, perk, plus

persecute *v* abuse, afflict, distress, harass, hound, hunt, ill-treat, maltreat, mistreat, oppress, pursue, torment, torture, victimize

persevere *v* carry on, continue, endure, go on, hammer away *inf*, hang on, hold on, hold out, keep at it *inf*, keep going, keep it up *inf*, maintain, persist, pursue, remain; ***opp*** give up

persist *v* carry on, continue, endure, go on, hammer away *inf*, hang on, hold on, hold out, keep at it *inf*, keep going, keep it up *inf*, maintain, persevere, pursue, remain; ***opp*** give up

persistent *adj* **1** (of a person) assiduous, determined, dogged, hard-working, immovable, insistent, obstinate, patient, persevering, relentless, resolute, steadfast, stubborn, tenacious, tireless, unflagging, untiring, unwavering. **2** (of a noise) ceaseless, constant, continual, continuous, endless, eternal, everlasting, incessant, interminable, lasting, long-lasting, never-ending, permanent, perpetual, relentless, unending, unrelenting, unrelieved; ***opp*** intermittent

person *n* being, body, character, figure, human, human being, individual, mortal, soul

personal *adj* **1** characteristic, distinctive, exclusive, idiosyncratic, individual, own, particular, peculiar, personalized, unique. **2** (a personal phone call) confidential, intimate, private

personality *n* **1** (sb's personality)

character, disposition, individuality, make-up, nature, persona, temperament. **2** (a TV personality) big name, celebrity, famous name, household name, idol, star, superstar, VIP

personnel *n* employees, helpers, human resources, labor, labor force, manpower, members, people, staff, workers, workforce

perspective *n* **1** (sb's perspective on sth) angle, approach, attitude, opinion, outlook, point of view, position, slant, stance, stand, standpoint, vantage point, view, viewpoint. **2** (in perspective) context, proportion, relation, relativity

perspiration *n* beads of sweat, moisture, sweat, wetness

perspire *v* drip with sweat, glow, pour with sweat, secrete, sweat, swelter

persuade *v* allure, cajole, coax, coerce, convince, entice, impel, induce, influence, press, prevail upon, prompt, sway, talk into, tempt, urge, wheedle *inf*, win over; ***opp*** dissuade

persuasion *n* **1** cajoling, coaxing, coercing, convincing, enticement, inducement, influencing, persuading, pressing, prompting, urging, wheedling. **2** (your political persuasion) attitude, belief, conviction, opinion, position, slant, stance, stand, standpoint, view, viewpoint

persuasive *adj* **1** (of evidence) compelling, conclusive, convincing, credible, impressive, plausible, sound, strong, telling, unarguable, watertight; ***opp*** unconvincing. **2** (of a person) effective, eloquent, forceful, impressive, influential, strong

pertinent *adj* admissible, applicable, apposite, appropriate, apt, fit, fitting, material, relevant, suitable, to the point; ***opp*** irrelevant

perturb *v* agitate, alarm, bother, disconcert, disquiet, distress, disturb, fluster, frighten, ruffle, scare, trouble, unnerve, unsettle, upset, worry

perturbed *adj* agitated, alarmed, anxious, bothered, disconcerted, disquieted, distressed, disturbed, flustered, ill at ease, nervous, restless, ruffled, scared, shaken, troubled, uncomfortable, uneasy, unnerved, unsettled, upset, worried; ***opp*** unconcerned

peruse *v* browse, check, examine, have a look at, inspect, look over, read, run your eye over, scan, scrutinize, study

pervade *v* diffuse, extend, fill, filter through, imbue, infuse, penetrate, percolate, permeate, saturate, spread through

pervasive *adj* common, extensive, inescapable, omnipresent, pervading, prevalent, rife, ubiquitous, universal, widespread; ***opp*** rare

perverse *adj* awkward, contrary, difficult, headstrong, inflexible, intractable, obstinate, pig-headed, rebellious, stubborn, uncooperative, unruly, wayward; ***opp*** reasonable

perversion *n* **1** aberration, abnormality, debauchery, depravity, deviance, deviation, immorality, unnaturalness, vice, wickedness. **2** (the perversion of sth) corruption, distortion, falsification, misrepresentation, twisting

pervert *n* degenerate, deviant, weirdo *sl*

pervert *v* abuse, bend, distort, falsify, misapply, misconstrue, misrepresent, misuse, twist, warp

perverted *adj* abnormal, amoral, corrupt, debased, debauched, depraved, deviant, immoral, sick, twisted, unhealthy, unnatural, warped; ***opp*** natural

pessimistic *adj* bleak, cynical, defeatist, fatalistic, gloomy, negative, resigned; ***opp*** optimistic

pest *n* **1** annoyance, bother, inconvenience, irritation, nuisance, pain, pain in the neck, trial. **2** (on plants) bug, creepy-crawly *inf*, insect, parasite

pester *v* annoy, badger, bother, disturb, harass, harry, hassle, hound, irk, nag, plague, torment, trouble, worry

pestilence *n* affliction, blight, cancer, curse, disease, epidemic, plague, scourge

pet *n* apple of your eye, blue-eyed boy, blue-eyed girl, darling, favorite, idol, jewel

pet *v* caress, fondle, pat, stroke

petition *n* **1** (sign a petition) list of signatures, protest document. **2** (file a petition) appeal, application, entreaty, plea, request, suit, supplication

petition *v* appeal, apply, ask, beg, beseech, entreat, plead, press, solicit, urge

petrify *v* **1** fill sb with fear, frighten, horrify, panic, paralyze, scare, scare sb out of his wits/skin, scare sb to death, stun, stupefy, terrify. **2** calcify, fossilize, turn to stone

petty *adj* **1** (petty squabbling) inconsequential, insignificant, little, minor, negligible, paltry, slight, small, trifling, trivial, unimportant; ***opp*** important, major. **2** (don't be so petty) grudging, mean, nit-picking, small-minded, spiteful, stingy, ungenerous; ***opp*** generous

phantom *n* apparition, ghost, phantasm, specter, spirit, spook

phase *n* chapter, period, part, point, season, spell, stage, step, time

phenomenal *adj* amazing, astonishing, astounding, exceptional, extraordinary, fabulous, fantastic, incredible, marvelous, mind-blowing *inf*, mind-boggling *inf*, miraculous, outstanding, remarkable, sensational, singular, staggering, stunning, unbelievable, unique, wondrous; ***opp*** unremarkable

phenomenon *n* **1** (a natural phenomenon) circumstance, event, happening, incident, occurrence, sight. **2** (a musical phenomenon) marvel, miracle, prodigy, rarity, sensation, wonder

philanthropist *n* altruist, humanitarian, giver, good Samaritan, provider

philistine *n* barbarian, ignoramus, lout; ***opp*** intellectual

philosopher *n* logician, metaphysician, sage, scholar, theorist, thinker

philosophical *adj* **1** (a philosophical discussion) abstract, erudite, learned, theoretical, thoughtful. **2** (be philosophical about sth) accepting, calm, collected, composed, cool, patient, rational, realistic, reasonable, resigned, stoical

philosophy *n* **1** (study philosophy) ideology, logic, metaphysics, rationalism, reason, thinking, thought.

2 (your philosophy on sth) attitude, belief, conviction, ideology, opinion, outlook, point of view, principle, thinking, view, viewpoint

phlegmatic *adj* 1 calm, cool, composed, imperturbable, philosophical, placid, serene, stoical, undemonstrative, unemotional; ***opp*** excitable. 2 apathetic, impassive, indifferent, unenthusiastic, unresponsive; ***opp*** enthusiastic

phobia *n* antipathy, aversion, dislike, distaste, dread, fear, hang-up *inf*, hatred, horror, loathing, neurosis, obsession, repulsion, terror

phone *n* car phone, mobile phone, telephone

phone *v* call, call up, dial, give sb a buzz, give sb a call, give sb a ring, make a phone call, ring, ring up, telephone

phony *adj* artificial, assumed, bogus, counterfeit, fake, false, fictitious, forged, fraudulent, imitation, mock, pretend, pseudo, put-on *inf*, sham, spurious, trick; ***opp*** real

photocopy *n* copy, duplicate, photostat

photocopy *v* copy, duplicate, photostat, reproduce, run off

photograph *n* enlargement, exposure, image, likeness, photo, picture, print, shot, snap *inf*, snapshot

photograph *v* capture on film, film, record, shoot, take a picture

photographic *adj* (a photographic memory) accurate, exact, pictorial, precise, retentive, visual

phrase *n* 1 catchphrase, expression, idiom, proverb, remark, saying, statement, utterance. 2 clause, group of words, sentence

phrase *v* express, formulate, frame, present, put, say, term, utter, voice, word

physical *adj* 1 (physical things) concrete, material, palpable, real, substantial, tangible, visible; ***opp*** intangible. 2 (physical activity) bodily, corporal, corporeal, physiological; ***opp*** mental

physician *n* consultant, doc *inf*, doctor, general practitioner, GP, medic *inf*, medical practitioner, quack *inf*, specialist

physique *n* body, build, figure, form, frame, shape

pick *n* best, cream, elite, favorite, flower, pride; ***opp*** worst

pick *v* 1 choose, decide, elect, favor, make a choice, opt for, plump for, prefer, select, settle on, single out, vote for; ***opp*** discard. 2 (pick flowers) collect, cut, gather, harvest, pluck, pull. 3 **pick on** browbeat, bully, give sb a hard time, harass, hector, persecute, push sb around *inf*; ***opp*** favor

picture *n* 1 drawing, illustration, image, likeness, painting, photograph, portrait, print, representation, sketch. 2 (a picture of what sth is like) account, depiction, description, image, impression, report. 3 (take a picture) photo, shot, snapshot. 4 (a motion picture) blockbuster, film, flick *inf*, movie, video

picture *v* call to mind, conceive, conjure up, envisage, evoke, imagine, see, think up, visualize

picturesque *adj* attractive, beautiful, charming, idyllic, lovely, pretty, quaint, scenic, striking; ***opp*** ugly

piece *n* 1 bit, bite, chunk, dollop *inf*,

fraction, fragment, hunk, length, lump, morsel, part, portion, quantity, scrap, section, segment, share, shred, slab, slice, sliver, unit. 2 (a piece in the newspaper) article, column, composition, item, report, review. 3 (a piece by a famous sculptor) creation, specimen, study, work, work of art

pier *n* breakwater, dock, jetty, landing stage, quay, wharf

pierce *v* bore, drill, impale, jab, penetrate, perforate, prick, puncture, spike, stab

piercing *adj* 1 (a piercing sound) ear-splitting, high-pitched, loud, sharp, shrieking, shrill; ***opp*** gentle, soft. 2 (a piercing wind) arctic, biting, bitter, cold, freezing, keen, numbing, wintry; ***opp*** warm

pigment *n* color, colorant, dye, stain, tincture, tint

pile *n* 1 accumulation, agglomeration, bundle, collection, heap, mass, mound, mountain, stack, stock, store, tower. 2 abundance, heaps *inf*, load, loads *inf*, mass, masses *inf*, lots *inf*, stacks *inf*

pile *v* accumulate, amass, assemble, collect, gather, heap, hoard, load, pile up, stack up, stockpile, stock up, store up

pile-up *n* accident, collision, crash, smash, smash-up

pilgrim *n* crusader, devotee, seeker, traveler, wanderer, wayfarer, worshiper

pilgrimage *n* crusade, expedition, journey, mission, quest, search

pill *n* capsule, drug, lozenge, medicine, pastille, pellet, tablet

pillage *n* looting, marauding, plunder, plundering, raiding, ransacking, rifling, robbery, robbing, sack

pillage *v* despoil, loot, plunder, raid, ransack, ravage, raze, rifle, rob, sack, strip

pillar *n* 1 column, pier, pilaster, pole, post, prop, shaft, stanchion, support, upright. 2 (pillar of society) backbone, mainstay, rock, supporter, upholder, worthy

pilot *n* 1 airman, aviator, captain, commander, director, driver, flier, helmsman, navigator. 2 experiment, model, prototype, test, trial

pilot *v* 1 conduct, convey, direct, drive, fly, guide, lead, navigate, point, shepherd, steer. 2 model, test, try out

pimple *n* acne, blackhead, boil, pustule, spot, swelling, zit *sl*

pin *n* bolt, brooch, clip, fastener, nail, peg, rivet, spike, staple, tack

pin *v* 1 affix, attach, clip, fasten, fix, join, nail, peg, rivet, secure, staple, stick, tack. 2 **pin down** constrain, hold down, immobilize, pinion, restrain

pinch *v* 1 compress, grasp, nip, press, squeeze, tweak. 2 chafe, confine, cramp, crush, hurt, rub, squeeze. 3 filch *inf*, lift *inf*, make off with *inf*, nick *inf*, plunder, poach, rob, shoplift, steal, swipe *inf*, walk off with

pine *v* ache, crave, hanker, hunger, long, miss, mourn, mope, sicken, yearn

pinnacle *n* acme, apex, apogee, cap, crest, crown, height, high point, peak, summit, top, zenith

pinpoint *v* define, discover, distinguish, find, home in on, identify, locate, specify, spot

pioneer *n* **1** colonist, discoverer, explorer, frontiersman, frontierswoman, settler. **2** architect, developer, discoverer, founder, frontrunner, groundbreaker, innovator, inventor, leader, originator, trailblazer, trendsetter

pioneer *v* begin, create, develop, discover, experiment with, found, initiate, instigate, institute, introduce, invent, lead the way, launch, originate, set up, start

pious *adj* **1** dedicated, devoted, devout, God-fearing, godly, holy, religious, reverent, righteous, saintly, spiritual, virtuous; ***opp*** impious. **2** goody-goody *inf*, holier-than-thou, hypocritical, sanctimonious, self-righteous, self-satisfied

pipe *n* channel, conduit, cylinder, duct, hose, line, main, passage, pipeline, tube

pipe *v* **1** channel, conduct, siphon, transmit. **2** cheep, chirp, flute, peep, shrill, squeak, trill, twitter, warble, whistle

piquant *adj* hot, peppery, pungent, salty, savory, sharp, spicy, tart, tasty; ***opp*** bland

pirate *n* **1** buccaneer, corsair, freebooter, hijacker, marauder, raider, rover. **2** copier, plagiarist

pirate *v* appropriate, copy, infringe copyright, plagiarize, poach, reproduce

pit *n* **1** abyss, cavity, chasm, crater, dent, depression, ditch, excavation, gulf, hole, hollow, indentation, pothole, trench. **2** coal-mine, colliery, mine, quarry, shaft, working

pitch *n* **1** arena, field, ground, park, playing field, stadium. **2** degree, extent, height, intensity, level, point. **3** angle, dip, gradient, incline, slant, slope, steepness, tilt

pitch *v* **1** bowl, cast, chuck *inf*, fling, heave, hurl, lob *inf*, sling, throw, toss. **2** (pitch a tent) erect, put up, raise, set up. **3 pitch in** assist, chip in *inf*, contribute, do your bit, help, join in, lend a hand, participate, play a part

pitch-black *adj* coal-black, ebony, jet-black, pitch-dark, raven

piteous *adj* affecting, distressing, grievous, heartbreaking, heartrending, lamentable, miserable, moving, pathetic, pitiable, pitiful, plaintive, poignant, sad, touching, upsetting, woeful, wretched

pitfall *n* catch, danger, difficulty, drawback, hazard, peril, snag, stumbling-block, trap

pitiful *adj* **1** affecting, distressing, grievous, heartbreaking, heartrending, lamentable, miserable, moving, pathetic, piteous, pitiable, plaintive, poignant, sad, touching, upsetting, woeful, wretched. **2** contemptible, hopeless, inadequate, laughable, mean, measly, miserable, paltry, pathetic *inf*, poor, ridiculous, risible, shabby, sorry, useless, worthless; ***opp*** good

pitiless *adj* brutal, callous, cold-blooded, cold-hearted, cruel, hard, hard-hearted, harsh, heartless, implacable, inexorable, inhuman, merciless, relentless, ruthless, sadistic, uncaring, unfeeling, unmerciful, unsympathetic; ***opp*** merciful

pittance *n* chicken-feed *inf*, drop, mite, peanuts *inf*, scrap, trifle

pity *n* **1** charity, clemency, commiseration, compassion, compunction, condolence, fellow-feeling, forbearance, kindness, mercy, quarter, sympathy, tenderness, understanding. **2** (a pity) bad luck, crime *inf*, crying shame *inf*, misfortune, shame

pity *v* commiserate, feel for, feel sorry for, show compassion, show mercy, sympathize, weep for; ***opp*** envy

pivot *n* **1** axis, axle, fulcrum, hinge, pin, spindle, swivel. **2** center, focus, heart, hub

pivot *v* revolve, rotate, swing, swivel, turn

placard *n* advertisement, bill, notice, poster, sign

placate *v* appease, assuage, calm, conciliate, humor, mollify, pacify, propitiate, satisfy, soothe

place *n* **1** area, location, point, position, scene, setting, site, situation, spot, station, venue, whereabouts. **2** city, country, county, district, locale, locality, neighborhood, quarter, region, state, town, vicinity, village. **3** (sb's home) abode, apartment, domicile, dwelling, house, flat, property, residence, rooms. **4** (second place in a race) grade, position, rank, role, standing, station, status. **5** (a job) employment, job, office, position, post, situation

place *v* **1** deposit, dump *inf*, lay, leave, locate, plant, position, put, rest, settle, situate, stand, station, stick *inf*. **2** arrange, categorize, class, classify, grade, group, order, put in order, rank, sort

placid *adj* calm, collected, composed, cool, easy-going, equable, even-tempered, gentle, imperturbable, mild, peaceful, phlegmatic, quiet, serene, steady, still, tranquil, unexcitable, unruffled; ***opp*** excitable

plagiarize *v* copy, crib *inf*, lift *inf*, pirate, reproduce, steal

plague *n* **1** disease, epidemic, infection, outbreak, pestilence. **2** affliction, bane, blight, blot, calamity, cancer, curse, evil, scourge, torment, trial

plague *v* afflict, annoy, badger, bedevil, bother, bug *inf*, disturb, harass, hassle *inf*, hound, molest, nag, persecute, pester, tease, torment, torture, trouble, vex

plain *adj* **1** apparent, audible, clear, comprehensible, distinct, evident, legible, lucid, manifest, obvious, patent, transparent, unambiguous, unmistakable, visible. **2** average, common, commonplace, everyday, homely, lowly, modest, ordinary, simple, typical, unaffected, unpretentious; ***opp*** sophisticated. **3** austere, bare, basic, discreet, modest, muted, pure, restrained, severe, simple, stark, unadorned, spartan; ***opp*** decorated, fancy. **4** (of sb's appearance) ordinary-looking, ugly, unattractive, unprepossessing; ***opp*** pretty. **5** artless, bluff, blunt, candid, frank, guileless, honest, open, outspoken, straightforward, unvarnished, upfront *inf*

plain *n* flatland, grassland, lowland, pampas, plateau, prairie, savannah, steppe, veld

plain-spoken *adj* artless, bluff, blunt, candid, direct, explicit, forthright, frank, guileless, honest, open, outspoken, straightforward, unvarnished, upfront *inf*; ***opp*** indirect

plaintive *adj* doleful, melancholy, mournful, pathetic, piteous, pitiful, plangent, rueful, sad, sorrowful, unhappy, wistful, woebegone, woeful; ***opp*** cheerful

plan *n* **1** aim, course, design, device, formula, idea, intention, method, plot, policy, procedure, program, project, proposal, proposition, scenario, scheme, strategy, suggestion, system. **2** bird's-eye view, blueprint, chart, diagram, drawing, layout, map, representation, sketch

plan *v* **1** arrange, concoct, contrive, design, devise, draft, draw up, formulate, map out, mastermind, organize, outline, plot, prepare, project, scheme, think up, work out. **2** aim, contemplate, envisage, foresee, intend, mean, propose, purpose, think of

plane *adj* even, flat, flush, horizontal, level, regular, smooth, uniform

plane *n* **1** flat surface, level, surface. **2** degree, footing, level, position, rank, stratum. **3** aeroplane, aircraft, airplane, jet, jumbo

planet *n* globe, orb, satellite, sphere, world

plant *n* **1** bush, flower, greenery, herb, shrub, vegetable, weed. **2** factory, foundry, mill, shop, works, workshop, yard. **3** apparatus, equipment, gear, machinery, machines, tools

plant *v* **1** implant, scatter, seed, sow, transplant. **2** locate, place, put, set, situate, station

plaster *n* **1** gypsum, mortar, plasterwork, stucco. **2** bandage, dressing, sticking-plaster

plaster *v* coat, cover, daub, overlay, smear, spread

plastic *adj* ductile, flexible, malleable, pliable, pliant, soft, supple, workable; ***opp*** rigid

plate *n* **1** dish, platter, salver. **2** illustration, lithograph, photo, photograph, picture, print

platform *n* **1** dais, podium, rostrum, stage, stand. **2** manifesto, objectives, plan, policy, program, proposals

platitude *n* banality, cliché, commonplace, stock phrase, truism

plausible *adj* believable, conceivable, credible, imaginable, likely, logical, persuasive, possible, probable, rational, reasonable, sensible, tenable; ***opp*** implausible

play *n* **1** comedy, drama, performance, piece, show, tragedy. **2** amusement, diversion, entertainment, frivolity, frolics, fun, games, horse-play, leisure, merry-making, playing, recreation, revelry, sport

play *v* **1** amuse yourself, caper, cavort, enjoy yourself, frisk, frolic, have a good time, have fun, gambol, romp, sport, trifle. **2** (in a game, match) compete, join in, participate, take part. **3** (play a character) act, impersonate, perform, play the part of, portray, represent, take the part of. **4 play down** belittle, downplay, gloss over, make light of, make little of, minimize, underplay, underrate, understate. **5 play on** abuse, capitalize on, exploit, impose on, make the most of, profit by, take advantage of, trade on. **6 play up** accentuate, emphasize, exaggerate, highlight, overstate, spotlight, stress, talk up, underline

playboy *n* hedonist, ladies' man, man-about-town, philanderer, pleasure-seeker, rake, roué, socialite, sybarite, womanizer

player *n* 1 competitor, contestant, participant, sportsman, sportswoman, team member. 2 (theater) actor, actress, artiste, entertainer, performer, thespian, trouper. 3 (music) artist, artiste, instrumentalist, musician, performer, soloist, virtuoso

playful *adj* cheerful, frisky, frolicsome, fun-loving, high-spirited, humorous, impish, jokey, kittenish, light-hearted, lively, merry, mischievous, puckish, roguish, spirited, sportive, sprightly, teasing, vivacious; ***opp*** serious

plea *n* 1 appeal, entreaty, petition, prayer, request, suit, supplication. 2 argument, claim, excuse, explanation, justification

plead *v* 1 appeal, beg, beseech, entreat, implore, petition, pray, solicit, supplicate. 2 allege, argue, assert, claim, declare, maintain, put forward, reason

pleasant *adj* 1 agreeable, amusing, delightful, enjoyable, fine, good, gratifying, lovely, nice, pleasing, pleasurable, satisfying, welcome; ***opp*** unpleasant. 2 (of a person) affable, agreeable, amiable, charming, cheerful, congenial, engaging, friendly, genial, good-humoured, likable, nice, sympathetic, winning; ***opp*** unpleasant

pleasantry *n* badinage, banter, greeting, jest, joke, quip, remark

please *v* 1 amuse, appeal, charm, cheer, content, delight, divert, entertain, give pleasure, gladden, gratify, indulge, make happy, satisfy, suit, tickle *inf*; ***opp*** displease. 2 (do as you please) choose, desire, like, prefer, see fit, want, will, wish

pleased *adj* charmed, content, contented, delighted, elated, euphoric, glad, gratified, happy, satisfied, thrilled, tickled *inf*; ***opp*** annoyed, unhappy

pleasing *adj* agreeable, amusing, attractive, beautiful, charming, delightful, enjoyable, fine, good, gratifying, lovely, nice, pleasant, pleasurable, satisfying

pleasure *n* amusement, bliss, comfort, contentment, delectation, delight, diversion, enjoyment, entertainment, ecstasy, euphoria, fulfillment, gratification, happiness, joy, recreation, satisfaction

pledge *n* 1 assurance, covenant, oath, promise, undertaking, vow, warrant, word. 2 bail, bond, collateral, deposit, gage, guarantee, security, surety

pledge *v* commit yourself, contract, covenant, give your word, guarantee, promise, swear, undertake, vouchsafe, vow, warrant

plentiful *adj* abounding, abundant, bounteous, bountiful, copious, generous, inexhaustible, lavish, liberal, overflowing, plenteous, profuse; ***opp*** rare

plenty *n* 1 abundance, loads *inf*, lots *inf*, masses *inf*, mountains, plethora, profusion, quantity, stacks *inf*, sufficiency, tons *inf*, wealth. 2 abundance, affluence, bounty, fruitfulness, luxury, opulence, plenitude, prosperity, wealth; ***opp*** scarcity

pliable *adj* **1** bendable, ductile, elastic, flexible, malleable, plastic, pliant, soft, stretchable, supple, workable; ***opp*** rigid. **2** (of a person) amenable, compliant, docile, flexible, impressionable, manageable, pliant, receptive, tractable, yielding; ***opp*** stubborn

plight *n* case, condition, difficulty, dilemma, hot water *inf*, jam *inf*, pickle *inf*, problem, predicament, scrape *inf*, situation, spot *inf*, state, straits, trouble

plod *v* clump, drag, lumber, plough, slog, stomp, tramp, tread, trudge

plot *n* **1** cabal, conspiracy, intrigue, machination, plan, scheme, stratagem. **2** (of a story) action, narrative, outline, scenario, story, story-line, thread. **3** (plot of land) acreage, allotment, garden, lot, parcel, patch, smallholding, tract

plot *v* **1** collude, conspire, cook up *inf*, devise, hatch, intrigue, maneuver, plan, scheme. **2** calculate, chart, compute, draft, draw, locate, map, mark, outline, record, sketch

plow *v* cultivate, dig, furrow, ridge, till, turn over, work

pluck *v* clutch, grab, grasp, jerk, pull, seize, snatch, tug, tweak, yank

plug *n* **1** bung, cork, seal, spigot, stopper. **2** advertisement, hype *inf*, mention, promotion, publicity, push

plug *v* **1** block, bung, close, cork, seal, stop, stopper, stuff. **2** advertise, hype *inf*, mention, promote, publicize, push

plume *n* feather, plumage, quill

plump *adj* ample, buxom, chubby, corpulent, dumpy, fat, fleshy, full, obese, portly, pudgy, roly-poly, rotund, round, stout, tubby; ***opp*** thin

plunder *n* **1** booty, contraband, ill-gotten gains, loot, pickings, prize, spoils, stolen goods, swag *inf*. **2** looting, marauding, pillage, plundering, raiding, ransacking, rifling, robbery, robbing, sack

plunder *v* despoil, lay waste, loot, pillage, raid, ransack, ravage, rifle, rob, sack, spoil, steal, strip

plunge *v* **1** descend, dip, dive, drop, fall, hurtle, nosedive, plummet, pitch, sink, swoop, tumble. **2** dip, douse, immerse, sink, submerge, thrust

ply *v* carry on, engage in, exercise, follow, practice, pursue, work at

poach *v* filch *inf*, lift *inf*, make off with *inf*, nick *inf*, pinch *inf*, plagiarize, plunder, rob, steal, swipe *inf*, thieve

pocket *n* bag, compartment, hollow, pouch, receptacle, sack

pocket *v* appropriate, filch *inf*, nick *inf*, pinch *inf*, steal, take, walk off with

pod *n* case, hull, husk, shell

poem *n* ditty *inf*, haiku, limerick, lyric, ode, rhyme, song, sonnet, verse

poet *n* bard, lyricist, rhymer, sonneteer, versifier

poetic *adj* flowery, imaginative, lyric, lyrical, musical, rhythmical

poetry *n* poems, rhymes, rhyming, verse

poignant *adj* affecting, bitter, distressing, emotional, evocative, heartbreaking, intense, moving, painful, pathetic, pitiful, sad, sentimental, tender, touching, tragic, upsetting

point *n* **1** (meet at a certain point) location, place, position, site, spot. **2** (a sharp point) apex, end, nib, prong, sharp end, spike, spur, tine, tip, top.

3 (point in time) instant, juncture, moment, second, stage, time. 4 (the point of doing sth) aim, goal, intention, motive, purpose, reason, use. 5 (the point of what sb is saying) crux, drift, essence, gist, meaning, relevance, significance, theme, thrust. 6 (sb's good points) attribute, characteristic, facet, feature, quality, trait

point *v* 1 (point sth at sb) aim, direct, level, train. 2 (point at sth) call attention to, draw attention to, indicate, point out, show, signal. 3 (point sb in the right direction) guide, lead, steer

pointed *adj* barbed, edged, sharp, spiky

pointer *n* 1 arrow, hand, indicator, needle. 2 advice, hint, recommendation, suggestion, tip, warning

pointless *adj* aimless, fruitless, futile, ineffective, in vain, irrelevant, meaningless, senseless, silly, stupid, unproductive, useless, worthless; ***opp*** useful

poise *n* aplomb, assurance, calmness, composure, cool, coolness, dignity, equanimity, sang-froid, self-assurance, self-possession

poised *adj* 1 calm, collected, composed, dignified, self-confident, self-possessed, unflappable *inf*. 2 balanced, hovering, in equilibrium, steady, teetering, wavering. 3 (poised for sth) all set, keyed up, prepared, ready, standing by, waiting

poison *n* toxin, venom

poison *v* 1 (poison sth) adulterate, blight, contaminate, infect, pollute, spoil. 2 (poison sb) give poison to, kill, murder. 3 (poison sb's mind) corrupt, deprave, pervert, subvert, warp

poisonous *adj* deadly, fatal, lethal, noxious, toxic, venomous, virulent

poke *v* dig, elbow, hit, jab, nudge, prod, punch, push, stab, stick, thrust

poky *adj* confined, cramped, narrow, small, tiny; ***opp*** spacious

pole *n* bar, column, mast, post, prop, rod, shaft, spar, stake, stick, upright

polarize *v* diverge, divide, separate, split

police *n* constabulary, police force, the fuzz *inf*, the law *inf*

police *v* control, guard, keep in order, oversee, patrol, protect, regulate, supervise, watch over

policeman *n* cop *inf*, copper *inf*, detective, inspector, officer, policeman, policewoman

policy *n* approach, code, course, guidelines, line *inf*, manifesto, plan, practice, procedure, program, protocol, rules, scheme, strategy, theory

polish *n* 1 brightness, brilliance, finish, glaze, gleam, gloss, luster, sheen, shine, sparkle, veneer. 2 beeswax, oil, shellac, varnish, wax. 3 (sb has polish) class *inf*, elegance, grace, refinement, sophistication, style

polish *v* brighten, buff, burnish, clean, rub, shine, smooth, wax

polished *adj* 1 (a polished surface) bright, gleaming, glossy, lustrous, shining, shiny, slippery, smooth. 2 (polished manners) civilized, classy *inf*, cultivated, elegant, polite, posh, refined, sophisticated, well-bred; ***opp*** rough. 3 (a polished performance) accomplished, expert, flawless, impeccable, masterly, perfect, proficient, skillful; ***opp*** bad, poor

polite *adj* **1** (of a person) attentive, chivalrous, civil, considerate, courteous, gracious, respectful, thoughtful, well-behaved, well-mannered, well-spoken; ***opp*** rude. **2** diplomatic, discreet, euphemistic, formal, proper, tactful

political *adj* administrative, civic, diplomatic, governmental, legislative, parliamentary, public, state

politician *n* congressman, legislator, senator, statesman

politics *n* affairs of state, civics, diplomacy, government, political science, public affairs, statesmanship

poll *n* **1** ballot, count, election, referendum, vote, voting. **2** canvass, census, market research, sampling, show of hands, survey

poll *v* ballot, canvass, interview, question, sample, survey

pollute *v* adulterate, contaminate, dirty, foul, infect, make dirty, poison, soil, spoil, stain, taint

pollution *n* adulteration, contamination, dirt, dirtiness, filth, filthiness

pomp *n* ceremony, display, glitter, glory, grandeur, magnificence, majesty, ostentation, pageantry, ritual, spectacle, splendor, show

pompous *adj* affected, arrogant, boastful, bombastic, conceited, grandiose, imperious, inflated, ostentatious, overbearing, pretentious, self-important, showy, smug, snooty *inf*, stuck-up *inf*, vain; ***opp*** modest

pond *n* lake, millpond, pool, puddle, tarn

ponder *v* brood, consider, contemplate, deliberate, meditate, mull over, muse, reflect, ruminate, study, think

ponderous *adj* **1** awkward, bulky, cumbersome, heavy, huge, massive, slow, unwieldy; ***opp*** light. **2** (a ponderous speech) boring, dreary, dull, humorless, labored, long-winded, plodding, slow, tedious, tiresome

pool *n* lagoon, lake, oasis, paddling pool, pond, puddle, swimming pool, tarn

pool *v* amalgamate, combine, merge, put together, share

poor *adj* **1** (of a person) badly off, broke *inf*, deprived, destitute, hard up *inf*, impoverished, needy, penniless, poverty-stricken, skint *inf*; ***opp*** rich. **2** (a poor amount) deficient, inadequate, insufficient, meager, miserable, reduced, scanty, sparse. **3** (poor quality) bad, cheap, defective, faulty, imperfect, inferior, rubbishy, shoddy, substandard; ***opp*** good. **4** (unlucky) ill-fated, luckless, miserable, pathetic, pitiable, unfortunate, unhappy, unlucky, wretched; ***opp*** lucky. **5** (a poor home) humble, lowly, mean, modest, simple. **6** (poor soil) arid, bare, barren, depleted, infertile, unproductive; ***opp*** rich

pop *v* bang, burst, crack, detonate, explode, go off, snap

populace *n* crowd, general public, masses, mob, multitude, people, public, rabble

popular *adj* **1** (liked by many people) accepted, approved, celebrated, famous, fashionable, favorite, in, in demand, liked, sought-after, well-known, well-liked; ***opp*** unpopular. **2** (believed by many people) common, conventional, current, general, predominant, prevailing, standard, universal, widespread

popularity *n* acceptance, acclaim, approval, currency, demand, fame, favor, renown, vogue

popularize *v* give credence to, give currency to, make accessible, make available, make popular, promote, spread

populate *v* colonize, dwell in, fill, inhabit, live in, occupy, overrun, people, settle

population *n* citizens, community, folk, inhabitants, people, populace, public, residents, society

populous *adj* crowded, densely populated, heavily populated, overpopulated, packed

porch *n* doorway, entrance, lobby, vestibule

pore over *v* **1** (pore over a book) examine, peruse, read, scrutinize, study. **2** (pore over a question) brood on, contemplate, dwell on, go over, meditate on, mull over, muse on, ponder, reflect on, think about

pornographic *adj* blue, dirty, erotic, explicit, filthy, indecent, obscene, porn *inf*, sexual, titillating

porous *adj* absorbent, cellular, penetrable, permeable, spongelike, spongy

port *n* dock, harbor, haven, seaport

portable *adj* compact, convenient, easy to carry, handy, light, lightweight, manageable, mobile, movable, pocket, pocket-sized, small, transportable

porter *n* caretaker, concierge, doorkeeper, doorman, gatekeeper, janitor, security-guard, watchman

portion *n* **1** bit, chunk, helping, piece, section, segment, serving, slice, sliver, wedge. **2** (sb's portion) allocation, allowance, cut *inf*, measure, percentage, quantity, quota, ration, share, whack *inf*

portrait *n* drawing, image, likeness, painting, photograph, picture, portrayal, representation, self-portrait, study

portray *v* **1** delineate, depict, draw, illustrate, paint, render, represent, sketch. **2** characterize, depict, describe, represent, show

pose *n* **1** attitude, bearing, position, posture, stance. **2** act, affectation, facade, front, masquerade, posture, pretense, role

pose *v* **1** (pose for your picture) model, sit, strike a pose. **2** act, be a poser *inf*, put on airs, put on an act, show off. **3** (pose a question) ask, put, submit, suggest. **4** (pose a problem) cause, create, present

poseur *n* fraud, poser *inf*, posturer, show-off

posh *adj* **1** (of a person) aristocratic, genteel, rich, snobbish, stuck-up *inf*, upper-class; ***opp*** common. **2** (of a restaurant, shop) classy *inf*, elegant, expensive, fancy, fashionable, swanky *inf*, swish *inf*, up-market *inf*, upscale *inf*; ***opp*** cheap

position *n* **1** (position on a map) bearings, location, reference, whereabouts. **2** (a house in a good position) area, locale, location, place, setting, site, situation, spot. **3** (a comfortable position for driving) angle, pose, posture, stance, way of sitting. **4** (put sb in an awkward position) plight, predicament, situation, state.

5 (opinion) attitude, belief, opinion, point of view, stance, view. 6 (position in society) caste, class, importance, place, rank, station, status. 7 (applying for a position in the company) job, post, situation. 8 (position in a league) grade, level, place, rank

position *v* arrange, array, lay out, locate, place, put, set, site, situate, stand, station

positive *adj* 1 absolute, actual, affirmative, categorical, certain, clear, clear-cut, decided, definite, emphatic, firm, incontrovertible, indisputable, real, undeniable, unmistakable. 2 certain, confident, convinced, sure; ***opp*** doubtful. 3 (some positive advice) constructive, helpful, practical, productive, useful, worthwhile; ***opp*** unhelpful. 4 (a positive approach) confident, hopeful, idealistic, optimistic; ***opp*** negative

possess *v* 1 be the owner of, enjoy, have, hold, own. 2 (possess a sense of humor) be blessed with, be endowed with, have. 3 (take by force) acquire, invade, occupy, seize, take over, take possession of. 4 (possess sb's mind) bewitch, captivate, cast a spell over, charm, control, dominate, enchant, enthrall, haunt, hypnotize, influence, obsess

possessions *n* assets, belongings, effects, property, things, worldly goods

possessive *adj* 1 clinging, controlling, dominating, domineering, jealous, overprotective, proprietorial, protective. 2 acquisitive, covetous, grasping, greedy, selfish; ***opp*** generous

possibility *n* chance, danger, likelihood, odds, potential, probability, prospect, risk

possible *adj* able to be done, attainable, conceivable, credible, feasible, imaginable, likely, plausible, potential, practicable, probable, realizable, reasonable, viable, within reach; ***opp*** impossible

possibly *adv* God willing, hopefully *inf*, if possible, maybe, perhaps

post *n* 1 (wooden post) column, pillar, pole, shaft, stake, support, upright. 2 (job) appointment, job, position, situation, vacancy. 3 (catch the mail) collection, delivery, mail, postal service. 4 (deal with your mail) correspondence, letters, mail

post *v* dispatch, mail, send, transmit

poster *n* advertisement, flyer, notice, placard, sign

posterity *n* 1 future, future generations. 2 children, descendants, offspring, heirs, successors

postpone *v* adjourn, defer, delay, hold over, put back, put off, put on ice *inf*, put on the back burner *inf*, shelve, suspend

postscript *n* addition, afterthought, appendix, codicil, PS

postulate *v* advance, assume, hypothesize, posit, propose, suppose

posture *n* attitude, bearing, carriage, deportment, pose, stance

pot *n* bowl, cauldron, container, dish, jar, pan, urn, vessel

potent *adj* effective, forceful, influential, mighty, overwhelming, powerful, strong, vigorous; ***opp*** weak

potential *adj* budding, developing,

embryonic, future, likely, possible, promising, would-be *inf*

potion *n* brew, concoction, dose, draft, drink, drug, elixir, liquid, mixture

potter *v* **1** (potter in the garden) dabble, do odd jobs, fiddle, mess about, tinker. **2** (potter along) dawdle, dilly-dally, move slowly

pottery *n* ceramics, china, crockery, earthenware, porcelain, stoneware, terracotta

pouch *n* bag, pocket, purse, sack, wallet

pounce *v* ambush, attack, drop, jump, lunge, snatch, spring, strike, swoop, take sb by surprise

pound *n* compound, corral, enclosure, pen, yard

pound *v* **1** batter, beat, knead, press, pummel, thump. **2** crush, grind, mash, powder, pulverize, smash. **3** (pounding along) clump, stamp, stomp, tramp. **4** (heart began to pound) bang, beat heavily, bump, palpitate, pulse, throb, thump

pour *v* **1** (liquid pouring) cascade, course, flood, flow, gush, jet, run, rush, spew, spill, splash, spout, spurt, stream. **2** (rain)rain hard, teem. **3** (pour the wine) decant, serve

poverty *n* destitution, distress, hardship, insolvency, need, penury, want; ***opp*** wealth

powder *n* dust, fine particles, talc

powder *v* crush, granulate, grind, pound, pulverize

power *n* **1** drive, energy, force, might, muscle, potency, powerfulness, strength, vigor. **2** (the power to do sth) ability, capability, competence, potential. **3** (power over sb) ascendancy, authority, clout *inf*, command, control, dominance, domination, influence, mastery, rule, sovereignty, supremacy, sway. **4** (power to grant sth) authority, authorization, license, prerogative, right

powerful *adj* **1** mighty, robust, strapping, strong, sturdy, tough; ***opp*** weak. **2** (a powerful ruler) authoritative, commanding, dominant, invincible, mighty, omnipotent, sovereign, strong, supreme; ***opp*** weak. **3** (a powerful argument) compelling, convincing, effective, eloquent, forceful, persuasive, telling; ***opp*** weak

powerless *adj* debilitated, defenseless, dependent, disabled, feeble, frail, helpless, impotent, incapable, incapacitated, ineffectual, paralyzed, unable, unarmed, vulnerable, weak; ***opp*** strong

practicable *adj* achievable, attainable, doable *inf*, feasible, possible, realistic, sensible, viable, workable; ***opp*** impracticable

practical *adj* **1** (a practical person) capable, competent, efficient, expert, hands-on, no-nonsense *inf*, practiced, proficient, skilled, trained. **2** (be practical about sth) businesslike, down-to-earth, hard-headed, hard-nosed *inf*, matter-of-fact, pragmatic, realistic, sensible. **3** (practical shoes) functional, sensible, utilitarian

practice *n* **1** drill, exercise, preparation, rehearsal, repetition, study, training. **2** (it's only a practice) rehearsal, run-through *inf*. **3** (a common practice) custom, habit, tradition, way.

4 (standard practice) method, procedure, tradition. 5 (put sth into practice) action, effect, operation

practice *v* 1 drill, exercise, go over, go through, polish, prepare, refine, rehearse, repeat, run through, study, train, warm up, work out. 2 (practice a religion) follow, observe

pragmatic *adj* businesslike, efficient, matter-of-fact, practical, realistic, sensible

praise *n* 1 acclaim, accolades, applause, approval, commendation, compliments, congratulations, ovation, thanks, tributes. 2 (praise of God) adoration, devotion, exaltation, glory, worship

praise *v* 1 (praise sb) acclaim, admire, applaud, cheer, clap, commend, compliment, congratulate, pay tribute to, rave about *inf*; ***opp*** criticize. 2 (praise God) adore, exalt, glorify, honor, offer praise to, worship

praiseworthy *adj* admirable, commendable, creditable, deserving, excellent, good, laudable

prance *v* bound, caper, cavort, dance, frisk, gambol, jump, leap, play, romp, skip

prank *n* jape, practical joke, stunt, trick

prattle *v* chatter, gabble, jabber, twitter, waffle *inf*

pray *v* 1 ask, beg, beseech, entreat, implore, petition, plead, request, urge. 2 (pray to God) commune with God, offer a prayer, say your prayers

prayer *n* communion, devotion, litany

preach *v* 1 evangelize, give a sermon, spread the gospel, teach. 2 advise, exhort, give advice, harangue, lay down the law, lecture, pontificate, urge

preacher *n* clergyman, cleric, evangelist, minister, missionary, parson, pastor, televangelist

preamble *n* foreword, introduction, opening remarks, overture, preface, prelude

precarious *adj* dangerous, dicey, dodgy *inf*, doubtful, dubious, hairy *inf*, hazardous, insecure, perilous, risky, treacherous, uncertain, unreliable, unsafe, unstable, unsure, vulnerable, wobbly; ***opp*** safe

precaution *n* 1 anticipation, care, caution, foresight, forethought, prudence, wariness. 2 preventive measure, protection, provision, safeguard, safety measure

precede *v* be in front, come before, come first, go ahead, go before, go in front, head, herald, introduce, lead, lead into, lead up to, preface, start, usher in

precedent *n* criterion, example, instance, model, patter, prototype, standard, yardstick

precious *adj* 1 (his precious baby) adored, beloved, cherished, darling, dear, favorite, irreplaceable, loved, treasured. 2 (precious stones) invaluable, priceless, prized, rare, valuable

precipice *n* bluff, brink, cliff, cliff face, crag, drop, escarpment, height, rock face

precipitate *adj* 1 abrupt, breakneck, brief, headlong, hurried, plunging, rapid, speedy, sudden, swift, unexpected, violent. 2 hasty, heedless, hurried, impetuous, impulsive, rash, reckless

precipitate *v* accelerate, advance, bring on, encourage, expedite, further, hasten, hurry, quicken, spark off, speed up, trigger

precise *adj* **1** accurate, clear, exact, explicit, specific, unambiguous. **2** (the precise meaning) actual, correct, faithful, literal, right, strict. **3** (at a precise time) definite, exact, fixed, particular, specific. **4** (precise movements) accurate, careful, exact, meticulous, scrupulous

preclude *v* debar, exclude, forestall, make impossible, prevent, prohibit, rule out, stop, thwart

precocious *adj* advanced, ahead, bright, developed, forward, gifted, intelligent, mature, quick

preconception *n* assumption, bias, expectation, notion, preconceived idea, prejudice, presumption

precursor *n* forerunner, harbinger, herald, predecessor

predatory *adj* hunting, marauding, pillaging, plundering, preying, rapacious, voracious

predecessor *n* ancestor, antecedent, forebear, forefather, forerunner, precursor

predetermined *adj* agreed, fixed, prearranged, set, settled

predicament *n* corner, crisis, difficult situation, dilemma, emergency, fix *inf*, hole *inf*, mess, pickle *inf*, plight, quandary, scrape *inf*, tight spot *inf*

predict *v* augur, divine, forebode, forecast, foresee, foreshadow, foretell, portend, presage, prophesy

predictable *adj* anticipated, certain, expected, foreseeable, foreseen, in the cards *inf*, likely, reliable, sure, unsurprising; ***opp*** unpredictable

prediction *n* forecast, prognosis, prophecy

predominant *adj* **1** ascendant, controlling, dominant, in control, leading, most powerful, principal, ruling, superior. **2** chief, main, most obvious, most noticeable, prevailing

predominate *v* be dominant, be in the majority, be most noticeable, be predominant, carry weight, have the upper hand, hold sway, outnumber, outweigh, overrule, prevail, rule

preeminent *adj* distinguished, excellent, famous, foremost, important, incomparable, outstanding, prominent, renowned, superior, unrivaled, unsurpassed

preempt *v* **1** acquire, appropriate, assume, commandeer, seize, take over, usurp. **2** anticipate, forestall, prevent

preen *v* **1** (of animals) arrange, clean, plume, smooth. **2** (of people) array, beautify, deck out, doll up *inf*, dress up, groom, prettify, primp, spruce up, titivate

preface *n* foreword, introduction, preamble, prelude, prologue

preface *v* begin, introduce, launch, lead into, open, precede, prefix, start

prefer *v* be partial to, choose, desire, elect, fancy, favor, go for *inf*, incline towards, like, like better, opt for, pick, select, vote for, want, wish

preferable *adj* advantageous, best, better, chosen, favored, more desirable, more suitable, nicer, preferred, superior, wanted

preference *n* 1 choice, desire, favorite, first choice, option, pick, selection, wish. 2 advantage, favoritism, partiality, precedence, preferential treatment, priority

preferential *adj* advantageous, better, biased, favorable, favored, partial, privileged, special, superior

pregnant *adj* carrying a child, expecting *inf*, having a baby, with child

prejudge *v* anticipate, presume, presuppose

prejudice *n* 1 agism, bigotry, chauvinism, discrimination, favoritism, intolerance, jingoism, narrow-mindedness, racism, sexism, unfairness, xenophobia. 2 bias, leaning, partiality, preconceived idea

prejudice *v* 1 (make sb prejudiced) bias, color, distort, influence, interfere with, jaundice, poison, predispose, slant, sway, warp. 2 (prejudice your case) be disadvantageous, be prejudicial, damage, harm, hurt, spoil, undermine

prejudiced *adj* biased, bigoted, discriminatory, intolerant, narrow-minded, unfair, unjust; ***opp*** impartial

prejudicial *adj* damaging, deleterious, detrimental, harmful, unfavorable

preliminary *adj* 1 first, initial, introductory, opening, prefatory, preparatory, prior. 2 early, experimental, exploratory, pilot, qualifying, tentative, test, trial

prelude *n* 1 introduction, introductory movement, overture, preface, prologue. 2 beginning, curtain-raiser *inf*, herald, precursor, start, warm-up *inf*

premature *adj* 1 early, immature, incomplete, raw, too early, too soon, undeveloped, unripe, untimely. 2 hasty, ill-considered, impulsive, rash

premeditated *adj* calculated, considered, deliberate, intended, intentional, planned, willful; ***opp*** spontaneous

premise *n* argument, assertion, assumption, basis, grounds, hypothesis, supposition

premises *n* building, establishment, place, property, site

premium *n* bonus, fee, payment, prize, remuneration, reward, surcharge

premonition *n* 1 apprehension, fear, feeling, foreboding, funny feeling, hunch *inf*, idea, intuition, misgiving, presentiment, suspicion. 2 indication, omen, portent, sign, warning

preoccupied *adj* absentminded, absorbed, distracted, engrossed, far-away, immersed, intent, lost in thought, oblivious, pensive, rapt, taken up, thoughtful, unaware

preparation *n* 1 arrangements, briefing, development, gearing up *inf*, getting ready, groundwork, making ready, making provision, organization, plans, practice, preparing, setting up, spadework, training. 2 (preparation for an exam) coaching, reading, revising, revision, study, studying, working

preparatory *adj* introductory, opening, prefatory, preliminary

prepare *v* 1 (prepare sth) arrange, assemble, draw up, get ready, make ready, put together. 2 (prepare to do sth) brace yourself, exercise, gear up *inf*, make preparations, plan, practice, psych yourself up *inf*, steel yourself, take steps, train, warm up. **3** (prepare for an exam) cram *inf*, practice, revise, study. **4** (prepare sb for sth) brief, coach, drill, educate, equip, groom, rehearse, teach, train, tutor. **5** (prepare a meal) cook, fix *inf*, get ready, make, put together

prepared *adj* **1** (prepared to do sth) able, disposed, inclined, minded, of a mind, predisposed, ready, willing. **2** (everything was prepared) arranged, in order, in readiness, ready, set

preposterous *adj* absurd, bizarre, crazy, excessive, impossible, incredible, ludicrous, monstrous, out of the question, outrageous, ridiculous, shocking, unbelievable, unthinkable

prerequisite *n* condition, must *inf*, necessity, precondition, qualification, requirement

prescribe *v* advise, commend, decree, direct, impose, instruct, lay down, order, recommend, specify, stipulate, suggest

presence *n* **1** (your presence is required) attendance, company. **2** (aware of sb's presence) closeness, nearness, proximity. **3** (sb has presence) charisma, magnetism, personality, poise, self-assurance, self-confidence, self-possession

present *adj* **1** contemporary, current, existing, immediate, instant, present-day, up-to-date. **2** accounted for, at hand, available, here, in attendance, nearby, ready, there, to hand

present *n* **1** (the present) here and now, now, the time being, today. **2** (a present) contribution, donation, gift, offering

present *v* **1** (present sb to people) announce, introduce, make known. **2** (present a gift) award, bestow, confer, donate, give, hand over, offer. **3** (present a proposal) advance, put forward, set forth, submit, suggest, tender. **4** (present a different side of your character) demonstrate, display, exhibit, reveal, show. **5** (present a TV show) host, introduce. **6** (present a show) act, give, mount, perform, put on, stage

presentable *adj* acceptable, all right, becoming, decent, fit to be seen, good enough, okay *inf*, passable, respectable, suitable, tidy, up to scratch *inf*, well-groomed

presentation *n* demonstration, display, exhibition, launch, performance, production, show

preserve *v* **1** care for, conserve, defend, guard, keep, look after, maintain, perpetuate, protect, safeguard, save, secure, uphold. **2** (preserve food) bottle, can, cure, dry, freeze, pickle, salt, smoke

preside *v* administer, be in charge, chair, conduct, control, direct, govern, head, lead, manage, officiate, run, take charge, take the chair

press *n* journalism, newspapers, magazines, papers, reporters, the media

press *v* **1** compress, condense, crush, jam, mash, push, reduce, squeeze, stuff. **2** (press sb close) clasp, crush, embrace, enfold, hold, hug, squeeze. **3** (press sb to do sth) ask, beg, compel, constrain, enjoin, entreat, exhort, implore, insist, persuade, put pressure on, urge. **4** (people press into a place) cluster, crowd, flock, gather, push, surge, swarm, throng. **5** (press clothes) flatten, iron, make flat, smooth

pressing *adj* critical, crucial, high priority, imperative, important, serious, urgent, vital; ***opp*** nonurgent, unimportant

pressure *n* **1** compression, crushing, force, heaviness, load, squeezing, stress, weight. **2** (pressure in your job) constraints, demands, difficulties, hassle *inf*, problems, strain, stress, tension. **3** (using pressure to make sb do sth) coercion, compulsion, duress, force, power

prestige *n* cachet, credit, distinction, eminence, esteem, fame, good name, honor, importance, influence, kudos *slang*, reputation, standing, status

prestigious *adj* acclaimed, celebrated, distinguished, eminent, famed, famous, glamorous, highly regarded, high-ranking, illustrious, important, influential, respected, well-known

presume *v* **1** assume, believe, conjecture, guess, imagine, infer, suppose, surmise, take for granted, take it, think. **2** be presumptuous, dare, go so far as, have the effrontery, have the temerity, make bold, take the liberty, venture

presumptuous *adj* arrogant, audacious, bold, cheeky, cocksure, forward, insolent, overconfident, pushy *inf*, too big for your britches *inf*; ***opp*** modest

presuppose *v* assume, imply, presume, suppose, take as read, take for granted

pretend *v* **1** affect, allege, bluff, deceive, dissemble, fake it, falsify, feign, impersonate, make out, pose, put on an act, simulate, trick. **2** (children like to pretend) act, fantasize, imagine, make believe, play, play-act, suppose

pretense *n* **1** act, affectation, appearance, artifice, charade, deceit, deception, dissembling, excuse, facade, falsehood, front, hypocrisy, insincerity, lying, mask, masquerade, pose, posing, posturing, pretext, ruse, sham, show, simulation, trickery, veneer. **2** fantasy, imagination, invention, make-believe, unreality

pretentious *adj* affected, conceited, exaggerated, flamboyant, grandiose, ostentatious, pompous, showy, snobbish, superficial; ***opp*** unpretentious

pretext *n* cover, excuse, lie, ploy, pretense, reason, red herring, ruse, wile

pretty *adj* **1** (of a person) appealing, attractive, beautiful, cute, fair, good-looking, lovely, nice-looking; ***opp*** ugly. **2** (of a place) attractive, charming, delightful, pleasant; ***opp*** ugly; ***opp*** unattractive

prevail *v* be victorious, conquer, overcome, overrule, prove superior, succeed, triumph, win, win out, win through

prevailing *adj* common, current, customary, established, fashionable, general, ordinary, popular, prevalent, usual, widespread

prevalent *adj* accepted, common, commonplace, current, established, extensive, frequent, rampant, rife, ubiquitous, universal, usual, widespread; ***opp*** rare

prevaricate *v* beat about the bush, be evasive, cavil, dodge, equivocate, evade, fence, fib, hedge, lie, quibble, shilly-shally, sidestep

prevent *v* avert, avoid, block, check, curb, deter, fend off, foil, forestall, frustrate, hamper, hinder, impede, nip in the bud, obstruct, put a stop to, restrain, stave off, stop, thwart, ward off; ***opp*** encourage

preventative *adj* deterrent, obstructive, precautionary, preemptive, preventive, protective

previous *adj* earlier, erstwhile, ex-, former, one-time, past, preceding, prior

prey *n* game, kill, quarry, victim

price *n* amount, bill, charge, cost, damage *inf*, estimate, expenditure, expense, fee, figure, offer, outlay, payment, quotation, rate, sum, terms, valuation, value, worth

priceless *adj* **1** costly, dear, expensive, invaluable, irreplaceable, precious, valuable, worth its weight in gold; ***opp*** worthless. **2** (hilarious) a scream *inf*, comic, funny, hilarious, killing *inf*

prick *v* **1** jab, nick, perforate, pierce, puncture, spike, stab. **2** (prickle) hurt, itch, prickle, smart, sting, tickle, tingle

prickle *n* barb, spike, spine, thorn

prickle *v* hurt, itch, prick, smart, sting, tickle, tingle

prickly *adj* **1** (with prickles) brambly, scratchy, sharp, spiky, spiny, thorny, vicious. **2** (of a person or situation) awkward, difficult, irritable, tetchy, thorny, touchy, tricky, waspish

pride *n* **1** dignity, ego, feelings, honor, self-esteem, self-respect. **2** arrogance, big-headedness *inf*, conceit, snobbery, vanity

priest *n* chaplain, clergyman, clergywoman, curate, deacon, ecclesiastic, father, member of the clergy, minister, padre, parson, pastor, priestess, rector, shaman, vicar

priggish *adj* goody-goody *inf*, moralistic, prim, sanctimonious, smug, strait-laced, stuffy *inf*

prim *adj* demure, fastidious, formal, prissy, proper, starchy, strait-laced

primarily *adv* basically, chiefly, essentially, first and foremost, in the main, largely, mainly, mostly, particularly, predominantly, principally

primary *adj* **1** earliest, elementary, first, initial, primitive. **2** chief, essential, foremost, main, most important, paramount, prime, principal

prime *adj* **1** best, choice, class-one, first-class, grade A, leading, superior, top-quality, top. **2** chief, essential, main, most important, paramount, primary, principal

prime *n* best part, height, heyday, peak, zenith

prime *v* brief, coach, get ready, groom, inform, prepare, train

primitive *adj* basic, crude, early, elementary, naive, rough, rudimentary, simple, uncivilized, unsophisticated

prince *n* monarch, ruler, sovereign

principal *adj* chief, first, foremost, fundamental, key, leading, main, major, most important, paramount, prime, top; ***opp*** minor

principal *n* boss *inf*, dean, director, head teacher, head, lead, leader, manager, star, top dog *inf*

principle *n* **1** axiom, canon, creed, doctrine, law, maxim, rule, theory. **2** decency, honor, integrity, morality, morals, probity, scruples, standards

print *n* 1 copy, engraving, etching, painting, photo, photograph, picture, reproduction, woodcut. 2 fingerprint, footprint, impression, indentation, mark. 3 characters, font, lettering, letters, text, type, typeface

print *v* 1 issue, publish, reproduce, run off, send to press, write. 2 engrave, etch, imprint, mark, stamp

priority *n* first place, first thing, main concern, main thing, most important thing, precedence, preference, prerogative

prison *n* 1 cell, cooler *inf*, detention center, dungeon, goal, jail, lock-up, penitentiary, place of detention. 2 confinement, custodial sentence, custody, detention, incarceration

prisoner *n* captive, convict, detainee, hostage, inmate, jailbird *inf*, POW

privacy *n* confidentiality, freedom from interference, isolation, peace and quiet, right to be left alone, seclusion, secrecy, solitude

private *adj* 1 (confidential) closed, confidential, off the record, restricted, secret, top secret, unofficial. 2 (secluded) concealed, hidden, isolated, secluded, solitary, withdrawn. 3 (personal) exclusive, intimate, own, personal, privately owned, secret

privilege *n* advantage, benefit, concession, entitlement, exemption, honor, license, perk *inf*, prerogative, right

privileged *adj* advantaged, elite, exempt, fortunate, immune, lucky, special

prize *adj* best, champion, prize-winning, special, top, winning

prize *n* accolade, award, cup, jackpot, medal, purse, reward, trophy, winnings

prize *v* cherish, idolize, revere, set great store by, treasure, value, worship

probability *n* chance, expectation, likelihood, odds, prospect

probable *adj* anticipated, apparent, expected, in the cards *inf*, likely, odds-on *inf*, plausible, very possible

probably *adv* doubtless, in all likelihood, in all probability, it is likely that, it is to be expected that, presumably

probe *n* examination, exploration, inquiry, investigation, study

probe *v* 1 examine, explore, feel, investigate, poke, prod. 2 check out, examine, investigate, look into, research, search

problem *adj* difficult, intractable, problematic, troublesome, unruly; ***opp*** easy

problem *n* brainteaser, can of worms *inf*, conundrum, difficulty, dilemma, headache *inf*, predicament, puzzle, quandary, snag, trouble

problematic *adj* awkward, complicated, delicate, thorny, tricky; ***opp*** simple

procedure *n* approach, drill, formula, means, method, operation, plan of action, policy, process, routine, step, system, technique, way

proceed *v* begin, carry on, continue, get going *inf*, go ahead, make progress, move on, press on, start; ***opp*** stop

proceedings *n* 1 affairs, business, events, goings-on *inf*, legal action, matters, measures, moves, steps. 2 account, annals, archives, minutes, report, transactions

proceeds *n* earnings, income, profit, receipts, revenue, takings

process *n* action, activity, method, operation, procedure, stages, steps, system, technique, way

process *v* administer, convert, deal with, handle, manufacture, prepare, produce, refine

procession *n* column, convoy, cortège, file, line, march, parade, string, succession

proclaim *v* **1** announce, declare, decree, make known, pronounce, publish. **2** be a sign of, herald, indicate, prove, reveal, show

proclamation *n* announcement, declaration, decree, edict, notice, publication

procrastinate *v* defer, dither, drag your feet, hesitate, play for time, prevaricate, put sth off, stall, vacillate

procure *v* acquire, buy, come by, get hold of, lay your hands on, obtain, pick up, secure, wangle *inf*

prod *v* **1** dig, jab, poke. **2** egg on *inf*, encourage, goad, motivate, rouse, spur, stimulate, urge

prodigal *adj* excessive, extravagant, imprudent, irresponsible, profligate, reckless, wanton, wasteful; ***opp*** careful, thrifty

prodigious *adj* enormous, gigantic, huge, immense, impressive, magnificent, massive, phenomenal, staggering, tremendous, vast

prodigy *n* genius, marvel, phenomenon, sensation, talent, wonder

produce *n* crops, fruit and vegetables, goods, groceries, merchandise, products, stock, stuff

produce *v* **1** (make) compose, construct, create, develop, form, generate, make, manufacture, put together, turn out. **2** (cause) bring about, cause, create, deliver, evoke, generate, give birth to, give rise to, give, initiate, result in, spark off, trigger, yield. **3** (produce information or evidence) disclose, present, provide, put forward, reveal, supply. **4** (produce a play) direct, do, mount, present, put on, stage

producer *n* **1** creator, grower, maker, manufacturer. **2** administrator, backer, director, impresario

product *n* **1** commodity, goods, item, merchandise, produce, wares. **2** by-product, consequence, effect, legacy, outcome, result, upshot

productive *adj* beneficial, effective, efficient, fertile, fruitful, profitable, prolific, rich, useful, worthwhile; ***opp*** fruitless, unproductive

productivity *n* capacity, efficiency, output, production rate, rate of work

profess *v* announce, assert, claim, declare, express, maintain, own, proclaim, state

profession *n* business, career, job, line of work, occupation, trade, vocation, work

professional *adj* **1** businesslike, competent, efficient, excellent, experienced, fine, polished, skillful; ***opp*** incompetent, unprofessional. **2** qualified, white-collar; ***opp*** unskilled. **3** doing sth for a living, paid; ***opp*** amateur

proficient *adj* accomplished, capable, competent, effective, efficient, experienced, expert, good, skillful, skilled, talented

profile *n* 1 outline, shape, side view, silhouette. 2 account, biography, CV, description, outline, portrait, review, sketch, study, summary, vignette

profit *n* 1 bottom line, dividend, earnings, gain, proceeds, receipts, return, revenue, takings, yield. 2 advantage, benefit, gain, good, return, value

profit *v* 1 (sth profits you) be an advantage to, be of use to, benefit, do sb good, help. 2 **profit from** benefit from, cash in on, exploit, use

profitable *adj* 1 cost-effective, lucrative, money-making, money-spinning, rewarding, successful; ***opp*** unprofitable. 2 advantageous, beneficial, constructive, useful, worthwhile; ***opp*** useless, worthless

profiteer *n* extortionist, racketeer, speculator, wheeler-dealer

profligate *adj* 1 excessive, extravagant, wasteful; ***opp*** careful. 2 degenerate, dissolute, immoral, shameless, unprincipled, wild

profound *adj* 1 (intense) deep, great, intense, keen, marked, passionate, sincere, strong. 2 (learned) difficult, erudite, impenetrable, intellectual, learned, scholarly, weighty

profuse *adj* abundant, copious, lavish, luxuriant, plentiful, prolific, unstinting

profusion *n* abundance, glut, loads *inf*, masses, mountain *inf*, plenty, superfluity, surplus, vast quantities, wealth; ***opp*** scarcity

program *n* 1 broadcast, edition, production, series, show, transmission. 2 agenda, bill, curriculum, listing, menu, order of events, order of the day, plan, schedule, scheme, syllabus

program *v* 1 arrange, line up, organize, plan, put together, schedule. 2 (program a video) adjust, set

progress *n* advance, advancement, development, evolution, growth, headway, improvement, movement, progression, step forward

progress *v* advance, come on, develop, get better, get on, forge ahead, improve, make headway, make progress, make strides, move, move forward, proceed

progression *n* 1 (headway) advancement, course, development, headway, progress. 2 (succession) chain, series, stream, string, succession

progressive *adj* advanced, avant-garde, contemporary, enlightened, go-ahead, innovative, liberal, modern, radical, trendy *inf*, up-to-date; ***opp*** old-fashioned

prohibit *v* ban, forbid, make illegal, make impossible, outlaw, preclude, prevent, proscribe, rule out, stop, veto; ***opp*** allow, permit

prohibition *n* ban, banning, embargo, injunction, outlawing, prevention, proscription, restriction

prohibitive *adj* 1 discouraging, preventive, restrictive. 2 (a prohibitive price) excessive, exorbitant, impossible, unreasonable; ***opp*** reasonable

project *n* enterprise, idea, job, operation, plan, program, proposal, scheme, task, undertaking, venture

project *v* 1 (stick out) bulge, extend, jut out, overhang, protrude, stick out. 2 (propel) cast, direct, fire, hurl, launch, propel, shoot, throw out, throw. 3 (forecast) calculate, compute, estimate, extrapolate, forecast, plan, predict

projectile *n* bullet, missile, rocket, shell, shot

projection *n* 1 bulge, ledge, overhang, protrusion, protuberance, shelf. 2 calculation, computation, estimate, extrapolation, forecast, prediction

proliferate *v* escalate, expand, flourish, grow, increase, multiply, mushroom, reproduce, rocket, snowball

prolific *adj* abundant, lush, luxuriant, plentiful, productive, profuse, riotous, vigorous

prolong *v* drag out, extend, lengthen, make longer, spin out, stretch, string out; ***opp*** shorten

prominent *adj* 1 bulging, conspicuous, jutting out, noticeable, obtrusive, protruding, sticking out. 2 distinguished, eminent, foremost, important, leading, main, major, top, well-known

promiscuous *adj* dissolute, fast, free, immoral, loose, sleeping around *inf*, wanton, wild

promise *n* 1 assurance, commitment, guarantee, oath, pledge, undertaking, vow. 2 hint, sign, suggestion. 3 (sb shows promise) ability, flair, potential, talent

promise *v* 1 give your word, guarantee, pledge, swear, undertake, vouch, vow. 2 (show signs of) augur, hint at, indicate, show signs of, suggest

promising *adj* 1 bright, encouraging, favorable, good, hopeful, optimistic, rosy; ***opp*** discouraging. 2 budding, gifted, rising, talented, up-and-coming

promote *v* 1 (encourage) back, boost, encourage, foster, further, nurture, push *inf*, stimulate, support; ***opp*** discourage. 2 (advertise) advertise, champion, endorse, market, plug *inf*, publicize, recommend, sell. 3 (give sb promotion) advance, give sb promotion, upgrade; ***opp*** demote

promotion *n* 1 backing, boost, encouragement, furtherance, nurturing, support. 2 advertising, advertising campaign, hype *inf*, marketing, publicity. 3 advancement, elevation, preferment, upgrading; ***opp*** demotion

prompt *adj* direct, early, immediate, instant, on time, punctual, quick, rapid, speedy, swift, timely; ***opp*** late, slow, sluggish

prompt *n* cue, hint, nudge, prod, reminder

prompt *v* 1 cause, encourage, induce, inspire, make, motivate, move, urge. 2 give sb a cue, help out, jog sb's memory, prod, remind

promulgate *v* advertise, announce, circulate, issue, make known, publicize, put about, spread

prone *adj* 1 (prone to sth) apt, disposed, given, inclined, liable, likely, subject, susceptible, tending, vulnerable. 2 (lying prone) face down, full-length, horizontal, prostrate, recumbent, stretched out

prong *n* branch, pin, point, spike, tine

pronounce *v* 1 articulate, enunciate, express, say, vocalize, voice. 2 announce, assert, declare, decree, proclaim, state

pronounced *adj* clear, definite, distinct, distinctive, evident, marked, noticeable, obvious, strong

pronouncement *n* announcement, declaration, decree, edict, judgment, proclamation, statement, verdict

pronunciation *n* accent, articulation, delivery, diction, enunciation, inflection, intonation, speech, stress, way of saying sth

proof *n* authentication, confirmation, corroboration, demonstration, evidence, facts, substantiation, verification

prop *n* brace, buttress, post, shaft, stanchion, stay, strut, support, truss

prop *v* 1 brace, buttress, hold up, shore up, support, underpin. 2 lean, rest, stand

propaganda *n* brainwashing, disinformation, hype *inf*, indoctrination, misinformation, promotion campaign, public relations exercise, publicity

propagate *v* 1 breed, generate, grow, increase, produce, reproduce, take cuttings. 2 (information) circulate, disseminate, promote, spread, transmit

propel *v* fling, hurl, launch, move, project, push, send, shoot, thrust

propensity *n* disposition, leaning, liability, proclivity, susceptibility, tendency

proper *adj* 1 acceptable, accepted, appropriate, conventional, correct, decent, decorous, fitting, respectable, right, seemly, suitable. 2 genuine, real, right, true; ***opp*** false

property *n* 1 (possessions) belongings, effects, gear *inf*, possessions, things. 2 building, land, real estate. 3 attribute, characteristic, feature, power, quality

prophecy *n* forecast, fortune-telling, prediction, prognosis, second sight

prophesy *v* forecast, foresee, foretell, predict

prophet *n* clairvoyant, oracle, seer, sibyl, soothsayer

prophetic *adj* far-seeing, inspired, prescient

propitious *adj* advantageous, auspicious, favorable, fortunate, lucky, opportune, promising, timely; ***opp*** inauspicious, unfavorable

proportion *n* 1 amount, distribution, fraction, part, percentage, portion, ratio, share. 2 balance, harmony, symmetry

proportional *adj* commensurate, comparable, corresponding, in proportion to, proportionate, relative

proposal *n* bid, offer, plan, project, proposition, recommendation, suggestion, tender

propose *v* 1 (suggest) offer, put forward, recommend, suggest, table. 2 (propose to do sth) aim, have in mind, intend, mean, plan. 3 (propose a motion or candidate) nominate, put forward, put up, sponsor

proposition *n* 1 (suggestion) offer, plan, proposal, recommendation, suggestion. 2 (undertaking) job, prospect, task, undertaking, venture

proprietor *n* landlady, landlord, landowner, owner

propriety *n* correctness, courtesy, decency, decorum, delicacy, etiquette, good form, good manners, politeness, protocol, rectitude, respectability, seemliness

prosaic *adj* dull, flat, lifeless, mundane,

pedestrian, stale, trite, unimaginative, uninteresting; ***opp*** interesting, novel

proscribe *v* ban, bar, forbid, make illegal, outlaw, prevent, prohibit; ***opp*** allow, permit

prosecute *v* accuse, bring an action against, bring before the courts, charge, haul up before the bench *inf*, indict, prefer charges against, put on trial, take to court, try

prospect *n* chance, expectation, future, hope, idea, likelihood, odds, outlook, possibility, probability, promise, thought

prospect *v* examine, explore, search, survey

prospective *adj* aspiring, expected, future, likely, possible, potential, probable, would-be

prospectus *n* advertising material, booklet, brochure, catalog, particulars, promotional material

prosper *v* blossom, boom, do well, flourish, get on, go from strength to strength, grow, succeed, thrive

prosperity *n* affluence, boom, plenty, prosperousness, success, wealth, well-being; ***opp*** adversity, bust *inf*, failure, poverty, recession

prosperous *adj* affluent, booming, comfortable, doing well, rich, thriving, wealthy, well-heeled, well-off, well-to-do; ***opp*** deprived, poor, struggling

prostitute *n* callgirl, courtesan, hooker *inf*, whore, woman of ill repute

prostitute *v* cheapen, debase, demean, lower, sell

protagonist *n* **1** advocate, champion, chief player, exponent, leader, leading light, prime mover, principal, proponent, standard-bearer. **2** competitor, contender, contestant, player

protect *v* conserve, cover, defend, guard, keep safe, look after, preserve, shelter, shield, take care of, watch over

protection *n* care, conservation, custody, defense, guard, guardianship, preservation, safe-keeping, security, shelter, shield

protective *adj* **1** fireproof, safety, waterproof. **2** overprotective, possessive, solicitous, vigilant, watchful

protector *n* bodyguard, champion, defender, guard, guardian, shield

protest *n* **1** complaint, dissent, objection, opposition, outcry. **2** demonstration, protest march, rally. **3** avowal, claim, declaration, protestation

protest *v* **1** appeal, argue, complain, kick up a fuss *inf*, make a stand against, object, take exception to. **2** campaign, demonstrate, lobby, march. **3** (protest your innocence) assert, declare, maintain, profess, state

protester *n* activist, campaigner, demonstrator, dissident, objector

protocol *n* **1** code of behavior, courtesies, custom, etiquette, formalities, good form, procedure, propriety. **2** agreement, concordat, convention, pact, treaty

prototype *n* model, original, precursor

protracted *adj* endless, extended, interminable, lengthy, long-winded, long, never-ending, prolonged; ***opp*** brief, short

protrude *v* bulge out, come through, extend, jut, jut out, poke out, project, stick out

protruding *adj* bulbous, bulging out, distended, jutting out, projecting, prominent, protuberant

proud *adj* **1** delighted, glad, gratified, happy, honored, pleased, satisfied, well pleased; ***opp*** ashamed. **2** arrogant, big-headed *inf*, boastful, cocky *inf*, conceited, disdainful, haughty, high-and-mighty *inf*, imperious, overbearing, self-important, snobbish, snooty *inf*, stuck up *inf*, supercilious, vain; ***opp*** modest. **3** distinguished, glorious, grand, honorable, illustrious, magnificent, noble, splendid, worthy. **4** dignified, independent, self-respecting. **5** (proud day) glorious, gratifying, happy, marvelous, satisfying

prove *v* **1** authenticate, bear out *inf*, confirm, corroborate, demonstrate, determine, establish, find proof, produce proof, show, substantiate, verify; ***opp*** disprove. **2** check, put to the test, test, try out. **3** (prove to be) emerge, end up, be found, turn out

proverb *n* adage, axiom, maxim, old saw, saying

proverbial *adj* **1** famous, infamous, legendary, notorious, renowned, well-known. **2** axiomatic, traditional, typical

provide *v* **1** endow, equip, fix up with *inf*, provision, stock up, supply. **2** contribute, donate, give, grant, lay on, present. **3** give, offer, produce, yield. **4 provide for** care for, keep, maintain, make provision for, support. **5 provide for/against** anticipate, be prepared for, guard against, get ready for, make arrangements, make plans, make preparations, make provisions, plan ahead, plan for, prepare for, take precautions

providence *n* **1** destiny, divine intervention, fate, fortune, God's will. **2** care, discretion, economy, foresight, good management, prudence, thrift; ***opp*** improvidence

provident *adj* careful, economical, farsighted, prudent, shrewd, thrifty; ***opp*** improvident

providential *adj* chance, fortuitous, happy, fortunate, lucky, opportune; ***opp*** unfortunate

province *n* **1** district, region, section, state, territory. **2** area of activity, area of responsibility, business, concern, field, part, responsibility, role, sphere

provincial *adj* **1** local, regional, state; ***opp*** national. **2** country, outlying, rural, rustic, small-town. **3** backward, insular, inward-looking, limited, narrow, narrow-minded, parochial, small-minded, unsophisticated; ***opp*** cosmopolitan

provision *n* **1** (the provision of sth) equipping, providing, supply, supplying. **2** (make provision for sth) arrangement, plan, precaution, precautionary measure, preparation. **3** (the provisions of a contract) condition, limitation, proviso, qualification, requirement, restriction, stipulation, term

provisional *adj* conditional, contingent, interim, limited, qualified, stopgap, temporary, tentative, transitional

provisions *n* food, food and drink, foodstuffs, food supplies, groceries, ration, stores, supplies

proviso *n* condition, exception, limitation, provision, qualification, requirement, restriction, stipulation

provocation *n* **1** affront, aggravation, annoyance, harassment, insult, irritation, offense, taunt, taunting, teasing. **2** goading, incitement, justification, motive, prompting, rousing, stimulus, stirring

provocative *adj* **1** aggravating, annoying, exasperating, goading, infuriating, insulting, offensive, provoking, stimulating. **2** alluring, erotic, raunchy *inf*, seductive, sexy, suggestive, titillating

provoke *v* **1** arouse, awaken, bring about, cause, elicit, evoke, excite, give rise to, incite, induce, inspire, kindle, occasion, produce, prompt, rouse, stimulate, stir up, work up. **2** (provoke sb) aggravate, anger, annoy, exasperate, gall, get on your nerves *inf*, harass, infuriate, insult, irritate, madden, make your blood boil *inf*, offend, outrage, pique, rile, rouse, tease, torment, upset, wind up *inf*

prowess *n* **1** ability, aptitude, competence, expertise, mastery, proficiency, skill, talent. **2** boldness, bravery, courage, gallantry, grit *inf*, guts *inf*, mettle, nerve, pluck, spirit, steadfastness, valor

prowl *v* creep, move stealthily, slink, sneak, stalk, steal

proximity *n* **1** closeness, nearness. **2** locality, neighborhood, vicinity

prudent *adj* **1** careful, cautious, circumspect, judicious, sagacious, sensible, shrewd, wary, wise; ***opp*** imprudent, unwise. **2** (prudent use of sth) canny, careful, economical, farsighted, provident, thrifty; ***opp*** wasteful

prudish *adj* easily shocked, goody-goody *inf*, old-fashioned, puritanical, priggish, prim, straitlaced, Victorian

prune *v* **1** clip, cut back, lop, shape, thin, thin out, trim. **2** curtail, cut, cut back, make cutbacks, make cuts, make reductions, pare down, reduce, retrench, shorten, trim

pry *v* be a busybody, be inquisitive, be nosy, interfere, intrude, meddle, nose about *inf*, poke your nose in *inf*, search, snoop, stick your nose in *inf*

prying *adj* curious, inquisitive, interfering, intrusive, meddlesome, meddling, nosy *inf*, snooping, spying

pseudonym *n* alias, assumed name, pen name, professional name, stage name

psyche *n* anima, individuality, inner being, personality, self, soul, spirit

psychiatrist *n* analyst, psychoanalyst, psychotherapist, shrink *inf*

psychic *adj* clairvoyant, extrasensory, mystic, occult, paranormal, preternatural, supernatural, supernormal, telepathic

psychological *adj* **1** cerebral, mental; ***opp*** physical. **2** emotional, in the mind, mental, irrational, subconscious, unconscious; ***opp*** physical

psychology *n* **1** science of the mind, study of the mental processes, study of personality. **2** (sb's phychology) attitude, mental processes, mind, mind-set *inf*, thought processes, way of thinking

psychopath *n* lunatic, madman, maniac, psycho *inf*

pub *n* bar, inn, saloon, tavern, wine bar

puberty *n* adolescence, pubescence, sexual maturity, teenage years, teens

public *adj* **1** (a public place) accessible, communal, open to all, open to the public, unrestricted. **2** (a public institution) civic, communal, community, national, nationalized, social, state. **3** (public awareness) collective, common, democratic, general, majority, popular, universal, widespread. **4** (make sth public) acknowledged, known, notorious, obvious, open, overt, plain, published, well-known, widely known. **5** (public figure) eminent, important, in the public eye, prominent, well-known

public *n* **1** citizens, community, electorate, everyone, ordinary people, people, people in general, populace, society, the country, the hoi polloi, the masses, the nation, the people. **2** (do sth to please your public) admirers, audience, clientele, fans, followers, patrons, supporters. **3 in public** for all to see, in full view, openly, publicly

publication *n* **1** book, booklet, brochure, leaflet, magazine, newspaper, pamphlet, periodical, title. **2** (the publication of information) announcement, broadcasting, declaration, disclosure, dissemination, notification, publicizing, reporting. **3** (the publication of a book) issuing, printing, production, publishing

publicity *n* **1** advertising, ballyhoo *inf*, hype *inf*, marketing, plug *inf*, promotion. **2** attention, limelight, public interest

publicize *v* **1** advertise, give publicity to, hype *inf*, market, plug *inf*, promote, push. **2** announce, broadcast, make known, make public, publish, spotlight

publish *v* **1** bring out, issue, print, produce, put out, release. **2** advertise, announce, break the news about, broadcast, circulate, declare, disclose, divulge, leak *inf*, make known, make public, publicize, report, reveal

puerile *adj* adolescent, childish, immature, infantile, juvenile

puff *n* blast, breath, draft, flurry, gust, whiff

puff *v* **1** blow, breathe heavily, exhale, gasp, pant, wheeze. **2** (a cigarette) drag *inf*, draw, inhale, inhale, pull on, smoke. **3 puff up** bloat, blow out, blow up, distend, inflate, swell

puffy *adj* bloated, distended, enlarged, puffed up, swollen

pugnacious *adj* aggressive, bellicose, belligerent, combative, irascible, quarrelsome; ***opp*** gentle, passive

pull *n* **1** jerk, tug, twitch, yank. **2** attraction, draw, force, lure, magnetism, power. **3** clout *inf*, influence, power

pull *v* **1** drag, draw, haul, tow, trail, tug, yank; ***opp*** push. **2** (pull flowers, vegetables) collect, cull, extract, pick, pluck, pull out, pull up, uproot. **3** (pull a muscle) sprain, strain, tear, wrench. **4** (pull the crowds) attract, bring in, draw, entice, lure. **5 pull down** demolish, destroy, knock down, level, raze. **6 pull through** come through, pull round, rally, recover, survive

pulp *n* **1** flesh, soft part. **2** mash, mush,

paste, puree

pulse *n* beat, beating, drumming, heartbeat, pounding, pulsation, rhythm, throb, throbbing, vibration

pump *v* 1 drive, force, inject, push, send. 2 (pump sb for information) cross-examine, give sb the third degree *inf*, grill *inf*, interrogate, question. 3 **pump up** blow up, inflate

pun *n* double entendre, play on words

punch *n* bash, blow, bop *inf*, clout, hit, hook, jab, smack, thump, wallop, whack

punch *v* 1 bash, belt *inf*, box, clout, hit, pound, pummel, slug, sock *inf*, strike, thump, wallop. 2 (punch a hole) bore, drill, hole, make a hole in, perforate, pierce, prick, puncture

punctual *adj* early, in good time, on the dot, on time, prompt, when expected; ***opp*** late

punctuate *v* 1 break, interrupt, intersperse, pepper, sprinkle. 2 insert punctuation, put in punctuation marks

puncture *n* 1 hole, leak, nick, opening, perforation, pin-prick, rupture. 2 blow out, burst tire, flat *inf*, flat tire

puncture *v* bore, deflate, hole, let down, make a hole in, penetrate, perforate, pierce, punch, rupture

pungent *adj* 1 (of a smell) acid, acrid, bitter, caustic, rank, sharp; ***opp*** gentle. 2 (of a taste) aromatic, hot, peppery, piquant, spicy, tangy; ***opp*** mild

punish *v* 1 castigate, chasten, chastise, correct, discipline, exact retribution from, inflict punishment on, make sb pay for sth, penalize, rap sb over the knuckles *inf*, take disciplinary action against, teach sb a lesson *inf*. 2 beat, cane, flog, scourge, spank, thrash, whip

punishable *adj* criminal, culpable, indictable

punishing *adj* arduous, backbreaking, exhausting, grueling, hard, strenuous, taxing, tiring, tough, wearing; ***opp*** easy, light

punishment *n* 1 chastening, chastisement, correction, disciplinary action, discipline, penalty, punitive measure, retribution, sanction. 2 beating, caning, flogging, hiding, pain, scourging, spank, spanking, thrashing, whipping

punitive *adj* 1 castigating, disciplinary, penal, penalizing, punishing. 2 cruel, harsh, savage, severe, stiff

puny *adj* feeble, frail, sickly, small, stunted, underdeveloped, undersized, weak, weakly; ***opp*** strong

pupil *n* 1 schoolboy, schoolgirl, scholar, student. 2 beginner, learner, novice, trainee. 3 apprentice, disciple, follower, protégé, protégée, student

puppet *n* 1 doll, dummy, marionette. 2 dupe, mouthpiece, pawn, stooge, tool

purchase *n* 1 acquisition, buy, investment. 2 foothold, grasp, grip, leverage, toehold

purchase *v* acquire, buy, get, invest in, obtain, pay for, pick up, procure, secure

pure *adj* 1 (pure gold) flawless, genuine, perfect, real, unadulterated, unalloyed, undiluted, true. 2 (pure air, water) clean, clear, germ-free, immaculate, spotless, sterile, uncontaminated, unpolluted, untainted, wholesome;

opp polluted. **3** (of a person) blameless, chaste, decent, good, immaculate, impeccable, innocent, irreproachable, uncorrupted, unsullied, virginal, virtuous. **4** (pure malice) absolute, downright, complete, out-and-out, perfect, sheer, total, utter. **5** (pure science) abstract, theoretical

purge *n* **1** cleansing, purging, purification. **2** clear out, dismissal, expulsion, ousting, rooting out, weeding out. **3** dose of salts, laxative, purgative

purge *v* **1** clean out, cleanse, purify, wash out. **2** clear out, depose, dismiss, eliminate, liquidate, expel, get rid of, oust, root out, weed out

purify *v* clean, cleanse, decontaminate, disinfect, fumigate, make pure, refine, sanitize, sterilize, wash

purist *n* dogmatist, pedant, stickler

puritanical *adj* ascetic, austere, goody-goody *inf*, narrow-minded, prim, prudish, self-denying, straitlaced, strict

purpose *n* **1** (have a purpose) aim, ambition, design, end, goal, intention, motivation, motive, object, objective, plan, target. **2** (sth lacks purpose) determination, direction, firmness, persistence, resoluteness, resolution, steadfastness, tenacity. **3** (the purpose of sth) point, reason, use, usefulness, value. **4 on purpose** by design, consciously, deliberately, intentionally, knowingly, willfully, with intent; *opp* accidentally

purposeful *adj* determined, dogged, firm, resolute, persistent, single-minded, steadfast, tenacious

purposeless *adj* aimless, meaningless, motiveless, pointless, senseless, useless

purse *n* **1** pocketbook, pouch, wallet. **2** coffers, exchequer, funds, means, money, resources, treasury, wealth. **3** award, prize, reward

pursue *v* **1** chase, dog, follow, give chase, go after, harry, hound, hunt, hunt down, run after, shadow, stalk, tail, track. **2** (pursue a goal) aim for, aspire to, been intent on, have as a goal, seek, strive for, work for, work towards. **3** (pursue a career, way of life) apply yourself to, carry on, conduct, continue, continue with, engage in, go for *inf*, go on with, persist in, proceed with, stick with

pursuit *n* **1** (the pursuit of a person, animal) chase, hue and cry, hunt, inquiry, pursuing, trail. **2** (leisure pursuits) activity, enthusiasm, hobby, interest, line, occupation, pastime, pleasure. **3** (the pursuit of knowledge) hunt, inquiry, quest, search, seeking after, striving for

push *n* **1** (give sb a push) butt, jolt, jostle, nudge, poke, prod, shove, thrust. **2** (military) advance, assault, attack, charge, offensive, sortie, thrust. **3** (have a lot of push) ambition, drive, energy, enterprise, enthusiasm, get-up-and-go, gumption *inf*, initiative

push *v* **1** (push sth) drive, press, propel, ram, shove, thrust. **2** (push past people) barge, bustle, elbow, hustle, jostle, manhandle, nudge, shoulder, shove, squeeze. **3** (push sth into a place) cram, force, jam, press in, ram, squash, squeeze, stuff. **4** (push sb into doing sth) browbeat, coerce, encourage, force, impel, incite, lean on *inf*, motivate, persuade, press, prompt, put pressure on, urge. **5** (push a product) advertise, hype *inf*, plug *inf*, promote, publicize, recommend. **6 push around** boss around, browbeat, bully, intimidate, lean on *inf*, tyrranize

pushed *adj* **1** busy, hurried, in a hurry, pressed, rushed, under pressure, up against it. **2 pushed for** feeling the need of, lacking, not having enough of, running short of, short of, without

pushover *n* **1** (a person) easy mark, easy prey, mug *inf*, soft touch, sucker *inf*, weakling, wimp. **2** (a task) breeze *inf*, child's play, cinch, doddle *inf*, easy task, piece of cake *inf*, walkover

pushy *adj* ambitious, assertive, brash, forceful, overbearing, presumptuous

put *v* **1** fix, install, locate, park, place, position, set, settle, situate, stand. **2** allocate to, assign to, consign, deploy, dispose, impose, station. **3 put down** (put sth down somewhere) deposit, lay, lay down, set down, settle. **4 put down** (put sb down) belittle, criticize, denigrate, deprecate, disparage, find fault with, knock, pick holes in, run down. **5 put down** (put down a rebellion) crush, defeat, put a stop to, quash, quell, repress stamp out, stop, suppress. **6 put down** (write down) enter, inscribe, jot down, log, make a note of, note, record, set down, take down, write down. **7 put down** (put an animal down) destroy, put out of its misery, put to sleep, kill. **8 put down to** ascribe, attribute, blame, chalk up to, impute, put the blame on. **9 put forward** advance, introduce, move, nominate, present, propose, recommend, submit, suggest. **10 put off** (put sth off) defer, delay, postpone, put back, put on ice, put on the back burner, reschedule, shelve. **11 put off** (put sb off an idea) discourage, dissuade, dishearten, offend, repel. **12 put off** (put sb off when they are working) distract, divert, divert the attention of, sidetrack. **13 put off** (put off the light) switch off, turn off. **14 put on** (put on clothes) change into, dress in, don, slip into. **15 put on** lay on, make available, provide, supply. **16 put on** (put on a play, an exhibition) do, mount, present, produce, stage. **17 put on** (pretend) affect, fake, feign, pretend, sham, simulate. **18 put on** (put on the light) switch on, turn on. **19 put on (put on weight)** gain, increase. **20 put up** (put up a building) build, construct, erect. **21 put up** (put sb up) accommodate, allow sb to stay, give sb a bed, give sb a place to stay, provide sb with accommodations, take sb in. **22 put up** (put up money) advance, donate, give, pledge, provide, supply. **23 put up to** (put sb up to sth) egg on, encourage, incite, persuade, talk sb into sthg, urge on. **24 put up with** accept, bear, endure, stand, swallow, take, tolerate

putrid *adj* bad, decayed, decomposed, fetid, foul, off, putrefied, rancid, rotten, rotting, spoiled, stale, stinking; ***opp*** fresh

puzzle *n* brainteaser, conundrum, dilemma, enigma, mystery, poser *inf*, quandary, question, riddle

puzzle *v* **1** baffle, bewilder, confuse, flummox *inf*, mystify, perplex, stump *inf*. **2** (puzzle over sth) brood, consider, muse, ponder, study, think about, think over, wonder about. **3 puzzle out** crack *inf*, decipher, figure out, find the answer to, solve, think out, unravel, work out

puzzled *adj* at a loss, at sea, baffled, bewildered, confused, flummoxed *inf*, mystified, perplexed, stumped

puzzling *adj* abstruse, baffling, bewildering, confusing, cryptic, enigmatic, incomprehensible, involved, mind-boggling *inf*, mysterious, mystifying, perplexing, unclear; ***opp*** clear

quail *v* back away, cower, cringe, falter, flinch, quake, recoil, shake, shrink, shy away, tremble, waver

quaint *adj* charming, curious, droll, eccentric, fanciful, odd, offbeat, olde worlde *inf*, old-fashioned, peculiar, queer, strange, sweet, unusual, whimsical

quake *v* quiver, rock, shake, shiver, shudder, tremble, vibrate

qualification *n* **1** ability, aptitude, capability, competence, eligibility, fitness, proficiency, skill, suitability, training. **2** condition, exception, limitation, modification, provision, proviso, restriction, stipulation

qualified *adj* **1** able, capable, certificated, competent, experienced, fit, proficient, skilled, trained. **2** (qualified acceptance) cautious, conditional, guarded, half-hearted, limited, modified, provisional, reserved, restricted; ***opp*** wholehearted

qualify *v* **1** be eligible, be entitled, have/gain the right, get through, go through, make the grade *inf*, meet the requirements, pass, reach the required standard, succeed. **2** (sth qualifies sb for a particular responsibility) authorize, empower, entitle, equip, fit, make eligible, make suitable, prepare, suit. **3** (qualify a statement) add a rider to, limit, mitigate, moderate, modify, modulate, nuance, restrict, soften, temper, tone down, weaken

quality *n* **1** (extent to which sth is good) caliber, excellence, merit, rating, standard, standing, status, value, worth. **2** (what sth is like) character, description, essence, kind, nature. **3** (the qualities of sth or sb) advantage, aspect, attribute, characteristic, feature, good point, hallmark, mark, property, trait

qualms *n* anxiety, apprehension, conscience, disinclination, disquiet, doubt, guilt, hesitancy, hesitation, misgivings, pangs, reluctance, remorse, reservations, reticence, scruples, second thoughts, uncertainty, uneasiness

quandary *n* difficulty, dilemma, fix *inf*, impasse, plight, predicament, problem, puzzle, uncertainty

quantity *n* aggregate, amount, lot, number, sum, total

quarrel *n* altercation, argument, battle, break, conflict, confrontation, difference of opinion, disagreement, dispute, falling-out, feud, fight, rivalry, row *inf*, squabble, tiff *inf*, vendetta, war, wrangle *inf*

quarrel *v* argue, battle, be estranged, be in conflict, bicker, cross, cross swords, dispute, fall out, feud, fight, row *inf*, spar, squabble, tangle, wrangle *inf*

quarrelsome *adj* aggressive, angry, argumentative, bad-tempered, bloody-minded, cantankerous, choleric, confrontational, contrary, disagreeable, disputatious, explosive, fractious, impatient, irascible, irritable, obstructive, pugnacious, querulous, quick-tempered, testy, truculent, unfriendly, vengeful, volatile

quarry *n* **1** excavation, hole in the ground, mine, open-cast mine, pit. **2** goal, objective, prey, prize, target, victim

quarter *n* **1** area, district, locality, neighborhood, part of town. **2** (advice from a particular quarter) direction, person, source

quarters *n* abode, accommodation, apartments, barracks, billet, digs *inf*, dwelling, home, house, lodgings, residence, rooms

quash *v* annul, cancel, nullify, invalidate, overrule, overthrow, overturn, rescind, reverse, revoke, suppress; ***opp*** uphold

quaver *v* falter, fluctuate, quake, shake, tremble, vibrate, waver

queasy *adj* bilious, ill, nauseous, queer *inf*, seasick, sick, unwell, woozy *inf*

queen *n* **1** Crown, head of state, Her Majesty, lady, matriarch, monarch, ruler, sovereign. **2** consort, dowager queen

queer *adj* aberrant, abnormal, bizarre, curious, deviant, eccentric, funny, inexplicable, odd, outlandish, peculiar, singular, strange, suspicious, unusual, weird

quell *v* allay, beat down, conquer, defeat, eliminate, extinguish, overcome, pacify, quash, stifle, subdue, suppress, vanquish

quench *v* end, extinguish, gratify, relieve, sate, satisfy, slake

query *n* **1** inquiry, problem, question. **2** (a query over sb's future) doubt, hesitation, problem, question, question mark, suspicion, uncertainty

query *v* call into question, challenge, contest, dispute, doubt, mistrust, question, suspect

quest *n* crusade, expedition, journey, mission, pursuit, search

question *n* **1** brainteaser *inf*, conundrum, demand, inquiry, query, riddle; ***opp*** answer. **2** (sth to be considered or decided) affair, controversy, debate, issue, mystery, point, problem, puzzle, situation

question *v* **1** ask, cross-examine, debrief, grill *inf*, inquire, interrogate, interview, poll, probe, pump *inf*, quiz. **2** (question whether sth is true) argue over, call into question, challenge, contest, dispute, doubt, impugn, object to, oppose, quarrel with, query

questionable *adj* arguable, borderline, contestable, controversial, debatable, disputable, doubtful, dubious, open to challenge, problematic, uncertain

queue *n* file, line, string, waiting line

queue *v* file, form a line, line up, queue up, stand in line, wait in line

quibble *n* argument, complaint, criticism, dispute, nit-picking, objection, pettifogging, point of contention, query

quibble *v* argue, carp, dispute, part company, nit-pick, pettifog, split hairs, take issue

quick *adj* **1** brisk, fast, fast-moving, fleet of foot, headlong, high-speed, nippy *inf*, rapid, speedy, swift; ***opp*** slow. **2** (not lasting long) abrupt, hasty, hurried, lightning, momentary, rapid, swift. **3** (not delayed) immediate, instant, instantaneous, prompt, rapid, spur-of-the-moment, swift. **4** (quick to do sth) hasty, in a hurry, precipitate, prompt. **5** (thinking quickly) alert, astute, bright, clever, intelligent, keen, perceptive, quick-thinking, quick-witted, sharp, shrewd, smart

quicken *v* **1** (sth quickens) accelerate, gather pace, gather speed, go faster, speed up; ***opp*** slow down. **2** (quicken sth) accelerate, expedite, hasten, hurry, speed up; ***opp*** slow down

quiet *adj* **1** calm, noiseless, peaceful, placid, restful, serene, silent, sleepy, soundless, still, tranquil, unexciting; ***opp*** noisy. **2** (of sb's voice) breathy, inaudible, hushed, low, muffled, murmuring, muted, small, soft, subdued, tiny, whispering; ***opp*** loud. **3** (of a person) docile, inactive, introverted, meek, passive, phlegmatic, placid, quiescent, reserved, retiring, silent, taciturn, uncommunicative, withdrawn; ***opp*** noisy. **4** (have a quiet word with sb) confidential, discreet, on the quiet *inf*, private, secret

quiet *n* calm, calmness, hush, peace, peacefulness, placidity, quietness, repose, rest, silence, stillness, tranquillity; ***opp*** noise

quip *n* bon mot, crack *inf*, epigram, gag *inf*, jest, joke, one-liner, wisecrack, witticism

quirk *n* **1** caprice, eccentricity, foible, idiosyncrasy, kink, oddity, peculiarity, whim. **2** (quirk of fate, nature) aberration, anomaly, exception, freak, reversal, turn, twist

quit *v* **1** depart, give notice, go away, hand in your notice, leave, resign, vacate, withdraw; ***opp*** stay on. **2** (stop doing sth) abandon, abstain, cease, cut out, desist, discontinue, drop, give up, refrain, renounce, stop; ***opp*** continue

quite *adv* **1** fairly, moderately, pretty *inf*, rather, relatively, somewhat. **2** absolutely, altogether, completely, entirely, fully, totally, wholly

quits *adj* equal, even, level, on equal terms, square

quiver *v* oscillate, palpitate, pulsate, shake, shiver, shudder, throb, tremble, vibrate

quiz *n* competition, contest, game show, questionnaire

quiz *v* cross-examine, fire questions at, grill *inf*, interrogate, interview, poll, pump, question

quota *n* allocation, allowance, amount, assignment, consignment, cut *inf*, measure, percentage, portion, proportion, quantity, ratio, ration, share, supply

quotation *n* **1** citation, excerpt, extract, line, verse, passage, quote *inf*, reference. **2** (a price) bid, estimate, figure, price, rate, tender

quote *v* **1** cite, instance, mention, recite, refer to, repeat, reproduce. **2** bid, cost, estimate, price, tender

rabble *n* 1 band, crowd, gang, horde, mob, rioters, troublemakers. 2 (lowest ranks of society) common people, commoners, hoi polloi, lower classes, masses, plebs *inf*, riff-raff

race *n* 1 chase, competition, contest, event, heat, match, pursuit, run. 2 (in particular sports) handicap, marathon, rally, sprint, stakes, steeplechase. 3 ethnic group, nation, nationality, people, tribe

race *v* 1 (in sport) be pitted against sb, chase, compete, contest, pursue, sprint. 2 (run, move quickly) bowl, career, dash, gallop, hasten, hurry, run, rush, scamper, speed, sprint, whizz *inf*

racial *adj* anthropological, communal, ethnic, ethnological, folk, national, tribal

rack *n* frame, framework, holder, pallet, stand, structure

rack *v* 1 (racked by pain, uncertainty) afflict, assail, besiege, crucify, harass, harrow, oppress, persecute, plague, torment, torture. 2 **rack your brains** search your memory, think hard, turn sth over in your mind, try to remember

racket *n* 1 cacophony, din, disturbance, fracas, noise, sound, tumult, uproar. 2 corruption, extortion, fraud, graft, scam *inf*, scheme

radiant *adj* 1 (giving off light) bright, brilliant, dazzling, glittering, luminous, resplendent, shining, shiny, sparkling. 2 (of a person) beaming, delighted, expansive, happy, serene, smiling, warm

radiate *v* 1 (radiate heat, energy) emanate, emit, exude, generate, give off, produce, send forth, shed, send out, shine, spread. 2 (lines radiating from a central point) branch, diverge, fan out, spread, spread out

radical *adj* 1 campaigning, left-of-center, left-wing, militant, progressive, revolutionary, socialist; ***opp*** conservative, reactionary. 2 (radical change) complete, extreme, fundamental, great, major, severe, thorough, thoroughgoing; ***opp*** minor

radio *n* 1 receiver, transistor radio, tuner, wireless. 2 (for sending and receiving messages) CB, transmitter, walkie-talkie

rage *n* anger, bile, frenzy, fulmination, fury, rampage, violence, vituperation

rage *v* 1 be angry, be beside yourself, be enraged, be furious, be hopping mad *inf*, be in a frenzy, be in a fury, be incensed, be infuriated, be mad, blow a fuse *inf*, blow a gasket *inf*, blow your top *inf*, boil over, explode *inf*, flip your lid *inf*, foam at the mouth, fume, go berserk, hit the roof *inf*, lose your temper, rail, rant, rave, roar, seethe, shout, swear, thunder. **2** (of a storm, controversy) be at its height, continue, continue unabated; ***opp*** abate

ragged *adj* **1** frayed, in ribbons, in shreds, in tatters, old, patched, ripped, shabby, tattered, tatty *inf*, threadbare, torn, worn through. **2** (not straight) irregular, jagged, serrated, uneven, untidy, wavy, zigzag

rags *n* castoffs, old clothes, remnants, shreds, tatters

raid *n* **1** assault, attack, foray, incursion, invasion, sally, sortie. **2** (by police) inspection, search, seizure, spot check

raid *v* **1** assault, attack, foray, invade, storm. **2** (involving robbery) loot, pillage, plunder, rob. **3** (police) descend on, inspect, search, spot-check

raider *n* **1** assailant, attacker, invader. **2** bandit, brigand, looter, marauder, robber, predator, thief

rain *n* cloudburst, deluge, downpour, drizzle, flood, precipitation, raindrops, rainfall, shower, storm, thunderstorm, torrent

rain *v* bucket *inf*, drizzle, pour, pour down, rain cats and dogs *inf*, spit

raise *v* **1** elevate, hoist, hold up, jack up, lift, lift up, pick up, pull up, push up, rear; ***opp*** lower. **2** augment, boost, increase, inflate, jack up *inf*, mark up, push up, put up, up *inf*; ***opp*** lower. **3** (raise the quality, status of sth) enhance, exalt, heighten, improve, promote, upgrade. **4** (sth raises fears, doubts, questions) activate, arouse, awaken, breed, cause, create, engender, evoke, excite, foment, foster, generate, incite, instigate, kindle, provoke, rouse, set off, spark, stimulate, trigger. **5** (sb raises a question, problem) ask, bring up, broach, express, introduce, mention, moot, pose, present, propose, put forward, state, suggest. **6** (raise cattle, children) breed, bring up, look after, nurture, rear. **7** (raise funds) amass, collect, generate, make, solicit

rally *n* **1** drive, race. **2** (large meeting) assembly, conference, congress, convention, convocation, gathering, mass meeting, meeting, public meeting, reunion. **3** (of stock prices) improvement, increase, recovery, resurgence, revival

rally *v* **1** be revitalized, be revived, bounce back, improve, make a comeback, recover, regroup, reorganize, resist, revive. **2** (rally the troops) inspire, mobilize, revitalize, revive, revivify, spur on, steel, stir up. **3 rally round** be supportive, come to the rescue, help, support

ram *v* batter, buffet, bump, butt, collide with, cram, crush, hit, impact, pound, strike

ramble *n* hike, stroll, walk

ramble *v* **1** (talk) chatter, digress, drone on, wander. **2** (walk) amble, hike, range, roam, rove, stroll, walk, wander

rampage *n* **on the rampage 1** (in an angry mood) angry, berserk, breathing fire, furious, on the warpath, raging. 2 looting, marauding, out of control, pillaging, rampaging, stampeding, violent

rampage *v* charge, go berserk, loot, pillage, run amok, run riot, stampede, storm

rampant *adj* out of control, raging, rampaging, riotous, stampeding, unbridled, uncontrollable, uncontrolled, unrestrained, wanton, wild

ramshackle *adj* decrepit, dilapidated, flimsy, jerry-built, rickety, shaky, unstable, unsteady, tumbledown

rancid *adj* curdled, festering *inf*, off, rank, putrid, rotting, sour, spoiled, stale

random *adj* accidental, arbitrary, casual, chance, disorganized, fortuitous, haphazard, hit-or-miss, indiscriminate, irregular, sporadic, spot, stray, unplanned, unsystematic

range *n* 1 (of sb's interests, responsibilities) area, breadth, compass, diversity, extent, gamut, scale, scope, span, spectrum, sphere, spread, sweep, variety. 2 (of vision, weapon) area, distance, extent, field, limit, reach

range *v* comprise, consist of, encompass, extend, include, reach, span, spread, stretch, vary

rank *adj* disgusting, fetid, foul, foul-smelling, putrid, rancid, revolting, smelly *inf*, stinking

rank *n* class, grade, level, place, position, ranking, rating, seniority, standing, station, status

rank *v* categorize, class, classify, grade, order, place, rate

ransack *v* plunder, rifle, rummage, scour, search, trash *inf*, turn upside-down

ransom *n* bribe, compensation, deliverance, liberation, pay-off, redemption

ransom *v* buy back, deliver, liberate, recover, redeem, rescue

rant *v* bawl, bellow, bluster, go on and one, harangue, rage, rail, rave, roar, shout, spout, swear, thunder, vociferate, yell

rape *n* abuse, assault, attack, indecent assault, molestation, sexual abuse, sexual assault, violation

rape *v* abuse, assault, attack, defile, deflower, force yourself on, indecently assault, molest, ravish, sexually abuse, sexually assault, violate

rapid *adj* 1 breakneck, brisk, fast, fast-moving, headlong, high-speed, lightning, nippy *inf*, quick, speedy, swift. 2 (not lasting long) hasty, hurried, momentary, quick, swift. 3 (not delayed) immediate, instant, instantaneous, lightning, prompt, quick, spur-of-the-moment, swift

rare *adj* 1 few and far between, infrequent, occasional, scarce, scattered, sporadic, ***opp*** common. 2 (having unusual qualities) atypical, exceptional, extraordinary, singular, uncommon, untypical, unique, unusual; ***opp*** common

rascal *n* 1 devil, imp, jackanapes, mischief-maker, rapscallion *inf*, scallywag *inf*, scamp *inf*, terror *inf*. 2 (wicked, criminal) blackguard, bounder, cad, rat, reprobate, rogue, scoundrel, villain

rash *adj* devil-may-care, foolhardy, harebrained, hasty, headlong, headstrong, heedless, hot-headed, hurried, ill-advised, ill-considered, impetuous, imprudent, impulsive, incautious, injudicious, madcap, overadventurous, precipitate, premature, reckless, spur-of-the-moment, unguarded, unthinking

rash *n* **1** allergic reaction, dermatitis, eczema, eruption, inflammation, irritation, psoriasis, redness, skin irritation, spots. **2** (a rash of burglaries) flood, outbreak, plague, rush, series, spate, wave

rate *n* **1** (rate of change, increase) degree, intensity, level, pace, ratio, scale, speed, tempo. **2** (money to be paid) amount, band, charge, cost, fare, fee, figure, payment, price, scale, sum, tariff, wage. **3 at any rate** anyhow, anyway, in any case, in any event, nevertheless, whatever the case may be

rate *v* **1** adjudge, appraise, assess, class, classify, estimate, evaluate, gauge, grade, judge, measure, put a value on, rank, regard, value. **2** be worth, be worthy of, deserve, merit

ratify *v* accredit, approve, certify, confirm, countersign, endorse, pass, sanction, sign, underwrite, validate

rating *n* category, class, classification, designation, grade, level, placing, rank, ranking, position, standard, standing, status, tariff, type, value

ratio *n* comparison, fraction, frequency, proportion, quotient, rate

ration *n* allocation, allowance, amount, assignment, dose, helping, measure, portion, provision, quantity, quota, share, supply

ration *v* allot, apportion, distribute, eke out, mete out, parcel out, share, share out

rational *adj* enlightened, intelligent, logical, lucid, reasonable, sane, sensible, sound; ***opp*** irrational

rationale *n* argument, case, grounds, justification, logic, motivation, philosophy, reason, reasoning, theory

rationalize *v* account for, clarify, elucidate, excuse, explain, justify, resolve, think through, vindicate

rattle *v* **1** (rattle sth) bang, clang, clank, clatter, jangle. **2** (rattle sb) alarm, disconcert, disturb, fluster, frighten, perturb, put off, scare, shake, unnerve, upset, worry; ***opp*** calm

raucous *adj* grating, harsh, hoarse, husky, jarring, loud, noisy, piercing, rasping, rough, shrill, squawking, strident; ***opp*** quiet

ravage *v* **1** demolish, destroy, devastate, lay waste, level, raze, ruin, spoil, wreak havoc on, wreck. **2** loot, pillage, plunder, raid, ransack

rave *v* **1** fume, go crazy, go mad, rage, rant, roar, splutter, storm, thunder. **2** (rave about sb) enthuse, go into raptures *inf*, gush *inf*

raving *adj* crazed, crazy, delirious, demented, deranged, frenzied, hysterical, insane, irrational, mad, rabid, raging, unbalanced, wild; ***opp*** sane

raw *adj* **1** (raw food) fresh, rare,

uncooked, underdone, unprepared; ***opp*** cooked, prepared. **2** (raw materials) basic, coarse, crude, natural, rough, unfinished, unprocessed, unrefined, untreated. **3** (a raw wound) bloody, chafed, grazed, inflamed, open, scraped, scratched, sensitive, sore, tender, unhealed; ***opp*** healed

ray *n* **1** (a ray of light) bar, beam, flash, gleam, glint, laser, shaft, streak, stream. **2** (a ray of hope) flicker, glimmer, hint, spark, trace

reach *n* **1** (beyond your reach) distance, extension, extent, grasp, spread, stretch. **2** (the reach of an organization) area, authority, command, control, influence, jurisdiction, power, range, scope, sphere, sway, territory

reach *v* **1** (reach a high standard) accomplish, achieve, arrive at, attain, gain, get, make. **2** (reach a place, an object) contact, extend to, get as far as, stretch to, touch. **3 reach for** extend, outstretch, put out your hand, stretch, try to get

react *v* **1** answer, reciprocate, reply, respond, retaliate, retort. **2** act, behave, function, operate, proceed, work

reaction *n* answer, reply, response, retaliation, retort, riposte

reactionary *adj* conservative, die-hard, old-fashioned, rightist, right-wing, traditionalist; ***opp*** progressive, radical

read *v* **1** (read a book) dip into, look at, peruse, pore over, scan, skim, study. **2** (read the news) announce, deliver, recite, speak, utter. **3** (read sth into sth) assume, comprehend, construe, infer, interpret, see, take sth to mean, understand

ready *adj* **1** (prepared) all set *inf*, arranged, completed, equipped, fit, organized, prepared, primed, set, waiting; ***opp*** unprepared. **2** (available) accessible, at hand, at your disposal, at your fingertips *inf*, available, convenient, handy, near, on call, present; ***opp*** unavailable. **3** (willing) agreeable, consenting, disposed, eager, game *inf*, glad, happy, pleased, willing; ***opp*** unwilling

real *adj* **1** (real leather) authentic, bona fide, genuine, true; ***opp*** artificial, fake. **2** (a real person) actual, corporeal, existing, genuine, ordinary, non-fictitious; ***opp*** fictitious

realistic *adj* **1** (of a person) clear-sighted, common-sense, down-to-earth, levelheaded, matter-of-fact, objective, practical, pragmatic, rational, sensible; ***opp*** unrealistic. **2** (a realistic copy) convincing, faithful, lifelike, true to life, truthful; ***opp*** unrealistic

reality *n* actuality, experience, fact, life, practice, real life, the real world, truth; ***opp*** theory

realize *v* **1** appreciate, catch on to *inf*, comprehend, conceive, grasp, imagine, recognize, take in, understand. **2** (realize a plan) accomplish, achieve, bring off, complete, do, effect, fulfill, implement, make happen

realm *n* country, domain, empire, kingdom, land, monarchy, principality, province, state

reap *v* **1** (reap rewards) acquire, collect, derive, gain, gather, get, obtain, realize, receive, win. 2 (reap a harvest) cut, gather in, harvest; ***opp*** sow

rear *adj* back, end, following, hind, hindmost, last, posterior; ***opp*** front

rear *n* back, back end, end, hind, rear end, stern, tail, tail end; ***opp*** front

reason *n* 1 (your reason for doing sth) aim, basis, cause, end, explanation, goal, grounds, impetus, incentive, intention, justification, motive, object, objective, pretext, purpose, rationale. 2 (a man of reason) brains, common sense, intellect, judgment, logic, reasonableness, sanity, sense, understanding, wisdom, wit

reason *v* calculate, conclude, consider, deduce, figure out, infer, judge, reckon, surmise, think, work out

reasonable *adj* 1 (of a person) calm, fair, intelligent, impartial, just, logical, practical, realistic, sane, sensible, sober, sound, thinking, unbiased, wise; ***opp*** irrational. 2 (quite good) average, fair, moderate, ordinary, passable, tolerable. 3 (of a price) acceptable, appropriate, cheap, competitive, fair, inexpensive, low, modest; ***opp*** high

reasoning *n* 1 (learn sth through reasoning) analysis, deduction, logic, rationalization, theorizing, thinking, thought. 2 (sb's reasoning) argument, case, hypothesis, line of thought, rationale

reassure *v* calm, cheer, comfort, encourage, hearten, put sb at ease, restore sb's confidence, set sb's mind at rest, support, uplift; ***opp*** worry

rebel *n* anarchist, dissenter, heretic, insurgent, nonconformist, revolutionary

rebel *v* defy, disobey, dissent, resist, revolt, rise up, take a stand; ***opp*** obey

rebellion *n* 1 mutiny, resistance, revolt, revolution, riot, rising, uprising. 2 (a mood of rebellion) defiance, disobedience, dissent, heresy, nonconformity; ***opp*** obedience

rebellious *adj* defiant, difficult, disloyal, disobedient, disorderly, insurgent, intractable, mutinous, nonconformist, obstinate, rebel, recalcitrant, revolutionary, turbulent, unruly, wild; ***opp*** obedient

rebound *n* boomerang, bounce, recoil, return, ricochet, spring back

rebound *v* boomerang, bounce, recoil, return, ricochet, spring back

rebuild *v* overhaul, reassemble, recondition, reconstruct, recreate, redevelop, refashion, regenerate, remake, renovate, restore

rebuke *v* blame, castigate, censure, chide, give sb a (good) talking to *inf*, haul sb over the coals, lecture, read sb the riot act, reprehend, reprimand, reproach, reprove, scold, take sb to task, tell off *inf*, tick off *inf*

rebuke *n* blame, censure, lecture, reprimand, reproach, reproof, scolding, talking-to *inf*, telling-off *inf*, ticking-off *inf*

recall *v* 1 (recall sb's name) recollect, remember, summon up, think of. 2 (recall a product) call in, summon, take back, withdraw

recede *v* 1 (a tide recedes) ebb, fall back, go back, regress, retreat, shrink back, subside, withdraw;

opp advance. **2** (a threat recedes) decline, decrease, dwindle, fade, lessen, peter out, subside, wane; ***opp*** increase

receipt *n* **1** (a train ticket receipt) acknowledgment, bill, proof of payment, sales slip, stub, voucher. **2** (on receipt of sth) acceptance, delivery, getting, obtaining, receiving, taking

receive *v* **1** acquire, be given, be sent, collect, gain, get, obtain, pick up, take; ***opp*** give, send. **2** (receive some news) apprehend, be informed, be notified, be told, find out, gather, hear, learn of; ***opp*** tell. **3** (receive bad treatment) be subjected to, encounter, endure, experience, go through, meet with, suffer, sustain, undergo; ***opp*** give. **4** (receive guests) entertain, greet, let in, meet, show in, welcome

recent *adj* brand new, contemporary, current, fresh, late, latest, modern, new, novel, up-to-date, up-to-the-minute, young; ***opp*** old

reception *n* **1** (get an enthusiastic reception) acknowledgment, greeting, reaction, response, treatment, welcome. **2** (attend a reception) bash *inf*, do *inf*, function, gathering, get-together *inf*, party, social

receptive *adj* amenable, flexible, interested, open, open-minded, sympathetic, responsive, well-disposed, willing; ***opp*** hostile

recess *n* **1** alcove, cavity, hollow, niche, nook. **2** adjournment, break, breather *inf*, closure, holiday, respite, rest, time off, time out, vacation

recession *n* decline, depression, downturn, drop, hard times, slump; ***opp*** boom

recipe *n* directions, formula, instructions, method, prescription, procedure, process, system, technique

reciprocal *adj* alternate, common, complementary, correlative, corresponding, equivalent, exchanged, give-and-take, interchangeable, mutual, returned, shared; ***opp*** one-way

reciprocate *v* do the same, give back, match, reply, requite, respond, return

recital *n* **1** concert, performance, program, show. **2** (a recital of sth you did) account, description, narration, narrative, recounting, relation, report, statement, telling

recite *v* articulate, deliver, narrate, perform, present, rattle off *inf*, recount, reel off *inf*, relate, repeat

reckless *adj* careless, crazy *inf*, daredevil, foolhardy, hasty, heedless, impetuous, imprudent, impulsive, irresponsible, mad *inf*, rash, thoughtless, wild; ***opp*** careful, cautious, prudent

reckon *v* (sb is reckoned to be the best) believe, consider, deem, hold, judge, rate, regard. **2** (reckon that sth is true) assume, believe, conjecture, fancy, guess, imagine, suppose, surmise, think

reclaim *v* get back, recapture, recover, regain, reinstate, retrieve, take back

recline *v* lean, lie, loll, lounge, rest, stretch out

recluse *n* hermit, loner, monk, nun

recognition *n* (in recognition of sb's

bravery) acceptance, admission, appreciation, avowal, endorsement, notice, respect. **2** (act of recognizing) identification, recollection, remembrance

recognize *v* **1** identify, know, place, recall, recollect, remember, spot. **2** (recognize sb's bravery) accept, admit, appreciate, avow, endorse, notice, respect

recoil *v* **1** fly back, rebound, return, ricochet, spring back. **2** (of a person) draw back, falter, flinch, jump, shrink, shy away, start, wince

recollect *v* recall, remember, summon up, think of

recollection *n* impression, memory, remembrance, reminiscence

recommend *v* **1** (recommend a course of action) advise, advocate, counsel, propose, put forward, suggest, urge. **2** (recommend sb for a job) back *inf*, commend, endorse, favor, push *inf*, put in a good word for, speak favorably/highly/well of, support, vouch for

recommendation *n* **1** advice, counsel, hint, proposal, suggestion, tip. **2** approval, backing, blessing, commendation, endorsement, reference, support

reconcile *v* **1** (reconcile yourself to sth) accept, get used to, make the best of, resign, submit, yield; ***opp*** resist. **2** (reconcile people) appease, bring together, conciliate, pacify, placate, restore harmony, reunite; ***opp*** divide

reconnaissance *n* examination, exploration, inspection, investigation, observation, patrol, reconnoitering, scrutiny, spying

reconnoiter *v* examine, explore, inspect, investigate, observe, patrol, scan, scrutinize, survey

reconsider *v* change your mind, have a change of heart, reassess, re-examine, rethink, review, revise, think again, think better of, think twice

record *n* **1** (a record of proceedings) account, chronicle, documentation, dossier, file, journal, log, register, report. **2** (have a good record in sales) background, career, curriculum vitae, history, performance. **3** (play a record) album, disk, LP, recording, release, single. **4 off the record** confidential, private, secret, unofficial; ***opp*** public

record *v* **1** catalog, chronicle, document, enter, file, log, minute, note, put down, note down, register, report, set down, transcribe, write down. **2** tape, tape-record, video

recording *n* album, cassette, CD, compact disc, disk, record, tape, video, videotape

recount *v* communicate, depict, describe, impart, narrate, portray, recite, relate, repeat, report, tell

recover *v* **1** be on the mend, convalesce, get back on your feet, get back to normal, get better, get well, improve, perk up *inf*, pick up, pull through, rally, recuperate, revive; ***opp*** deteriorate. **2** (recover property) get back, reclaim, recoup, redeem, regain, repossess, retrieve, salvage, win back

recovery *n* **1** convalescence,

improvement, progress, rally, recuperation, revival. **2** (recovery of property) reclaiming, recouping, redeeming, regaining, repossession, retrieval, salvage

recreation *n* amusement, distraction, diversion, enjoyment, exercise, fun, hobby, leisure, pastime, play, pleasure, relaxation, relief, sport; ***opp*** work

recrimination *n* accusation, comeback *inf*, counterattack, countercharge, reprisal, retaliation, retort, retribution, vengeance

recruit *n* apprentice, beginner, convert, initiate, learner, new boy *inf*, newcomer, new girl *inf*, novice, trainee

recruit *v* draft, employ, engage, enlist, enroll, sign on, sign up, take on

rectify *v* correct, cure, fix, improve, put right, redress, remedy, repair, right, square

recuperate *v* be on the mend, convalesce, get back on your feet, get back to normal, get better, get well, improve, perk up *inf*, pick up, pull through, rally, recover, revive; ***opp*** deteriorate

recur *v* come back, happen again, persist, reappear, return

recurrent *adj* continued, frequent, habitual, intermittent, periodic, persistent, recurring, repeated, returning; ***opp*** one-off

recycle *v* reclaim, reprocess, retrieve, reuse, salvage, save, use again

red *adj* crimson, rosy, ruby, ruddy, scarlet, vermilion

redden *v* blush, flush, glow, go red

redeem *v* **1** (redeem a voucher) cash in, exchange for cash, use. **2** (redeem property) get back, reclaim, recoup, recover, regain, repossess, retrieve, salvage, win back. **3** (redeem sb) deliver, emancipate, free, liberate, release, rescue, save, set free

reduce *v* contract, cut, decrease, diminish, lessen, limit, lower, minimize, moderate, shorten, shrink, slash, truncate; ***opp*** increase

reduction *n* contraction, cut, cutback, decline, decrease, drop, lessening, limit, lowering, minimizing, moderation, shortening, shrinking, slashing, truncating; ***opp*** increase

redundant *adj* **1** nonessential, superfluous, supernumerary, surplus, unnecessary, unneeded, unwanted; ***opp*** essential. **2** (be made redundant) dismissed, jobless, laid-off, sacked, unemployed; ***opp*** employed

reel *v* falter, lurch, pitch, rock, roll, stagger, stumble, sway, totter, wobble

refer *v* **1** (refer to sth) allude, cite, hint, make reference to, mention, speak of. **2** (refer sb to sth) direct, guide, pass on, point, recommend, send. **3** (refer to a dictionary) consult, go to, look at, study, turn to

referee *n* adjudicator, arbiter, arbitrator, judge, ref *inf*, umpire

reference *n* **1** (make reference to) allusion, mention, note, remark. **2** (in reference to) concern, connection, consideration, regard, relation, respect. **3** (write a reference) endorsement, recommendation, testimonial

refine *v* **1** decontaminate, distill, filter, process, purify, treat. **2** civilize, cultivate, elevate, improve, perfect, polish, temper

refined *adj* civilized, courteous, cultivated, cultured, dignified, discerning, discriminating, elegant, genteel, gracious, ladylike, polished, polite, sophisticated, urbane, well-bred; ***opp*** common

refinement *n* 1 breeding, civility, courtesy, cultivation, culture, dignity, discernment, elegance, finesse, gentility, graciousness, polish, politeness, sophistication, taste. 2 (make a refinement) alteration, change, enhancement, improvement, modification

reflect *v* 1 echo, mirror, reproduce, return, send back, scatter, throw back. 2 (reflect on sth) consider, contemplate, deliberate, meditate, mull over, muse, ponder, ruminate, think, wonder

reflection *n* 1 echo, reproduction, image. 2 consideration, contemplation, deliberation, meditation, musing, pondering, thought, wondering

reform *n* change, conversion, correction, improvement, rebuilding, reconstruction, regeneration, remodeling, renovation, reorganization, repair, restoration, revision

reform *v* change, convert, correct, improve, mend, rebuild, reclaim, reconstruct, refashion, regenerate, remodel, renovate, reorganize, repair, restore, revamp, revise

refrain *v* abstain, avoid, cease, desist, do without, eschew, forbear, give up, leave off, quit *inf*, renounce, stop

refresh *v* 1 brace, cheer, cool, energize, enliven, fortify, freshen, invigorate, perk up *inf*, pick up, reanimate, renew, restore, revitalize, revive, revivify, stimulate. 2 (refresh sb's memory) activate, awaken, jog, prod, prompt, renew, rouse, stimulate

refreshing *adj* 1 bracing, cheering, cooling, energizing, fortifying, fresh, invigorating, restorative, revitalizing, reviving, stimulating, tonic. 2 different, fresh, original, new, novel, stimulating, welcome

refreshments *n* drinks, eatables, food, nibbles *inf*, snacks, titbits

refuge *n* 1 asylum, haven, hideaway, hideout, hiding place, protection, retreat, safety, sanctuary, security, shelter, stronghold. 2 expedient, recourse, resort, stratagem, strategy, tactic

refugee *n* displaced person, émigré, escapee, exile, fugitive, runaway

refund *n* rebate, reimbursement, repayment, return

refund *v* give back, make good, pay back, reimburse, repay, restore, return

refurbish *v* do up *inf*, fix up *inf*, make over, overhaul, recondition, redecorate, refit, remodel, renovate, restore, revamp, spruce up

refuse *n* debris, detritus, dregs, dross, garbage, junk, litter, rubbish, trash, waste

refuse *v* decline, deny, rebuff, reject, repudiate, say no, spurn, turn down, withhold

refute *v* counter, discredit, disprove, negate, overthrow, prove wrong, rebut, silence

regain *v* find, get back, recapture, reclaim, recoup, recover, recuperate, retake, retrieve, win back

regard *n* 1 attention, consideration, heed, interest, mind, notice, thought. 2 admiration, affection, appreciation, deference, esteem, honor, love, respect. 3 gaze, look, observation, scrutiny, stare

regard *v* 1 adjudge, believe, consider, deem, esteem, hold, imagine, judge, look upon, perceive, rate, reckon, see, suppose, think, treat, value, view. 2 (watch) eye, keep an eye on, look at, observe, scrutinize, stare at, study, watch, view

regarding *prep* about, apropos, as regards, as to, concerning, in regard to, in respect of, in the matter of, on the subject of, pertaining to, re, respecting, with reference to, with regard to

regime *n* dictatorship, government, junta, leadership, order, reign, rule, system

regiment *v* bring into line, control, discipline, order, organize, regulate, systematize

region *n* area, county, department, district, division, locality, part, place, province, quarter, section, sector, state, territory, tract, zone

regional *adj* district, local, parochial, provincial, sectional

register *n* annals, archives, catalog, chronicle, diary, directory, file, index, inventory, journal, ledger, list, log, record, roll

register *v* 1 archive, catalog, chronicle, enter, file, index, inscribe, list, log, note, record, take down, write down. 2 (register an emotion) betray, display, exhibit, express, indicate, manifest, reflect, reveal, show

regress *v* backslide, degenerate, deteriorate, go back, lapse, lose ground, recede, relapse, retreat, retrogress, return, revert, slip back; ***opp*** improve

regret *n* 1 compunction, conscience, contrition, guilt, penitence, remorse, repentance, ruefulness, self-reproach, sorrow. 2 bitterness, disappointment, grief, sadness, sorrow

regret *v* 1 accuse yourself, feel guilty, feel remorse, feel sorry, repent, reproach yourself, rue. 2 bemoan, bewail, deplore, deprecate, grieve, lament, miss, mourn, weep over

regrettable *adj* deplorable, disappointing, disgraceful, reprehensible, sad, shameful, unfortunate; ***opp*** fortunate

regular *adj* 1 (a regular pattern) consistent, constant, equal, even, fixed, measured, ordered, periodic, predictable, recurring, repeated, rhythmic, set, steady, symmetrical, systematic, uniform, unvarying. 2 (a regular route, procedure) common, conventional, customary, daily, established, everyday, familiar, frequent, habitual, known, normal, ordinary, orthodox, prevailing, routine, standard, typical, usual. 3 (a regular job) dependable, reliable, safe, steady

regulate *v* adjust, administer, arrange, balance, control, direct, govern, guide, handle, manage, monitor, order, oversee, rule, run, settle, steer, superintend, supervise

regulation *n* **1** bylaw, commandment, decree, dictate, directive, edict, law, order, ordinance, precept, requirement, restriction, rule, ruling, statute. **2** (the regulation of sth) adjustment, administering, administration, control, controlling, directing, direction, government, handling, management, monitoring, ordering, overseeing, running, steering, supervising, supervision

rehearsal *n* drill, dry run, practice, preparation, reading, run-through, try-out

rehearse *v* drill, go over, go through, practice, prepare, read through, repeat, run through, try out

reign *n* administration, command, control, dominion, empire, government, monarchy, power, rule, sovereignty

reign *v* administer, be in power, be on the throne, command, govern, rule

reincarnation *n* rebirth, transmigration

reinforce *v* back up, bolster, brace, buttress, emphasize, fortify, harden, prop, shore up, stiffen, strengthen, stress, support, toughen, underline

reinforcements *n* auxiliaries, back-up, help, reserves, support

reinstate *v* recall, rehabilitate, replace, restore, return, take back

reject *n* cast-off, discard, failure, second

reject *v* **1** (reject a person, thing) cast out, discard, dismiss, disown, eliminate, exclude, jettison, jilt, rebuff, renounce, repudiate, scrap, send back, send packing *inf*, shun, spurn, throw away, throw out. **2** (reject a request, offer) decline, deny, refuse, say no, turn down, veto; ***opp*** accept

rejection *n* **1** brush-off *inf*, casting out, discarding, dismissal, disowning, elimination, exclusion, jilting, renunciation, repudiation, scrapping, spurning, throwing away, throwing out. **2** denial, no, refusal, thumbs down *inf*, veto; ***opp*** acceptance

rejoice *v* celebrate, delight, exult, glory, revel, triumph

rejoicing *n* celebration, delight, elation, euphoria, exultation, gladness, happiness, jubilation, merry-making, revelry, triumph

relapse *n* degeneration, deterioration, lapse, regression, retrogression, reversion, setback, weakening, worsening

relapse *v* backslide, degenerate, deteriorate, fail, have a relapse, lapse, regress, revert, sink, weaken, worsen

relate *v* **1** communicate, describe, detail, impart, make known, narrate, present, recount, report, set forth, tell. **2** (establish a connection) ally, associate, connect, correlate, couple, join, link. **3 relate to** (be relevant) apply, be relevant, concern, have to do with, pertain, refer to

related *adj* affiliated, akin, allied, associated, connected, correlated, coupled, interconnected, linked, relevant, similar

relation *n* **1** association, bearing, bond, connection, correlation, interconnection, link, relevance, similarity. **2** family member, kin, kith and kin, relative

relations *n* **1** affairs, communication,

connections, contact, dealings, interaction, liaison, links. 2 family, kin, kindred, kinsfolk, relatives

relationship *n* 1 affinity, association, bond, conjunction, connection, correlation, interconnection, kinship, link. 2 affair, alliance, friendship, intrigue, liaison, partnership, romance

relative *adj* comparable, comparative, parallel, respective

relative *n* family member, kin, kith and kin, relation

relax *v* 1 calm down, chill out *sl*, cool down, laze around, loosen up, put your feet up *inf*, slow down, take it easy, unwind. 2 (relax a control) diminish, ease, lessen, let up, loosen, reduce, slacken, soften, weaken; ***opp*** tighten

relaxation *n* 1 amusement, diversion, enjoyment, fun, leisure, pleasure, recreation, refreshment, repose, rest. 2 (relaxation of a control) diminishing, easing, lessening, letting up, loosening, slackening, softening, weakening; ***opp*** tightening

relaxed *adj* at ease, at home, calm, carefree, casual, comfortable, cool, easy, easygoing, informal, insouciant, laid-back *inf*, leisurely, light-hearted, nonchalant, peaceful, serene, tranquil, unconcerned, untroubled; ***opp*** uptight

relay *n* 1 relief, shift, turn. 2 broadcast, dispatch, program, transmission

relay *v* broadcast, carry, communicate, hand on, pass on, send, spread, televise, transmit

release *n* 1 acquittal, deliverance, discharge, emancipation, freeing, liberating, setting free, unchaining, unfastening, unshackling, untying. 2 (a press release) announcement, bulletin, communication, proclamation, publication

release *v* 1 acquit, deliver, discharge, emancipate, extricate, free, let go, let out, liberate, loose, set free, unchain, unfasten, unshackle, untie. 2 (release news) announce, break, circulate, communicate, disseminate, distribute, issue, make available, make known, make public, present, publish, put out, send out

relent *v* be merciful, capitulate, forbear, give way, melt, show mercy, soften, yield

relentless *adj* harsh, implacable, inexorable, merciless, pitiless, remorseless, ruthless, unbending, unrelenting, unyielding

relevant *adj* applicable, apposite, appropriate, apt, connected, germane, material, pertinent, related, salient, significant, to the point; ***opp*** irrelevant

reliable *adj* certain, consistent, constant, dependable, faithful, loyal, predictable, proven, regular, responsible, safe, secure, solid, sound, stable, staunch, sure, true, trusty, trustworthy, unfailing; ***opp*** unreliable

relic *n* fragment, keepsake, memento, remains, reminder, remnant, scrap, token, trace, vestige

relief *n* aid, alleviation, assistance, balm, comfort, cure, deliverance, diversion, ease, help, letup *inf*, remedy, remission, rescue, respite, solace, succour, support

relieve *v* 1 aid, allay, alleviate, assist, assuage, calm, comfort, deliver, ease, help, lessen, lift, lighten, mitigate, moderate, palliate, reduce, release, remedy, rescue, soothe, succour, support. **2** (relieve sb at work) fill in for, stand in for, substitute for, replace, take over from, take the place of

religion *n* belief, creed, denomination, divinity, doctrine, dogma, faith, sect, theology

religious *adj* devotional, devout, faithful, God-fearing, godly, holy, pious, pure, reverent, righteous, spiritual

relish *v* appreciate, delight in, enjoy, like, love, revel in, savor, take pleasure in

reluctant *adj* averse, disinclined, grudging, hesitant, loath, slow, unenthusiastic, unwilling; ***opp*** keen, willing

rely *v* **rely on** bank on, be sure of, bet on, count on, depend on, have confidence in, lean on, put your trust in, reckon on, swear by, trust

remain *v* abide, be left, carry on, continue, endure, keep on, last, linger, live on, persist, prevail, stand, stay, survive

remainder *n* balance, excess, leavings, leftovers, remains, remnants, residue, rest, surplus

remaining *adj* left, lingering, outstanding, persisting, surviving, unfinished

remains *n* **1** balance, crumbs, debris, dregs, leavings, leftovers, pieces, relics, remnants, residue, rest, scraps, traces, vestiges. **2** ashes, body, bones, cadaver, carcass, corpse

remark *n* assertion, comment, declaration, observation, pronouncement, reflection, statement, utterance

remark *v* **1** assert, comment, declare, mention, note, observe, pass comment, reflect, say, state. **2** discern, espy, heed, mark, note, notice, observe, perceive, regard, see

remarkable *adj* amazing, astonishing, astounding, considerable, distinctive, distinguished, exceptional, extraordinary, impressive, notable, noteworthy, outstanding, phenomenal, preeminent, rare, singular, strange, striking, surprising, uncommon, unforgettable, unusual; ***opp*** ordinary, unremarkable

remedy *n* antidote, corrective, countermeasure, cure, drug, medication, medicine, palliative, panacea, relief, therapy, treatment

remedy *v* alleviate, assuage, control, correct, counter, counteract, cure, ease, heal, help, rectify, relieve, soothe, treat

remember *v* be mindful of, call up, keep in mind, recall, recognize, recollect, reminisce, retain

remind *v* bring to mind, call up, give a reminder, jog your memory, prompt

reminder *n* **1** cue, hint, memo *inf*, memorandum, mnemonic, note, nudge, prompt. **2** keepsake, memento, relic, remembrance, souvenir

reminiscent *adj* evocative, redolent, similar, suggestive

remiss *adj* careless, forgetful, heedless, inattentive, lax, neglectful, negligent, slack, slipshod, sloppy *inf*, thoughtless, unmindful, unthinking

remission *n* **1** absolution, amnesty, discharge, exemption, exoneration, forgiveness, parole, pardon, release, repeal, reprieve. **2** abatement, alleviation, lull, moderation, reduction, relaxation, respite, suspension

remittance *n* allowance, fee, payment, transfer

remnant *n* bit, crumbs, debris, dregs, fragment, leavings, leftovers, relic, remnant, residue, rest, scrap, trace, vestige

remonstrate *v* argue, challenge, complain, dispute, dissent, expostulate, object, oppose, protest, take exception, take issue

remorse *n* compunction, conscience, contrition, guilt, mortification, penitence, regret, repentance, self-reproach, shame, sorrow

remorseful *adj* ashamed, conscious-stricken, contrite, guilt-ridden, guilty, mortified, penitent, regretful, repentant, sorry

remorseless *adj* cruel, harsh, implacable, inexorable, inhumane, merciless, pitiless, relentless, ruthless, unrelenting, unremitting

remote *adj* **1** cut off, distant, far, faraway, far-off, inaccessible, in the middle of nowhere, isolated, lonely, off the beaten track, out of the way, secluded. **2** aloof, chilly, cool, detached, distant, haughty, removed, reserved, standoffish, unapproachable, unfriendly, withdrawn; ***opp*** friendly

removal *n* **1** carrying away, moving, relocating, removing, taking away, transfer, transportation. **2** abolition, deletion, effacing, elimination, eradication, erasure, extermination, liquidation, obliteration, withdrawal. **3** (of a person) deposition, dislodging, dismissal, ejection, expulsion, eviction, firing, ousting, replacement, sacking

remove *v* **1** carry away, convey, move, relocate, take away, transfer, transport. **2** abolish, banish, delete, do away with, eliminate, efface, eradicate, erase, excise, expunge, exterminate, get rid of, kill, liquidate, obliterate, withdraw. **3** (remove a person) depose, dislodge, dismiss, eject, expel, evict, fire, oust, replace, sack. **4** (remove clothes) doff, peel off, shed, slip off, strip off, take off

render *v* **1** cause to be, get, leave, make. **2** (give) cede, contribute, deliver, furnish, give, hand over, make available, offer, present, provide, submit, supply, surrender, tender, turn over, yield. **3** (give a performance of) act, depict, do, execute, interpret, perform, present, portray, represent

renege *v* back out, break your promise, cop out *inf*, default, go back on your word, pull out

renew *v* **1** modernize, overhaul, recondition, refit, refurbish, regenerate, rejuvenate, remodel, renovate, repair, replace, restore, resurrect, revamp, revitalize, revive, transform. **2** (renew efforts) come back to, continue, pick up, recommence, restart, resume, return to. **3** (renew a pledge) confirm, reaffirm, reiterate, repeat, restate

renounce *v* abandon, abstain, cast off, deny, discard, disown, eschew, forgo, forsake, forswear, give up, quit, reject, relinquish, repudiate, spurn, waive

renovate *v* fix up *inf*, modernize,

overhaul, recondition, refit, refurbish, remake, remodel, repair, restore, revamp

renowned *adj* acclaimed, celebrated, distinguished, eminent, famed, famous, illustrious, known, noted, prominent, well-known

rent *n* fee, hire, lease, payment, rental, tariff

rent *v* charter, lease, let

repair *n* darn, fixing, mending, overhaul, patch, restoration

repair *v* darn, fix, heal, mend, patch, patch up, put right, renovate, restore

repay *v* **1** (repay money) compensate, pay back, recompense, refund, reimburse, settle up, square. **2** (repay a wrong) avenge, get back at, get even, get your own back *inf*, hit back, reciprocate, retaliate, revenge, settle the score

repeal *v* (repeal a law) abolish, annul, cancel, invalidate, rescind, revoke, withdraw

repeat *n* recap *inf*, repetition, replay, reproduction, rerun

repeat *v* **1** (say sth again) echo, parrot, quote, recap *inf*, recite, reiterate, retell, say again. **2** (do sth again) copy, do again, duplicate, rehearse, replay, replicate, reproduce, rerun, show again

repel *v* **1** (repel invaders) beat back, confront, drive back, fend off, fight, force back, hold off, keep at bay, resist, ward off. **2** (sth repels you) be repellent, disgust, make your flesh creep, make you sick, nauseate, offend, put off *inf*, revolt, shock, sicken, turn your stomach. **3** (repel water) be impermeable to, keep out, resist; ***opp*** attract

repellent *adj* abhorrent, disgusting, distasteful, foul, horrid, loathsome, nauseating, obnoxious, obscene, odious, offensive, off-putting, repugnant, repulsive, revolting, sickening, vile

repent *v* atone, be contrite, be penitent, be sorry, feel remorse, regret, reproach yourself, rue

repentance *n* compunction, contrition, grief, guilt, penitence, regret, remorse, self-accusation, self-reproach, shame, sorrow

repentant *adj* apologetic, ashamed, chastened, conscience-stricken, contrite, guilt-ridden, penitent, remorseful, sorry; ***opp*** unrepentant

repercussion *n* backlash, consequence, effect, result, sequel

repetition *n* **1** (too much repetition) copying, duplication, redundancy, repeating, repetitiousness. **2** (a repetition) duplication, echo, recurrence, repeat, restatement, retelling

repetitive *adj* boring, dull, mechanical, monotonous, recurrent, repeated, tedious, unchanging

replace *v* **1** (replace sth) change, make good, put back, renew, restore, substitute. **2** (replace sb) come after, cover for, fill in for, follow, oust, stand in for, succeed, supersede, take the place of, understudy

replacement *n* double, locum, proxy, stand-in, substitute, successor, surrogate, understudy

replenish *v* fill, refill, renew, replace, restock, stock up

replica *n* carbon copy, clone, copy, duplicate, facsimile, imitation, likeness, model, reproduction

reply *n* acknowledgement, answer, comeback *inf*, reaction, rejoinder, response, retort, riposte

reply *v* **1** (reply to what sb says) answer, counter, rejoin, respond, retort, riposte. **2** (reply to a letter) acknowledge, answer, write back. **3** (reply to what sb does) react, reciprocate, respond, retaliate

report *n* **1** account, announcement, article, description, message, news, note, paper, piece, statement, story, write-up. **2** (a loud report) backfire, bang, blast, boom, crack, crash, discharge, echo, explosion, noise, sound

report *v* **1** (tell people about sth) announce, broadcast, circulate, communicate, describe, disclose, document, publish, recount, reveal, tell, write about, write up. **2** (report sb) accuse, complain about, denounce, inform against, inform on, rat on *inf*, squeal on *inf*, tell on *inf*. **3** (report for duty) announce yourself, arrive, be present, check in, come, present yourself, sign in, turn up

reporter *n* correspondent, journalist, newscaster, newsman, newspaperman, newspaperwoman, newswoman, presenter, writer

repose *n* calmness, ease, peace, peacefulness, quietness, relaxation, rest, serenity, sleep, slumber, stillness, tranquillity

reprehensible *adj* bad, blameworthy, culpable, delinquent, deplorable, disgraceful, inexcusable, shameful, unpardonable, wicked, wrong

represent *v* **1** correspond to, embody, exemplify, express, mean, stand for, symbolize, typify. **2** (sb must represent the people) act for, be the representative of, be the spokesperson for, speak for. **3** (represent sb in a picture) depict, draw, evoke, illustrate, paint, portray, render, show, sketch. **4** (represent sb on stage) act out, assume the guise of, enact, impersonate, personify, pose as, pretend to be, show

representation *n* account, depiction, description, figure, icon, illustration, image, likeness, model, painting, picture, portrait, portrayal, statue

representative *adj* **1** (of a sample) archetypal, average, characteristic, illustrative, indicative, normal, symbolic, typical. **2** (of a government) authorized, chosen, delegated, democratic, elected, elective, official, popular

representative *n* **1** ambassador, consul, councillor, delegate, deputy, emissary, envoy, ombudsman, spokesman, spokesperson, spokeswoman, stand-in, substitute. **2** (a representative for a company) agent, rep *inf*, salesman, salesperson, saleswoman

repress *v* **1** (repress people) control, crush, dominate, intimidate, keep down, oppress, overpower, quash, quell, restrain, subdue, subjugate. **2** (repress feelings) bottle up *inf*, control, inhibit, hold in, keep in, smother, stifle, suppress; ***opp*** show

repressed *adj* **1** (of people) frustrated, inhibited, restrained, tense, unbalanced, uptight *inf*, withdrawn. **2** (of feelings) hidden, subconscious, suppressed, unconscious

repression *n* control, domination, oppression, subjugation, totalitarianism, tyranny

repressive *adj* absolute, authoritarian, brutal, despotic, dictatorial, fascist, harsh, oppressive, tyrannical, undemocratic; ***opp*** liberal

reprieve *n* amnesty, pardon, postponement, stay of execution

reprieve *v* forgive, let off, pardon, rescue, save, set free, spare

reprimand *n* condemnation, criticism, dressing-down *inf*, lecture *inf*, rebuke, reproach, scolding, slap on the wrist *inf*, talking-to *inf*, telling-off *inf*, ticking-off *inf*

reprimand *v* castigate, criticize, lecture *inf*, rebuke, reproach, scold, tell off *inf*, tick off *inf*

reprisal *n* redress, retaliation, retribution, revenge, vengeance

reproach *n* blame, contempt, criticism, disapproval, discredit, disgrace, scorn, shame, stigma

reproach *v* blame, censure, condemn, criticize, find fault, reprimand, scold, show disapproval; ***opp*** praise

reproachful *adj* censorious, critical, disappointed, disapproving, disparaging, reproving, scolding, scornful

reproduce *v* **1** clone, copy, echo, forge, imitate, match, mirror, parallel, recreate, redo, remake, repeat, replicate. **2** copy, duplicate, make a copy of, photocopy, print, reprint. **3** bear young, breed, give birth, increase, multiply, procreate, produce offspring, spawn

reproduction *n* copy, duplicate, facsimile, fake, fax, forgery, imitation, photocopy, picture, print, replica

repudiate *v* contradict, deny, disagree with, disclaim, dispute, rebuff, reject

repugnant *adj* abhorrent, disagreeable, disgusting, distasteful, hateful, horrible, nauseating, objectionable, offensive, repellent, revolting, sickening, unpleasant

repulsive *adj* abominable, disgusting, distasteful, foul, gross *slang*, hateful, hideous, loathsome, nasty, nauseating, odious, off-putting *inf*, repellent, repugnant, revolting, sick *inf*, sickening, ugly, vile

reputable *adj* (a reputable company) aboveboard, excellent, good, highly regarded, honorable, legitimate, of good repute, prestigious, reliable, respectable, respected, trustworthy, upright, well-thought-of; ***opp*** disreputable

reputation *n* character, good name, name, position, prestige, recognition, renown, repute, respectability, standing, status

reputed *adj* alleged, believed, considered, deemed, judged, reckoned, regarded, rumored, said, supposed, thought

request *n* appeal, call, demand, desire, entreaty, petition, plea, prayer, question

request *v* apply for, ask, ask for, beg, beseech, call for, claim, demand, desire, implore, invite, pray, seek

require *v* **1** (need) be missing, be short of, crave, desire, lack, miss, need, want, wish. **2** (require sb to do sth) ask, bid, command, compel, force, insist upon, instruct, oblige, order, put pressure on, request. **3** (require a lot of strength) call for, demand, depend on, necessitate, need, take

requirement *n* condition, demand, essential, necessity, need, precondition, qualification, stipulation

requisite *adj* called for, compulsory, essential, indispensable, mandatory, necessary, needed, obligatory, required, vital

rescue *n* deliverance, freeing, liberation, recovery, release, rescuing, salvage, saving

research *n***rescue** *v* deliver, free, get back, get out, liberate, recover, redeem, release, retrieve, salvage, save, set free

analysis, enquiry, examination, experimentation, exploration, fact-finding, inquiry, investigation, study, tests

research *v* analyze, examine, experiment, explore, investigate, look into, review, study, test

resemblance *n* analogy, comparison, conformity, congruity, correspondence, kinship, likeness, similarity

resemble *v* bear a resemblance to, be like, duplicate, echo, look like, mirror, put you in mind of, sound like, remind you of, take after

resent *v* begrudge, be resentful about, dislike, envy, feel aggrieved at, feel bitter about, grudge, grumble at, object to, take exception to, take offense at, take umbrage at

resentful *adj* aggrieved, angry, bitter, disgruntled, in a huff *inf*, indignant, irate, irked, irritated, jealous, miffed *inf*, offended, peeved *inf*, piqued, put out *inf*, spiteful, vindictive

resentment *n* anger, animosity, bitterness, displeasure, fury, hard feelings, hurt, ill-will, indignation, malice, pique, rancor, spite

reservation *n* **1** (have reservations about sth) doubt, hesitation, misgiving, qualm, reluctance, skepticism, scruple. **2** (live on a reservation) enclave, homeland, preserve, reserve, sanctuary, territory, tract. **3** (a reservation at a restaurant) appointment, arrangement, booking

reserve *adj* auxiliary, extra, fall-back, in reserve, spare, substitute

reserve *n* **1** (kept a reserve for emergencies) fund, hoard, savings, stock, stockpile, store, supply. **2** (known for his reserve) aloofness, coolness, detachment, formality, modesty, remoteness, restraint, reticence, self-effacement, shyness. **3** (animals on a reserve) area, game park, park, protected area, reservation, sanctuary, tract. **4** (an extra person) backup *inf*, reinforcements, replacement, stand-in *inf*, substitute

reserve *v* **1** (reserve a ticket) book, order, pay in advance for, prearrange. **2** (reserve sth for later) conserve, earmark, hang on to *inf*, hoard, keep, keep back, lay aside, put away, save, set aside, stockpile, store up, withhold

reserved *adj* **1** (of a person) aloof, cautious, cold, cool, demure, diffident, modest, quiet, remote, restrained, reticent, self-effacing, shy, silent, undemonstrative, unfriendly, unsociable. **2** (of a table, seat) booked, engaged, held, kept, retained, taken

reside *v* abide, dwell, inhabit, live, lodge, occupy, settle, stay

residence *n* address, dwelling, flat, home, house, lodgings, quarters

resident *n* citizen, householder, inhabitant, local, lodger, occupant, occupier, tenant

residue *n* dregs, excess, extra, leftovers, remainder, remains, remnant, rest, surplus

resign *v* abdicate, give notice, give up, hand in your notice, hand over, leave, quit, retire, step down *inf*

resigned *adj* **1** compliant, forbearing, long-suffering, passive, patient, philosophical, stoical, subdued, tolerant, unresisting. **2** (resigned to sth) accepting, acquiescent, reconciled, submitting, yielding

resilient *adj* **1** (of materials) bouncy, elastic, firm, flexible, plastic, pliable, pliant, rubbery, springy, supple; ***opp*** brittle. **2** (of a person) adaptable, buoyant, irrepressible, quick to recover, strong, tough, unstoppable

resist *v* **1** (stop sth) block, check, counteract, curb, frustrate, halt, hinder, inhibit, keep at bay, obstruct, prevent, rebuff, stop. **2** (resist an enemy) battle against, combat, confront, defy, fight, oppose, repel, stand up to, thwart. **3** (resist moisture) be resistant to, repel, withstand. **4** (try to resist a cake) abstain from, avoid, desist from, do without, refrain from

resistant *adj* **1** immune to, impervious to, proof against, strong, tough, unaffected by; ***opp*** susceptible to. **2** (resistant to change) antagonistic, defiant, hostile, intransigent, obstinate, opposed, recalcitrant, stubborn, uncooperative, unyielding

resolute *adj* adamant, bold, committed, decided, decisive, determined, dogged, immovable, obstinate, persistent, resolved, set, singleminded, staunch, steadfast, stubborn, tenacious, unbending, undaunted, unwavering

resolution *n* **1** boldness, commitment, courage, dedication, determination, persistence, purpose, resolve, staying power, steadfastness, willpower. **2** (a resolution) aim, decision, declaration, intent, intention, judgment, motion, plan, pledge, promise, resolve, undertaking, verdict, vow

resolve *v* **1** (resolve to do sth) agree, decide, determine, intend, make up your mind, undertake. **2** (resolve a difficulty) clear up, figure out, settle, sort out, solve, unravel, work out

resort *n* haunt, refuge, retreat, spot, vacation spot

resort to *v* employ, exercise, fall back on, make use of, turn to, use, utilize

resource *n* **1** fund, reserve, stock, stockpile, supply. **2** course, device, expedient, means, way

resourceful *adj* able, bright, capable, clever, creative, enterprising, imaginative, ingenious, inspired, inventive, quick-witted, skillful, talented

resources *n* assets, capital, funds, holdings, money, possessions, reserves, supplies, wealth

respect *n* **1** (respect for sb) admiration, approval, awe, consideration, esteem, honor, recognition, regard, reverence. **2** (in this/that respect) aspect, attribute, characteristic, detail, feature, matter, particular, point, quality, sense, trait, way. **3** (show respect) consideration, courtesy, deference, politeness, thoughtfulness. **4** (with respect to your letter) reference, regard

respect *v* **1** (respect sb) admire, adore, defer to, esteem, have a high opinion of, honor, look up to, revere, think highly of, venerate. **2** (respect rules) abide by, adhere to, comply with, follow, heed, obey, observe; ***opp*** break. **3** (respect sb's views) recognize, show consideration for, take into account, value

respectable *adj* **1** (of a person) decent, dignified, genteel, good, honest, honorable, law-abiding, of good repute, proper, reputable, trustworthy, upright, venerable, virtuous, worthy. **2** (of an amount) adequate, ample, appreciable, considerable, decent, fair, goodly, presentable, reasonable, satisfactory, sizable, substantial, tolerable

respectful *adj* admiring, civil, considerate, courteous, deferential, dutiful, humble, polite, reverential, subservient; ***opp*** disrespectful

respective *adj* individual, own, particular, personal, relevant, special, specific, various

respite *n* break, breather *inf*, cessation, halt, hiatus, holiday, interval, letup *inf*, lull, pause, relief, rest, time off, time out

respond *v* **1** (respond to a letter) acknowledge, answer, reply, write back. **2** (respond to speech or action) answer, counter, react, reciprocate, reply, retort, return

response *n* answer, comeback *inf*, feedback, reaction, reply

responsibility *n* **1** (have a responsibility) accountability, answerability, authority, duty, importance, liability, obligation, onus, power, trust. **2** (responsibility for sth going wrong) accountability, blame, burden, fault, guilt, liability

responsible *adj* **1** (having responsibility) accountable, in charge, in control, liable. **2** (responsible for sth going wrong) accountable, answerable, at fault, culpable, guilty, to blame; ***opp*** innocent. **3** (behaving in a responsible way) adult, conscientious, dependable, levelheaded, mature, reasonable, reliable, sensible, steady, trustworthy; ***opp*** irresponsible. **4** (a responsible job) decision-making, executive, front-line *inf*, high, important, managerial, powerful; ***opp*** menial

rest *n* **1** (stop for a rest) break, breather *inf*, halt, interlude, intermission, interval, lull, pause, respite, time off, time out. **2** (a well-earned rest) break, vacation. **3** (a sleep) forty winks *inf*, nap, siesta, sleep. **4** (need plenty of rest) calmness, ease, hush, inactivity, peace, quiet, relaxation, repose, sleep, tranquillity. **5** (throw away the rest) balance, excess, leftovers, others, remainder, remnants, residue, surplus

rest *v* **1** be still, catnap, doze, have a nap, have a rest, have a sleep, lie down, nod off, put your feet up, snooze *inf*, take it easy *inf*, unwind. **2** (rest on a surface) lean, lie, place, prop, set, sit, stand, steady, support. 3 (everything rests on your answer) depend, hang, hinge, rely, turn

restful *adj* calm, calming, leisurely, peaceful, placid, quiet, relaxed, relaxing, serene, sleepy, soothing, still, tranquil

restless *adj* 1 (not staying in one place) itinerant, nomadic, roaming, roving, transient, traveling, unsettled, wandering; ***opp*** settled. 2 (constantly moving) active, busy, changable, changing, in motion, moving, on the move, turbulent; ***opp*** still. 3 (not getting much sleep) disturbed, fitful, fretful, sleepless, uncomfortable, uneasy, wakeful; ***opp*** restful. 4 (not patient or calm) agitated, edgy, excitable, fidgeting, fidgety, ill at ease, impatient, jittery *inf*, jumpy, nervous, restive, uneasy, unruly, unsettled, worked up, worried; ***opp*** calm, relaxed

restore *v* 1 (restore sth old) clean, fix, fix up *inf*, mend, recondition, redecorate, refurbish, renew, renovate, repair, revamp. 2 (restore a person) build up, refresh, rejuvenate, revive, revitalize, strengthen. 3 (restore stolen property) bring back, give back, hand back, recover, replace, return, send back

restrain *v* 1 (restrain feelings) control, curb, hold in check, inhibit, rein in, repress, stifle, subdue, suppress; ***opp*** show. 2 (restrain a prisoner) chain up, confine, detain, handcuff, imprison, lock up, manacle, tie up; ***opp*** let loose. 3 (restrain sb from doing sth) hinder, hold back, keep, obstruct, prevent, save, stop; ***opp*** encourage

restrained *adj* 1 (of a person) calm, controlled, mild, moderate, reticent, undemonstrative, unemotional. 2 (of colors) discreet, muted, soft, subtle, tasteful, understated, unobtrusive

restraint *n* 1 (show restraint) inhibition, moderation, prudence, self-control, self-discipline. 2 (a restraint on sth) ban, check, constraint, curb, deterrent, embargo, limit, rein, restriction

restrict *v* circumscribe, confine, contain, control, hamper, handicap, hinder, impede, imprison, limit, moderate, regulate, restrain

restriction *n* ban, check, condition, control, curb, handicap, limit, limitation, proviso, qualification, regulation, restraint, rule, stipulation

result *n* 1 (the result of sth happening) conclusion, consequence, effect, outcome, repercussion, sequel, upshot. 2 (the wrong result) answer, decision, judgment, solution, verdict

result *v* appear, arise, come about, derive, develop, emerge, ensue, follow, happen, occur, proceed, spring, stem, take place, turn out

resume *v* begin again, carry on, continue, proceed, recommence, reopen, restart, take up

resurrect *v* breathe new life into, bring back, raise from the dead, reawaken, reintroduce, renew, restore to life, revive

resuscitate *v* bring round, give the kiss of life to, revive, save

retain *v* 1 absorb, contain, hang on to *inf*, hold, keep, keep hold of, keep in, maintain, preserve, reserve, save, soak up; ***opp*** lose. **2** keep in mind, learn, memorize, recall, recollect, remember; ***opp*** forget

retaliate *v* avenge yourself, get even *inf*, get your own back, give as good as you get, hit back, reciprocate, repay, settle a score, strike back, take revenge

retard *v* arrest, delay, handicap, hinder, hold back, impede, obstruct, set back, slow down

reticent *adj* quiet, reserved, retiring, secretive, shy, silent, tight-lipped, uncommunicative

retire *v* **1** give up work, leave, quit, stop working. **2** depart, exit, go away, go out, leave, withdraw. **3** call it a day, go to bed, go to sleep, turn in *inf*

retiring *adj* bashful, coy, demure, diffident, meek, modest, quiet, reserved, reticent, shrinking, shy, timid, unassertive; ***opp*** outgoing

retort *n* answer, rejoinder, reply, response, riposte

retort *v* answer, answer back, come back at, counter, reply, riposte, say in reply

retract *v* **1** draw in, pull back, pull in, sheathe. **2** backtrack on, cancel, deny, disclaim, disown, renounce, repudiate, reverse, revoke, take back, withdraw

retreat *n* **1** asylum, den, haunt, haven, hideaway, hideout, hiding place, refuge, sanctuary, shelter. **2** departure, evacuation, exit, flight, withdrawal

retreat *v* **1** back away, back down, back off, depart, draw back, evacuate, fall back, flee, give way, go away, go back, leave, move back, pull back, recoil, retire, run away, take flight, take to your heels *inf*, turn tail, withdraw; ***opp*** advance. **2** ebb, flow back, recede, shrink back; ***opp*** advance

retribution *n* compensation, justice, punishment, reckoning, recompense, redress, reparation, repayment, reprisal, retaliation, revenge, reward, vengeance

retrieve *v* bring back, fetch, find, get back, recall, recapture, recover, regain, repossess, rescue, salvage, trace, track down, win back

retrospective *adj* backward-looking, looking back, with hindsight

return *n* **1** arrival, coming home, homecoming, reappearance. **2** (a good return on your investment) earnings, gain, income, interest, profit, revenue, yield

return *v* **1** come again, come back, go back, reappear. **2** (return to look for sth) backtrack, double back, go back, retrace your steps. **3** (return a library book) give back, put back, replace, restore, send back, take back. **4** (return a favor) pay back, reciprocate, repay

reveal *v* **1** (reveal a secret) announce, betray, broadcast, confess, disclose, divulge, give away, leak, let on, let out, let slip, make known, publicize, tell. **2** (show sth) bare, display, expose, show, uncover, unmask, unveil

revel *v* **1** celebrate, have fun, live it up *inf*, make merry, paint the town red *inf*, party. **2** (revel in sth) bask, delight, gloat, luxuriate, relish, savor, take pleasure, wallow

revelation *n* admission, betrayal, confession, disclosure, discovery, leak *inf*, publishing, revealing, telling

revelry *n* celebrations, festivities, fun,

gaiety, jollification, jollity, living it up *inf*, merrymaking, party

revenge *n* 1 (get your revenge) redress, reprisal, retaliation, retribution, vengeance. 2 (feelings of revenge) hate, hatred, hostility, malice, spite, spitefulness, vindictiveness

revenue *n* gain, income, interest, money, proceeds, profits, receipts, returns, takings, rewards, yield

reverberate *v* boom, echo, rebound, resonate, resound, ring, thunder, vibrate

revere *v* adore, exalt, glorify, honor, idolize, pay homage to, praise, respect, venerate, worship

reverent *adj* adoring, awed, deferential, devout, humble, pious, religious, respectful, reverential, solemn, submissive, worshipful

reverse *adj* back-to-front, backward, backwards, contrary, converse, inverted, opposite, transposed

reverse *n* 1 contrary, converse, inverse, opposite. 2 back, other side, rear, wrong side

reverse *v* 1 (in a vehicle) back, go backwards, move backwards. 2 (reverse a judgment) annul, cancel, change, countermand, invalidate, overrule, overturn, quash, repeal, revoke, set aside, undo, upset. 3 (reverse an image) invert, put back to front, transpose, turn over, turn round, turn upside down, up-end

review *n* 1 analysis, assessment, fresh look, reassessment, reconsideration, re-examination, rethink. 2 (write a review) appreciation, commentary, criticism, critique, evaluation, judgment, report, study, write-up

review *v* 1 (review a decision) look again at, reassess, reconsider, reexamine, rethink, think over. 2 (review a performance) analyze, appraise, assess, criticize, evaluate, judge, write a review of. 3 (review the year) look back on, look back over, recall, recollect, reflect on, remember, survey

reviewer *n* commentator, critic, judge

revise *v* 1 (revise your opinion) alter, amend, change, modify, reconsider, review. 2 (revise your work) correct, edit, improve, redraft, rephrase, rewrite, update. 3 (revise for a test) brush up, cram *inf*, learn, read, reread, study

revision *n* 1 alteration, amendment, change, correction, modification, rewriting, updating. 2 homework, reading, studying

revival *n* reawakening, rebirth, renaissance, renewal, resurgence, resurrection, return, upsurge

revive *v* 1 (revive a person) bring round, give the kiss of life to *inf*, resuscitate, rouse. 2 (sb revives) come back to life, come round, come to, rally, recover, regain consciousness. 3 (a drink to revive you) cheer, invigorate, refresh, revitalize, strengthen. 4 (revive memories) awaken, call forth, rekindle, stir up

revolt *n* civil war, coup, insurgency, insurrection, mutiny, rebellion, revolution, rising, uprising

revolt *v* 1 defect, disobey, mutiny, rebel, resist, riot, rise up, take to the streets. 2 (sth revolts you) appall, disgust, make your flesh creep, make you sick, nauseate, offend, repel, sicken, turn your stomach

revolting *adj* abhorrent, disgusting, distasteful, foul, horrible, nasty, nauseating, obnoxious, obscene, offensive, repellent, repugnant, repulsive, shocking, sickening, vile

revolution *n* **1** coup, coup d'état, insurgency, mutiny, putsch, rebellion, revolt, rising, uprising. **2** change, reorganization, shift, transformation, upheaval, U-turn *inf*. **3** circle, circuit, cycle, gyration, orbit, rotation, round, spin, turn

revolutionary *adj* **1** (revolutionary methods) avant-garde, different, drastic, experimental, groundbreaking, innovative, new, novel, progressive, radical; ***opp*** conservative. **2** (revolutionary forces) extremist, insurgent, mutinous, rebel, subversive

revolve *v* circle, go round, gyrate, orbit, rotate, spin, swivel, turn, turn round, twist, wheel, whirl

revulsion *n* abhorrence, aversion, disgust, distaste, hate, hatred, loathing, repugnance

reward *n* award, bonus, decoration, gift, honor, medal, payment, present, prize, remuneration, tribute

reward *v* compensate, decorate, give a reward to, honor, pay, recompense, remunerate, tip

rewarding *adj* beneficial, fulfilling, gratifying, productive, profitable, satisfying, useful, valuable, worthwhile; ***opp*** unrewarding

rhetoric *n* eloquence, expressiveness, gift of the gab *inf*, oratory, rhetorical language, speechifying, verbosity

rhetorical *adj* bombastic, extravagant, flamboyant, florid, flowery, high-flown, insincere, longwinded, ostentatious, pretentious, showy, verbose, wordy

rhyme *n* ditty, doggerel, jingle, ode, poem, poetry, song, verse

rhythm *n* accent, beat, cadence, flow, lilt, meter, movement, pattern, pulse, stress, swing, tempo, time

rhythmic *adj* flowing, harmonious, lilting, measured, melodious, metrical, musical, pulsating, regular, repeated, rhythmical, steady, throbbing

rich *adj* **1** affluent, flush *inf*, loaded *inf*, made of money *inf*, moneyed, prosperous, wealthy, well-heeled *inf*, well-off, well-to-do; ***opp*** poor. **2** (rich furnishings) costly, elaborate, elegant, expensive, exquisite, fine, gorgeous, grand, lavish, opulent, palatial, precious, splendid, sumptuous, valuable; ***opp*** simple. **3** (rich ground) abundant, ample, copious, fertile, fruitful, lush, luxurious, plentiful, productive, prolific; ***opp*** poor. **4** (an area rich in wildlife) abounding, full, overflowing, replete, rife, teeming, well-provided, well-stocked, well-supplied. **5** (rich food) cloying, creamy, delicious, fattening, fatty, full-flavored, heavy, savory, spicy, succulent, sweet, tasty; ***opp*** light. **6** (rich sounds) deep, full, mellow, melodious, resonant; ***opp*** thin. **7** (a rich red) brilliant, deep, intense, strong, vivid, warm

riches *n* affluence, assets, fortune, gold, money, possessions, property, resources, treasure, wealth; ***opp*** poverty

rid *v* 1 cleanse, clear, deliver, free, purge, purify, relieve, rescue, save, unburden. 2 **get rid of** destroy, dispose of, do away with, dump, eject, eliminate, expel, jettison, remove, throw away, unload

riddle *n* brainteaser *inf*, conundrum, enigma, mystery, poser, problem, puzzle, question

ride *n* drive, journey, joyride *inf*, lift, outing, spin *inf*, trip

ride *v* 1 float, gallop, go, journey, move, progress, travel, trot. 2 (ride a bicycle) be mounted on, control, handle, manage, mount, pedal, sit on, steer

ridicule *n* derision, irony, laughter, mockery, sarcasm, satire, scorn, sneering, teasing, taunting

ridicule *v* be sarcastic about, caricature, deride, humiliate, jeer at, laugh at, make jokes about, mock, parody, poke fun at, satirize, sneer at, taunt, tease

ridiculous *adj* 1 (a ridiculous story) amusing, crazy, droll, farcical, funny, humorous, illogical, incredible, ludicrous, nonsensical, preposterous, surreal, unbelievable. 2 (you look ridiculous) absurd, comical, foolish, funny, hilarious, silly, weird. 3 (a ridiculous price) crazy, derisory, laughable, ludicrous, outrageous, shocking, stupid, unreasonable; ***opp*** reasonable

rife *adj* abundant, common, general, predominant, prevalent, rampant, ubiquitous, universal, widespread; ***opp*** rare

rift *n* 1 (a physical rift) breach, break, chink, cleft, crack, crevice, fault, fissure, opening, split. 2 (a rift in a family) breach, difference, disagreement, division, feud, quarrel, separation

rig *v* 1 equip, fit, fit out, furnish, provide, set up, supply. 2 (rig the results) arrange, engineer, fake, falsify, fix *inf*, manipulate, tamper with. 3 **rig up** assemble,build, cobble together, construct, improvise, knock up, put together, throw together

right *adj* 1 (what you did was right) correct, decent, equitable, ethical, fair, good, honest, honorable, just, lawful, moral, proper, virtuous; ***opp*** wrong. 2 (the right time) accurate, correct, exact, precise, true; ***opp*** wrong. 3 (at the right moment) appropriate, convenient, ideal, opportune, proper; ***opp*** wrong. 4 (the right thing to wear) appropriate, decent, fit, proper, seemly, suitable; ***opp*** inappropriate. 5 (do sth the right way) best, good, normal, preferable, preferred, recommended, sensible, usual; ***opp*** wrong

right *n* 1 (fight for your rights) claim, due, entitlement, freedom, interest, privilege. 2 (have the right to do sth) authority, license, permission, power, prerogative. 3 (have right on your side) decency, good, goodness, honor, justice, lawfulness, morality, reason, truth, virtue; ***opp*** wrong

right *v* 1 (make sth right) amend, correct, fix, make amends for, put right, put to rights, rectify, redress, remedy, repair, settle, sort out, straighten out. 2 (right a fallen chair) pick up, set upright, stand upright, straighten up

right *adv* 1 directly, in a straight line, straight. 2 directly, immediately, promptly, quickly, straightaway. **3** (it fell right off the table) all the way, altogether, completely, quite, totally, utterly. **4** (right on the nose) exactly, slap-bang *inf*, precisely, squarely. **5** (not doing it right) appropriately, correctly, properly, satisfactorily, suitably. **6** (treating her right) equitably, fairly, honestly, honorably, justly. **7** (work out right) advantageously, favorably, for the best, fortunately, to your advantage, well

righteous *adj* blameless, ethical, fair, God-fearing, good, honest, honorable, just, law-abiding, moral, pure, sanctimonious, upright, upstanding, virtuous; ***opp*** immoral

rightful *adj* authorized, bona fide, correct, lawful, legal, legitimate, proper, real, true

rigid *adj* **1** (rigid ideas) firm, fixed, hard and fast, harsh, inflexible, rigorous, set, strict, unalterable, unrelenting; ***opp*** flexible. **2** (rigid materials) hard, inelastic, inflexible, solid, stiff, strong, taut, unbending; ***opp*** flexible

rigor *n* **1** hardship, harshness, rigidity, severity, sternness, strictness, toughness. **2** (do sth with rigor) accuracy, meticulousness, precision, thoroughness

rigorous *adj* challenging, demanding, exacting, hard, harsh, meticulous, painstaking, scrupulous, severe, strict, stringent, thorough, tough

rim *n* border, brim, brink, circumference, edge, lip, margin, perimeter, verge

rind *n* crust, husk, outer layer, peel, skin

ring *n* **1** band, circle, circlet, disk, halo, loop, round. **2** arena, enclosure, rink. **3** alliance, band, clique, gang, gathering, group, knot, league, mob, organization, syndicate. **4** (telephone call) bell *inf*, buzz *inf*, call, phone call *inf*, telephone call. **5** (sound of bells) buzz, chime, clang, clink, jangle, jingle, peal, ping, ringing, tinkle, tolling

ring *v* **1** buzz, chime, clang, clink, ding-dong, jangle, jingle, peal, ping, sound, toll. **2** echo, resonate, resound, reverberate. **3** (telephone) call, phone *inf*, telephone. **4** (make a ring around sth) circle, encircle, enclose, fence in, hem in, put a ring around, surround

rinse *v* bathe, clean, cleanse, dip, flush, sluice, swill, wash, wash out, wet

riot *n* **1** anarchy, chaos, confusion, disorder, lawlessness, pandemonium, rioting, tumult, turbulence, upheaval, uproar, violence. **2** brawl, demonstration, fight, fracas, free-for-all, mutiny, protest, scuffle, rebellion, revolt, uprising

riot *v* brawl, fight, go berserk, go wild, mutiny, rampage, rebel, revolt, rise up, run amok, run wild, take to the streets

riotous *adj* **1** (a riotous crowd) anarchic, disorderly, lawless, mutinous, rebellious, rowdy, uncontrollable, unruly, violent. **2** (a riotous evening) boisterous, hilarious, loud, noisy, unrestrained, uproarious, wild

rip *n* gash, hole, opening, slit, split, tear

rip *v* **1** (rip sth to shreds) cut, gash, lacerate, pull apart, rupture, shred, slit, split, tear. **2** (rip sth out of sb's hands) grab, pull, snatch, wrench, yank

ripe *adj* **1** full-grown, mature, mellow, ready, ready to eat. **2** auspicious, favorable, ideal, opportune, right, suitable, timely

ripen *v* age, become ripe, come to maturity, develop, grow ripe, mature, mellow

rise *n* **1** advance, escalation, improvement, increase, jump, leap, upsurge, upswing, upturn; ***opp*** drop, fall. **2** ascent, bank, elevation, hill, incline, ramp, ridge, upward slope. **3** increment, pay increase

rise *v* **1** get to your feet, get up, leap up, stand up, surface *inf*, wake up. **2** (go upward) ascend, climb, come up, go up, levitate, lift, mount, move up, take off; ***opp*** descend. **3** (of prices) escalate, go up, increase, rocket, soar, spiral; ***opp*** fall. **4** (of sounds) become louder, grow, increase, intensify, soar, swell; ***opp*** fall. **5** (rise in the firm) advance, be promoted, do well, progress, prosper. **6** (of a road) climb, get steeper, go uphill, slope upward; ***opp*** descend. **7** (of a tower) loom, soar, stand out, tower. **8** (of water) come up, get deeper, get higher, swell; ***opp*** fall. **9** (of a river) begin, flow from, issue from, originate, spring

risk *n* **1** chance, danger, likelihood, possibility. **2** danger, hazards, jeopardy, peril, speculation, uncertainty. **3** (it's a risk) gamble, venture

risk *v* **1** (risk losing) chance, dare, hazard, take the risk of, venture. **2** (risk your life) endanger, gamble with, imperil, jeopardize, put at risk

risky *adj* chancy *inf*, dangerous, fraught with danger, hazardous, perilous, precarious, touch-and-go, tricky, uncertain, unsafe; ***opp*** safe

rite *n* ceremony, custom, observance, practice, ritual, service, tradition

ritual *adj* **1** ceremonial, customary, formal, prescribed, traditional. **2** (habitual) customary, habitual, prescribed, regular, routine, set

ritual *n* **1** ceremony, custom, observance, practice, rite, tradition. **2** (routine) ceremony, habit, procedure, routine

rival *adj* competing, conflicting, enemy, opposing, opposite, warring; ***opp*** friendly

rival *n* adversary, antagonist, challenger, competitor, contender, contestant, enemy, opponent, opposition; ***opp*** friend, helper, teammate

rival *v* be as good as, challenge, compete with, equal, match up to, measure up to, oppose, parallel, vie with

rivalry *n* adversary, competition, competitiveness, conflict, contention, hostility, opposition; ***opp*** cooperation, friendliness

road *n* avenue, bypass, drive, expressway, freeway, highway, lane, roadway, route, street, thoroughfare

roam *v* prowl, ramble, range, tramp, travel, walk, wander

roar *v* **1** bawl, bellow, blare, boom, crash, cry, rumble, shout, thunder, yell. **2** (laugh) guffaw, hoot, howl with laughter, kill yourself laughing, laugh, split your sides *inf*

rob *v* **1** break into, burgle, hold up, loot, mug, pick sb's pocket, raid, ransack, rifle, steal from, steal, thieve. **2** cheat, con, rip off *inf*, swindle

robber *n* bandit, burglar, cat burglar, housebreaker, looter, mugger, pickpocket, shoplifter, thief

robbery *n* breakin, burglary, embezzlement, fraud, holdup, housebreaking, larceny, looting, misappropriation, mugging, pilfering, raid, shoplifting, stealing, theft

robe *n* attire, ceremonial dress, costume, gown, vestment

robot *n* android, automaton, computer-controlled machine, humanoid, machine

robust *adj* **1** hardy, powerful, rugged, strong, sturdy, tough, vigorous, well-made. **2** practical, pragmatic, realistic, sensible, sound, strong

rock *n* boulder, crag, outcrop, reef, stone

rock *v* **1** lurch, move to and fro, pitch, sway, teeter, totter, wobble. **2** astound, shake, shock, stagger, startle, stun, take by surprise

rocky *adj* **1** bumpy, craggy, pebbly, rough, rugged, stony. **2** iffy *inf*, shaky, uncertain, unstable, unsteady, wobbly

rod *n* bar, baton, pole, shaft, stick, wand

rogue *n* cheat, con-man, crook, fraud, rascal, scoundrel, sharper

role *n* **1** capacity, contribution, function, job, position, task. **2** (in a play) character, part

roll *n* **1** ball, bobbin, cylinder, furl, round, scroll, spool, tube, tube, twist. **2** (rolling movement) cycle, revolution, rotation, spin, turn, twirl. **3** (register) census, directory, inventory, list, listing, record, register, schedule. **4** (rumble) boom, reverberation, roar, rumble

roll *v* **1** coil, curl, furl, go round, revolve, rotate, somersault, spin, tumble, turn, twirl, wheel, wind. **2** (of a ship) lurch, pitch, reel, rock, toss. **3** (flatten) compact, compress, flatten, level out, press down, press, smooth

romance *n* **1** intrigue, love affair, love, passion, relationship. **2** love story, romantic fiction. **3** adventure, fascination, glamour

romantic *adj* **1** affectionate, amorous, emotional, lovey-dovey *inf*, loving, passionate, sentimental, soppy *inf*, tender; ***opp*** unromantic. **2** dreamy, exciting, fabulous, fairy-tale, glamorous, idealistic, impractical, starry-eyed; ***opp*** down-to-earth, practical

room *n* **1** capacity, elbow-room, space, volume. **2** (scope) capacity, freedom, latitude, leeway, margin, opportunity, scope. **3** accommodation, bedroom, place to stay

roomy *adj* baggy, big, extensive, large, sizable, spacious, voluminous; ***opp*** small

root *n* **1** rhizome, taproot, tuber. **2** (the root of a problem) basis, bottom, cause, core, crux, germ, origin, seat, source, starting point

root *v* **1** germinate, sprout, take root. **2** (search) forage, root around, rummage, scrabble, search. **3 root out** cut out, destroy, dig out, discover, eliminate, eradicate, get rid of, remove, search out, unearth, uproot, weed out

rope *n* cable, cord, guy, halter, hawser, line, tether, towrope

rot *n* **1** canker, decay, decomposition, mold, putrefaction. **2** (nonsense) drivel *inf*, garbage *inf*, gibberish, nonsense, rubbish, tripe *inf*

rot *v* crumble, decay, decompose, disintegrate, fester, go bad, go off, go

sour, mold, perish, putrefy
rota *n* list, roster, schedule, timetable
rotate *v* **1** go round, pivot, revolve, spin, swirl, swivel, turn, twirl, wind. **2** alternate, come round, do in turn, recur, share, take turns at
rotten *adj* **1** (decaying) addled, bad, decaying, foul, moldering, off *inf*, perished, putrid, rotting, sour; ***opp*** fresh. **2** (terrible) awful, bad, disappointing, dismal, foul *inf*, inferior, lousy *inf*, miserable, nasty, poor, terrible; ***opp*** terrific, wonderful. **3** (ill) bad, ill, off color, poorly, rough *inf*, sick, under the weather, unwell; ***opp*** fine, well
rough *adj* **1** bumpy, coarse, jagged, rocky, rugged, scratchy, stony, uneven; ***opp*** smooth. **2** (a rough estimate) approximate, crude, estimated, general, quick, raw, rudimentary, sketchy, vague; ***opp*** detailed, exact, precise. **3** (of a person) badly behaved, brusque, curt, ill-mannered, loutish, rowdy, rude, surly; ***opp*** refined. **4** (of work, conditions) arduous, hard, heavy-handed, severe, spartan, tough, unfair, unjust, violent. **5** (of a voice) grating, gruff, harsh, hoarse, husky, rasping; ***opp*** smooth, soft. **6** (of the sea) choppy, heavy, stormy, wild; ***opp*** calm. **7** (ill) bad, ill, off color, poorly, rotten *inf*, sick, under the weather, unwell; ***opp*** fine, well
round *adj* ball-shaped, bulbous, circular, curved, cylindrical, disk-shaped, globular, rounded, spherical, spheroid
round *n* **1** ball, band, circle, disk, globe, ring, sphere. **2** (in sport or competitions) bout, cycle, game, heat, level, series, session, stage. **3** (of a doctor or guard) beat, circuit, lap, route, tour, turn
round *v* (go round) circle, circumnavigate, come round, go round, skirt, turn
roundabout *adj* circuitous, devious, evasive, indirect, longwinded, meandering, oblique, rambling, tortuous; ***opp*** direct
rouse *v* **1** (stir up) arouse, awaken, egg on *inf*, galvanize, incite, inflame, kindle, provoke, rally, stimulate, stir up, whip up, work up; ***opp*** calm, discourage. **2** (rouse sb) awaken, wake up, waken
rousing *adj* electrifying, energetic, exciting, fervent, lively, moving, spirited, stimulating, stirring, vigorous; ***opp*** dull, flat, lifeless, uninspiring
rout *n* conquest, defeat, drubbing, overthrow, thrashing; ***opp*** victory
rout *v* conquer, crush, defeat, drive off, hammer *inf*, overthrow, thrash, trounce
route *n* course, crossing, itinerary, journey, path, run, way
routine *adj* **1** common, everyday, familiar, habitual, ordinary, regular, standard, usual; ***opp*** special, unusual. **2** (dull) boring, dull, monotonous, predictable, run-of-the-mill, tedious, unexciting; ***opp*** exciting
routine *n* **1** custom, drill, formula, habit, pattern, procedure, program, system. **2** act, patter, performance, piece, set
row *n* (line) chain, column, file, line, procession, queue, rank, series, string, tier
row *n* **1** (argument) altercation, argument, controversy, disagreement, dispute, quarrel, scrap, spat, squabble,

tiff, wrangle. **2** (noise) commotion, din, fracas, hubbub, hullabaloo, noise, racket, rumpus, uproar

row *v* argue, bicker, quarrel, squabble, wrangle

rowdy *adj* badly behaved, boisterous, loutish, noisy, rough, unruly, wild; ***opp*** quiet, well-behaved

royal *adj* imperial, majestic, princely, regal, sovereign, stately

rub *v* **1** buff, clean, polish, scour, scrub, shine, smooth, wipe. **2** (stroke) caress, fondle, massage, stroke. **3** (chafe) abrade, chafe, scrape, wear away. **4** apply, put on, smear, spread. **5 rub out** cancel, delete, efface, erase, remove, rub off, wipe out

rubbish *adj* **1** (nonsense) balderdash, claptrap, drivel, gobbledegook, nonsense, rot *inf*. **2** (refuse) debris, detritus, dross, garbage, junk, litter, rubble, scrap, trash, waste, refuse

ruddy *adj* blushing, crimson, florid, flushed, healthy, pink, red, rosy, scarlet

rude *adj* **1** abusive, bad-mannered, cheeky, discourteous, disrespectful, impertinent, impolite, insolent, insulting, offensive, offhand, short, uncivil, uncouth; ***opp*** polite. **2** (of a joke) blue, coarse, crude, dirty, naughty, obscene, risqué, smutty, vulgar; ***opp*** clean

rudeness *n* bad manners, cheek, cheekiness, coarseness, discourtesy, disrespect, impertinence, impudence, insolence, offensiveness, vulgarity; ***opp*** courtesy, good manners, politeness

rudimentary *adj* basic, crude, early, elementary, primitive, simple; ***opp*** sophisticated

rudiments *n* basic principles, basics, essentials, foundations, fundamentals, nuts and bolts

ruffian *n* bully, hooligan, lout, rowdy, scamp, thug, tough

ruffle *v* **1** disturb, mess up, ripple, rumple, stir, tousle. **2** agitate, annoy, disconcert, disturb, fluster, irritate, nettle *inf*, put out, rattle *inf*, unsettle, upset

rugged *adj* barren, craggy, hard, harsh, rocky, rough, tough, weatherbeaten, weathered

ruin *n* bankruptcy, collapse, defeat, destitution, destruction, downfall, end, failure, havoc, insolvency, undoing, wreck, wreckage

ruin *v* bankrupt, bring down, defeat, demolish, destroy, devastate, mess up, shatter, smash, spoil, wreck

ruined *adj* bankrupt, crumbling, derelict, destroyed, dilapidated, in ruins, insolvent, ramshackle, spoiled, uninhabitable, wrecked

ruinous *adj* catastrophic, crippling, crushing, devastating, dire, disastrous, fatal, injurious, shattering

rule *n* **1** axiom, code, direction, formula, guideline, law, maxim, order, principle, regulation, ruling, standard, statute, tenet. **2** (control) administration, authority, command, control, dominion, government, management, power, regime, reign, sovereignty, supervision

rule *v* **1** decide, decree, determine, find, judge, lay down, order, pronounce. **2** (govern) administer, be in power, be on the throne, control, govern, hold the reigns, lead, manage, reign, run.

3 rule out disallow, discount, dismiss, disqualify, eliminate, exclude, preclude, prohibit, reject

ruler *n* chief, dictator, emperor, governing body, government, governor, head of state, king, leader, monarch, potentate, president, queen, regent, sovereign

ruling *adj* controlling, dominant, in power, leading, reigning, supreme

ruling *n* adjudication, decision, decree, finding, judgment, pronouncement, verdict

rumor *n* dirt *inf*, gossip, grapevine, hearsay, lowdown *inf*, news, scandal, story, talk, the latest

run *n* **1** canter, gallop, jog, sprint, trot. **2** (a journey) drive, journey, outing, ride, route, spin *inf*, trip. **3** (a series) period, round, series, spell, stretch, succession. **4** enclosure, pen

run *v* **1** bolt, charge, dash, gallop, hotfoot it *inf*, hurry, jog, race, scurry, sprint, tear. **2** (run a company) administer, control, direct, govern, head, lead, manage, operate, supervise. **3** (function) behave, function, go, operate, perform, work. **4** (trains run every hour) go, move, operate, pass, travel. **5** (extend) continue, extend, go, last, lie, reach, stretch. **6** (run for office) apply, be a candidate, compete, go in for, put your name forward, stand, take part. **7** (flow) cascade, discharge, dribble, flow, gush, pour, spill, spout, stream, trickle. **8** (drip) dissolve, drip, go soft, melt. **9 run away** abscond, escape, leave home, bolt, run off, make off. **10 run over** (look at sth again) go through, look through, recap, recapitulate, repeat, run through. **11 run over** (knock down) hit, knock down, knock over, run down. **12 run over** (of liquid) overflow, spill over

runner *n* **1** athlete,harrier, jogger, sprinter. **2** shoot, sprout, sucker, tendril

running *adj* **1** consecutive, continual, continuous, in a row, incessant, on the trot, ongoing, perpetual, successive, uninterrupted. **2** (running water) flowing, moving; ***opp*** still

rupture *n* **1** breach, break, cleft, fracture, split, tear. **2** hernia. **3** (disagreement) break, disagreement, division, feud, quarrel, rift, schism

rupture *v* breach, break, burst, divide, fracture, separate, sever, split, tear

rural *adj* agrarian, agricultural, countrified, country, countryside, pastoral, rustic; ***opp*** urban

rush *n* bustle, charge, dash, flood, haste, hurry, panic, race, scramble, speed, sprint, stampede, surge, urgency

rush *v* bolt, charge, dart, dash, flood, fly, get a move on, hotfoot it *inf*, hurry, move fast, race, run, scramble, shoot, speed, sprint, stampede, surge, tear, zoom

rust *n* corrosion, oxidation

rust *v* corrode, oxidize

rustic *adj* agrarian, agricultural, countrified, country, countryside, pastoral, rural

rustle *n* crackle, hiss, swish, whisper

rustle *v* crackle, hiss, swish, whisper

rusty *adj* **1** corroded, oxidized, rusted. **2** (out of practice) below par, neglected, not up to scratch *inf*, out of practice, poor, stale, weak. **3** brick-red, chestnut, coppery, reddish-brown, rust-colored

rut *n* **1** furrow, gouge, groove, gutter, hollow, track, trough, wheel mark.
2 in a rut at a dead end, bored, in a routine, on the treadmill, stuck in the daily grind

ruthless *adj* brutal, callous, cold, cruel, harsh, heartless, inhuman, merciless, pitiless, savage, severe, unfeeling, unrelenting, violent

sabotage *n* damage, destruction, subversion, vandalism, wrecking
sabotage *v* attack, damage, destroy, disable, put out of action, thwart, vandalize, wreck
sack *n* **1** dismissal, notice, redundancy, the ax, the boot *inf*, your cards. **2** bag, totebag
sack *v* ax, discharge, dismiss, downsize, fire, give sb the boot *inf*, give sb the push *inf*, give sb the sack, give sb his marching orders *inf*, lay off, make redundant, terminate sb's contract
sacred *adj* blessed, consecrated, devotional, divine, godly, hallowed, heavenly, holy, inviolate, religious, revered, sacrosanct, sanctified, spiritual
sacrifice *n* **1** loss, relinquishment, renunciation, surrender. **2** offering
sacrifice *v* forfeit, forego, give up, lose, offer, relinquish, renounce, surrender
sacrilege *n* blasphemy, desecration, disrespect, godlessness, heresy, irreverence, profanity, violation
sacrosanct *adj* inviolable, non-negotiable, protected, sacred, untouchable
sad *adj* **1** (unhappy) brokenhearted, crestfallen, dejected, depressed, desolate, despondent, disappointed, distressed, down in the dumps *inf*, down *inf*, grief-stricken, heartbroken, low, miserable, tearful, unhappy, upset; ***opp*** cheerful, happy. **2** (a sad story) depressing, distressing, heartbreaking, heartrending, moving, poignant, touching, tragic, upsetting; ***opp*** cheerful, heartwarming. **3** (unsatisfactory) bad, deplorable, disastrous, disgraceful, miserable, pitiful, regrettable, sorry, unfortunate, unsatisfactory, wretched; ***opp*** excellent
sadden *v* break sb's heart, depress, disappoint, dishearten, dismay, distress, make unhappy, upset; ***opp*** cheer
sadistic *adj* barbarous, brutal, cruel, heartless, inhuman, perverted, savage
sadness *n* dejection, depression, despondency, disappointment, grief, heartache, misery, regret, sorrow, unhappiness; ***opp*** happiness
safe *adj* **1** (unharmed) all right, in one piece, intact, out of danger, safe and sound, unharmed, unhurt, uninjured. **2** (of a place) impregnable, protected, secure; ***opp*** dangerous. **3** (harmless) fit for human consumption, good, harmless, healthy, nontoxic, pure, tried and tested, uncontaminated, wholesome; ***opp*** dangerous, harmful. **4** (reliable) careful, cautious, conservative, dependable, prudent, reliable, trustworthy, unadventurous

safe *n* repository, safety deposit box, strongbox, vault
safeguard *n* defense, guarantee, insurance, precaution, protection, security, shield, surety
safeguard *v* foster, guard, keep safe, look after, preserve, protect, secure, watch over
safety *n* dependability, protection, reliability, sanctuary, security, shelter
sag *v* bend, dip, droop, drop, fall, flop, give, hang down, sink, slump, wilt
sail *v* **1** cruise, go sailing, put to sea, set sail, steam, tack. **2** captain, navigate, pilot, skipper. **3** (sail into the room) drift, float, fly, glide, skim, soar, sweep, waltz
sailor *n* marine, mariner, seafarer, seaman, skipper
saintly *adj* angelic, blessed, devout, God-fearing, godly, good, holy, pious, pure, religious, righteous, virtuous
sake *n* account, advantage, benefit, good, interest, purpose, reason
salary *n* earnings, fee, income, pay, remuneration, stipend, take-home pay, wage
sale *n* auction, deal, marketing, retailing, selling, trade, traffic, transaction
salient *adj* chief, conspicuous, important, main, noticeable, obvious, principal, prominent, striking; ***opp*** irrelevant, minor
sallow *adj* pale, pallid, pasty, sickly, unhealthy-looking, wan, yellowish; ***opp*** rosy, ruddy
salt *adj* brackish, saline, salted, salty
salute *n* acknowledgment, greeting, homage, recognition, salutation, tribute
salute *v* acknowledge, greet, honor, pay tribute to, praise, take your hat off to *inf*
salvage *v* reclaim, recover, redeem, rescue, restore, resurrect, retrieve, save
salvation *n* reclamation, recovery, redemption, rescue, saving
same *adj* **1** alike, corresponding, duplicate, equal, equivalent, identical, interchangable, like, matching, parallel, similar, twin; ***opp*** different. **2** changeless, consistent, constant, unchanging, uniform, unvarying
sample *n* example, foretaste, specimen, swatch, taster, trailer, trial pack
sample *v* taste, try out, try
sanctify *v* **1** anoint, bless, canonize, consecrate, dedicate, make holy, purify. **2** approve, authorize, legitimize, license, permit, sanction, support; ***opp*** forbid
sanctimonious *adj* goody-goody *inf*, holier-than-thou, pious, self-righteous, smug, superior
sanction *n* **1** agreement, approval, authority, authorization, backing, consent, endorsement, the go-ahead, permission, seal of approval, support, the green light *inf*, the thumbs up *inf*. **2** penalty, punishment, sentence. **3** ban, boycott, embargo, penalty, restriction
sanction *v* allow, approve, authorize, back, endorse, give sth the thumbs up *inf*, give the go-ahead to, give sth the green light *inf*, okay *inf*, permit, support; ***opp*** forbid, prevent
sanctity *n* devotion, godliness, holiness, righteousness, sacredness, saintliness, spirituality, virtue
sanctuary *n* **1** asylum, cover, haven, protection, refuge, safety, shelter.

2 animal sanctuary, conservation area, nature reserve, protected area, reservation, reserve. 3 altar, chapel, church, holy place, sanctum, temple

sane *adj* all there *inf*, balanced, in possession of all your faculties, in your right mind, lucid, of sound mind, rational, reasonable, right-minded, stable; ***opp*** insane, mad

sanitary *adj* clean, germfree, healthy, hygienic, pure, salubrious, sterile, uncontaminated; ***opp*** dirty, unhealthy, unhygienic

sanity *n* common sense, good sense, level-headedness, normality, rationality, reason

sap *n* life force, life-blood, vigor, vitality

sarcasm *n* derision, irony, mockery, satire, scoffing, scorn

sarcastic *adj* caustic, derisive, ironic, mocking, sardonic, satirical, scoffing, scornful

satire *n* burlesque, caricature, irony, mockery, parody, ridicule, sarcasm, skit, spoof *inf*, take-off *inf*

satirical *adj* caustic, ironical, irreverent, mocking, sarcastic, sardonic

satirize *v* caricature, make fun of, mock, parody, poke fun at, take off *in*

satisfaction *n* 1 comfort, contentment, enjoyment, fulfillment, gratification, pleasure, pride; ***opp*** dissatisfaction. 2 compensation, justice, redress, reparation, vindication

satisfactory *adj* acceptable, adequate, all right, average, fair, good enough, not bad, okay, passable, quite good, reasonable, sufficient, suitable, up to scratch *inf*; ***opp*** poor, unacceptable, unsatisfactory

satisfy *v* 1 (satisfy a need or requirement) answer, comply with, fulfill, meet, resolve, supply. 2 (satisfy sb's hunger or thirst) assuage, gratify, quench, satiate, suffice. 3 (convince sb) convince, make happy, persuade, placate, put sb's mind at rest, reassure

saturate *v* douse, drench, permeate, soak, steep, suffuse, wet

sauce *n* dressing, coulis, condiment, gravy

saucy *adj* cheeky, nervy, sauciness

savage *adj* 1 (wild) fierce, primitive, uncivilized, untamed, wild; ***opp*** tame. 2 (vicious) barbaric, brutal, cruel, ferocious, ruthless, vicious, violent

save *v* 1 (keep) collect, conserve, hoard, hold on to, invest, keep, put aside, put away, put back, reserve, stash away, stockpile, store. 2 (economize) cut costs, cut expenditures, economize, find savings, make cuts, make economies. 3 (rescue) bail out, conserve, defend, deliver, free, preserve, protect, rescue, safeguard, salvage, screen, shield. 4 (save you from having to do sth) make unnecessary, prevent, spare, stop

savings *n* capital, funds, investments, nest egg, piggy bank *inf*, reserves

savior *n* champion, fairy godmother, friend in need, Good Samaritan, guardian angel, knight in shining armor, rescuer

savor *v* appreciate, enjoy, luxuriate in, relish, revel in, wallow in

savory *adj* 1 piquant, salty, spicy, tangy. 2 appetizing, delicious, mouthwatering, scrumptious *inf*, tasty

say *n* **1** (have your say) chance to speak, opinion, right to speak, two cents' worth. **2** (have no say) authority, influence, input, part, sway, voice, vote

say *v* **1** (refuse to say the word) enunciate, mention, mouth, pronounce, utter, voice. **2** (say that sth is true) affirm, allege, announce, assert, claim, come out with *inf*, declare, maintain, put about *inf*, report, state, suggest. **3** (say how you feel) articulate, communicate, convey, enunciate, express, intimate, make known, put into words, tell. **4** answer, comment, declare, exclaim, remark, reply, respond, retort. **5** (say a prayer) deliver, read, read out, recite, repeat

saying *n* **1** adage, axiom, dictum, maxim, motto, precept, proverb. **2** catchphrase, cliché, expression, formula, slogan

scale *n* **1** calibration, gradation, graduation, measuring system, steps. **2** hierarchy, ladder, order, pecking order *inf*, ranking, spectrum, spread. **3** (on a large/small/grand scale) degree, extent, range, scope, way. **4** (in music) octave, sequence, series. **5** (rough skin) dandruff, flake, plate, scurf

scale *v* ascend, clamber up, climb, climb up, go up, mount, scramble up

scamper *v* dart, dash, frisk, frolic, gambol, romp, run, scoot, scuttle

scan *v* **1** check, examine, gaze at, investigate, look at, pore over, scrutinize, search, stare at, study, survey, sweep. **2** (look at writing) flick through, flip through, have a look at, leaf through, glance over, look over, read, read through, run your eye over, skim, skim through

scandal *n* **1** crime, impropriety, misconduct, offense, sin, transgression. **2** (a political scandal) outrage, sensation. **3** (cause a scandal) disgrace, dishonor, disrepute, embarrassment, ignominy, infamy, notoriety, reproach, shame. **4** (gossip) backbiting, defamation, dirt, gossip, muckraking, rumor, slander, slur, talk, tittle-tattle

scandalize *v* affront, appall, cause raised eyebrows, disgust, horrify, offend, outrage, shock, upset

scandalous *adj* **1** disgraceful, disgusting, odious, immoral, indecent, outrageous, shameful, shocking, sordid. **2** defamatory, libelous, scurrilous, slanderous

scanty *adj* inadequate, insufficient, limited, meager, measly, paltry, poor, restricted, scant, skimpy

scar *n* **1** blemish, brand, discoloration, disfigurement, mark. **2** (emotional scar) damage, injury, trauma

scar *v* **1** blemish, brand, discolor, deface, disfigure, mark. **2** (mentally) affect, damage, injure, leave its mark, leave scars, traumatize, upset

scarce *adj* at a premium, few and far between, hard to come by *inf*, hard to find *inf*, inadequate, infrequent, in short supply, insufficient, lacking, rare, scanty, seldom seen, short, sparse, uncommon, unusual, wanting

scarcely *adv* barely, hardly, only just

scare *n* alarm, alert, fright, horror, shock, terror

scare *v* alarm, daunt, frighten, give sb a fright, intimidate, make sb afraid, make sb jump *inf*, panic, petrify, put the fear of God into sb *inf*, startle, terrify, terrorize, unnerve

scared *adj* alarmed, fearful, frightened, nervous, panicky, panicstricken, petrified, shaken, startled, terrified

scary *adj* alarming, frightening, hair-raising, horrifying, petrifying, terrifying

scathing *adj* biting, caustic, critical, cutting, harsh, sarcastic, scornful, severe, stinging, trenchant, withering

scatter *v* **1** (scatter things) diffuse, disseminate, fling, litter, shower, sow, spread, sprinkle, strew, toss about. **2** (people scatter) break up, disband, disperse, go off in all directions, separate

scene *n* **1** area, locality, location, place, position, setting, site, spot. **2** landscape, panorama, prospect, scenery, view, vista. **3** backdrop, background, location, set, setting. **4** (make a scene) carry-on *inf*, commotion, disturbance, furor, fuss, row, tantrum, to-do, upset. **5** picture, sight, spectacle. **6** (not my scene) area of interest, field, interest, milieu, sphere, world. **7** (of a play or film) act, clip, episode, part, section, sequence

scenery *n* **1** landscape, panorama, surroundings, terrain, view, vista. **2** backdrop, set, stage set, setting

scenic *adj* beautiful, breathtaking, lovely, picturesque, pretty, spectacular

scent *n* **1** aroma, bouquet, fragrance, odor, perfume, smell. **2** (an animal's scent) spoor, track, trail. **3** (perfume) cologne, fragrance, perfume, toilet water

scent *v* **1** be on the trail of, follow the scent of, nose out, smell, sniff, sniff out. **2** become aware of, detect, discern, get wind of, recognize, sense, sniff out

schedule *n* **1** agenda, calendar, diary, itinerary, plan, program, timetable. **2** catalog, inventory, list, register

schedule *v* arrange, arrange a time, book, fix a time, organize, plan, program, slot in, time, timetable

scheme *n* **1** course of action, plan, procedure, program, project, strategy, system, tactics. **2** blueprint, design, draft, layout, outline, plan, project, proposal. **3** arrangement, organization, system. **4** conspiracy, intrigue, machinations, plot, ploy, racket *inf*, ruse, stratagem

scheme *v* collude, conspire, intrigue, maneuver, plan, plot

scheming *adj* artful, calculating, conniving, cunning, Machiavellian, sly, underhand, wily

scholar *n* **1** academic, egghead *inf*, intellectual, learned person, man of letters, pundit, woman of letters. **2** pupil, schoolboy, schoolgirl, student

scholarly *adj* **1** (of a person) academic, bookish, erudite, intellectual, learned, lettered, studious, well-read. **2** (of a piece of work) academic, rigorous, scientific, well-documented, well-argued, well-researched

scholarship *n* **1** academic achievement, education, erudition, knowledge, learning, letters. **2** bursary, endowment, exhibition, fellowship, grant

school *n* **1** academy, college, educational establishment, educational institution, seminary. **2** adherents, circle, devotees, disciples, followers, group, movement, pupils, set. **3** (school of thought) belief, creed, faith, outlook, persuasion, opinion, point of view, school of thought, way of thinking

schooling *n* **1** education, formal education, instruction, learning, teaching, tuition. **2** coaching, drill, grounding, instruction, preparation, training

science *n* **1** branch of knowledge, discipline, organized knowledge, systematic study. **2** art, skill, technique

scientific *adj* analytical, controlled, methodical, rational, regulated, rigorous, systematic

scintillating *adj* bright, brilliant, dazzling, flashing, flickering, lively, sparkling, stimulating, vivacious

scoff *v* **1** be sarcastic, be scornful, gibe, jeer, sneer. **2** (eat) bolt, devour, finish off, guzzle, polish off *inf*. **3 scoff at** belittle, deride, despise, disparage, flout, laugh at, mock, poke fun at, pooh-pooh *inf*, ridicule, scorn

scold *v* bawl out *inf*, berate, blame, castigate, chide, give sb a talking-to, haul over the coals, lecture, nag, rap over the knuckles, read the riot act to, rebuke, reprimand, reproach, reprove, tell off, tick off

scoop *v* bail, dig, excavate, gouge, hollow, ladle, scrape, shovel, spoon

scoop *n* **1** dipper, ladle, spoon. **2** (in a newspaper) exclusive, exposé, inside story, revelation

scope *n* **1** area, compass, competence, extent, field, limit, range, reach, span, sphere, terms of reference. **2** capacity, chance, elbow-room, freedom, latitude, leeway, liberty, opportunity, room, room to maneuver

scorch *v* blacken, blister, burn, char, dry up, parch, sear, singe, shrivel

scorching *adj* baking, boiling, fiery, flaming, red-hot, roasting, searing, sizzling, sweltering, very hot; ***opp*** freezing

score *n* **1** count, marks, points, result, sum, tally, total. **2** (on a surface) gash, gouge, groove, mark, scrape, scratch. **3** (a score to settle) a bone to pick, grievance, grudge. **4 know the score** be aware of the situation, know the facts, know what's what

score *v* **1** achieve, chalk up, gain, gain a point, get a goal, notch up, win. **2** add up, count, keep count, keep a record, keep score, record. **3** (score the surface of sth) gash, gouge, mark, scrape, scratch

scorn *n* contempt, derision, disdain, disparagement, mockery, sarcasm

scorn *v* **1** be above, deride, disdain, disparage, flout, look down on, mock, scoff at, slight, treat with contempt; ***opp*** admire. **2** (scorn sb) rebuff, refuse, reject, spurn, turn down, turn your nose up at *inf*; ***opp*** accept

scornful *adj* contemptuous, derisive, disdainful, haughty, insolent, mocking, sarcastic, slighting, sneering, snide *inf*, supercilious, superior; ***opp*** respectful

scoundrel *n* good-for-nothing, heel *slang*, miscreant, rascal, reprobate, rogue, ruffian, villain

scour *v* **1** abrade, clean, rub, scrub, wash.

2 (search) comb, go over, hunt through, ransack, rummage through, search, turn upside down *inf*

scourge *n* affliction, bane, burden, curse, evil, infliction, misery, misfortune, plague, punishment, terror, torment, visitation

scout *n* advance guard, escort, lookout, outrider, spy, vanguard

scowl *v* frown, glare, glower, grimace

scramble *v* 1 clamber, climb, crawl, scurry, struggle. 2 compete, contend, jockey, jostle, push, rush, strive, struggle, vie

scrap *n* 1 bit, fragment, grain, offcut, part, particle, piece, remnant, snippet, trace. 2 (of food) bit, bite, crumb, grain, morsel, mouthful, scraping. 3 (scrap merchant) junk, rejects, rubbish, waste. 4 (fight) argument, brawl, clash, fight, quarrel, row, scuffle, set-to, squabble, tiff

scrap *v* 1 chuck *inf*, demolish, discard, drop, get rid of, jettison, shed, throw away, throw on the scrap heap, write off. 2 (fight) argue, bicker, fall out *inf*, fight, quarrel, scuffle, squabble

scrape *n* 1 abrasion, graze, laceration, scratch, wound. 2 grating, grinding, rasping, scratch, scratching, squeak. 3 mark, scuff, scratch. 4 (awkward situation) escapade, mischief, prank, trouble. 5 difficulty, fix *inf*, mess, plight, predicament, tight corner, tight spot, trouble

scrape *v* 1 abrade, bark, graze, lacerate, rub, scratch, scuff, skin. 2 grate, grind, rasp, scratch, squeak. 3 clean, erase, file, remove, rub, scour, scrub

scratch *v* 1 abrade, bark, claw, cut, graze, mark, score, scrape, wound. 2 delete, eliminate, pull out, withdraw

scratch *n* 1 abrasion, cut, graze, wound. 2 line, mark, scrape. 3 **up to scratch** acceptable, adequate, competent, good enough, okay *inf*, satisfactory, up to standard

scream *v* bawl, cry, howl, screech, shriek, squall, squeal, wail, yell, yowl

scream *n* 1 cry, howl, screech, shriek, squeal, wail, yell, yowl. 2 (a real scream) barrel of laughs *inf*, hoot *inf*, laugh, riot

screen *n* 1 awning, blind, canopy, curtain, shade. 2 guard, protection, shelter, shield. 3 camouflage, cloak, cover, disguise, facade, front, shield, veil. 4 divider, partition

screen *v* 1 guard, protect, shade, shelter, shield. 2 camouflage, conceal, disguise, hide, mask, veil. 3 (of people) check, examine, investigate, test, vet

screw *v* rotate, tighten, turn, twist, work

scribble *v* dash off, doodle, jot down, scrawl

script *n* 1 (of a play or film) book, libretto, lines, screenplay, text, words. 2 hand, handwriting, writing

scripture *n* Bible, good book, gospel, holy writ, sacred writings, word of God

scrounge *v* beg, cadge, sponge

scrounger *n* beggar, cadger, freeloader, parasite, sponger

scrub *v* 1 clean, rub, scour, wash. 2 abandon, call off, cancel, do away with, drop, give up

scruffy *adj* 1 (of a person) disheveled, ragged, shabby, slovenly, tattered, unkempt, untidy. 2 (of a place) disreputable, rundown, shabby, squalid, untidy

scruples *n* compunction, conscience, doubt, hesitation, misgiving, qualm, second thought, twinge of conscience

scrupulous *adj* 1 ethical, fair, honest, honorable, moral, principled, proper, upright. 2 careful, conscientious, diligent, fastidious, finicky, meticulous, painstaking, precise, punctilious, rigorous, strict, thorough

scrutinize *v* check, examine, explore, inspect, investigate, look at closely, peruse, scan, search, study

scrutiny *n* check, checking, examination, exploration, inspection, investigation, perusal, search, study

scum *n* 1 dross, film, froth, grime. 2 dregs of society, rabble, riffraff

scurrilous *adj* 1 abusive, defamatory, insulting, libelous, slanderous. 2 coarse, foul, gross, indecent, low, obscene, offensive, vile, vulgar

sea *n* 1 ocean, the briny, the deep, the waves. 2 (a sea of people) expanse, host, mass, multitude, plethora, profusion, sheet. 3 **at sea** at a loss, baffled, bewildered, confused, lost, mystified, perplexed

seal *v* 1 close up, cork, fasten, make airtight, make watertight, plug, secure, stick down, stop, stopper, stop up. 2 (decide sth) clinch, decide, finalize, secure, settle. 3 **seal off** close off, cordon off, isolate, quarantine, segregate

seal *n* 1 badge, crest, emblem, insignia, mark, sign, symbol. 2 (seal of approval) assurance, authentication, confirmation, guarantee, ratification, warrant, warranty

seam *n* 1 stitching. 2 layer, lode, stratum, thickness, vein

search *n* 1 check, examination, inspection, look, probe, scrutiny. 2 hunt, inquiry, investigation, pursuit, quest. 3 **in search of** hunting for, in pursuit of, looking for, on the lookout for, on the track of, seeking

search *v* 1 comb, examine, explore, go over, go over with a fine-tooth comb, go through, hunt through, investigate, poke about, pry, ransack, rummage through, sift through, turn inside out, turn upside down. 2 (search sb) check, examine, frisk, inspect, scrutinize. 3 **search for** ferret about for, hunt for, look for, seek, try to find

searching *adj* 1 (a searching look) discerning, intense, intent, keen, penetrating, piercing, sharp. 2 (searching questions) analytic, close, penetrating, probing, thorough

season *n* period, phase, spell, term, time, time of year

season *v* 1 add flavoring to, add seasoning to, flavor, salt, spice. 2 add spice to, add zest to, color, enliven, leaven, liven up, pep up

seasonable *adj* appropriate, opportune, suitable, timely, well-timed

seasoning *n* condiment, dressing, flavoring, herbs, herbs and spices, pepper, salt, salt and pepper, spice

seat *n* 1 bench, chair, pew, settle, stool. 2 (place where sth is based) capital, center, headquarters, heart, hub, location, place, site, situation

seat *v* 1 place, put, settle. 2 (the room seats 50) accommodate, have room for, have seating for, hold, take

seating *n* accommodation, chairs, places, room, seats

secluded *adj* 1 concealed, cut off, hidden, inaccessible, isolated, lonely, off the beaten track, out of the way, remote, solitary, tucked away. 2 cloistered, private, sequestered, sheltered, shut away

second *adj* 1 (in time, sequence) added, additional, duplicate, extra, following, further, later, next, other, repeated, subsequent, succeeding. 2 (in importance) assistant, deputy, inferior, junior, lesser, lower, secondary, second-best, second-class, subordinate, supporting, vice-

second *n* 1 flash, instant, jiffy *inf*, minute *inf*, moment, split second, twinkling of an eye, wink of an eye. 2 assistant, backer, helper, right-hand man, supporter

second *v* 1 approve, back, endorse, side with, support, take sb's side. 2 assign, move, post, relocate, transfer

secondary *adj* 1 inferior, less important, lesser, minor, subordinate, subsidiary. 2 (not happening or experienced directly) auxiliary, by-, at one remove, derivative, derived, indirect, second-hand; ***opp*** primary. 2 (of schools) high, senior; ***opp*** primary

secret *adj* clandestine, concealed, confidential, covert, esoteric, hidden, mysterious, private, undercover, undisclosed, unknown

secret *n* coded message, confidence, mystery, skeleton in the closet

secretary *n* administrative assistant, clerk, gofer *inf*, PA, personal assistant, typist

secrete *v* 1 discharge, exude, generate, produce. 2 conceal, hide, hoard, palm, put away, salt away *inf*, sequester, spirit away, tuck away

secretive *adj* enigmatic, furtive, mysterious, reticent, sly, sneaky *inf*, surreptitious, suspicious, uncommunicative; ***opp*** open

sect *n* 1 cult, denomination, faith, religion. 2 camp, caucus, clique, faction, grouping, party, splinter group

sectarian *n* bigot, extremist, partisan, racist, segregationist, zealot

section *n* 1 area, division, part, portion, region, segment, sector, unit. 2 (of an organization) branch, department, division, group, subdivision, unit. 3 (of text) paragraph, part, passage, stretch, subsection

sector *n* 1 area, district, division, section, territory, ward, zone. 2 (sector of industry) area, branch, division, part, section, subdivision, type

secular *adj* 1 civil, humanist, lay, non-religious, profane, temporal, worldly; ***opp*** religious

secure *adj* 1 (of objects, goods) fastened, locked, locked up, secured, tight, unbreakable. 2 (in a particular position) fast, firm, fixed, held in place, stable, supported; ***opp*** insecure. 3 (of a person, place) impregnable, invulnerable, protected, safe, unassailable, untouchable; ***opp*** insecure

secure *v* 1 (secure an object) anchor,

batten down, bind, bolt, fasten, fix, fortify, lock, make safe, padlock, reinforce, tie, tighten. **2** (keep a place secure) defend, guard, protect, safeguard. **3** (get sth) achieve, acquire, gain, get, get hold of, insure, make certain, obtain, procure

security *n* asylum, defense, protection, refuge, safety, shelter

sedate *adj* calm, composed, decorous, deliberate, dignified, majestic, slow, solemn, staid, stately, unhurried; ***opp*** frantic

sedative *adj* anodyne, calming, hypnotic, narcotic, relaxing, sleep-inducing, soothing, tranquilizing

sedentary *adj* desk-bound, inactive, seated, sitting, stationary; ***opp*** active

sediment *n* alluvium, deposit, dregs, grounds, lees, residue, silt

seduce *v* **1** (attract sb) attract, charm, entice, flirt with, flutter her eyelashes at *inf*, tempt. **2** (sexually) bed, corrupt, debauch, deflower, get sb into bed, have your evil way with *inf*, lead sb astray

seductive *adj* alluring, appealing, attractive, bedroom, charming, come-hither, enticing, erotic, flirtatious, ravishing, sexy, tempting

see *v* **1** behold, catch sight of, descry, discern, distinguish, espy, glimpse, have before your eyes, look, make out, note, notice, observe, perceive, sight, spot, spy, view, watch, witness. **2** (have an image, idea in your mind) conceive, foresee, imagine, picture, visualize. **3** (understand) appreciate, apprehend, comprehend, fathom, follow, grasp, perceive, realize, understand. **4** (see many things during your life) bear witness to, encounter, experience, go through, meet, meet with. **5** (have a meeting with sb) consult, go out with, go to, have a date with, have an appointment with, interview, meet, rendezvous with, spend time with, visit. **6** (see sb somewhere) accompany, come with, conduct, drive, escort, go with, run *inf*, take. **7 see about** consider, inquire, investigate, look into, think about. **8 see through** (see through sb) be wise to, have no illusions about, not be deceived by, not be taken in by, penetrate, unmask. **9 see through** (see sth through) complete, endure, finish, go all the way, keep at, persevere with, persist with, see out, stick out *inf*. **10 see to** attend to, busy yourself with, concern yourself with, concentrate on, deal with, occupy yourself with, organize, see about, turn your attention to

seed *n* **1** ear, germ, grain, pip, stone. **2** (the seeds of sth) beginning, cause, germ, origin, root, source

seedy *adj* decaying, dilapidated, faded, disreputable, dubious, gone to seed, grubby, rundown, shabby, sleazy *inf*, squalid

seek *v* be after, be on the lookout for, chase after, go in search of, hunt, look for, pursue, search for, want

seem *v* appear, feel, give the impression, look, sound

seethe *v* be agitated, be angry, be furious, be in a rage, be incensed, be livid, boil, foam at the mouth, fume, rage, simmer

segment *n* chunk *inf*, part, portion, section, sector, share
segregate *v* divide, keep apart, isolate, quarantine, separate, sort; ***opp*** mix
seize *v* **1** grab, lay hands on, pick up, snatch, take hold of. **2** (seize a criminal) apprehend, arrest, capture, catch, nab *inf*, take, take away. **3** (seize goods) confiscate, sequestrate, take, take away. **4 seize up** crash, freeze, get stuck, give out, grind to a halt, stick, stiffen
seizure *n* **1** (of a criminal) arrest, capture. **2** (of goods) confiscation. **3** (medical) apoplexy, attack, convulsion, fit, paroxysm, spasm, stroke, turn *inf*
select *v* choose, cull, draw, elect, pick, pick out, prefer, sample
selection *n* assortment, choice, collection, range, sample, set
selective *adj* **1** careful, choosy, discriminating, discerning, fastidious, finicky *inf*, fussy *inf*, particular, picky *inf*. **2** (a selective account of events) biased, discriminatory, edited, incomplete, misleading, unbalanced; ***opp*** balanced
self-centered *adj* egoistic, egotistical, selfish, self-absorbed, self-interested, self-obsessed, self-regarding, self-seeking, smug, vain
self-confident *adj* assured, brash, cocky *inf*, confident, self-assured, sure of yourself, swaggering
self-conscious *adj* discomfited, embarrassed, ill at ease, shy, uncomfortable
self-esteem *n* confidence, dignity, pride, self-confidence, self-image, self-respect
self-evident *adj* axiomatic, clear, natural, obvious, plain, self-explanatory
selfish *adj* egoistic, egotistical, greedy, mean, mercenary, miserly, self-centered, self-interested, self-seeking; ***opp*** altruistic, generous
selfless *adj* altruistic, generous, heroic, magnanimous, modest, self-effacing, self-sacrificing; ***opp*** selfish
self-respect *n* confidence, dignity, pride, self-confidence, self-esteem, self-image
self-righteous *adj* holier-than-thou, pious, pompous, pontificating, sanctimonious, sententious, vain
sell *v* **1** cash in, dispose of, export, find a buyer for, get rid of, offload *inf*; ***opp*** buy. **2** (have sth to sell) advertise, deal in, dispense, have for sale, hawk *inf*, put on sale, offer, stock, trade in, vend
seller *n* commercial traveler, hawker, merchant, sales rep *inf*, sales representative, salesman, shopkeeper, vendor; ***opp*** buyer
send *v* **1** (send a letter, parcel) consign, despatch, export, forward, mail, post, put in the mail, relay, send off, ship; ***opp*** receive. **2** (send sth into the air) drive, force, kick, propel, throw. **3** (send sb somewhere) assign, force, order, post, second, throw. **4** (send a signal, electronic message) beam, broadcast, emit, send out, transmit; ***opp*** receive. **5 send for** ask for, call, call in, call up, order, request, summon; ***opp*** send away
senile *adj* confused, demented, doddering, forgetful, gaga *inf*, in their dotage, in their second childhood, old, soft in the head *inf*, rambling, raving, suffering from Alzheimer's disease
senior *adj* elder, first, high, outranking,

ranking, superior, top; ***opp*** junior

sensation *n* 1 experience, feeling, impression, perception, sense. 2 animation, commotion, controversy, excitement, shock, stir, surprise

sensational *adj* 1 amazing, astonishing, extraordinary, incredible, surprising, unexpected. 2 brilliant *inf*, excellent, exciting, fabulous *inf*, fantastic *inf*, great, magnificent, marvelous, stupendous *inf*, thrilling, wonderful. 3 (sensational journalism) exaggerated, lurid, melodramatic, over-the-top, sensationalist, tabloid, titillating

sense *n* 1 (physical, mental attribute) ability, faculty, feel, feeling, instinct, gift, perception, reflex, sensitivity, talent. 2 (a sense of sth about to happen) awareness, feeling, gut feeling, hunch, instinct, intuition, perception, sensation, sixth sense. 3 (have the sense to do sth) common sense, foresight, gumption *inf*, intelligence, judgment, understanding, wisdom, wit. 4 (the sense of a word) connotation, denotation, implication, import, meaning, reference

sense *v* be aware of, be conscious of, detect, experience, feel, intuit, perceive

senseless *adj* 1 asleep, comatose, out cold *inf*, unconscious. 2 absurd, crazy, daft *inf*, fatuous, foolish, futile, half-witted, idiotic, illogical, inane, irrational, ludicrous, mad, meaningless, mindless, nonsensical, pointless, ridiculous, silly, stupid, useless; ***opp*** sensible

sensibility *n* delicacy, emotions, feelings, finer feelings, sensitivity

sensible *adj* intelligent, judicious, logical, meaningful, practical, rational, sober, wise; ***opp*** foolish, stupid

sensitive *adj* 1 (feeling emotions deeply) delicate, easily hurt, emotional, feeling, highly strung, touchy. 2 (sensitive to the problems involved) alert, attuned, aware, conscious, in tune, perceptive, responsive, sympathetic; ***opp*** insensitive. 3 (of a measuring instrument) accurate, delicate, finely tuned, reactive, responsive

sensual *adj* 1 (of pleasure) bodily, carnal, fleshly, material, physical, sexual, tactile; ***opp*** intellectual. 2 (arousing pleasure) arousing, attractive, exciting, sensuous, sexy, titillating, voluptuous. 3 (seeking pleasure) debauched, decadent, hedonistic, lascivious, lustful, pleasure-seeking

sensuous *adj* curvaceous *inf*, curvy, sensual, sinuous, sleek, slinky, smooth, voluptuous, sexy

sentence *n* 1 proposition, question, statement. 2 decree, decision, edict, judgment, order, penalty, punishment, term of imprisonment, verdict

sentence *v* condemn, decree, imprison, judge, order, penalize, pronounce sentence, punish

sentiment *n* 1 attitude, feeling, judgment, opinion, view, way of thinking, wish. 2 compassion, emotion, pathos, pity, sadness, sensibility, sympathy, tenderness

sentimental *adj* emotional, exaggerated, gooey *inf*, gushing, pathetic, sad, sickly, sloppy, tear-jerking

sentry *n* guard, lookout, sentinel,

soldier, watchman

separable *adj* detachable, divisible, removable, separate; ***opp*** inseparable

separate *adj* **1** (two separate parts) detached, disconnected, discrete, distinct, divided, independent, individual, separable, separated, unattached. **2** (a separate subject) different, in its own right, other, unconnected, unrelated

separate *v* **1** (separate two things) break up, cut off, divide, detach, disconnect, dissociate, divorce, isolate, part, pull apart, segregate, sever, sort, split, sunder, take apart, tear asunder. **2** (sth separates into two) break up, come apart, diverge, divide, fork, split. **3** (of a couple) become estranged, break up, divorce, go their separate ways, lead separate lives, live apart, part, part company, split, split up

separated *adj* divorced, estranged, living apart

separation *n* break, breakup, divorce, estrangement, parting, parting of the ways, rift, split

septic *adj* festering, gangrenous, infected, poisoned, suppurating

sequel *n* aftermath, consequence, continuation, fall-out, follow-up, repercussion

sequence *n* continuation, list, order, procedure, progression, series, succession

serene *adj* calm, content, happy, peaceful, placid, quiet, untroubled

series *n* array, column, group, list, row, sequence, set, succession

serious *adj* **1** (a serious matter, decision) critical, crucial, far-reaching, grave, important, life-and-death, major, momentous, of consequence, pressing, significant, urgent, vital, weighty; ***opp*** trivial. **2** (a serious illness) acute, bad, chronic, critical, dangerous, grave, grievous, life-threatening, severe; ***opp*** mild. **3** (not laughing) austere, dour, earnest, grave, humorless, long-faced, pensive, poker-faced *inf*, prim and proper, severe, sober, solemn, somber, stern, thoughtful, unsmiling. **4** (not joking) earnest, genuine, honest, in earnest, sincere, truthful. **5** (serious about doing sth) determined, earnest, firm, in earnest, resolute, resolved

sermon *n* **1** (in church) address, discourse, homily, preaching, speech. **2** admonishment, homily, lecture, lesson, reprimand, scolding, talking-to *inf*

servant *n* assistant, butler, companion, drudge *inf*, employee, factotum, flunkey, footman, housekeeper, lackey, maid, menial, minion, retainer, secretary, slave, valet; ***opp*** master, mistress

serve *v* **1** (serve a customer) assist, attend to, deal with, help, see to, wait on. **2** (serve food) bring, dole out *inf*, give out, ladle, serve up, spoon. **3** (be a servant to) assist, be employed by, be in sb's employ, help, work for. **4** (serve a purpose) aid, answer, help, be useful for, fulfill, satisfy

service *n* **1** (official, public) authority, body, brigade, bureau, department, force, institution, network, office, organization, unit, utility. **2** (offered by an organization) aid, amenity, assistance, benefit, facility, help, opportunity, product, support, system. **3** (in a shop, restaurant) assistance, attentiveness, help. **4** (in a particular job or cause) assistance, dedication, devotion, duty, employment, help, labor, record, work. **5** (in a church) ceremony, rite, ritual, sacrament. **6** (for a car) adjustment, check, examination, maintenance, overhaul, repairs

service *v* adjust, check, check over, examine, give sth the once-over *inf*, maintain, overhaul, repair

serviceable *adj* adequate, in good repair, practicable, usable, useful

servile *adj* cringing, groveling, humble, ingratiating, obsequious, slavish, submissive, unctuous

session *n* **1** period, sitting, spell, stretch, time. **2** assembly, conference, discussion, hearing, meeting, sitting

set *adj* **1** definite, definitive, determinate, firm, fixed, inflexible, permanent, pre-arranged, pre-ordained, prescribed, rigid, unalterable, unchanging; ***opp*** vague. **2** (set to do sth) about to, on the point of, prepared to, primed to, ready to, soon to. **3** (set on doing sth) bent, determined, earnest, intent, resolute, resolved, stubborn

set *n* **1** array, assemblage, assortment, batch, collection, combination, lot, group, series, suite. **2** (type) category, class, genus, group, kind, range, type

set *v* **1** apply, arrange, locate, lodge, put, place, plant, position, rest, situate, station. **2** (set a clock, machine) adjust, calibrate, prepare, regulate, start, synchronize. **3** (set a time, date) agree, appoint, arrange, decide, determine, fix, schedule, specify. **4** (set sb a task) allocate, assign, designate, give, prescribe, present. **5** (a substance sets) coagulate, congeal, crystallize, gel, harden, solidify, stiffen, thicken. **6** (of the sun, moon) descend, go down, sink; ***opp*** rise. **7 set about** approach, begin, deal with, do, get on with, get to grips with, go about, organize, plan, start, tackle. **8 set in** become established, begin, establish itself, start, take hold, take root. **9 set off** (start a journey) depart, leave, set forth, set out, set sail, start, start off. **10 set off** (an explosion, an argument) cause, explode, ignite, initiate, instigate, provoke, spark, spark off, trigger, trigger off. **11 set out** (set things out) arrange, display, exhibit, lay out, present. **12 set out** (set out to do sth) aim, aspire, attempt, intend, plan, set your sights on, try. **13 set up** arrange, construct, equip, establish, install, organize, prepare, put in place

setback *n* complication, delay, difficulty, disappointment, failure, holdup, obstacle, problem, tribulation, vicissitude

setting *n* **1** backdrop, background, context, decor, location, milieu, scene, scenery, situation, surroundings. **2** (the settings of a machine) adjustment, attribute, calibration, option, property, timing

settle *v* **1** agree, arrange, conclude, decide, resolve, reconcile, sort *inf*, sort out. **2** (settle a bill, debt) clear, defray, discharge, liquidate, pay, pay off, redeem, repay, square. **3** (settle in a place) camp, colonize, ensconce yourself *inf*, establish yourself, go to live, install yourself, occupy, people, populate, put down roots, set up home. **4** (of snow) be precipitated, come to rest, lie, stick. **5 settle down** calm down, make yourself at home, make yourself comfortable, relax. **6 settle for** accept, agree to, be content with, be satisfied with

settlement *n* **1** agreement, compact, concordat, pact, reconciliation, resolution. **2** colony, community, encampment, habitation, hamlet, township, village

sever *v* break, chop, cut, cut off, disconnect, dissociate, part, pull apart, separate, snip, split

severe *adj* **1** bad, bitter, dangerous, drastic, extreme, fierce, great, heavy, intense, serious, violent; ***opp*** mild, minor. **2** (severe test) arduous, demanding, difficult, exacting, hard, rigorous, stringent, taxing, tough. **3** (of punishment) cruel, hard, harsh, oppressive, pitiless, rigid, rigorous, strict, stringent; ***opp*** lenient. **4** (of sb's character, appearance) austere, cold-hearted, dour, forbidding, grim, humorless, intimidating, serious, sober, solemn, stern, unsmiling; ***opp*** friendly

sew *v* crochet, embroider, darn, knit, mend, stitch

sex *n* **1** femininity, masculinity, gender, sexuality. **2** coitus, copulation, fornication, hanky-panky *inf*, intercourse, intimacy, it *inf*, love-making, mating, penetration, physical love, roll in the hay *inf*, sexual activity, sexual intercourse, sexuality

sexual *adj* erotic, genital, marital, physical, reproductive, sensual, sex-related

sexuality *n* **1** eroticism, libido, lust, sensuality, sex, sex drive. **2** inclinations, proclivities, sexual orientation, sexual preference, tastes

sexy *adj* alluring, arousing, attractive, enticing, erotic, ravishing, seductive, sensual, sensuous

shabby *adj* **1** dilapidated, dingy, dirty, dowdy, drab, faded, frayed, gone to seed, grubby, moth-eaten, ragged, rundown, old, scruffy, seedy, tatty *inf*, threadbare, worn; ***opp*** neat, smart. **2** base, contemptible, deceitful, despicable, discreditable, dishonest, dishonorable, disreputable, grubby, ignoble, lowdown *inf*, mean, nasty, shameful, shoddy, sordid, squalid, treacherous, unfair, ungenerous, unkind, unscrupulous, unworthy; ***opp*** noble

shade *n* **1** dark, darkness, gloom, penumbra, shadow, shelter; ***opp*** light. **2** (of color) degree, intensity, nuance, tinge, tint, variation

shade *v* cloud, conceal, cover, darken, dim, hide, mask, obscure, screen, shadow, shield, shroud, veil; ***opp*** expose

shadow *n* **1** outline, shape, silhouette. **2** (in the shadows) darkness, dimness, gloom, obscurity, shade; ***opp*** daylight. **3** (no shadow of a doubt) hint, suggestion, suspicion, touch, trace. **4** (cast a shadow over sb) cloud, gloom, sadness, unhappiness

shadowy *adj* **1** dark, dim, dusky, gloomy, murky, obscure, shaded; ***opp*** well-lit. **2** (a shadowy figure) dreamlike, faint, ghostly, nebulous, obscure, phantom, unreal, vague; ***opp*** distinct

shady *adj* **1** cool, leafy, shaded, sheltered; ***opp*** sunny. **2** (a shady character) crooked, disreputable, dubious, fishy *inf*, shifty, slippery, suspicious, untrustworthy; ***opp*** trustworthy

shaft *n* **1** (a mine shaft) duct, flue, mine, passage, pit, tunnel, well. **2** (shaft of light) beam, gleam, laser, pencil, ray, streak. **3** (shaft of a golf club) handle, pole, post, rod, shank, stem, upright

shaggy *adj* bushy, disheveled, hairy, hirsute, long-haired, tousled, unkempt, unshorn, woolly; ***opp*** clean-shaven

shake *v* **1** agitate, bump, convulse, jar, quiver, rattle, rock, shiver, shudder, sway, totter, tremble, vibrate, waver, wobble. **2** (shake your fist) brandish, flourish, wave. **3 shake up** alarm, distress, disturb, frighten, perturb, rattle, ruffle, shock, throw *inf*, unnerve, unsettle, upset; ***opp*** comfort, reassure

shaky *adj* **1** (take your first shaky steps) doddering, faltering, feeble, insecure, precarious, quivery, shaking, staggering, teetering, tottering, trembling, unstable, unsteady, weak, wobbly; ***opp*** confident. **2** decrepit, dilapidated, flimsy, precarious, ramshackle, rickety, rocky, unstable, unsteady, weak, wobbly; ***opp*** robust

shallow *adj* empty-headed, facile, foolish, frivolous, glib, ignorant, insincere, puerile, silly, simple, superficial, unintelligent, unthinking; ***opp*** thinking

sham *n* counterfeit, fake, forgery, fraud, hoax, imitation, pretense

shambles *n* chaos, confusion, disarray, disorder, disorganization, mess, muddle; ***opp*** order

shame *n* condemnation, discredit, disgrace, dishonor, disrepute, humiliation, ignominy, infamy, loss of face, reproach, scandal, smear, stigma, vilification; ***opp*** pride

shame *v* condemn, discredit, disgrace, dishonor, humiliate, lose face, reproach, smear, stigmatize, vilify

shamefaced *adj* ashamed, embarrassed, guilty, humiliated, mortified, penitent, red-faced *inf*, remorseful, repentant, shamed, sorry; ***opp*** proud

shameful *adj* atrocious, base, contemptible, deplorable, despicable, disgraceful, indecent, low, mean, outrageous, reprehensible, scandalous, wicked; ***opp*** noble

shameless *adj* audacious, brash, brazen, corrupt, depraved, immodest, improper, indecent, unabashed, unashamed, undisguised, unprincipled, unselfconscious, wanton; ***opp*** modest

shape *n* **1** configuration, contours, cut, figure, form, format, formation, lines, model, mold, outline, pattern. **2** (of a person) body, build, figure, physique, profile, silhouette. **3** (in good shape) condition, fettle, health, kilter, state

shape *v* **1** (shape an object) carve, cast, create, cut, fashion, form, make, model, mould, produce. **2** (shape a plan) define, develop, devise, organize, plan, prepare

shapeless *adj* amorphous, formless, irregular, nebulous, undeveloped, unshaped, unstructured, vague; ***opp*** well-defined

share *n* allocation, allotment, allowance, assignment, cut, division, helping, part, percentage, portion, proportion, quota, ration, serving

share *v* allocate, allot, apportion, assign, deal out, distribute, divide, halve, quarter, split

sharp *adj* **1** (of a knife) jagged, pointed, serrated, spiky; ***opp*** blunt. **2** (a sharp bend) abrupt, acute, angular, hairpin, sudden, tight; ***opp*** wide. **3** (of a person) alert, astute, bright, clever, incisive, intelligent, observant, perceptive, quick, quick-witted, shrewd, smart; ***opp*** slow. **4** (a sharp pain) acute, cutting, intense, piercing, severe, shooting, stabbing, stinging, violent; ***opp*** nagging, slight. **5** (a sharp image) clear, crisp, distinct, focused, well-defined; ***opp*** unclear. **6** (a sharp tongue) bitter, critical, curt, cutting, harsh, hurtful, sarcastic, sardonic, scathing, severe, venomous, vitriolic; ***opp*** kind. **7** (a sharp taste) acid, acrid, caustic, hot, piquant, pungent, tangy, tart; ***opp*** bland

sharpen *v* file, grind, hone; ***opp*** blunt

shatter *v* blast, break, burst, crack, crush, demolish, disintegrate, explode, fracture, smash, splinter, split, wreck

shed *v* **1** (shed leaves, skin) cast off, discard, drop, molt, slough; ***opp*** grow. **2** (shed workers) dismiss, fire *inf*, get rid of, make redundant, sack *inf*; ***opp*** take on

sheen *n* brightness, glaze, gleam, glint, gloss, luster, polish, reflection, shimmer, shine, sparkle; ***opp*** dullness

sheepish *adj* bashful, coy, embarrassed, guilty, meek, reticent, self-conscious, shy, timid, uncomfortable; ***opp*** brazen

sheer *adj* **1** (a sheer drop) abrupt, perpendicular, precipitous, sharp, steep, vertical; ***opp*** gradual. **2** (sheer stupidity) complete, downright, out-and-out, plain, pure, total, unqualified, utter. **3** (sheer material) filmy, fine, flimsy, gauzy, see-through, thin, translucent, transparent; ***opp*** thick

sheet *n* **1** (a sheet of snow) blanket, coat, covering, film, layer, veneer. **2** (a sheet of glass) pane, panel, piece, plate, slab. **3** (a sheet of paper) folio, leaf, page, piece

shell *n* **1** case, casing, covering, husk, pod. **2** (of a ship) chassis, framework, hull, structure

shell *v* attack, barrage, blitz, bomb, bombard, strike, torpedo

shelter *n* **1** (a shelter for the homeless) haven, refuge, retreat, sanctuary. **2** (look for shelter) defense, protection, refuge, safety, sanctuary, security

shelter *v* conceal, defend, enclose, guard, harbour, hide, keep safe, protect, safeguard, shield

sheltered *adj* **1** (of a place) protected, screened, secluded, shaded, shady, shielded,; ***opp*** exposed. **2** (of sb's life) cloistered, protected, quiet, unadventurous, unexciting, withdrawn; ***opp*** full

shelve *v* defer, delay, postpone, put off, put on ice, put on the back burner, suspend; ***opp*** continue

shield *n* barrier, cover, defense, guard, protector, safeguard, screen

shield *v* cover, defend, guard, keep safe, protect, safeguard, screen; ***opp*** expose

shift *n* **1** (in your opinion) about-turn, adjustment, alteration, change, modification, reversal, sea change, switch, transfer, variation. **2** (the night shift) crew, gang, group, team, workforce

shift *v* **1** budge, displace, move, relocate, reposition; ***opp*** remain. **2** (shift your opinion) adjust, alter, change, modify, reverse, switch, transfer, vary; ***opp*** maintain

shifty *adj* crooked, disreputable, dodgy *inf*, dubious, fishy *inf*, shady, slippery, suspicious, untrustworthy; ***opp*** trustworthy

shimmer *v* flicker, gleam, glint, glisten, glow, sparkle, twinkle

shine *n* brightness, glare, gleam, glisten, glitter, glow, shimmer, sparkle, twinkle; ***opp*** dullness

shine *v* **1** beam, blaze, dazzle, flash, glare, gleam, glisten, glitter, glow, radiate, shimmer, sparkle, twinkle. **2** (shine at sth) be excellent, be exceptional, be outstanding, do well, excel, stand out

shiny *adj* bright, burnished, gleaming, glistening, glittering, glossy, lustrous, polished, shimmering, shinning, sparkling, twinkling; ***opp*** dull

ship *n* boat, craft, cruiser, destroyer, ferry, frigate, liner, steamer, tanker, trawler, vessel, yacht

ship *v* carry, convey, deliver, ferry, send, transport

shirk *v* avoid, dodge, duck, evade, get out of, play truant, shun, sidestep, skive

shiver *v* quake, quiver, shake, shudder, tremble

shock *n* **1** (come as a shock) blow, bombshell, thunderbolt, trauma, upset. **2** (a feeling of shock) astonishment, distress, fright, offense, outrage, revulsion

shock *v* astonish, astound, daze, disquiet, distress, frighten, give sb a turn *inf*, horrify, jar, jolt, offend, outrage, revolt, shake, sicken, stagger, startle, stun, stupefy, traumatize, unsettle

shocking *adj* appalling, astounding, atrocious, awful, disgraceful, distressing, foul, ghastly, hideous, horrific, obscene, offensive, outrageous, revolting, scandalous, sickening, terrible, upsetting

shoddy *adj* cheap, inferior, poor, rubbishy *inf*, second-rate, shabby, slipshod, tacky *inf*, trashy *inf*; ***opp*** quality

shoot *v* **1** (shoot sb) bag, bring down, gun down, hit, injure, kill, shell, snipe at, wound. **2** (shoot a gun) aim, discharge, fire, launch. **3** (shoot out of the room) bolt, charge, dart, dash, fly, hurtle, leap, race, rush, speed, streak, tear; ***opp*** saunter

shop *n* boutique, chain store, department store, outlet, retailer, seller, store, supermarket, wholesaler

shore *n* bank, beach, coast,oceanfront, oceanside, sands, water's edge, waterside

short *adj* **1** (a short speech) abbreviated, abridged, brief, compact, compressed, concise, pithy, succinct, summarized, terse, truncated; ***opp*** long. **2** (of a person) diminutive, little, midget, petite, pint-sized *inf*, slight, small, squat; ***opp*** tall. **3** (a short break) brief, cursory, fleeting, momentary, passing, quick, short-lived, transitory; ***opp*** long. **4** (in short supply) deficient, inadequate, insufficient, lacking, low, scarce, sparse, tight, wanting; ***opp*** plentiful

shortage *n* dearth, deficiency, deficit, inadequacy, insufficiency, lack, scarcity, shortfall, want; ***opp*** excess

shortcoming *n* bad thing, defect, drawback, failing, fault, flaw, frailty, imperfection, limitation, weakness, weak point; ***opp*** strength

shorten *v* abbreviate, abridge, compress, condense, contract, curtail, cut, decrease, dock, lessen, prune, reduce, shrink, summarize, trim, truncate; ***opp*** lengthen

short-sighted *adj* **1** myopic, near-sighted; ***opp*** long-sighted. **2** careless, ill-advised, ill-considered, imprudent, injudicious, rash, unthinking, unwary, unwise; ***opp*** sensible

short-tempered *adj* crabby *inf*, fiery, hot-tempered, impatient, irascible, irritable, quick-tempered, touchy; ***opp*** patient

shot *n* **1** (take a shot) fling, hurl, lob, pot shot, throw. **2** (fire a shot) ammunition, bullet, lead, missile, pellet, slug *inf*. **3** (hear a shot) blast, crack, explosion, gun fire. **4** (have a shot at sth) attempt, bash *inf*, crack *inf*, effort, endeavor, go *inf*, guess, stab *inf*, try, turn

shout *v* ball, bellow, call, cheer, clamor, cry, holler *inf*, rant, roar, scream, screech, shriek, yell; ***opp*** whisper

shove *v* barge, drive, elbow, force, nudge, press, prod, push, shoulder, thrust

shovel *v* clear, dig, excavate, ladle, scoop, shift, spoon

show *n* **1** (go to see a show) concert, drama, gig *inf*, pageant, parade, performance, play, production. **2** (a car show) demonstration, display, exhibition, expo *inf*, exposition, fair, presentation. **3** (for show) affectation, appearance, display, facade, illusion, ostentation, pose, pretense

show *v* **1** (sth shows) appear, be in view, be seen, be visible, catch the eye, make an appearance, materialize, stand out, stick out. **2** (show sth is true) demonstrate, divulge, explain, expose, express, indicate, make known, make plain, prove, reveal, teach, uncover. **3** (show symptoms) display, exhibit, manifest, present. **4** (show sb to their seat) accompany, conduct, direct, escort, guide, lead, steer, usher. **5 show off** be full of yourself *inf*, boast, blow your own horn *inf*, brag, crow, swagger around. **6 show up** embarrass, humiliate, let down, mortify, shame

showdown *n* clash, climax, confrontation, crisis, face-off, moment of truth *inf*

shower *n* **1** (of rain) deluge, downpour, fall, flurry, rainstorm, sprinkling, torrent. **2** (of bullets) barrage, stream, volley

shower *v* deluge, heap, inundate, lavish, load, overwhelm, pour

show-off *n* big-head, braggart, egotist, exhibitionist, poser *inf*

showy *adj* conspicuous, elaborate, fancy, flamboyant, flashy, fussy, garish, gaudy, lavish, loud *inf*, lurid, ornate, ostentatious, pretentious, vulgar; ***opp*** modest

shred *n* **1** bit, fragment, piece, rag, scrap, sliver, tatter. **2** (a shred of evidence) grain, iota, jot, scintilla, scrap, speck, trace

shred *v* cut, grate, rip, scrap, tear

shrewd *adj* astute, canny, clever, crafty, cunning, intelligent, keen, knowing, observant, perceptive, quick-witted, sharp, sly, smart, wily; ***opp*** ignorant

shriek *v* cry, holler *inf*, howl, scream, screech, squawk, squeal, wail, whoop, yell; ***opp*** whisper

shrill *adj* acute, ear-splitting, high, jarring, penetrating, piercing, screeching, sharp, shrieking; ***opp*** soft

shrink *v* **1** contract, decrease, diminish, dwindle, lessen, reduce; ***opp*** grow. **2** (shrink from sth) back off, cower, draw back, flinch, recoil, retreat, shy away, wince, withdraw

shrivel *v* curl, dehydrate, droop, dry out, dry up, wilt, wither, wizen, wrinkle

shroud *n* blanket, cloak, cloud, cover, mantle, mask, screen, swathe, veil

shroud *v* blanket, cloak, cloud, conceal, cover, envelop, hide, mask, screen, swathe, veil, wrap

shudder *n* convulsion, jerk, quake, quiver, rattle, shake, shiver, spasm, tremble, tremor, vibration

shudder *v* convulse, jerk, quake, quiver, rattle, shake, shiver, tremble, vibrate

shuffle *v* **1** (shuffle somewhere) drag your feet, hobble, limp, scrape your feet, slide; ***opp*** stride. **2** (shuffle cards) confuse, disarrange, intermix, jumble, mix, rearrange, reorganize

shun *v* avoid, elude, evade, flee, give sb a wide berth *inf*, give sb the cold shoulder *inf*, rebuff, reject, spurn, turn away from; ***opp*** welcome

shut *v* **1** bolt, close, draw, fasten, lock, seal, secure, slam; ***opp*** open. **2 shut up** gag, hush, keep quiet, make silent, muzzle, silence

shy *adj* bashful, coy, diffident, hesitant, inhibited, introverted, nervous, reserved, reticent, retiring, self-conscious, self-effacing, sheepish, shrinking, timid, wary, withdrawn; ***opp*** self-confident

sick *adj* **1** (feel sick) nauseated, nauseous, queasy. **2** (ill) ailing, bedridden, diseased, feeble, ill, indisposed, infirm, poorly, sickly, under the weather *inf*, unwell, weak; ***opp*** well. **3** (sick humor) black, ghoulish, grim, macabre, morbid, perverted, sadistic, unhealthy

sicken *v* appall, disgust, gross out *inf*, make you sick, nauseate, offend, repel, revolt, turn your stomach

sickening *adj* abhorrent, disgusting, distasteful, foul, gross, hideous, loathsome, nauseating, objectionable, offensive, repugnant, repulsive, revolting, vile

sickly *adj* ailing, delicate, feeble, frail, ill, infirm, languid, puny, unhealthy, weak; ***opp*** healthy

side *n* **1** (a side of a field) border, boundary, division, edge, fringe, limit, margin, perimeter, periphery, rim, verge. **2** (a side of a cube) aspect, face, facet, flank, part, surface, view. **3** (be on opposing sides) camp, faction, group, party, sect, team, wing

side with *v* ally with, back, be on the

side of, form an alliance with, join up with, partner, prefer, support, take the side of, team up with; ***opp*** oppose

sidestep *v* avoid, bypass, circumvent, dodge, duck *inf*, elude, evade, find a way around, skirt, steer clear of; ***opp*** confront

sidetrack *v* deflect, distract, divert, send off track

sieve *v* filter, screen, separate, sift, strain

sift *v* **1** filter, screen, separate, sieve, strain. **2** (sift evidence) analyze, examine, investigate, probe, screen, scrutinize, sort out, study, pore over, work over

sigh *n* breath, exhalation, murmur

sight *n* **1** (have good sight) eyes, eyesight, seeing, vision. **2** (a wonderful sight) appearance, display, scene, spectacle, view, vista

sight *v* behold, discern, distinguish, glimpse, make out, notice, observe, perceive, recognize, see, spot

sign *n* **1** clue, evidence, hint, indication, manifestation, mark, proof, suggestion, symptom, token, trace. **2** board, marker, notice, placard, signpost. **3** gesticulation, gesture, indication, motion, movement, signal. **4** cipher, code, device, emblem, hieroglyph, insignia, logo, mark, symbol

signal *n* **1** cue, gesticulation, gesture, indication, motion, movement, sign. **2** evidence, hint, indication, mark, proof, token

signal *v* beckon, gesticulate, gesture, give a signal, indicate, motion, nod, sign, wave

signature *n* autograph, mark, name

significance *n* **1** idea, import, meaning, message, point, purpose, sense, signification. **2** consequence, importance, magnitude, moment, seriousness, value, weight

significant *adj* considerable, important, meaningful, momentous, noteworthy, of consequence, of note, serious, valuable, weighty; ***opp*** insignificant

signify *adj* be a sign of, betoken, connote, denote, imply, indicate, mean, point to, portend, represent, stand for, suggest, symbolize

silence *n* calm, hush, lull, peace, quiet, quietness, soundlessness, stillness, tranquillity; ***opp*** noise

silent *adj* **1** calm, hushed, noiseless, peaceful, quiet, soundless, still, tranquil; ***opp*** noisy. **2** dumb, mum, mute, speechless, taciturn, tight-lipped, tongue-tied, voiceless, wordless; ***opp*** talkative

silhouette *n* contour, form, outline, profile, shape

silly *adj* absurd, asinine, brainless, childish, crazy, daft *inf*, fatuous, foolish, frivolous, giddy, idiotic, immature, inane, infantile, meaningless, mindless, pointless, puerile, ridiculous, simple-minded, stupid; ***opp*** sensible

similar *adj* akin, alike, analogous, close, comparable, corresponding, equivalent, like, matching, parallel, related, resembling, the same, uniform; ***opp*** different

similarity *n* affinity, agreement, closeness, correspondence, equivalence, kinship, likeness, match, relation, resemblance, similitude, uniformity;

opp difference

simmer *v* **1** boil, bubble, cook, poach, stew. **2** fume, rage, seethe, smart, smolder

simple *adj* **1** clear, comprehensible, easy, intelligible, lucid, obvious, plain, straightforward, uncomplicated, understandable; ***opp*** complicated. **2** austere, basic, classic, clean, modest, natural, plain, pure, restrained, unadorned, unfussy; ***opp*** elaborate. **3** artless, candid, childlike, frank, guileless, gullible, ingenuous, innocent, naive, natural, sincere, unaffected, unsophisticated; ***opp*** sophisticated

simplicity *n* **1** clarity, clearness, comprehensibility, ease, intelligibility, lucidity, obviousness, straightforwardness. **2** austerity, cleanness, modesty, naturalness, plainness, purity, restraint. **3** artlessness, candor, frankness, gullibility, ingenuousness, innocence, naiveté, naturalness, sincerity

simplify *v* abridge, clarify, cut, make simpler, edit, prune, shorten, streamline

simplistic *adj* facile, glib, inadequate, naive, oversimplified, shallow, superficial

simultaneous *adj* at the same time, coinciding, concurrent, contemporaneous, parallel, synchronized, synchronous

sin *n* corruption, crime, depravity, error, evil, guilt, immorality, iniquity, misdeed, misdemeanor, offense, peccadillo, transgression, trespass, vice, wickedness, wrong, wrongdoing

sin *v* do wrong, err, fall, go astray, lapse, offend, stray, transgress, trespass

sincere *adj* candid, earnest, frank, genuine, guileless, heartfelt, honest, open, real, serious, truthful, unaffected, unfeigned, wholehearted; ***opp*** insincere

sincerity *n* candor, earnestness, frankness, genuineness, good faith, honesty, openness, seriousness, truth, truthfulness; ***opp*** insincerity

sinful *adj* bad, corrupt, criminal, depraved, erring, evil, fallen, guilty, immoral, iniquitous, wicked, wrong; ***opp*** virtuous

sing *v* chant, chirp, croon, hum, pipe, serenade, trill, warble, yodel

singe *v* blacken, burn, char, scorch, sear

single *adj* **1** distinct, individual, isolated, lone, one, only, separate, sole, solitary, singular, unique. **2** bachelor, celibate, free, lone, unattached, unmarried, unwed; ***opp*** married

single-handed *adj* alone, by yourself, independent, on your own, solitary, solo, unaided, unassisted

single-minded *adj* dedicated, determined, dogged, fixed, focused, persevering, purposeful, resolute, set, steadfast, stubborn, tireless, unswerving, unwavering

singular *adj* **1** distinct, individual, isolated, lone, one, only, separate, sole, solitary, single, unique. **2** abnormal, curious, different, distinctive, exceptional, extraordinary, notable, noteworthy, odd, outstanding, peculiar, rare, remarkable, strange, striking, unique, unusual; ***opp*** normal, usual

sinister *adj* dark, dire, disquieting, disturbing, evil, forbidding, foreboding, frightening, malevolent, malign, malignant, menacing, nefarious, ominous, threatening, villainous

sink *v* 1 collapse, decline, descend, diminish, dip, droop, drop, ebb, fade, fall, flag, founder, lapse, lessen, lower, plummet, plunge, sag, slip, subside, weaken, worsen. 2 be engulfed, be submerged, founder, go down, go under, plummet

sip *v* drink, lap, sample, sup, taste, try

sit *v* 1 be seated, perch, rest, settle, squat, take a seat. 2 (a court sits) assemble, be in session, convene, gather, meet

site *n* area, ground, location, place, plot, position, setting, situation, spot

site *v* install, locate, place, position, put, set, situate

situate *v* install, locate, place, position, put, set, site

situation *n* 1 background, case, circumstances, condition, position, state of affairs. 2 environment, locale, location, place, plot, position, setting, site, spot. 3 employment, job, place, position, post

sizable *adj* ample, big, considerable, decent, generous, large, significant, substantial, worthwhile; ***opp*** small

size *n* 1 amount, area, capacity, dimensions, extent, gauge, measurements, proportions, range, scale, scope, volume. 2 (large size) bulk, expanse, hugeness, immensity, largeness, magnitude, mass, vastness, volume

skeptic *n* agnostic, cynic, doubter, doubting Thomas, unbeliever

skeptical *adj* cynical, disbelieving, distrustful, doubting, dubious, hesitant, incredulous, mistrustful, suspicious, uncertain, unconvinced, unsure

sketch *n* depiction, doodle, draft, drawing, outline, plan, representation

sketch *v* delineate, depict, doodle, draft, draw, indicate, outline, plot, portray, represent, rough out

sketchy *adj* cursory, patchy, provisional, imprecise, inadequate, incomplete, inexact, perfunctory, rough, skimpy, superficial, undeveloped, vague; ***opp*** detailed

skill *n* ability, accomplishment, adeptness, adroitness, aptitude, artistry, cleverness, competence, craft, deftness, dexterity, efficiency, expertise, facility, finesse, flair, gift, knack, mastery, proficiency, prowess, quickness, talent, technique, workmanship

skilled *adj* able, accomplished, adept, adroit, clever, competent, consummate, deft, dexterous, efficient, experienced, expert, handy, masterful, masterly, nimble, practiced, proficient, qualified, quick, skillful, trained; ***opp*** unskilled

skillful *adj* able, accomplished, adept, adroit, clever, competent, consummate, deft, dexterous, efficient, expert, handy, masterful, masterly, nimble, practiced, proficient, quick, skilled, trained

skim *v* 1 coast, fly, glide, graze, plane, sail, skate, slide, soar. 2 flick through, flip through, glance at, leaf through, scan, skip

skimp *v* be economical with, be mean with, be sparing with, cut corners, economize, pinch, scrimp, save, stint

skin *n* 1 epidermis, fleece, fur, hide, pelt. 2 casing, coat, coating, covering, crust, exterior, film, husk, membrane, outside, peel, rind, shell, surface

skin *v* flay, pare, peel, shell, strip

skip *v* 1 bob, bound, caper, cavort, dance, frisk, gambol, hop, jump, leap, prance, romp, spring, trip. 2 avoid, bypass, forget, ignore, leave out, miss, miss out, omit, overlook, pass over, skim through

skirmish *n* affray, battle, brush, clash, combat, conflict, confrontation, contest, engagement, fight, fracas, fray, incident, melee, set-to, spat, tussle

skirmish *v* battle, clash, confront, contend, fight, tussle

skirt *v* avoid, border, bypass, circle, circumvent, dodge, evade, go around, pass round, sidestep, steer clear of

sky *n* air, atmosphere, blue, firmament, heavens, space, stratosphere

slab *n* block, chunk, hunk, lump, piece, slice, wedge

slack *adj* 1 baggy, drooping, droopy, limp, loose, sagging, saggy, soft, relaxed; ***opp*** tight. 2 careless, disorganized, idle, inattentive, indolent, lax, lazy, neglectful, negligent, remiss, slapdash, slipshod, sloppy, undisciplined. 3 (business is slack) inactive, quiet, slow, sluggish; ***opp*** busy

slack *n* excess, leeway, play, room

slacken *v* 1 (a rope) droop, loosen, sag, soften, relax. 2 (pressure) abate, decrease, diminish, drop, ease off, lessen, loosen, moderate, reduce, relax, release

slam *v* 1 bang, crash, dash, fling, hurl, smash, throw, thump. 2 attack, blast *inf*, criticize, lambast, pillory, vilify

slander *n* calumny, defamation, libel, misrepresentation, muckraking, slur, smear

slander *v* blacken the name of, calumniate, defame, disparage, libel, malign, misrepresent, muckrake, slur, smear, traduce, vilify

slanderous *adj* calumnious, damaging, defamatory, disparaging, false, libelous, malicious, scurrilous, untrue, vicious

slant *n* 1 angle, camber, diagonal, gradient, incline, list, pitch, rake, ramp, slope, tilt. 2 angle, approach, attitude, perspective, point of view, standpoint, take, view, viewpoint. 3 bias, distortion, emphasis, leaning, prejudice, twist, weight

slant *v* 1 be at an angle, be skewed, incline, lean, list, slope, tilt. 2 angle, bias, color, distort, prejudice, skew, twist, weight

slanting *adj* angled, aslant, at an angle, diagonal, inclined, leaning, listing, oblique, shelving, skewed, sloping, tilted, tilting; ***opp*** straight

slap *v* clout, cuff, hit, smack, spank, strike, whack

slapdash *adj* careless, clumsy, disorganized, hasty, hurried, inattentive, lax, messy, neglectful, negligent, remiss, slack, slipshod, sloppy, slovenly, undisciplined, untidy; ***opp*** careful

slash *n* cut, gash, hack, incision, laceration, rent, rip, slit

slash *v* 1 cut, gash, hack, knife, lacerate, rend, rip, score, slit. 2 (slash prices) cut, decrease, drop, lower, mark down, reduce

slaughter *n* bloodshed, butchery, carnage, extermination, killing, massacre, murder, slaying

slaughter *v* butcher, exterminate, kill, massacre, murder, slay
slave *n* drudge, serf, servant, vassal
slave *v* drudge, labor, slog, sweat, toil, work your fingers to the bone
slavery *n* bondage, captivity, enslavement, serfdom, servitude, subjugation, thralldom
slavish *adj* 1 abject, cringing, deferential, fawning, groveling, gushing, obsequious, servile, submissive, subservient, sycophantic. 2 (slavish imitation) close, strict, sycophantic, uncritical, unimaginative, unoriginal, unthinking
slay *v* assassinate, bump off *inf*, butcher, do away with *inf*, exterminate, get rid of *inf*, kill, massacre, murder, put to death, slaughter
sleazy *adj* cheap, disreputable, dirty, low, seedy, sordid, squalid, unwholesome
sleek *adj* gleaming, glossy, lustrous, satiny, shiny, silky, smooth, well-groomed
sleep *n* catnap, doze, forty winks *inf*, nap, repose, rest, siesta, slumber, snooze
sleep *v* be asleep, catnap, doze, drop off *inf*, drowse, fall asleep, nap, nod off *inf*, slumber, snooze, snore
sleepless *adj* awake, conscious, insomniac, restless, wakeful, wide awake
sleepy *adj* dopey, drowsy, dull, heavy, lethargic, sluggish, somnolent, tired, torpid, weary
slender *adj* 1 fine, graceful, lean, narrow, slight, slim, svelte, sylph-like, willowy; ***opp*** fat. 2 (slender means) inadequate, insubstantial, insufficient, little, meager, paltry, scanty, slight, small. 3 (a slender hope) faint, feeble, flimsy, fragile, frail, slight, slim, tenuous, thin, weak; ***opp*** strong
slice *n* layer, piece, portion, segment, share, shaving, sliver, wedge
slice *v* carve, cut, divide, segment
slick *adj* 1 glib, oily, plausible, polished, smooth, specious, suave, unctuous. 2 (doing sth well) adroit, deft, dexterous, efficient, polished, skillful, smooth, streamlined, well organized
slide *v* coast, glide, plane, skate, skid, skim, slip, slither, veer
slight *adj* 1 imperceptible, inconsequential, insignificant, meager, minor, minute, modest, negligible, small, tiny; ***opp*** large. 2 delicate, frail, petite, slender, slim, small; ***opp*** big
slight *n* affront, discourtesy, disregard, disrespect, insult, neglect, rebuff, rudeness, snub
slight *v* affront, disdain, disregard, disrespect, ignore, insult, neglect, put down, rebuff, scorn, snub
slightly *adv* a bit, a little, moderately, somewhat, to a small extent
slim *adj* 1 fine, lean, narrow, slender, slight, svelte, sylph-like, trim, willowy; ***opp*** fat. 2 (slim hope) faint, feeble, flimsy, fragile, frail, remote, slight, slim, tenuous, thin, weak; ***opp*** strong
slimy *adj* 1 clammy, glutinous, greasy, mucous, muddy, oily, slippery, slithery, squishy *inf*, viscous, wet. 2 (of a person) creepy *inf*, gushing, obsequious, oily, smooth, sycophantic, unctuous
sling *v* cast, chuck *inf*, fling, heave, hurl, lob, pelt, pitch, throw, toss
slink *v* creep, prowl, skulk, slide, slip, sneak, steal
slinky *adj* clinging, close-fitting,

sexy *inf*, sinuous, sleek

slip *v* **1** coast, glide, plane, skate, skid, skim, slide, slither. **2** creep, edge, slide, sneak, steal

slip *n* blunder, boob *inf*, bungle, error, failure, lapse, miscalculation, mistake, oversight, slip-up

slippery *adj* **1** glassy, greasy, icy, oily, perilous, slimy, smooth, wet. **2** (of a person) crafty, cunning, devious, dishonest, evasive, shifty, sneaky, tricky, two-faced, unreliable, wily

slit *n* aperture, cleft, crack, cut, gash, hole, incision, opening, rent, slash, slot, split, tear, vent

slit *v* cut, cut open, gash, knife, lance, pierce, rip, slash, slice, tear

slither *v* creep, glide, slide, slink, slip, snake, undulate, worm

slog *n* **1** (hard work) effort, exertion, hard task, struggle. **2** (hard going) hike, trek, trudge. **3** (a hard hit) hit, slug *inf*, sock *inf*, stroke, wallop *inf*, whack *inf*

slog *v* **1** (hit sth) hit, punch, slug, sock *inf*, strike, thump, wallop *inf*, whack. **2** (slog away at sth) labor, persevere, plod, plow, slave. **3** (slog through the mud) plod, tramp, trek, trudge

slogan *n* catchphrase, catchword, jingle, motto, saying

slope *n* angle, ascent, camber, descent, dip, drop, fall, gradient, incline, hill, mountain, pitch, ramp, rise, slant, tilt

slope *v* dip, drop away, fall, incline, lean, pitch, rise, slant, tilt, tip

sloping *adj* angled, diagonal, dipping, inclined, inclining, leaning, listing, oblique, slanted, slanting, tilting

sloppy *adj* **1** liquid, runny, sludgy, slushy, soggy, splashy, watery, wet; ***opp*** firm. **2** (of work) careless, clumsy, disorganized, hurried, lax, messy, slapdash, untidy, weak; ***opp*** careful. **3** (a sloppy film) mawkish, schmaltzy *inf*, sentimental, soppy *inf*, trite

slot *n* **1** aperture, crack, gash, groove, hole, notch, opening, slit, vent. **2** opening, period, place, position, space, spot, time, vacancy

slouch *v* droop, hunch, loll, sag, slump, stoop

slovenly *adj* careless, dirty, disheveled, disorderly, lax, loose, messy, negligent, slack, slapdash, slatternly, slipshod, sloppy *inf*, unmethodical, untidy; ***opp*** careful

slow *adj* **1** (slow movement) careful, cautious, creeping, dawdling, lazy, leaden, leisurely, measured, painstaking, ponderous, sluggish, snail-like, steady, unhurried, unwilling; ***opp*** fast. **2** (a slow death) gradual, lingering, long-drawn-out, prolonged, protracted; ***opp*** quick. **3** (a slow learner) backward, behind, late, retarded, with special needs. **4** dense, dim, dull, stupid

slow *v* decelerate, ease up *inf*, go slower, put the brakes on, reduce speed, slow down

sluggish *adj* drowsy, dull, heavy, inactive, inert, languid, lazy, lethargic, listless, slothful, slow, torpid, unresponsive; ***opp*** lively

slump *v* collapse, crash, drop, fall, go down, nosedive, plummet, plunge, sink, slip, subside

slump *n* collapse, crash, depression,

devaluation, dip, downturn, drop, failure, fall, falling-off, low, nosedive, recession, trough; ***opp*** boom

slur *n* affront, aspersion, disgrace, insinuation, insult, libel, slander, slight, smear, stain, stigma

sly *adj* artful, crafty, cunning, deceitful, devious, foxy, furtive, mischievous, scheming, secret, secretive, shifty, shrewd, sneaky, stealthy, surreptitious, tricky, underhand, wily

smack *v* belt *inf*, clout, cuff, hit, pat, slap, spank, strike, swipe

small *adj* **1** baby *inf*, dwarf, little, microscopic, mini, miniature, minute, pocket-sized *inf*, teeny, teeny-weeny, tiny, wee, young; ***opp*** big. **2** (of a person) petite, pint-sized *inf*, puny, short, slender, slight, thin, undersized; ***opp*** big. **3** (a small problem) inconsequential, insignificant, minor, petty, trivial, unimportant; ***opp*** big. **4** (a small amount) inadequate, insufficient, meager, mean, measly, scanty, stingy, unsatisfactory; ***opp*** large

small-minded *adj* bigoted, grudging, intolerant, mean, narrow-minded, petty, prejudiced, selfish, ungenerous

smart *adj* **1** chic, dapper, dashing *inf*, elegant, fashionable, neat, snazzy *inf*, stylish, tidy, well-dressed, well-groomed, well turned-out; ***opp*** scruffy. **2** (clever) astute, bright, clever, gifted, intelligent, quick, quick-witted, sharp

smart *v* burn, hurt, sting, throb, tingle

smash *n* accident, car crash, collision, crash, pile-up *inf*

smash *v* **1** break, crack, demolish, shatter. **2** (smash into sth) bash, bump, collide, crash, knock, pound, slam, strike

smashing *adj* brilliant, excellent, fabulous, first-class, great, marvelous, out of this world, sensational, super, terrific, wonderful; ***opp*** awful

smattering *n* bit, dash, small amount, sprinkling

smear *n* **1** blot, blotch, daub, mark, smudge, splotch, spot, streak. **2** (a smear on sb's name) blot, slur, stain, stigma

smear *v* **1** (smear sth with paint) bedaub, coat, cover, dirty, mark, soil, stain, streak. **2** (smear paint on sth) dab, daub, plaster, slap, smudge, wipe. **3** (smear sb's reputation) blacken, sully, tarnish, vilify

smell *n* **1** (the smell of roses) aroma, bouquet, fragrance, odor, perfume, redolence, scent. **2** (the smell of old socks) reek, stench, stink, whiff

smell *v* **1** (be able to smell sth) get a whiff of, scent, sniff out. **2** (sth smells) reek, stink, whiff

smelly *adj* foul-smelling, high *inf*, malodorous, rank, reeking, stinking

smile *n* beam, grin, laugh, smirk, sneer

smile *v* beam, grin, laugh, leer, simper, smirk

smirk *v* grin, leer, look smug, simper, sneer

smitten *adj* **1** (smitten with a disease) affected, afflicted, laid low, plagued, struck down, suffering. **2** (smitten with sb) beguiled, bewitched, bowled over *inf*, captivated, charmed, entranced, infatuated, swept off your feet, taken

smoke *n* exhaust, fumes, pollution, smog, steam, vapor

smoke *v* **1** (give off smoke) burn, emit

smoke, smolder. **2** (smoke a cigarette) have a cigarette, inhale, puff

smooth *adj* **1** even, flat, flush, horizontal, level, plane, unwrinkled; ***opp*** bumpy. **2** burnished, glossy, polished, satiny, shiny, silken, silky, sleek, soft, velvety; ***opp*** rough. **3** (smooth surface of a lake) calm, glassy, mirrorlike, peaceful, still, tranquil, unbroken, undisturbed, unruffled. **4** (a smooth person) debonair, glib, insincere, persuasive, slick, smug, suave, urbane. **5** (smooth movements) comfortable, easy, effortless, flowing, fluent, fluid, regular, rhythmic, steady; ***opp*** jerky. **6** (smooth sounds) agreeable, bland, mellow, mild, pleasant, soft, soothing; ***opp*** harsh

smooth *v* brush, buff up, burnish, comb, even out, file, flatten, iron, level, plane, polish, press, press down, roll out, sand down

smother *v* **1** (smother a person) asphyxiate, choke, stifle, suffocate. **2** (smother a sound) hide, keep back, muffle, stifle, suppress. **3** (smother flames) damp down, extinguish, put out, stamp out

smudge *n* blotch, mark, smear, smut, spot, streak

smudge *v* blur, dirty, mark, soil, smear, streak

smug *adj* complacent, conceited, pleased with yourself, priggish, self-important, self-righteous, self-satisfied, superior

snack *n* bite, light meal, nibbles, nosh, refreshments

snag *n* catch, complication, disadvantage, drawback, hitch, obstacle, problem, setback, stumbling block

snap *n* **1** click, crack, crackle, pop. **2** (a cold snap) interval, period, spell, time. **3** (a holiday snap) photo, photograph, picture, snapshot

snap *v* **1** break, come apart, crack, fracture, give way, separate, split. **2** (of a dog) bite, catch, nip, seize, snatch. **3** (snap at sb) bark, flash, growl, jump down sb's throat *inf*, retort, snarl, speak sharply

snare *n* ambush, net, noose, trap

snare *v* capture, catch, ensnare, entrap, net, seize, trap

snatch *n* (a snatch of a tune) bit, fragment, part, piece, snippet

snatch *v* **1** catch, clutch, grab, grasp, grip, pluck, pull, seize, take, win, wrench. **2** abduct, hold ransom, kidnap, make off with, nab *inf*, steal, take as a hostage

sneak *n* informer, snitch *inf*, telltale

sneak *v* **1** (sneak through the bushes) cower, creep, lurk, pad, prowl, sidle, skulk, slink, stalk, steal. **2** (sneak sth in) slip, smuggle, spirit, whisk. **3** (sneak on sb) inform against, report, snitch *inf*, tell *inf*, tell tales

sneaky *adj* deceitful, furtive, mean, shady, shifty *inf*, sly, stealthy, surreptitious, treacherous, underhand

sneer *v* be contemptuous, be scornful, deride, hiss, jeer, laugh, mock, ridicule, scoff, smirk, snigger, taunt

sniff *v* breathe, breathe in, get a whiff of, inhale, scent, smell, snuffle

snigger *v* chuckle, giggle, laugh, sneer, titter

snip *n* bit, clipping, cutting, fragment, piece, scrap, shred, tatter

snip *v* clip, crop, cut, dock, nick, notch, prune, shave, trim
snivel *v* blubber, cry, grizzle, moan, sniff, sniffle, snuffle, sob, whimper, whine
snobbish *adj* arrogant, condescending, haughty, hoity-toity, patronizing, pompous, posh *inf*, proud, smug, snobby, snooty *inf*, stuck-up *inf*, superior
snoop *v* interfere, meddle, nose about *inf*, poke your nose in *inf*, pry, sneak, spy
snub *n* affront, insult, rebuff, slap in the face *inf*, slight
snub *v* be rude to, give the cold shoulder to, humiliate, ignore, insult, rebuff, shun, slight, spurn
snug *adj* comfortable, comfy *inf*, cozy, intimate, sheltered, soft, warm
snuggle *v* cuddle, curl up, nestle, nuzzle
soak *v* **1** drench, saturate, wet through. **2** (soak sth) immerse, marinate, steep. **3** (soak into sth) infuse, penetrate, permeate
soaking *adj* drenched, dripping, saturated, soaked, soaked to the skin, sodden, sopping, waterlogged, wringing wet; ***opp*** dry
soar *v* **1** (of a bird) ascend, fly, hover, rise, take flight, take off. **2** (of prices) climb, escalate, go up, increase, rise, shoot up, spiral; ***opp*** plummet, tumble
sob *v* bawl, cry, gasp, howl, shed tears, snivel, weep
sober *adj* **1** abstinent, moderate, teetotal. **2** (sober clothing) dark, drab, dull, plain, restrained, somber, subdued. **3** (a sober expression) grave, serious, solemn, thoughtful. **4** (a sober look at sth) calm, clear-headed, level-headed, rational, sensible
sociable *adj* affable, companionable, convivial, cordial, extroverted, friendly, gregarious, outgoing, social, warm, welcoming; ***opp*** unsociable
social *adj* **1** collective, communal, community, general, group, popular, public. **2** civilized, organized. **3** communicative, friendly, gregarious, outgoing, sociable; ***opp*** antisocial
social *n* do *inf*, gathering, get-together *inf*, party
socialize *v* be sociable, entertain, get together, go out, join in, mix
society *n* **1** civilization, community, culture. **2** mankind, people, the community, the public. **3** (club) association, circle, club, group, guild, league, union
sodden *adj* boggy, drenched, saturated, soaked, soggy, sopping, swampy, waterlogged; ***opp*** dry
soft *adj* **1** doughy, elastic, flexible, gelatinous, gooey *inf*, malleable, mushy, plastic, pliable, pulpy, spongy, springy, squashy, supple, tender, yielding; ***opp*** hard. **2** (a soft coat) downy, feathery, fleecy, fluffy, furry, silky, smooth, velvety; ***opp*** rough. **3** (soft light) diffuse, dim, faint, gentle, low, restful, subdued; ***opp*** harsh. **4** (soft sounds) dulcet, faint, gentle, hushed, inaudible, low, mellow, murmured, muted, quiet, soothing, subdued, whispered. **5** (soft colors) light, muted, pale, pastel; ***opp*** vivid. **6** (a soft breeze) balmy, gentle, light, mild, pleasant; ***opp*** strong. **7** (of a person) compassionate,

easygoing, feeble, forgiving, gentle, kind, lenient, loving, sensitive, soft-hearted, sympathetic, tender-hearted, tolerant, weak. **8** (soft ground) boggy, marshy, muddy, swampy, waterlogged; ***opp*** firm

soften *v* alleviate, calm down, cushion, deaden, decrease, diminish, lower, make softer, moderate, muffle, quell, quiet, subdue, tone down, turn down

soggy *adj* boggy, sodden, soft, sopping, swampy, waterlogged, wet; ***opp*** dry

soil *n* clay, dirt, dust, earth, ground, loam, topsoil

soil *v* contaminate, dirty, foul, make dirty, muddy, pollute, smear, smudge, spatter, spot, stain, tarnish

soldier *n* commando, fighter, gunner, officer, paratrooper, private, serviceman, servicewoman, warrior

sole *adj* **1** (the sole survivor) lone, only, single, solitary. **2** (for your sole use) exclusive, individual

solemn *adj* **1** (looking solemn) earnest, grave, grim, long-faced, serious, sober, thoughtful, unsmiling. **2** (a solemn ceremony) ceremonial, ceremonious, dignified, formal, grand, holy, important, imposing, impressive, religious, stately. **3** (a solemn vow) genuine, honest, serious, sincere, wholehearted

solicit *v* (solicit advice) appeal for, ask for, request, seek

solid *adj* **1** compact, compressed, concrete, dense, firm, hard, impermeable, rigid, thick, unmoving. **2** durable, robust, sound, stable, strong, sturdy, substantial, well-made; ***opp*** flimsy. **3** (solid gold) genuine, pure, real, unalloyed, unmixed. **4** (a solid shape) cubic, rounded, spherical, three-dimensional; ***opp*** flat. **5** (solid support) complete, dependable, effective, reliable, stalwart, trustworthy, undivided, united, unwavering

solidarity *n* accord, camaraderie, cohesion, harmony, like-mindedness, stability, team spirit, unanimity, unity

solidify *v* become hard, clot, coagulate, congeal, crystallize, go hard, harden, jell, set, thicken; ***opp*** liquefy

solitary *adj* **1** (of a thing) alone, by itself, lone, one, single, sole. **2** (of a person) friendless, isolated, lonely, lonesome, unsociable. **3** (of a place) desolate, hidden, lonely, out-of-the-way, private, remote, secluded

solitude *n* isolation, loneliness, privacy, remoteness, retirement, seclusion

solo *adj, adv* alone, by yourself, individually, on your own, unaccompanied

soluble *adj* (soluble in water) dispersing, dissolving, melting

solution *n* **1** answer, clarification, conclusion, explanation, key, result, solving, working out. **2** blend, compound, emulsion, infusion, mixture, solvent, suspension

solve *v* **1** (solve a mystery) clear up, explain, figure out, find the solution to, unravel. **2** (solve your problems) find the answer to, resolve, sort out. **3** (solve a clue) crack *inf*, decipher, interpret

solvent *adj* creditworthy, debt-free, in credit, in the black, solid, sound, viable

somber *adj* black, bleak, cheerless, dark,

dim, dismal, doleful, funereal, gloomy, joyless, melancholy, morose, mournful, sad, sepulchral

song *n* anthem, ballad, carol, ditty, hymn, lullaby, pop song, tune

soon *adv* any minute now *inf*, before long, before you know it *inf*, in a minute, in a moment, in a while, in the near future, in two shakes of a lamb's tail *inf*, quickly, shortly, straightaway

soothe *v* **1** alleviate, appease, assuage, calm, ease, relieve, soften. **2** (soothe a baby) calm, comfort, lull, pacify, quiet, settle

sophisticated *adj* **1** (of people) cool *inf*, cosmopolitan, cultivated, cultured, grown-up *inf*, mature, refined, suave, urbane, worldly, worldly wise; ***opp*** unsophisticated. **2** (of technology) advanced, complex, complicated, elaborate, highly developed, intricate, involved; ***opp*** simple

soppy *adj* **1** (a soppy film) corny *inf*, mawkish, schmaltzy, sentimental, slushy *inf*. **2** (a soppy person) daft *inf*, foolish, overemotional, sentimental, silly, soft *inf*, wet

sorcerer *n* enchanter, enchantress, magician, sorceress, warlock, witch, wizard

sorcery *n* black magic, charms, incantations, magic, spells, voodoo, witchcraft, witchery, wizardry

sordid *adj* **1** dingy, dirty, filthy, foul, mean, miserable, seedy, shabby, sleazy, slovenly, squalid, ugly, unpleasant, vile, wretched. **2** corrupt, dishonorable, disreputable, immoral, mercenary, shabby *inf*, unethical

sore *adj* **1** aching, angry, bruised, burning, inflamed, irritated, painful, raw, red, sensitive, smarting, tender, wounded. **2** (feel sore about sth) aggrieved, annoyed, hurt, irritated, peeved *inf*, put out *inf*, resentful, upset

sorrow *n* anguish, dejection, desolation, disappointment, distress, grief, heartache, melancholy, misery, regret, sadness, tearfulness, unhappiness, woe, wretchedness; ***opp*** happiness, joy

sorrowful *adj* brokenhearted, dejected, grief-stricken, heartbroken, melancholy, miserable, sad, saddened, tearful, unhappy, upset, woebegone; ***opp*** happy

sorry *adj* **1** apologetic, ashamed, contrite, penitent, remorseful, repentant, shamefaced; ***opp*** unrepentant. **2** distressed, grieved, sad, sorrowful, unhappy, upset; ***opp*** glad. **3** (sorry for sb) compassionate, concerned, full of pity, moved, pitying, sympathetic; ***opp*** uncaring

sort *n* **1** brand, kind, make, type. **2** breed, family, kind, race, species, strain, type, variety. **3** category, class, classification, description, genre, kind, nature, style, type

sort *v* **1** (put things into groups) class, divide, grade, put in groups, rank, select. **2** (put things in order) arrange, catalog, categorize, classify, group, put in order, systematize, tidy. **3** (sort papers) file, organize, tidy. **4 sort out** (put in order) organize, tidy up. **5 sort out** (sort out a problem) deal with, find a solution to, handle, resolve

soul *n* **1** being, body, creature, individual, mortal, person. **2** inner self, spirit, true being

sound *adj* **1** complete, entire, firm, fit, hale and hearty, healthy, in good health, in good shape, intact, perfect, unhurt, uninjured, whole. **2** (strong) robust, solid, strong, sturdy, substantial, tough, undamaged; ***opp*** flimsy. **3** (sound reasoning) convincing, correct, logical, plausible, proper, reasonable, right, sane, sensible, true, valid, wise

sound *n* bang, blare, crash, creak, cry, din, hoot, music, noise, scream, shout, squeak, thud, yelp, voice

sound *v* **1** be heard, echo, make a noise, resonate, resound, reverberate. **2** (you sound desperate) appear, look, seem. **3** (sound the words carefully) articulate, pronounce, say, utter, voice. **4 sound out** canvass, examine, inquire into, investigate, look into, probe, research, test

soup *n* bouillon, broth, consommé, stock

sour *adj* **1** (a sour taste) acid, bitter, lemony, pungent, sharp, tangy, tart, vinegary. **2** (sour milk) bad, curdled, off, rancid, turned; ***opp*** fresh. **3** (of a person) bad-tempered, bitter, cross, crotchety, discontented, grouchy *inf*, grumpy, irritable, jaundiced, nasty, unpleasant; ***opp*** pleasant

source *n* **1** author, beginning, cause, creator, origin, starting point. **2** (source of a river) head, spring, start, wellhead, wellspring

souvenir *n* keepsake, memento, memorabilia, relic, reminder

sovereign *adj* absolute, all-powerful, chief, dominant, highest, imperial, predominant, principal, royal, ruling, supreme, unlimited

sovereign *n* crowned head, emperor, empress, king, monarch, prince, princess, queen, ruler, tsar

sow *v* **1** (sow seeds) plant, scatter, strew. **2** (sow confusion) instigate, promote, spread

space *n* **1** emptiness, infinity, nothingness, vacuum, void. **2** (fired a rocket into space) outer space, the galaxy, the solar system, the stratosphere, the universe. **3** (need more space) capacity, elbow room *inf*, freedom, leeway, margin, room, scope, spaciousness. **4** (a large space) area, expanse, volume. **5** (gap) blank, empty space, gap, hole, opening

spacious *adj* ample, broad, capacious, comfortable, extensive, huge, large, open, roomy, sizable, vast, wide; ***opp*** small

span *n* distance, extent, length, reach, spread, stretch, width

span *v* arch over, bridge, cover, cross, extend across, go over, straddle, stretch over, vault over

spank *v* belt, cuff, give a hiding to *inf*, put over your knee, slap, smack, wallop

spare *adj* additional, emergency, extra, free, in reserve, leftover, odd, remaining, surplus, unoccupied, unused, unwanted

spare *v* **1** afford, do without, manage, sacrifice. **2** (spare some change) donate, give, provide. **3** (spare sb or sth) be merciful, free, have mercy, let off *inf*, pardon, release, reprieve, save

sparing *adj* careful, economical, frugal, miserly, parsimonious, prudent, stingy *inf*, thrifty, tight-fisted *inf*; ***opp*** lavish

spark *n* flare, flash, flicker, gleam, glint, sparkle
spark *v* ignite, kindle, provoke, set off, touch off, trigger
sparkle *v* **1** beam, flash, gleam, glint, glisten, glitter, glow, shimmer, shine, twinkle, wink. **2** bubble, effervesce, fizz
sparse *adj* light, meager, scanty, scarce, slight, thin
spasm *n* attack, bout, contraction, convulsion, cramp, fit, jerk, outburst, seizure, twitch
spasmodic *adj* convulsive, erratic, fitful, intermittent, irregular, jerky, occasional, periodic, sporadic
spate *n* deluge, flood, flow, rush, torrent
spatter *v* daub, pepper, shower, splash, splatter, spray, sprinkle
speak *v* **1** argue, communicate, converse, express yourself, give a lecture, have a chat, have a word, hold forth, pipe up *inf*, recite, say sth, talk, tell sth, use your voice. **2** (speak Spanish) converse in, pronounce, talk in. **3 speak out** have your say, make yourself heard, raise your voice, sound off, speak up, speak your mind
speaker *n* lecturer, orator, public speaker, spokesperson
spearhead *v* initiate, launch, lead, pioneer, set in motion
special *adj* **1** different, distinctive, exceptional, extraordinary, noteworthy, odd, out-of-the-ordinary, peculiar, strange, unique, unmistakable, unusual; ***opp*** ordinary. **2** (a special day) festive, gala, important, memorable, momentous, red-letter, significant, unique, unusual; ***opp*** ordinary
specialist *n* authority, buff *inf*, connoisseur, consultant, expert, professional
specialize *v* be a specialist in, be best at, concentrate on, focus on, have a reputation for, have special knowledge in
specialty *n* claim to fame *inf*, field, forte, gift, special skill, strength, strong point, talent
species *n* breed, class, genus, kind, sort, type, variety
specific *adj* **1** definite, especial, exact, individual, particular, special, specified. **2** (be specific about what you want) definite, detailed, explicit, firm, particular, precise, unambiguous, unequivocal
specification *n* conditions, description, details, instructions, particulars, requirements
specify *v* define, detail, enumerate, indicate, list, mention, name, set out, spell out, state, stipulate
specimen *n* example, illustration, instance, model, pattern, representative sample, sample
speck *n* dot, fleck, smudge, speckle, spot
speckled *adj* dappled, dotted, flecked, freckled, mottled, patchy, spotted, stippled
spectacle *n* **1** display, event, extravaganza, pageant, parade, performance, scene, show, sight. **2** (make a spectacle of yourself) curiosity, fool, laughing-stock
spectacular *adj* beautiful, breathtaking, daring, dazzling, dramatic, eye-catching, impressive,

magnificent, sensational, striking

spectator *n* beholder, bystander, eyewitness, observer, onlooker, viewer, watcher, witness

specter *n* apparition, ghost, phantom, spirit, wraith

speculate *v* conjecture, consider, hypothesize, make a guess, meditate, muse, reflect, suppose, think, wonder

speech *n* **1** (make a speech) address, discourse, lecture, monologue, oration, sermon, soliloquy, talk. **2** (human speech) communication, conversation, dialogue, discussion, talk. **3** (way of speaking) articulation, delivery, diction, elocution, pronunciation, way of speaking

speechless *adj* **1** dumb, inarticulate, mum, mute, silent, struck dumb, tongue-tied, wordless. **2** (too shocked to speak) aghast, amazed, astounded, dazed, dumbstruck, shocked, thunderstruck

speed *n* **1** briskness, haste, hurry, quickness, rapidity, speediness, swiftness, velocity. **2** pace, rate, tempo

speed *v* **1** flash, hurtle, race, streak, tear, whizz, zoom. **2** (run) career, dash, fly, gallop, hurry, race, run, rush, scamper, sprint. **3** break the speed limit, exceed the speed limit, go too fast. **4 speed up** accelerate, gather momentum, get moving *inf*, hurry up, increase speed, put on speed, put your foot down *inf*, rush, step on it *inf*

speedy *adj* fast, hasty, hurried, immediate, prompt, quick, rapid, swift

spell *n* **1** charm, enchantment, incantation, magic formula, sorcery, witchcraft. **2** (a spell of wintry weather) interval, patch, period, time

spellbound *adj* bewitched, captivated, charmed, enthralled, entranced, fascinated, gripped, hooked *inf*, mesmerized, overcome, rapt, riveted, transported, under a spell

spend *v* **1** (spend money) fork out *inf*, fritter away, pay out, shell out *inf*, splurge *inf*, squander, use up, waste. **2** (spend time) fill, occupy, pass, while away

sphere *n* **1** ball, circle, globe, globule, orb. **2** area, department, domain, field, jurisdiction, province, realm, specialty, subject, territory

spherical *adj* ball-shaped, globe-shaped, globular, round

spice *n* **1** flavor, flavoring, kick *inf*, piquancy, punch *inf*, relish, savor, seasoning, spiciness. **2** (in life) color, excitement, interest, zest, zing *inf*

spicy *adj* aromatic, flavorsome, fragrant, highly flavored, hot, peppery, pungent, seasoned, sharp, well-seasoned; ***opp*** bland

spike *n* barb, nail, pin, point, prong, skewer, spine, stake

spill *v* **1** (spill a drink) knock over, overturn, slop, splash, tip over, upset. **2** (spill the contents of sth) drop, scatter, shed, upset. **3** (spill over) brim over, discharge, disgorge, overflow, pour, slop over, spill over

spin *n* gyration, revolution, roll, rotation, turn, twist, whirl

spin *v* **1** circle, gyrate, pirouette, reel, revolve, rotate, swivel, turn, twirl, twist, wheel, whirl. **2** (your head spins) be giddy, go round, grow dizzy, reel, swim

spine *n* **1** backbone, spinal column, vertebrae. **2** barb, bristle, needle, quill, spike

spine-chilling *adj* bloodcurdling, creepy *inf*, eerie, frightening, hair-raising, horrifying, scary *inf*, spooky *inf*, terrifying

spineless *adj* cowardly, faint-hearted, feeble, gutless *inf*, soft *inf*, timid, weak, weak-willed, wimpish *inf*, yellow *inf*, yellow-bellied *inf*; ***opp*** courageous

spiral *adj* circular, coiled, corkscrew, helical, scrolled, twisting, winding

spirit *n* **1** apparition, ghost, phantom, poltergeist, specter, vision. **2** (admire sb's spirit) attitude, bravery, courage, determination, enterprise, enthusiasm, guts *inf*, mettle, optimism, pluck, resolution, vigor, willpower

spirited *adj* animated, assertive, brave, daring, energetic, enthusiastic, gutsy *inf*, heroic, lively, passionate, vigorous

spiritual *adj* devotional, devout, divine, heavenly, holy, pure, religious, sacred

spit *n* dribble, drool, saliva, slaver, slobber, spittle

spit *v* dribble, hiss, salivate, slobber, splutter

spite *n* animosity, bitterness, envy, hate, hatred, ill-feeling, malice, maliciousness, pique, resentment, spitefulness, vindictiveness

spiteful *adj* barbed, catty *inf*, cruel, cutting, hurtful, ill-natured, malevolent, malicious, snide, venomous, vicious, vindictive

splash *n* **1** (splash of color) burst, dash, patch, spattering, spot, streak. **2** (making a splash) impact, sensation. **3** (having a splash in the pool) dip, paddle, plunge, swim, wallow

splash *v* **1** (splash sb with water) shower, slop, slosh, spatter, splatter, spray, sprinkle, squirt, wash, wet. **2** (splash around) bathe, dabble, paddle, wallow. **3** (splash the news over all the papers) blazon, broadcast, headline, plaster, publicize, trumpet

splendid *adj* **1** admirable, awe-inspiring, glorious, grand, heroic, magnificent, outstanding, sublime, superb. **2** beautiful, costly, dazzling, elegant, fabulous, gorgeous, impressive, lavish, magnificent, opulent, rich, sumptuous. **3** beautiful, excellent, fantastic *inf*, fine, glorious, great *inf*, marvelous, super *inf*, wonderful

splendor *n* beauty, brightness, brilliance, dazzle, glitter *inf*, grandeur, luxury, magnificence, pomp, radiance, richness, sumptuousness

splice *v* braid, entwine, intertwine, interweave, join, overlap, plait, tie together

splinter *n* chip, flake, fragment, needle, shard, shaving, sliver

splinter *v* break, chip, crack, fracture, shatter, smash, split

split *n* **1** breach, cleft, crack, division, fissure, gap, gash, opening, rip, slash, slit, tear. **2** (between people) breakup, difference of opinion, division, divorce, estrangement, rift, separation

split *v* **1** break, burst, crack, disintegrate, rip, separate, snap, splinter. **2** (split sth) bisect, break, chop, cleave, cut, divide, rip, separate, slash, slice, slit, tear (split the proceeds) distribute, divide, dole out, parcel out, share out. **3** (split into two) branch, diverge, divide, fork. **4 split up** break up, disband, divorce, go your separate ways, part, separate

spoil *v* **1** blemish, blight, damage, deface, destroy, disfigure, harm, impair, injure, mar, mess up, ruin, undermine, undo, upset, wreck. **2** (spoil sb) baby, coddle, cosset, indulge, make a fuss of, mollycoddle, overindulge, pamper. **3** (of food) addle, curdle, decay, go bad, go off *inf*, go sour, rot, turn

sponsor *n* backer, benefactor, patron, promoter, supporter

sponsor *v* back, finance, fund, promote, subsidize, support, underwrite

spontaneous *adj* automatic, impromptu, impulsive, instinctive, off-the-cuff, reflex, spur-of-the-moment, unhesitating, unplanned, unrehearsed, voluntary; ***opp*** planned

spooky *adj* creepy, eerie, frightening, ghostly, hair-raising, scary, spine-chilling, supernatural, uncanny, unearthly, weird

sporadic *adj* erratic, every now and then, intermittent, irregular, occasional, on and off, patchy, periodic, random, scattered, spasmodic

sport *n* athletics, ball games, games, hunting, PE, physical activity, physical exercise, team games, water sports, winter sports

sport *v* carry, display, flaunt, show off, wear

sporting *adj* decent, fair, generous, gentlemanly, honorable; ***opp*** unsporting

sportsman *n* athlete, competitor, contestant, participant, player, sportswoman, team member

sporty *adj* active, athletic, energetic, fit, healthy, muscular, outdoor

spot *n* **1** blackhead, freckle, mole, pimple, pockmark, pustule, rash, whitehead, zit *inf*. **2** blob, blotch, dot, drop, fleck, mark, patch, speck, splash, stain. **3** area, location, place, position, site, situation. **4** bit, drop, little, smidgen, touch

spot *v* **1** catch sight of, glimpse, make out, notice, recognize, see. **2** mark, spatter, splash, stain

spotless *adj* **1** clean, gleaming, hygienic, immaculate, shining, spick and span, sterile; ***opp*** dirty. **2** (of sb's reputation) above reproach, faultless, flawless, squeaky-clean *inf*, unsullied, untarnished; ***opp*** tarnished

spotty *adj* **1** blotchy, dappled, dotty, flecked, mottled, polka-dot, speckly, spotted. **2** acned, pimply

spouse *n* husband, mate, missis *inf*, old man *inf*, other half *inf*, partner, wife

spout *v* **1** erupt, flow, gush, jet, pour, shoot, spew, spurt, squirt, stream. **2** expound, go on, harangue, hold forth, rabbit on *inf*, rant, rattle on *inf*

sprawl *v* **1** flop, languish, loll, lounge, recline, slouch, slump, spread out, stretch out. **2** be scattered, ramble, spill over, spread, straggle, tumble over

spray *n* **1** droplets, fountain, mist, shower, spatter. **2** aerosol, atomizer, pump, sprinkler, vaporizer

spray *v* mist, shower, spatter, splash, sprinkle, wet

spread *n* **1** (the spread of sth) advance, expansion, growth, increase, proliferation. **2** (span) expanse, extent, range, reach, span. **3** (in a newspaper) article, feature, piece, story. **4** (sth to put on bread) butter, conserve, jam, margarine, paste, pâté, preserve. **5** feast, meal

spread *v* **1** (open out) expand, extend, fan out, open out, stretch, unfold, unfurl. **2** (grow) broaden, develop, disperse, distribute, expand, get bigger, grow, increase, multiply, mushroom, proliferate, swell. **3** (reach) cover, extend, reach, sprawl, stretch. **4** (lay out) arrange, distribute, lay out, scatter. **5** (spread butter) apply, coat, cover with, plaster on *inf*, put on, rub over, smear on. **6** (spread news) advertise, broadcast, circulate, disseminate, give out, make known, pass round, promulgate, publicize

spree *n* bender *inf*, binge, bout, day out, fling, junket *inf*, night out, splurge *inf*

sprightly *adj* active, agile, alert, brisk, chipper *inf*, energetic, jaunty, lively, nimble, perky *inf*, spry

spring *n* **1** bounce, bound, hop, jump, leap, vault. **2** elasticity, flexibility, give, springiness. **3** springtime. **4** geyser, spa, water source, well

spring *v* **1** bounce, bound, jump, leap, pounce, recoil, vault. **2** (spring from) come from, derive, emanate, originate, spring from, start, stem from. **3** (spring up) appear, develop, emerge, grow, mushroom, pop up, shoot up, spring up, sprout

sprinkle *v* dribble, drizzle, pepper, scatter, shower, spatter, spray, strew

sprinkling *n* dribble, dusting, few, handful, scattering, splash, trickle

sprint *v* charge, dash, hotfoot it *inf*, race, run, rush, tear

sprout *v* come into bud, come up, germinate, grow, put out shoots, shoot

spur *n* encouragement, impetus, incentive, inducement, motivation

spur *v* drive, encourage, give sb the incentive, goad, incite, motivate, pressurize, prod, prompt, stimulate, urge

spurious *adj* artificial, bogus, false, insincere, mock, phony *inf*, pretended, pseudo, sham; ***opp*** genuine, real

spurn *v* give sb the cold shoulder, rebuff, reject, repulse, shun, turn away; ***opp*** encourage

spy *n* agent, double agent, foreign agent, informer, member of the secret service, mole *inf*, secret agent, snooper, undercover agent, 007 *inf*

spy *v* **1** catch sight of, discover, glimpse, notice, see, spot. **2** follow, gather intelligence, keep an eye on, keep under observation, trail, keep under surveillance, snoop *inf*, tail *inf*, watch

squabble *n* argument, difference of opinion, disagreement, fight, row, spat, tiff, wrangle

squabble *v* argue, bicker, fall out, fight, have a tiff, row, wrangle

squalid *adj* **1** deprived, dingy, dirty, filthy, foul, nasty, neglected, rundown, seedy, slovenly, wretched; ***opp*** smart. **2** corrupt, disreputable, indecent, shameful, sleazy, sordid

squalor *n* decay, deprivation, dilapidation, dirt, filth, neglect, seediness, wretchedness

squander *v* blow *inf*, fritter away, misuse, pour down the drain *inf*, splurge *inf*, throw away, waste

square *adj* 1 quadrilateral, rectangular, right-angled, true. 2 (honest) above board, decent, fair, honest, on the level, straight

squash *v* 1 compress, crush, flatten, mash, pound, press, pulp, pulverize, squeeze. 2 (squash things in) cram, crowd, jam, pack, ram, squeeze, wedge

squawk *v* call, caw, croak, screech, shriek, squeak, squeal

squeak *v* cheep, cry, peep, pipe, scream, screech, shrill, squeal, yelp

squeal *v* cry, howl, scream, screech, shout, shriek, squawk, wail, yelp

squeamish *adj* delicate, faint, funny *inf*, groggy *inf*, nauseated, queasy, sick

squeeze *v* 1 (press) clasp, compress, crush, grip, mash, nip, pinch, press, pulp, squash. 2 (squeeze things in) cram, crowd, force, jam, pack, ram, squash, stuff, wedge. 3 (squeeze sth to get out water) extract, press, twist, wring

squirm *v* fidget, flounder, thrash about, twist, wriggle, writhe

squirt *v* eject, gush, jet, shoot, shower, spew out, spray, spurt

stab *v* cut, gash, gore, jab, knife, pierce, run through, skewer, slash, spear, spike

stability *n* equilibrium, firmness, permanence, reliability, security, solidity, soundness, steadiness, strength, sturdiness; ***opp*** insecurity, shakiness, unsteadiness

stabilize *v* balance, keep steady, make stable, settle, steady

stable *adj* balanced, constant, established, fast, firm, lasting, on a firm footing, permanent, reliable, secure, solid, sound, steadfast, steady, sturdy, unchanging, unvarying, well founded; ***opp*** shaky, unstable

stack *n* heap, hoard, mass, mound, mountain, pile, tower

stack *v* heap, load, pile up, pile, put, stow

staff *n* 1 baton, cane, crook, mace, scepter, stave, stick, walking stick, wand. 2 crew, employees, members of staff, personnel, workers, workforce

stage *n* 1 (phase) juncture, lap, leg, level, phase, point, step. 2 (platform) dais, platform, podium, proscenium, rostrum. 3 (the stage) acting, footlights, repertory, show business, theater

stagger *v* 1 careen, lurch, pitch, reel, rock, roll, totter. 2 amaze, astound, flabbergast, overwhelm, shake, stun, surprise, take sb's breath away. 3 alternate, interlace, vary

stagnant *adj* brackish, foul, lethargic, sluggish, stale, standing, static, still; ***opp*** flowing, fresh

stagnate *v* decay, deteriorate, fester, go nowhere, become stagnant, languish, rot, vegetate

staid *adj* demure, fuddy-duddy *inf*, prim, proper, quiet, reserved, sedate, serious, solemn, stiff, straitlaced, stuffy *inf*, unadventurous; ***opp*** adventurous

stain *n* 1 blotch, discoloration, mark, spot. 2 coloring, dye, varnish

stain *v* 1 dirty, discolor, make dirty, mark, splash, spot. 2 blacken, damage, disgrace, spoil, taint, tarnish. 3 color, dye, varnish

stair *n* escalator, flight of stairs, riser, rung, staircase, stairway, steps, tread

stake *n* 1 pole, post, rod, shaft, spike,

stave, stick, support. **2** bet, money, wager. **3** claim, concern, interest, investment, share

stake *v* **1** brace, hold up, prop up, support. **2** bet, chance, gamble, risk, wager

stale *adj* **1** dry, hard, musty, off *inf*, old, past its expiration date, sour; ***opp*** fresh. **2** clichéd, dry-as-dust, dull, hackneyed, jaded, tedious, tired, worn-out; ***opp*** fresh, new

stalk *v* **1** follow, hound, hunt, pursue, shadow, tail, track, trail. **2** flounce, march, prance, stride, strut

stall *n* booth, kiosk, stand, table

stall *v* delay, drag your feet, hedge, hesitate, hold off, play for time, prevaricate, put off, stonewall

stamina *n* dynamism, endurance, energy, fortitude, go *inf*, guts *inf*, resilience, staying power, strength, vigor

stammer *v* fumble your words, hesitate, splutter, stumble, stutter, trip over your tongue

stamp *n* authorization, brand, die, impression, mark, print, seal

stamp *v* **1** (stamp on sth) crush underfoot, squash, step on, trample, tread on. **2** brand, emboss, impress, label, mark, mark, print. **3 stamp out** abolish, destroy, eliminate, eradicate, exterminate, get rid of, put an end to, quash, suppress

stampede *n* charge, dash, headlong dash, rout, rush

stance *n* **1** angle, approach, attitude, line, position, stand, standpoint. **2** attitude, bearing, carriage, pose, posture

stand *n* **1** base, holder, pedestal, rack, support, tripod. **2** (stall) booth, kiosk, stall, table. **3** grandstand, terraces. **4** (take a stand) angle, approach, attitude, line, position, stance

stand *v* **1** (stand sth somewhere) erect, lean, place, position, put, set. **2** (stand up) get to your feet, get up, rise. **3** (be situated) be, be found at, be located, be situated, lie, sit. **4** (tolerate) abide, bear, cope with, endure, handle, put up with, stomach, take, tolerate, withstand

standard *adj* average, basic, normal, orthodox, regular, set, staple, typical, usual

standard *n* **1** benchmark, criterion, example, guideline, ideal, level, measure, model, norm, principle, quality, requirement, spec *inf*, specification, yardstick. **2** banner, colors, ensign, flag, pennant

standardize *v* bring into line, equalize, make consistent, regularize, regulate, systematize

standpoint *n* angle, approach, attitude, line, opinion, perspective, philosophy, point of view, position, school of thought, stance, stand, way of seeing things

staple *adj* basic, essential, key, main, normal, primary, standard, usual

star *adj* brilliant, leading, principal, prominent, well known

star *n* **1** celebrity, film star, leading actor, leading light, name, personality, pop star, rock star, superstar. **2** celestial body. **3** asterisk

star *v* appear, feature, take the lead

stare *v* gape, gawp, gaze, glare, look, peer, scrutinize, watch

stark *adj* **1** (bleak) austere, barren, bleak, desolate, drab, grim, harsh, plain, severe. **2** (stark contrast) clear, glaring, obvious, sharp. **3** (stark terror) absolute, complete, downright, pure, sheer, total, unmitigated, utter

start *n* **1** beginning, birth, commencement, creation, dawn, early stages, foundation, inception, introduction, launch, onset, opening, origin, outset, root, source. **2** advantage, edge, head start, lead. **3** jerk, jump, spasm, wince

start *v* **1** (start doing sth) begin, commence, get cracking *inf*, get down to it, get going, get the show on the road *inf*, kick off *inf*, make a start, set the ball rolling, set out, take the plunge. **2** (set sth up) create, establish, form, found, get off the ground, inaugurate, initiate, instigate, introduce, launch, open, pioneer, set up, start up, trigger. **3** (sth starts) appear, arise, begin, come into being, start up. **4** (start a journey) depart, get going, get the show on the road *inf*, get under way, hit the road *inf*, leave, push off *inf*, set off, set out. **5** (start a machine) activate, boot, get going, start up, switch on, turn on. **6** (jump) flinch, jerk, jump, jump out of your skin *inf*, shy away, wince

startle *v* alarm, frighten, give sb a fright, give sb a turn, make sb jump out of hisskin, make sb jump, shock, surprise

starvation *n* famine, hunger, lack of food, malnutrition, undernourishment

starve *v* deprive of food, die of hunger, die of starvation, fast, go hungry, go on hunger strike, refuse food

starving *adj* could eat a horse *inf*, dying of hunger *inf*, famished, hungry, malnourished, ravenous, starved, undernourished

state *n* **1** circumstances, condition, mode, position, shape, situation, status. **2** (in a real state) chaos, condition, fluster, frame of mind, mess, mood, panic, plight, predicament, tizzy *inf*. **3** country, kingdom, land, nation, republic, territory. **4** (the state) civil authorities, establishment, government

state *v* affirm, announce, articulate, assert, declare, express, proclaim, pronounce, put into words, say, specify, voice

stately *adj* ceremonial, dignified, formal, grand, imperial, imposing, magnificent, majestic, regal, royal

statement *n* account, announcement, assertion, bulletin, comment, communiqué, declaration, disclosure, explanation, press release, proclamation, report, testimony

static *adj* **1** (still) immobile, inert, motionless, stationary, still, unmoving; ***opp*** active, in motion. **2** (of pressure or costs) constant, fixed, frozen, level, stable, steady, unvarying; ***opp*** changeable, fluctuating, varying

station *n* **1** (for trains or buses) bus station, depot, railroad station, stop, terminus. **2** (TV or radio station) channel, company, radio station, TV station. **3** base, center, depot, headquarters, post

station *v* install, locate, place, post,

put, send, set, situate

stationary *adj* at a standstill, fixed, moored, motionless, parked, standing, static, still, stockstill, unmoving; ***opp*** moving

statistics *n* data, facts and figures, figures, numbers, records

status *n* 1 class, grade, importance, level, position, prestige, rank, standing. 2 condition, position, state

staunch *adj* faithful, firm, loyal, steadfast, strong, true, unswerving

stay *n* holiday, stop, stopover, vacation, visit

stay *v* 1 (wait) hang on, linger, remain, wait. 2 (persist) continue, go on, keep, last, persist, remain. 3 (stay with friends) be put up, crash *inf*, live, lodge, move in with, sleep at, stop over, stop, visit

steadfast *adj* dependable, faithful, firm, loyal, reliable, stalwart, staunch, unswerving; ***opp*** fickle

steady *adj* 1 balanced, firm, safe, secure, solid, stable, still, sure; ***opp*** shaky, unstable, wobbly. 2 consistent, constant, continuous, even, nonstop, perpetual, regular, rhythmic, round-the-clock, unbroken, unfaltering, uniform, uninterrupted, unvarying. 3 (a steady climb) gentle, gradual; ***opp*** steep

steady *v* 1 balance, brace, hold steady, keep still, secure, stabilize, support. 2 calm, compose, control

steal *v* 1 burglarize, embezzle, hijack, lift, misappropriate, nick *inf*, pilfer, pinch *inf*, pirate, poach, pocket, rob, shoplift, snatch, swipe *inf*, take, walk off with. 2 creep, glide, pussyfoot, slink, slip, sneak, tiptoe

stealth *n* cunning, furtiveness, secrecy, sleight of hand, slyness

stealthy *adj* clandestine, concealed, covert, cunning, furtive, inconspicuous, secretive, sly, sneaky, surreptitious, undercover

steep *adj* 1 abrupt, perpendicular, precipitous, sharp, sheer, sudden, vertical. 2 (of a price) excessive, extortionate, high, unreasonable

steer *v* 1 be at the wheel, be in the driving seat, direct, drive, guide, navigate, pilot. 2 (steer to the left of sth) direct, drive, go, head, turn, veer

stem *n* branch, shoot, stalk, trunk, twig

stem *v* check, contain, cut off, halt, staunch, stop

step *n* 1 footfall, footstep, gait, pace, print, stride, tramp, tread, walk. 2 (stair) doorstep, rung, stair, threshold, tread. 3 level, point, position, rank

step *v* move, pace, stamp, stride, tramp, trample, tread, walk

stereotype *n* conventional idea, formula, model, mold, pattern

stereotype *v* label, pigeonhole, typecast

sterile *adj* 1 antiseptic, aseptic, clean, disinfected, germ-free, hygienic, pure, spotless, sterilized, uncontaminated. 2 barren, infertile, sterilized, unproductive; ***opp*** fruitful, productive. 3 fruitless, futile, pointless, unimaginative, unproductive, useless

sterilize *v* 1 clean, disinfect, make sterile. 2 castrate, give a man a vasectomy, make infertile, make sterile, neuter, spay

stern *adj* austere, cruel, forbidding, grave, grim, hard, harsh, serious, severe, somber, strict

stew *n* casserole, goulash

stick *n* baton, branch, cane, crook, piece of wood, pole, rod, staff, stake, twig, walking stick, wand

stick *v* **1** (stick sth in) insert, jab, poke, push, stab, thrust. **2** (stick things together) attach, bond, cement, fasten, fix, fuse, glue, join, paste, secure, tape. **3** be unable to move, get bogged down, get clogged up, get stuck, jam, seize up. **4** (stick sth somewhere) chuck, drop, dump, put. **5** (stick sth out) endure, linger, persist, remain, stay

sticky *adj* **1** adhesive, glutinous, gooey, gummed, self-adhesive, tacky, viscous. **2** clammy, close, humid, moist, muggy, oppressive, steamy, sultry. **3** (a sticky situation) awkward, delicate, difficult, embarrassing, tricky

stiff *adj* **1** arthritic, firm, hard, rheumatic, rigid, solid, solidified, taut, tense, unbending; ***opp*** bendable, supple. **2** challenging, determined, difficult, hard, resolute, rigorous, strict, strong, tough

stiffen *v* become stiff, brace, clot, coagulate, congeal, harden, gel, make rigid, reinforce, set, solidify, tense, thicken

stifle *v* **1** asphyxiate, choke, muffle, smother, suffocate. **2** check, control, crush, curb, keep back, quash, quell, repress, silence, suppress

stigma *n* blemish, blot, disgrace, dishonor, scar, shame, stain

still *adj* at rest, calm, flat, motionless, peaceful, quiet, restful, serene, silent, stagnant, static, stationary, tranquil, undisturbed, unmoving

still *v* calm, hush, lull, quiet, settle, soothe, subdue

stilted *adj* artificial, forced, labored, stiff, unnatural, wooden; ***opp*** flowing, fluent, fluid, smooth

stimulant *n* antidepressant, pick-me-up *inf*, restorative, tonic; ***opp*** depressant, downer *inf*

stimulate *v* animate, arouse, encourage, excite, fire up, foment, induce, inflame, instigate, invigorate, motivate, prompt, provoke, stir up, trigger; ***opp*** discourage

stimulating *adj* arousing, challenging, dynamic, exciting, exhilarating, inspiring, invigorating, motivating, stirring, thought-provoking; ***opp*** dull

stimulus *n* encouragement, goad, incentive, inducement, provocation, shot in the arm *inf*, spur

sting *v* **1** (of an insect) bite, hurt, nip, prick. **2** (hurt) burn, hurt, prickle, smart

stink *v* be high, reek, smell bad, smell

stint *n* session, share, shift, spell, stretch, time, turn

stipulate *v* demand, insist on, lay down, require, specify, state

stir *n* commotion, disturbance, excitement, flurry, furor, fuss, to-do, tumult, uproar

stir *v* **1** (with a spoon) agitate, blend, churn, mingle, mix. **2** (move) budge, come round, move, show signs of life, wake up. **3** (stir feelings) arouse, excite, fire up, inflame, inspire, kindle, provoke, rouse, touch

stirring *adj* dramatic, electrifying, emotive, exciting, gripping, heady, invigorating, moving, rousing, spirited, thrilling

stock *n* **1** (merchandise) goods, merchandise, range, supply, variety, wares. **2** (reserve) cache, fund, hoard, reserve, reservoir, store, supply. **3** (family) ancestry, blood, descent, extraction, family, line, lineage, parentage, pedigree, race, strain. **4** (farm animals) animals, beasts, farm animals, livestock. **5** (of a gun) handle, shaft, grip

stock *v* carry, deal in, handle, have available, have on sale, keep in stock, keep, sell, supply

stock *adj* **1** banal, cliched, conventional, formulaic, hackneyed, ready, routine, set-piece, set, standard, traditional, trite; ***opp*** original. **2** average, basic, common, regular, standard; ***opp*** special

stocky *adj* chunky, dumpy, solid, squat, sturdy, thickset; ***opp*** slender

stodgy *adj* **1** (of food) filling, heavy, indigestible, solid, substantial, thick; ***opp*** light. **2** (of writing) dry, dull, heavy-going, stuffy, tedious, turgid, unimaginative; ***opp*** lively

stoical *adj* accepting, cool, dispassionate, impassive, imperturbable, long-suffering, phlegmatic, resigned, self-disciplined, unemotional

stolid *adj* bovine, impassive, slow, unemotional, unimaginative, unresponsive, wooden

stomach *n* **1** abdomen, belly, guts *inf*, insides *inf*, paunch, tummy. **2** (desire) appetite, desire, hunger, inclination, liking, taste

stomach *v* **1** abide, bear, endure, put up with, stand, take, tolerate. **2** digest, eat, swallow

stone *n* **1** boulder, pebble, rock. **2** gem, jewel, precious stone, rock *inf*. **3** gravestone, headstone, memorial stone, monument, obelisk, tombstone

stony *adj* **1** gravelly, pebbly, rocky, shingly. **2** adamant, callous, hard, hardhearted, harsh, indifferent, pitiless, severe, unfeeling, unforgiving, unsympathetic. **3** blank, chilly, cold, expressionless, fixed, frigid, frosty, icy

stoop *v* **1** bend, bend down, bow, lean down. **2** be round-shouldered, hunch your shoulders. **3** (stoop to sth) condescend, deign, demean yourself, descend to, humble yourself, lower yourself to, resort to, sink to

stop *n* **1** cessation, conclusion, discontinuation, end, finish, halt, termination. **2** ban, bar, block, check, control, curb, hindrance, impediment. **3** break, pause, rest. **4** break, sojourn, stay, stop-off, stopover, visit. **5** depot, station, terminal, terminus

stop *v* **1** (stop moving) come to a halt, come to a standstill, come to a stop, draw up, halt, pause, pull up, stop moving. **2** (stop sth happening) abolish, ax, ban, bring to an end, call off, crack down on, cut short, discontinue, end, finish, interrupt, nip in the bud, put a stop to, put down, quell, suppress, terminate, wind up. **3** (sth stops happening) be over, cease, come to an end, conclude; finish, pause, peter out. **4** (stop for lunch) break off, cease, desist, knock off *inf*, leave off, quit *inf*, refrain from. **5** (prevent) block, check, curb, foil, frustrate, hamper, hinder, hold back, impede, obstruct, prevent, repress, restrain, thwart. **6** (the police stop sb) arrest, capture, catch, detain, hold, intercept, seize. **7** (stop the flow of sth) block, bung up, plug, seal, stem, staunch, stop up. **8** (stop off somewhere) interrupt your trip, lodge, put up, stay, stop off, stop over, visit

stoppage *n* close, closure, halt, pause, interruption, shutdown, standstill, strike, walkout

store *n* **1** cache, fund, hoard, provision, reserve, reservoir, stock, stockpile, supply. **2** depository, repository, storehouse, storeroom, warehouse. **3** chain store, department store, emporium, outlet, retail outlet, shop, supermarket, superstore

store *v* hoard, keep, lay in, preserve, put away, put by, reserve, save, set aside, squirrel away *inf*, stash *inf*, stockpile, stock up

storm *n* **1** cyclone, gale, hurricane, tempest. **2** clamor, commotion, furor, outcry, row, rumpus, to-do *inf*, tumult, turmoil

storm *v* **1** attack, charge, make a raid on, rush, take by storm. **2** blow your top *inf*, bluster, complain, fly off the handle *inf*, fume, rage, rant, rave, scold, thunder

stormy *adj* blustery, gusty, rainy, squally, tempestuous, thundery, turbulent, wild, windy

story *n* **1** allegory, anecdote, fable, legend, myth, narrative, parable, romance, tale, yarn. **2** account, chronicle, history, record, report, saga. **3** (a news story) article, dispatch, feature, news item, piece, report. **4** plot, story-line. **5** falsehood, fib *inf*, lie, tall tale, untruth, white lie. **6** (in a building) floor, level

stout *adj* **1** big, beefy *inf*, burly, corpulent, fat, heavy, overweight, plump, portly, rotund, thickset, tubby; ***opp*** slender, slim. **2** robust, solid, strong, sturdy, substantial, thick, tough; ***opp*** flimsy. **3** brave, courageous, determined, firm, gallant, resolute, staunch, steadfast, tough, unswerving, valiant; ***opp*** cowardly

straight *adj* **1** direct, unbending, unswerving. **2** aligned, erect, even, in line, level, square, symmetrical, true, upright. **3** in order, neat, orderly, organized, put to rights, shipshape, sorted out. **4** consecutive, in a row, one after another, successive, unbroken, uninterrupted. **5** decent, fair, honest, honorable, right-minded, upright. **6** (straight talking) blunt, candid, direct, forthright, frank, honest, plain-speaking, sincere, straightforward. **7** (of alcoholic drinks) neat, pure, unadulterated, undiluted. **8** conventional, orthodox

straightaway *adv* at once, immediately, instantly, now, pronto *inf*, right away, without delay

straighten *v* **1** make straight, neaten, put straight, tidy, unbend, uncurl, untwist. **2 straighten out** clear up, disentangle, put in order, put right, resolve, settle, sort out

straightforward *adj* **1** blunt, candid, direct, forthright, frank, honest, plain-speaking, sincere. **2** easy, intelligible, simple, uncomplicated; ***opp*** complicated, difficult

strain *n* 1 tautness, tension. 2 sprain, wrench. 3 anxiety, burden, demands, pressure, stress, tension, worry. 4 exertion, exhaustion, overwork. 5 breed, species, variety

strain *v* 1 distend, draw tight, extend, pull tight, stretch, tighten. 2 (a muscle) pull, sprain, tear, twist, wrench. 3 (strain sb) be too much for, overtax, overwork, push to the limit, tax, tire, tire out, wear out, weary. 4 (strain to do sth) bend over backwards *inf*, do your utmost, drive yourself to the limit, exert yourself, give your all, knock yourself out *inf*, labor, make every effort, strive, struggle. 5 filter, purify, separate, sieve, sift

strained *adj* 1 artificial, awkward, embarrassed, false, forced, labored, put-on, self-conscious, stiff, uncomfortable, unnatural, wooden. 2 drawn, stressed, tense, troubled, weary. 3 (of relations) hostile, tense, troubled, uneasy, under a strain

strand *n* 1 fiber, filament, thread. 2 lock, tress, wisp. 3 beach, coast, seashore, shore, waterfront

stranded *adj* 1 aground, beached, high-and-dry, stuck. 2 abandoned, forsaken, left high and dry, marooned, stuck, unable to leave

strange *adj* 1 abnormal, bizarre, curious, funny, mystifying, odd, peculiar, perplexing, puzzling, quaint, queer, remarkable, surreal. 2 eerie, grotesque, sinister, uncanny, weird. 3 (strange lands) alien, exotic, foreign, remote, unexplored, unknown. 4 (of a person) crazy, eccentric, funny, odd, unconventional, way out *inf*, zany

stranger *n* alien, foreigner, new arrival, newcomer, outsider, visitor

strangle *v* 1 asphyxiate, choke, garrote, throttle. 2 check, curb, gag, repress, restrain, silence, stifle, suppress

strap *n* band, belt, leash, thong, tie

strap *v* bind, buckle, fasten, lash, secure, tie, truss

stratagem *n* maneuver, plan, plot, ploy, ruse, scheme, subterfuge, tactic, trick

strategic *adj* 1 calculated, deliberate, planned, politic, tactical. 2 critical, crucial, important, key, vital

strategy *n* approach, design, game plan, master plan, plan, plan of action, policy, program

stray *adj* 1 abandoned, homeless, lost, wandering. 2 casual, chance, haphazard, isolated, odd, random

stray *v* 1 drift, meander, move aimlessly, ramble, range, roam, wander. 2 deviate, digress, err, get lost, go astray, go wrong, wander

streak *n* 1 band, bar, line, striation, strip, stripe. 2 mark, smear, smudge. 3 (mean streak) dash, element, touch, trace, vein. 4 (winning streak) period, run, series, stretch, time

streak *v* 1 mark with streaks, smear, smudge, striate. 2 dart, dash, flash, fly, gallop, hurtle, rush, speed, sprint, tear, whiz, zoom

stream *n* 1 brook, channel, creek, rill, rivulet, tributary, watercourse. 2 flow, gush, jet, rush, surge, torrent

stream *v* 1 cascade, course, flood, flow, gush, pour, run, spill, spout. 2 (of people) flood, pour, surge, swarm. **3** (in the wind) flap, float, flutter, swing

streamlined *adj* **1** aerodynamic, sleek, smooth. **2** efficient, organized, rationalized, slick, well-run

street *n* avenue, crescent, cul-de-sac, drive, lane, row, road, terrace

strength *n* **1** brawn, might, muscle, power, robustness, stamina, staying power, sturdiness, toughness, vigor. **2** effectiveness, efficacy, force, intensity, potency, power, validity, weight. **3** backbone *inf*, commitment, courage, determination, firmness, fortitude, grit, resolution, resolve, spirit, tenacity. **4** (strength of feeling) ardor, fervency, force, forcefulness, intensity, vehemence. **5** (the strengths of sth) advantage, asset, forte, strong point

strengthen *v* **1** (give more strength to) bolster, brace, buttress, consolidate, fortify, make stronger, prop up, reinforce, toughen. **2** (make sth more successful) boost, build up, encourage, make stronger, stiffen, support. **3** (sth strengthens) become strong, build up, gain strength, get stronger, grow stronger, heighten, intensify. **4** (strengthen a belief) authenticate, back up, bear out, confirm, corroborate, reinforce, substantiate, support. **5** (strengthen a person) build up, invigorate, make healthy, make strong, nourish, tone up, toughen up

strenuous *adj* **1** arduous, backbreaking, demanding, grueling, hard, heavy, laborious, taxing, tiring, tough; ***opp*** easy, light. **2** active, determined, energetic, forceful, resolute, spirited, tenacious, vigorous, zealous

stress *n* **1** anxiety, pressure, strain, tension, worry. **2** difficulty, distress, trauma. **3** emphasis, importance, significance, weight. **4** accent, beat, emphasis

stress *v* **1** accentuate, dwell on, emphasize, harp on, lay stress on, point up, rub in, spotlight, underline. **2** accentuate, emphasize, place the accent on, put the stress on. **3** (stress sb) overtax, overwork, pressurize, push too far, subject to stress, subject to strain

stressful *adj* anxious, difficult, taxing, tiring, traumatic, worrying

stretch *v* **1** distend, draw out, elongate, expand, extend, inflate, lengthen, pull out, pull taut, pull tight. **2** be elastic, be stretchy, enlarge, expand, get bigger, get loose. **3** extend, range, spread, unfold. **4** (stretch sb's mind) challenge, overtax, push to the limit, strain, tax. **5 stretch out** (offer sth to sb) extend, hold out, offer, reach out. **6 stretch out** (lie) lie down, lie flat, recline, sprawl

stretch *n* **1** area, expanse, extent, spread, sweep, tract. **2** period, spell, stint, term, time

strict *adj* **1** authoritarian, firm, harsh, inflexible, rigid, severe, stern, stringent; ***opp*** lenient, soft. **2** accurate, close, exact, faithful, meticulous, precise, scrupulous, true. **3** absolute, complete, total, utter

strident *adj* discordant, grating, harsh, jarring, raucous, shrill

strife *n* animosity, bickering, conflict, contention, disagreement, discord, dissension, friction, hostility, quarreling, wrangling

strike *n* **1** industrial action, stoppage, walkout. **2** assault, attack, bombardment

strike *v* **1** beat, clout *inf*, hit, punch, slap, smack, smite, sock *inf*, thump, wallop, whack. **2** bang into, bump into, collide with, dash against, hit, run into, smash into. **3** (disaster strikes) affect, afflict, hit, reach, smite. **4** (attack sb) assault, attack, fall upon, launch an attack on, set upon, storm. **5** (strike a ball) drive, force, hit, impel, propel, swipe. **6** (strike a bargain) achieve, arrive at, attain, reach. **7** (go on strike) go on strike, mutiny, stop work, walk off job, walk out, walk picket line. **8** (sth strikes you) appear, come to, dawn on, impress, occur to, seem

striking *adj* **1** arresting, dazzling, extraordinary, impressive, memorable, outstanding, splendid, stunning. **2** conspicuous, evident, noticeable, obvious, prominent, visible

string *n* **1** cord, line, rope, twine, yarn. **2** chain, sequence, series, succession. **3** column, file, line, row, queue, stream

stringent *adj* exacting, inflexible, rigid, rigorous, severe, strict, tight; ***opp*** loose

strip *n* band, bar, belt, piece, ribbon, shred, slip

strip *v* **1** disrobe, get undressed, strip off, take sb's clothes off, take your clothes off, undress, unclothe. **2** (strip sb of sth) confiscate, deprive, divest, take away. **3** (strip a place) clean out, clear out, empty, gut, loot, plunder, ransack, rob. **4** (strip sth off) pare, peel, peel off, remove, skin, take off

striped *adj* banded, barred, striated

strive *v* attempt, bend over backwards *inf*, do everything you can, do your utmost, endeavor, give it your best shot *inf*, labor, make a real effort, strain, struggle, toil, try, try your hardest. **2** compete, contend, fight, grapple with, struggle

stroke *n* **1** blow, clout *inf*, hit, slap, smack, swipe, thump, wallop, whack. **2** achievement, coup, feat. **3** (pen stroke) flourish, line, mark, sweep. **4** (medical) apoplexy, cardiovascular accident, CVA, embolism, seizure, thrombosis

stroke *v* caress, fondle, massage, pet, run your hand over, rub, soothe

stroll *n* airing, amble, ramble, turn, walk

stroll *v* amble, dawdle, go for a stroll, go for a walk, ramble, saunter, stretch your legs, take a walk, wander

strong *adj* **1** athletic, brawny, burly, hardy, mighty, muscular, powerful, resilient, robust, rugged, strapping, sturdy, tough, vigorous. **2** hale and hearty, healthy, sound, vigorous, well. **3** brave, courageous, decisive, dependable, determined, firm, forceful, formidable, resolute, strong-minded, tough. **4** durable, hard-wearing, heavy, impenetrable, indestructible, long-lasting, solid, sturdy, tough, well-made, well-built. **5** (a strong supporter) dedicated, eager, enthusiastic, fervent, fierce, keen, loyal, passionate, staunch, steadfast, vehement, zealous. **6** (a strong argument) cogent, compelling, convincing, persuasive, plausible, powerful, valid, weighty. **7** (strong measures) draconian, drastic, extreme, firm, forceful, harsh, severe, tough. **8** (a strong light) bright, brilliant, dazzling, glaring, gleaming, intense, radiant, vivid. **9** (a strong flavor) full, highly flavored, pungent, savory, spicy, sharp, well-flavored. **10** (a strong solution) concentrated, undiluted. **11** (strong drink) alcoholic, intoxicating

structure *n* **1** arrangement, configuration, conformation, constitution, design, form, formation, makeup, organization. **2** building, construction, edifice, erection, framework, pile

structure *v* arrange, build, construct, design, form, frame, organize, put together, shape

struggle *n* **1** brush, clash, conflict, contest, encounter, fight, scrap, skirmish, tussle. **2** battle, difficulty, effort, fight, grind, hassle, labor, problem, trouble. **3** competition, contention, fight, rivalry

struggle *v* **1** bend over backward *inf*, do everything you can, do your utmost, endeavor, give it your best shot *inf*, labor, make a real effort, strain, toil, try, try your hardest. **2** clash, compete, contend, fight, vie. **3** brawl, fight, grapple, scuffle, wrestle

strut *v* parade, swagger, walk proudly

stubborn *adj* **1** (of a person) adamant, defiant, determined, dogged, headstrong, inflexible, intractable, obdurate, obstinate, pig-headed, rigid, uncompromising, unreasonable, unyielding, willful. **2** (of a stain) hard to get rid of, long-lasting, persistent, tenacious

stuck *adj* **1** bogged down, fast, fixed, immovable, rooted, unable to move. **2** fastened, fixed, glued. **3** at a loss, baffled, beaten, stumped, stymied *inf*, up against a brick wall *inf*

student *n* **1** pupil, scholar, undergraduate. **2** apprentice, learner, trainee

studied *adj* affected, artificial, calculated, conscious, contrived, deliberate, false, feigned, planned

studious *adj* **1** academic, attentive, bookish, earnest, hard-working, industrious, serious, scholarly, thoughtful. **2** assiduous, attentive, careful, diligent, meticulous, painstaking, thorough

study *n* **1** analysis, examination, inquiry, investigation, review, scrutiny, survey. **2** academic work, education, learning, lessons, reading, research, scholarship, schoolwork. **3** essay, paper, review

study *v* **1** analyze, consider, contemplate, inquire into, investigate, look into, research, survey, think about. **2** examine, inspect, look closely at, peruse, pore over, read carefully, scrutinize. **3** (study a subject) learn, learn about, major in, read, read about, read up on, take a course in, take lessons in. **4** (study hard) burn the midnight oil *inf*, cram *inf*, read up on, revise

stuff *n* **1** baggage, fabric, material, raw material, substance. **2** baggage, belongings, bits and pieces, effects, gear, impedimenta, junk, paraphernalia, possessions, things. **3** articles, bits and pieces, garbage, items, junk, objects, things

stuff *v* **1** cram, crowd, fill, force, jam, load, pack, push, ram, shove, squeeze, stow, wedge. **2** fill, line, pack, pad

stuffy *adj* **1** airless, close, muggy, oppressive, stifling, suffocating, sultry. **2** conventional, dreary, dull, formal, fuddy-duddy *inf*, priggish, prim, sedate, staid, starchy, stiff, stodgy

stumble *v* **1** fall, flounder, lose your balance, lurch, reel, slip, stagger, trip. **2** blunder, falter, flounder, hesitate, stutter. **3 stumble on** come across, discover, encounter, find, run across, turn up

stun *v* **1** astonish, astound, devastate, dumbfound, flabbergast *inf*, overcome, overwhelm, shock, stagger. **2** daze, knock out, paralyze, stupefy

stunning *adj* **1** beautiful, brilliant, dazzling, fabulous, gorgeous, lovely, marvelous, ravishing, sensational, smashing *inf*, wonderful. **2** astonishing, extraordinary, impressive, incredible, remarkable, spectacular, splendid, striking, stupendous

stunt *n* act, deed, exploit, feat, trick

stunted *adj* diminutive, dwarf, dwarfish, little, small, tiny, undersized

stupendous *adj* **1** amazing, astounding, breathtaking, marvelous, overwhelming, phenomenal, prodigious, sensational, staggering, superb, wonderful. **2** colossal, enormous, gigantic, huge, massive, vast; ***opp*** tiny

stupid *adj* **1** (of a person) brainless, clueless, daft, dense, dim, foolish, gullible, half-witted, moronic, naive, silly, simple, thick *inf*, unintelligent; ***opp*** clever, intelligent. **2** (of an idea) absurd, asinine, crackpot, crazy, futile, half-baked, idiotic, ill-advised, inane, irrational, ludicrous, mindless, pointless, rash, senseless, silly, unwise; ***opp*** good, sensible

stupidity *n* **1** (of a person) brainlessness, foolishness, gullibility, lack of intelligence, naivety; ***opp*** intelligence. **2** (of an idea) absurdity, folly, foolishness, futility, idiocy, inanity, lunacy, madness, mindlessness, pointlessness, silliness; ***opp*** cleverness

stupor *n* coma, daze, oblivion, torpor, trance, unconsciousness

sturdy *adj* **1** (of a person) brawny, healthy, husky, muscular, powerful, powerfully built, robust, strapping, strong, tough, vigorous, well built; ***opp*** slight. **2** (of an object) durable, solid, substantial, tough, well made; ***opp*** delicate, flimsy

stutter *v* falter, hesitate, stammer, stumble

style *n* **1** (sb has style) dash, élan, elegance, flair, panache, polish, smartness, sophistication, stylishness. **2** approach, custom, habit, manner, method, way. **3** (a style of sth) design, kind, pattern, type, variety. **4** (fashion) cut, design, fashion, look, mode, pattern, shape, vogue. **5** (literary style) diction, language, mode of expression, sentence structure, wording. **6** (live in style) affluence, comfort, elegance, luxury

style *v* design, fashion, make, produce, tailor

stylish *adj* chic, classy *inf*, elegant, fashionable, modish, smart, snazzy *inf*, sophisticated, trendy; ***opp*** unfashionable

subconscious *adj* hidden, inner, intuitive, latent, repressed, subliminal; ***opp*** conscious

subdue *v* **1** conquer, crush, defeat, dominate, humble, master, overcome, overpower, quell, subjugate, tame, trample, vanquish. **2** (a feeling) check, control, curb, hold back, keep under control, repress, restrain, suppress. **3** mellow, moderate, quiet, restrain, tone down

subdued *adj* **1** chastened, crestfallen, dejected, down in the mouth, quiet, sad, serious, solemn; ***opp*** vivacious. **2** dim, hushed, low-key, muted, quiet, restrained, sober, soft, subtle, toned down, unobtrusive; ***opp*** bright, loud

subject *n* **1** affair, business, gist, issue, matter, point, question, subject matter, substance, theme, topic. **2** area of study, branch of knowledge, course, discipline, field. **3** (in an experiment) case, client, guinea pig, participant, patient. **4** (of a country) citizen, national. **5** (of a king) liege, subordinate, underling, vassal

subject *v* expose to, lay open to, put through, submit to

subjective *adj* biased, emotional, individual, personal, prejudiced; ***opp*** objective

subjugate *v* beat down, break, bring to heel, bring sb to his knees, conquer, crush, defeat, enslave, gain ascendancy over, gain control over, gain mastery over, humble, overcome, quell, subdue, suppress, tame, vanquish

sublime *adj* awe-inspiring, exalted, excellent, exquisite, fine, ideal, lofty, magnificent, majestic, marvelous, out of this world *inf*, rarefied, refined, subtle, superb, superior, wonderful

submerge *v* **1** (sth submerges) dive, go down, go under, plunge, sink; ***opp*** surface. **2** (submerge sth) dip, dunk *inf*, engulf, immerse, plunge, sink

submission *n* **1** acquiescence, capitulation, compliance, surrender. **2** (submissive attitude) boot-licking *inf*, deference, docility, meekness, obedience, passivity, self-effacement, servility, subjection, submissiveness, subservience, unassertiveness. **3** (a document submitted) application, bid, paper, presentation, proposal, tender

submissive *adj* acquiescent, boot-licking *inf*, deferential, docile, groveling, humble, masochistic, meek, obedient, passive, self-effacing, servile, subservient, unassertive; ***opp*** dominant

submit *v* **1** bend the knee, bow, capitulate, cede, concede, give in, give way, knuckle under, lay down your arms, succumb, surrender, wave the white flag, yield; ***opp*** resist. **2** (submit a piece of work) give in, hand in, present, put in, put forward, register, send in, surrender, tender

subordinate *adj* **1** inferior, lesser, junior, lower, lower-ranking; ***opp*** superior. **2** dependent, less important, low priority, secondary, subsidiary

subordinate *n* assistant, deputy, inferior, junior, minion, underling; ***opp*** superior

subscribe *v* **1** enlist, enroll, join, register, sign up, take out a subscription. **2 subscribe to** (a magazine) buy, have sth delivered, take. 3 **subscribe to** (a belief, principle) agree with, approve of, back, be in favor of, believe in, endorse, favor, hold, hold to, sign up to *inf*, support; ***opp*** oppose

subscription *n* 1 enrollment, membership, registration. 2 (money paid) charge, contribution, dues, fee

subsequent *adj* 1 consequent, ensuing, following, further, later, resulting, succeeding; ***opp*** preceding, prior. 2 **subsequent to** after, as a result of, following, further to, in the wake of; ***opp*** prior to

subside *v* 1 cave in, collapse, crumble, fall down, settle, sink. 2 abate, calm down, die down, diminish, lessen, let up, quiet down, slacken off, peter out, recede

subsidence *n* collapse, crumbling, sinking

subsidiary *adj* additional, ancillary, auxiliary, less important, lesser, minor, secondary, subordinate, supplementary; ***opp*** main

subsidize *v* bail out, contribute to, finance, financially support, foot the bill for, fund, invest in, pay for, pick up the tab for *inf*, prop up *inf*, underwrite

subsidy *n* aid, contribution, financial support, finance, funding, grant, investment, loan

substance *n* chemical, gas, fluid, liquid, material, matter, mineral, ore, stuff *inf*

substandard *adj* below par, below standard, inadequate, mediocre, shoddy, unacceptable, unsatisfactory; ***opp*** satisfactory

substantial *adj* ample, considerable, extensive, great, large, important, marked, meaningful, notable, significant, sizable, valuable, weighty; ***opp*** insubstantial, negligible

substantiate *v* authenticate, back up, bear out, confirm, corroborate, demonstrate, establish, give substance to, illustrate, prove, support, uphold, validate

substitute *n* 1 replacement, stopgap, surrogate. 2 (person) deputy, locum, proxy, relief, reserve, stand-in, stopgap, surrogate, understudy

substitute *v* 1 exchange, replace, swap, switch. 2 **substitute for** cover for, deputize for, fill in for, hold the fort for *inf*, relieve, replace, stand in for, take over from, take the place of

subtle *adj* 1 complex, delicate, elusive, exquisite, fine, intricate, nice, nuanced, refined, sublime, understated; ***opp*** overstated. 2 adroit, artful, astute, clever, crafty, cunning, devious, diplomatic, discerning, discreet, discriminating, guileful, ingenious, perceptive, sensitive, shrewd, skillful, tactful, wily

subtlety *n* 1 complexity, delicacy, elusiveness, intricacy, nicety, nuance, refinement. 2 adroitness, artfulness, astuteness, cleverness, cunning, deviousness, diplomacy, discernment, discretion, ingenuity, guile, perceptiveness, sensitivity, shrewdness, skill, tact, tactfulness, wiles

subtract *v* deduct, knock off *inf*, remove, take away, take off; ***opp*** add

suburbs *n* bedroom communities, outlying areas, outskirts, periphery, satellite towns, sprawl, suburbia

subversive *adj* **1** avant-garde, challenging, mischievous, questioning, radical, revolutionary. **2** corrupting, deceitful, destructive, disruptive, seditious, treasonable, underhand

subvert *v* corrupt, disrupt, pervert, sabotage, turn, undermine, vitiate, weaken

succeed *v* **1** achieve success, arrive *inf*, be successful, come up trumps *inf*, do well, flourish, get a result *inf*, get your name in lights *inf*, hit the jackpot *inf*, make good *inf*, make it *inf*, prosper, score *inf*, thrive, win, win through; ***opp*** fail. **2** (in doing or getting sth) accomplish, achieve, attain, be able, be successful, bring off, gain, manage, realize, win; ***opp*** fail. **3** (of a plan) be successful, come to fruition, do the trick *inf*, have the desired effect, turn out well, work, work out; ***opp*** fail. **4** (succeed sb in office) accede, be next in line, come after, come next, follow, follow in sb's footsteps, inherit, replace, take over, take sb's place; ***opp*** precede

success *n* **1** fame, fortune, fruition, mastery, prosperity, triumph, victory; ***opp*** failure. **2** accomplishment, achievement, attainment, gain, hit *inf*, triumph, victory, win; ***opp*** failure. **3** (a person) celebrity, somebody *inf*, star, VIP, winner; ***opp*** failure

successful *adj* **1** all-conquering, booming, flourishing, profitable, prosperous, rich, strong, thriving, top, triumphant, victorious. **2** (a successful attempt) effective, fruitful, lucky, lucrative, profitable, rewarding, victorious, winning; ***opp*** failed, unsuccessful

succession *n* **1** catalog, chain, continuation, course, list, litany, sequence, series. **2** (the succession to the throne) accession, descent, inheritance, line, lineage, order of precedence

successive *adj* consecutive, following, in succession, on the run, one after the other, running, succeeding, unbroken, uninterrupted

successor *n* heir, inheritor, next in line, replacement; ***opp*** predecessor

succinct *adj* brief, clear, compact, concise, condensed, laconic, pithy, short, short and sweet *inf*, snappy, terse; ***opp*** long, wordy

succulent *adj* delicious, juicy, luscious, lush, ripe, sappy, tasty

succumb *v* capitulate, crumble, die, fall, fall victim, give up, go under, submit, yield; ***opp*** survive

sudden *adj* **1** (quick) abrupt, hurried, instant, instantaneous, momentary, quick. **2** (unexpected) impromptu, impulsive, spontaneous, unexpected

sue *v* drag sb through the courts, proceed against, prosecute, serve a writ on, summons, take legal action against, take sb to court

suffer *v* **1** ache, ail, be in distress, be in pain, grieve, hurt *inf*, struggle, writhe. **2** (suffer from an illness) be a victim of, be affected by, be afflicted by, be cursed with, be troubled with, have. **3** (suffer hardship) bear, endure, experience, feel, go through, live through, put up with, sustain, undergo

suffering *n* affliction, agony, anguish, discomfort, distress, grief, hardship, harm, heartache, hurt, misery, pain, torment, torture
suffice *v* be sufficient, do, satisfy, serve
sufficient *adj* adequate, ample, decent, enough, plenty, satisfactory; ***opp*** insufficient
suffocate *v* asphyxiate, choke, smother, stifle, strangle, throttle
suggest *v* **1** advise, move, propose, recommend. **2** hint, imply, indicate, insinuate, intimate. **3** conjure up, connote, evoke, recall
suggestion *n* **1** idea, motion, plan, proposal, proposition. **2** hint, indication, intimation, remark, whisper
suggestive *adj* **1** evocative, indicative, reminiscent. **2** (sexually suggestive) bawdy, blue *inf*, improper, indelicate, indecent, lewd, ribald, rude, risqué, smutty, titillating
suit *v* **1** (of clothes) become, fit, flatter, go with, match, set off. **2** be suitable for, befit, conform to, please, satisfy
suitable *adj* acceptable, adequate, applicable, apposite, appropriate, apt, befitting, convenient, due, fit, fitting, opportune, pertinent, proper, relevant, right, satisfactory, to your liking; ***opp*** unsuitable
suitor *n* admirer, beau, swain
sulk *v* brood, fume, pout, seethe
sulky *adj* aloof, angry, bitter, brooding, broody, churlish, cross, fuming, gloomy, glum, grouchy *inf*, grumpy *inf*, in a huff *inf*, huffy *inf*, irascible, irritable, moody, morose, peeved *inf*, peevish, petulant, querulous, resentful, seething, sour, sullen, surly, truculent, uncommunicative, uncooperative, unhappy, unsociable, vexed; ***opp*** cheerful
sullen *adj* angry, ashen-faced, brooding, broody, cheerless, depressed, gloomy, hostile, moody, morose, obstinate, peeved *inf*, peevish, resentful, seething, somber, sour, sulky, surly, tight-lipped, uncommunicative, uncooperative, unfriendly, unhappy, unsociable
sultry *adj* close, heavy, humid, muggy, oppressive, sticky, stifling, sweltering
sum *n* **1** addition, aggregate, tally, total. **2** (sum of money) amount, payment, quantity. **3** addition, calculation, division, multiplication, problem, subtraction
summarize *v* abridge, condense, encapsulate, outline, précis, put in a nutshell, round up, sum up
summary *n* abridgment, abstract, digest, outline, précis, resume, round-up, rundown, synopsis
summit *n* **1** brow, crest, peak, pinnacle, top. **2** (of sb's career, achievements) acme, apex, consummation, crowning glory, height, peak, pinnacle, top, zenith; ***opp*** nadir
summon *v* beckon, bid, call, call for, call up, convene, convoke, invite, send for
sumptuous *adj* de luxe, glorious, gorgeous, grand, lavish, luxurious, magnificent, opulent, rich, splendid, superb; ***opp*** poor
sundry *adj* assorted, different, diverse, miscellaneous, odd, several, some, varied, various
sunny *adj* bright, brilliant, clear,

cloudless, fine, glorious, radiant, summery, sunlit

sunrise *n* crack of dawn, dawn, daybreak, first light; ***opp*** sunset

sunset *n* dusk, evening, sundown, twilight; ***opp*** sunrise

superb *adj* admirable, brilliant, excellent, exquisite, fabulous, fantastic, fine, first-class, first-rate, glorious, gorgeous, magnificent, marvelous, outstanding, splendid, sublime, superior, superlative, unrivaled, wonderful, world-class; ***opp*** awful, dreadful

superficial *adj* **1** (done quickly) casual, cursory, desultory, hasty, hurried, perfunctory, quick, rushed, sketchy, slapdash. **2** (without deep thought) facile, shallow, skin deep, silly, slight, trite, trivial; ***opp*** profound. **3** (on the surface) apparent, external, surface

superfluous *adj* excess, excessive, extra, left over, needless, redundant, remaining, residual, spare, surplus, unnecessary, unwanted

superhuman *adj* divine, godlike, heroic, miraculous, mythic, Olympian, supernatural; ***opp*** subhuman

superior *adj* **1** better, choice, classy *inf*, elegant, excellent, exclusive, fine, first-class, first-rate, high-quality, preferable, quality *inf*, refined, select, sophisticated, superlative, top, top-notch *inf*, up-scale *inf*; ***opp*** inferior. **2** (in hierarchy) chief, commanding, higher, more important, outranking, ranking, senior; ***opp*** subordinate. **3** (of sb's character, attitude) arrogant, boastful, condescending, contemptuous, disdainful, elitist, haughty, high and mighty, lofty, paternalistic, patronizing, pretentious, scornful, self-important, smug, snobbish, snooty *inf*, stuck-up *inf*, supercilious

superior *n* boss, chief, commander, commanding officer; ***opp*** subordinate

superlative *adj* beyond compare, brilliant, excellent, fine, first-class, first-rate, glorious, great, incomparable, magnificent, marvelous, matchless, outstanding, peerless, perfect, second to none, superb, superior, tiptop *inf*, top-notch *inf*, unrivaled, unsurpassed, wonderful; ***opp*** awful, dreadful

supernatural *adj* eerie, ghostly, inexplicable, magical, miraculous, mysterious, mystic, occult, out of the ordinary, paranormal, phantom, preternatural, psychic, spectral, spiritual, strange but true, uncanny, unearthly, unexplained, unnatural, weird

superstition *n* belief, folklore, legend, myth, old wives' tale

superstitious *adj* credulous, irrational

supervise *v* administer, be in charge of, conduct, control, direct, govern, invigilate, keep an eye on, look after, manage, mind, monitor, organize, oversee, preside over, regulate, run, watch over

supervision *n* care, charge, control, direction, governance, management, monitoring, organization, regulation, running, surveillance

supervisor *n* boss, controller, director, foreman, head, inspector, instructor, leader, manager, monitor, organizer, overseer, prefect, regulator, teacher, timekeeper, trainer, tutor, warden

supple *adj* **1** bendable *inf*, elastic, flexible, malleable, plastic, pliable, pliant, soft, yielding; ***opp*** rigid. **2** (of a person) agile, double-jointed, graceful, lithe, nimble

supplement *n* **1** addendum, addition, add-on, appendix, continuation, extra, postscript. **2** (payment) bonus, excess, surcharge. **3** (to a newspaper) glossy *inf*, insert, magazine, pull-out, special issue

supplement *v* add to, augment, back up, bolster, boost, complement, enhance, extend, increase, reinforce, strengthen, support

supplementary *adj* accompanying, added, additional, ancillary, auxiliary, backup, complementary, excess, extra, further, subsidiary, supporting

supplier *n* dealer, distributor, exporter, importer, merchant, provider, purveyor, retailer, seller, shopkeeper, source, trader, vendor, wholesaler

supply *n* **1** (the supply of goods) donation, delivery, distribution, export, provision, sale. **2** (a supply of sth) amount, cache, consignment, delivery, hoard, quantity, provision, ration, reserve, reservoir, stock, stockpile, store. **3 supplies** (for soldiers, explorers) equipment, essentials, food, necessities, provisions, rations

supply *v* **1** (supply goods) contribute, deal in, deliver, distribute, donate, export, furnish, give, hand over, offer, procure, provide, purvey, retail, sell, trade in. **2** (supply a person) cater to, endow, equip, keep sb in sth

support *n* **1** aid, assistance, backing, backup, endorsement, help; ***opp*** opposition. **2** advocacy, agreement, approval, backing, endorsement, favor; ***opp*** opposition. **3** (financial) aid, assistance, backing, finance, funding, grant, investment, loan, maintenance, provision, relief, sponsorship, subsidy. **4** (an object giving support) brace, bracket, buttress, column, frame, mounting, pillar, prop, strut, truss

support *v* **1** aid, assist, back, back up, bolster, defend, endorse, get behind, give strength to, help, protect, reinforce, second, speak up for, sponsor, stick up for; ***opp*** oppose. **2** advocate, agree with, approve of, back, be in favor of, believe in, endorse, favor, hold to, subscribe to; ***opp*** oppose. **3** (support a football team) cheer on, follow, get behind, root for, stick up for *inf*, worship *inf*. **4** (evidence that supports a theory) agree with, be consistent with, bear out, bolster, boost, buttress, confirm, corroborate, demonstrate, illustrate, prove, reinforce, strengthen, substantiate, underpin; ***opp*** contradict. **5** (financially) back, bail out, contribute to, donate to, finance, fund, invest in, keep, maintain, provide for, sponsor, subsidize, underwrite. **6** (physically) bear, carry, hold, hold up, keep in place, prop, prop up, shore up, withstand

supporter *n* **1** adherent, advocate, backer, believer, champion, defender, disciple, proponent, seconder, subscriber, voter; ***opp*** opponent. **2** (of a voluntary organization) benefactor, contributor, donor, friend, helper, member, patron, subscriber, volunteer. **3** (of a football team) cheerleader, devotee, fan, fanatic, follower. **4** (of a financial venture) backer, benefactor, contributor, donor, funder, investor, patron, sponsor, subscriber, underwriter

supportive *adj* approving, caring, encouraging, helpful, reassuring, understanding, sympathetic

suppose *v* assume, conjecture, expect, guess, infer, presume, speculate, surmise, think

supposition *n* assumption, conjecture, hypothesis, guess, guesswork, presumption, speculation, theory

suppress *v* **1** beat down, bring to heel, conquer, crush, curb, defeat, destroy, eliminate, eradicate, extinguish, oppress, put down, quell, repress, snuff out, subdue, subjugate, terminate, vanquish, wipe out. **2** (suppress information) bury, censor, conceal, cover up, hide, keep back, keep secret, sit on *inf*; ***opp*** disclose. **3** (suppress feelings) conceal, control, hide, mask, repress, stifle; ***opp*** show

suppression *n* **1** conquest, defeat, destruction, elimination, eradication, extinction, oppression, repression, subjugation, terminate. **2** concealment, secrecy; ***opp*** disclosure

supremacy *n* ascendancy, command, dominance, domination, dominion, hegemony, leadership, mastery, pre-eminence, sovereignty, superiority

supreme *adj* **1** absolute, best, consummate, excellent, exquisite, extreme, greatest, highest, perfect, pre-eminent, prime, ultimate. **2** most important, overriding, paramount, prime, uppermost

sure *adj* **1** certain, confident, in no doubt, positive; ***opp*** uncertain. **2** (be sure of getting sth) assured, certain, destined, guaranteed. **3** (a sure method of doing sth) infallible, reliable, trusty, unerring, unfailing

surface *n* **1** covering, crust, epidermis *tech*, exterior, face, skin, top, topsoil, upper layer. **2 on the surface** apparently, at first glance, on the face of it, outwardly, superficially, to the casual eye, to the untrained eye

surface *v* appear, break the surface, come to the surface, come up, emerge, rise; ***opp*** submerge

surfeit *n* excess, glut, overabundance, profusion, superfluity, surplus

surge *v* **1** (of water) gush, pour out, rush, stream. **2** (of the ocean) billow, heave, rise, roll, swell, swirl. **3** (of a crowd) drive, force their way, move, press, push, rush. **4** (of emotions) grow, rise up, surge up, well up

surly *adj* bad-tempered, churlish, crusty *inf*, gruff, grumpy *inf*, hostile, ill-natured, irascible, irritable, rude, sulky, sullen, uncivil, unfriendly

surmise *v* assume, believe, conjecture, deduce, fancy, gather, guess, hypothesize, imagine, infer, judge, postulate, presume, speculate, suppose; ***opp*** know

surpass *v* beat, better, do better than, eclipse, exceed, leave behind, leave standing, outclass, outdo, outshine, outstrip, top

surplus *n* balance, excess, extra, glut, oversupply, remainder, residue, superfluity, surfeit; ***opp*** shortage

surprise *n* **1** (a feeling of surprise)

amazement, astonishment, incredulity, wonder. 2 (be a complete surprise) bolt from the blue *inf*, bombshell, revelation, shock

surprise *v* 1 amaze, astonish, astound, bewilder, dumbfound, faze, flabbergast, nonplus, rock, take sb aback, take sb by surprise, shock, startle, stun, throw *inf*. 2 (surprise a burglar) burst in on, catch, catch sb in the act, catch sb red-handed, detect, discover, spring upon, startle, take sb by surprise, take sb unawares

surprised *adj* amazed, astonished, astounded, bewildered, dumbfounded, fazed, flabbergasted, incredulous, nonplussed, shocked, speechless, staggered, startled, struck dumb, stunned, thrown *inf*, thunderstruck; ***opp*** unsurprised

surprising *adj* amazing, astonishing, astounding, bewildering, extraordinary, incredible, mind-blowing, remarkable, shocking, staggering, startling, unexpected, unusual; ***opp*** unsurprising

surrender *n* 1 capitulation, giving in, giving up, submission. 2 abandoning, giving up, handing over, relinquishment, waiving, yielding

surrender *v* 1 capitulate, concede, give in, give up, lay down your arms, submit, throw in the towel *inf*, yield; ***opp*** fight on. 2 (surrender sth) abandon, give up, hand over, part with, relinquish, waive, yield; ***opp*** keep

surreptitious *adj* clandestine, covert, crafty, furtive, hidden, secret, sly, shifty, sneaky, stealthy, underhand; ***opp*** open

surround *v* encircle, enclose, encompass, envelop, go round, girdle, ring, skirt

surrounding *adj* adjacent, adjoining, bordering, nearby, neighboring; ***opp*** distant

surroundings *n* background, environment, environs, location, milieu, setting, vicinity

surveillance *n* inspection, observation, reconnaissance, scrutiny, vigilance, watch

survey *n* examination, inquiry, inspection, overview, scrutiny, study

survey *v* 1 (survey the view) contemplate, examine, inspect, look at, observe, scan, scrutinize, view. 2 (survey a building) appraise, do a survey of, map out, measure, plan out, plot

survive *v* carry on, continue, endure, keep going, last, live, live on, persist, remain, subsist, succeed; ***opp*** fail

susceptible *adj* 1 (susceptible to sth) disposed, given, inclined, liable, open, predisposed, prone, subject, vulnerable; ***opp*** resistant. 2 (susceptible teenagers) gullible, impressionable, innocent, sensitive, suggestible, vulnerable

suspect *adj* doubtful, dubious, iffy *inf*, questionable, shady *inf*, suspicious; ***opp*** trustworthy

suspect *v* 1 believe, conjecture, consider, fancy, feel, guess, have a feeling, have a hunch, imagine, suppose, surmise, think; ***opp*** know. 2 (suspect sb) be skeptical about, distrust, doubt, have doubts about, have suspicions about, mistrust; ***opp*** trust

suspend *v* 1 (suspend sth from the ceiling) attach, dangle, hang, swing. 2 (suspend proceedings) adjourn, cut short, defer, delay, discontinue, freeze, interrupt, postpone, put off, put on ice, put on the back burner, shelve; ***opp*** continue

suspense *n* anticipation, anxiety, apprehension, drama, expectancy, expectation, not knowing, tension, uncertainty, waiting

suspicion *n* **1** caution, distrust, doubt, dubiousness, misgiving, mistrust, wariness; ***opp*** trust. **2** (have a suspicion) belief, feeling, funny feeling, hunch, idea, impression, notion, supposition

suspicious *adj* **1** (a suspicious character) dubious, fishy *inf*, funny, shady *inf*, shifty, suspect, unreliable, untrustworthy; ***opp*** trustworthy. **2** (a suspicious husband) doubtful, jealous, unbelieving; ***opp*** trusting

sustain *v* **1** continue, keep going, keep up, maintain, prolong; ***opp*** lose. **2** (sustain the weight of sth) bear, buttress, carry, keep up, prop, reinforce, shore up, support

sustained *adj* constant, continuous, long-term, nonstop, perpetual, prolonged, steady; ***opp*** short-term

swallow *v* down *inf*, gulp, guzzle, wash down

swamp *n* bog, fen, marsh, mire, mud, quagmire

swamp *v* drench, flood, immerse, submerge

swampy *adj* boggy, marshy, muddy, soggy, spongy, waterlogged; ***opp*** dry

swap *v* barter, exchange, interchange, switch, trade

swarm *n* army, bevy, crowd, drove, flock, herd, horde, mass, multitude, pack, stream, throng

swarm *v* **1** (people swarm) cluster, congregate, crowd, flock, gather, mass, stream, throng; ***opp*** trickle. **2** (swarming with people) be crowded with, be full of, be overrun with, bristle, crawl, seethe, teem

sway *n* authority, command, control, government, jurisdiction, power, rule, sovereignty

sway *v* **1** bend, incline, lean, lurch, oscillate, rock, swing, wave. **2** (sway sb's decision) affect, bias, change sb's mind, control, convert, govern, guide, induce, influence, persuade

swear *v* **1** blaspheme, curse, use bad language. **2** (swear to do sth) avow, declare, give your word, promise, vouchsafe, vow

swearing *n* bad language, blasphemy, cursing, foul language

swearword *n* curse, expletive, four-letter word *inf*, obscenity

sweat *n* (in a sweat) fluster, fuss, lather *inf*, panic, state *inf*

sweat *v* **1** break out in a sweat, drip with sweat, glow, have a hot flush, perspire. **2** (sweat over sth) agonize, fret, lose sleep, panic, torture yourself, worry

sweaty *adj* clammy, damp, moist, perspiring, sticky, sweating; ***opp*** dry

sweep *v* **1** (sweep the floor) brush, clean, clear. **2** (sweep past) flounce, fly, glance, glide, sail, stride, tear, zoom

sweeping *adj* **1** (sweeping changes) across-the-board, all-embracing, all-inclusive, blanket, broad, comprehensive, extensive, far-ranging, far-reaching, global, wide, wide-ranging, universal; ***opp*** localized. **2** (a sweeping statement) exaggerated, indiscriminate, overstated, superficial, unqualified, wholesale; ***opp*** considered

sweet *adj* **1** (sweet food) sugared, sugary, sweetened; ***opp*** savory. **2** (a sweet child) agreeable, amiable, appealing, attractive, charming, cute, endearing, engaging, good-natured, likable, lovable, winning; ***opp*** disagreeable. **3** (a sweet smell) aromatic, balmy, fragrant, fresh, perfumed, pure; ***opp*** acrid

sweeten *v* add sugar to, honey, make sweeter, sugar

sweetheart *n* admirer, boyfriend, girlfriend, love, lover, suitor

swell *n* escalation, increase, rise, surge; ***opp*** reduction

swell *v* **1** balloon, billow, bloat, blow up, bulge, distend, enlarge, expand, extend, inflate; ***opp*** shrink. **2** (swell the population) add to, augment, boost, escalate, increase, raise; ***opp*** reduce

swelling *n* bulge, bump, enlargement, inflammation, lump, protrusion, protuberance, tumor

swerve *v* bend, deflect, deviate, diverge, careen, dodge, sheer, shift, skew, swing, turn, veer, wander

swift *adj* brisk, fast, flying, hasty, hurried, prompt, quick, rapid, speedy; ***opp*** slow

swimsuit *n* bathing suit, swimwear

swindle *v* cheat, con *inf*, deceive, defraud, double-cross, dupe, fleece, pull a fast one, rip sb off *inf*, take sb for a ride, trick

swindler *n* cheat, con artist *inf*, con man *inf*, fraud, shark *inf*

swing *n* change, fluctuation, shift, sway, turnaround, variation

swing *v* **1** (swing from the ceiling) dangle, hang, suspend. **2** (swing from side to side) oscillate, rock, sway, veer, wave

swirl *v* churn, circulate, revolve, spin, turn, twirl, twist, whirl

switch *n* button, control, dial, knob

switch *v* **1** (switch brands) change, exchange, replace, substitute, swap, trade. **2** (switch direction) change, deflect, deviate, divert, redirect, reverse, turn

swivel *v* gyrate, pirouette, pivot, revolve, rotate, spin, swing, turn, twirl

swollen *adj* bloated, blown-up, bulging, distended, enlarged, inflamed, puffed-up, puffy

swoop *v* descend, dive, drop down, lunge, plunge, sweep down; ***opp*** rise

syllabus *n* course, curriculum, program

symbol *n* badge, crest, emblem, insignia, logo, sign, token

symbolic *adj* **1** meaningful, significant; ***opp*** meaningless. **2** (symbolic of sth) allegorical, figurative, metaphorical, representative

symbolize *v* denote, indicate, mean, represent, signify, stand for, suggest

symmetrical *adj* balanced, even, proportional, regular; ***opp*** asymmetrical

sympathetic *adj* caring, compassionate, concerned, feeling, friendly, humane, interested, kind, responsive, supportive, understanding, warm; ***opp*** unsympathetic

sympathize *v* **1** agree, be on the same wave length, empathize, identify, see eye to eye, understand. **2** be sorry for, commiserate, feel pity

sympathizer *n* advocate, ally, backer, partisan, supporter; ***opp*** opponent

sympathy *n* **1** caring, compassion, concern, friendliness, humanity, kindness, responsiveness, support, understanding; ***opp*** hostility. **2** (sympathy with sb's point of view) agreement, empathy, understanding; ***opp*** opposition

symptom *n* characteristic, evidence, indication, manifestation, sign, signal, warning, warning sign

synthesis *n* amalgamation, blend, combination, compound, fusion, union

synthetic *adj* artificial, fake, man-made, manufactured, mock, simulated; ***opp*** natural

system *n* **1** (a filing system) arrangement, classification, network, setup *inf*, structure. **2** (a system for dealing with complaints) approach, means, method, procedure, process, routine, scheme, technique, way

systematic *adj* efficient, logical, methodical, orderly, organized, precise, structured, well organized; ***opp*** haphazard, random

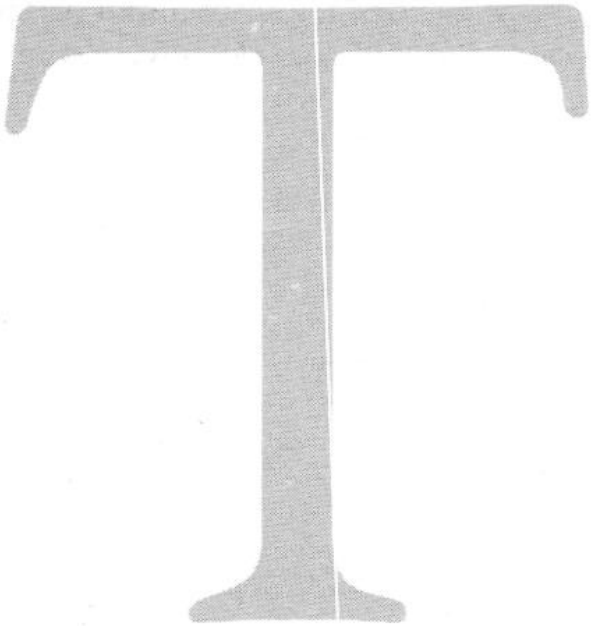

table *n* **1** bench, counter, desk, trestle, worktop. **2** (a mathematical table) chart, diagram, figure, graph, index, inventory, list, plan, register, roll, schedule

tablet *n* capsule, drug, medication, medicine, pill

taboo *n* anathema, ban, prohibition, veto

tacit *adj* implicit, implied, inferred, taken for granted, understood, unexpressed, unspoken, unstated, unvoiced; ***opp*** expressed

taciturn *adj* antisocial, quiet, reserved, reticent, uncommunicative, unforthcoming, unsociable, withdrawn; ***opp*** chatty

tack *n* **1** nail, pin, pushpin, staple. **2** (change tack) approach, course, direction, line, method, plan, policy, procedure, strategy, tactic, way

tack *v* **1** affix, attach, fasten, fix, nail, pin, staple. **2** (tack cloth) sew, stitch

tackle *n* **1** (fishing tackle) apparatus, equipment, gear *inf*, stuff *inf*, things *inf*, tools. **2** (in sport) block, challenge, grapple, interception

tackle *v* **1** (tackle a job) attempt, begin, have a go at *inf*, have a stab at *inf*, set about, take on, undertake. **2** (tackle a problem) confront, cope with, deal with, face up to, grapple with, handle, sort out. **3** (in sport) block, challenge, grapple with, intercept, take on

tact *n* care, delicacy, diplomacy, discretion, judgment, perception, savoir-faire, sensitivity, tactfulness; ***opp*** tactlessness

tactful *adj* careful, delicate, diplomatic, discreet, perceptive, sensitive; ***opp*** tactless

tactic *n* approach, course, line, maneuver, means, method, policy, procedure, scheme, strategy, tack, way

tactical *adj* clever, cunning, planned, shrewd, skillful, smart, strategic

tactless *adj* blundering, blunt, bungling, careless, clumsy, gauche, inconsiderate, indiscreet, insensitive, thoughtless, undiplomatic, unfeeling, unsubtle; ***opp*** tactful

tail *n* back, brush, end, extremity, rear, train

taint *n* blemish, blot, defect, fault, flaw, smear, spot, stain, stigma

taint *v* adulterate, contaminate, corrupt, dirty, foul, infect, pollute, soil, spoil; ***opp*** enrich

take *v* **1** (take sth from sb) get, grab, grasp, grip, obtain, receive, seize, snatch; ***opp*** give. **2** (take sth to sb) carry, cart, convey, ferry, transport. **3** (take sb to the door) accompany, escort, guide, lead, usher. **4** (buy or rent) buy, hire, lease, pay for, pick, purchase, rent, reserve, select. **5** (I can't take it anymore) abide, bear, endure, put up with, stand, stomach, suffer, tolerate, undergo. **6** (take a pill) consume, drink, eat, swallow. **7** (take 3 from 10) deduct, subtract, take away; ***opp*** add. **8 take down** make a note of, note, record, set down, transcribe, write. **9 take off** (run away) abscond, depart, disappear, go, go off *inf*, leave, run away, split *inf*. **10 take off** (clothing) remove, slip off, throw off; ***opp*** put on. **11 take on** employ, engage, enlist, enroll, hire, sign; ***opp*** dismiss. **12 take over** assume control, become leader, come to power, seize control, take command, usurp. **13 take up** adopt, become involved in, embark on, get into, start

takeoff *n* ascent, departure, launch, liftoff; ***opp*** landing

takeover *n* amalgamation, merger; ***opp*** sell-off

takings *n* earnings, income, profit, receipts, returns, revenue, yield; ***opp*** outgoings

tale *n* **1** fable, legend, myth, story. **2** (a tale about sb's exploits) account, anecdote, report, story. **3** (tell tales) fabrication, falsehood, fib, lie, story *inf*, untruth, yarn *inf*; ***opp*** truth

talent *n* ability, aptitude, brilliance, capacity, expertise, flair, genius, gift, prowess

talented *adj* able, accomplished, brilliant, gifted, skillful

talk *n* **1** chat, chit-chat *inf*, conversation, gossip. **2** conference, consultation, dialogue, discussion, negotiation, parley. **3** (give a talk) address, lecture, oration, presentation, sermon, speech

talk *v* **1** babble, chat, chatter, converse, gossip, have a conversation, say, speak, tell, utter, verbalize. **2** confer, discuss, hold negotiations, negotiate, parley. **3** blab *inf*, confess, crack, inform, spill the beans *inf*, squeal *inf*, tell all

talkative *adj* chatty, communicative, effusive, expansive, garrulous, gossipy, long-winded, loquacious, open, verbose, vocal, wordy; ***opp*** taciturn

tall *adj* big, gangling, giant, high, lanky, lofty, soaring, towering

tally *n* addition, count, reckoning, record, score, sum, total

tally *v* **1** accord, agree, coincide, concur, conform, correspond, fit, harmonize, match up, square. **2** add up, calculate, compute, count, reckon, total, work out

tame *adj* **1** amenable, broken, disciplined, docile, domesticated, gentle, house-trained, manageable, obedient, submissive, tamed, tractable. **2** bland, boring, dull, feeble, flat, insipid, safe, uncontroversial, vapid, weak, wishy-washy *inf*

tame *v* break in, discipline, domesticate, house-train, master, pacify, subdue, train

tamper *v* adjust, alter, fiddle, interfere, meddle, mess, tinker

tangible *adj* actual, concrete, corporeal, definite, material, palpable, perceptible, physical, positive, real, solid, substantial, unmistakable

tangle *n* **1** coil, jumble, knot, mass, mat, mesh, mess, scramble, snarl, twist, web. **2** confusion, imbroglio, jumble, labyrinth, maze, mess, mix-up

tangle *v* catch, enmesh, ensnare, entangle, knot, scramble, snarl, trap, twist

tangled *adj* 1 caught, enmeshed, ensnared, entangled, jumbled, knotted, matted, scrambled, snarled, twisted. 2 complex, complicated, confused, jumbled, knotty, messy, mixed up, muddled, scrambled; ***opp*** simple

tank *n* 1 cistern, container, receptacle, reservoir, vat, vessel. 2 armored car, combat vehicle

tanned *adj* bronzed, brown, sunburned, suntanned, weather-beaten

tantalize *v* entice, fascinate, frustrate, keep sb on tenterhooks, lead sb on, make sb's mouth water, provoke, tease, tempt, titillate, torment

tantrum *n* display of temper, fit, outburst, storm

tap *n* 1 blow, knock, pat, rap, touch. 2 faucet, spigot, spout, valve

tap *v* 1 drum, hit, knock, pat, rap, strike, touch. 2 bleed, drain, draw off, siphon off. 3 draw on, exploit, extract, make use of, milk, mine, use, utilize

tape *n* 1 band, binding, ribbon, strip. 2 audiotape, cassette, recording, tape-recording, video, videotape

tape *v* 1 bind, fasten, fix, seal, secure, stick. 2 record, tape-record, video, video-record

target *n* 1 aim, ambition, end, goal, hope, intention, mark, object, objective, purpose. 2 (target of abuse, jokes) butt, object, prey, quarry, scapegoat, victim

tariff *n* 1 charges, menu, price list, rate, schedule. 2 duty, excise, levy, tax, toll

tarnish *v* 1 blacken, blemish, corrode, dirty, discolor, rust, soil, spoil, stain, taint. 2 (tarnish sb's reputation) blacken, blemish, blot, disgrace, dishonor, mar, ruin, spoil, stain, sully, taint

tart *adj* 1 acid, astringent, citrus, piquant, sharp, sour, tangy. 2 (tart remark) acid, astringent, biting, caustic, cutting, mordant, scathing, sharp, stinging, trenchant

task *n* activity, assignment, charge, chore, duty, enterprise, errand, exercise, job, mission, undertaking, work

taste *n* 1 flavor, relish, savor, smack, tang. 2 (have a taste of sth) bit, bite, dash, drop, morsel, mouthful, nibble, nip, sample, sip, swallow, touch. 3 (have a taste for sth) appetite, bent, desire, fondness, inclination, leaning, liking, love, partiality, penchant, predilection, preference, relish. 4 (good taste) class *inf*, cultivation, culture, discernment, discrimination, elegance, judgment, grace, polish, refinement, style, stylishness

taste *v* bite, nibble, sample, savor, sip, swallow, test, try

tasteful *adj* artistic, classy *inf*, cultivated, cultured, decorous, discerning, discriminating, elegant, graceful, in good taste, polished, refined, restrained, subtle, stylish, understated, well judged; ***opp*** tasteless

tasteless *adj* 1 cheap, crude, flashy *inf*, garish, gaudy, graceless, in bad taste, indecorous, inelegant, in poor taste, kitsch, loud, tacky *inf*, tawdry, uncouth, undiscriminating, vulgar; ***opp*** tasteful.

2 (of food) bland, dull, flavorless, insipid, mild, uninteresting, vapid, watery; ***opp*** tasty

tasty *adj* appetizing, delectable, delicious, flavorful, flavorsome, luscious, mouth-watering, palatable, piquant, savory, scrumptious *inf*, yummy *inf*; ***opp*** tasteless

tattered *adj* battered, frayed, ragged, raggedy, ripped, shredded, tatty, torn, worn out

tatty *adj* battered, frayed, old, ragged, raggedy, scruffy *inf*, shabby, shoddy, tattered, threadbare, worn

taunt *n* barb, catcall, dig, gibe, insult, jeer, sneer

taunt *v* deride, gibe, goad, insult, jeer, laugh at, make fun of, mock, poke fun at, revile, ridicule, sneer, tease, torment

taut *adj* firm, flexed, rigid, strained, stretched, tense, tight; ***opp*** slack

tawdry *adj* cheap, common, flashy *inf*, garish, gaudy, showy, tacky *inf*, tasteless, tatty, vulgar

tax *n* charge, due, duty, excise, imposition, levy, tariff, tithe, toll

tax *v* 1 assess, charge, exact, impose, levy, put duty on. 2 exhaust, make demands on, pressure, pressurize, push, strain, stretch, try, wear out

teach *v* advise, coach, direct, drill, educate, enlighten, give lessons, guide, impart, inculcate, inform, instill, instruct, lecture, school, show, train, tutor

teacher *n* adviser, coach, don, educator, governess, guide, guru, instructor, lecturer, master, mentor, mistress, pedagogue, professor, schoolmaster, schoolmistress, schoolteacher, trainer, tutor

team *n* band, bunch, company, crew, gang, group, lineup, party, set, side, squad, troupe

team up *v* band together, cooperate, form an alliance, join, get together, unite, work together

tear *n* gash, hole, laceration, opening, rent, rip, rupture, scratch, slit, split

tear *v* claw, gash, gore, lacerate, mangle, pull apart, rend, rip, rupture, scratch, shred, split, sunder

tearful *adj* blubbering *inf*, crying, emotional, in tears, lachrymose, sniveling, sobbing, weeping, weepy *inf*

tease *v* bait, goad, laugh at, make fun of, mock, needle *inf*, pester, plague, poke fun at, provoke, pull sb's leg *inf*, rib *inf*, tantalize, taunt, torment

technical *adj* complicated, esoteric, expert, scientific, skilled, specialist, specialized, technological

technique *n* 1 course, manner, means, method, mode, procedure, system, way. 2 ability, art, artistry, craft, facility, knack, proficiency, skill, touch, workmanship

technological *adj* advanced, automated, computerized, electronic, high-tech *inf*, scientific

tedious *adj* banal, boring, drab, dreary, dull, endless, humdrum *inf*, laborious, long-drawn-out, long-winded, mind-numbing, monotonous, repetitive, prosaic, tiresome, uninteresting, vapid, wearisome; ***opp*** interesting

tedium *n* banality, boredom, drabness, dreariness, dullness, laboriousness, monotony, repetitiousness, routine, tediousness; ***opp*** interest

teem with *v* alive with, be full of, be infested with, be overrun with, brim with, crawl with, overflow with, seethe with, swarm with

teenager *n* adolescent, boy, girl, juvenile, minor, pubescent, young person, youth

teetotaler *n* abstainer, nondrinker

telegram *n* cable, telex, wire

telephone *n* mobile, phone

telephone *v* call, dial, give sb a buzz *inf*, give sb a call, give sb a ring, phone, ring

televise *v* broadcast, film, relay, send out, show, transmit

television *n* tube *inf*, TV

tell *v* **1** (give information) advise, announce, communicate, describe, disclose, divulge, explain, express, impart, inform, let sb know, make known, mention, narrate, notify, recite, recount, relate, reveal, say, speak, state, utter. **2** (tell sb to do sth) bid, call upon, command, direct, enjoin, instruct, order, require. **3** (make known sth secret) blab *inf*, blow the whistle, give the game away, inform, open your mouth *inf*, rat *inf*, snitch *inf*, spill the beans *inf*, squeal *sl*, talk, tell tales. **4** (tell what sth is) appreciate, calculate, comprehend, deduce, differentiate, discern, distinguish, identify, make out, notice, perceive, recognize, see

telling *adj* considerable, decisive, effective, important, influential, marked, meaningful, potent, powerful, revealing, significant, sizable, solid, striking, substantial, weighty

temper *n* **1** attitude, character, disposition, humor, makeup, mind, mood, nature, personality, temperament. **2** anger, annoyance, fury, hot-headedness, ill-humor, irascibility, irritability, passion, peevishness, petulance, rage, tantrum, wrath. **3 lose your temper** blow up, blow your top *inf*, explode, flip *inf*, fly into a rage, fly off the handle *inf*, get angry, get mad *inf*, go crazy *inf*, go mad *inf*, go nuts *inf*, have a fit *inf*, hit the roof *inf*, lose your composure, lose your cool *inf*, see red

temper *v* allay, assuage, lessen, mitigate, moderate, modify, modulate, reduce, soften, soothe, tone down

temperament *n* attitude, character, constitution, disposition, humor, make-up, mind, mood, nature, personality, temper

temperamental *adj* capricious, changeable, emotional, erratic, excitable, fickle, highly strung, inconsistent, moody, sensitive, touchy, unpredictable, unreliable, volatile

temperance *n* abstemiousness, abstinence, continence, moderation, self-control, self-discipline, self-restraint, sobriety, teetotalism

temperate *adj* **1** (of weather) agreeable, balmy, clement, fair, mild, moderate, pleasant. **2** (of a person) abstemious, calm, continent, controlled, disciplined, moderate, reasonable, restrained, sensible, sober; ***opp*** wild

tempest *n* cyclone, gale, hurricane, storm, tornado, typhoon, whirlwind

tempestuous *adj* fierce, furious, heated, intense, passionate, stormy, tumultuous, turbulent, uncontrolled, violent, wild

temple *n* church, house of god, place of

worship, sanctuary, shrine

tempo *n* beat, pace, rate, rhythm, pulse, speed, timing

temporary *adj* brief, ephemeral, fleeting, impermanent, interim, momentary, passing, provisional, short-lived, short-term, transient, transitory; ***opp*** permanent

tempt *v* allure, attract, bait, bribe, cajole, coax, dare, decoy, draw, entice, inveigle, invite, lure, persuade, provoke, seduce, tantalize, woo

temptation *n* allure, appeal, attraction, bait, bribe, decoy, draw, enticement, inducement, lure, provocation, pull, seduction, snare

tempting *adj* alluring, appetizing, attractive, enticing, inviting, mouth-watering, persuasive, seductive, tantalizing

tenacious *adj* adamant, determined, dogged, firm, fixed, immovable, inflexible, obstinate, persistent, resolute, set, single-minded, staunch, steadfast, strong, stubborn, unshakable, unswerving, unwavering, unyielding

tenant *n* inhabitant, leaseholder, lodger, occupant, occupier, renter, resident

tend *v* **1** be disposed, be inclined, be liable, be prone, gravitate, have a tendency, incline, lean. **2** (look after) attend, care for, cultivate, guard, keep, look after, maintain, manage, minister to, nurse, protect, take care of, wait on, watch over

tendency *n* bent, bias, disposition, drift, inclination, leaning, partiality, penchant, predilection, predisposition, preference, proclivity, proneness, propensity, susceptibility, trend

tender *adj* **1** dainty, delicate, fragile, frail, sensitive, soft, vulnerable, weak; ***opp*** tough. **2** affectionate, amorous, caring, compassionate, concerned, emotional, fond, gentle, kind, loving, sentimental, solicitous, soft-hearted, sympathetic, tender-hearted, warm. **3** aching, bruised, inflamed, irritated, painful, raw, sensitive, smarting, sore, throbbing

tenderness *n* affection, caring, compassion, concern, fondness, gentleness, kindness, love, sentiment, solicitude, sympathy, warmth

tense *adj* **1** anxious, apprehensive, edgy, highly strung, jittery, jumpy, keyed-up *inf*, nervous, on edge, on tenterhooks, strained, stressed, under pressure, uptight *inf*, worked up *inf*, worried; ***opp*** relaxed. **2** (a tense situation) exciting, fraught, nail-biting *inf*, nerve-racking, strained, stressful, worrying. **3** (keep a rope tense) firm, flexed, rigid, strained, stretched, taut, tight; ***opp*** slack

tension *n* **1** anxiety, apprehension, excitement, nervousness, pressure, stress, suspense, unease, worry. **2** (in a rope) firmness, pull, rigidity, strain, tautness, tightness

tentative *adj* cautious, diffident, doubtful, experimental, exploratory, faltering, hesitant, indecisive, indefinite, nervous, preliminary, provisional, shy, speculative, timid, uncertain, uncommitted, unsure, wavering; ***opp*** definite

tenuous *adj* doubtful, dubious, flimsy, fragile, insubstantial, shaky, sketchy, slender, slight, slim, uncertain; ***opp*** clear

tepid *adj* **1** lukewarm, warmish. **2** apathetic, cool, half-hearted, indifferent, lukewarm, unenthusiastic

term *n* **1** appellation, denomination, designation, epithet, expression, name, phrase, title, word. **2** duration, period, season, space, span, spell, time. **3** (in a school, college) course, semester, session

term *v* call, denominate, designate, dub, entitle, express, label, name, style, tag

terminal *adj* deadly, fatal, final, incurable, killing, lethal, mortal

terminal *n* **1** airport, depot, port, station, terminus. **2** keyboard, monitor, workstation

terminate *v* bring to an end, cease, conclude, cut off, end, discontinue, finish, interrupt, put an end to, put a stop to, stop, wind up; ***opp*** start

terminology *n* argot, cant, expressions, jargon, language, lexicon, nomenclature, phraseology, vocabulary, words

terms *n* **1** conditions, particulars, provisions, provisos, qualifications, specifications, stipulations. **2** charges, fee, payments, price, rates, schedule, tariff

terrain *n* country, ground, land, landscape, territory, topography, turf

terrible *adj* **1** abysmal, appalling, awful, bad, dire, dreadful, no good, poor, rotten, useless; ***opp*** brilliant, wonderful. **2** appalling, awful, dreadful, fearsome, frightful, ghastly, gruesome, harrowing, hateful, horrible, horrific, horrendous, horrifying, hideous, loathsome, nasty, nauseating, outrageous, revolting, shocking, unbearable, unspeakable, unthinkable, vile

terrific *adj* **1** amazing, brilliant, excellent, fabulous, fantastic, fine, good, great, marvelous, outstanding, superb, wonderful; ***opp*** awful, dreadful. **2** (a terrific noise) considerable, enormous, extraordinary, extreme, great, huge, tremendous, vast

terrify *v* alarm, frighten, horrify, make sb's blood run cold *inf*, make sb's hair stand on end *inf*, paralyze, petrify, scare sb to death, shock, terrorize

terrifying *adj* alarming, appalling, fearsome, frightening, frightful, horrendous, horrific, horrifying, petrifying

territory *n* area, country, county, district, enclave, land, neighborhood, patch, precinct, province, region, space, state, terrain, zone

terror *n* alarm, dread, fear, fright, horror, panic, shock, trepidation

terrorize *v* browbeat, bully, coerce, frighten, intimidate, menace, oppress, persecute, scare, threaten, torment

terse *adj* **1** (a terse account) brief, concise, incisive, pithy, short, succinct, to the point; ***opp*** lengthy. **2** (a terse reply) abrupt, blunt, brusque, curt, short

test *n* analysis, appraisal, assessment, check, checkup *inf*, evaluation, exam, examination, investigation, questionnaire, quiz, research, trial

test *v* analyze, appraise, assess, check, evaluate, experiment, investigate, prove, put to the test, question, research, study, try, try out, verify

testament *n* attestation, demonstration, evidence, proof, testimony, witness

testify *v* **1** (testify in a court) be a witness, give evidence, state on oath. **2** (testify that you have done sth) affirm, assert, attest, avow, certify, declare, swear

testimonial *n* certificate, character reference, commendation, endorsement, recommendation, reference, tribute

testimony *n* affidavit, attestation, avowal, corroboration, evidence, protestation, statement, submission, sworn statement

text *n* **1** book, textbook, work. **2** chapter, paragraph, passage, verse. **3** story, words, writing

texture *n* appearance, composition, consistency, feel, grain, quality, structure, surface, touch, weave

thank *v* offer thanks, say thank you, show appreciation, show gratitude

thankful *adj* appreciative, glad, grateful, happy, indebted, obliged, pleased, relieved

thankless *adj* (a thankless task) futile, unappreciated, unrecognized, unrewarded, unrewarding, useless, vain

thanks *n* acknowledement, appreciation, credit, gratefulness, gratitude, recognition

thaw *v* defrost, de-ice, heat up, liquefy, melt, soften, warm, warm up

theater *n* **1** acting, drama, dramatic art, show business, the stage. **2** auditorium, hall, playhouse

theatrical *adj* affected, artificial, dramatic, exaggerated, melodramatic, overdone, showy, stagy, unnatural

theft *n* burglary, embezzlement, fraud, larceny, pilfering, robbery, shoplifting, stealing, swindling, thieving

theme *n* argument, idea, matter, subject, text, topic

theoretical *adj* abstract, academic, hypothetical, notional, not practical, speculative, unproven, untested

theorize *v* conjecture, form a theory, guess, hypothesize, speculate, suppose

theory *n* argument, assumption, belief, conjecture, explanation, guess, hypothesis, notion, speculation, view

therapeutic *adj* beneficial, curing, good, healing, health-giving, helpful, medicinal, remedial

therapist *n* analyst, counselor, healer

therapy *n* cure, healing, remedy, treatment

thesis *n* **1** argument, assertion, contention, hypothesis, idea, opinion, proposition, theory, view. **2** (write a thesis) composition, dissertation, essay, paper, treatise

thick *adj* **1** broad, bulky, chunky, deep, fat, large, solid, stout, wide; ***opp*** thin. **2** (a thick mixture) clotted, coagulated, concentrated, firm, dense, solid, sticky, stiff, viscous; ***opp*** thin. **3** (thick fog) dense, heavy, impenetrable, murky. **4** (a thick coat) heavy, padded, quilted, warm; ***opp*** thin. **5** (thick hair) abundant, bushy, luxuriant, plentiful. **6** (thick forest) close-packed, dense, impassable, impenetrable. **7** (not clever) brainless, dim *inf*, dull, obtuse, slow, stupid, unintelligent; ***opp*** bright

thicken *v* cake, clot, coagulate, condense, congeal, firm up, gel, set, solidify

thief *n* bandit, burglar, cheat, embezzler,

housebreaker, looter, mugger, pickpocket, pirate, robber, shoplifter, stealer, swindler

thieving *adj* dishonest, light-fingered

thin *adj* **1** (a thin line) fine, narrow. **2** (thin material) delicate, diaphanous, filmy, fine, flimsy, gauzy, gossamer, see-through, sheer; ***opp*** thick. **3** (of a person) bony, gaunt, lanky, lean, scraggy, skinny, slender, slight, slim, svelte, underweight, wiry; ***opp*** fat. **4** (a thin mixture) dilute, diluted, runny, sloppy, watery, weak

thing *n* **1** apparatus, article, device, gadget, implement, instrument, invention, item, machine, mechanism, object, thingumajig, tool, utensil. **2** (a thing that happens) affair, circumstance, deed, episode, event, happening, incident, occurrence, phenomenon, proceeding. **3** (a thing you think) feeling, idea, notion, theory, thought. **4** (a thing you do) act, action, chore, exploit, job, responsibility, task, undertaking. **5** (have a thing about heights) (*inf*) aversion, dislike, fear, fixation, hang-up *inf*, horror, mania, neurosis, obsession, phobia, preoccupation. **6** (have a thing about chocolate) liking, love, partiality, passion, penchant, weakness

think *v* **1** believe, be under the impression, conclude, consider, feel, guess *inf*, have an opinion, imagine, judge, presume, reckon, suppose. **2** (have time to think) brood, chew things over, concentrate, daydream, deliberate, meditate, mull things over, muse, ponder, rack your brains, reflect, reminisce, worry. **3** (try to think what might happen) anticipate, envisage, expect, foresee, imagine, plan, visualize, work out. **4 think over** consider, contemplate, mull over, ponder, weigh up. **5 think up** come up with, concoct, create, devise, dream up, imagine, improvise, invent

thinker *n* innovator, intellect, inventor, philosopher, sage, scholar

thinking *adj* intelligent, logical, philosophical, rational, reflective, sensible, thoughtful

thirst *n* **1** dehydration, dryness, thirstiness. **2** (a thirst for sth) appetite, craving, desire, eagerness, hunger, longing, yearning

thirsty *adj* **1** dehydrated, dry, gasping *inf*, parched. **2** (wanting sth badly) avid, eager, greedy, hankering, longing, yearning

thorn *n* barb, needle, prickle, spike, spine

thorny *adj* **1** (with thorny stems) barbed, pointed, prickly, sharp, spiky, spiny. **2** (a thorny problem) awkward, bothersome, complicated, difficult, tough, troublesome, worrying; ***opp*** simple

thorough *adj* **1** (a thorough examination) careful, complete, comprehensive, conscientious, deep, detailed, exhaustive, full, in-depth *inf*, intensive, methodical, meticulous, painstaking, scrupulous. **2** (a thorough waste of time) absolute, complete, downright, out-and-out, outright, perfect, sheer, thoroughgoing, total, unqualified, utter

thoroughfare *n* access, highway,

passage, passageway, road, roadway, street, way

thought *n* 1 (require some thought) concentration, consideration, contemplation, deliberation, meditation, musing, reflection, rumination, thinking, worrying. 2 (have a thought) idea, notion, observation, opinion, plan. 3 (have thought for sb) compassion, concern, consideration, kindness, regard, sympathy, thoughtfulness

thoughtful *adj* 1 absorbed, contemplative, lost in thought, pensive, reflective, ruminative, serious, solemn, wistful, worried. 2 (a thoughtful person) attentive, caring, compassionate, considerate, helpful, kind, kindly, solicitous, unselfish

thoughtless *adj* 1 careless, foolish, ill-advised, irresponsible, mindless, rash, reckless, silly, stupid, unthinking, unwise. 2 cruel, impolite, inconsiderate, indiscreet, insensitive, rude, tactless, undiplomatic, unfeeling, unkind

thrash *v* 1 beat, belt *inf*, cane, flog, give sb a hiding, lash, punish, spank, whip. 2 (defeat) beat, defeat, hammer *sl*, lick *inf*, run rings around *inf*, trounce, wipe the floor with *inf*. 3 (thrash around in your bed) squirm, toss and turn, twist, twitch, wriggle, writhe

thread *n* cotton, fiber, filament, hair, strand, yarn

threadbare *adj* frayed, holey, old, ragged, scruffy, shabby, tattered, tatty, used, worn, worn-out

threat *n* danger, foreboding, forewarning, hazard, menace, omen, portent, risk, warning

threaten *v* 1 endanger, imperil, jeopardize, put at risk, put in jeopardy. 2 (threaten sb) bully, intimidate, issue threats to, lean on *inf*, make threats to, pressurize, terrorize. 3 (black clouds threatening rain) forebode, foreshadow, forewarn of, give warning of, portend, warn of

threatening *adj* bullying, intimidatory, menacing, warning

three *n* threesome, triad, trinity, trio, triumvirate

threshold *n* 1 door, doorstep, doorway, entrance, entry, sill. 2 (on the threshold of sth) beginning, brink, opening, outset, start, verge

thrift *n* carefulness, economizing, economy, frugality, miserliness, penny-pinching, saving

thrifty *adj* careful, economical, economizing, frugal, mean, miserly, parsimonious, penny-pinching, prudent, sparing

thrill *n* 1 flutter, frisson, quiver, shudder, tingle, tremble, tremor, vibration. 2 delight, joy, pleasure. 3 buzz *inf*, kick *inf*

thrill *v* arouse, electrify, excite, stir, titillate

thrilling *adj* electrifying, exciting, gripping, hair-raising *inf*, riveting, rousing, sensational, stimulating, stirring

thrive *v* 1 be vigorous, bloom, do well, grow, shoot up. 2 develop, flourish, grow, increase, prosper, succeed

thriving *adj* 1 blooming, doing well, flourishing, growing, healthy, prolific. 2 booming, burgeoning, developing, growing, prospering, prosperous, successful, wealthy

throb *v* beat, palpitate, pound, pulsate, pulse, thump, vibrate

throng *n* crowd, flock, horde, host, mass, mob, multitude, swarm

throttle *v* asphyxiate, choke, smother, stifle, strangle, suffocate

throw *n* fling, heave, lob, shot, shy, toss

throw *v* **1** cast, chuck *inf*, fling, heave, hurl, launch, lob, pitch, project, propel, shy, sling, toss. **2 throw away** (throw away the garbage) chuck out *inf*, discard, dispense with, dispose of, dump *inf*, jettison, reject, scrap, throw out. **3 throw away** (throw away your chance) blow *inf*, lose, squander, waste. **4 throw out** (throw out garbage) chuck out *inf*, discard, jettison, junk *inf*, scrap. **5 throw out** (throw sb out of their home) chuck out *inf*, evict, expel, kick out *inf*. **6 throw out** (throw out light) emit, give off, radiate, send out

thrust *n* **1** force, impetus, momentum, pressure. **2** drive, jab, lunge, poke, prod, push, shove, stab

thrust *v* drive, elbow, force, impel, jostle, lunge, plunge, poke, press, prod, push, shove, stab, urge

thud *n* bang, clunk, crash, smack, thump

thud *v* bang, clump, crash, knock, smack, thump

thug *n* assassin, delinquent, gangster, heavy *sl*, hoodlum, hooligan, killer, murderer, ruffian, tough *inf*, troublemaker, vandal, yob

thump *n* bang, clunk, crash, knock, rap, slap, smack, thud

thump *v* **1** bang, batter, beat, clobber *sl*, crash, hit, knock, pound, punch, rap, smack, strike, thrash, thud, whack *inf*. **2** pound, pulse, throb

thunder *n* boom, booming, clap, crack, crash, roar, roaring, roll, rumble, rumbling

thunder *v* bellow, blast, boom, clap, crack, crash, peal, resound, reverberate, roar, rumble, shout, yell

thwart *v* check, defeat, foil, frustrate, hinder, impede, obstruct, oppose, outwit, prevent, stand in the way of, stop, stump

ticket *n* card, coupon, docket, label, pass, permit, slip, sticker, tab, tag, token, voucher

tide *n* course, current, drift, ebb, flow, stream, tidal flow, tidewater, tideway, undertow

tidy *adj* **1** (a tidy person) careful, house-proud, methodical, neat, organized, presentable, systematic, well-groomed; ***opp*** untidy. **2** (a tidy room) clean, in good order, shipshape, spick and span, spruce, trim, uncluttered, well-kept, well-ordered; ***opp*** untidy

tie *n* **1** catch, clip, cord, fastening, link. **2** (have no ties) bond, commitment, obligation, responsibility. **3** (in a game) dead heat, draw, stalemate. **4** (wear a tie) bow tie, cravat, necktie

tie *v* **1** attach, bind, chain, connect, couple, fasten, hitch, join, knot, lash, link, moor, rope, secure, splice, tether, tie up. **2** (in a game) be even, be equal, be level, be neck and neck, draw

tier *n* bank, file, layer, level, line, order, rank, row, story

tight *adj* **1** fast, firm, fixed, rigid, secure, stiff, strained, stretched, taut, tense.

2 (a tight space) compact, constricted, cramped, inadequate, limited, restricted, small. 3 (a tight sweater) close-fitting, figure-hugging, snug, tight-fitting, too small; ***opp*** loose. 4 (a tight lid) airtight, impermeable, leakproof, sealed, waterproof, watertight. 5 (not generous) mean, miserly, stingy, tight-fisted; ***opp*** generous. 6 (a tight match) close, even, well-matched

tighten *v* become tighter, close, close up, constrict, fasten, harden, make taut, make tight, narrow, pull tight, secure, squeeze, stiffen, stretch, tense

tilt *n* angle, inclination, incline, pitch, slant, slope

tilt *v* bank, heel over, incline, keel over, lean, list, slant, slope, tip

timber *n* beams, boards, firewood, forest, logs, planks, trees, tree trunks, wood

time *n* 1 (in the time of Jefferson) age, days, epoch, era, period. 2 (do sth for a time) interval, period, spell, stretch, term, while. 3 (the right time to do sth) juncture, moment, occasion, opportunity, point. 4 (clap in time) beat, measure, meter, rhythm, tempo

time *v* 1 (time your arrival) choose a time for, fix a time for, plan, schedule. 2 (time how long sth takes) clock, count, measure

timeless *adj* ageless, deathless, endless, eternal, everlasting, immortal, lasting, permanent, unchanging, undying

timely *adj* appropriate, convenient, fitting, judicious, opportune, prompt, punctual, suitable, well-timed; ***opp*** untimely

timetable *n* agenda, calendar, diary, list, program, rota, schedule

timid *adj* afraid, apprehensive, bashful, coy, fearful, nervous, scared, shy, spineless, unadventurous, wimpish *inf*; ***opp*** bold

tingle *n* 1 itch, pins and needles *inf*, prickling, stinging, tickle, tingling. 2 quiver, sensation, shiver, thrill, tremor

tingle *v* itch, prickle, sting, tickle

tinker *v* dabble, fiddle, meddle, mess about, play, potter, tamper, toy

tint *n* color, coloring, dye, hue, shade, stain, tone, wash

tint *v* color, dye, rinse, stain, wash

tiny *adj* diminutive, infinitesimal, insignificant, little, microscopic, mini *inf*, miniature, minute, negligible, small, teeny-weeny *inf*, wee; ***opp*** huge, large

tip *n* 1 (the end of sth) apex, cap, cover, crown, end, head, nib, peak, pinnacle, point, summit, top. 2 (a useful tip) hint, piece of advice, pointer, recommendation, suggestion, tip-off. 3 (leave a tip) gift, gratuity, money, reward

tip *v* 1 capsize, incline, keel, lean, list, overturn, slant, spill, tilt, tip over, topple, upend, upset. 2 (tip sth somewhere) dump, empty, pour out, unload. 3 (tip sb) give a tip to, leave a tip for, reward

tire *v* 1 (tire sb) exhaust, overtire, take it out of *inf*, wear out, weary. 2 (feel tired) droop, flag, get tired. 3 (tire of sth) be fed up with *inf*, be sick of *inf*, be weary of, get bored with

tired *adj* dead on your feet *inf*, dog-tired *inf*, done in *inf*, drained, drowsy, exhausted, fatigued, shattered *inf*, sleepy, weary, worn out, zonked *sl*

tireless *adj* determined, dogged, energetic, industrious, unflagging, untiring, vigorous

tiresome *adj* annoying, boring, dull, exasperating, irritating, laborious, maddening, monotonous, tedious, troublesome, trying, wearing

tiring *adj* arduous, exacting, exhausting, fatiguing, strenuous, taxing, tough, wearying

tissue *n* **1** gauze, netting, webbing. **2** paper handkerchief. **3** tissue paper

title *n* **1** caption, credit, heading, headline, inscription, label, name. **2** designation, form of address, name, nickname, position, rank, status. **3** (title to sth) claim, entitlement, ownership, possession, privilege, right. **4** (win a title) championship, crown

titled *adj* aristocratic, noble, upper-class

toast *n* drink, salute, tribute

toast *v* **1** drink a toast to, drink the health of, drink to, raise your glass to, salute. **2** (toast sth under the grill) brown, crisp, cook, grill, heat, warm

together *adv* **1** (work together) closely, collectively, cooperatively, jointly, side by side. **2** (do sth together) all at once, at the same time, in chorus, in unison, simultaneously

toil *n* drudgery, effort, exertion, grind *inf*, hard work, industry, labor, slaving, work

toil *v* drudge, keep at it *inf*, labor, push yourself, slave, slog, strive, struggle, sweat *inf*, work

toilet *n* bathroom, latrine, lavatory, privy, urinal, washroom

token *adj* nominal, notional, superficial, symbolic

token *n* **1** (a token of sth) demonstration, emblem, evidence, expression, indication, keepsake, mark, memento, proof, reminder, sign, symbol. **2** counter, coupon, disk, voucher

tolerable *adj* **1** acceptable, bearable, endurable; ***opp*** intolerable, unbearable. **2** acceptable, adequate, all right, average, fair, good enough, O.K. *inf*, not bad *inf*, satisfactory

tolerance *n* **1** acceptance, endurance, forbearance, fortitude, resilience, stamina, toughness. **2** fairness, forgiveness, indulgence, lenience, open-mindedness, patience, understanding

tolerant *adj* charitable, easygoing, forbearing, magnanimous, open-minded, patient, sympathetic, understanding, unprejudiced; ***opp*** intolerant

tolerate *v* accept, allow, bear, condone, countenance, endure, permit, put up with, sanction, stand, stomach, submit to, suffer, swallow, take, undergo

toll *n* **1** (pay a toll) charge, customs, dues, duty, fee, levy, payment, tariff, tax. **2** (a heavy toll) cost, damage, loss, penalty

toll *v* **1** chime, clang, knell, peal, ring, sound, strike. **2** (toll the hour) announce, call, herald, signal

tomb *n* burial chamber, catacomb, crypt, grave, mausoleum, monument, sepulchre, tombstone, vault

tone *n* **1** (of voice) accent, emphasis, force, inflection, intonation, modulation, phrasing, pitch, sound, sound quality, stress, timbre, tone of voice, volume. **2** (mood) air, atmosphere, attitude, character, drift, effect, feel, feeling, manner, mood, note, quality, spirit, style, temper, vein. 3 (color) cast, color, hue, shade, tint

tone *v* 1 blend, go, go well, harmonize, match, suit. 2 **tone down** dampen, moderate, modulate, play down, reduce, restrain, soften, subdue, temper

tongue *n* dialect, idiom, language, lingo *inf*, parlance, patois, speech, talk, vernacular

tongue-tied *adj* at a loss for words, dumb, dumbfounded, dumbstruck, inarticulate, mute, silent, speechless, struck dumb

tonic *n* boost, pick-me-up, refresher, shot in the arm *inf*, stimulant

tool *n* aid, appliance, contrivance, device, gadget, implement, instrument, machine, utensil

top *adj* 1 (top score) best, high, highest, maximum, most, winning. 2 (the top step) highest, topmost, uppermost. 3 (a top athlete) ace *inf*, fine, great, topnotch *inf*. 4 (top people in society) elite, important, influential, superior. 5 (top quality) best, choicest, first, finest, supreme

top *n* 1 apex, crest, crown, head, height, highest point, peak, pinnacle, summit, tip, vertex, zenith. 2 (top of a container) cap, cork, cover, covering, lid, stopper. 3 (top of the line) head, lead. 4 (piece of clothing) blouse, shirt, sweater, sweatshirt, T-shirt

top *v* 1 (top the dish with tomatoes) coat, complete, cover, decorate, finish, garnish, spread. 2 (do better than sth or sb) beat, do better than, eclipse, exceed, excel, outdo, outstrip, surpass, transcend

topic *n* issue, matter, point, question, subject, text, theme

topical *adj* contemporary, current, in the news, recent, up-to-date

topple *v* 1 (topple sth) fell, knock down, knock over, push over, tip over, upset. 2 (sth topples) capsize, collapse, fall, fall over, keel over, overbalance, overturn, totter, tumble. 3 (topple a government) bring down, oust, overthrow, overturn, unseat

torch *n* brand, flashlight, lamp

torment *n* 1 agony, anguish, distress, hell, misery, ordeal, pain, persecution, suffering, torture, wretchedness. 2 annoyance, bane, bother, curse, hassle *inf*, irritation, nuisance, worry

torment *v* 1 afflict, cause pain to, distress, harrow, hurt, pain, persecute, plague, torture, victimize. 2 aggravate *inf*, annoy, bother, harass, hassle *inf*, irritate, nag, persecute, pester, provoke, tease

torn *adj* 1 cut, lacerated, ragged, slit, split, tattered. 2 (feel torn) of two minds *inf*, split, uncertain, undecided, unsure, wavering

tornado *n* cyclone, gale, hurricane, squall, storm, tempest, twister *inf*, typhoon, whirlwind

torpid *adj* apathetic, dull, heavy, inert, languid, lethargic, listless, sleepy, slothful, slow, slow-moving, sluggish

torrent *n* cascade, current, deluge, downpour, flood, flow, gush, rush, spate, stream, tide

tortuous *adj* circuitous, complicated, convoluted, curling, curvy, indirect, meandering, turning, twisted, twisting, twisty, wandering, winding; ***opp*** direct

torture *n* abuse, agony, anguish, cruelty, distress, hell, humiliation, martyrdom, misery, pain, persecution, punishment, suffering, torment

torture *v* **1** abuse, be cruel to, bully, cause pain to, hurt, ill-treat, inflict pain on, persecute, torment, victimize. **2** afflict, agonize, distress, nag, plague, trouble, worry

toss *n* **1** (a toss of the head) jerk, jiggle, movement, shake. **2** (the toss of a coin) flip, throw, tossing

toss *v* **1** chuck *inf*, fling, hurl, sling, throw. **2** (ships being tossed by the waves) bob, disturb, jolt, lurch, pitch, plunge, rock, roll, shake. **3** (tossing and turning) move restlessly, squirm, wriggle, writhe, thrash, tumble. **4** (toss your head) jerk, throw back. **5** (toss a pancake) flip, throw, turn. **6** (toss a coin) flick, flip, spin, throw

total *n* amount, answer, mass, sum, sum total, totality, whole

total *v* **1** add up to, amount to, come to, make, reach. **2** add up, calculate, compute, count up, find the sum of, reckon, work out

totalitarian *adj* absolute, authoritarian, autocratic, despotic, dictatorial, fascist, one-party, oppressive, tyrannical, undemocratic

totter *v* be unsteady, dodder, falter, lurch, quiver, reel, rock, shake, stagger, stumble, sway, teeter, walk unsteadily, wobble

touch *n* **1** blow, brush, caress, contact, hit, pat, pressure, stroke, tap. **2** (a touch of sth) bit, dash, drop, hint, jot, pinch, smattering, speck, spot, suggestion, taste, trace. **3** (do sth by touch) feel, feeling, sense of touch, touching. **4** (sb's touch) ability, artistry, capability, expertise, flair, gift, knack, skill, technique, way

touch *v* **1** (touch sth) brush, caress, feel, finger, fondle, handle, pat, push, rub, stroke, tap. **2** (things touch) abut, border, come into contact, come together, converge, join, meet. **3** (touch sb emotionally) affect, disturb, get to *inf*, influence, make sad, move, soften, stir, upset. **4** (don't touch) fiddle with, interfere with, mess about with, move, play with, toy with. **5 touch up** enhance, finish off, improve, patch up, perfect, put the finishing touches to, repair, retouch

touching *adj* affecting, emotional, heart-rending, heart-warming, moving, poignant, sad, stirring, tender, upsetting

touchy *adj* bad-tempered, cross, easily offended, grouchy *inf*, grumpy, hypersensitive, irritable, oversensitive, quick-tempered, sensitive, short-tempered, thin-skinned

tough *adj* **1** durable, firm, hard, hard-wearing, indestructible, lasting, leathery, rigid, rugged, solid, sound, stiff, stout, strong, sturdy, substantial, unbreakable, well-made; ***opp*** delicate, flimsy. **2** (a tough decision) difficult, hard, troublesome; ***opp*** easy. **3** (a tough climb) arduous, challenging, demanding, difficult, grueling, hard, strenuous; ***opp*** gentle. **4** (tough meat) chewy, hard, gristly, leathery, rubbery, stringy; ***opp*** tender. **5** (of a person) hard, macho, rough, rowdy, strong, vicious, violent, wild. **6** (a tough life) grim, hard, harsh, rough, severe, strict; ***opp*** easy. **7** (be tough with sb) firm, merciless, severe, stern, strict, unbending, unsympathetic; ***opp*** lenient. **8** (that's tough) regrettable, too bad *inf*, unfortunate, unlucky

tough *n* brute, bully, heavy *sl*, hooligan, ruffian, thug

tour *n* excursion, jaunt, journey, outing, ride, trip

tour *v* explore, go around, go sightseeing, journey through, travel around, vacation in, visit

tourist *n* globetrotter *inf*, sightseer, traveler, visitor, voyager

tournament *n* championship, competition, contest, event, match, meeting, series

tow *v* drag, draw, haul, lug, pull, trail, tug

tower *n* **1** belfry, bell tower, column, minaret, obelisk, pillar, skyscraper, spire, steeple, turret. **2** castle, citadel, fort, fortress, keep, stronghold

tower *v* dominate, loom, mount, overlook, rear, rise, soar, stand out, stick up

towering *adj* **1** (very high) colossal, gigantic, high, huge, lofty, sky-high, soaring. **2** (very intense) extreme, fiery, frenzied, intense, mighty, overpowering, terrible, vehement, violent

town *n* borough, city, hamlet, settlement, township, village

toxic *adj* dangerous, deadly, harmful, lethal, noxious, poisonous

toy *n* game, plaything

trace *n* **1** evidence, indication, mark, record, relic, remnant, sign, survival, token, vestige. **2** (a trace of sth) bit, dash, drop, hint, iota, shadow, suggestion, touch, trifle, whiff. **3** footprint, mark, print, spoor, track, trail

trace *v* **1** detect, dig up, discover, find, get back, recover, retrieve, track down, turn up, uncover, unearth. **2** follow, pursue, track, track down, trail, tail. **3** (trace sth on paper) chart, copy, draw, go over, make a copy of, map, mark out, record, show, sketch

track *n* **1** footmark, footprint, footstep, mark, path, print, scent, spoor, trace, trail. **2** bridle path, bridleway, footpath, path, road, route, trail, way. **3** course, flight path, orbit, route, slipstream, trajectory, wake. **4** line, rail, rails. **5** circuit, dirt-track, racecourse, racetrack

track *v* chase, dog, follow, hound, pursue, shadow, stalk, tail, trace, trail

tracks *n* impressions, imprints, marks, wheel marks

tractable *adj* amenable, compliant, controllable, docile, dutiful, manageable, obedient, submissive, tame, willing

trade *n* **1** barter, business, buying and selling, commerce, dealing, exchange, marketing, merchandising, trading, traffic, trafficking, transactions. **2** (learn a trade) business, calling, career, job, line of work, occupation, profession, skill. **3** (arrange a trade) deal, exchange, swap

trade *v* bargain, barter, buy and sell, deal, do business, exchange, market, peddle, traffic, swap, switch

trader *n* broker, buyer, dealer, merchant, retailer, salesman, seller, shopkeeper, storekeeper, supplier

tradesman *n* **1** merchant, retailer, seller, shopkeeper, storekeeper, supplier. **2** craftsman, skilled worker, workman

tradition *n* **1** belief, folklore. **2** custom, habit, institution, practice, rite, ritual, usage

traditional *adj* **1** conventional, customary, established, familiar, fixed, habitual, time-honored, usual. **2** (traditional legends) folk, historic, old, oral, popular, unwritten

traffic *n* **1** cars, vehicles. **2** freight, movement of goods, movement of passengers, shipping, transport, transportation. **3** (traffic in drugs) barter, business, commerce, dealings, peddling, smuggling, trade, trading, trafficking

traffic *v* deal, do business, peddle, smuggle, trade

tragedy *n* **1** blow, calamity, catastrophe, disaster, misfortune, shock. **2** adversity, misfortune, sad events, sadness

tragic *adj* **1** appalling, awful, calamitous, catastrophic, dire, disastrous, dreadful, fatal, ill-fated, ill-starred, miserable, sad, shocking, unfortunate, unlucky; ***opp*** fortunate. **2** doleful, grief-stricken, hurt, pathetic, pitiful, sad, sorrowful, unhappy, woeful

trail *n* **1** evidence, footmarks, footprints, marks, scent, signs, slipstream, spoor, traces, wake. **2** path, pathway, road, route, track

trail *v* **1** (pull sth behind you) drag, draw, haul, pull, tow. **2** (hang down) dangle, drag, droop, hang, sweep. **3** (go after sb) chase, follow, pursue, shadow, stalk, tail, trace, track, track down. **4** (go along a surface) crawl, creep. **5** (go slowly) dawdle, drag, lag, linger, loiter, plod, straggle

train *n* **1** carriage, diesel, steam train. **2** caravan, column, convoy, line, file, procession. **3** (sth that follows) path, stream, wake, wash, tail, trail

train *v* **1** (train sb) coach, drill, educate, guide, indoctrinate, instruct, prepare, school, teach, tutor. **2** (train to do sth) learn, prepare, rehearse, study. **3** (train before a race) exercise, practice, work out. **4** (train a rifle on sb) aim, direct, level, point

trainer *n* coach, instructor, teacher, tutor

training *n* **1** exercise, practice, preparation. **2** discipline, education, guidance, instruction, schooling, teaching, upbringing

trait *n* attribute, characteristic, feature, idiosyncrasy, mannerism, peculiarity, quality, quirk

traitor *n* back-stabber, betrayer, deceiver, deserter, double-crosser, informer, Judas, renegade

tramp *n* bag lady, beggar, bum *inf*, dosser *inf*, down-and-out, drifter, homeless person, vagrant, wanderer

tramp *v* **1** (go for a walk) hike, march, ramble, roam, rove, stride, trek, walk. **2** (walk heavily) march, plod, stamp, stomp, stump, toil, traipse, trudge

trample *v* crush, flatten, squash, squish *inf*, stamp on, stand on, step on, tread on, walk on

trance *n* daze, dream, hypnotic state, rapture, reverie, semi-consciousness, spell, stupor

tranquil *adj* **1** calm, peaceful, placid, quiet, restful, serene, still, undisturbed. **2** (of a person) composed, cool, even-tempered, placid, serene, unemotional, unflappable

tranquilize *v* calm, calm down, pacify, quieten, relax, sedate, settle, soothe

tranquilizer *n* barbiturate, downer *inf*, narcotic, sedative, ***opp*** stimulant

tranquillity *n* calm, calmness, composure, coolness, equanimity, peace, peacefulness, placidity, quiet, quietness, restfulness, serenity, stillness

transaction *n* agreement, arrangement, deal, item, negotiation, purchase, sale, settlement

transcend *v* exceed, go beyond, leave behind, outdo, rise above, surpass, top

transcribe *v* copy, record, rewrite, transliterate, write out

transfer *n* **1** change, changeover, conveyance, delivery, move, relocation, transport, transmission. **2** change of ownership, conveyancing, handover, sale

transfer *v* **1** carry, change over, convey, ferry, move, relocate, transplant, transport. **2** give, hand over, pass on, pass over, sell

transfix *v* **1** fix, hold, hypnotize, mesmerize, paralyze, petrify, root to the spot. **2** impale, run through, skewer, spear, spike, stab

transform *v* alter, change, convert, make over, metamorphose, remodel, reshape, restructure, revolutionize

transformation *n* change, alteration, conversion, makeover, metamorphosis, remodeling, reshaping, restructuring, revolution, sea change, transition

transgress *v* **1** break the law, do wrong, misbehave, offend, sin; ***opp*** behave. **2** breach, break, contravene, defy, disobey, infringe, overstep, violate; ***opp*** abide by, keep, obey

transgression *n* **1** crime, disobedience, error, misbehavior, misdemeanor, mistake, offense, sin, wrong, wrongdoing. **2** breach, contravention, infringement, violation

transient *adj* brief, ephemeral, fleeting, passing, short-lived, short, temporary, transitory; ***opp*** long-lasting, permanent

transition *n* change, conversion, development, evolution, progress, progression, shift, transformation

transitional *adj* **1** (a transitional government) caretaker, provisional, temporary. **2** changeover, changing, conversion, developing, developmental, evolutionary, evolving

transitory *adj* brief, ephemeral, fleeting, passing, short-lived, short, temporary, transient; ***opp*** long-lasting, permanent

translate *v* **1** decipher, decode, explain, interpret, paraphrase, transcribe. **2** alter, change, convert, rephrase, transform, turn

transmission *n* **1** broadcast, edition, program, repeat, show, showing. **2** broadcasting, carriage, communication, dispatch, dissemination, relaying, sending, shipment, spread, transfer, transport

transmit *v* broadcast, carry, convey,

dispatch, disseminate, emit, forward, mail, pass on, post, put on air, put out, relay, send, ship, spread, transfer, transport

transparent *adj* **1** blatant, clear, evident, obvious, open, patent, plain, unambiguous, unequivocal, unmistakable, visible; ***opp*** obscure. **2** clear, crystal-clear, glassy, see-through, sheer, translucent; ***opp*** cloudy, opaque

transpire *v* **1** arise, come about, happen, occur. **2** emerge, become apparent, become known, come to light

transport *n* carriage, conveyance, dispatch, freight, haulage, movement, moving, shipment, shipping, transfer

transport *v* bring, carry, convey, fetch, move, shift, ship, take, transfer

transpose *v* **1** change, exchange, invert, reorder, reverse, swap, switch. **2** convert, rewrite

trap *n* ambush, booby-trap, pitfall, ploy, ruse, snare, trick

trap *v* block, catch, catch out, confine, corner, cut off, hold back, imprison, inveigle, lure, shut in, snare, trick, trip up

trapped *adj* blocked, caught, cornered, cut off, imprisoned, in a tight spot, locked in, shut in, snared, stuck, with your hands tied; ***opp*** free

trappings *n* accessories, apparatus, bits and pieces, extras, finery, frills, gear *inf*, paraphernalia, things, trimmings

trash *n* **1** garbage, junk, litter, refuse, rubbish, waste.**2** drivel, hot air, nonsense, rot *inf*, rubbish, tripe *inf*, twaddle *inf*

trashy *adj* cheap, poor, shoddy, tacky, useless, worthless

traumatic *adj* difficult, distressing, frightening, harrowing, nerve-racking, painful, stressful, upsetting; ***opp*** easy

travel *v* backpack, cross, fly, go, go on a trip, go on vacation, journey, move, proceed, sail, tour, trek, vacation, visit, walk

traveler *n* backpacker, commuter, explorer, gypsy, holidaymaker, itinerant, migrant, nomad, passenger, pilgrim, tourist, vacationer, visitor

traveling *adj* itinerant, migrant, migratory, mobile, nomadic, touring, wandering

travesty *n* caricature, distortion, farce, misrepresentation, mockery, parody, perversion, send-up, sham

treacherous *adj* **1** dangerous, dicey *inf*, hazardous, perilous, tricky, unsafe; ***opp*** safe. **2** deceitful, disloyal, double-crossing, double-dealing, faithless, false, unfaithful, untrustworthy; ***opp*** loyal

treachery *n* back-stabbing, betrayal, deceit, deception, disloyalty, double-dealing, duplicity, treason; ***opp*** loyalty

tread *n* footfall, footstep, step, tramp, walk

tread *v* **1** go, march, pace, step, stride, tramp, walk. **2** crush underfoot, press, squash, stamp on, stand on, trample, walk on

treason *n* betrayal, disloyalty, high treason, rebellion, sedition, subversion, treachery

treasure *n* **1** booty, cache, gold, hoard, jewels, riches, treasure trove, valuables. **2** (a person) darling, gem, star

treasure *v* cherish, guard, idolize,

love, prize, revere, value

treat *n* amusement, indulgence, luxury, outing, pleasure, present, surprise

treat *v* **1** consider, deal with, handle, manage, regard, tackle, think of, view. **2** (give treatment to) attend to, care for, cure, dress, give treatment to, minister to, nurse, tend. **3** (give sb a treat) buy sth for sb, entertain, give sb a treat, pay for, take sb out

treatise *n* article, dissertation, essay, monograph, paper, study, thesis, tract

treatment *n* **1** conduct, coverage, handling, management, usage, use. **2** care, cure, first aid, healing, medication, medicine, operation, prescription, remedy, surgery, therapy

treaty *n* agreement, alliance, concordat, contract, convention, deal, pact, protocol, settlement

trek *n* expedition, hike, journey, march, safari, slog *inf*, trip, walk

trek *v* backpack, hike, march, slog *inf*, traipse, travel, trudge, walk

tremble *n* judder, quaking, quiver, shaking, shiver, shudder, vibration, wobble

tremble *v* judder, quake, quiver, shake, shiver, shudder, vibrate, wobble

tremendous *adj* **1** ace *inf*, amazing, brilliant, excellent, fantastic, marvelous, sensational, superb, terrific, wonderful; ***opp*** awful, dire. **2** colossal, enormous, giant, gigantic, great, huge, massive, vast; ***opp*** minute, tiny

tremor *n* earthquake, judder, quake, quiver, shaking, shiver, tremble, trembling, vibration, wobble

trench *n* channel, ditch, furrow, hole, trough

trend *n* **1** bias, development, direction, inclination, movement, shift, tendency. **2** craze, fad *inf*, fashion, look, style, vogue

trendy *adj* all the rage, fashionable, in fashion, in vogue, latest, smart, stylish, up-to-date, up-to-the-minute

trespass *v* encroach, intrude

trial *adj* experimental, exploratory, pilot, probationary, provisional, test

trial *n* **1** case, court case, court-martial, court proceedings, hearing, inquiry, lawsuit, legal action, legal proceedings, litigation, prosecution, tribunal. **2** (test) check, dry run *inf*, probation, test, test run, testing, trial period, trial run. **3** (hardship) adversity, difficulty, hardship, misery, nuisance, ordeal, pain *inf*, problem, suffering, tribulation, trouble, woe, worry

tribe *n* clan, ethnic group, family, group, people, race

tribute *n* accolade, acknowledgment, appreciation, compliment, honor, praise, recognition; ***opp*** criticism

trick *n* **1** cheat, con *inf*, deception, dodge, hoax, ploy, practical joke, prank, ruse, scam *inf*, stunt, swindle. **2** art, gift, knack, secret, skill, technique. **3** conjuring, magic, sleight of hand

trick *v* cheat, con *inf*, deceive, diddle, double-cross, fool, pull a fast one *inf*, pull sb's leg, pull the wool over sb's eyes *inf*, swindle, take sb in

trickery *n* cheating, con *inf*, deceit, deception, dishonesty, double-dealing, duplicity, fraud, hoax, sleight-of-hand, swindle

trickle *n* dribble, drip, leak, leakage, seepage
trickle *v* dribble, drip, filter, leak, ooze, percolate, run, seep
tricky *adj* awkward, complicated, delicate, dicey *inf*, difficult, risky, sticky *inf*, touch-and-go; ***opp*** simple, straightforward
trifle *n* 1 bauble, irrelevance, knick-knack, nothing, rubbish, sth of little consequence, trinket, trivia, triviality. 2 bit, drop, little bit, tad *inf*, touch
trifle *v* fiddle, fool, meddle, mess about *inf*, play, toy, treat lightly
trifling *adj* frivolous, inconsequential, insignificant, irrelevant, minor, negligible, paltry, petty, silly, trivial, unimportant, worthless; ***opp*** important, major
trim *adj* 1 neat, neat and tidy, orderly, smart, spick and span, tidy, well-groomed; ***opp*** untidy. 2 in good shape, shapely, slender, slim, willowy; ***opp*** fat, overweight
trim *v* 1 clip, cut, cut back, even up, lop, pare, peel, prune, shape, snip, tidy up. 2 decorate, dress, garnish
trimmings *n* accompaniments, decorations, extras, garnish, ornaments, trappings
trip *n* business trip, day trip, excursion, expedition, holiday, journey, outing, ride, tour, visit
trip *v* fall, fall over sth, lose your footing, slip, stagger, stumble
trite *adj* banal, cliched, dull, hackneyed, insincere, overused, stale, tired, unimaginative, uninteresting, uninspired, unoriginal, worn-out; ***opp*** original
triumph *n* 1 (a victory) achievement, coup, feat, sensation, success, victory, win. 2 (joy) elation, exultation, joy, jubilation, pride
triumph *v* carry the day, come out on top, come through, defeat, overcome, prevail, succeed, vanquish, win; ***opp*** fail, lose
triumphant *adj* 1 elated, exultant, gleeful, joyful, joyous, jubilant, pleased, proud. 2 successful, victorious, winning
trivia *n* minutiae, rubbish, trifles, trivialities
trivial *adj* inconsequential, insignificant, minor, paltry, petty, trifling, unimportant, worthless; ***opp*** important
troop *n* band, bunch, company, contingent, crowd, flock, gang, group, horde, pack, squad, team, unit
troop *v* crowd, flock, go, march, stream, surge, swarm
trophy *n* award, cup, prize, shield
tropical *adj* hot, humid, steamy, sticky, sultry, sweltering, torrid
trot *n* jog, lope, run, scamper
trot *v* go, jog, run, scamper, scuttle, toddle, trundle
trouble *n* 1 (difficulty) affliction, anxiety, difficulty, hassle, heartache, misfortune, nuisance, problem, suffering, tribulation, worry. 2 (unrest) bother, commotion, discontent, disorder, disturbance, fighting, fuss, rioting, row, unrest; ***opp*** calm, peace. 3 (heart trouble) complaint, condition, defect, disorder, illness, problem
trouble *v* afflict, bother, concern, distress,

disturb, plague, torment, upset, worry; ***opp*** reassure

troublemaker *n* agitator, hooligan, mischief-maker, rabble-rouser, rowdy, stirrer

troublesome *adj* **1** annoying, difficult, distressing, hard, irritating, problematic, tiresome, tricky, trying, upsetting, worrying; ***opp*** easy, straightforward. **2** (of a person) badly behaved, disobedient, disorderly, naughty, rowdy, undisciplined, unruly; ***opp*** obedient, placid, well-behaved

trousers *n* chinos, cords, denims, jeans, pants, slacks

truant *n* **1** absconder, absentee, dodger, runaway. **2 play truant** be absent without leave, go AWOL, play hooky *inf*

truce *n* armistice, ceasefire, cessation, letup, pact, peace, respite, suspension of hostilities

trudge *n* haul, hike, march, slog *inf*, struggle, traipse, tramp, trek, walk

trudge *v* hike, march, plod, slog *inf*, stomp, struggle, traipse, tramp, trek, walk

true *adj* **1** (a true story) correct, factual, honest, legitimate, right, truthful, valid. **2** (genuine) actual, authentic, bona fide, genuine, proper, real. **3** (the true meaning) accurate, close, correct, exact, precise. **4** (loyal) constant, dedicated, dependable, devoted, faithful, firm, loyal, staunch, trustworthy

trunk *n* **1** (of a tree) main stem, stalk, stem. **2** box, case, chest, crate. **3** (of an animal) nose, snout. **4** body, torso

trust *n* **1** (faith) belief, confidence, expectation, faith, reliance. **2** (custody) care, charge, custody, guardianship, protection, responsibility, safekeeping

trust *v* **1** bank on, be sure of, count on, depend on, have confidence in, have faith in, put your faith in, rely on. **2** anticipate, assume, expect, hope, presume, suppose

trusting *adj* credulous, gullible, innocent, unquestioning, unsuspecting, unwary; ***opp*** skeptical, suspicious, wary

trustworthy *adj* dependable, honest, loyal, reliable, responsible, true; ***opp*** dishonest, unreliable

trusty *adj* dependable, faithful, loyal, reliable, staunch, trusted, trustworthy

truth *n* accuracy, authenticity, candor, correctness, fact, genuineness, honesty, legitimacy, reality, truthfulness, validity, veracity; ***opp*** falsehood, fallacy

truthful *adj* accurate, candid, correct, frank, honest, realistic, reliable, right, sincere, straight; ***opp*** deceitful

try *n* attempt, bash *inf*, effort, go, shot *inf*, stab *inf*

try *v* **1** aim, attempt, do your best, endeavor, have a go, have a stab at *inf*, make an attempt, make an effort, undertake. **2** (judge) adjudicate, hear, judge, put on trial. **3** (test) appraise, check out, evaluate, sample, test, trial, try out. **4** annoy, put to the test, strain, tax

trying *adj* annoying, arduous, demanding, difficult, exasperating, irritating, stressful, taxing, tiresome, tiring, tough; ***opp*** easy

tub *n* barrel, bath, butt, cask, container, jar, keg, pot

tube *n* conduit, cylinder, duct, hose, pipe, roll
tug *n* haul, heave, jerk, pluck, pull, wrench, yank
tug *v* drag, haul, heave, jerk, lug, pluck, pull, tow, wrench, yank
tuition *n* coaching, education, instruction, lessons, teaching, training, tutelage
tumble *n* **1** fall, somersault. **2** collapse, crash, drop, fall, nosedive, plunge, slump
tumble *v* **1** fall, fall over, lose your footing, overbalance, pitch, roll, somersault, topple. **2** (of prices or numbers) collapse, crash, dive, drop, fall, nosedive, plummet, plunge, slump; ***opp*** rise
tumult *n* bedlam, chaos, commotion, confusion, disorder, free-for-all, hubbub, hullabaloo, noise, pandemonium, racket, rumpus, turmoil, upheaval, uproar; ***opp*** calm, peace
tumultuous *adj* chaotic, confused, disorderly, frenzied, hectic, noisy, rowdy, stormy, turbulent, unruly, uproarious, wild; ***opp*** calm, peaceful
tune *n* ditty, melody, music, song
tune *v* adapt, adjust, pitch, regulate, set, suit
tuneful *adj* attractive, catchy, easy listening, easy on the ear, lilting, lyrical, melodic, melodious, musical, pleasant, sweet; ***opp*** discordant, harsh
tuneless *adj* atonal, discordant, dissonant, flat, harsh, monotonous, out of tune, unmusical; ***opp*** harmonious, melodic
tunnel *n* burrow, hole, passage, shaft, subway, underpass
tunnel *v* bore, burrow, dig, mine
turbulent *adj* confused, disorderly, in turmoil, rough, rowdy, seething, stormy, tempestuous, troubled, tumultuous, unruly, unsettled, unstable, violent, volatile, wild; ***opp*** calm, orderly, peaceful
turf *n* **1** grass, grassland, green, lawn, pitch. **2** clod, divot
turgid *adj* flowery, grand, highfalutin, ornate, pompous, pretentious, wordy; ***opp*** plain, simple
turmoil *n* bedlam, chaos, commotion, confusion, disorder, hubbub, pandemonium, tumult, turbulence, upheaval, uproar; ***opp*** calm, peace
turn *n* **1** (in a game) go, move, period, round, shot, stint, try. **2** coil, cycle, loop, pirouette, revolution, roll, spin, twirl, twist. **3** (change of direction) angle, bend, change of direction, corner, curve, deviation, hairpin, junction, loop, swerve, turning, U-turn. **4** (events have taken a new turn) change, development, direction, drift, shift, tendency, trend, variation. **5** (a comedy turn) act, performance, performer, routine, set
turn *v* **1** (spin) circle, coil, curl, go around, gyrate, loop, pivot, revolve, roll, rotate, spin, spiral, swivel, twirl, wind. **2** bend, flip, fold, invert, reverse. **3** (change direction) change course, change direction, go, head, move, steer, swerve, swing round, veer, wheel. **4** (turn a corner) go round, negotiate, round, take. **5** (turn a hose on sb) aim, direct, point, train. **6** (change to) alter, become, change to, convert, get, go, mutate, transform. **7 turn down** (reject) decline, refuse, reject, say no to, throw

out, veto. **8 turn down** (turn down the volume) decrease, lower, make softer, make quieter, muffle, mute, reduce, soften; ***opp*** turn up. **9 turn off** (switch off) disconnect, put off, shut down, shut off, stop, switch off, turn out; ***opp*** start, switch on, turn on. **10 turn off** (turn off the main road) leave, take a side road, take a turning, turn left, turn right; ***opp*** join. **11 turn off** (put sb off) alienate, deter from, discourage, disgust, offend, put off, repel, sicken; ***opp*** attract. **12 turn on** (switch on) activate, boot, get going, start, start up, switch on; ***opp*** stop, switch off, turn off. **13 turn on** (depend on) be dependent on, depend on, hang on, hinge on, rest on, revolve around. **14 turn on** (attack) assault, attack, lay into, set upon. **15 turn on** (excite) attract, enthuse, excite, interest, stimulate, thrill; ***opp*** turn off. **16 turn up** (arrive) appear, arrive, attend, come, get here, get there, put in an appearance, show up. **17 turn up** (turn up the volume) amplify, increase, make louder, raise; ***opp*** turn down . **18 turn up** (discover) come across, dig up, discover, expose, find, uncover, unearth. **19 turn up** (come to light) arise, be found, come to light, crop up, happen, occur, transpire. **20 turn up** (turn up a hem) shorten, take up; ***opp*** lengthen, let down

turning *n* crossroads, exit, fork, junction, left turn, right turn, road, side road, turn, turn-off

turning point *n* change, crisis, crossroads, decisive moment, eleventh hour, juncture, key moment, moment of truth, point of no return, turn of the tide, watershed

turnover *n* business, flow, movement, output, production, profits, revenue, sales figures, takings, thoughput, receipts

tutor *n* coach, guru, instructor, lecturer, mentor, supervisor, teacher

tutor *v* coach, educate, instruct, lecture, supervise, teach, train

twilight *n* dusk, early evening, half-light, sundown, sunset, the end of the day

twin *adj* corresponding, dual, duplicate, identical, matching, symmetrical, twofold

twin *n* clone, counterpart, double, duplicate, match, mate, other half, pair, partner, spitting image, twin brother, twin sister

twine *n* cord, string, thread

twine *v* climb, coil, entwine, intertwine, snake, spiral, twist, weave, wind, worm, wrap

twinkling *n* flash, instant, jiffy, moment, second, split second, trice

twirl *n* coil, pirouette, revolution, rotation, spin, spiral, swirl, turn, twiddle, twist, whirl, whorl

twirl *v* coil, gyrate, pirouette, pivot, revolve, rotate, spin, spiral, turn, twiddle, twist, whirl, wind

twist *n* **1** coil, curl, screw, spin, spiral, swivel, turn, twiddle, twirl, wind, wring. **2** (bend) angle, bend, curve, hairpin, turn, zigzag. **3** (distortion) bend, buckle, contortion, distortion, kink, warp, wrinkle. **4** (turn of events) complication, development, oddity, quirk, revelation, slant, turn of events, variation

twist *v* **1** coil, corkscrew, curl, meander, screw, snake, spin, spiral, swivel, turn, twine, weave, wind, worm, wrap, wring, zigzag. **2** (contort) bend, buckle, contort, distort, kink, screw up, warp, wrinkle. **3** squirm, wriggle, writhe. **4** (twist your ankle) hurt, pull, sprain, strain, turn, wrench. **5** (twist sb's words) change, distort, falsify, misinterpret, misquote, misrepresent, pervert, warp

twisty *adj* bendable, contorted, crooked, curving, meandering, rambling, serpentine, sinuous, snaking, tortuous, twisting, winding, zigzag

twit *n* clot, clown, dimwit *inf*, dingbat *inf*, dope *inf*, fool, idiot, nerd *inf*, nitwit *inf*, twerp *inf*

twitch *n* **1** convulsion, jerk, jump, spasm, tic, tremor. **2** jerk, pull, tug, tweak, yank

twitch *v* **1** flutter, go into spasm, jerk, jump, shake, tremble. **2** jerk, pull, snatch, tug, tweak, yank

two *n* brace, couple, duet, duo, pair, twosome

tycoon *n* baron, businessperson, capitalist, entrepreneur, fat cat *inf*, financier, industrialist, magnate, millionaire, mogul, wheeler-dealer

type *n* **1** category, character, class, genre, group, kind, nature, order, sort, species, variety. **2** characters, font, lettering, letters, print, text, typeface, words

typical *adj* **1** average, normal, ordinary, regular, routine, run-of-the-mill, usual; ***opp*** unusual. **2** archetypal, classic, conventional, model, orthodox, representative, quintessential, standard, stock; ***opp*** unusual. **3** characteristic, in character, normal, predictable, unsurprising, usual, to be expected; ***opp*** unusual

typify *v* be a good example of, characterize, epitomize, exemplify, personify, represent, sum up, symbolize

tyrannical *adj* authoritarian, autocratic, despotic, dictatorial, domineering, high-handed, oppressive, overbearing, severe, totalitarian, undemocratic, unjust

tyranny *n* **1** absolutism, authoritarianism, autocracy, despotism, dictatorship. **2** coercion, cruelty, harshness, oppression, severity

tyrant *n* **1** absolute ruler, authoritarian, autocrat, despot, dictator. **2** bully, martinet, oppressor, slavedriver

ugly *adj* **1** (of a person) not much to look at *inf*, plain, unattractive; ***opp*** good-looking. **2** (of a thing) grotesque, hideous, horrible, inelegant, misshapen, nasty, unprepossessing, unsightly. **3** (an ugly sight) disagreeable, distasteful, foul, frightful, hideous, horrible, monstrous, nasty, nauseating, obnoxious, offensive, repulsive, shocking, sickening, vile. **4** (an ugly situation) dangerous, menacing, nasty, ominous, sinister, threatening. **5** (an ugly mood) angry, hostile, sullen, surly

ulterior *adj* concealed, covert, hidden, private, secret, underlying, undisclosed; ***opp*** overt

ultimate *adj* **1** closing, concluding, eventual, extreme, final, last, terminal. **2** basic, fundamental, primary, root, underlying. **3** greatest, highest, paramount, supreme, unsurpassed

umpire *n* adjudicator, arbitrator, judge, ref *inf*, referee

unabashed *adj* blatant, bold, brazen, shameless, unconcerned, undismayed

unable *adj* **1** incapable, incompetent, ineffectual, not equal to, not up to, unfit, unqualified; ***opp*** able. **2** impotent, without the power to, not in a position to, powerless; ***opp*** able

unabridged *adj* complete, entire, full-length, unexpurgated, whole; ***opp*** abridged

unacceptable *adj* **1** inadequate, inadmissible, invalid, unsatisfactory; ***opp*** acceptable. **2** disagreeable, improper, inappropriate, intolerable, objectionable, obnoxious, offensive, taboo, undesirable, unpleasant, unsuitable

unaccompanied *adj* alone, by yourself, lone, on your own, solitary, solo, unescorted, unattended

unaccustomed *adj* **1** new, novel, out of the ordinary, special, unfamiliar, unusual; ***opp*** accustomed, usual. **2 unaccustomed to** green, inexperienced, new to, not practiced in, not used to, unfamiliar with, unversed in; ***opp*** accustomed to

unafraid *adj* bold, confident, daring, fearless, intrepid, undaunted; ***opp*** afraid

unanimous *adj* **1** collective, common, concerted, united. **2** agreed, at one, in complete agreement, like-minded, of one mind, united, with one voice

unappetizing *adj* flavorless, insipid, not very nice, off-putting *inf*, tasteless, unattractive, uninteresting, unpalatable, unpleasant, yucky *inf*; ***opp*** appetizing

unapproachable *adj* **1** aloof, chilly, cold, cool, detached, distant, frigid, remote, reserved, standoffish, unfriendly, unsociable, withdrawn; ***opp*** approachable. **2** inaccessible, out of reach, out of the way, remote; ***opp*** accessible

unarmed *adj* defenseless, exposed, helpless, unprotected, vulnerable, weaponless; ***opp*** armed

unassuming *adj* diffident, humble, modest, natural, reticent, retiring, self-effacing, simple, unaffected, unassertive, unpretentious

unattached *adj* **1** available, footloose and fancy free, free, independent, on your own, single, unmarried, without a partner. **2** autonomous, independent, nonaligned. **3** detached, disconnected, loose; ***opp*** attached

unattended *adj* **1** abandoned, left alone, unguarded. **2** alone, by yourself, on your own, unaccompanied, unescorted

unattractive *adj* **1** (of a person) not much to look at *inf*, plain, ugly; ***opp*** attractive. **2** (of a thing) inelegant, unprepossessing, ugly, unsightly; ***opp*** attractive. **3** disagreeable, distasteful, foul, nasty, objectionable, off-putting *inf*, repellent, repulsive, unpleasant, vile. **4** dull, plain, uninteresting, uninviting; ***opp*** attractive

unauthorized *adj* illegal, illicit, irregular, unlawful, unlicensed, unofficial

unavoidable *adj* **1** bound to happen, certain, destined, fated, inescapable, inevitable, inexorable, predestined, sure, unalterable; ***opp*** avoidable. **2** compulsory, mandatory, necessary, obligatory

unaware *adj* ignorant, ill-informed, oblivious, unconscious, uninformed, unknowing, unsuspecting; ***opp*** aware

unbalanced *adj* **1** asymmetrical, irregular, lopsided, out of balance, unstable, unsteady, wobbly; ***opp*** balanced. **2** crazy, demented, deranged, eccentric, insane, irrational, mad, mentally ill, out of your mind, out to lunch *inf*, unstable *inf*; ***opp*** sane. **3** biased, bigoted, one-sided, partial, prejudiced; ***opp*** balanced, fair

unbearable *adj* insufferable, intolerable, more than flesh and blood can stand *inf*, too much *inf*, unacceptable, unendurable

unbelievable *adj* beyond belief, far-fetched, implausible, impossible, improbably, inconceivable, incredible, preposterous; ***opp*** believable

unbiased *adj* disinterested, equitable, even-handed, fair, impartial, just, neutral, objective, unprejudiced; ***opp*** biased

unbreakable *adj* indestructible, shatter-proof, rugged, solid, tough, toughened

uncalled-for *adj* gratuitous, needless, undeserved, unjustified, unnecessary, unwarranted

uncanny *adj* **1** creepy *inf*, eerie, mysterious, queer, spooky *inf*, strange, supernatural, weird. **2** astonishing, astounding, extraordinary, incredible, remarkable, striking

uncertain *adj* **1** ambivalent, distrustful, doubtful, dubious, hesitant, indecisive, not convinced, not sure, of two minds, skeptical, tentative, unconvinced, undecided, unsure, vague, wavering; ***opp*** certain, sure. **2** chancy, dicey *inf*, doubtful, iffy *inf*, in the balance, precarious, questionable, risky, unclear, undecided, unpredictable, up in the air. 3 changeable, erratic, fitful, inconstant, not dependable, unpredictable, unreliable, unsettled, variable

uncertainty *n* 1 ambivalence, confusion, distrust, doubt, hesitance, indecision, lack of confidence, perplexity, skepticism, vacillation, vagueness; ***opp*** certainty. 2 doubtfulness, unpredictability, unreliability. 3 doubt, misgiving, qualm

uncharitable *adj* censorious, hard, harsh, insensitive, intolerant, stern, unchristian, uncompromising, unforgiving, unkind, unsympathetic; ***opp*** charitable

uncharted *adj* not mapped, strange, undiscovered, unexplored, unfamiliar, unknown, unsurveyed

uncivilized *adj* 1 barbarian, barbaric, barbarous, primitive, savage, wild; ***opp*** civilized. 2 boorish, churlish, coarse, philistine, uncouth, uncultured, uncultivated, uneducated, unsophisticated

unclean *adj* 1 corrupt, defiled, lewd, licentious, sinful, unchaste; ***opp*** pure. 2 dirty, filthy, foul, impure, polluted, soiled, stained, tainted; ***opp*** clean

unclear *adj* 1 dim, blurred, faint, fuzzy, hazy, indistinct, out of focus, opaque; ***opp*** clear. 2 ambiguous, confused, garbled, imprecise, muddled, obscure, vague; ***opp*** clear. 3 not known, uncertain, unknown, unpredictable; ***opp*** clear

uncomfortable *adj* 1 cold, comfortless, cramped, hard, lumpy, painful, spartan; ***opp*** comfortable. 2 anxious, awkward, edgy, embarrassed, ill-at-ease, nervous, self-conscious, troubled, worried; ***opp*** comfortable. 3 awkward, embarrassing, strained, unpleasant

uncommon *adj* 1 distinctive, exceptional, out of the ordinary, rare, special, strange, unusual. 2 few and far between *inf*, not common, rare, scarce, unusual. 3 extraordinary, outstanding, remarkable, striking

uncommunicative *adj* 1 close, curt, secretive, short, silent, taciturn, tight-lipped, unforthcoming. 2 aloof, reserved, reticent, retiring, shy, standoffish, unsociable, withdrawn

uncomplimentary *adj* deprecatory, derogatory, disparaging, insulting, pejorative, rude, scathing, unfavorable, unflattering; ***opp*** complimentary

uncompromising *adj* firm, hard-line, implacable, inflexible, intransigent, obstinate, stiff-necked, strict, stubborn, unbending

unconditional *adj* absolute, categorical, complete, entire, full, outright, total, unlimited, unqualified, unreserved, unrestricted, wholehearted, with no strings attached *inf*

unconnected *adj* 1 detached, divided, independent, separate; ***opp*** connected. 2 disjointed, illogical, incoherent, irrelevant, rambling, unrelated

unconscious *adj* 1 comatose, dead to the world *inf*, in a coma, insensible, knocked out, out cold *inf*, out for the count *inf*, senseless; ***opp*** conscious. 2 ignorant, insensible, oblivious, unaware, unsuspecting. 3 accidental, inadvertent, unintended, unpremeditated, unwitting; ***opp*** deliberate. 4 automatic, instinctive, involuntary, reflex, spontaneous, unthinking. 5 repressed, subconscious, subliminal, suppressed; ***opp*** conscious

uncontrollable *adj* 1 incorrigible, out of control, recalcitrant, undisciplined, ungovernable, unmanageable, unruly, untameable, untamed, wild. 2 frantic, frenzied, furious, ungovernable, violent

uncontrolled *adj* 1 furious, rampant, riotous, undisciplined, untamed, wild. 2 unbridled, unchecked, uninhibited, unrestrained

unconventional *adj* 1 atypical, bizarre, different, idiosyncratic, irregular, odd, offbeat, peculiar, queer, strange, unorthodox, unusual, way-out *inf*, weird, zany; ***opp*** conventional. 2 bohemian, eccentric, independent, individual, unorthodox, wayward, zany; ***opp*** conventional. 3 futuristic, new, novel, original, progressive, revolutionary, unorthodox

unconvincing *adj* dubious, far-fetched, hard to believe, implausible, improbable, inconclusive, questionable, specious, unlikely; ***opp*** convincing

uncooperative *adj* lazy, not lifting a finger *inf*, obstinate, obstructive, recalcitrant, resistant, selfish, self-willed, unhelpful, unruly; ***opp*** cooperative, helpful

uncoordinated *adj* all thumbs *inf*, awkward, blundering, bungling, clumsy, inept, lumbering, maladroit, ungainly, ungraceful

uncouth *adj* bad-mannered, boorish, churlish, coarse, crude, loutish, rough, rude, uncivilized; ***opp*** polite

uncover *v* 1 bare, expose, lay bare, show, strip. 2 open, unwrap. 3 bring to light, detect, disclose, discover, reveal, unearth, unmask

undecided *adj* 1 indefinite, in the balance, not decided, not known, not settled, pending, uncertain, unresolved. 2 ambivalent, dithering, doubtful, hesitant, indecisive, in two minds, not convinced, uncertain, unsure

undefined *adj* 1 imprecise, indeterminate, unclear, unexplained, unspecified, vague. 2 blurry, formless, hazy, indefinite, nebulous, shadowy, vague

undeniable *adj* 1 certain, clear, evident, manifest, obvious. 2 indisputable, irrefutable, proven, sound, sure, unquestionable

underclothes *n* lingerie, undergarments, underwear, undies *inf*

undercover *adj* clandestine, concealed, covert, furtive, hidden, hush-hush *inf*, secret, stealthy, surreptitious

undercurrent *n* 1 feeling, hint, murmur, suggestion, tendency, undertone, vibes *inf*. 2 rip, rip tide, undertow

underdog *n* little fellow *inf*, loser, victim, weaker party

underestimate *v* 1 look down on, not appreciate, not do justice to, sell short *inf*, underrate, undervalue; ***opp*** overestimate. 2 (a cost or price) minimize, miscalculate, misjudge, set too low, undervalue

undergo *v* be subjected to, endure, experience, go through, submit to, suffer

underground *adj* 1 below ground, below the surface, buried, covered, subterranean sunken. 2 clandestine, concealed, covert, hidden, secret, surreptitious, undercover, unofficial. 3 alternative, revolutionary, subversive

undergrowth *n* brush, brushwood, ground cover, scrub

underhand *adj* crafty, crooked, deceitful, devious, dishonest, double-dealing, fraudulent, sly, sneaky, treacherous, unscrupulous

underline *v* 1 draw a line under, underscore. 2 accentuate, call attention to, emphasize, highlight, stress

underlying *adj* 1 basic, fundamental, intrinsic, primary, prime, root. 2 concealed, hidden, masked, veiled

undermine *v* 1 damage, impair, sabotage, sap, subvert, threaten, weaken. 2 burrow under, dig under, excavate, tunnel under. 3 erode, wear away

underrate *v* not appreciate, not do justice to, sell short *inf*, underestimate, undervalue; ***opp*** overrate

understand *v* 1 appreciate, apprehend, catch on *inf*, comprehend, fathom, figure out, follow, get, get sb's drift *inf*, get the hang of *inf*, get the message *inf*, get the picture *inf*, get to the bottom of, grasp, interpret, see, take in, tumble to, work out. 2 empathize with, feel compassion towards, know how sb feels, sympathize with. 3 assume, believe, conclude, gather, hear, learn, presume, suppose, think

understanding *n* 1 appreciation, apprehension, comprehension, grasp, interpretation. 2 acumen, awareness, discernment, insight, judgment, intelligence, knowledge, perceptiveness, percipience, sense, wisdom. 3 compassion, empathy, insight, kindness, sympathy, tolerance. 4 assumption, belief, conclusion, feeling, idea, perception, supposition, view. 5 arrangement, bargain, compact, contract, gentleman's agreement, pact. 6 consensus, harmony, sympathy

understanding *adj* compassionate, considerate, forgiving, kind, patient, perceptive, sensitive, sympathetic, tolerant

understood *adj* implicit, implied, inferred, tacit, unspoken, unstated

undertake *v* accept responsibility for, begin, embark on, give an undertaking, promise to do, set about, shoulder, start, tackle

undertaking *n* 1 affair, assignment, business, enterprise, operation, project, task, venture. 2 assurance, pledge, promise, vow, word

undertone *n* 1 low tone, low voice, murmur, whisper. 2 atmosphere, feeling, hint, suggestion, trace, undercurrent

undervalue *v* not appreciate, think too little of, underestimate, underrate

underwear *n* lingerie, underclothes, undergarments, undies *inf*

underweight *adj* all skin and bones *inf*, bony, emaciated, half-starved, scrawny, skinny, thin, undernourished; ***opp*** overweight

underwrite *v* 1 back, finance, fund, guarantee, insure, sponsor, subsidize, support. 2 agree to, approve, confirm, consent to, endorse, okay *inf*, ratify, sanction. 3 countersign, endorse, initial, sign

undesirable *adj* 1 disagreeable, disliked, nasty, unacceptable, unpleasant, unwanted. 2 disagreeable, nasty, objectionable, obnoxious, offensive, unattractive, unpleasant, unsavory

undisciplined *adj* 1 anarchic, disobedient, disorderly, naughty, rebellious, uncontrollable, unmanageable, unruly, untrained, wild. 2 capricious, erratic, willful. 3 chaotic, disorderly, disorganized, lax, uncontrolled, unsystematic

undisputed *adj* accepted, acknowledged, certain, indisputable, recognized, unchallenged, uncontested, undeniable, undoubted

undistinguished *adj* average, commonplace, everyday, indifferent, mediocre, nothing special *inf*, nothing to write home about *inf*, ordinary, unexceptional, unimpressive, unremarkable; ***opp*** special

undo *v* 1 detach, disconnect, disentangle, loosen, open, uncouple, unfasten, unlock, untie, unwrap. 2 annul, cancel, invalidate, nullify, quash, repeal, rescind, reverse, revoke, set aside. 3 defeat, destroy, overthrow, overturn, ruin, shatter, undermine, wreck

undoing *n* 1 collapse, defeat, destruction, disgrace, downfall, overthrow, reversal, ruin, shame. 2 blight, curse, misfortune, trouble, weakness

undone *adj* 1 detached, disconnected, free, loose, open, unbuttoned, uncoupled, unfastened, untied. 2 ignored, incomplete, left, neglected, not attended to, not done, omitted, outstanding, unfinished. 3 defeated, overthrown, ruined, shattered

undoubted *adj* 1 beyond doubt, certain, incontrovertible, indubitable, irrefutable, proved, proven, sure, undeniable, unquestionable. 2 certain, uncontested, undisputed

undress *v* 1 change, get changed, get undressed, peel off, strip, strip off, take your clothes off, tear your clothes off. 2 (undress sb) get sb undressed, strip, take sb's clothes off, tear sb's clothes off

undue *adj* disproportionate, excessive, extreme, inappropriate, inordinate, undeserved, unjustified, unnecessary, unreasonable, unwarranted

unduly *adv* disproportionately, excessively, inordinately, unnecessarily, unreasonably

undying *adj* constant, deathless, eternal, everlasting, immortal, perpetual, unceasing, without end

unearth *v* 1 bring to light, discover, expose, ferret out, find, reveal, uncover. 2 dig up, disinter, dredge up, excavate, exhume

unearthly *adj* 1 eerie, ghastly, ghostly, spooky *inf*, strange, uncanny, weird. 2 absurd, preposterous, ridiculous

uneasy *adj* 1 agitated, anxious, apprehensive, disturbed, edgy, jittery, nervous, on edge, perturbed, tense, troubled, twitchy, upset, worried. 2 awkward, insecure, precarious, strained, tense, uncomfortable, unstable

uneconomic *adj* inefficient, loss-making, uneconomical, unproductive, unprofitable, wasteful

uneducated *adj* ignorant, ill-informed, illiterate, lowbrow, nonacademic, uncultivated, uninformed, unschooled, unskilled, untaught, untrained, untutored; ***opp*** educated

unemotional *adj* aloof, calm, cold, controlled, cool, deadpan, detached, dispassionate, distant, emotionless, expressionless, frigid, hard-nosed, heartless, icy, impassive, impersonal, indifferent, inscrutable, insensitive, passionless, phlegmatic, poker-faced, reserved, soulless, stoical, stolid, stony-faced, unconcerned, undemonstrative, unfeeling, unmoved, unresponsive, unruffled, unsentimental

unemployed *adj* idle, jobless, laid off, on the dole *inf*, out of a job, out of work, redundant, resting, unemployable, unoccupied; ***opp*** employed

unending *adj* ceaseless, constant, endless, eternal, everlasting, imperishable, incessant, never-ending, nonstop, perennial, permanent, perpetual, interminable, undying, unrelenting, unremitting, without end

unequal *adj* **1** asymmetrical, different, differing, disproportionate, dissimilar, uneven, unmatched, unvarying. **2** (of a society) class-ridden, hierarchical, inequitable, prejudiced, undemocratic, unfair, unjust; ***opp*** egalitarian

unequaled *adj* best, beyond compare, greatest, highest, incomparable, matchless, peerless, record, record-breaking, second to none, supreme, unbeaten, unique, unparalleled, unrivaled, unsurpassed

unequivocal *adj* absolute, certain, clear, definite, plain, unambiguous, unmistakable

unethical *adj* dishonest, dishonorable, unconscionable, unfair, unprincipled, unprofessional, unscrupulous, wrong; ***opp*** ethical

uneven *adj* **1** bumpy, jagged, lumpy, pitted, pockmarked, rough, rutted, undulating, up-and-down; ***opp*** even. **2** erratic, fitful, inconsistent, intermittent, irregular, spasmodic, up-and-down, variable, varying

uneventful *adj* boring, humdrum, ordinary, quiet, routine, unexciting, uninteresting; ***opp*** eventful

unexceptional *adj* average, indifferent, mediocre, middling, ordinary, regular, uneventful; ***opp*** exceptional

unexpected *adj* like a bolt from the blue, sudden, surprising, unannounced, unanticipated, unforeseen, unheralded, unpredicted; ***opp*** expected

unfailing *adj* absolute, constant, dependable, regular as clockwork, reliable, surefire *inf*

unfair *adj* **1** arbitrary, dishonest, sneaky *inf*, undeserved, unethical, unjust, unjustifiable, unmerited, unreasonable, wrong, wrongful; ***opp*** fair. **2** (favoring some people and not others) biased, discriminatory, inequitable, one-sided, partial, partisan, prejudiced, unbalanced, unequal, uneven; ***opp*** fair, just. **3** (victimizing sb) cruel, hard, harsh, unkind

unfaithful *adj* **1** adulterous, flighty, flirtatious, inconstant, philandering, promiscuous, two-timing; ***opp*** faithful. **2** deceitful, disloyal, double-crossing, double-dealing, faithless, false, perfidious, traitorous, treacherous; ***opp*** loyal

unfashionable *adj* behind the times, dated, dowdy, old-fashioned, out of date, out of fashion, out of favor, outdated, outmoded, square *inf*, unhip *inf*, unpopular; ***opp*** fashionable

unfasten *v* detach, free, loose, release, separate, unclip, uncouple, undo, unhitch, unhook, unlock, untie; ***opp*** fasten

unfavorable *adj* **1** (of circumstances) adverse, disadvantageous, inauspicious, unfortunate, unpromising. **2** (of comments, opinion) adverse, damning, critical, disapproving, hostile, negative; ***opp*** favorable

unfeeling *adj* callous, cold, cold-blooded, cold-hearted, cruel, emotionless, hard, impassive, indifferent, insensitive, hard-hearted, heartless, inhuman, inhumane, insensitive, pitiless, uncaring, unconcerned, unemotional, unmoved, unsentimental, unsympathetic; ***opp*** sympathetic

unfit *adj* **1** below par, ill, injured, out of shape *inf*, sick, unhealthy, unwell, weak; ***opp*** fit, healthy. **2** ill-adapted, ill-suited, inadequate, inappropriate, incapable, incompetent, unacceptable, unequipped, unsuitable, unsuited, unsatisfactory, useless

unflinching *adj* bold, brave, constant, courageous, determined, nerveless, resolute, steadfast, steady, unflagging, unwavering

unfold *v* **1** extend, open out, spread out, straighten out, unfurl, unroll. **2** (of story, events) be revealed, become known, continue, develop, evolve, progress, take place, take shape

unforeseen *adj* sudden, surprising, unanticipated, unexpected, unplanned, unscheduled

unfortunate *adj* **1** hapless, ill-fated, ill-starred, luckless, out of luck, unlucky, unsuccessful. **2** annoying, deplorable, regrettable, infelicitous, lamentable, untimely

unfounded *adj* baseless, false, groundless, idle, invalid, unjustified, unproven, unsupported, untenable, untrue, without foundation

unfriendly *adj* aloof, antagonistic, churlish, cold, distant, hostile, impolite, rude, stand-offish *inf*, surly, unkind, unpleasant; ***opp*** friendly

ungainly *adj* awkward, clumsy, gangling, heavy-footed, hulking, lumbering, shambling, uncoordinated; ***opp*** graceful

ungodly *adj* **1** blasphemous, corrupted, depraved, evil, heathen, profane, sacrilegious, sinful, unholy, wicked. **2** (at this ungodly hour) improper, inappropriate, indecent, uncivilized, unseemly

ungrateful *adj* churlish, discourteous, impolite, mercenary, rude, ungracious, unthankful; ***opp*** grateful

unhappy *adj* **1** depressed, disconsolate, distressed, downcast, downhearted, inconsolable, melancholy, miserable, sad; ***opp*** happy. **2** (unhappy about a decision) aggrieved, annoyed, discontented, disgruntled, dissatisfied, resentful; ***opp*** happy. **3** (of event, circumstances) deplorable, lamentable, regrettable, sad, tragic, unfortunate; ***opp*** fortunate

unharmed *adj* intact, safe, safe and sound, undamaged, unhurt, unscathed, untouched, whole

unhealthy *adj* **1** ailing, delicate, frail, ill, in poor health, infirm, invalid, sick, unfit, unwell, weak; ***opp*** healthy. **2** (unhealthy conditions) detrimental, harmful, insalubrious, insanitary, noxious, unwholesome

unheard-of *adj* inconceivable, original, unknown, unfamiliar, unimaginable, unimagined, unprecedented, without precedent

unidentified *adj* mysterious, nameless, unfamiliar, unknown, unnamed, unrecognized

uniform *adj* **1** common, comparable, consistent, equal, homogeneous, identical, invariable, same, similar, unified, universal. **2** (of speed, rate) constant, even, regular, same, smooth, unchanging, unvarying

uniform *n* costume, dress, livery, outfit, regalia, robes, suit

uniformity *n* consistency, evenness, homogeneity, monotony, regularity, sameness, similarity, unity

unify *v* amalgamate, bind, bring together, combine, fuse, harmonize, join, merge, unite

unimaginable *adj* beyond belief, fantastic, impossible, inconceivable, incredible, unbelievable

unimportant *adj* insignificant, irrelevant, meaningless, minor, obscure, paltry, petty, secondary, trifling, trivial, two-bit *inf*, worthless; ***opp*** important

uninhabited *adj* barren, desert, deserted, empty, unoccupied, unpopulated, vacant; ***opp*** inhabited

unintelligent *adj* brainless *inf*, daft *inf*, dim *inf*, foolish, hare-brained *inf*, impractical, mindless, obtuse, senseless, silly, slow, slow-witted, stupid, thoughtless, unimaginative, unwise, witless; ***opp*** intelligent

unintentional *adj* accidental, casual, chance, coincidental, inadvertent, subconscious, unconscious, unintended; ***opp*** deliberate, intentional

uninterested *adj* apathetic, bored, distracted, fed up, incurious, indifferent, listless, tired, unconcerned; ***opp*** interested

union *n* **1** (act of coming together) amalgamation, association, combination, conjunction, fusion, intermingling, marriage, merger, unification, uniting. **2** (organization) alliance, association, brotherhood, coalition, confederacy, confederation, federation, fellowship, fraternity, guild, league, partnership, society

unique *adj* incomparable, inimitable, matchless, one of a kind, original, peerless, unequaled, unparalleled, unprecedented, unrepeatable, unrivaled

unison *n* **in unison** collectively, in agreement, in concert, in harmony, together, unanimously, with one accord, with one voice

unit *n* **1** agency, corps, department, detachment, detail, group, section, squad, task-force. **2** building block, component, constituent, element, item, member, module, part, piece

unite *v* **1** (unite things, groups) ally, amalgamate, associate, blend, bring together, combine, fuse, harmonize, join, link, marry, meld, merge, unify, wed; ***opp*** separate. **2** (people unite) ally, associate, band together, close ranks, collaborate, cooperate, come together, gang up, join forces, pool your resources, work together

united *adj* **1** (of people) agreed, at one, collaborative, collective, combined, concerted, cooperative, coordinated, in harmony, in unison, together, unanimous. **2** (of organizations) amalgamated, affiliated, allied, combined, in alliance, in association, unified

unity *n* **1** (within a structure, a text) agreement, coherence, cohesion, completeness, consistency, harmony, oneness, regularity, uniformity. **2** (within a group of people) accord, agreement, collaboration, concord, consensus, cooperation, harmony, like-mindedness, rapport, solidarity, sweetness and light *inf*, togetherness *inf*, unanimity; ***opp*** disunity

universal *adj* all-embracing, all-inclusive, common, comprehensive, constant, general, global, ubiquitous, uniform, unvarying, widespread

universe *n* cosmos, creation, ether, heavens, outer space, space, void

unjust *adj* immoral, indefensible, inequitable, undeserved, unequal, unfair, unjustifiable, unjustified, unmerited, wrong, wrongful; ***opp*** fair, just

unjustifiable *adj* excessive, illegitimate, indefensible, inexcusable, unacceptable, unconscionable, unforgivable, unjust, unjustified, unreasonable, unwarranted; ***opp*** justifiable

unkind *adj* beastly *inf*, callous, churlish, cruel, harsh, impolite, inconsiderate, insensitive, malevolent, malicious, mean, nasty *inf*, pitiless, rough, rude, sadistic, savage, severe, sharp, spiteful, uncaring, uncharitable, unchristian, unfair, unfriendly, unpleasant, unsympathetic, vicious; ***opp*** kind

unknown *adj* anonymous, mysterious, nameless, obscure, strange, uncharted, undiscovered, unexplored, unheard-of, unfamiliar, unidentified, unnamed, unrecognized, unspecified, unsung; ***opp*** famous, well-known

unlawful *adj* against the law, banned, criminal, forbidden, illegal, illicit, outlawed, prohibited, unauthorized, wrongful; ***opp*** legal

unlike *prep* **be unlike** be different from, be dissimilar to, bear no resemblance to, have nothing in common with

unlikely *adj* **1** (sth is unlikely to happen) doubtful, impossible, improbable, inconceivable. **2** (of a story) dubious, farfetched, implausible, improbable, incredible, suspect, unbelievable, unconvincing; ***opp*** believable, convincing

unlimited *adj* boundless, endless, immeasurable, infinite, limitless, unbounded

unload *v* clear out, deposit, empty, remove, set down, take out, unpack

unlock *v* open, release, unbolt, unfasten; ***opp*** lock

unloved *adj* disliked, detested,

emotionally deprived, forsaken, friendless, hated, jilted, loathed, neglected, rejected, shunned, starved of affection, uncared-for, unpopular, unwanted

unlucky *adj* down on your luck, hapless, ill-fated, ill-starred, luckless, out of luck, star-crossed, unfortunate, unhappy, unsuccessful; ***opp*** lucky

unmarried *adj* **1** bachelor, celibate, divorced, engaged, single, unattached, unwed, widowed; ***opp*** married. **2** (of a couple, partner) cohabiting, common-law, living in sin

unmistakable *adj* blatant, categorical, clear, conspicuous, glaring, indisputable, manifest, obvious, plain, striking, unambiguous, unequivocal

unmitigated *adj* absolute, complete, downright, out-and-out, thorough, total, unqualified, utter, veritable

unmoved *adj* aloof, cold, impassive, impervious, indifferent, stony-faced, unaffected, uncaring, unconcerned, unfeeling, unperturbed; ***opp*** moved

unnatural *adj* **1** (unnatural phenomena) abnormal, bizarre, extraordinary, paranormal, strange, supernatural; ***opp*** natural. **2** (of feelings, relationships) abnormal, against nature, deviant, perverted, unhealthy, unwholesome; ***opp*** natural, normal. **3** (of behavior) affected, artificial, contrived, false, feigned, forced, insincere, mannered, stagy, strained, studied; ***opp*** natural

unnecessary *adj* **1** dispensable, expendable, gratuitous, needless, pointless, redundant, superfluous, surplus to requirements, unwanted, useless; ***opp*** necessary. **2** excessive, gratuitous, inappropriate, injudicious, inopportune, out of place, uncalled-for, undesirable, unhelpful, unseasonable, unsuitable, untimely, untoward, unwelcome

unnerve *v* agitate, alarm, daunt, demoralize, deter, disconcert, discourage, dishearten, disquiet, frighten, fluster, perturb, put off, rattle *inf*, scare, shake, stop sb in his tracks, take aback, throw off balance, trouble, unman, unsettle, worry

unobtrusive *adj* discreet, low-key, low-profile, modest, self-effacing, unassuming, unnoticeable, unostentatious

unoccupied *adj* deserted, empty, uninhabited, unpopulated, vacant

unofficial *adj* casual, informal, unauthorized, unconfirmed, unsanctioned, wildcat; ***opp*** official

unorthodox *adj* abnormal, creative, different, irregular, noncomformist, non-standard, original, strange, unconventional, unusual; ***opp*** conventional, orthodox

unpaid *adj* amateur, free of charge, gratis, honorary, voluntary, volunteer; ***opp*** paid

unpleasant *adj* **1** bad, disagreeable, disgusting, distasteful, foul, nasty, nauseating, offensive, repellent, repugnant, unpalatable, unsavory, unspeakable *inf*; ***opp*** pleasant. **2** (of a person) bad-tempered, churlish, cruel, disagreeable, hostile, ill-natured, insulting, nasty, nauseating, obnoxious, offensive, repulsive, rude, surly, ugly, unattractive, unfriendly, unkind, unspeakable *inf*; ***opp*** nice

unpopular *adj* disliked, out of favor, unfashionable, unloved, unwanted, unwelcome; ***opp*** popular

unpredictable *adj* **1** chance, erratic, haphazard, in the balance, irregular, random, uncertain, unforeseeable, up in the air *inf*. **2** (of a person) capricious, enigmatic, erratic, fickle, full of surprises, inconsistent, mercurial, temperamental, unreliable, unstable, volatile

unproductive *adj* fruitless, futile, idle, ineffective, pointless, time-wasting, unprofitable, unrewarding, useless, vain, wasted, worthless; ***opp*** productive

unravel *v* disentangle, untangle, straighten out, unpick, untie

unreal *adj* **1** artificial, fabricated, false, fictitious, hypothetical, illusory, imaginary, imagined, invented, made-up, make-believe, nonexistent, untrue; ***opp*** real. **2** (causing surprise, bewilderment) absurd, bizarre, paradoxical, strange, surreal, topsy-turvy, unnatural

unrealistic *adj* foolish, half-baked *inf*, impossible, impracticable, impractical, improbable, unreasonable, unworkable, wild; ***opp*** realistic

unreasonable *adj* **1** absurd, illogical, irrational, ludicrous, meaningless, nonsensical, senseless; ***opp*** reasonable. **2** (of demands, expectations, prices) disproportionate, excessive, exorbitant, extortionate, extreme, inordinate, extravagant, outrageous, preposterous, steep, unconscionable, unfair; ***opp*** fair, reasonable. **3** (of a person) cruel, harsh, inflexible, intolerant, obdurate, obstinate, opinionated, pig-headed *inf*, prejudiced, stubborn, unfair; ***opp*** reasonable

unrelated *adj* coincidental, disparate, independent, separate, unconnected; ***opp*** related

unreliable *adj* dubious, fallible, questionable, suspect, uncertain, unsafe, unsound, untrustworthy; ***opp*** reliable

unrest *n* agitation, discontent, discontentment, discord, dissatisfaction, dissension, dissent, protest, rebellion, rioting, strife, trouble, turmoil, violence; ***opp*** calm, peace

unruly *adj* badly behaved, disobedient, disorderly, insubordinate, misbehaving, mischievous, mutinous, naughty, obstreperous, rebellious, rowdy, uncontrollable, undisciplined, ungovernable, unmanageable, wayward, wild; ***opp*** quiet, well-behaved

unsafe *adj* **1** (of a person) at risk, in danger, insecure, unprotected, vulnerable; ***opp*** safe. **2** (of an activity, vehicle, equipment) dangerous, faulty, reckless, risky, unreliable, unsound; ***opp*** safe. **3** (of a criminal conviction) doubtful, dubious, questionable, unreliable, unsound, wrongful

unsatisfactory *adj* bad, disappointing, inadequate, poor, unacceptable, unfit, unsatisfying; ***opp*** satisfactory

unsavory *adj* **1** disagreeable, distasteful, disgusting, gross, nasty, offensive, repellent, repulsive, unpleasant; ***opp*** pleasant. **2** (an unsavory character) criminal, crooked, doubtful, dubious, low-life, questionable, seedy, shady, sleazy *inf*, suspect, suspicious, underworld, untrustworthy

unscrupulous *adj* amoral, bad, corrupt, deceitful, devious, dishonest, evil, exploitative, immoral, ruthless, unconscionable, unethical, unprincipled, untrustworthy, wicked

unsettle *v* agitate, bother, confuse, discomfit, disconcert, disturb, make sb feel uncomfortable, perturb, rattle *inf*, ruffle, shake, throw, throw sb off balance, trouble, unnerve, upset, worry; ***opp*** reassure

unsettled *adj* 1 agitated, anxious, dissatisfied, edgy *inf*, fidgety, on edge, perturbed, restive, restless, shaken, rattled *inf*, tense, troubled, uneasy. 2 (of weather) changeable, rainy, showery, wet; ***opp*** settled

unsightly *adj* hideous, obtrusive, out of place, repulsive, ugly, unattractive, unpleasant; ***opp*** attractive

unsound *adj* defective, doubtful, dubious, erroneous, fallacious, faulty, flawed, ill-founded, illogical, questionable, shaky, specious, spurious, uncertain, unreasonable, unreliable, unsafe, weak

unspoiled *adj* as good as new, conserved, in its natural state, intact, natural, perfect, preserved, unadulterated, unblemished, unchanged, undamaged, unimpaired, undefiled, untouched

unspoken *adj* implicit, implied, tacit, taken for granted, unarticulated, undeclared, understood, unstated

unstable *adj* 1 (of a structure) flimsy, insecure, precarious, rickety, rocky, shaky, tottering, unsafe, unsteady, wobbly; ***opp*** stable. 2 (of a situation) changeable, erratic, fitful, fluctuating, inconsistent, shifting, unpredictable, variable, volatile; ***opp*** stable. 3 (of a person) capricious, irrational, temperamental, unbalanced, unhinged, unpredictable, unreliable; ***opp*** stable

unsteady *adj* 1 (of a structure) flimsy, insecure, precarious, rickety, rocky, shaky, tottering, unsafe, unstable, wobbly; ***opp*** steady. 2 (of sb's voice) changeable, erratic, fluctuating, inconstant, irregular, up and down, variable, wavering; ***opp*** steady

unsuccessful *adj* 1 failed, fruitless, futile, unprofitable, useless, vain; ***opp*** successful. 2 (in a game) beaten, defeated, hapless, losing, unlucky, vanquished; ***opp*** successful

unsuitable *adj* ill-chosen, ill-judged, inappropriate, inapt, incompatible, incongruous, out of keeping, out of place, unacceptable, unfitting, unsuited; ***opp*** suitable

unsure *adj* doubtful, dubious, hesitant, irresolute, of two minds, skeptical, suspicious, unconvinced, undecided, wavering; ***opp*** sure

unsuspecting *adj* credulous, green *inf*, gullible, naive, off guard, trusting, unwary; ***opp*** skeptical

untangle *v* 1 (untangle a rope) disentangle, straighten, unravel; ***opp*** tangle. 2 (untangle a mystery) clear up, explain, solve, sort out

unthinkable *adj* 1 beyond the bounds of possibility, implausible, impossible, inconceivable; ***opp*** possible. 2 (unthinkable cruelty) incredible, outrageous, terrible, unbelievable, unimaginable

untidy *adj* cluttered, disorderly, in a mess, in a state, in disarray, jumbled, like a pig sty, littered, messy, rumpled; ***opp*** tidy

untie *v* disentangle, free, loosen, release, undo, unfasten, unhitch; ***opp*** fasten

untimely *adj* 1 (untimely death) early, premature. 2 (an untimely visit) ill-timed, inconvenient, inopportune; ***opp*** well-timed

untold *adj* 1 (untold damage) indescribable, inexpressible, unimaginable, unspeakable, unthinkable, unutterable. 2 (untold millions) countless, immeasurable, incalculable, innumerable, uncountable, uncounted

untoward *adj* improper, inappropriate, indecorous, unacceptable, unbecoming, unseemly, unsuitable; ***opp*** acceptable

untrue *adj* erroneous, fallacious, false, inaccurate, incorrect, mistaken, spurious, wrong; ***opp*** true

untrustworthy *adj* crooked, deceitful, devious, dishonest, disloyal, shady *inf*, slippery *inf*, tricky, two-faced, undependable, unreliable; ***opp*** trustworthy

unusual *adj* abnormal, atypical, bizarre, curious, different *inf*, extraordinary, irregular, odd, out of the ordinary, queer, rare, remarkable, strange, surprising, uncommon, unexpected, unfamiliar, weird *inf*; ***opp*** normal, usual

unwelcome *adj* 1 (make sb feel unwelcome) excluded, rejected, uninvited, unwanted; ***opp*** welcome. 2 (an unwelcome intrusion) disagreeable, displeasing, unacceptable, undesirable, uninvited, unpleasant, unwanted; ***opp*** welcome

unwell *adj* ailing, groggy *inf*, ill, in poor health, not very well, off-color, out of sorts, poorly, sick, sickly, under the weather; ***opp*** well

unwieldy *adj* 1 (of an object) bulky, cumbersome, hefty, hulking, massive, unmaneuverable. 2 (of a system) awkward, cumbersome, inconvenient, unmanageable; ***opp*** efficient

unwilling *adj* 1 (an unwilling helper) grudging, reluctant, resistant, uncooperative, unenthusiastic, unhelpful; ***opp*** willing. 2 (unwilling to do sth) averse, disinclined, indisposed, loath, slow; ***opp*** willing

unwind *v* 1 disentangle, slacken, uncoil, undo, unravel, unreel, unroll, untwist; ***opp*** wind. 2 (relax) chill out *inf*, relax, take it easy, wind down

unwise *adj* daft *inf*, foolhardy, foolish, ill-advised, ill-judged, improvident, imprudent, inadvisable, injudicious, irresponsible, rash, reckless, senseless, silly, stupid, thoughtless; ***opp*** wise

unwitting *adj* 1 innocent, unaware, unknowing, unsuspecting. 2 (an unwitting blunder) accidental, chance, inadvertent, involuntary, unintended, unintentional; ***opp*** intentional

unworthy *adj* base, contemptible, despicable, disgraceful, disreputable, reprehensible, shameful; ***opp*** worthy

unyielding *adj* adamant, firm, hardline, inflexible, intransigent, obstinate, pig-headed, resolute, rigid, steadfast, stubborn, tough, uncompromising;

opp flexible

upbringing *n* breeding, cultivation, education, instruction, nurture, raising, rearing, training

upgrade *v* (upgrade sth) enhance, expand, improve, make better, refurbish; ***opp*** downgrade. **2** (upgrade sb) advance, elevate, promote, raise; ***opp*** downgrade

upheaval *n* chaos, commotion, confusion, difficulty, disorder, disruption, disturbance, revolution, to-do *inf*, turmoil, upset

uphill *adj* **1** (an uphill climb) ascending, climbing, rising, upward; ***opp*** downhill. **2** (an uphill struggle) arduous, difficult, exhausting, grueling, hard, laborious, onerous, punishing, strenuous, taxing, tough; ***opp*** easy

uphold *v* advocate, back, champion, defend, encourage, endorse, maintain, stand by, stick up for *inf*, support; ***opp*** reject

upkeep *n* care, maintenance, repair, running, support

uplifting *adj* cheering, encouraging, feel-good, heartening, inspiring; ***opp*** depressing

upper *adj* elevated, high, highest, superior, top, topmost, uppermost; ***opp*** lower

upright *adj* **1** erect, on end, perpendicular, straight, vertical; ***opp*** leaning. **2** decent, fair, good, honest, principled, respectable, righteous, straight *inf*, upstanding, virtuous; ***opp*** dishonest

uprising *n* coup, coup d'état, disturbance, insurgence, insurrection, mutiny, rebellion, revolt, revolution, riot, rising

uproar *n* bedlam, chaos, commotion, hullabaloo *inf*, mayhem, outcry, pandemonium, riot, rumpus *inf*, tumult, turbulence, turmoil

uproarious *adj* **1** chaotic, boisterous, disorderly, loud, noisy, rowdy, riotous, tumultuous, turbulent, unruly, wild; ***opp*** calm. **2** (an uproarious show) hilarious, hysterical, rip-roaring, side-splitting

upset *adj* anxious, bothered, dismayed, distressed, disturbed, hurt, ruffled, saddened, shaken, troubled, worried

upset *n* **1** bother, dismay, distress, disturbance, hurt, sadness, worry. **2** (a stomach upset) complaint, disturbance, illness, sickness

upset *v* **1** (upset sb) bother, dismay, distress, disturb, hurt, ruffle, sadden, shake, trouble, worry. **2** (upset sb's plans) disrupt, disturb, hinder, interfere with, jeopardize, mess up, spoil. **3** (upset sth) overturn, tip over, topple, turn over, upend

upshot *n* conclusion, culmination, denouement, issue, outcome, result

upside down *adj* inverted, overturned, the wrong way up, topsy-turvy, upended, upturned

upstanding *adj* decent, fair, good, honest, principled, respectable, righteous, straight *inf*, upstanding, virtuous; ***opp*** dishonest

upward *adj* ascending, climbing, rising, uphill; ***opp*** downward

urban *adj* built-up, city, civic, inner city, metropolitan, municipal, suburban, town; ***opp*** rural

urge *n* compulsion, desire, drive, hunger,

impulse, itch, longing, need, thirst, wish, yearning

urge *v* 1 (urge sb to do sth) compel, drive, egg on *inf*, encourage, entreat, force, goad, impel, incite, induce, persuade, prompt, spur, stimulate. 2 (urge restraint) advise, advocate, back, counsel, endorse, recommend, suggest

urgency *n* haste, hurry, importance, necessity, need, seriousness, top priority

urgent *adj* compelling, crucial, high priority, imperative, important, pressing, top priority

use *n* 1 employment, exploitation, operation, usage, utilization. 2 (have several uses) application, function, purpose. 3 (be of no use) advantage, benefit, good, help, point, service, usefulness, value, worth

use *v* 1 employ, exploit, make use of, operate, ply, put into service, utilize, wield, work. 2 (use all of sth) consume, deplete, exhaust, expend, fritter away, get through, spend, waste

used *adj* cast-off, hand-me-down, nearly-new, second-hand, worn; ***opp*** new

useful *adj* advantageous, beneficial, effective, fruitful, helpful, of help, of use, productive, profitable, rewarding, successful, valuable, worthwhile; ***opp*** useless

useless *adj* 1 fruitless, futile, hopeless, ineffective, of no help, of no use, pointless, unavailing, unproductive, unprofitable, unrewarding, unsuccessful, vain; ***opp*** useful. 2 (not good at sth) hopeless, inadequate, incapable, incompetent, inept, no good *inf*, poor; ***opp*** talented

usual *adj* common, conventional, customary, established, expected, familiar, habitual, normal, ordinary, orthodox, regular, routine, set, standard, stock, traditional, typical; ***opp*** unusual

utilize *v* employ, have recourse to, make the most of, make use of, put to use, resort to, take advantage of, turn to, use

utmost *adj* extreme, greatest, highest, maximum, paramount, supreme

utmost *n* 1 (do sth to the utmost) extreme, greatest, highest, max *inf*, maximum. 2 (try your utmost) best, hardest

utter *adj* absolute, complete, downright, out-and-out, outright, perfect, sheer, total, unmitigated, unqualified

utter *v* articulate, come out with *inf*, express, put sth into words, say, speak, verbalize, vocalize, voice

utterly *adv* absolutely, completely, entirely, perfectly, thoroughly, totally

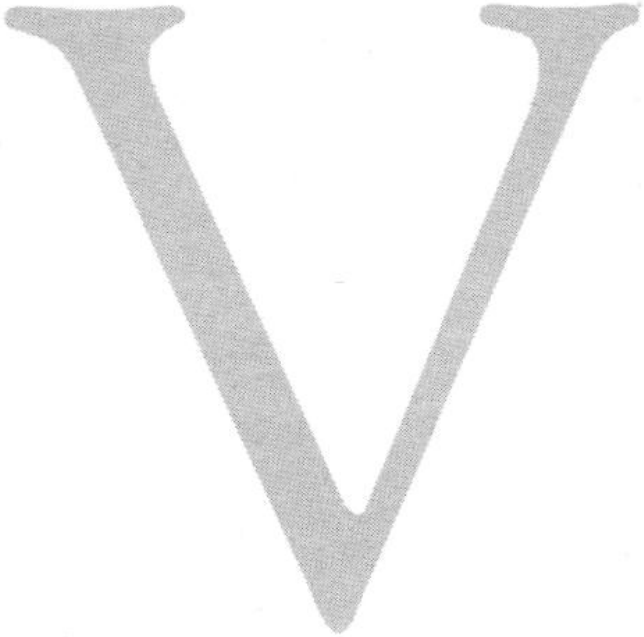

vacancy *n* job, opening, position, post, slot

vacant *adj* **1** (a vacant room) available, empty, free, idle, unfilled, unused; ***opp*** occupied. **2** (a vacant expression) absent-minded, blank, dreamy, faraway, inane, inattentive, vacuous; ***opp*** attentive

vacate *v* abandon, depart from, desert, evacuate, get out of, leave, quit, withdraw from

vacuum *n* emptiness, gap, nothingness, space, void

vagabond *n* beggar, bum *inf*, tramp, vagrant

vagrant *n* beggar, bum *inf*, vagabond

vague *adj* **1** (a vague image) blurred, dim, fuzzy, hazy, ill-defined, indistinct, misty, nebulous, obscure, out of focus, shadowy, unclear; ***opp*** clear. **2** (a vague answer) ambiguous, confused, doubtful, hazy, imprecise, inexact, loose, uncertain, unclear, woolly *inf*; ***opp*** precise

vain *adj* **1** (of a person) arrogant, big-headed *inf*, boastful, cocky *inf*, conceited, egotistical, narcissistic, proud, self-admiring, swaggering; ***opp*** modest. **2** (a vain attempt) fruitless, futile, hopeless, ineffective, of no help, of no use, pointless, unavailing, unproductive, unprofitable, unrewarding, unsuccessful, useless; ***opp*** successful

valiant *adj* bold, brave, courageous, gallant, heroic, plucky *inf*, worthy; ***opp*** faint-hearted

valid *adj* acceptable, approved, authentic, authorized, bona fide, current, genuine, legitimate, official; ***opp*** invalid

validate *v* approve, authenticate, authorize, certify, endorse, legitimize, make valid, ratify, sanction; ***opp*** invalidate

valley *n* canyon, chasm, dale, dell, depression, glen, gorge, gully, hollow, ravine, vale; ***opp*** hill

valuable *adj* **1** costly, dear *inf*, expensive, irreplaceable, precious, priceless; ***opp*** worthless. **2** (valuable advice) advantageous, beneficial, helpful, of help, of use, useful, worthwhile; ***opp*** useless

value *n* **1** cost, price, rate, worth. **2** (the value of sb's advice) advantage, benefit, help, importance, merit, profit, use, usefulness, worth

value *v* **1** (value a house) assess, estimate, evaluate, price, put a figure on *inf*, rate. **2** (value sb's friendship) appreciate, cherish, hold dear, prize, respect, treasure

vandal *n* hooligan, looter, raider,

ruffian, thug, troublemaker

vanish *v* disappear, disperse, dissolve, dwindle, evaporate, fade, go away; ***opp*** appear

vanity *n* arrogance, big-headedness *inf*, boastfulness, cockiness *inf*, conceit, egotism, narcissism, pride, self-admiration; ***opp*** modesty

vanquish *v* beat, clobber *inf*, conquer, crush, defeat, lick *inf*, master, overcome, overpower, overthrow, put down, quash, quell, triumph over, wipe the floor with *inf*

vapor *n* fog, fumes, gas, haze, mist, smoke, steam

variable *adj* changeable, erratic, fickle, fitful, fluctuating, fluid, inconstant, shifting, unpredictable, unstable, unsteady, up and down *inf*, volatile, wavering; ***opp*** constant

variation *n* **1** (a variation from the norm) departure, deviation, difference, discrepancy, divergence, variant. **2** (every day without variation) alteration, change, modification

varied *adj* assorted, different, diverse, heterogeneous, miscellaneous, mixed, sundry, various

variety *n* **1** (enjoy variety) change, diversity, variation. **2** (a variety of different things) assortment, collection, combination, mixture, range. **3** (a variety of flower) brand, breed, category, class, classification, kind, make, sort, species, strain, type

various *adj* assorted, different, diverse, heterogeneous, miscellaneous, mixed, sundry, varied

vary *v* **1** (vary sth) adapt, adjust, alter, change, diversify, modify, transform. **2** (vary in quality) be different, differ

vast *adj* colossal, enormous, extensive, gigantic, great, huge, immense, infinite, limitless, mammoth, massive, monstrous, unlimited; ***opp*** tiny

vault *n* basement, cavern, cellar, crypt, repository

vault *v* bound, clear, hurdle, jump, leap, spring

veer *v* change course, change direction, dodge, sheer, shift, swerve, swing, turn

vegetate *v* go to seed *inf*, idle, languish, laze around, stagnate

vegetation *n* flora, foliage, greenery, growth, plant life, plants, undergrowth

vehement *adj* ardent, eager, earnest, enthusiastic, fervent, fierce, intense, keen, passionate, vigorous; ***opp*** half-hearted

veil *n* blanket, cloak, cover, covering, curtain, film, mantle, mask, screen, shade, shroud

veil *v* cloak, conceal, cover, disguise, hide, mask, obscure, screen, shroud

vein *n* **1** (in a lighter vein) humor, mode, mood, spirit, style, temper, tenor, tone. **2** (a vein of humor) dash, hint, strain, streak, thread. **3** (a vein of coal) bed, deposit, seam, stratum, streak, stripe

vendetta *n* conflict, feud, quarrel

veneer *n* **1** (a veneer of respectability) appearance, facade, front, guise, pretense, semblance, show. **2** (a veneer of lacquer) coating, covering, finish, surface

venerable *adj* esteemed, hallowed, honored, respected, venerated

venerate *v* adore, esteem, hero-worship,

idolize, pay homage to, respect, revere, reverence, worship

vengeance *n* an eye for an eye, pay-back *inf*, reprisal, retaliation, retribution, revenge, tit for tat

venom *n* **1** poison, toxin. **2** acrimony, bitterness, grudge, hate, hatred, malevolence, malice, rancor, spite, viciousness, vindictiveness, virulence

venomous *adj* **1** deadly, noxious, poisonous, toxic. **2** acrimonious, bitter, grudging, malevolent, malicious, rancorous, savage, spiteful, vicious, vindictive, virulent

vent *n* aperture, cut, duct, flue, gap, hole, opening, orifice, outlet, passage, slit, slot, split

vent *v* air, articulate, emit, express, give vent to, let out, make known, pour out, utter, voice

ventilate *v* aerate, air, air-condition, freshen, oxygenate

venture *n* chance, endeavor, enterprise, experiment, gamble, project, risk, speculation, undertaking

venture *v* **1** bet, chance, dare, gamble, risk, speculate, stake, wager. **2** (venture an opinion) advance, dare, hazard, put forward, risk, volunteer

venue *n* location, place, setting

verbal *adj* oral, said, spoken, word-of-mouth

verbose *adj* garrulous, long-winded, loquacious, prolix, talkative, voluble, wordy; ***opp*** brief, concise

verdict *n* adjudication, assessment, conclusion, decision, finding, judgment, opinion, ruling

verge *n* border, boundary, brink, edge, limit, lip, margin, side, threshold

verge on *v* approach, border on, come close, come near, tend towards

verify *v* affirm, attest, authenticate, check, confirm, corroborate, establish, prove, substantiate, support, testify to, validate, vouch for

versatile *adj* adaptable, all-round, flexible, handy, multipurpose, resourceful, variable

verse *n* **1** canto, couplet, lines, stanza, strophe. **2** lyric, ode, poem, poetry, rhyme, sonnet

version *n* account, description, interpretation, portrayal, reading, rendering, rendition, report, translation

vertical *adj* erect, on end, perpendicular, standing, straight, upright; ***opp*** horizontal

vertigo *n* dizziness, giddiness, light-headedness, loss of balance

very *adv* awfully *inf*, decidedly, deeply, eminently, enormously, especially, exceedingly, extremely, greatly, highly, hugely, most, outstandingly, particularly, really, remarkably, to a great extent, terribly *inf*, truly, unbelievably, unusually, vastly

vessel *n* **1** boat, craft, ship. **2** container, pot, receptacle, tank, vat

vet *v* check out, examine, inspect, investigate, review, scan, scrutinize

veteran *adj* adept, experienced, expert, old, practiced, seasoned

veteran *n* master, old hand, old soldier, past master, pro *inf*, trouper; ***opp*** novice

veto *n* ban, bar, block, boycott, embargo, interdict, prohibition, refusal, rejection, thumbs down *inf*

veto *v* ban, bar, block, boycott, dismiss, forbid, prohibit, proscribe, refuse, reject, rule out, turn down, vote against; ***opp*** allow

vex *v* aggravate, annoy, bother, disturb, exasperate, get on sb's nerves *inf*, harass, hassle *inf*, infuriate, irk, irritate, plague, provoke, rile, torment, trouble, upset, worry

viable *adj* achievable, feasible, operable, possible, practicable, realistic, reasonable, sound, sustainable, usable, valid, workable; ***opp*** impossible

vibrant *adj* alive, animated, colorful, dynamic, electric, energetic, lively, sparkling, spirited, throbbing, vivacious, vivid; ***opp*** dull

vibrate *v* oscillate, pulsate, quiver, resonate, reverberate, shake, shiver, throb, tremble, wobble

vibration *n* oscillation, pulse, quivering, resonance, reverberation, shaking, shivering, throbbing, trembling, wave, wobble

vice *n* **1** badness, corruption, depravity, evil, immorality, iniquity, sin, turpitude, wickedness, wrongdoing; ***opp*** virtue. **2** bad habit, defect, failing, flaw, foible, imperfection, peccadillo, shortcoming, weakness; ***opp*** virtue

vicinity *n* area, district, environs, locale, locality, neighborhood, proximity, region, territory, zone

vicious *adj* **1** atrocious, barbaric, barbarous, bloodthirsty, brutal, callous, cruel, diabolical, fiendish, foul, heinous, inhuman, merciless, monstrous, pitiless, ruthless, sadistic, savage, vile, violent. **2** bitchy *inf*, catty, cruel, cutting, malicious, mean, nasty, poisonous, rancorous, savage, sharp, spiteful, venomous, vindictive, vitriolic; ***opp*** kind

victim *n* casualty, fatality, injured party, martyr, prey, scapegoat, sufferer, target

victimize *v* bully, discriminate against, exploit, intimidate, oppress, persecute, pick on, prey on, single out, take advantage of, terrorize, torment

victor *n* champion, conqueror, first, number one, prizewinner, vanquisher, winner

victorious *adj* champion, conquering, first, prizewinning, successful, top, triumphant, vanquishing, winning; ***opp*** defeated, vanquished

victory *n* conquest, mastery, success, triumph, win; ***opp*** defeat

view *n* **1** aspect, landscape, outlook, panorama, picture, prospect, scene, scenery, sight, vision, vista. **2** attitude, belief, conviction, feeling, idea, notion, opinion, perception, position, sentiment, thought

view *v* behold, check out *inf*, consider, contemplate, examine, eye, gaze at, inspect, look at, observe, regard, scan, survey, watch, witness

viewer *n* audience, observer, onlooker, spectator, watcher

viewpoint *n* angle, attitude, opinion, perception, perspective, point of view, position, slant, stance, standpoint

vigilant *adj* alert, attentive, careful, cautious, eagle-eyed, observant, on your guard, on your toes *inf*, sharp-eyed, unsleeping, wakeful, wary, watchful

vigor *n* activity, animation, dash,

dynamism, energy, fitness, force, forcefulness, gusto, health, heartiness, life, liveliness, power, robustness, soundness, spirit, stamina, strength, sturdiness, verve, virility, vitality

vigorous *adj* active, animated, brisk, dynamic, effective, energetic, fit, flourishing, forceful, full-blooded, hale, hardy, healthy, hearty, intense, lively, lusty, potent, powerful, robust, sound, spirited, strong, sturdy, thriving, virile, vital

vile *adj* **1** bad, base, contemptible, debased, degenerate, depraved, despicable, detestable, evil, ignoble, immoral, impure, loathsome, low, perverted, shocking, sinful, ugly, vicious, wicked; ***opp*** good. **2** disgusting, foul, horrible, horrid, loathsome, nasty, nauseating, repellent, repugnant, repulsive, revolting, unpleasant, yucky *inf*; ***opp*** lovely

villain *n* criminal, crook *inf*, evil-doer, malefactor, miscreant, reprobate, rogue, ruffian, scoundrel, wretch, wrong-doer

villainous *adj* bad, base, corrupt, criminal, debased, dishonest, evil, fiendish, hateful, heinous, infamous, sinful, treacherous, vicious, vile, wicked

vindicate *v* confirm, corroborate, justify, prove sb right, substantiate, verify

vindication *n* confirmation, corroboration, justification, proof, substantiation, verification

vindictive *adj* avenging, bitter, malevolent, malicious, malignant, rancorous, resentful, revengeful, spiteful, unforgiving, vengeful

vintage *adj* choice, classic, fine, good, high quality, mature, mellowed, old, prime, quality, seasoned, select, superior, venerable

violate *v* **1** (violate a law) breach, break, contravene, defy, disobey, disregard, flout, ignore, infringe, transgress. **2** (violate sb) abuse, assault, attack, defile, desecrate, dishonor, force oneself upon, outrage, pollute, rape, ravish

violation *n* **1** (of a law) abuse, breach, breaking, contravention, defiance, disobedience, disregard, flouting, ignoring, infraction, infringement, offense, transgression. **2** (of a person) abuse, assault, attack, defilement, desecration, dishonoring, outrage, rape

violence *n* **1** aggression, assault, attack, bloodshed, brutality, fighting, ferocity, force, roughness, savagery. **2** (of feelings) passion, power, ferocity, force, forcefulness, intensity, power, strength, tempestuousness, vehemence, wildness

violent *adj* **1** aggressive, attacking, bellicose, belligerent, bloodthirsty, brutal, destructive, ferocious, fierce, hot-headed, hot-tempered, intemperate, savage, vicious, warlike. **2** passionate, powerful, fierce, fiery, forceful, intense, powerful, raging, strong, tempestuous, unbridled, uncontrollable, uncontrolled, unrestrained, vehement, wild

VIP *n* celebrity, dignitary, official, personality, star

virgin *adj* chaste, immaculate, inexperienced, maidenly, pure, uncorrupted, undefiled, untouched, vestal, virtuous

virgin *n* girl, maid, maiden

virile *adj* lusty, macho, male, manly, masculine, potent, red-blooded, rugged, strong, vigorous; ***opp*** effeminate

virtue *n* **1** goodness, honesty, honor, innocence, integrity, morality, probity, rectitude, righteousness, uprightness; ***opp*** vice. **2** advantage, asset, attribute, credit, good point, merit, quality, strength; ***opp*** weakness. **3** chastity, honor, innocence, purity, virginity; ***opp*** vice

virtuoso *adj* bravura, brilliant, dazzling, masterly, outstanding, stunning

virtuoso *n* artist, genius, maestro, master, prodigy

virtuous *adj* **1** blameless, decent, ethical, exemplary, good, honest, honorable, incorruptible, moral, principled, pure, righteous, upright, worthy. **2** chaste, innocent, maidenly, pure, uncorrupted, undefiled, untouched, vestal, virginal

virulent *adj* **1** dangerous, deadly, lethal, life-threatening, noxious, pernicious, poisonous, venomous. **2** acrimonious, bitter, hate-filled, hostile, malevolent, malicious, malignant, savage, vicious, vindictive

visible *adj* apparent, clear, conspicuous, detectable, discernible, distinct, distinguishable, evident, manifest, noticeable, observable, obvious, open, palpable, perceivable, plain, recognizable, unconcealed, undisguised, unmistakable; ***opp*** invisible

vision *n* **1** eyes, eyesight, perception, sight, view. **2** (sth imagined) apparition, daydream, delusion, dream, fantasy, hallucination, illusion, image, mental image, mental picture. **3** (a person with vision) far-sightedness, foresight, imagination, insight, intuition, perception, perceptiveness, prescience, understanding

visionary *adj* farseeing, farsighted, futuristic, idealistic, imaginative, insightful, intuitive, perceptive, prescient, prophetic, Utopian

visit *n* call, stay, stopover, visitation

visit *v* call on, drop in on *inf*, go to see, look up *inf*, pay a call on, pay a visit to, pop in on *inf*, see, stay with, stop by

visitor *n* **1** caller, company, guest. **2** pilgrim, sightseer, tourist, traveler, vacationer

visual *adj* **1** optic, optical. **2** discernible, observable, perceivable, perceptible, visible

visualize *v* conceive, dream up, envisage, have an image of, imagine, picture, think of

vital *adj* **1** basic, cardinal, critical, crucial, decisive, essential, fundamental, imperative, important, indispensable, key, mandatory, requisite, urgent; ***opp*** inessential. **2** alive, animated, dynamic, energetic, forceful, lively, sparkling, spirited, vigorous, vivacious; ***opp*** lifeless

vitality *n* animation, dynamism, energy, go *inf*, life, liveliness, sparkle, spirit, stamina, strength, vigor, vivacity, zest

vitriolic *adj* acerbic, acid, bitchy *inf*, bitter, caustic, cruel, hostile, malicious, poisonous, sardonic, savage, scathing, spiteful, venomous, vicious, vindictive, virulent, withering

vivacious *adj* alive, animated, bubbly, cheerful, ebullient, high-spirited, light-hearted, lively, sparkling, spirited, sprightly; ***opp*** dull

vivid *adj* **1** bright, brilliant, clear, colorful, dazzling, glowing, intense, rich, strong, vibrant; ***opp*** dull. **2** detailed, evocative, graphic, lifelike, memorable, powerful, realistic, stirring, striking

vocabulary *n* **1** lexicon, lexis, words. **2** dictionary, glossary, lexicon, phrase book, word-list

vocal *adj* **1** oral, said, spoken, verbal, vocalized, voiced. **2** blunt, forthright, loud, noisy, outspoken, strident, vociferous

vocation *n* calling, career, employment, job, mission, niche, occupation, profession, role, work

vociferous *adj* blunt, forthright, insistent, loud, noisy, outspoken, strident, vehement, vocal

vogue *n* craze, fad, fashion, latest thing *inf*, in thing *inf*, mode, rage, style, taste, trend

voice *n* **1** accent, articulation, inflection, intonation, singing, speaking, speech, tone, utterance. **2** (the voice of the people) opinion, say, view, vote, will, wish

voice *v* air, articulate, assert, communicate, declare, divulge, enunciate, explain, express, give voice to, put into words, speak, tell, utter

void *n* blank, emptiness, gap, lacuna, nothingness, space, vacuum

volatile *adj* capricious, changeable, erratic, explosive, fickle, flighty, inconstant, mercurial, moody, temperamental, unpredictable, unstable, unsteady, up and down *inf*, variable; ***opp*** stable

volley *n* barrage, battery, blast, bombardment, burst, discharge, explosion, fusillade, hail, salvo, shower

volume *n* **1** amount, body, bulk, capacity, dimensions, mass, quantity, size. **2** book, title, tome, treatise, work

voluntary *adj* elective, free, optional, noncompulsory, unforced; ***opp*** compulsory

volunteer *n* benefactor, helper, voluntary assistant

volunteer *v* be willing, offer, propose, put yourself forward, step forward

voluptuous *adj* **1** ample, buxom, curvaceous, curvy *inf*, plump, rounded, sexy, shapely, well-endowed. **2** carnal, hedonistic, luxurious, pleasure-seeking, self-indulgent, sensual

vomit *v* be sick, bring sth up, chuck *inf*, disgorge, heave *inf*, hurl *inf*, puke *inf*, regurgitate, retch, spew *inf*, throw up *inf*

voracious *adj* avid, devouring, eager, famished, gluttonous, greedy, hungry, insatiable, keen, ravenous

vote *n* **1** ballot, election, plebiscite, poll, referendum. **2** franchise, say, suffrage, voice

vote *v* cast your vote, choose, elect, have your say, nominate, opt, pick, return, select

vouch for *v* affirm, answer for, assert, attest to, bear witness, certify, confirm, endorse, guarantee, sponsor, uphold, validate, verify

vow *n* oath, pledge, promise, undertaking, word of honor

vow *v* affirm, declare, give your word, guarantee, pledge, promise, swear, take an oath

voyage *n* crossing, cruise, expedition, journey, passage, travels, trip

vulgar *adj* **1** coarse, common, crude, dirty, foul, gross, ill-bred, ill-mannered, impolite, improper, indecent, naughty, offensive, rude, uncouth, unseemly; ***opp*** polite. **2** flashy, gaudy, in bad taste, inelegant, nasty, showy, tasteless, tawdry; ***opp*** tasteful

vulnerable *adj* at risk, defenseless, easily hurt, exposed, helpless, open, powerless, sensitive, susceptible, tender, unguarded, unprotected, weak, wide open; ***opp*** strong

wad *n* ball, bundle, lump, mass, pad, plug, roll
wade *v* **1** paddle, splash. **2** (wade through sth) plow, work your way
waffle *n* evasiveness, padding, prattle, verbiage, wordiness
waffle *v* babble, blather *inf*, jabber, prattle, ramble
waft *v* **1** bear, carry, puff, transport. **2** be borne, be carried, drift, float, glide, travel
wag *v* **1** bob, flap, nod, waggle, wave, wiggle, wobble. **2** rock, shake, sway, swing, twitch, undulate, vibrate
wage *n* allowance, earnings, fee, income, pay, payment, remuneration, salary, stipend, wages
wager *n* bet, gamble, stake
wager *v* bet, chance, gamble, lay odds, place a bet, put money on, stake
waggle *n* shake, wag, wave, wiggle, wobble
waggle *v* flutter, oscillate, shake, sway, wag, wave, wiggle, wobble
wail *n* complaint, cry, howl, moan, sob
wail *v* bawl, caterwaul, cry, howl, lament, shriek, sob, weep
wait *n* delay, halt, holdup, interval, pause, rest, stop
wait *v* **1** be patient, bide your time, delay, hang fire, hang on *inf*, hesitate, hold back, hold your horses *inf*, linger, pause, sit tight *inf*, stay, stop. **2 wait on** attend to, minister to, serve
waive *v* forgo, give up, relinquish, renounce, sign away, surrender, yield
wake *v* **1** (wake sb) disturb, rouse, waken, wake up. **2** (sb wakes) get up, rise, stir, wake up
wakeful *adj* **1** restless, sleepless. **2** alert, attentive, observant, on the lookout, vigilant, wary, watchful
waken *v* awaken, stir, wake up
walk *n* **1** hike, promenade, ramble, stroll, trek. **2** (way of walking) gait, step, stride, way of walking. **3** (a tree-lined walk) alley, avenue, drive, footpath, lane, path, pavement
walk *v* **1** go by foot, go walking, hike, ramble. **2** amble, plod, saunter, stroll, traipse, tramp, troop, trudge. **3** (walk on the grass) stand, step, trample, tread. **4 walk out** (leave) flounce out, get up and go, leave suddenly, storm out. **5 walk out** (go on strike) go on strike, picket, put down tools, quit, stop work, strike. **6 walk out on** abandon, desert, leave
walker *n* hiker, pedestrian, rambler
walkout *n* labor action, protest, stoppage, strike
wall *n* **1** panel, partition, room divider,

screen. 2 barricade, embankment, fortification, parapet, rampart

wallet *n* case, holder, pouch, purse

wallow *v* 1 (wallow in the mud) lie, roll, splash around, tumble, wade. 2 (wallow in emotions) bask, delight, enjoy, glory, indulge, luxuriate, revel, take delight

wan *adj* ashen, bloodless, colorless, pale, pasty, peaky, tired, washed out, waxen, white

wand *n* baton, rod, sprig, staff, stick, twig

wander *v* 1 cruise, drift, meander, ramble, range, roam, rove, saunter, stray, stroll, walk. 2 curve, wind, zigzag. 3 deviate, digress, drift, go off at a tangent, swerve, veer

wane *v* decrease, diminish, dwindle, ebb, fade, fail, grow less, lessen, shrink, subside, taper off, weaken; ***opp*** wax

want *n* 1 (sth wanted) craving, demand, desire, fancy, hankering, longing, need, requirement, thirst, wish. 2 (sth needed) absence, dearth, deficiency, insufficiency, lack, need, scarcity, shortage. 3 (living in want) destitution, famine, hunger, need, neediness, poverty; ***opp*** plenty, wealth

want *v* 1 aspire to, covet, crave, desire, fancy, hanker after, like, long for, pine for, prefer, set your heart on *inf*, wish, yearn for. 2 (need sth) be in need of, be short of, call for, demand, lack, miss, need, require

wanton *adj* 1 (wanton destruction) gratuitous, malicious, motiveless, needless, pointless, senseless, spiteful, unjustified, unprovoked, willful. 2 (having no morals) immoral, loose, promiscuous, shameless

war *n* 1 battle, campaign, conflict, crusade, fight, hostilities, military action. 2 combat, fighting, warfare

ward *n* 1 compartment, cubicle, room. 2 area, district, division, quarter, zone. 3 charge, dependant

warden *n* administrator, caretaker, curator, guard, guardian, janitor, keeper, supervisor, watchman

warehouse *n* depository, depot, stockroom, store, storehouse

wares *n* goods, merchandise, produce, stock, stuff

warfare *n* armed conflict, combat, fighting, hostilities, strife

warlike *adj* aggressive, belligerent, combative, hostile, martial, militant, militaristic, warmongering, warring; ***opp*** peaceful

warm *adj* 1 (warm weather) balmy, hot, mild, pleasant, summery, sunny, temperate; ***opp*** cold. 2 (warm water) heated, lukewarm, tepid; ***opp*** cold. 3 (a warm embrace) effusive, emotional, enthusiastic, friendly, heartfelt, hearty, passionate, sincere; ***opp*** cold, cool. 4 (a warm nature) affectionate, caring, friendly, genial, happy, loving, warm-hearted; ***opp*** cold. 5 (a warm sweater) cozy, thick, woolly; ***opp*** thin

warm *v* heat, heat up, make warm, melt, reheat, thaw, thaw out, warm up; ***opp*** cool

warmth *n* 1 heat. 2 (warmth of feeling) affection, animation, ardor, eagerness, enthusiasm, fervor, heartiness, intensity, love, passion, sincerity, spirit, tenderness, zeal

warn *v* admonish, advise, alert, caution, counsel, forewarn, give notice, inform, let sb know, tell, tip off *inf*

warning *n* **1** advice, caution, forewarning, notice, notification, threat, tip, tipoff *inf*. **2** (a warning of what was to come) omen, portent, premonition, sign, signal, token

warrant *n* authority, authorization, document, license, papers, permission, permit, sanction, written order

warrant *v* **1** affirm, assure, attest, certify, declare, endorse, guarantee, pledge, swear to, vouch for. **2** be a reason for, deserve, excuse, justify. **3** authorize, commission, empower, entitle, license, permit, sanction

warrior *n* fighter, soldier

wary *adj* alert, attentive, careful, cautious, distrustful, guarded, on the lookout, on your guard, prudent, suspicious, vigilant, watchful

wash *n* bath, clean, cleaning, rinse, scrub, shampoo, shower, washing

wash *v* **1** bath, bathe, clean, cleanse, flush, launder, moisten, mop, rinse, scrub, shampoo, shower, soap, sponge, swab, swill, wet, wipe. **2** (of waves) beat, break, dash, lap, splash

washout *n* debacle, disappointment, disaster, failure, fiasco, flop *inf*

waste *adj* **1** extra, left over, superfluous, unusable, unused, unwanted, useless, worthless. **2** arid, bare, barren, bleak, derelict, desolate, empty, uncultivated, uninhabited, unproductive, wild

waste *n* **1** debris, dregs, dross, excess, garbage, junk, leavings, leftovers *inf*, litter, refuse, remnants, rubbish, scrap, trash. **2** extravagance, loss, misuse, squandering, wastage, wastefulness. **3** (frozen wastes) desert, wasteland, wilderness

waste *v* **1** be wasteful with, blow *inf*, fritter away, misspend, misuse, splurge, squander, throw away, use up. **2** (wasting away) become emaciated, grow weak, waste away, weaken, wither

wasteful *adj* excessive, extravagant, lavish, needless, profligate, spendthrift, thriftless, uneconomical; ***opp*** economical

watch *n* **1** chronometer, clock, digital watch, timepiece, wristwatch. **2** (keep a watch) guard, lookout, surveillance, vigil

watch *v* **1** check out *inf*, eye, gaze at, look, note, observe, peer at, regard, see, stare at, view. **2** keep tabs on *inf*, keep watch on, spy on. **3** (watch what you're doing) attend to, be watchful, keep your eyes on, pay attention, take care. **4** (supervise sb) guard, keep an eye on, look after, mind, protect, supervise, take care of. **5 watch out** be alert, be careful, be on your guard, be vigilant, be watchful, keep your eyes open, look out, mind, take care

watchful *adj* alert, attentive, eagle-eyed, guarded, observant, sharp-eyed, suspicious, vigilant, wary, wide awake

watchman *n* caretaker, guard, lookout, security man, sentry

water *v* dampen, douse, drench, flood, hose, irrigate, moisten, saturate, soak, spray, sprinkle, wet

waterfall *n* cascade, cataract, falls

waterproof *adj* damp-proof, water-repellent, water-resistant, watertight, weatherproof

watertight *adj* sealed, sound, waterproof

watery *adj* **1** (like water) aqueous, fluid, liquid. **2** (too thin) dilute, diluted, runny, tasteless, thin, watered down, weak, wishy-washy *inf*. **3** (containing water) boggy, damp, moist, sodden, soggy, squelchy, waterlogged, wet. **4** (full of tears) moist, tear-filled, tearful, weepy, wet

wave *n* **1** (a wave of sth) current, flood, movement, outbreak, rush, stream, surge, tide, trend, upsurge. **2** (in the ocean) billow, breaker, crest, ripple, roller, surf, swell, tidal wave. **3** (a wave of your hand) flourish, gesture, shake, sign, signal

wave *v* **1** (wave a stick) brandish, flourish, shake, swing, wag, waggle, wield. **2** (wave in the wind) billow, flap, flutter, ripple, stir, undulate. **3** (wave to sb) beckon, gesticulate, gesture, indicate, signal

waver *v* **1** be indecisive, be of two minds, dither, falter, hesitate, shilly-shally *inf*, vacillate. **2** become unsteady, flicker, fluctuate, quiver, reel, shake, sway, teeter, totter, tremble, undulate, vary, wave, weave, wobble

wavy *adj* **1** (wavy hair) curling, curly; ***opp*** straight. **2** (a wavy line) curving, curvy, squiggly, undulating, winding; ***opp*** straight

wax *v* broaden, develop, expand, get bigger, grow, increase, mount, rise, swell, widen; ***opp*** wane

way *n* **1** (way of doing sth) approach, manner, means, method, mode, plan, procedure, scheme, system, technique. **2** (the way to a place) access, avenue, channel, course, direction, lane, path, pathway, road, roadway, route, street, track, trail. **3** (sb's way) behavior, conduct, custom, eccentricity, habit, manner, mannerism, nature, personality, routine, style, temperament, trait, wont. **4** (different in some ways) aspect, circumstance, detail, feature, particular, point, respect, sense

waylay *v* accost, ambush, attack, buttonhole, hold up, intercept, lie in wait for, pounce on, surprise

weak *adj* **1** anemic, debilitated, decrepit, delicate, exhausted, faint, feeble, fragile, frail, infirm, puny, sickly, tender, tired, unsteady, wasted, weedy, worn out; ***opp*** strong. **2** breakable, brittle, fragile, inadequate, insubstantial, rickety, shaky, thin, unsafe; ***opp*** strong. **3** (a weak position) defenseless, exposed, open, unguarded, unprotected, vulnerable; ***opp*** strong. **4** (a weak ruler) cowardly, fearful, impotent, indecisive, ineffective, ineffectual, powerless, spineless, timid, unassertive; ***opp*** powerful. **5** (a weak sound) distant, dull, faint, low, muffled, quiet, small, soft; ***opp*** loud. **6** (a weak light) dim, fading, faint, poor, small; ***opp*** bright. **7** (a weak excuse) feeble, flimsy, hollow, lame, pathetic, unconvincing, unsatisfactory; ***opp*** good. **8** (a weak mixture) diluted, insipid, runny, tasteless, thin, thinned down, watery; ***opp*** strong

weaken *v* **1** (weaken sth) destroy, dilute, diminish, erode, exhaust, lessen, lower, make weaker, reduce, sap, soften, thin down, tire, undermine, water down, wear out. **2** (sth weakens) abate, become weaker, decline, decrease, dwindle, ease up, ebb, fade, flag, give in, give way, let up, tire, wane

weakling *n* coward, doormat *inf*, drip *inf*, mouse, sissy, wimp *inf*

weakness *n* **1** cowardliness, feebleness, frailty, impotence, powerlessness, spinelessness, vulnerability; ***opp*** strength. **2** Achilles' heel *inf*, defect, failing, fault, flaw, imperfection, shortcoming, weak point; ***opp*** strength. **3** (a weakness for sth) fondness, liking, partiality, penchant, soft spot, taste

wealth *n* **1** affluence, assets, capital, cash, funds, means, money, opulence, prosperity, resources, riches, treasure; ***opp*** poverty. **2** (a wealth of sth) abundance, bounty, fullness, mine, plenty, profusion, richness, store, treasury

wealthy *adj* affluent, comfortable, flush *inf*, loaded *inf*, prosperous, rich, well-heeled *inf*, well-off, well-to-do; ***opp*** poor

weapon *n* bomb, chemical weapon, firearm, gun, missile, nuclear weapon

wear *n* **1** (show signs of wear) damage, depreciation, erosion, friction, use. **2** (get more wear out of sth) mileage *inf*, use. **3** (leisure wear) attire, clothes, clothing, dress, garments, outfit

wear *v* **1** be clothed in, be dressed in, clothe yourself in, have on, put on, sport *inf*. **2** (wear glasses) have, need, use. **3** (wear away) become worn, corrode, damage, erode, fray, grind away, injure, mark, scuff, wash away, weaken, wear away, wear out, wear thin. **4 wear off** become weaker, decrease, diminish, fade, lose effect, peter out, subside, wane, weaken. **5 wear out** deteriorate, fray, wear thin. **6 wear out** (wear sb out) drain, exhaust, fatigue, sap, tire, weary

wearing *adj* draining, exasperating, exhausting, fatiguing, irksome, stressful, tiresome, tiring, trying, wearisome

wearisome *adj* annoying, boring, bothersome, burdensome, dreary, dull, exhausting, fatiguing, monotonous, repetitive, tedious, trying

weary *adj* **1** dead on your feet *inf*, dog-tired *inf*, exhausted, fatigued, flagging, jet-lagged *inf*, shattered *inf*, sleepy, tired, worn out. **2** (weary of sth) bored, fed up, impatient, jaded, lethargic, listless, sick and tired *inf*

weather *n* climate, conditions, temperature, the elements

weather *v* **1** (come through sth successfully) brave, come through, endure, overcome, resist, surmount, survive, withstand. **2** (change because of the weather) be exposed, color, erode, harden, toughen, wear

weave *v* **1** (weave threads) blend, braid, criss-cross, entwine, interlace, intermingle, intertwine, knit, merge, plait, sew, twist, unite. **2** (weave a web) build, construct, create, make, spin. **3** (weave between the cars) dodge, tack, wind your way, zigzag

web *n* cobweb, knot, lattice, mesh, net, network, tangle

wedding *n* marriage, nuptials, union

wedge *n* block, chock, chunk, lump

wedge *v* block, cram, crowd, force, jam, pack, squeeze, stick, stuff, thrust

weep *v* bawl, blubber, cry, lament, moan, mourn, shed tears, sob, wail, whimper

weigh *v* **1** (weigh sth) measure the weight of, put on the scales. **2** (weigh a certain amount) have a weight of, tip the scales at *inf*. **3** (weigh things up) assess, balance, compare, consider, contemplate, evaluate, judge, mull over, think about, think over, weigh up

weight *n* **1** (a heavy weight) burden, load. **2** (the weight of sth) density, heaviness, mass. **3** (what she says carries weight) authority, credibility, force, importance, influence, power, significance, value, worth. **4** (a weight off my mind) burden, load, strain, trouble, worry

weighty *adj* **1** burdensome, dense, heavy. **2** crucial, important, momentous, serious, substantial, vital; ***opp*** trivial. **3** burdensome, onerous, oppressive, stressful, troublesome

weird *adj* bizarre, creepy *inf*, eerie, funny, ghostly, grotesque, mysterious, odd, queer, spooky *inf*, strange, supernatural, uncanny, unearthly, unnatural, unusual, zany

welcome *adj* **1** (a welcome break) acceptable, agreeable, cheering, delightful, desirable, much-needed, pleasant, pleasurable, refreshing, wanted; ***opp*** unwelcome. **2** (make sb feel welcome) appreciated, wanted; ***opp*** unwelcome

welcome *n* greeting, hospitality, reception, salutation

welcome *v* **1** (welcome sb) give a welcome to, greet, meet, receive. **2** (welcome sth) accept, appreciate, be pleased by, like, want

welfare *n* comfort, good fortune, happiness, health, prosperity, success, well-being

well *adj* **1** (fit and well) fit, healthy, hearty, in good health, sound, strong, thriving; ***opp*** unwell. **2** (if all is well) all right, fine, O.K. *inf*, satisfactory

well *n* fount, fountain, pool, reservoir, shaft, source, spring, waterhole

well *adv* **1** (everything went well) nicely, pleasantly, satisfactorily, smoothly, successfully; ***opp*** badly. **2** (do sth well) ably, carefully, conscientiously, correctly, effectively, excellently, expertly, proficiently, properly, skillfully, thoroughly, with skill; ***opp*** badly. **3** (eat well) abundantly, amply, fully, heartily, sufficiently, very much. **4** (live well) comfortably, in comfort, prosperously. **5** (know sb well) deeply, fully, intimately, personally, thoroughly. **6** (treat sb well) civilly, fairly, generously, hospitably, kindly, nicely, politely; ***opp*** badly. **7** (speak well of sb) admiringly, favorably, glowingly, highly, warmly, with praise; ***opp*** ill

well-balanced *adj* balanced, elegant, graceful, harmonious, proportional, symmetrical, well-proportioned

well-behaved *adj* cooperative, disciplined, dutiful, good, hard-working, law-abiding, obedient, well-trained

well-fed *adj* **1** healthy, in good condition, well-nourished; ***opp*** malnourished. **2** chubby, fat, plump, pudgy, stout; ***opp*** thin

well-known *adj* celebrated, eminent, familiar, famous, illustrious, notable, noted, notorious, popular, prominent, renowned, widely known; ***opp*** unknown

well-off *adj* **1** affluent, comfortable, prosperous, rich, wealthy, well-to-do; ***opp*** poor. **2** fortunate, lucky

wet *adj* **1** bedraggled, clammy, damp, dank, dewy, dripping, moist, saturated, soaking, sodden, soggy, sopping, waterlogged, watery, wet through, wringing wet; ***opp*** dry. **2** (of weather) drizzling, humid, pouring, raining, rainy, showery; ***opp*** dry. **3** (the paint is still wet) runny, sticky, tacky; ***opp*** dry

wet *v* dampen, dip, douse, drench, irrigate, moisten, put water on, saturate, soak, splash, spray, sprinkle

wharf *n* dock, jetty, landing stage, pier, quay

wheel *n* circle, disk, hoop, ring

wheel *v* **1** circle, go round, move in circles, pivot, revolve, rotate, spin, swerve, swing, swivel, turn, veer, whirl. **2** (wheel sth along) pull, push, trundle

wheeze *v* breathe noisily, cough, gasp, hiss, pant, puff, rasp, whistle

whiff *n* **1** aroma, blast, hint, odor, scent, smell, stink. **2** (a whiff of air) breath, gust, puff

whim *n* craze, desire, fancy, idea, impulse, notion, urge

whimper *n* cry, groan, moan, sob, whine

whimper *v* cry, moan, sniffle, snivel, sob, weep, whine

whimsical *adj* bizarre, capricious, curious, fanciful, mischievous, odd, peculiar, playful, quaint, unusual

whine *n* cry, groan, moan, sob, wail, whimper

whine *v* bleat, complain, cry, fuss, gripe *inf*, groan, grouch *inf*, grumble, moan, sob, wail, whimper

whip *n* birch, bull whip, cane, crop, horsewhip, lash, switch

whip *v* **1** beat, cane, flog, horsewhip, lash, tan *inf*, thrash. **2** (whip sth away) jerk, pull, snatch, yank. **3** (whip cream) beat, stir, whip up, whisk

whirl *n* confusion, daze, dither, flurry, muddle, spin

whirl *v* **1** circle, gyrate, pirouette, pivot, reel, revolve, roll, rotate, spin, swirl, turn, twist, wheel. **2** (my head starting to whirl) go round, reel, spin

whirlwind *n* hurricane, tornado, typhoon

whisper *n* low voice, murmur, quiet voice, undertone

whisper *v* breathe, murmur, mutter, say under your breath, speak softly, talk quietly

white *adj* **1** cream, ivory, off-white, snow-white. **2** (of sb's face) ashen, bloodless, pale, pallid, pasty, wan, white as a sheet. **3** (clean) bright, clean, immaculate, spotless

whiten *v* blanch, bleach, fade, lighten, make pale, make white

whole *adj* **1** complete, entire, full, solid, total, unabbreviated, unabridged, uncut. **2** flawless, good, in one piece, intact, perfect, sound, unbroken, undamaged, unharmed, unhurt, uninjured

wholesale *adj* broad, comprehensive, extensive, far-reaching, global, indiscriminate, mass, sweeping, universal, widespread

wholesome *adj* **1** beneficial, good, good for you, healthy, nourishing, nutritious, strengthening. **2** clean, decent, innocent, nice, pure, respectable, virtuous

wicked *adj* amoral, bad, blasphemous, corrupt, criminal, diabolical, dishonorable, evil, foul, immoral, malicious, mischievous, murderous, naughty, obscene, perverted, scandalous, shameful, sinful, unholy, unscrupulous, vicious, vile, villainous, violent, wrong; ***opp*** good

wickedness *n* evil, depravity, immorality, sin, sinfulness, villainy, wrong, wrongdoing; ***opp*** virtue

wide *adj* **1** ample, broad, expansive, full, large, roomy, spacious, vast, yawning. **2** all-embracing, broad, encyclopedic, far-ranging, general, inclusive, wide-ranging. **3** dilated, extended, open, outspread, outstretched. **4** (wide of the mark) off-course, off-target

widen *v* broaden, dilate, enlarge, expand, extend, flare, make wider, open out, open wide, spread, stretch

widespread *adj* common, extensive, far-reaching, general, pervasive, popular, prevalent, rife, sweeping, universal

width *n* breadth, broadness, diameter, extent, girth, range, reach, scope, span, thickness, wideness

wield *v* **1** brandish, employ, flourish, swing, use, wave. **2** (wield power) command, exercise, exert, have, hold, possess

wife *n* bride, mate, partner, spouse

wild *adj* **1** (a wild animal) feral, ferocious, fierce, free, savage, unbroken, untamed; ***opp*** tame. **2** (wild country) desolate, godforsaken, natural, overgrown, remote, uncivilized, uncultivated, unpopulated, unsettled, waste; ***opp*** cultivated. **3** (wild behavior) barbaric, boisterous, disorderly, excited, noisy, out of control, riotous, rough, rowdy, uncivilized, uncontrolled, undisciplined, unmanageable, unruly, violent; ***opp*** calm. **4** (drive sb wild) angry, berserk, crazy, delirious, demented, deranged, frantic, hysterical, incensed, mad, seething; ***opp*** calm. **5** (a wild guess) arbitrary, crazy, foolish, ill-considered, impulsive, inaccurate, random, reckless, silly, uninformed; ***opp*** sensible. **6** (of weather) blustery, rough, stormy, windy; ***opp*** calm. **7** (wild about sb) crazy *inf*, daft, mad *inf*, nuts *inf*, passionate. **8** (a wild appearance) disheveled, tousled, unkempt, untidy, wind-blown; ***opp*** neat

wilderness *n* desert, jungle, waste, wasteland, wilds

wile *n* **1** artfulness, cheating, craftiness, cunning, guile, slyness, trickery. **2** gambit, maneuver, ploy, ruse, stratagem, trick

will *n* **1** (the will to succeed) determination, resolve, single-mindedness, willpower. **2** (do sth against sb's will) desire, wish. **3** (make a will) testament

will *v* (to will sth to happen) bid, cause, command, decree, effect, force, influence, order, persuade, wish

willful *adj* **1** determined, dogged, headstrong, inflexible, obstinate, perverse, pigheaded, self-willed, stubborn. **2** calculated, conscious, deliberate, intentional, premeditated

willing *adj* **1** (willing to do sth) happy, pleased, prepared, ready. **2** (a willing volunteer) cooperative, eager, enthusiastic, helpful, keen, obliging

willpower *n* commitment, determination, drive, nerve, purposefulness, resolution, resolve, self-control, self-discipline, strength of will, will

wilt *v* **1** (of flowers) become limp, droop, flop, sag, shrivel, wither. **2** (of courage) diminish, fade, fail, lessen, melt away, wane; ***opp*** grow

wily *adj* artful, clever, crafty, cunning, deceitful, furtive, scheming, shifty, shrewd, sly, tricky, underhand

win *n* conquest, success, triumph, victory

win *v* **1** be the winner, be victorious, come first, overcome, prevail, succeed, triumph. **2** (win sth) achieve, acquire, attain, catch, collect, earn, gain, get, pick up *inf*, receive, secure, walk away with *inf*

wince *v* blench, cower, cringe, draw back, flinch, grimace, quail, recoil, shrink, start

wind *n* **1** air, blast, breath, breeze, current, draft, gale, gust, hurricane, monsoon, squall, tornado, whirlwind, zephyr. **2** breath, puff *inf*, respiration

wind *v* **1** coil, curl, furl, loop, reel, roll, spiral, twine, twist, wrap, wreathe. **2** bend, curve, loop, meander, ramble, snake, turn, twist, zigzag

windfall *n* bonanza, godsend, jackpot, stroke of good luck

winding *adj* bending, circuitous, convoluted, crooked, curving, indirect, looping, meandering, rambling, roundabout, spiraling, twisting, wandering

windy *adj* blowy, blustery, breezy, drafty, fresh, gusting, gusty, squally, stormy, tempestuous, wild, windswept

wing *n* **1** (of a building) annex, extension. **2** (of a political party) branch, faction, group, grouping, section, side

wink *v* **1** bat, blink, flutter. **2** flash, gleam, glitter, sparkle, twinkle

winner *n* champ *inf*, champion, conquering hero, conqueror, prizewinner, title-holder, victor

winning *adj* **1** conquering, leading, successful, top, triumphant, unbeaten, victorious; ***opp*** losing. **2** (winning ways) alluring, attractive, beguiling, bewitching, captivating, charming, cute, delightful, disarming, endearing, lovely, sweet

winnings *n* booty, gains, proceeds, profits, spoils, takings

wintry *adj* arctic, biting, bleak, cheerless, chilly, cold, desolate, frozen, harsh, icy, snowy; ***opp*** summery

wipe *v* **1** brush, clean, dry, dust, mop, polish, rub, sponge, swab, wash. **2 wipe out** annihilate, blot out, destroy, eradicate, erase, exterminate, obliterate

wipe *n* brush, clean, dust, rub, wash

wiry *adj* **1** (of a person) lean, muscular, sinewy, spare, strong, thin, tough. **2** (wiry hair) bristly, coarse, kinky, stiff

wisdom *n* cleverness, common sense, good sense, insight, intelligence, judgment, knowledge, learning, perception, sense, understanding

wise *adj* **1** (of a person) clever, deep-thinking, educated, experienced, fair, informed, intelligent, just, knowledgeable, perceptive, philosophical, well-informed, well-read; ***opp*** stupid. **2** (a wise choice) clever, diplomatic, good, logical, prudent, sensible, smart, thoughtful; ***opp*** unwise

wish *n* ambition, aspiration, craving, desire, fondness, hope, liking, longing, request, requirement, want, yearning

wish *v* **1** (wish for sth) covet, crave, desire, fancy, hanker after, hope for, hunger for, long for, need, set your heart on, thirst for, want, yearn for. **2** (if you wish) ask, bid, command, desire, direct, order, require, want. **3** (wish them Merry Christmas) bid

wistful *adj* disconsolate, dreaming, longing, melancholy, mournful, nostalgic, pensive, regretful, sad, yearning

wit *n* **1** banter, fun, funniness, humor, jokes, puns, quips, repartee, witticisms, wittiness. **2** (a wit) comedian, comic, funny person, humorist, joker, wag. **3** (have the wit to do sth) common sense, intellect, intelligence, sense, wisdom

witch *n* crone, enchantress, magician, sorceress

witchcraft *n* black magic, charms, enchantment, incantations, magic, sorcery, spells, the occult, voodoo, wizardry

withdraw *v* **1** cancel, extract, pull back, pull out, remove, retract, take back, take out. **2** (withdraw from the contest) back away, back down, back out, drop out, go, leave, pull out, quit, retire, retreat, run away

withdrawal *n* **1** extraction, removal. **2** departure, evacuation, exit, leaving, retreat

withdrawn *adj* aloof, detached, distant, introverted, private, quiet, reserved, shy, silent, taciturn, timid, uncommunicative, unsociable; ***opp*** outgoing

wither *v* decay, decline, die, disintegrate, droop, dry out, dry up, fade, go limp, languish, perish, shrink, shrivel, waste away, wilt

withering *adj* cruel, cutting, devastating, hurtful, scornful, wounding

withhold *v* check, control, curb, hide, hold back, keep, keep back, refuse, repress, reserve, retain, suppress

withstand *v* bear, brave, cope with, defy, endure, face, hold out against, put up with *inf*, resist, stand up to, survive, take, thwart, tolerate

witness *n* bystander, eyewitness, observer, onlooker, spectator, viewer, watcher

witness *v* behold, be present at, notice, observe, see, view, watch

wits *n* brains, common sense, ingenuity, intelligence, judgment, reason, sense, understanding

witticism *n* clever remark, crack *inf*, joke, one-liner, play on words, pun, quip, wisecrack *inf*, witty remark

witty *adj* amusing, brilliant, clever, comic, droll, facetious, funny, humorous, sarcastic

wizard *n* conjurer, enchanter, magician, sorcerer, warlock

wobble *v* be unsteady, quake, quaver, quiver, rock, see-saw, shake, stagger, sway, teeter, totter, tremble, vibrate, waver

wobbly *adj* **1** (a wobbly tooth) insecure, loose. **2** (a wobbly voice) quavering, shaking, shaky, trembling. **3** (feeling wobbly) rocky, teetering, tottering, unstable, unsteady

woe *n* affliction, anguish, despair, distress, grief, heartache, misery, misfortune, pain, sadness, sorrow, suffering, unhappiness

woeful *adj* **1** (unhappy) dismal, gloomy, miserable, mournful, remorseful, sad, sorrowful, sorry, unhappy; ***opp*** cheerful, happy. **2** heart-breaking, piteous, pitiful, sad, tragic, wretched. **3** (deplorable) abysmal, appalling, awful, deplorable, disgraceful, hopeless, miserable, poor, sorry, terrible; ***opp*** excellent

woman *n* female, girl, lady

womanizer *n* Casanova, Don Juan, ladies' man, philanderer

womanly *adj* female, feminine, ladylike, matronly, motherly

wonder *n* **1** amazement, astonishment, awe, fascination, reverence, surprise. **2** curiosity, marvel, miracle, mystery, phenomenon, sensation, sight, spectacle

wonder *v* **1** ask yourself, conjecture, deliberate, ponder, puzzle, reflect, speculate, think. **2** be amazed, be flabbergasted, be surprised, marvel

wonderful *adj* brilliant, excellent, fantastic, great, incredible, magnificent, marvelous, outstanding, remarkable, sensational, smashing, stunning, superb, terrific; ***opp*** awful, dreadful

woo *v* **1** be after, chase, court, pursue, seduce. **2** attract, chase after, cozy up to *inf*, cultivate, find favor with, pursue, seek the support of

wood *n* **1** boards, chipboard, hardwood, lumber, planks, plywood, softwood, timber. **2** coppice, copse, forest, grove, jungle, orchard, rain forest, tree plantation, trees, woodland. **3** firewood, fuel, kindling, logs

wooden *adj* **1** made of wood, timber, wood. **2** awkward, clumsy, dead, deadpan, expressionless, flat, lifeless, stiff, stilted, unnatural; ***opp*** emotional, lively

wool *n* **1** coat, fleece, fur, hair. **2** fiber, yarn

woolly *adj* **1** curly, fleecy, fluffy, frizzy, furry, shaggy, soft, woolen. **2** confused, hazy, ill-defined, muddled, unclear, unfocused, unstructured, vague; ***opp*** crystal-clear

word *n* **1** expression, name, term. **2** (have a word with sb) chat, talk, discussion, conversation, brief exchange. **3** (news) comment, information, lowdown *inf*, message, news, notice, remark, rumor, statement. **4** (give the word to go ahead) command, go-ahead, green light, order, signal. **5** (promise) guarantee, pledge, promise, undertaking, vow

word *v* couch, express, phrase, put, say, state

wordy *adj* discursive, long-winded, loquacious, never-ending, rambling, roundabout, verbose, waffly; ***opp*** brief, concise, succinct

work *n* **1** business, career, employment,

field, job, line, livelihood, living, occupation, post, profession, trade. **2** (effort) drudgery, effort, elbow grease *inf*, exertion, graft *inf*, grind *inf*, hassle *inf*, slog *inf*, trouble. **3** (task) assignment, charge, chore, duty, housework, job, project, responsibility, task, undertaking. **4** (composition) book, composition, creation, oeuvre, opus, piece, production, writing

work *v* **1** be busy, be employed, earn a living, go to work, have a job, labor, make an effort, slave, toil. **2** (the machine won't work) function, go, operate, perform, run. **3** (to work a machine) control, drive, handle, operate, use. **4** (the plan worked) be effective, have the desired effect, succeed, be successful, go according to plan. **5** (maneuver) ease, edge, guide, maneuver, push, wiggle. **6** (work loose, work free) become, get. **7** (arrange) accomplish, achieve, arrange, bring about, bring off, contrive, fix, produce, pull off, sort *inf*, swing it *inf*. **8** (work the soil) cultivate, dig, till. **9 work out** (work out a sum or total) calculate, estimate, solve. **10 work out** (the total works out to be $5) add up to, amount to, be, come to, total. **11 work out** (work out why sth happened) clear up, decide, figure out, puzzle out, resolve, solve, sort out, understand. **12 work out** (work out a plan) construct, develop, devise, formulate, plan, put together. **13 work out** (it worked out well/badly) develop, go, pan out *inf*, turn **14 work out** (things didn't work out) be successful, go as planned, go well, succeed, turn out well. **15 work out** do exercises, exercise, get fit, train

worker *n* breadwinner, craftsperson, employee, laborer, member of staff, operative, staff, trader, troops *inf*, wage-earner, workaholic

workforce *n* crews, employees, labor force, labor pool, personnel, staff, team, troops *inf*

workman *n* laborer, tradesman, worker

workmanship *n* art, craft, craftsmanship, expertise, finish, handiwork, skill, work

works *n* **1** factory, foundry, industrial unit, mill, plant, workshop. **2** (of an author or musician) books, compositions, oeuvre, output, writings. **3** (good works) actions, acts, deeds. **4** (working parts) action, innards, insides, mechanism, working parts, workings. **5 the works** the full treatment, the lot, the whole caboodle, the whole shebang,

workshop *n* **1** atelier, garage, industrial unit, production room, studio, workroom. **2** class, discussion group, practical session, seminar

world *n* **1** earth, globe, planet. **2** everybody, human race, humanity, international community, people, public, whole world. **3** (the academic world) domain, field, province, realm, sphere. **4** (the world of steam) age, days, era, life and times, period, time

worldly *adj* **1** earthly, material, materialistic, physical, secular, temporal, terrestrial; ***opp*** spiritual. **2** cosmopolitan, experienced, shrewd, smart, sophisticated, streetwise *inf*, worldly wise; ***opp*** naive

worldwide *adj* global, international, transnational, ubiquitous, universal, widespread; ***opp*** local

worn *adj* decrepit, frayed, moth-eaten, old, ragged, scruffy, shabby, tattered, tatty *inf*, threadbare, tired, weary, worn-out; ***opp*** new

worn-out *adj* **1** all in *inf*, exhausted, ready to drop *inf*, shattered *inf*, tired out, weary. **2** broken-down, decrepit, moth-eaten, on its last legs, shabby, tatty *inf*, threadbare, useless, wrecked

worried *adj* agitated, anxious, apprehensive, bothered, concerned, distraught, distressed, fearful, fretful, nervous, on edge, perturbed, stressed-out *inf*, tense, troubled, uneasy, uptight *inf*, worked-up; ***opp*** calm, laid-back *inf*, relaxed

worry *n* **1** (anxiety) agitation, anxiety, apprehension, bother, concern, disquiet, distress, nervousness, stress, tension, trouble, uneasiness. **2** (a problem) bother, burden, doubt, irritation, nuisance, pest, problem

worry *v* **1** (worry about sth) agonize, be agitated, be anxious, be concerned, bother, feel uneasy, fret, get worked up. **2** (sth/sb worries you) bother, concern, disturb, hassle, irritate, nag, pester, torment, trouble, unsettle, upset

worsen *v* **1** (get worse) decline, degenerate, deteriorate, get worse, go downhill, go from bad to worse; ***opp*** improve. **2** (make sth worse) aggravate, damage, exacerbate, make worse; ***opp*** improve

worship *n* deification, devotion, prayer, reverence, service, veneration

worship *v* **1** idolize, pray to, revere, venerate. **2** go to church, pray. **3** admire, adore, dote on, idolize, look up to, love, put on a pedestal

worth *n* **1** excellence, importance, merit, profit, significance, usefulness, value, virtue. **2** cost, price, value

worthless *adj* **1** futile, ineffective, insignificant, meaningless, not worth the paper it's written on, of no value, pointless, poor, trashy, useless, valueless; ***opp*** useful, valuable. **2** (good-for-nothing) despicable, good-for-nothing, useless, no-good *inf*

worthwhile *adj* advantageous, beneficial, constructive, fruitful, good, helpful, productive, profitable, rewarding, useful, valuable; ***opp*** useless

worthy *adj* commendable, deserving, excellent, good, honorable, laudable, praiseworthy, respectable

wound *n* **1** cut, gash, graze, injury, laceration, lesion, scar. **2** anguish, blow, damage, distress, grief, hurt, injury, scar, shock, trauma

wound *v* **1** cut, damage, harm, hurt, injure, lacerate, stab. **2** (distress) damage, distress, hurt, injure, offend, shock, traumatize

wrangle *n* argument, difference of opinion, disagreement, dispute, fight, quarrel, row, spat *inf*, squabble, tiff

wrangle *v* argue, bicker, disagree, fall out, fight, quarrel, row *inf*, squabble

wrap *v* **1** bind, cover, encase, enfold, envelop, fold, lag, muffle, package, shroud. **2 wrap up** gift-wrap, package, wrap. **3 wrap up** dress warmly, keep warm, muffle up, put warm things on.

4 wrap up bring to an end, close, conclude, finish off, round off, summarize, wind up. **5 wrap up** be quiet, pipe down, shut up. **6 wrapped up in** engrossed, hooked on, in another world, involved, obsessed, preoccupied

wrath *n* anger, annoyance, displeasure, fury, indignation, irritation, rage; ***opp*** delight, pleasure

wreath *n* **1** bouquet, floral tribute, tribute. **2** band, coronet, crown, garland

wreathe *v* coil, cover, encircle, envelop, festoon, smother, twist, wind, wrap

wreck *n* **1** (wreckage) mess, remains, ruin, ruins, shipwreck, wreckage, write-off. **2** (destruction) annihilation, destruction, devastation, loss, ruin, shattering, spoiling, wrecking

wreck *v* dash, demolish, destroy, devastate, play havoc with,ruin, scuttle, smash, spoil, write off

wreckage *n* debris, pieces, remains, rubble

wrench *v* **1** jerk, pull, rip, tear, tug, twist, yank. **2** dislocate, pull, put out, sprain, strain, twist

wrestle *v* contend with, fight, grapple, struggle, tussle

wretch *n* **1** down-and-out, miserable creature, poor soul, unfortunate. **2** louse *inf*, pig *inf*, rat *inf*, rogue

wretched *adj* **1** miserable, poor, sorry, unfortunate. **2** (bad) appalling, atrocious, bad, deplorable, grim, miserable, terrible; ***opp*** excellent, good, wonderful. **3** (unhappy) dejected, depressed, distressed, down, downcast, gloomy, miserable, sad, unhappy; ***opp*** cheerful, happy

wriggle *n* squirm, twist, wiggle

wriggle *v* snake, squirm, twist, wiggle, worm, writhe

wring *v* **1** (wring out clothes) squeeze, twist. **2** (wring sb's hand) grasp, grip, press, pump, shake, squeeze. **3** (wring a confession from sb) exact, extract, force, wrest

wrinkle *n* crease, crinkle, crow's foot, fold, line, pucker

wrinkle *v* crease, crinkle, crumple, fold, pucker, ruck up, rumple; ***opp*** smooth

writ *n* court order, decree, injunction, instruction, order, summons

write *v* **1** (put in writing) jot down, note down, put down, put in writing, record, scrawl, scribble, sign. **2** (create) compile, compose, create, dash off, draft, draw up, pen, produce, put together. **3** (correspond) communicate, correspond, drop sb a line, write sb a letter. **4 write off** cancel, discount, dismiss, disregard, forget about, wipe out

writer *n* author, biographer, columnist, compiler, contributor, correspondent, creator, diarist, dramatist, editor, essayist, ghostwriter, hack, journalist, novelist, playwright, poet, scribbler, scriptwriter, wordsmith

writhe *v* flail, snake, squirm, thrash about, twist, worm, wriggle

writing *n* **1** article, book, composition, document, essay, letter, piece, publication, work. **2** calligraphy, hand, handwriting, inscription, lettering, letters, print, scribble, script, text

wrong *adj* **1** (incorrect) false, inaccurate, incorrect, mistaken, untrue; ***opp*** correct, right, true. **2** against the law, bad, criminal, dishonest, evil, ill-advised, illegal, illicit, ill-judged, immoral, improper, inappropriate, misguided, unacceptable, unethical, unfair, unlawful, unsuitable, wicked; ***opp*** good, legal, right. **3** (there's sth wrong with this) amiss, awry, defective, faulty, funny, out of order, strange

wrong *n* abuse, atrocity, bad deed, crime, error, evil, immorality, iniquity, injustice, mistake, offense, outrage, sin, unfairness, wickedness, wrong-doing; ***opp*** right

wrongful *adj* criminal, dishonorable, illegal, improper, incorrect, unethical, unfair, unjust, unjustified, unlawful, unwarranted, wrong

wry *adj* caustic, cynical, derisive, ironic, mocking, quizzical, sarcastic, sardonic, twisted

yard *n* **1** area, back yard, compound, court, courtyard, enclosure, farmyard, garden, quadrangle. **2** dockyard, factory, steelyard, works, workshop

yardstick *n* benchmark, criterion, gauge, guide, measure, standard

yarn *n* **1** anecdote, story, tale, tall story. **2** fiber, silk, strand, thread, wool

yawning *adj* cavernous, deep, gaping, huge, massive, vast, wide

yearly *adj, adv* annual, annually, each year, every year, once a year, per annum, per year

yearn *v* covet, crave, desire, eat your heart out *inf*, hanker after, hunger for, long for, pine for, want

yell *n* bellow, cry, howl, roar, scream, screech, shout, whoop, yelp, yowl

yell *v* bawl, bellow, cry, howl, roar, scream, screech, shout, whoop, yelp, yowl

yield *n* crop, earnings, harvest, income, proceeds, profit, return, revenue

yield *v* **1** bear, bring in, earn, generate, pay, produce, provide, return. **2** accede, acquiesce, admit defeat, capitulate, comply, give in, give up, give way, relinquish, submit, surrender, throw in the towel *inf*; ***opp*** fight on, resist, stick to your guns

young *adj* adolescent, baby, fledgling, growing, immature, infant, junior, juvenile, newborn, new, teenage, youthful

youth *n* **1** adolescence, childhood, formative years, younger days. **2** (a young person) adolescent, teenager, young man, young person, young woman. **3** (young people) children, kids *inf*, the young, young adults, the younger generation, young people

youthful *adj* childish, fresh, sprightly, well-preserved, young at heart, young-looking, young; ***opp*** old

zany *adj* absurd, crazy, daft *inf*, eccentric, mad, off the wall *inf*, wacky *inf*, wild

zeal *n* ardor, dedication, determination, enthusiasm, fanaticism, fervor, gusto, passion, vehemence, zest; ***opp*** apathy, lethargy

zealous *adj* ardent, dedicated, determined, devoted, enthusiastic, fanatical, fervent, passionate, vehement; ***opp*** apathetic, half-hearted, lethargic

zenith *n* climax, culmination, height, high point, peak, pinnacle, summit, top; ***opp*** nadir

zero *n* love, nil, nothing, nought, zilch *inf*, zip *inf*

zest *n* **1** (enthusiasm) determination, enthusiasm, gusto, keenness, relish, zeal. **2** (spice) excitement, flavor, kick *inf*, spice, tang

zone *n* area, belt, district, locality, quarter, region, section, sector

zoom *v* bolt, caree, charge, dash, flash, fly, gallop, hurry, hurtle, run, rush, shoot, speed, tear, whiz, zip